WINDO\

API HOW-TO

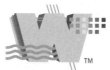

Waite Group Press™
A Division of Sams Publishing
Corte Madera, CA

Publisher: *Mitchell Waite*
Editor-in-Chief: *Charles Drucker*

Acquisitions Editor: *Jill Pisoni*

Editorial Director: *John Crudo*
Managing Editor: *Lisa Goldstein*
Content Editor: *Heidi Brumbaugh*
Copy editor: *Judith Brown*
Technical Reviewer: *Paul Thurrott*

Production Director: *Julianne Ososke*
Production Manager: *Cecile Kaufman*
Production Editor: *Mark Nigara*
Cover Design: *Karen Johnston*
Design: *Sestina Quarequio*
Production: *Christi Fryday, Judith Levinson*

Printed in the United States of America
96 97 98 99 • 10 9 8 7 6 5 4 3 2 1

Library of Congress Cataloging-in-Publication Data
Telles, Matthew A.
    Windows 95 API how-to : the definitive Windows API problem solver
    / Matthew Telles, Andrew Cooke.
       p.   cm.
    Includes index.
    ISBN: 1-57169-060-3 : $44.99
    1. Microsoft Windows (Computer file)   2. Operating systems
(Computers)   3. Application software--Development.   I. Title.
QA76.76.063T433   1996
005.265--dc20   96-6019
                                                                      CIP

Message from the
Publisher

WELCOME TO OUR NERVOUS SYSTEM

Some people say that the World Wide Web is a graphical extension of the information superhighway, just a network of humans and machines sending each other long lists of the equivalent of digital junk mail.

I think it is much more than that. To me, the Web is nothing less than the nervous system of the entire planet—not just a collection of computer brains connected together, but more like a billion silicon neurons entangled and recirculating electro-chemical signals of information and data, each contributing to the birth of another CPU and another Web site.

Think of each person's hard disk connected at once to every other hard disk on earth, driven by human navigators searching like Columbus for the New World. Seen this way the Web is more of a super entity, a growing, living thing, controlled by the universal human will to expand, to be more. Yet, unlike a purposeful business plan with rigid rules, the Web expands in a nonlinear, unpredictable, creative way that echoes natural evolution.

We created our Web site not just to extend the reach of our computer book products but to be part of this synaptic neural network, to experience, like a nerve in the body, the flow of ideas and then to pass those ideas up the food chain of the mind. Your mind. Even more, we wanted to pump some of our own creative juices into this rich wine of technology.

TASTE OUR DIGITAL WINE

And so we ask you to taste our wine by visiting the body of our business. Begin by understanding the metaphor we have created for our Web site—a universal learning center, situated in outer space in the form of a space station. A place where you can journey to study any topic from the convenience of your own screen. Right now we are focusing on computer topics, but the stars are the limit on the Web.

If you are interested in discussing this Web site or finding out more about the Waite Group, please send me e-mail with your comments, and I will be happy to respond. Being a programmer myself, I love to talk about technology and find out what our readers are looking for.

Sincerely,

Mitchell Waite

Mitchell Waite, C.E.O. and Publisher

200 Tamal Plaza
Corte Madera, CA 94925
415-924-2575
415-924-2576 fax

Internet e-mail:
Support@waite.com

Website:
http://www.waite.com/waite

CREATING THE HIGHEST QUALITY COMPUTER BOOKS IN THE INDUSTRY

Waite Group Press
Waite Group New Media

Come Visit
WAITE.COM
Waite Group Press
World Wide Web Site

Now find all the latest information on Waite Group books at our new Web site, **http://www.waite.com/waite**. You'll find an online catalog where you can examine and order any title, review upcoming books, and send e-mail to our authors and editors. Our FTP site has all you need to update your book: the latest program listings, errata sheets, most recent versions of Fractint, POV Ray, Polyray, DMorph, and all the programs featured in our books. So download, talk to us, ask questions, on **http://www.waite.com/waite**.

The New Arrivals Room has all our new books listed by month. Just click for a description, Index, Table of Contents, and links to authors.

The Backlist Room has all our books listed alphabetically.

The People Room is where you'll interact with Waite Group employees.

Links to Cyberspace get you in touch with other computer book publishers and other interesting Web sites.

The FTP site contains all program listings, errata sheets, etc.

The Order Room is where you can order any of our books online.

The Subject Room contains typical book pages, which show description, Index, Table of Contents, and links to authors.

World Wide Web:

COME SURF OUR TURF—THE WAITE GROUP WEB

http://www.waite.com/waite
Gopher: gopher.waite.com
FTP: ftp.waite.com

Matt Telles is a professional programmer with over 10 years in the industry. He works for Dataware Technologies in Boulder, Colorado. He began programming in FORTRAN on DEC 1091s back in the late 70s and early 80s and decided to move to PCs when it became apparent that it was his only hope of getting a job. Today, he programs in Windows in C, C++, Visual Basic, and Delphi and longs for his old DEC 10.

Andrew Cooke is a professional analyst programmer from New Zealand. He has used Turbo Pascal and a number of BASICs in the past years. He now programs extensively using C and C++ with the Windows API, as well as object-oriented encapsulations of it, such as ObjectWindows. Andrew particularly enjoys experimenting with the possibilities of new APIs as Microsoft releases them, and browses the Internet regularly to enhance his understanding.

CONTENTS

TABLE OF CONTENTS

ACKNOWLEDGMENTS

Thanks to my wife and children, my friends at Dataware who didn't give me enough to do to stop me from writing more books, my mother and father, and my cats.

—Matt Telles

Thanks first to the dedicated people at Waite Group Press. Although Matt and I did the writing, it is their efforts that bought this book to completion. I would like to acknowledge the comprehensive reviews of the text by Heidi Brumbaugh, for her suggestions and encouragement. Thanks also to Paul Thurrott for his careful technical review of the code examples that accompany this book. Lisa Goldstein managed the project, keeping us on track, and providing encouragement and assistance when the going got tough.

Thanks to Paul Marshall, my colleague at AgResearch, New Zealand's Pastoral Agriculture Research Institute. Paul provided enthusiastic support and a willingness to help. He also was the voice for the "Ni!" sound effect used in the example code. Those of you who recognise the British comedy that used that word will also have a handle on Paul's sense of humor. Bevan Diprose composed the music that we use for the MIDI demo, and modified it when we found that some sound cards couldn't play it. Finally, to my wife Adelle, who patiently supported me through the long hours and late nights it took to produce this book. Thank you.

—Andrew Cooke

INTRODUCTION

In the beginning, there was the Windows Application Programming Interface (API). And the programmers looked upon the API and said, "It is good." Unto the API, they rendered Windows programs. And the users looked upon the Windows programs and said, "They are pretty cool." Beneath it all was the API, which consisted of hundreds and hundreds of magic pieces called "functions." And then corporate America looked upon the API and said, "Yuck!"

When the world of Windows programming was new, all that was available to Windows programmers were the API functions. These functions were hard to understand, easy to misuse, and prone to error.

All of that changed with the advent of visual programming environments. Suddenly, programmers could drag and drop their way to beautiful, fully functional applications that looked good and worked well. Class libraries from Borland and Microsoft replaced the arcane functionality of the API. Much as a pearl grows around an ugly pebble, the class libraries and custom controls that make up today's applications grew up around the Windows API. These class libraries and functions sped up the development of Windows application programming. For the first time, programmers could concentrate on what they wanted to implement without worrying about the thousands of lines of code necessary to make that dream a reality. Unfortunately, too many programmers were "weaned" on the class libraries and are unaware of the power of the API functions underneath. Like the pearl analogy, the pebble was forgotten in the shine of the new functionality.

That common pebble in the center is still there, however. Today, it is more important than ever that programmers understand the capabilities of the API if they are to write programs that meet contemporary standards. The class libraries and custom controls make laying out your application much easier. But they barely scratch the surface of the functionality that awaits you with Microsoft Windows.

The purpose of this book is to teach you how to do all the tricks that can only be accomplished by using API calls. Not only will you learn how to interface to the internals of Windows, but you will appreciate the power and flexibility of this graphical user interface. Only by really understanding the inside of the Windows API can you extend those class libraries and visual environments successfully.

This book is laid out in a cookbook approach. You can simply jump to the specific How-To's related to your task and take what you need to make your current application do what you need it to do.

The *Windows 95 API How-To* is divided into 15 chapters, each of which covers a single part of the application programmer interface function set.

Chapter 1: Getting System Information. Here you will learn simple tricks for determining what computer processor is running, what version of Windows is running, and how much memory is available to your application. In addition, we will cover little programming tricks such as finding out which keys are pressed and turning off the NUMLOCK key. In this chapter you will discover how to determine the network name of your computer (if it has one) and how to find out the name of the user who is currently logged in. Finally, we will take a look at one of the new extensions built into Windows 95, the Registry, and how you can use it in your applications.

Chapter 2: Files and Directories. You will find out how to handle critical errors under Windows 95 as well as how to get information about disks, drives, and directories. We will show you how to determine whether a CD is a music, photo, or plain data disc. In addition, there are How-To's to flush the disk cache and copy files.

Chapter 3: Application and Task Control. This chapter contains tricks and tips that will let you find out what other programs or tasks are currently running on the system and the steps you need to take to start or stop a task. We will show you how to ensure that only a single instance of your application runs at any given time, how to do background processing, and how to terminate and restart windows from your application.

Chapter 4:Drawing and the Graphics Device Interface. This chapter will take you through the ins and outs of the GDI and how you can use the Windows 95 API to make the world a prettier place. There are discussions of loading, displaying, scaling, and rotating bitmaps, as well as "rubber-band" drawing with the mouse. You will find out how to draw charts and graphs and even learn how to perform animation, using both simple methods and the new WinG graphics library.

Chapter 5: Dialog Boxes. You will learn how you can use a dialog box as the main window of your application and how to process accelerator keys within that dialog. Find out how to change the font and color of dialogs as well as individual controls on a dialog. We will take you through the process of enabling and disabling controls in a dialog as well as changing a dialog by showing and hiding controls. One of the central pillars of Windows 95 is extensive use of property sheets in dialogs, and we will show you how you can include these features in your applications.

Chapter 6: Edit Controls. You will learn how to make an edit control read-only, as well as how you can get passwords, find and replace text, add text, undo user actions, and validate input.

Chapter 7: List Boxes. You will learn how you can maximize the usefulness of list boxes in your applications. You will learn how to scroll a list box vertically and horizontally, add multiple columns to a list box, and how to create a list box that you can draw yourself! In addition, we will look at the new Tree control for Windows 95 and how you can use it effectively in your applications.

Chapter 8: Menus. You will learn how you can enable, disable, add, and remove menu items. You will learn how to check items in menus and how to change the appearance of the check box. Finally, we will examine the system menu for your application windows and how you can modify it as well.

Chapter 9: Documents and Editors. You will learn how to create new MDI windows automatically, how to use dialogs as MDI child windows, and how you can implement the basic functionality of a complete text editor using simple Windows 95 API commands. In this chapter we also look at the new Rich Text Edit control in Windows 95 and what is necessary to use it in your application.

Chapter 10: Printing. Just a few of the tidbits covered here include finding out what printers are installed and determining their capabilities. You will learn how to let the user print to a file and how to find out what fonts are available for any given printer.

Chapter 11: Communicating with Other Applications. This involves learning about DDE, OLE, and the Windows Clipboard. Extensive examples are given of these difficult concepts in Windows 95.

Chapter 12: Sound Effects and Music. How-To information such as playing sounds, reading compact disc information, and recording MIDI information is presented in this chapter.

Chapter 13: Working with Windows. You will learn the basics of writing a screen saver. Also, keeping your windows always on top or bottom and moving and resizing them will be covered in this chapter. You will find out how to load icon information from other applications and how to change your own program icon.

Chapter 14: Programming Tips and Tricks. Validating pointers, placing version information in files, and using and loading dynamic link libraries are all covered here.

Chapter 15: The Polished Application. This chapter contains information on using status bars, toolbars, "fly-over" hints, and splash screens among others. You will find out how to animate a program icon and how to display a bitmap in the background of your dialog or window.

Who Is This Book Intended For?

This book is intended to serve as a reference for intermediate to advanced programmers who wish to continue using the visual environments to which they have become accustomed. The book is meant to solve problems that occur in the normal development of Windows applications. If you are creating a new application in Visual C++, Visual Basic, or Delphi, and would like the capability to go beyond what is given you by the MFC, VB controls, and Delphi components, then this book is for you.

In addition, this book is an excellent reference for those students and hobbyists who wish to further their knowledge of Windows programming. Specific examples are given of programming problems and techniques needed by programmers at all levels. Only by studying advanced code can you as a beginning programmer ever hope to improve your skills.

Finally, this book is divided into two "styles" of coding. First, raw API functions are used in a plain C environment for those people who are more comfortable without a high-level library to insulate them from the "real" operating system. Second, examples are given using the MFC environment of Visual C++. These examples are for programmers who want the power of the MFC but need to go beyond the functionality exposed by Microsoft. By combining these two differing styles in a single book, we give you the best of all possible worlds.

About the CD

All of the files and projects introduced in this book can be found on the accompanying CD-ROM. The projects are all laid out on the disc under directories of the form CHAPTxx\SAMPLES\CHyyy, where xx is the chapter number (1, 2, 10, 11, etc.) and yyy is the project number made up of the chapter and the How-To. For example, you will find the third How-To listed in Chapter 9 (How-To 9.3) on the disk in directory CHAPT9\CH93.

All of the code in this book was developed using Visual C++ 2.x, Delphi 1.0, and Visual Basic 4.0. In addition to the 32-bit code in the book and on the disk, 16-bit versions (using Visual C++ 1.5 and Visual Basic 3.0) can be found on the accompanying CD-ROM. You will find this code under the WIN16 directory on the disk. Although Windows 95 will eventually become the major player in the Windows operating system wars, there is still the need to maintain and enhance existing Windows 3.x applications. The How-To's done using Visual C++ 1.5 will work under Windows 3.x.

Copying Source Code from the CD-ROM

To copy the source code projects from the CD-ROM to your hard disk for compiling or modifications, you may use either MS-DOS, the DOS shell under Windows 95, or the Explorer Window.

To copy using MS-DOS or the DOS shell under Windows 95 or Windows NT, simply create a new directory on your hard drive and copy the files into it. You may need to copy subdirectories as well. The aforementioned project structure does not need to be maintained on your hard drive. However, any subdirectories found under the main directory for a project need to be copied as well.

When using File Manager or Windows Explorer, simply copy the entire directory tree you are interested in to a new directory on your hard drive. Visual C++, Delphi, and Visual Basic will all make the necessary changes to the project files to ensure that everything is found correctly.

CHAPTER 1
GETTING SYSTEM INFORMATION

GETTING SYSTEM INFORMATION

How do I...

Designing an application for any version of the Windows operating system involves much more than simply designing some data entry screens and creating some menus. Users of today's programs expect your program to be aware of its surroundings. They expect applications to know what version of Windows is running without being told. Windows and data entry forms are supposed to center themselves on the users' screens without being told how big those screens are. Users expect that the information they pass on to the network under Windows will somehow be reflected where appropriate in your application. Most importantly, users don't want to have to do things that the program is supposed to do for itself. There is no need to configure the keyboard for each application, or to make sure that the [CAPSLOCK] and [NUMLOCK] keys are turned on or off for each application if that is what should happen.

It is the programmer's responsibility to make all of these small adjustments to his or her application and to ensure that user errors or setup errors do not cause the user untold confusion and grief.

1.1   Determine the Current Version of Windows

If your program makes use of special features that depend on the version of Windows that is running, you need to know if that version of Windows is installed on the user's machine. Here you will learn how to determine whether the user's operating system is Windows 3.x, Windows 95, or Windows NT.

1.2   Get Equipment Information about the Monitor, Mouse, and System

It is often crucial to know whether the user is using a mouse (since double-clicking with the keyboard is a difficult procedure!), how many disk drives he or she is using and what type they are, and what the size of the monitor is. All of this information is available through the Windows API. You will learn how to show the number of disk drives and the probable type of each one. You will learn how to find out if a mouse is installed and whether the current user has reversed the right and left buttons. Finally, you will learn how to get the size of the screen and how to center your windows or dialogs within that space.

1.3   Determine the Type of Processor in the Computer

It can be useful to know what processor is in a user's computer. This information can be stored for later retrieval by a profiling application, or it might be used for help desk information. Imagine that the user can simply press a key when the help desk asks him or her all sorts of application-specific information. This key would then display a dialog box that shows the user all of the information needed for that application. This is an excellent way to make your application truly user friendly!

1.4   Determine How Much System Memory Is Available

When creating an application that uses large amounts of system memory, it is best to verify that those resources are available before proceeding. Also, in an application that is trying to protect against serious memory or disk corruption, it is nice to occasionally reassure yourself that your program is not "eating" system memory or using up system resources. You will learn how to defend yourself against memory and disk corruption by validating the amount of system memory available.

1.5 Get Information about the User Registration on the System

Have you ever noticed that the "professional" programs somehow automatically "know" who the Windows software on a given machine was originally registered to? That information is available to anyone who wants to know, but it takes a bit of API trickery to get at the good stuff. You will learn how to extract that information from Windows and, in the process, learn how to "steal" other programs' resources to use in your own applications.

1.6 Get the Network Name of the Computer

In any network environment, it is nice to know the name of the computer to which you are attached. With the Windows API, you can find out this information for display purposes, or for use in your own user logging scheme. You will learn how to get the current network name of the computer you are running on.

1.7 Find Out What User Is Currently Logged into the Network on the Computer

It almost goes without saying that once you have the name of the computer, you would naturally want the name of the user who is currently logged in. This information can be displayed or used in your own applications to customize options based on the user's name. Imagine being able to simply log into the computer and have all of the programs running know exactly how the user likes things to work. This is possible if you know the API "code" to do it!

1.8 Find Out Which Keys Are Currently Pressed on the Keyboard

If you are trying to scroll through a complex document, you know the frustration of programs that do not check to see if the [CTRL] or [SHIFT] key is pressed while the [↓] is being held. Furthermore, you can imagine how it must feel to press several keys at once only to have one of them not register in the application. You will find out how to detect the state of all keys on the keyboard, active or not.

1.9 Use the Windows 95 Registry to Store and Retrieve Information

If you are accustomed to programming for the Windows 3.x API, you have probably worked extensively with initialization (.INI) files. These files are prone to user corruption, either by users simply editing them with a text editor or by other applications overwriting your data. Windows 95 solves this problem by bringing in the idea of a registry file. This file is maintained by the application through the Windows registry functions. You will learn how to add new entries to a registry file and how to read existing entries from the files.

1.10   Find Out the Version Number of a Program or DLL on the System

Sooner or later, all programmers will be bitten by the problem of an outdated copy of a file being used by their applications. Sometimes, the results are simply annoying; the application refuses to do what it is supposed to do. Other times, the results are catastrophic. Data is destroyed, programs corrupt memory, or they simply won't run anymore. You will learn how to detect the version of a file and how to place that information in your own files so that it can be verified at runtime.

Table 1-1 lists the Windows 95 API functions used in this chapter.

GetVersionEx	VerQueryValue	GetFileVersionInfoSize	GetFileVersionInfo
GetSystemInfo	GetDriveType	GetSystemMetrics	
RegOpenKeyEx	GlobalMemoryStatus	RegOpenKey	
WNetGetConnection	RegEnumValue	RegCloseKey	
RegEnumKey	WNetGetUser	GetKeyboardState	
RegCreateKey	RegQueryValue	RegSetValue	

Table 1-1 Windows 95 API functions used in Chapter 1

COMPLEXITY
EASY

1.1   How do I...
Determine the current version of Windows?

Problem

I would like to be able to determine which version of Windows is running so that I can take special steps depending on the version number.

Technique

The documented Windows API function GetVersionEx does the job of determining which version of the Microsoft Windows operating system is currently running. Windows NT is denoted as 3.51, for the current release of Windows NT 3.51, and Windows 95 is indicated as Windows 4.0.

Steps

Open and run the Visual C++ application CH11.MAK from the CHAPT1\SAMPLES\CH11 directory on the CD that comes with this book. Select Windows Version from the SysInfo menu option. A dialog box appears and shows you the Windows version number.

To duplicate this functionality, follow these steps:

1. Create a new project in Visual C++ using AppWizard. Give the new project the name CH11.MAK.

2. Enter AppStudio and add a new menu to the IDR_MAINFRAME menu. This top-level menu should be called SysInfo. Add a new option to the menu called &Windows Version, and give it the dialog ID of ID_WIN_VERSION.

3. Bring up ClassWizard and select the CMainFrame object from the drop-down list. Select ID_WIN_VERSION from the object list, and select COMMAND for the message to process. Click on the Add Function button. Type

```
OnWinVersion
```

for the function name and select Edit Code.

4. Enter the following code into the OnWinVersion method in the editor:

```
void CMainFrame::OnWinVersion()
{
        char buffer[80];
        OSVERSIONINFO osinfo;

        // Get version info

        osinfo.dwOSVersionInfoSize = sizeof(OSVERSIONINFO);
        GetVersionEx(&osinfo);

        // Break into the major and minor versions of Windows

    sprintf(buffer, "Version %ld.%ld", osinfo.dwMajorVersion,
osinfo.dwMinorVersion);

    MessageBox(buffer, "Windows", MB_ICONINFORMATION | MB_OK);

}
```

How It Works

The Windows API function GetVersionEx will return a structure containing version information to the application. In this case, we are interested in using the dwMajorVersion and dwMinorVersion elements of the structure. These elements contain DWORD values (or double integer values).

Note that you must set the size of the structure into the dwOSVersionInfoSize before making the call to GetVersionEx. This is necessary so that future changes to the structure will not break existing code. All later elements will be appended to the structure, and the function will only return the portion that you have allocated.

Comments

The currently supported version of Windows 95 will return 4.0 as the value from GetVersionEx. In addition, Windows NT will return 3.51 for the current version of that operating system. This function is 32-bit specific and cannot be used in Windows 3.x. To get the version number in Windows 3.x, use the 16-bit GetVersion function.

COMPLEXITY
MODERATE

1.2   How do I...
Get equipment information about the monitor, mouse, and system?

Problem

I would like to be able to determine what equipment the user is operating at present. This information should include the number and type of drives and whether he or she is using a mouse. It would also be nice to determine what kind of monitor he or she is using, as well as its resolution.

Technique

Several steps are involved in determining all of this information. Determining which drives are installed on a machine and what type they are (hard drive, CD-ROM, floppy drive, or network drive) can be accomplished through calls to the Windows API function GetDriveType.

The second part of getting the information–determining whether the mouse is present and the size of the monitor–is accomplished by using the Windows API function GetSystemMetrics. This function returns a wealth of information to the programmer, only a portion of which we will use in this example.

Steps

Open and run the Visual C++ application CH12.MAK from the CHAPT1\SAMPLES\CH12 directory on the CD that comes with this book. Select the SysInfo menu and the Drives menu option. You will see a dialog (shown in Figure 1-1) that contains all of the possible drive letters (A-Z) and the type of that drive. The type will be one of the following:

- Undetermined: This drive probably does not exist on the system.

- Removable Drive: Normally a floppy drive.

- Fixed Drive: Normally a hard drive or CD-ROM.

- Network or CD-ROM: Although network drives normally show up here, certain CD-ROM drivers will also indicate their status in this category.

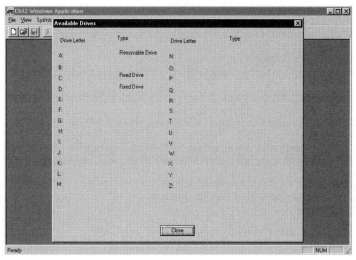

Figure 1-1 Available drives on the system

1. Create a new project in Visual C++ using AppWizard. Give the new project the name CH12.MAK. Using AppStudio, create a new menu called SysInfo, and add a menu item to it called Drives. Give this menu the identifier ID_DRIVE_INFO.

2. Create a new dialog called IDD_DIALOG1 in AppStudio. Add 26 static controls containing text representing the drive letters (A:, B:, C:, and so on). Add 26 other static controls aligned with the first set and assign them IDs of 1001, 1002, and so on, in the same order as the drive letters.

3. Create a new dialog class by selecting ClassWizard in AppStudio and selecting New Class. Give the new class the name CDriveDlg and accept all other defaults. Add a function handler for the WM_INITDIALOG message (called OnInitDialog).

4. Add the following code to the OnInitDialog message handler you just created:

```
BOOL CDriveDlg::OnInitDialog()
{
   CDialog::OnInitDialog();
   char buffer[10];

   for ( int i=0; i<26; ++i ) {
      sprintf(buffer, "%c:\\", 'A' + i );
       WORD ret = GetDriveType(buffer);
       switch ( ret ) {
           case 1:    // This indicates this is beyond the last drive
                      // defined.
```

continued on next page

9

continued from previous page

```
                      break;
              case 0:   // Non-determined drive type
                  GetDlgItem(1001+i)->SetWindowText("Undetermined");
                  break;
              case DRIVE_REMOVABLE: // Floppy drives
                  GetDlgItem(1001+i)->SetWindowText("Removable Drive");
                  break;
              case DRIVE_FIXED:     // Hard drive OR mapped drive on
                                    // hard drive
                  GetDlgItem(1001+i)->SetWindowText("Fixed Drive");
                  break;
              case DRIVE_REMOTE:    // Network drive OR CD-ROM
                  GetDlgItem(1001+i)->SetWindowText("Network or CDROM");
                  break;
              default:
                  GetDlgItem(1001+i)->SetWindowText("");
                  break;

         }
     }

   return TRUE;  // return TRUE  unless you set the focus to a control
}
```

5. Enter ClassWizard and select the CMainFrame object from the drop-down list. Select the ID_DRIVE_INFO object from the object list and the COMMAND message from the message list. Click on the Add Function button and give the new function the name OnDriveInfo. Add the following code for the OnDriveInfo function of CMainFrame:

```
void CMainFrame::OnDriveInfo()
{
    CDriveDlg dlg;

    dlg.DoModal();
}
```

6. Add the following include file line to the include file list at the top of MAIN-FRM.CPP:

```
#include "drivedlg.h"
```

7. Compile and run the application.

How It Works

The GetDriveType API function is used to determine the type of drive installed. Although it can be "fooled" by certain CD-ROM drives and network drivers, as well as by software that emulates a disk drive, it is a reasonable way to determine which drive letters are valid on the current system. These drives can then be used by your application.

The GetSystemMetrics function is used to determine a wide variety of information about the system and its capabilities. This How-To only touches on the possible information available from this API function. You can use the function to center your windows on the screen. It will work for centering dialogs and information messages as well.

Comments

You can accomplish the same tasks described in this How-To using Delphi. To view the mouse and screen size information, open the SYSINFO.DPR project from the CHAPT1\SAMPLES\CH11 directory on the enclosed CD-ROM and run it. A form will display with the information you have requested. The form also uses the GetSystemMetrics call to center the window on the screen, a likely candidate for getting the screen size.

To duplicate this functionality, do the following:

1. Create a new project called SYSINFO.DPR. Add three text fields to the form, with the captions, Mouse Present, Screen Width, and Screen Height. Add three other text fields and give them the names MousePresent, ScreenWidth, and ScreenHeight.

2. Add the following code to the FormCreate method of the form by double-clicking anywhere in the form area (except in one of the text fields you defined earlier):

```
procedure TForm1.FormCreate(Sender: TObject);
var
    screen_height, screen_width : Integer;
    ht, wt : Integer;
begin
    screen_width := GetSystemMetrics(SM_CXSCREEN);
    screen_height := GetSystemMetrics(SM_CYSCREEN);

    form1.top := (screen_height div 2) - (form1.height div 2);
    form1.left := (screen_width div 2) - (form1.width div 2);

    if ( GetSystemMetrics(SM_MOUSEPRESENT) <> 0  ) then
        begin
            MousePresent.Caption := 'Yes';
        end
    else
        MousePresent.Caption := 'No';
    ScreenWidth.Caption := IntToStr(screen_width);
    ScreenHeight.Caption := IntToStr(screen_height);
end;
```

3. Run the application. The form shown in Figure 1-2 will appear on the screen.

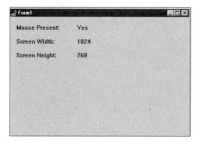

Figure 1-2 Centered form containing the screen size and mouse installation information

COMPLEXITY
EASY

1.3   How do I...
Determine the type of processor in the computer?

Problem

I would like to know what processor is installed in the machine on which my program is running. I can use this information for help desk information, or simply to determine whether my application will run adequately given the equipment provided by the user.

Technique

You can use the GetSystemInfo Windows API function to determine the processor information. This function returns a variety of information, including the processor type. It will identify the current processor(s) (since Windows NT can run on multiprocessor machines) as either a 386, 486, or Pentium. The 80286 and lower processors are not identified, as Windows NT and Windows 95 will not run on them.

Steps

Open and run the Visual C++ application CH13.MAK from the CHAPT1\SAMPLES\CH13 directory on the CD that comes with this book. Select the SysInfo menu. Select the option Processor Type. A message box will be displayed, indicating the type of processor installed in the current machine. This message box will be one of the following selections: 80386, 80486, or Pentium.

1. Create a new project in Visual C++ using AppWizard. Give the new project the name CH13.MAK. Add a menu option for SysInfo to the main menu. Add a new menu item to the SysInfo menu called &Processor Type, and give it an ID of ID_PROCESSOR.

2. Open ClassWizard and select the CMainFrame object. Select the object ID for ID_PROCESSOR and the message ID for COMMAND. Choose the Add Function button. Name the method OnProcessor.

3. Select the Edit Code button and enter the following code into the OnProcessor method body:

```
void CMainFrame::OnProcessor()
{
    SYSTEM_INFO sinfo;

    GetSystemInfo( &sinfo );
    if ( sinfo.dwProcessorType == PROCESSOR_INTEL_386 )
        MessageBox ( "80386 Processor", "Information",
                MB_ICONINFORMATION | MB_OK );
```

```
    if ( sinfo.dwProcessorType == PROCESSOR_INTEL_486 )
        MessageBox ( "80486 Processor", "Information",
                MB_ICONINFORMATION | MB_OK );
    if ( sinfo.dwProcessorType == PROCESSOR_INTEL_PENTIUM )
        MessageBox ( "Pentium Processor", "Information",
                MB_ICONINFORMATION | MB_OK );
}
```

COMPLEXITY

MODERATE

1.4 How do I...
Determine how much system memory is available?

Problem

I would like to be able to display the amount of free system memory in my About box the same way Program Manager does from Windows 3.1. How can I do this?

Technique

The GlobalMemoryStatus function was designed for Windows 95 (and Windows NT) to supply the programmer with information necessary to determine whether a program will run under the current system configuration. Both physical memory and virtual memory can be determined using this function so that the program can also determine whether the system will swap memory during operation.

Steps

Open and run the Visual C++ application CH14.MAK from the CHAPT1\SAMPLES\CH14 directory on the CD that comes with this book. Select the Help | About menu item and look at the dialog box that is displayed. The two numbers shown at the bottom of the dialog box represent the number of bytes of physical and virtual memory available.

To accomplish the same functionality in your own application, do the following:

1. Create a new project in Visual C++ using AppWizard. Give this new project the name CH14.MAK.

2. Modify the IDD_ABOUTDLG dialog resource in AppStudio to add two new static text fields with the captions Free System Memory and Free Virtual Memory. Add two new static text fields next to the two captions you just added. Give these text fields a blank caption and the IDs, ID_MEM_AVAIL and ID_VIRTUAL_AVAIL, respectively.

3. Enter ClassWizard and select the CAboutDlg class from the drop-down combo box. Click on the CAboutDlg object in the object list and the WM_INITDIALOG message in the message list. Click on the Add Function button and add the following code in the OnInitDialog method of CAboutDlg:

```
BOOL CAboutDlg::OnInitDialog()
{
  CDialog::OnInitDialog();
  MEMORYSTATUS memStatus;

  memStatus.dwLength = sizeof(MEMORYSTATUS);

  GlobalMemoryStatus(&memStatus);

  // Get the physical memory free
  DWORD mem = memStatus.dwAvailPhys;
  // Get the virtual memory free
  DWORD res = memStatus.dwAvailVirtual;
  // Set the dialog items
  char buffer[80];
  sprintf(buffer, "%ld", mem );
  GetDlgItem(ID_MEM_AVAIL)->SetWindowText ( buffer );
  sprintf(buffer, "%ld", res );
  GetDlgItem(ID_VIRTUAL_AVAIL)->SetWindowText ( buffer );
  return TRUE;  // return TRUE  unless you set the focus to a control
}
```

4. Compile and run the application.

How It Works

The total amount of memory that is available to your program is a combination of the real memory in the machine and the virtual memory available to the operating system. By using the GlobalMemoryStatus function, you can determine how large a program can run on the current system.

Note that when using the GlobalMemoryStatus function, you must pass in the address of a structure (MEMORYSTATUS) that contains information fields about the global memory status of the machine. Before you call the function, however, it is necessary to initialize a single field of the structure (dwLength) with the size of the structure. This will ensure that future changes to the structure will not break existing programs.

It is also worth noting that in addition to the dwAvailPhys and dwAvailVirtual fields in the MEMORYSTATUS structure, there are fields with the names dwTotalPhys and dwTotalVirtual, which can be examined to determine the actual amount of memory installed in the machine and the amount of virtual memory allocated.

Note: The number of bytes available in Windows is the combination of both real and virtual memory and may not be the same as the largest contiguous block that you can allocate. Always check the return value of any allocation function for an allocation failure!

COMPLEXITY
DIFFICULT

1.5 How do I... Get information about the user registration on the system?

Problem

I would like to be able to display the information about who the currently installed version of Windows is registered to. This information includes the user's name and organization. I can't seem to find a Windows API function that accomplishes this goal.

Technique

You can't find a single Windows API function to display registration information because there isn't a direct way to do this. Only by combining several Windows API functions with a certain amount of sleight-of-programming hand can you accomplish your task.

The information concerning whom Windows is registered to and what organization they belong to is actually stored as part of the Windows registry. To get at this information, you need to be able to open the registry, navigate to the correct entry, and retrieve the value of the key you are looking for.

This How-To will show you how you can accomplish the job of retrieving user information by finding the proper keys and values within the new Windows 95 registry database.

Steps

Open and run the Visual C++ application CH15.MAK from the CHAPT1\SAMPLES\CH15 directory on the CD that comes with this book. Select the User Registration option from the SysInfo menu. A dialog will appear (as shown in Figure 1-3) showing you the user name registered to this version of Windows, as well as his or her organization.

Figure 1-3 User Registration Information dialog containing current user information

To duplicate this functionality, perform the following steps:

1. Create a new project in Visual C++ using AppWizard. Give this project the name CH15.MAK.

2. Enter AppStudio and create a new dialog. Add two static text fields with IDs of ID_STATIC that contain the phrases, "User Name: " and "Organization."

3. Create two additional static fields aligned with the first two. Give these two static fields the names ID_USER_NAME and ID_ORGANIZATION.

4. Change the name of the dialog to ID_USER_INFO. Change the title of the dialog to User Registration Information.

5. Enter ClassWizard and select the Add Class button. Call the class CUserRegDlg and select CDialog as the base class. Accept the defaults for the source and header file names.

6. Select the CUserRegDlg object in the object ID section of ClassWizard. Select the WM_INITDIALOG message and click the Add Function button. Select the Edit Code button and enter the following code into the OnInitDialog function:

```
BOOL CUserRegDlg::OnInitDialog()
{
  HKEY hkRoot, hSubKey;

  CDialog::OnInitDialog();

  if (RegOpenKey(HKEY_LOCAL_MACHINE, NULL, &hkRoot) == ERROR_SUCCESS) {
  if ( RegOpenKeyEx (hkRoot, "SOFTWARE\\MICROSOFT\\Windows\\CurrentVersion\\",
                     0,
                     KEY_ENUMERATE_SUB_KEYS |
                     KEY_EXECUTE |
                     KEY_QUERY_VALUE,
                     &hSubKey) == ERROR_SUCCESS ) {
    char ValueName[256];
    unsigned char DataValue[256];
    unsigned long cbValueName = 256;
    unsigned long cbDataValue = 256;
    DWORD dwType;

    if ( RegEnumValue (hSubKey,
              4,
              ValueName,
              &cbValueName,
              NULL,
              &dwType,
              DataValue,
              &cbDataValue) == ERROR_SUCCESS ) {

        GetDlgItem(ID_USER_NAME)->SetWindowText ( (char *)DataValue );
    }
```

```
        cbValueName = 256;
        cbDataValue = 256;

        if ( RegEnumValue (hSubKey,
                  5,
                  ValueName,
                  &cbValueName,
                  NULL,
                  &dwType,
                  DataValue,
                  &cbDataValue) == ERROR_SUCCESS ) {

          GetDlgItem(ID_ORGANIZATION)->SetWindowText ( (char *)DataValue );
          }

          // Don't forget to close the open subkey...

          RegCloseKey(hSubKey);
        }

        // And certainly don't forget to close the root key.

        RegCloseKey(hkRoot);
    }

    return TRUE;   // return TRUE  unless you set the focus to a control
}
```

7. Go back to AppStudio and select the IDR_MAINFRAME menu. Add a new menu item called User Registration to a main menu with the caption SysInfo, and give it the ID, ID_USER_REGISTRATION.

8. Enter ClassWizard and select the CMainFrame object. Select ID_USER_REG-ISTRATION from the object ID list and COMMAND from the message list. Click on the Add Function button. Accept OnUserRegistration as the function name.

9. Select the Edit Code button and enter the following code into the OnUserRegistration method.

```
void CMainFrame::OnUserRegistration()
{
    CUserRegDlg dlg;
    dlg.DoModal();
}
```

10. At the same time, add the line

```
#include "userregd.h"
```

to the top of the MAINFRM.CPP file.

11. Compile and run the application.

How It Works

The process of retrieving the user information begins with the job of opening and navigating the Windows 95 registration database. Within this database is a hierarchical set of keys that contain information about various aspects of the Windows 95 system. One of these keys, which can be found along the path

```
SOFTWARE\\MICROSOFT\\Windows\\CurrentVersion\
```

contains the information needed to retrieve the user's name and organization.

First, you must open the registration database. To do this, you select a root-level key in the database and then open it. In our case, the root-level key is the HKEY_LOCAL_MACHINE root. This root is then opened using the RegOpenKey (or RegOpenKeyEx) function of the API. The subkey is then found using the RegOpenKeyEx function (to show both of them in action, either could have been used for both cases), and a handle to the CurrentVersion segment is found.

Once the handle is retrieved from the registration database, the RegEnumValue function is called to retrieve a specific value within that key. In our case, the two values we are interested in are numbered 4 and 5. Once they are retrieved, the values are placed in the dialog's static text fields and the database is closed by closing all of the open keys. Closing the registration key handles is accomplished using the RegCloseKey API function.

COMPLEXITY
DIFFICULT

1.6   How do I...
Get the network name of
the computer?

Problem

I would like to be able to know the network name of the drives on my computer. Knowing that they are network drives is useful, but I must be able to show users the "expanded" network name of the files they wish to open. How can I accomplish this using the Windows API functions?

Technique

Users appreciate being able to see the "real" name of files that they are working on. More importantly, they would like to be sure that the network name of the file is the same as what they believe it should be. Nothing is more frustrating for a user than to work on a file for some time only to discover that it was actually a copy of the correct file on another network drive. Displaying the network name of the drive is an excellent way to aid in fixing this problem.

Windows 95 provides an excellent set of networking functions that you can use in your application. This How-To builds on the example in How-To 1.2 of getting all of the drives on the computer so users can check each one at their discretion. This allows them to see what its network name might be, if there is one associated with that drive.

To this end, we will use the GetDriveType API function that we used earlier to discover which drives are available for this machine. We will assume that only potential network drives and fixed drives are available for network use. Floppy drives and nonexistent drives will be ignored. Once the user specifies a drive letter to check, we will use the network function, WNetGetConnection, to find out the network name for that drive.

Steps

Open and run the Visual C++ application CH16.MAK from the CHAPT1\SAMPLES\CH16 directory on the CD that comes with this book. Select the Get Network Name option from the Networks menu. A dialog will appear (as shown in Figure 1-4) showing you the drives attached to this machine. As you select a drive from the list, a text field will be updated with the name of the network associated with that drive or with the string "Not network drive" if this is simply a local drive.

To duplicate this functionality, perform the following steps:

1. Create a new project in Visual C++ using AppWizard. Give this project the name CH16.MAK.

2. Enter AppStudio and create a new dialog. Add a text field that reads Drive Letter: to the dialog. Add another that reads Network Name: . Add a combo box to the dialog and set its style to be Drop Down List. Add a static text field to the dialog and give it the name ID_NET_NAME.

3. Change the ID of the dialog to ID_NETWORK_CONNECTION and set the title of the dialog to View Network Connections. Save the dialog.

4. Add a new menu item to the IDR_MAINFRAME menu that reads Networks. Add a menu item to the Networks menu that reads Get Network Name and assign it the ID, ID_NETWORK_NAME.

5. Go into ClassWizard and select the Add Class button. Enter the name

`CNetworkConnectDlg`

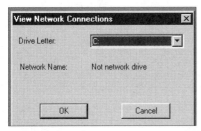

Figure 1-4 View Network Connections dialog

into the name field, and select CDialog as the base class. Select ID_NET-
WORK_CONNECTION as the dialog ID.

6. Select the CNetworkConnectDlg from the drop-down list in ClassWizard,
then select the CNetworkConnectDlg object in the object ID list and the
WM_INITDIALOG message from the message list. Click on the Edit Code
button.

7. Enter the following code into the OnInitDialog method of the
CNetworkConnectDlg:

```
BOOL CNetworkConnectDlg::OnInitDialog()
{
 CDialog::OnInitDialog();

 CComboBox *combo = (CComboBox *)GetDlgItem(IDC_COMBO1);

 for ( int i=0; i<26; ++i ) {
  char buffer[10];
   sprintf(buffer, "%c:\\", 'A'+i);
  WORD ret = GetDriveType(buffer);
  switch ( ret ) {
    case DRIVE_FIXED:    // Hard drive OR mapped drive on hard-drive
      sprintf(buffer, "%c:", 'A'+i);
      combo->AddString ( buffer );
      break;
    case DRIVE_REMOTE:  // Network drive OR CD-ROM
      sprintf(buffer, "%c:", 'A'+i);
      combo->AddString ( buffer );
      break;

  }
 }

 // Set to first entry in combo box

 combo->SetCurSel(0);
 OnNewDrive();

 return TRUE; // return TRUE  unless you set the focus to a control
}
```

8. Select the IDC_COMBO1 object in the object ID list of ClassWizard and select
the command CBN_SELCHANGE. Click on the Add Function button and
name the method OnNewDrive. Click on Edit Code and enter the following
code into the OnNewDrive method of CNetworkConnectDlg:

```
void CNetworkConnectDlg::OnNewDrive()
{
    char drive_letter[20];
    char network_name[256];
    unsigned int  size;
```

```
    // Update the data

    UpdateData();

    // Get the selection from the combo box


    CComboBox *combo = (CComboBox *)GetDlgItem(IDC_COMBO1);
    int sel = combo->GetCurSel();

    // Get the text associated with the item

    combo->GetLBText ( sel, drive_letter );

    if ( WNetGetConnection(drive_letter, network_name, &size) == 0 ) {
        GetDlgItem(ID_NET_NAME)->SetWindowText ( network_name );
    }
    else
        GetDlgItem(ID_NET_NAME)->SetWindowText ( "Not network drive" );
}
```

9. Select the CMainFrame object from the drop-down list and select the ID_NETWORK_NAME object in the object list. Select COMMAND from the message list. Click on the Add Function button and name the method OnNetworkName. Click on the Edit Code button and enter the following code into the OnNetworkName method of CMainFrame:

```
void CMainFrame::OnNetworkName()
{
    CNetworkConnectDlg dlg;
    dlg.DoModal();
}
```

10. Add the following line to the top of the MAINFRM.CPP file:

```
#include "networkc.h"
```

11. Compile and run the application.

How It Works

The GetDriveType function discussed earlier in How-To 1.2 identifies all of the possible drives on the system that Windows 95 recognizes. The WNetGetConnection function uses those drive letters to inquire of the servers the network names associated with that drive letter. Mapped drives that are simply logical extensions of the drive mapping system show up as the correct network name, whereas local drives will return an error and be marked as local.

COMPLEXITY
MODERATE

1.7 How do I...
Find out what user is currently logged into the network on the computer?

Problem

I would like to be able to show the user what name he or she is currently logged in under. This will allow me to identify the user who is presently attempting an operation as well as notify users that someone is already logged into the current machine under a different user name. How can I accomplish this using the networking functions of Windows 95?

Technique

The previous How-To showed you how to find out the network connection information. In Windows 95 and Windows NT, the user information is tied directly to the network connection as well. In Windows for Workgroups, a more roundabout method is necessary.

You can determine the user who is currently logged in using the WNetGetUser Windows API function. In Win32 systems (Windows 95 and Windows NT) this function accepts the name of a local drive and returns a user name and size (of the user name buffer). In Windows 3.x systems, WNetUser takes simply a user_name and a size (of the user_name buffer).

Steps

Open and run the Visual C++ application CH17.MAK from the CHAPT1\SAMPLES\CH17 directory on the CD that comes with this book. Select the menu option Networks. Select the menu item User Names. A dialog will appear (as shown in Figure 1-5) showing you the drives attached to this machine. As you select a drive from the list, a text field will be updated with the name of the user associated with that drive or with the string "Not network drive" if this is simply a local drive.

1. Create a new project in Visual C++ using AppWizard. Give this project the name CH17.MAK.

2. Enter AppStudio and create a new dialog. Add a text field that reads Drive Letter: to the dialog. Add another that reads Network name:. Add a combo box to the dialog and set its style to be Drop Down List. Add a static text field to the dialog and give it the name ID_NET_NAME.

3. Change the ID of the dialog to ID_NETWORK_USER and set the title of the dialog to View Network Users. Save the dialog.

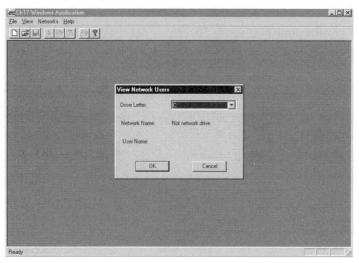

Figure 1-5 View Network Users dialog

4. Create a new dialog class for the new dialog by entering ClassWizard and selecting the Add Class button. Use CNetworkUserDlg for the class name, CDialog for the base class type, and ID_NETWORK_USER for the dialog's ID.

5. Select CNetworkUserDlg from the drop-down list in ClassWizard. Select the CNetworkUserDlg object in the object ID list and the WM_INITDIALOG message from the message list. Click on the Edit Code button.

6. Enter the following code into the OnInitDialog method of the CNetworkUserDlg:

```
BOOL CNetworkUserDlg::OnInitDialog()
{
  CDialog::OnInitDialog();

  char buffer[20];

  CComboBox *combo = (CComboBox *)GetDlgItem(IDC_COMBO1);

  for ( int i=0; i<26; ++i ) {
      sprintf(buffer, "%c:\\", 'A'+i);
    WORD ret = GetDriveType(buffer);
    switch ( ret ) {
      case DRIVE_FIXED:   // Hard drive OR mapped drive on hard-drive
          sprintf(buffer, "%c:", 'A'+i);
          combo->AddString ( buffer );
          break;
      case DRIVE_REMOTE:  // Network drive OR CD-ROM
          sprintf(buffer, "%c:", 'A'+i);
          combo->AddString ( buffer );
          break;
```

continued on next page

continued from previous page

```
        }
    }

    combo->SetCurSel(0);
    OnDriveChange();

    return TRUE;   // return TRUE  unless you set the focus to a control
}
```

7. Select the IDC_COMBO1 object in the object ID list of ClassWizard and select the command CBN_SELCHANGE. Click on the Add Function button and name the method OnDriveChange. Click on Edit Code and enter the following code into the OnDriveChange method of CNetworkUserDlg:

```
void CNetworkUserDlg::OnDriveChange()
{
    char drive_letter[20];
    char network_name[256];
    char user_name[256];
    unsigned int  size=256;

    // Update the data

    UpdateData();

    // Get the selection from the combo box


    CComboBox *combo = (CComboBox *)GetDlgItem(IDC_COMBO1);
    int sel = combo->GetCurSel();

    // Get the text associated with the item

    combo->GetLBText ( sel, drive_letter );

    if ( WNetGetConnection(drive_letter, network_name, &size) == 0 ) {
        GetDlgItem(ID_NET_NAME)->SetWindowText ( network_name );
    }
    else
        GetDlgItem(ID_NET_NAME)->SetWindowText ( "Not network drive" );

    if ( WNetGetUser(drive_letter, user_name, &size) ) {
        GetDlgItem(ID_NET_USER)->SetWindowText ( user_name );
    }
    else
        GetDlgItem(ID_NET_USER)->SetWindowText ( "None" );

}
```

8. Enter AppStudio and add a new main menu item with the caption Networks. Add a menu item to the Networks menu with the caption User Names and the ID, ID_NETWORK_USERS.

9. Select the CMainFrame object from the drop-down list and select the ID_NETWORK_USERS object in the object list. Select COMMAND from the message list. Click on the Add Function button and name the method

OnNetworkUsers. Click on the Edit Code button and enter the following code into the OnNetworkUsers method of CMainFrame:

```
void CMainFrame::OnNetworkUsers()
{
    CNetworkUserDlg dlg;
    dlg.DoModal();
}
```

10. Add the following line to the top of the MAINFRM.CPP file:

```
#include "networku.h"
```

11. Compile and run the application.

How It Works

For the most part, the code is quite straightforward. The check is made to see if a drive is valid, and if so, the drive letter is added to the combo box. When the user makes a selection from the combo box, the code then inquires of the network software the name of the network to which that drive is logically connected. Finally, since multiple user names can be used to log into several different networks from the same workstation, the network software is asked for the name of the user connected through that drive.

COMPLEXITY
EASY

1.8   How do I...
Find out which keys are currently pressed on the keyboard?

Problem

I would like to be able to identify all of the keys pressed on the keyboard in order to process them correctly in my application. Specifically, I am interested in knowing whether the user has pressed [SHIFT], [CTRL], [NUM LOCK], or [CAPS LOCK]. For the [SHIFT] and [CTRL] keys, I am obviously interested in whether the user is currently pressing them down. For the [NUM LOCK] and [CAPS LOCK] keys, I am simply interested in whether the user has selected them to be on before my application gets control.

Technique

This is a fairly interesting problem. How can you determine which keys on the keyboard have been pressed in a multitasking, multiwindow operating system such that the keyboard state is consistent for all applications? You cannot simply trap for the keypresses, since they may happen in another window. You cannot simply watch globally for the NUM LOCK key to be pressed, since it could have been pressed before your application was ever started.

What is necessary to complete this task, therefore, is a way to interpret the keyboard state at any given time. Fortunately, the Windows API provides an easy solution to this problem in the GetKeyboardState API function.

Steps

Open and run the Visual C++ application CH18.MAK from the CHAPT1\SAM-PLES\CH18 directory on the CD that comes with this book. Select the menu option Keyboard. Select the menu item Keys Pressed from the drop-down list. A dialog will appear showing you a list of keys with no text next to them. Press several of the keys listed and click on the Show button. The list will be updated on the right-hand side to show the current states of those keys. The dialog is shown in Figure 1-6.

To duplicate this functionality, perform the following steps:

1. Create a new project in Visual C++ using AppWizard. Give this project the name CH18.MAK.

2. Enter AppStudio and create a new dialog. Add four text fields that have the captions Control Key, Shift Key, Num Lock Key, and Caps Lock Key.

3. Create four additional text fields with blank captions directly across from the four captioned fields you just created. Give these fields the IDs, ID_CON-TROL_KEY, ID_SHIFT_KEY, ID_NUM_LOCK_KEY, and ID_CAPS_LOCK_KEY.

4. Change the title of the dialog to View Key States.

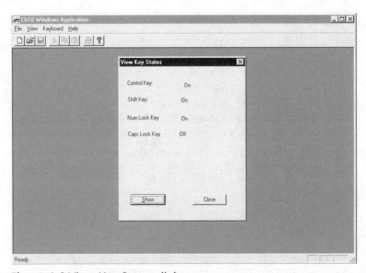

Figure 1-6 View Key States dialog

5. Select ClassWizard and click on the Add Class button. Name the dialog CKeyShowDlg.

6. Click on the CKeyShowDlg object in the drop-down list in ClassWizard. Select the IDC_BUTTON1 object from the object list and select the COM-MAND message from the message list. Click on the Add Function button. Accept OnButton1 as the name of the function.

7. Enter the following code into the OnButton1 method in the CKeyShowDlg object:

```
void CKeyShowDlg::OnButton1()
{
    unsigned char kbuf[256];
    GetKeyboardState( kbuf );

    if ( kbuf[VK_CAPITAL] & 1 )
        GetDlgItem(ID_CAPS_LOCK_KEY)->SetWindowText("On");
    else
        GetDlgItem(ID_CAPS_LOCK_KEY)->SetWindowText("Off");

    if ( kbuf[VK_SHIFT] & 128 )
        GetDlgItem(ID_SHIFT_KEY)->SetWindowText("On");
    else
        GetDlgItem(ID_SHIFT_KEY)->SetWindowText("Off");

    if ( kbuf[VK_CONTROL] & 128 )
        GetDlgItem(ID_CTRL_KEY)->SetWindowText("On");
    else
        GetDlgItem(ID_CTRL_KEY)->SetWindowText("Off");

    if ( kbuf[VK_NUMLOCK] & 1 )
        GetDlgItem(ID_NUM_LOCK_KEY)->SetWindowText("On");
    else
        GetDlgItem(ID_NUM_LOCK_KEY)->SetWindowText("Off");

}
```

8. Add a new menu item to the Keyboard menu with the caption Keys Pressed. Give the menu the identifier ID_KEYS_PRESSED. Enter ClassWizard and add a new function to the CMainFrame object for the ID_KEYS_PRESSED object and the COMMAND message. Call this new function OnKeysPressed and add the following code for that method:

```
void CMainFrame::OnKeysPressed()
{
    CKeyShowDlg dlg;
    dlg.DoModal();
}
```

9. Add the following line to the top of the MAINFRM.CPP file:

```
#include "keyshowd.h"
```

10. Compile and run the application.

How It Works

The GetKeyboardState function of the Windows API returns the current state of each key on the keyboard. For keys that can be pressed and released, such as SHIFT, CTRL, TAB, and all of the alphanumeric keys, the value of the "state" of that key will either have the high bit set (indicating that it is down) or will have the high bit cleared (indicating that it is not pressed, or up). Keys that toggle a selection, such as NUM LOCK or CAPSLOCK, will have the low bit set to indicate that the key is currently toggled (on) or cleared to indicate that the key is not currently toggled (off).

By checking the keyboard at a predetermined time in a consistent state, you can identify any and all keys that are pressed at any given time. If the user presses CTRL-ALT-SHIFT-F10, for example, the keyboard buffer array will have the high bit set for the following key values:

```
VK_SHIFT
VK_CONTROL
VK_MENU (for the ALT key)
VK_F10
```

All of these keyboard virtual key codes are listed in the WINDOWS.H include file or in the online help.

Comments

It is possible to accomplish the same task using Visual Basic. To do the same job in a Visual Basic form, perform the following steps. The form is shown in Figure 1-7.

1. Create a new Visual Basic project and create a new form. Add label fields containing the strings Control Key:, Shift Key:, Num Lock Key:, and Caps Lock Key. At the same time create an additional label field next to each of these fields with a blank caption. Add two buttons to the form labeled, Show and Close.

2. Double-click on the Show button and add the following code to the method:

```
Sub Command1_Click
```

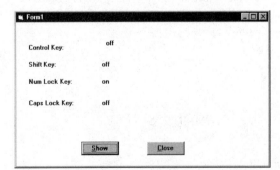

Figure 1-7 Visual Basic form showing keys pressed

```
Dim keys As String
keys = Space$(256)
GetKeyboardState keys

If &H1 = (Asc(Mid(keys, VK_CONTROL + 1, 1)) And &H1) Then
    label2.Caption = "on"
Else
 label2.Caption = "off"
End If

If &H1 = (Asc(Mid(keys, VK_SHIFT + 1, 1)) And &H1) Then
    label4.Caption = "on"
Else
 label4.Caption = "off"
End If

If &H1 = (Asc(Mid(keys, VK_NUMLOCK + 1, 1)) And &H1) Then
    label6.Caption = "on"
Else
 label6.Caption = "off"
End If

If &H1 = (Asc(Mid(keys, VK_CAPITAL + 1, 1)) And &H1) Then
    label8.Caption = "on"
Else
 label8.Caption = "off"
End If
End Sub
```

3. Add the following code to the Close button on the form:

```
Sub Command2_Click

    End
End Sub
```

4. Finally, add the following lines to the General section of the form:

```
Const VK_SHIFT = &H10
Const VK_CAPITAL = &H14
Const VK_NUMLOCK = &H90
Private Declare Sub GetKeyboardState Lib "User32" (ByVal lpKeyState As String)
```

COMPLEXITY
DIFFICULT

1.9 How do I...
Use the Windows 95 registry to store and retrieve information?

Problem

I have heard quite a bit about the new Windows 95 registry, which is used in place of the old Windows 3.1 initialization (.INI) files. How do I go about using this registry, and how do I store information in it to retrieve later? Should I put all of my information for my application into the registry, or can I continue using my .INI files?

Technique

The Windows 95 registry is actually just an extension of the registry functions that existed previously in Windows 3.1. These functions were used to define OLE (Object Linking and Embedding) information for the OLE server to use when launching applications in response to OLE commands.

In Windows 95, however, Microsoft has extended the functionality of the registry to allow applications to store much more information at the system level. Since the majority of Windows 95 is drag-and-drop enabled and OLE compliant, it is much more important that you be able to gather the information for OLE applications.

While OLE command information is beyond the scope of this How-To, it is important that you be aware of what information is available in the registry and how to get at it. Also, you will learn how to add your own application-specific information to the registry and how to get it back.

Steps

Open and run the Visual C++ application CH110.MAK from the CHAPT1\SAMPLES\CH110 directory on the CD that comes with this book. Select the menu option Registry and the menu item Show Keys. A dialog will appear showing you the registry's main level keys and their values. For each main level key, zero or more subkeys that are defined for that main key will be listed. Subkeys are denoted in the list box by a double dash (- -) preceding the key name. The Show Keys dialog is shown in Figure 1-8.

Figure 1-8 Show Registry Keys dialog

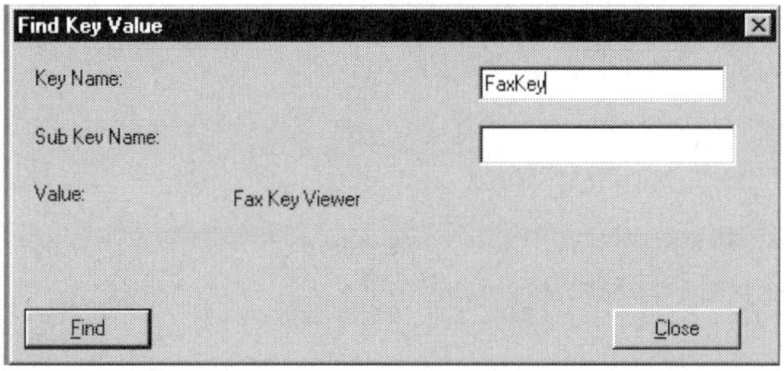

Figure 1-9 Find Key Value dialog

Two other menu items have been defined in the Registry main menu. The first, Find Key, lets you look for a specific main level key and, optionally, for a subkey for that main level key. Select Find Key under the Registry menu. A dialog will appear (shown in Figure 1-9) with two edit boxes. Select the first edit box and type in the name of a key in the registry. Keys are usually just the name of the application. You may go through the Show Keys list box to find the name of an application for this purpose, or you may enter one of your own. The second edit box is for the subkey name. If you have noted a key in the Show Keys dialog that contains subkeys, you may enter the name of the subkey here. The dialog will then display the value of the key and sub-key combination in the Value field below the two edit boxes.

To reproduce these dialogs, follow these steps:

1. Create a new project in Visual C++ using AppWizard. Give the new project the name CH110.MAK.

2. Go into AppStudio and add a new dialog. To this dialog add a list box control. Enter ClassWizard and generate a new dialog class for this dialog template. Call the dialog CRegistryDlg. Accept the defaults for all other parts.

3. Enter ClassWizard and select the CRegistryDlg class. Select the WM_INITDI-ALOG message and add the following code to the OnInitDialog method:

```
ShowKeys ();
```

4. Add the following code to the class source file (.CPP):

```
void CRegistryDlg::ShowKeys()
{
  HKEY hkRoot;
  HKEY   hSubKey;
  char buffer[256];
  char szBuff[80], szValue[80];
  char szBuff1[80], szValue1[80];
  DWORD i, i1;
  LONG cb;

  // Get the list box from the dialog in which to store the information

  CListBox *list = (CListBox *)GetDlgItem(IDC_LIST1);
```

continued on next page

continued from previous page

```
// Clear out existing entries

list->ResetContent();

// Loop through the keys in the registration database, beginning with
// the top level (HKEY_CLASSES_ROOT) and moving through the rest.

if (RegOpenKey(HKEY_CLASSES_ROOT, NULL, &hkRoot) == ERROR_SUCCESS) {
   for (i = 0; RegEnumKey(hkRoot, i, szBuff,
         sizeof(szBuff)) == ERROR_SUCCESS; ++i) {

      // Ignore system keys

      if (*szBuff == '.')
         continue;
      cb = sizeof(szValue);

      // Get the value of this key

      if (RegQueryValue(hkRoot, (LPSTR) szBuff, szValue,
            &cb) == ERROR_SUCCESS) {

         // Add the key and value to the list box

         sprintf(buffer, "%s: %s", szBuff, szValue );
         list->AddString ( buffer );
      }
      // Do the subkeys

      if (RegOpenKey(hkRoot, szBuff, &hSubKey) == ERROR_SUCCESS) {
         for (i1 = 0; RegEnumKey(hSubKey, i1, szBuff1,
            sizeof(szBuff1)) == ERROR_SUCCESS; ++i1) {
         if (*szBuff1 == '.')
            continue;
           cb = sizeof(szValue);

           // Get the value of this subkey

           if (RegQueryValue(hSubKey, (LPSTR) szBuff1, szValue1,
                 &cb) == ERROR_SUCCESS) {
              sprintf(buffer, "--%s: %s", szBuff1, szValue1 );
              list->AddString ( buffer );
           }
         }
      }

      // Don't forget to close all open keys...

      RegCloseKey(hSubKey);
   }
}

// And certainly don't forget to close the root key.

RegCloseKey(hkRoot);
}
```

5. Add the following code to the header file (.H):

```
void ShowKeys(void);
```

6. Now, go back into AppStudio and create a new dialog. To this dialog, add three text fields labeled Key Name:, Sub Key Name, and Value. Add a new text field next to the Value text field and give it the identifier ID_KEY_VALUE. Add two edit fields next to the Key Name and SubKey Name fields.

7. Change the title of the IDOK button to Find and the IDCANCEL button to Close.

8. Generate a new dialog class from this dialog template using ClassWizard. Select the IDOK object ID and the BN_CLICKED message. Add the following code to the OnOK method of the class:

```
void CFindRegKey::OnOK()
{
    char keyName[256];
    char subKeyName[256];
    HKEY hkRoot, hSubKey;
    char szValue[80];
    char szValue1[80];
    LONG cb;

    // Get the key name from the edit box

    GetDlgItem(IDC_EDIT1)->GetWindowText ( keyName, 256 );

    // Get the subkey name (if any) from the edit box

    GetDlgItem(IDC_EDIT2)->GetWindowText ( subKeyName, 256 );

    // Look them up.

    if (RegOpenKey(HKEY_CLASSES_ROOT, NULL, &hkRoot) == ERROR_SUCCESS) {

            // Get the value of this key

            cb = sizeof(szValue);
            if (RegQueryValue(hkRoot, (LPSTR) keyName, szValue, &cb) ==
ERROR_SUCCESS) {

                // If they asked for a subkey, ask for it.

                if ( strlen(subKeyName) ) {
                    if (RegOpenKey(hkRoot, keyName, &hSubKey) ==
ERROR_SUCCESS) {
                        cb = sizeof(szValue1);
                        if (RegQueryValue(hSubKey, (LPSTR) subKeyName,
szValue1, &cb) == ERROR_SUCCESS) {
                            // Put it in the value string
                            GetDlgItem(ID_KEY_VALUE)->SetWindowText (
szValue1 );
                        }
```

continued on next page

continued from previous page

```
                        // Don't forget to close the open subkey...

                        RegCloseKey(hSubKey);

                }
            }
            else {
                // Put this value in the value string.

                GetDlgItem(ID_KEY_VALUE)->SetWindowText ( szValue );

            }

        }

    }

    // And certainly don't forget to close the root key.

    RegCloseKey(hkRoot);
}
```

9. Finally, go into AppStudio one last time. Add a new dialog and put in three text fields, labeled Key Name, Sub Key Name, and Value, again. Add three edit fields next to the three text fields so that each lines up horizontally with a given text field.

10. Change the IDOK button caption to read Add and the IDCANCEL button caption to read Close.

11. Enter ClassWizard and generate a class for this dialog. Name the class CAddKeyDlg. Accept all other defaults.

12. Select the IDOK object ID from the object list and the BN_CLICKED message from the message list. Click on the Add Function button and add the following code into the generated OnOK method:

```
void CAddKeyDlg::OnOK()
{
    char keyName[256];
    char subKeyName[256];
    HKEY hkRoot, hKey, hSubKey;
    char value[80];
    LONG cb;

    // Get the key name from the edit box

    GetDlgItem(IDC_EDIT1)->GetWindowText ( keyName, 256 );

    // Get the subkey name (if any) from the edit box

    GetDlgItem(IDC_EDIT2)->GetWindowText ( subKeyName, 256 );

    // And get the value (if any) from the edit box

    GetDlgItem(IDC_EDIT3)->GetWindowText ( value, 80 );
```

```
    cb = strlen(value);

    // Look them up. First, open the root key

    if (RegOpenKey(HKEY_CLASSES_ROOT, NULL, &hkRoot) == ERROR_SUCCESS) {

        // Open the main key here.

        if (RegOpenKey(hkRoot, keyName, &hKey) == ERROR_SUCCESS) {

            // If they asked for a subkey, ask for it.

            if ( strlen(subKeyName) ) {

                if (RegOpenKey(hKey, subKeyName, &hSubKey) ==
                    ERROR_SUCCESS) {

                    // Key already exists -- Error

                    RegCloseKey(hSubKey);
                    RegCloseKey(hKey);
                    RegCloseKey(hkRoot);
                    MessageBox("Key Already Exists!", "Error", MB_OK );
                }
                else {
                 // Add sub key here.

                    if (RegCreateKey(hKey, subKeyName, &hSubKey) ==
                        ERROR_SUCCESS) {
                        RegSetValue(hSubKey,NULL, REG_SZ,value, cb);
                    }
                    else
                        MessageBox("Unable to create sub key",
                        "Error",MB_OK);

                }
            }
            else {
             // Key already exists -- Error
             RegCloseKey(hkRoot);
             RegCloseKey(hKey);
             MessageBox("Key Already Exists!", "Error", MB_OK );
            }
    }   // End of open of main key.
    else {

        // Create main key

        if (RegCreateKey(hkRoot, keyName, &hKey) == ERROR_SUCCESS) {

            // Create sub key

            if (RegCreateKey(hKey, subKeyName, &hSubKey) ==
                ERROR_SUCCESS) {

            // And set the value as requested.
```

continued on next page

continued from previous page

```
                        RegSetValue(hSubKey,NULL, REG_SZ,value, cb);

                        RegCloseKey(hKey);
                        RegCloseKey(hSubKey);
                        RegCloseKey(hkRoot);
                 }
                 else
                  MessageBox("Unable to create sub key", "Error",MB_OK);

            }
            else
                MessageBox("Cannot create main key", "Error", MB_OK);
        }
    }
    else
        MessageBox( "Can't open root key!", "Error", MB_OK );
        CDialog::OnOK();
}
```

13. Add a new menu item to the Registry menu with the caption Show Keys. Give the menu the identifier ID_SHOW_KEYS. Enter ClassWizard and add a new function to the CMainFrame object for the ID_SHOW_KEYS object and the COMMAND message. Call this new function OnShowKeys and add the following code for that method:

```
void CMainFrame::OnShowKeys()
{
 CRegistryDlg dlg;

 dlg.DoModal();
}
```

14. Add a new menu item to the Registry menu with the caption Find Keys. Give the menu the identifier ID_FIND_KEYS. Enter ClassWizard and add a new function to the CMainFrame object for the ID_FIND_KEYS object and the COMMAND message. Call this new function OnFindKeys and add the following code for that method:

```
void CMainFrame::OnFindKeys()
{
    CFindRegKey    dlg;

    dlg.DoModal();
}
```

15. Add a new menu item to the Registry menu with the caption Add Keys. Give the menu the identifier ID_ADD_KEYS. Enter ClassWizard and add a new function to the CMainFrame object for the ID_ADD_KEYS object and the COMMAND message. Call this new function OnAddKeys and add the following code for that method:

```
void CMainFrame::OnAddKeys()
{
    CAddKeyDlg dlg;
```

```
    dlg.DoModal();
}
```

16. Add the following lines to the top of the MAINFRM.CPP source file:

```
#include "registry.h"
#include "findregk.h"
#include "addkeydl.h"
```

How It Works

The Windows 95 registry is simply a hierarchical tree of keys. Each key is stored as a child of a parent key, forming an inverted tree structure. The roots of the top of the tree are the predefined Microsoft keys including HKEY_CLASSES_ROOT. All of the user keys descend from the root key and can be navigated to by using the root.

To get to a given key in the tree, you open the root key and navigate downward through the parents of the key you are interested in. Adding a key works similarly, by finding the parent of the position where you wish to insert a new key and adding a key at that position.

The Windows 95 API functions RegOpenKey and RegCreateKey actually do exactly the same thing. They position you at a given location in the tree and return a "handle" to that key location. In the case of RegCreateKey, the position will be created if it does not already exist. If it does exist, it will simply be opened.

The API function RegSetValue associates a value with a key. If the key is a subkey of another tree node, you will need to navigate to it in order to set its value. RegCloseKey simply closes the key access and invalidates the handle.

It should be noted that although all of these functions work quite well in Windows 95 (and Windows NT), they have been superseded by 32-bit versions of the functions. RegOpenKey has been replaced by RegOpenKeyEx, RegCreateKey by RegCreateKeyEx, and so forth. For Windows 95, the differences in these functions are slight and not worth worrying about. For Windows NT, however, the security issues of the operating system make it worth your while to use the newer brand of functions.

COMPLEXITY
DIFFICULT

1.10   How do I...
Find out the version number of a program or DLL on the system?

Problem

I would like to ensure that my program is running with only a specific release of a DLL. In addition, I would like to know which version of a program is running so that I know whether certain functionality is available to me. How can the Windows 95 API help me accomplish these tasks?

Technique

The version information functions of Windows are found in the VERSION.DLL file in the Windows system directory. The version functions include the ability to find out if there is any version information in a file as well as ways to find out what that version information is.

A little backtracking might be in order here. Version information is stored in your application via the VERSIONINFO resource statement. This statement creates resources that are bound into your application at link time and are available to any application that needs to use them. The information available includes the version number of the executable or DLL, as well as the company that created it.

The relevant Windows 95 API calls are GetFileVersionInfoSize, GetFileVersionInfo, and VerQueryValue. Note that the VERSION.DLL dynamic link library is required to use these functions, and the export library VERSION.LIB must be linked into your application.

Steps

Open and run the Visual C++ application CH111.MAK from the CHAPT1\SAMPLES\CH111 directory on the CD that comes with this book. Select the menu SysInfo and the menu item File Version Info. A dialog will appear with an edit box and numerous text fields. Enter the fully qualified path name of a windows executable or .DLL file (a good one to try is \WINDOWS\SYSTEM\DDEML.DLL) and click on the Inspect button. Notice the information presented to you. The dialog itself is shown in Figure 1-10.

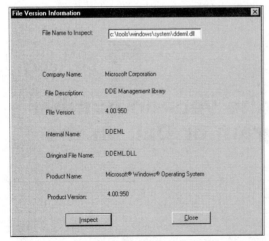

Figure 1-10 File Version Information dialog

To reproduce this functionality, follow this procedure:

1. Create a new project in Visual C++ using AppWizard. Give the new project the name CH111.MAK.

2. Create a new dialog using AppStudio that contains the following controls:

- Text fields with the captions: Company Name:, File Description:, File Version:, Internal Name:, Original File Name:, Product Name:, Product Version:, and File Name to Inspect:.

- Blank text fields with the following identifiers: ID_VER_COMPANY_NAME, ID_VER_FILE_DESC, ID_VER_FILE_VERSION, ID_VER_INTERNAL_NAME, ID_VER_ORIG_FILENAME, ID_VER_PRODUCT_NAME, and ID_VER_PRODUCT_VERSION.

3. Change the caption of the IDCANCEL button to Close and delete the IDOK button. Add a new button with the identifier ID_INSPECT and the caption Inspect. Next, add another button horizontally aligned with the edit field that has the caption &Browse.

4. Set the dialog caption to File Version Information.

5. Using ClassWizard, generate a new dialog class for this template. Call the class CVersionDlg and accept all other defaults.

6. Select the ID_INSPECT object from the object ID list and the BN_CLICKED message from the message list. Click on the Add Function button and accept OnInspect as the function name.

7. Enter the following code into the OnInspect button handler:

```
void CVersionDlg::OnInspect()
{
    UpdateData();

    // Get the edit field value

    char ebuffer[256];
    GetDlgItem(IDC_EDIT1)->GetWindowText ( ebuffer, 256 );

    BYTE        block[1024];
    DWORD FAR *translation;
    DWORD FAR *buffer;
    DWORD       handle;
    DWORD       bytes;

    char        name     [2048];        // StringFileInfo data block.
    char        data[256];

    // Get the actual size of the information block.

    bytes = GetFileVersionInfoSize(ebuffer, &handle);

    if (bytes)
```

continued on next page

continued from previous page

```
    {
        // Get the actual block for the version information

        bytes = 2048;

        if (GetFileVersionInfo(ebuffer, handle, bytes, block))
        {
            // Good. First, get the Product Version information

            if (VerQueryValue(block, "\\VarFileInfo\\Translation",
                    (VOID FAR * FAR *)&translation, (UINT FAR *)&bytes))
            {
            wsprintf(name,"\\StringFileInfo\\%04x%04x\\ProductVersion",
                    LOWORD(*translation), HIWORD(*translation));

            if (VerQueryValue(block, name, (VOID FAR * FAR *)&buffer,
                    (UINT FAR *)&bytes))
                lstrcpy(data, (char far *)buffer);
                GetDlgItem(ID_VER_PRODUCT_VERSION)->SetWindowText(data);
            }
            else {
                MessageBox ("Unable to get translation type", "Error",
                    MB_OK );
            }

            // Next, get the Company name information

            wsprintf(name, "\\StringFileInfo\\%04x%04x\\CompanyName",
                    LOWORD(*translation), HIWORD(*translation));

            if (VerQueryValue(block, name, (VOID FAR * FAR *)&buffer,
                    (UINT FAR *)&bytes)) {
                lstrcpy(data, (char far *)buffer);
                GetDlgItem(ID_VER_COMPANY_NAME)->SetWindowText(data);
            }

            // The Original File name for this file

            wsprintf(name, "\\StringFileInfo\\%04x%04x\\OriginalFilename",
                    LOWORD(*translation), HIWORD(*translation));

            if (VerQueryValue(block, name, (VOID FAR * FAR *)&buffer,
                    (UINT FAR *)&bytes)) {
                lstrcpy(data, (char far *)buffer);
                GetDlgItem(ID_VER_ORIG_FILENAME)->SetWindowText(data);
            }

            // The File Description name for this file

            wsprintf(name, "\\StringFileInfo\\%04x%04x\\FileDescription",
                    LOWORD(*translation), HIWORD(*translation));

            if (VerQueryValue(block, name, (VOID FAR * FAR *)&buffer,
                    (UINT FAR *)&bytes)) {
                lstrcpy(data, (char far *)buffer);
                GetDlgItem(ID_VER_FILE_DESC)->SetWindowText(data);
```

```
        }

        // The File Version for this file

        wsprintf(name, "\\StringFileInfo\\%04x%04x\\FileVersion",
                LOWORD(*translation), HIWORD(*translation));

        if (VerQueryValue(block, name, (VOID FAR * FAR *)&buffer,
                (UINT FAR *)&bytes)) {
            lstrcpy(data, (char far *)buffer);
            GetDlgItem(ID_VER_FILE_VERSION)->SetWindowText(data);
        }

        // The Internal Name for this file

        wsprintf(name, "\\StringFileInfo\\%04x%04x\\InternalName",
                LOWORD(*translation), HIWORD(*translation));

        if (VerQueryValue(block, name, (VOID FAR * FAR *)&buffer,
                (UINT FAR *)&bytes)) {
            lstrcpy(data, (char far *)buffer);
            GetDlgItem(ID_VER_INTERNAL_NAME)->SetWindowText(data);
        }

        // The Product Name for this file

        wsprintf(name, "\\StringFileInfo\\%04x%04x\\ProductName",
                LOWORD(*translation), HIWORD(*translation));

        if (VerQueryValue(block, name, (VOID FAR * FAR *)&buffer,
                (UINT FAR *)&bytes)) {
            lstrcpy(data, (char far *)buffer);
            GetDlgItem(ID_VER_PRODUCT_NAME)->SetWindowText(data);
        }

        }
    }
    UpdateData();

}
```

8. Select the IDC_BUTTON1 object from the object list and the BN_CLICKED message from the message list in ClassWizard. Select the Add Function button and give the new function the name OnBrowse. Enter the following code into the OnBrowse function of CVersionDlg:

```
void CVersionDlg::OnBrowse()
{
    // Put up a file open dialog

    static char szFilter[] = "DLLs (*.dll) | *.DLL | Executables
(*.exe) | *.exe | All Files (*.*) | *.* ||";
    CFileDialog dlg ( TRUE, "DLL", NULL, OFN_HIDEREADONLY, szFilter,
                this );

    if ( dlg.DoModal() == IDOK ) {
```

continued on next page

continued from previous page

```
        GetDlgItem(IDC_EDIT1)->SetWindowText ( dlg.GetPathName() );
    }
}
```

9. Add a new menu item to the SysInfo menu using AppStudio. Call the menu item File Version Info and give it the identifier ID_FILE_VERSION_INFO. Using ClassWizard, select the CMainFrame object in the drop-down list. Select the ID_FILE_VERSION_INFO identifier from the object list and the COMMAND message from the message list. Click on the Add Function button. Accept the OnFileVersionInfo as the method name for the function.

10. Add the following code to the OnFileVersionInfo method:

```
void CMainFrame::OnFileVersionInfo()
{
    CVersionDlg dlg;
    dlg.DoModal();
}
```

11. Add the following line to the MAINFRM.CPP file after the #include "stdafx.h" line:

```
#include "versiond.h"
```

12. Compile and run the application.

How It Works

When the user selects the File Version Info menu item from the menu, the dialog is launched. When the user enters a file name into the edit box and clicks on the Inspect button, several other things occur.

First, the GetFileVersionInfoSize function is called. This function will find out how big a buffer is required to hold all of the information in the VERSIONINFO resource for the specified file. What the function is really doing is opening the file, seeking to the start of the version information in the file, and reading the size of the header for the resource. The size of the actual resource is stored internally in this structure. This number is then returned to the caller. Note that if there is no version information or if the file does not exist, 0 will be returned by GetFileVersionInfoSize.

Next, the function GetFileVersionInfo is called. This function actually loads the block of version information out of the file and into the buffer, copying at most the number of bytes specified by the GetFileVersionInfoSize function. This block is in a "raw" state. This means that it is not a simple structure to access, but rather a complex variable-sized buffer of data.

The VerQueryValue function uses that raw information to extract pieces out by name. The function accepts the buffer that was obtained by the GetFileVersionInfo function and a name of a "block" of data to extract. The data is then stored in the user-supplied buffer. The first time the VerQueryValue function is called, it is asking for a block called the \\VarFileInfo\\Translation block. This information will be used to translate the other blocks found in the version resource. After specifying the translation table, the function is called again, this time with a string represented by the expression:

```
wsprintf(name, "\\StringFileInfo\\%04x%04x\\ProductVersion",
    LOWORD(*translation), HIWORD(*translation));.
```

This function call makes a new "key" for the version block, which represents the ProductVersion key entry using the translation obtained in the first call.

The buffer returned by the second and succeeding VerQueryValue function calls is the actual information stored in the version resource, which is displayed on the screen.

CHAPTER 2
FILES AND DIRECTORIES

FILES AND DIRECTORIES

How do I...

In earlier versions of Windows, most file and device functions were carried out using calls to DOS. In Windows 95, these functions are encapsulated in the Windows operating system. In this chapter you will learn the important disk and directory methods that make your application more robust and easier to use.

Table 2-1 lists the Windows 95 APIs covered in this chapter.

GetWindowsDirectory	GetSystemDirectory
GetTempPath	SetErrorMode
MessageBox	GetLastError
GetLogicalDrives	CopyFile
MoveFile	FillMemory
GetOpenFileName	GetSaveFileName
CreateDirectory	RemoveDirectory

 **Table 2-1** Windows APIs covered in Chapter 2

2.1   Find the Windows and System Directories

At some stage, almost all applications need to find out something about the environment in which they run. This How-To shows you the method of finding out the Windows directory, the System directory, and the temporary files directory.

2.2   Display My Own I/O Error Messages

If your application does anything more than the most simple file or device I/O, there will come a time when something goes wrong. Depending on the circumstances, it can be useful to handle hardware error messages within your application and supply the user with a message that makes sense to your application. In this How-To, you'll see how to stop the system from displaying the default error messages and how to replace them with your own.

2.3   Test Whether There Is a Disk in the Drive

Whether you are writing the definitive backup utility, producing your own installation program, or merely writing a few bytes to a disk, it makes sense to check that there is a disk in the drive before you do so. One means of achieving this is to access the drive and catch the error message, using the method described in How-To 2.2. However, Windows supplies a more elegant method of checking for a disk in a removable drive, and this How-To describes this method.

2.4   Copy Files Simply

Many programmers wish that there was a simpler method of copying files than spawning a DOS shell or writing a byte-by-byte copy function. The Windows 95 API provides two new functions for copying and renaming files. This How-To introduces you to these functions.

COMPLEXITY
EASY

2.1   How do I...
Find the Windows and System directories?

Problem

An application frequently needs to determine the location of files on a computer system. Many programmers simply hard-code the required directory locations within their applications. This can cause problems if a user has installed Windows to directories other than the defaults. In addition, many network setups may store the System directory on a shared file server. As a programmer, you need a way to determine the location of these directories.

Technique

The Windows 95 API provides a number of directory-oriented functions. The sample application discussed here uses three of the most useful ones. The GetWindowsDirectory function returns the location of the Windows directory. The GetSystemDirectory function returns the path of the Windows System directory, and the GetTempPath function is used to determine the best place to store temporary files.

Note that although all three of these functions take the same parameters, the order of the parameters is reversed in the newer GetTempPath function.

Steps

Open and run the WINDIR.EXE example application. You will find this application in the CHAPTER2\WINDIR directory on the CD that accompanies this book. This small application opens a single dialog box. It displays the Windows directory, the System directory, and the temporary path. Figure 2-1 shows this dialog.

Follow these steps to reproduce this sample application:

1. Create a working directory for this exercise called WINDIR. You will use this directory to hold all the source files for this application.

2. You will also need an icon for this application. Copy the file APP.ICO from the CHAPTER2\WINDIR directory on the CD into your working directory. Alternatively, if you do not have access to a CD-ROM drive, you can use a resource editor to create the icon. Create a 32-by-32-pixel icon with 16 colors or less. Save the icon as WINDIR.ICO.

3. Now create the resource file for the example application. The resource file includes the application icon and defines the dialog that will be displayed when the application is run. Use a text editor to create a new file and call it WINDIR.RC. Type the following text into this file:

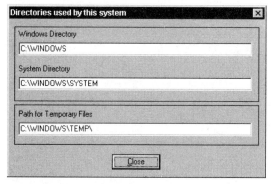

Figure 2-1 Displaying the Windows and System directories and temporary paths

```
/* ------------------------------------------------------------------ */
/*                                                                    */
/* MODULE: WINDIR.RC                                                  */
/* PURPOSE: Defines the dialog and application icon for the sample.   */
/*                                                                    */
/* ------------------------------------------------------------------ */

#include <windows.h>
#include "windir.rh"

IDD_WINDIRMAIN DIALOG 6, 15, 262, 144
STYLE DS_MODALFRAME | DS_3DLOOK | WS_POPUP | WS_VISIBLE |
      WS_CAPTION | WS_SYSMENU
CAPTION "Directories used by this system"
FONT 8, "MS Sans Serif"
{
    DEFPUSHBUTTON "&Close", IDOK, 106, 124, 50, 14
    CONTROL "", -1, "static", SS_BLACKFRAME | WS_CHILD | WS_VISIBLE,
           5, 7, 251, 69
    LTEXT "Windows Directory", -1, 9, 9, 90, 8
    EDITTEXT IDE_WINDOWSDIR, 9, 21, 240, 12, ES_AUTOHSCROLL | ES_READONLY |
           WS_BORDER | WS_TABSTOP
    LTEXT "System Directory", -1, 9, 41, 90, 8
    EDITTEXT IDE_SYSTEMDIR, 9, 53, 240, 12, ES_AUTOHSCROLL | ES_READONLY |
           WS_BORDER | WS_TABSTOP
    CONTROL "", -1, "static", SS_BLACKFRAME | WS_CHILD | WS_VISIBLE,
           5, 79, 251, 37
    LTEXT "Path for Temporary Files", -1, 9, 83, 90, 8
    EDITTEXT IDE_TEMPPATH, 9, 95, 240, 12, ES_AUTOHSCROLL | ES_READONLY |
           WS_BORDER | WS_TABSTOP
}

IDI_WINDIR ICON "windir.ico"
```

4. The next file that you will need to create is called WINDIR.RH. The following code defines the numbers and identifier values of the resource components, so that the dialog, icon, and edit controls can be referred to from within the application. Type the following code into a new file and save it as WINDIR.RH:

```
#ifndef __WINDIR_RH
/* ------------------------------------------------------------------ */
/*                                                                    */
/* MODULE: WINDIR.RH                                                  */
/* PURPOSE: Defines resource identifiers for the application.         */
/*                                                                    */
/* ------------------------------------------------------------------ */

// Our application icon.
#define IDI_WINDIR        201

// The dialog and its control IDs.
#define IDD_WINDIRMAIN    1001
#define IDE_WINDOWSDIR    101
#define IDE_SYSTEMDIR     102
#define IDE_TEMPPATH      104

#endif
```

5. Create a new file and call it WINDIR.C. Type the following code fragment at the top of this file. This code fragment includes the Windows header files and the resource header file that you created in step 3. It also defines the pre-processor symbol STRICT, which causes the Windows files to enforce strict type checking of menu and window handles.

```
/* ----------------------------------------------------------------- */
/*                                                                   */
/* MODULE: WINDIR.C                                                  */
/* PURPOSE: This C program demonstrates Windows 95 API calls which   */
/*          can be used to find out the location of the Windows,     */
/*          System, and Temp directories.                           */
/*                                                                   */
/* ----------------------------------------------------------------- */

#define STRICT
#include <windows.h>
#include <winnt.h>
#include <stdlib.h>
#include "windir.rh"
```

6. Now add the SetupDialog function. This function will be called in response to the WM_INITDIALOG message that is sent when a dialog is created. This function calls GetWindowsDirectory to retrieve the path of the Windows directory. The code passes a buffer to receive the path and specifies the maximum size of the buffer, in this case using the MAX_PATH constant that is defined by Windows.

The next function call is to the GetSystemDirectory function, using the same parameters to retrieve the name of the Windows System directory. Finally, the code calls the GetTempPath function to retrieve the name of a directory for temporary files. Notice that in this function the order of the buffer and size arguments are reversed. The three path names are placed into read-only edit controls within the dialog.

```
/* ----------------------------------------------------------------- */
/* This little function demonstrates our API routines. It calls the  */
/* GetWindowsDirectory() function, the GetSystemDirectory() function,*/
/* and the GetTempPath() function. Note that the arguments for the   */
/* latter are in the opposite order to the first two. All three      */
/* functions return the length the string, or 0 if they fail. If     */
/* the length of the string is greater than the size of the buffer   */
/* supplied, the functions return the length of the buffer required. */
/* We use MAX_PATH to make sure that the buffer is large enough.     */
/* ----------------------------------------------------------------- */
void SetupDialog(HWND hWnd)
{
    char *dirbuf;
    UINT  size;

    if ((dirbuf = malloc(MAX_PATH)) == NULL)
        return;
```

continued on next page

continued from previous page

```
    if (((size = GetWindowsDirectory(dirbuf,MAX_PATH)) != 0) && (size
        < MAX_PATH))
        SetDlgItemText(hWnd,IDE_WINDOWSDIR,dirbuf);

    if (((size = GetSystemDirectory(dirbuf,MAX_PATH)) != 0) && (size
        < MAX_PATH))
        SetDlgItemText(hWnd,IDE_SYSTEMDIR,dirbuf);

    if (((size = GetTempPath(MAX_PATH,dirbuf)) != 0) && (size
        < MAX_PATH))
        SetDlgItemText(hWnd,IDE_TEMPPATH,dirbuf);

    free(dirbuf);
}
```

7. Now add the HandleDialog function. This is a callback function that receives
messages sent to the dialog and processes them. It handles the WM_INITDIA-
LOG message to initialize the dialog, calling SetupDialog. The code also
responds to the WM_COMMAND message IDCLOSE, which is generated
when the user clicks the Close button. Finally, the code responds to a closing
dialog by shutting down the application.

```
/* ------------------------------------------------------------- */
/*  This function receives messages for the Dialog box. It processes */
/*  the WM_INITDIALOG message, and the ID_CLOSE dialog message.    */
/* ------------------------------------------------------------- */
BOOL CALLBACK HandleDialog(HWND hWnd, UINT message,
                           WPARAM wparam, LPARAM lparam)
{
    switch (message)
    {
        case WM_INITDIALOG:
                SetupDialog(hWnd);
                return TRUE;
        case WM_COMMAND:
                if (wparam == IDOK)
                {
                    DestroyWindow(hWnd);
                    return TRUE;
                }
                break;
        case WM_CLOSE:
                DestroyWindow(hWnd);
                return TRUE;
        case WM_DESTROY:
                PostQuitMessage(0);
                return TRUE;
    }
    return FALSE;
}
```

8. The final piece of code to add is the WinMain function. In a traditional C program such as this, the WinMain function is the entry point for the application.
This function creates and displays the dialog and processes messages until the

application is closed. Once you have added this code to the source file, you can compile and test the application.

```
/* ---------------------------------------------------------------- */
/* Our main function - set up and run the application.              */
/* ---------------------------------------------------------------- */
int PASCAL WinMain(HINSTANCE hInstance, HINSTANCE hPrevInstance,
                   LPSTR lpCmdLine, int nCmdShow)
{
    MSG  msg;
    HWND hWnd;

    if ((hWnd = CreateDialog(hInstance,
                             MAKEINTRESOURCE(IDD_WINDIRMAIN),
                             NULL,(DLGPROC)HandleDialog)) == NULL)
        return FALSE;

    while (GetMessage(&msg,NULL,0,0))
        if (!IsDialogMessage(hWnd, &msg))
        {
            TranslateMessage(&msg);
            DispatchMessage(&msg);
        }

    return msg.wParam;
}
```

9. Compile and run the application.

Comments

It is important to use the Windows directory system carefully. Applications are not encouraged to place any files in the Windows directory. Dynamic link libraries and other shared files can be placed into the System directory, but you will need network privileges to do this if the directory is stored on a network disk. Instead, you should place shared files into the Common Files directory that is defined in the registry. Private or application-specific files should be placed in a System subdirectory beneath the application's home directory. The registry functions described in Chapter 1 provide a mechanism to access the wealth of system and application location information stored in the Windows registry.

COMPLEXITY
EASY

2.2 How do I...
Display my own I/O error messages?

Problem

I would like to stop the system from displaying the default messages for I/O hardware errors and handle the errors within my application instead. Is there an easy way to display my own messages?

Technique

The Windows API function SetErrorMode allows applications to control whether hardware error messages are displayed. If your application calls an I/O function and an error occurs, Windows normally warns the user and asks what action to take before the function returns to your application. Figure 2-2 shows this taking place as the user tries to access a drive without a floppy disk using the Windows Explorer. By telling Windows not to handle critical errors, your application can force such function calls to fail without displaying a dialog, and it can interpret the error code returned.

Steps

Open and run the GETERRS.EXE application. You can find this application in the CHAPTER2\GETERRS directory on the CD that comes with this book. The application displays a list of available disk drives in a list box. When you double-click on a drive, or click the Write File button, the application attempts to create a file in the root directory of that drive. If the Handle Errors check box is unchecked, error handling is left to Windows. Attempting to write to a write-protected disk, or to a floppy disk drive with no disk in it, will display an error message generated by Windows 95.

Now check the Handle Errors check box and click the Write File button again. This time, any errors are handled directly by the application, and a message will be displayed such as that shown in Figure 2-3.

You can experiment with different error conditions by running the application with no disk in the drive, using a full disk, a write-protected disk, or an unformatted disk.

Figure 2-2 Standard Windows error message box

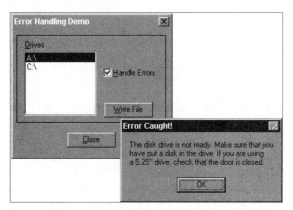

Figure 2-3 Error message caught by the application

The application will use SetErrorMode and handle its own errors, depending on whether the Handle Errors check box is checked or not.

Follow these steps to build this example application:

1. Create a new directory and call it GETERRS. Use this directory as your working directory while developing this application.

2. Now create the resource script for this application. Use a text editor to create a new file and call it GETERRS.RC. Add the following code. This resource script defines the menu and icon for the application.

```
/* ------------------------------------------------------------------ */
/*                                                                    */
/* MODULE: GETERRS.RC                                                 */
/* PURPOSE: Resource script for use in the GETERRS application.       */
/*          The application uses SetErrorMode to control the display  */
/*          of errors.                                                */
/*                                                                    */
/* ------------------------------------------------------------------ */

#include <windows.h>
#include "geterrs.rh"

IDD_TESTDIALOG DIALOG 6, 15, 162, 119
STYLE DS_MODALFRAME | DS_3DLOOK | WS_POPUP | WS_VISIBLE |
      WS_CAPTION | WS_SYSMENU
CAPTION "Error Handling Demo"
FONT 8, "MS Sans Serif"
{
    CONTROL "", -1, "static", SS_BLACKFRAME | WS_CHILD | WS_VISIBLE,
            3, 6, 154, 81
    LTEXT "&Drives", -1, 12, 11, 34, 8
    LISTBOX IDL_DRIVELIST, 12, 23, 73, 59, LBS_STANDARD | WS_TABSTOP
    AUTOCHECKBOX "&Handle Errors", IDC_HANDLEERRORS, 93, 35, 60, 12
    DEFPUSHBUTTON "&Write File", IDTEST, 94, 68, 50, 14
    PUSHBUTTON "&Close", IDCLOSE, 56, 96, 50, 14
}

IDI_ERRICON ICON "geterrs.ico"
```

55

3. You will need an icon file for the application. If you have a CD-ROM drive, copy the file GETERRS.ICO from the CHAPTER2\GETERRS directory on the CD. If you don't have a CD drive, you can use a resource editor to create a 32-by-32-pixel icon and save it as GETERRS.ICO in the working directory.

4. The resource script that you have created refers to an include file, GETERRS.RH. This file contains resource definitions of the menu items so that they can be used by the resource script, and also within the application source code. Create a new file and save it as GETERRS.RH. Place the following definitions into this file:

```
#ifndef __GETERRS_RH
/* ------------------------------------------------------------ */
/*                                                              */
/* MODULE: GETERRS.RH                                           */
/* PURPOSE: Defines resource identifiers.                       */
/*                                                              */
/* ------------------------------------------------------------ */
#define __GETERRS_RH

#define IDD_TESTDIALOG      200
#define IDC_HANDLEERRORS    101
#define IDL_DRIVELIST       102
#define IDTEST              103
#define IDCLOSE             104

#define IDI_ERRICON         201

#endif // not __GETERRS_RH.
```

5. Now create the main C source file for the application. This example program is written in straight C, so it should compile with most C and C++ compilers. Create a new file called GETERRS.C and insert the following code at the top of the file. This code includes the files necessary to compile a Windows application. In addition, it defines the name of the test file and two lines of text to be written to the file.

```
/* ------------------------------------------------------------ */
/*                                                              */
/* MODULE: GETERRS.C                                            */
/* PURPOSE: This C program demonstrates a method of avoiding the */
/*          default system display of critical errors, and receiving */
/*          the results in the application instead. The application */
/*          uses SetErrorMode to control the display of errors.  */
/*                                                              */
/* ------------------------------------------------------------ */
/*                                                              */
/* Copyright © 1995, Andrew Cooke. All rights reserved.         */
/*                                                              */
/* ------------------------------------------------------------ */

#define STRICT
#include <windows.h>
```

```
#include <winnt.h>
#include <windowsx.h>
#include <stdio.h>
#include "geterrs.rh"

static char *FileNameToWrite = "x:TestFile.txt";
static char *DataToWrite = "Sample data file\r\n"
                           "Created by GETERRS example\n"
                           "application\r\n";
```

6. Add the following code to the same file. The DisplayErrorMessages function
interprets the error code supplied into a string for display and looks for the
errors commonly encountered when writing to a file. The final condition of
the switch statement handles all errors that are not specifically recognized
with a default error message.

```
/* ------------------------------------------------------------- */
/* This function displays a dialog with an error message. It uses a */
/* large switch statement to generate useful messages for a group  */
/* of common I/O errors.                                           */
/* ------------------------------------------------------------- */
void DisplayErrorMessages(HWND hParent, DWORD errorCode)
{
    char *errMsg;

    switch (errorCode)
    {
        case ERROR_WRITE_PROTECT:
        case ERROR_ACCESS_DENIED:
            errMsg = "The disk that you have inserted is\n"
                     "write-protected. Move the write-protect\n"
                     "tab and reinsert the disk.";
            break;
        case ERROR_BAD_DEVICE:
        case ERROR_BAD_UNIT:
        case ERROR_INVALID_DRIVE:
            errMsg = "The requested disk device does not appear to\n"
                     "be available. Perhaps the device is not\n"
                     "properly installed on your system.";
            break;
        case ERROR_CRC:
        case ERROR_SECTOR_NOT_FOUND:
            errMsg = "A CRC error was encountered when writing to\n"
                     "the disk. Please use ScanDisk to check the\n"
                     "surface of this disk for errors.";
            break;
        case ERROR_DISK_CHANGE:
        case ERROR_FILE_INVALID:
        case ERROR_WRONG_DISK:
            errMsg = "You appear to have changed the disk while\n"
                     "this application had a file open on it.";
            break;
        case ERROR_DISK_CORRUPT:
        case ERROR_FLOPPY_UNKNOWN_ERROR:
        case ERROR_GEN_FAILURE:
```

continued on next page

continued from previous page

```
                    case ERROR_NOT_DOS_DISK:
                        errMsg = "This disk does not appear to be formatted. Use\n"
                                 "Explorer to format the disk, or insert \n"
                                 "another disk.";
                        break;
                    case ERROR_DISK_FULL:
                    case ERROR_HANDLE_DISK_FULL:
                        errMsg = "There is no room on this disk to write any more\n"
                                 "data. Please insert another disk.";
                        break;
                    case ERROR_NOT_READY:
                        errMsg = "The disk drive is not ready. Make sure that you\n"
                                 "have put a disk in the drive. If you are using\n"
                                 "a 5.25\" drive, check that the door is closed.";
                        break;
                    default:
                        errMsg = "The application caught an error message which\n"
                                 "there is not an explanation for. A complete\n"
                                 "example would handle this instance.";
                        break;
                }
                MessageBox(hParent,errMsg,"Error Caught!",MB_OK);
            }
```

7. Now add the TestFileIO function to the file. This code attempts to write a small text file to the selected drive. The code first looks to see if the Handle Errors check box is currently checked. If it is, the code calls SetErrorMode with the SEM_FAILCRITICALERRORS argument. This suppresses the display of error messages by Windows and causes the I/O routines to return an error instead. The old mode is saved in the variable oldErrorState so that it can be restored afterwards.

The function then attempts to open, write, and close a file on the selected drive. The drive letter is retrieved from the list box. If an error is encountered while the default error handling is turned off, this function uses GetLastError to retrieve a numeric error code, then displays the result by calling DisplayErrorMessages.

```
/* -------------------------------------------------------------- */
/* This function attempts to write a few lines to a file on the    */
/* specified disk drive. It retrieves the error code (if any). If  */
/* the handleErrors argument is non-zero, the function uses the    */
/* SetErrorMode API function to SEM_FAILCRITICALERRORS, and displays */
/* a message box depending upon the result of the I/O functions.   */
/* -------------------------------------------------------------- */
void TestFileIO(HWND hWnd)
{
    UINT    oldErrorState;
    BOOL    handleErrors, hadErrors;
    DWORD   errorCode;
    char    fileName[14], filePath[8];
    int     selItem;
    FILE    *fileHandle;
```

```
// Find out if we should handle errors or not.
handleErrors = SendDlgItemMessage(hWnd,IDC_HANDLEERRORS,
                                  BM_GETCHECK,0,0);

// Disable the default Windows error handler, if required.
if (handleErrors)
    oldErrorState = SetErrorMode(SEM_FAILCRITICALERRORS);

// Make up the file name to open.
selItem = SendDlgItemMessage(hWnd,IDL_DRIVELIST,
                             LB_GETCURSEL,0,0);
if (selItem == LB_ERR)
    MessageBox(hWnd,"Please select a drive to write to.",
               "Warning",MB_OK | MB_ICONEXCLAMATION);
SendDlgItemMessage(hWnd,IDL_DRIVELIST,LB_GETTEXT,
                   selItem,(LPARAM)filePath);
lstrcpy(fileName,FileNameToWrite);
fileName[0] = filePath[0];

// Attempt to open and write to a file.
hadErrors = FALSE;
fileHandle = fopen(fileName,"wt");
if (fileHandle)
{
    if (fwrite(DataToWrite,1,lstrlen(DataToWrite),fileHandle) == 1)
        hadErrors = (fclose(fileHandle) != 0);
}
else
    hadErrors = TRUE;

// Test for errors.
if ((hadErrors) && (handleErrors))
{
    errorCode = GetLastError();
    DisplayErrorMessages(hWnd,errorCode);
}

if (!hadErrors)
    MessageBox(hWnd,"File written successfully.",
               "No Errors",MB_ICONINFORMATION | MB_OK);

// Restore the original error mode.
if (handleErrors)
    SetErrorMode(oldErrorState);
}
```

8. Now add the SetupDialog function to the same source file. This code uses the
GetLogicalDrives API function to retrieve a DWORD mask that defines what
drives are available on this system. The first 26 bits in the value each correspond
to a drive. A bit is set (1) if that drive is available and clear, (0) if the drive is not
available. The code iterates through the DWORD mask and generates a string
for each valid drive, such as "A:\". The strings are inserted into the list box.

```
/* ------------------------------------------------------------------ */
/* The SetupDialog function is called in response to the              */
/* WM_INITDIALOG message. It uses GetLogicalDrives() to retrieve a     */
/* mask specifying the available drives, then converts that mask to    */
/* strings, placing each string into the list box.                    */
/* ------------------------------------------------------------------ */
static void SetupDialog(HWND hWnd)
{
    char    driveString[8];
    DWORD   drives;
    int     i;
    HWND    hWndList;

    // Get a handle to the list box.
    hWndList = GetDlgItem(hWnd,IDL_DRIVELIST);

    // Retrieve a mask of drives.
    drives = GetLogicalDrives();

    // Test 26 bits in the mask, to see if those drives are available.
    for (i = 0; i < 26; i++)
        if (drives & (1L << i))
        {
            wsprintf(driveString,"%c:\\",i + 'A');
            SendMessage(hWndList,LB_ADDSTRING,0,(LPARAM)driveString);
        }
}
```

9. The HandleDialog function receives messages that are sent to the dialog box. In response to WM_INITDIALOG, it retrieves the list of drives and displays them in the list box. In response to the IDCLOSE message sent when the Close button is clicked, this function stores the selected drive letter and closes the dialog. The code responds to the IDTEST message, or a double-click notification from the list box, by calling the TestFileIO function that you added previously.

```
/* ------------------------------------------------------------------ */
/* This callback function handles the messages sent to the dialog.    */
/* ------------------------------------------------------------------ */
LRESULT CALLBACK HandleDialog(HWND hWnd, UINT message,
                              WPARAM wParam, LPARAM lParam)
{
    UINT notifycode, idcode;

    switch (message)
    {
        case WM_INITDIALOG:
            SetupDialog(hWnd);
            return TRUE;
        case WM_COMMAND:
            idcode = GET_WM_COMMAND_ID(wParam,lParam);
            notifycode = GET_WM_COMMAND_CMD(wParam,lParam);
```

```
                    if (idcode == IDCLOSE)
                    {
                        DestroyWindow(hWnd);
                        return TRUE;
                    }
                    else
                        if ((idcode == IDTEST) ||
                            ((idcode == IDL_DRIVELIST) &&
                             (notifycode == LBN_DBLCLK)))
                        {
                            TestFileIO(hWnd);
                            return TRUE;
                        }
                    break;
            case WM_DESTROY:
                    PostQuitMessage(0);
                    return TRUE;
        }
        return FALSE;
}
```

10. Finally, add the WinMain function to the file. This function creates and displays
the dialog, then processes messages until the application is closed. Once you
have added this code, you can compile and test the application.

```
/* ---------------------------------------------------------------- */
/* The Windows entry point of the application. Initialize the dialog */
/* and process messages until the application is closed.             */
/* ---------------------------------------------------------------- */
int PASCAL WinMain(HINSTANCE hInstance, HINSTANCE hPrevInstance,
                   LPSTR lpCmdLine, int nCmdShow)
{
    MSG   msg;
    HWND  hWnd;

    if ((hWnd = CreateDialog(hInstance,
                             MAKEINTRESOURCE(IDD_TESTDIALOG),
                             NULL,(DLGPROC)HandleDialog)) == NULL)
        return FALSE;

    while (GetMessage(&msg,NULL,0,0))
        if (!IsDialogMessage(hWnd, &msg))
        {
            TranslateMessage(&msg);
            DispatchMessage(&msg);
        }

    return msg.wParam;
}
```

11. Compile and run the application.

Comments

The SetErrorMode API provides a useful mechanism for replacing the default system messages with your own and, more importantly, for changing your application's behavior to help the user deal with problems. If you are displaying your own error messages, it is important that the messages are specific enough and in clear enough language for users to understand.

COMPLEXITY
EASY

2.3   How do I...
Test whether there is a disk in the drive?

Problem

Before writing to a floppy disk, I would like my application to check that the user has put a disk into the drive. Is there any way to accomplish this without Windows telling the user that there is no disk in the drive?

Technique

The easiest way to find out if there is a disk in a drive is to access the drive. This is fine, but you will get a message from Windows if there is no disk in the drive, or if the disk is not formatted. To avoid this, you can frame your access attempt by calls to the SetErrorMode API function. Use the SEM_FAILCRITICALERRORS argument to turn off the message box that Windows displays, and instead, retrieve the error code using GetLastError.

The example application that you will see shortly also makes use of the GetLogicalDrives function to retrieve a list of drives. It then displays this list in the dialog for you to select from. The GetLogicalDrives function returns a DWORD with a bit for each of the 26 possible drive letters. If a bit is set in the return value, there is a drive with that letter on the computer. For instance, if bit 0 is set, the A: drive exists, and bit 3 being set tells you that the C: drive exists.

Steps

Open and run the DISKRDY application. You will find this application in the CHAPTER2\DISKRDY directory on the CD that comes with this book. A dialog should appear, containing a list of logical disk drives. Click on any drive and click the Test Drive button. The application will display a message box indicating whether any media was detected in that drive. Figure 2-4 shows this application in action.

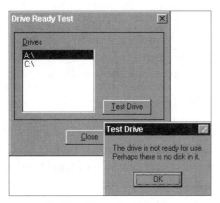

Figure 2-4 Testing whether there is a
disk in the drive

The following steps will show you how to implement this example application. Along
the way, you will learn how to find out the available drives and how you can tell if there
is a disk in the drive.

1. Create a new directory and call it DISKRDY. Use this directory to hold the
source files while you build this application.

2. Next, create the resource script that defines the dialog used in this application.
Use a text editor to create a new file and call it DISKRDY.RC. Add the following lines of code to the file:

```
/* -------------------------------------------------------------- */
/*                                                                */
/* MODULE: DISKRDY.RC                                             */
/* PURPOSE: This resource script defines the dialog and icon.     */
/*                                                                */
/* -------------------------------------------------------------- */

#include <windows.h>
#include "diskrdy.rh"

IDD_DISKRDYMAIN DIALOG 6, 15, 162, 119
STYLE DS_MODALFRAME | DS_3DLOOK | WS_POPUP | WS_VISIBLE |
      WS_CAPTION | WS_SYSMENU
CAPTION "Drive Ready Test"
FONT 8, "MS Sans Serif"
{
    CONTROL "", -1, "static", SS_BLACKFRAME | WS_CHILD | WS_VISIBLE,
            3, 6, 154, 81
    LTEXT "&Drives", -1, 12, 11, 34, 8
    LISTBOX IDL_DRIVELIST, 12, 23, 73, 59, LBS_STANDARD | WS_TABSTOP
    DEFPUSHBUTTON "&Test Drive", IDTEST, 94, 68, 50, 14
    PUSHBUTTON "&Close", IDCLOSE, 56, 96, 50, 14
```

continued on next page

continued from previous page

```
}
```

```
IDI_APPICON ICON "diskrdy.ico"
```

3. The resource script includes another file, DISKRDY.RH, that defines the identifier values of the dialog and controls. Use a text editor to create this file also, and enter the following definitions:

```
#ifndef __DISKRDY_RH
/* ------------------------------------------------------------------ */
/*                                                                    */
/* MODULE: DISKRDY.RH                                                 */
/* PURPOSE: Defines resource identifiers for use in the application. */
/*                                                                    */
/* ------------------------------------------------------------------ */
#define __DISKRDY_RH

#define IDD_DISKRDYMAIN         301
#define IDL_DRIVELIST           101
#define IDTEST                  102
#define IDCLOSE                 103

#define IDI_APPICON             302

#endif // not __DISKRDY_RH.
```

4. Now create the main source file for the application and save it as DISKRDY.C. Add the following code fragment to the top of this file. This code includes the Windows header files and also defines the preprocessor symbol STRICT, causing strict type checking to be enforced over the program's use of Windows handles and types.

```
/* ------------------------------------------------------------------ */
/*                                                                    */
/* MODULE: DISKRDY.C                                                  */
/* PURPOSE: This small application demonstrates how to test if there */
/*          is a formatted disk in the drive.                        */
/*                                                                    */
/* ------------------------------------------------------------------ */

#define STRICT
#include <windows.h>
#include <windowsx.h>
#include <io.h>
#include "diskrdy.rh"
```

5. Add the function SetupDialog to the same source file. This function will be called in response to the WM_INITDIALOG message that is sent when the dialog is first created. The code calls the GetLogicalDrives API function, then steps through the first 26 bits of the return code. If a bit is turned on (1), the drive letter (A to Z) is placed in the list box to be displayed.

```
/* ------------------------------------------------------------- */
/* The SetupDialog function is called in response to the         */
/* WM_INITDIALOG message. It uses GetLogicalDrives() to get a mask */
/* of available drives, then converts the mask to strings, placing */
/* each string in the list box.                                  */
/* ------------------------------------------------------------- */
static void SetupDialog(HWND hWnd)
{
    char    driveString[8];
    DWORD   drives;
    int     i;
    HWND    hWndList;

    // Get a handle to the list box.
    hWndList = GetDlgItem(hWnd,IDL_DRIVELIST);

    // Retrieve a mask of drives.
    drives = GetLogicalDrives();

    // Test 26 bits in the mask, to see if those drives are available.
    for (i = 0; i < 26; i++)
        if (drives & (1L << i))
        {
            wsprintf(driveString,"%c:\\",i + 'A');
            SendMessage(hWndList,LB_ADDSTRING,0,(LPARAM)driveString);
        }
}
```

6. Add the following code to the same file. Here is how it works: The
TestDriveReady function uses the C runtime library *access* function to test
whether the root directory of the specified drive is accessible. If the drive is
not accessible for some reason, access returns a non-zero code. Normally,
Windows will display a dialog if your application attempts to access a drive
that is not ready. To circumvent this, the following code calls the function
SetErrorMode before attempting to access the drive. The SEM_FAILCRITI-
CALERRORS flag causes Windows to fail operations when an error occurs,
without displaying an error message. This way, the application can test the
result of the access call and determine whether the drive is available or not
without any intervention from the user.

When you use SetErrorMode, you should always store the old error mode and
restore this when you have finished. This function stores the old mode in the
oldErrorMode variable and restores it with another call to SetErrorMode. The
code displays a message box to indicate whether it could access the drive or not.

```
/* ------------------------------------------------------------- */
/* The TestDriveReady function uses a DeviceIoControl API to test if */
/* the specified drive is ready. It puts up a message box to show  */
/* the result. If the user has not selected a list box item, they  */
/* are asked to.                                                  */
/* ------------------------------------------------------------- */
```

continued on next page

continued from previous page

```
void TestDriveReady(HWND hWnd)
{
    int     curItem;
    char    name[8];
    UINT    oldErrorMode;

    // Find the selected item in the listbox.
    if ((curItem = SendDlgItemMessage(hWnd,IDL_DRIVELIST,
                                      LB_GETCURSEL,0,0)) == LB_ERR)
    {
        MessageBox(hWnd,"You have not selected a drive to test.\n"
                        "Please select one of the drives in the\n"
                        "list, then choose Test Drive.",\n"
                        "Test Error",MB_OK);
        return;
    }

    // Retrieve the root directory path from the listbox.
    SendDlgItemMessage(hWnd,IDL_DRIVELIST,LB_GETTEXT,curItem,(LPARAM)name);

    // Turn on error handling.
    oldErrorMode = SetErrorMode(SEM_FAILCRITICALERRORS);

    // Use the C runtime library function access to check the drive.
    if (access(name,0) == 0)
        MessageBox(hWnd,"The drive is ready for use.\n",
                   "Test Drive",MB_OK);
    else
        MessageBox(hWnd,"The drive is not ready for use.\n"
                        "Perhaps there is no disk in it.",
                   "Test Drive",MB_OK);

    // Restore the old error mode.
    SetErrorMode(oldErrorMode);
}
```

7. Now add the following functions. The HandleDialog function handles messages sent to the dialog. In particular, it uses the WM_INITDIALOG message as its cue to set up the list of available drives. It also responds to the IDTEST and IDCLOSE command messages, testing the drive or closing the application.

The WinMain function is the main entry point of the application. This function creates and displays the dialog, then processes messages until the application is closed.

```
/* ----------------------------------------------------------------- */
/* This callback function handles the messages sent to the dialog.   */
/* ----------------------------------------------------------------- */
LRESULT CALLBACK HandleDialog(HWND hWnd, UINT message,
                              WPARAM wParam, LPARAM lParam)
{
    UINT notifycode, idcode;

    switch (message)
    {
```

TEST WHETHER THERE IS A DISK IN THE DRIVE?

```
        case WM_INITDIALOG:
                SetupDialog(hWnd);
                return TRUE;
        case WM_COMMAND:
                idcode = GET_WM_COMMAND_ID(wParam,lParam);
                notifycode = GET_WM_COMMAND_CMD(wParam,lParam);
                if (idcode == IDCLOSE)
                {
                    DestroyWindow(hWnd);
                    return TRUE;
                }
                else
                    if ((idcode == IDTEST) ||
                        ((idcode == IDL_DRIVELIST) &&
                         (notifycode == LBN_DBLCLK)))
                    {
                        TestDriveReady(hWnd);
                        return TRUE;
                    }
                break;
        case WM_DESTROY:
                PostQuitMessage(0);
                return TRUE;
    }
    return FALSE;
}



/* ------------------------------------------------------------------ */
/* The Windows entry point of the application. Initialize the dialog */
/* and process messages until the application is closed.             */
/* ------------------------------------------------------------------ */
int PASCAL WinMain(HINSTANCE hInstance, HINSTANCE hPrevInstance,
                   LPSTR lpCmdLine, int nCmdShow)
{
    MSG  msg;
    HWND hWnd;

    if ((hWnd = CreateDialog(hInstance,
                             MAKEINTRESOURCE(IDD_DISKRDYMAIN),
                             NULL,(DLGPROC)HandleDialog)) == NULL)
        return FALSE;

    while (GetMessage(&msg,NULL,0,0))
        if (!IsDialogMessage(hWnd, &msg))
        {
            TranslateMessage(&msg);
            DispatchMessage(&msg);
        }

    return msg.wParam;
}
```

8. You will need an icon file for the application. If you have a CD-ROM drive, copy the file DISKRDY.ICO from the CHAPTER2\DISKRDY directory on the CD. If you don't have a CD drive, you can use a resource editor to create a 32-by-32-pixel icon, and save it as DISKRDY.ICO in the working directory.

Comments

This How-To demonstrates a reasonably efficient method for checking that a drive is ready before attempting to use it. Future versions of Windows bring the promise of even better detection for such occasions. Windows NT implements a DeviceIoControl function, IOCTL_DISK_CHECK_VERIFY, that allows you to check the status of a drive transparently. Unfortunately, this Win32 functionality is not implemented in Windows 95. It remains to be seen whether it will arrive in the future.

COMPLEXITY
EASY

2.4 How do I...
Copy files simply?

Problem

I know that I can use the rename function in my language's runtime library to rename files, provided that the source and destination file names are on the same drive. How can I copy and move files from one disk to another, without having to write my own code?

Technique

Windows 95 provides two functions for copying and moving files. The CopyFile function creates a copy of a single file. The MoveFile function moves a file to another location and can also be used to rename a file. You can use MoveFile to move a file from one disk to another, for example, and to rename or move a directory and all its contents, provided that the destination is on the same disk.

Steps

Open and run the COPY application. Select the Copy File menu item from the File menu. The application will prompt you to choose the file to copy, using a standard Open File dialog box. You will then be prompted for the new name to copy the file to. This uses a standard File Save dialog box. You can choose to overwrite an existing file, or create a new file, provided that the file is not read-only or in a write-protected disk or directory. The file will then be copied. The application stops you from copying the file back on itself. Figure 2-5 demonstrates the application being used to copy a file.

Now choose the Move File menu item from the File menu. The application will prompt you for the source and destination files as before. In this case, the file will be moved or renamed, and the file with the old name will have disappeared. You can use the Explorer to verify that the application has performed as you expect.

Follow these steps to reproduce this example application:

1. Start by creating a working directory for this application. Call the directory COPY. Use this directory to hold all the source files while you build this application.

2. Now define the dialog for the application. Use a text editor to create a new file and call it COPY.RC. Add the following resource script to the file:

```
/* ------------------------------------------------------------------ */
/*                                                                    */
/* MODULE: COPY.RC                                                    */
/* PURPOSE: Resource script for use in the COPY application.          */
/*          Supplies the menu and the application icon.               */
/*                                                                    */
/* ------------------------------------------------------------------ */


#include <windows.h>
#include "copy.rh"

IDM_COPYMENU MENU
{
    POPUP "&File"
    {
        MENUITEM "&Copy File", CM_FILECOPY
        MENUITEM "&Move File", CM_FILEMOVE
        MENUITEM SEPARATOR
        MENUITEM "E&xit", CM_EXIT
    }
}


IDI_COPY ICON "copy.ico"
```

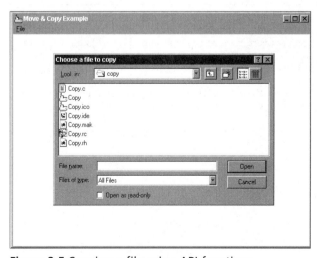

Figure 2-5 Copying a file using API functions

3. You will need an include file that defines the identifiers used in the resource
script. This file will also be used by the main source code to refer to the dialog
and its controls. Create a new file called COPY.RH. Type the following definitions into this file:

```
#ifndef __COPY_RH
/* ------------------------------------------------------------------- */
/*                                                                     */
/* MODULE: COPY.RH                                                     */
/* PURPOSE: Defines resource identifiers for use in the COPY          */
/*          application. The identifiers are used to display the      */
/*          menu and respond to commands, and to set the app icon.    */
/*                                                                     */
/* ------------------------------------------------------------------- */
#define __COPY_RH

#define IDM_COPYMENU    201
#define CM_FILECOPY     101
#define CM_FILEMOVE     102
#define CM_EXIT         103

#define IDI_COPY        202

#endif // not __COPY_RH.
```

4. Now you are ready to create the main source file for the application. Create a
new file and save it as COPY.C. Add the following code to the top of the file.
This code includes the necessary Windows header files, then declares the filter
that will be used in the file dialogs. The filter requests "All Files" with the file
specification *.*. The filter string uses null characters (\0) to separate the
strings. The C compiler will add an extra null character onto the end of this
string when it is compiled. Two null characters in a row will tell the Windows
File dialog that the list of filters is at an end.

```
/* ------------------------------------------------------------------- */
/*                                                                     */
/* MODULE: COPY.C                                                      */
/* PURPOSE: This application demonstrates the use of two Windows API  */
/*          functions. CopyFile copys a file from one name, device   */
/*          or directory to another. MoveFile renames a file, or     */
/*          directory, or moves the file or directory to another     */
/*          location. MoveFile can move files across devices, but    */
/*          cannot move directories across devices.                  */
/*                                                                     */
/* ------------------------------------------------------------------- */

#define STRICT
#include <windows.h>
#include <windowsx.h>
#include <commdlg.h>
#include "copy.rh"
```

```
static char *WindowClassName = "SampleCopyWindow";
static char *FilterStrings = "All Files\0*.*\0";
```

5. Now add the Copy function. This code initializes an OPENFILENAME structure and uses it to retrieve the old file name, oldName, from the user. It does this using the GetOpenFileName API function. It then reinitializes the same structure for use in the GetSaveFileName API call. This call retrieves the name for the destination file and stores it in newName.

Note that the structure used in the GetOpenFileName call only has the OFN_FILEMUSTEXIST flag set, while the flags used in the GetSaveFileName call specify that the path must exist and that users must be warned if they try to overwrite an existing file. The flags also specify that the file chosen must not be read-only or in a write-protected directory.

The code now calls the API function CopyFile, supplying the names of the source and destination files. The third fFailIfExists argument is set to FALSE, because the user will have already been warned if the destination file exists.

```
/* ---------------------------------------------------------------- */
/* This function uses GetOpenFileName and GetSaveFileName common    */
/* dialog box API functions to get the old and new names for the    */
/* file to copy. It then uses CopyFile to perform the operation. The*/
/* fFailIfExists argument is always set to FALSE, because the user  */
/* will have already been warned if an old file would be overwritten.*/
/* ---------------------------------------------------------------- */
void Copy(HWND hWnd)
{
    char            oldName[MAX_PATH], newName[MAX_PATH];
    char            extension[4];
    OPENFILENAME    ofn;

    oldName[0] = newName[0] = 0;
    FillMemory(&ofn,sizeof(OPENFILENAME),0);
    ofn.lStructSize = sizeof(OPENFILENAME);
    ofn.hwndOwner = hWnd;
    ofn.lpstrFilter = FilterStrings;
    ofn.nFilterIndex = 1;
    ofn.lpstrFile = oldName;
    ofn.nMaxFile = MAX_PATH;
    ofn.lpstrTitle = "Choose a file to copy";
    ofn.Flags = OFN_FILEMUSTEXIST;
    if (GetOpenFileName(&ofn))
    {
        lstrcpy(newName,oldName);
        if (ofn.nFileExtension)
            lstrcpy(extension,&oldName[ofn.nFileExtension]);
        else
            extension[0] = 0;
        FillMemory(&ofn,sizeof(OPENFILENAME),0);
        ofn.lStructSize = sizeof(OPENFILENAME);
        ofn.hwndOwner = hWnd;
        ofn.lpstrFilter = FilterStrings;
        ofn.nFilterIndex = 1;
```

continued on next page

continued from previous page

```
          ofn.lpstrFile = newName;
          ofn.nMaxFile = MAX_PATH;
          ofn.lpstrTitle = "Choose a name to copy the file to";
          if (extension[0])
              ofn.lpstrDefExt = extension;
          ofn.Flags = OFN_HIDEREADONLY | OFN_PATHMUSTEXIST |
          OFN_OVERWRITEPROMPT | OFN_NOREADONLYRETURN;
          if (GetSaveFileName(&ofn))
              if (lstrcmp(oldName,newName) != 0)
              {
                  if (MoveFile(oldName,newName,FALSE))
                      MessageBox(hWnd,"Copy completed",NULL,
                              MB_ICONINFORMATION | MB_OK);
                  else
                      MessageBox(hWnd,"Error during copy",NULL,
                              MB_ICONSTOP | MB_OK);
              }
              else
                  MessageBox(hWnd,"Old and new file names cannot\n"
                              "be the same.",
                              NULL,MB_ICONSTOP | MB_OK);
      }
}
```

6. The Move function that you will add next is very similar; the code for retrieving file names works in essentially the same way as that for the Copy function. An exception is that the source file name (retrieved using the GetOpenFileName API) must also not refer to a read-only file or a file in a write-protected directory. This is because the original file is removed by a call to MoveFile. The MoveFile function is then called. It takes the same arguments as the CopyFile function—the source name, a destination name, and a fFailIfExists flag. The flag is set to FALSE in this argument, because users will have already been warned if they attempt to overwrite an existing file.

```
/* ------------------------------------------------------------- */
/* This function uses GetOpenFileName and GetSaveFileName common  */
/* dialog box API functions to get the old and new names for the  */
/* file to copy. It then uses MoveFile to perform the operation. The*/
/* fFailIfExists argument is always set to FALSE, because the user */
/* will have already been warned if an old file would be overwritten.*/
/* Note that MoveFile can also be used to move directories (and all*/
/* their files and subdirectories in the same operation), providing*/
/* that the destination is on the same device.                    */
/* ------------------------------------------------------------- */
void Move(HWND hWnd)
{
    char         oldName[MAX_PATH], newName[MAX_PATH];
    char         extension[4];
    OPENFILENAME ofn;

    oldName[0] = newName[0] = 0;
    FillMemory(&ofn,sizeof(OPENFILENAME),0);
    ofn.lStructSize = sizeof(OPENFILENAME);
    ofn.hwndOwner = hWnd;
```

```
ofn.lpstrFilter = FilterStrings;
ofn.nFilterIndex = 1;
ofn.lpstrFile = oldName;
ofn.nMaxFile = MAX_PATH;
ofn.lpstrTitle = "Choose a file to move";
ofn.Flags = OFN_FILEMUSTEXIST | OFN_HIDEREADONLY |
OFN_NOREADONLYRETURN;
if (GetOpenFileName(&ofn))
{
    strcpy(newName,oldName);
    if (ofn.nFileExtension)
        lstrcpy(extension,&oldName[ofn.nFileExtension]);
    else
        extension[0] = 0;
    memset(&ofn,0,sizeof(OPENFILENAME));
    ofn.lStructSize = sizeof(OPENFILENAME);
    ofn.hwndOwner = hWnd;
    ofn.lpstrFilter = FilterStrings;
    ofn.nFilterIndex = 1;
    ofn.lpstrFile = newName;
    ofn.nMaxFile = MAX_PATH;
    ofn.lpstrTitle = "Choose a name to move the file to";
    if (extension[0])
        ofn.lpstrDefExt = extension;
    ofn.Flags = OFN_HIDEREADONLY | OFN_PATHMUSTEXIST |
OFN_OVERWRITEPROMPT | OFN_NOREADONLYRETURN;
    if (GetSaveFileName(&ofn))
        if (lstrcmp(oldName,newName) != 0)
        {
            if (MoveFile(oldName,newName,FALSE))
                MessageBox(hWnd,"Move completed",NULL,
                        MB_ICONINFORMATION | MB_OK);
            else
                MessageBox(hWnd,"Error during move",NULL,
                        MB_ICONSTOP | MB_OK);
        }
        else
            MessageBox(hWnd,"Old and new file names cannot\n"
                        "be the same.",
                    NULL,MB_ICONSTOP | MB_OK);
}
}
```

7. The next function to add is the MainWndProc function, which handles messages that are sent to the main window of the application. In particular, the code responds to the CM_FILECOPY and CM_FILEMOVE commands from the menu, calling Copy or Move functions as appropriate.

```
/* ------------------------------------------------------------- */
/* This callback function handles the messages for the window class. */
/* ------------------------------------------------------------- */
LRESULT CALLBACK MainWndProc(HWND hWnd, UINT message,
                        WPARAM wParam, LPARAM lParam)
{
    switch (message)
```

continued on next page

continued from previous page

```
        {
            case WM_COMMAND:
                switch(GET_WM_COMMAND_ID(wParam, lParam))
                {
                    case CM_EXIT:
                        DestroyWindow(hWnd);
                        break;
                    case CM_FILECOPY:
                        Copy(hWnd);
                        break;
                    case CM_FILEMOVE:
                        Move(hWnd);
                        break;
                    default:
                        break;
                }
                break;
            case WM_QUIT:
            case WM_DESTROY:
                PostQuitMessage(0);
                break;
            default:
                return (DefWindowProc(hWnd, message, wParam, lParam));
        }
        return 0;
}
```

8. Finally, add the framework functions for the application. These three functions set up and run the application. The InitApplication function registers the main window class and will be called only if a window of that class does not already exist. The InitInstance function creates and displays the main window. The final function, WinMain, is the entry point for this application. It calls the other functions to set up the application, then processes messages until the application is closed.

```
/* ---------------------------------------------------------------- */
/* Register the window class for the application's main window.    */
/* ---------------------------------------------------------------- */
BOOL InitApplication(HINSTANCE hInstance)
{
    WNDCLASS  wndClass;

    wndClass.style = 0;
    wndClass.lpfnWndProc = (WNDPROC)MainWndProc;
    wndClass.cbClsExtra = 0;
    wndClass.cbWndExtra = 0;
    wndClass.hInstance = hInstance;
    wndClass.hIcon = LoadIcon(hInstance,MAKEINTRESOURCE(IDI_COPY));
    wndClass.hCursor = LoadCursor(NULL, IDC_ARROW);
    wndClass.hbrBackground = (HBRUSH)(COLOR_WINDOW + 1);
    wndClass.lpszMenuName = MAKEINTRESOURCE(IDM_COPYMENU);
    wndClass.lpszClassName = WindowClassName;

    return (RegisterClass(&wndClass));
}
```

```
}
/* ------------------------------------------------------------------- */
/* Perform initialization specific to this instance of the            */
/* application. In this case, creation and display of the main window. */
/* ------------------------------------------------------------------- */
BOOL InitInstance(HINSTANCE hInstance, int nCmdShow)
{
    HWND   hWnd;

    // Create a main window for this instance of the application.
    hWnd = CreateWindow(WindowClassName,"Move & Copy Example",
                    WS_OVERLAPPEDWINDOW,CW_USEDEFAULT,CW_USEDEFAULT,
                    CW_USEDEFAULT,CW_USEDEFAULT,NULL,NULL,
                    hInstance,NULL);
    if (!hWnd)
        return FALSE;

    // Display the window and force it to be repainted.
    ShowWindow(hWnd, nCmdShow);
    UpdateWindow(hWnd);
    return TRUE;
}


/* ------------------------------------------------------------------- */
/* The main entry point for the application. This function starts      */
/* the application, then processes messages until it is closed.        */
/* ------------------------------------------------------------------- */
int PASCAL WinMain(HINSTANCE hInstance, HINSTANCE hPrevInstance,
                    LPSTR lpCmdLine, int nCmdShow)
{
    MSG msg;

    if (!FindWindow(WindowClassName,NULL))
        if (!InitApplication(hInstance))
            return FALSE;

    if (!InitInstance(hInstance, nCmdShow))
        return FALSE;

    // Loop, pumping messages.
    while (GetMessage(&msg,NULL,0,0))
    {
        TranslateMessage(&msg);
        DispatchMessage(&msg);
    }
    return msg.wParam;  // Return the value from PostQuitMessage.
}
```

Comments

With the CopyFile and MoveFile API functions, you can add advanced features to your application, providing functionality similar to that of the Windows Explorer. The MoveFile API does not support moving a directory to another device. To implement this feature, you would need to recurse through the directory structure to be moved, using CreateDirectory to create a destination directory, then using MoveFile to move each file within the directory. Once empty, the source directories could then be removed using the RemoveDirectory API function.

CHAPTER 3
APPLICATION AND TASK CONTROL

APPLICATION AND TASK CONTROL

How do I...

One of the hardest things for new Windows programmers to grasp is the concept that theirs is not the only program that the user is running at one time. Multitasking, and all of the joys associated with it, is one of the major bones of contention for beginning Windows programmers.

When you are within your own application, it is quite normal to expect others to use it as though it is the only application on the system. Most applications don't worry about the "outside" world, with the exception of dealing with the Windows Clipboard to copy text in and out or the Print Manager to spool a file off to the printer. Some programmers have grown accustomed to writing installation programs that require interfaces to the Program Manager; other programs need to be able to "launch" Windows Notepad or Windows Write to read and write user documentation.

It helps to think of Windows 95 as a "component-based" operating system or, sometimes, an "object-oriented" operating system. This is because of the large numbers of controls, utilities, and other programmatic devices available within Windows 95. Other programs, however, are as rich a source of functionality as Windows itself. Imagine launching a "zip" program to compress your files or a multimedia viewer to show the user an animated selection from your program. All these things are possible within the Windows operating environment.

Before you can start using other programs, however, it is important to understand how Windows views programs. Windows 95 considers each program running on the system to be a *task*. Each task is given a fixed slice of time to run itself and then must yield control back to the operating system. This idea is referred to as *time slicing*, because the time periods are "sliced" into smaller sections for each program to use. Because Windows has an intimate knowledge of what each program is doing at any given time, it knows when it is safe to interrupt that program and swap time to another program.

In this chapter you will learn how to take advantage of the knowledge that is built into the operating system and to exploit that knowledge for your own uses. You will learn how to start other programs, how to stop other programs, and how to find out what programs are available to the user. You will learn things about your own program, from Windows' viewpoint. Where am I running from? How many copies of me already exist? These are some of the questions that will be answered in this chapter.

3.1 Find Out What Other Tasks Are Running on the System

This How-To will show you several ways to find out what other programs, tasks, and DLLs are running in Windows 95 at any given time. You will see how you can determine the main-level windows that are on the screen, as well as the actual tasks running (which may or may not have a window on the screen) and the DLLs that are loaded by programs.

Using this methodology, you could easily write a task manager replacement for Windows for Workgroups or Windows 3.1, or even a task toolbar replacement for Windows 95.

3.2 Activate Another Task

One of the things that users are most likely to want is the ability to start another program from your program in order to accomplish a given task. This requires either starting an existing program or bringing a program that is already running to the front. This How-To will show you how to do the latter. You will learn, by using the previous How-To, how to find out whether the task you want is already running. If it is, you will be able to activate it from your own application.

3.3   Shut Down Another Application

Just as you would like the ability to start another task, you must be able to *stop* another task from running. Whether this is because you know that your application will not run with another task active, or because you would like to shut down any tasks you started during the running of your application, this How-To will show you how to do it.

3.4   Find Out the Executable File Name of My Application

Programmers frequently need to know where their programs are running from. If you would like to store information for a program in the same directory as the program itself, you will need to know what that directory is at runtime. Users get justifiably irate when configuration files for hundreds of applications clutter their System directory. Furthermore, since the drive on which your application is running is not necessarily the same as the Windows System directory, you may be using up disk space that is needed for other things. If the user specifically puts your program on the D: drive and their Windows System directory is on the C: drive, it is not your business to decide where your configuration files should go. Use this How-To to determine where your program is running from and to be user-friendly.

3.5   Allow Only One Copy of My Executable to Run at a Time

Although Windows 95 goes a long way toward easing the memory constraints that made it necessary to restrict programs to a single instance in Windows 3.x, there are still excellent reasons why you might not want to allow this functionality.

If your program needs exclusive access to a database or other file or resource, it is necessary to force the user to run only one copy of the program at a time. This How-To will show you the necessary steps not only to determine whether another instance of your application is running, but to activate it instead of starting a new one, if it is.

3.6   Perform Other Tasks in the Background

It is useful to be able to run other tasks in the background while continuing user processing in the foreground. This How-To will show you how to start another program and monitor its progress while the user continues to use the functionality of your own program. This capability can be very nice for running "unzip" programs to install something in the system while the user continues to view other information.

3.7   Run Another Program and Wait for It to Finish

Similar to the previous How-To, this How-To shows you how to start another Windows application and then wait until it has finished before going on. How-To 3.6 allows the user to continue working while another program does its job, but this How-To will show you how to force the user to wait until another program has completed its processing. Any system that requires calling to external programs will require this sort of functionality at some point.

3.8 Terminate and Restart Windows from within My Application

Windows installation programs often require you to restart Windows before continuing. This is necessary if new drivers are installed, or if the PATH statement has been modified, or even if a startup program is necessary to work with that program. Rather than asking users to stop what they are doing and restart Windows, you can do it under program control. This is not only more user-friendly, but it is safer, since you can guarantee that Windows is restarted before your program is run again.

Table 3-1 lists the Windows 95 API functions used in this chapter.

Process32First	Process32Next	Module32First
Module32Next	EnumWindows	MakeProcInstance
FreeProcInstance	BringWindowToTop	GetWindow
GetWindowTextLength	GetWindowText	PostMessage
GetModuleFileName	FindWindow	GetLastActivePopup
ShowWindow	CreateThread	PeekMessage
TranslateMessage	DispatchMessage	PostQuitMessage
WinExec	CreateProcess	WaitForSingleObject
NotifyRegister	NotifyUnregister	ExitWindowsEx

 Table 3-1 Windows 95 API functions used in Chapter 3

COMPLEXITY
MODERATE

3.1 How do I... Find out what other tasks are running on the system?

Problem

I would like to be able to list the current running tasks for users, but I'm not quite certain of the difference between a task and a window. Can I list both at the same time, or is it necessary to decide which one I would like to display?

Technique

It is not only possible to list both tasks and windows separately, it is probably quite useful to do so. A task is any running Windows application, whether it is displaying a window on the screen or not. A task may have several windows associated with it. The main window is the "parent" window on the desktop, and all other windows are "children" of the parent. Child windows normally are displayed within the borders of the main window but can appear outside of it. In either case, all child windows belong to a task as well.

This How-To will show you how to display not only all of the tasks running at the current time, but also the main windows that are being displayed on the desktop.

Steps

Open and run the CH31.MAK file in Visual C++. Select the Tasks main menu item and then the View Tasks drop-down menu selection. You will see a dialog that displays a list box and four buttons, as shown in Figure 3-1. Select the Processes button, and the list box will be filled with the process name of each of the currently running tasks.

If you investigate the desktop, you will probably find that not all of these windows appear on the screen. Select the second button, Windows, and the list box will be filled with the names of the windows that are currently displayed. Select the Modules button, and the list box will be filled with the modules that are loaded by the currently running tasks. When you have finished inspecting the various options, the Close button will close the dialog.

To duplicate this functonality in your own program, open the CH31.MAK file or create your own new project. Then follow this procedure to create the dialog:

1. Create a new project in Visual C++ using AppWizard. Give the project the name CH31.MAK.

2. Enter AppStudio and create a new dialog with a list box and three buttons. Label the buttons Processes, Windows, and Modules. Delete the Cancel button from the dialog and change the caption on the Ok button to read Close.

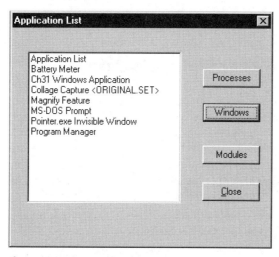

Figure 3-1 View Tasks dialog

3. Select ClassWizard and generate a new dialog class for this dialog template. Call the class CTaskDialog. Select the CTaskDialog object in the object list and the WM_INITDIALOG message. Click on the Add Function button and enter the following code into the OnInitDialog member function:

```
BOOL CTaskDialog::OnInitDialog()
{
    CDialog::OnInitDialog();

    // Make the dialog window centered in our application

    CenterWindow();

    // Init toolhelp 32 functions

    if ( !InitToolhelp32 () ) {
        MessageBox("Unable to initialize toolhelp functions!", "Error",
                MB_OK );
        EndDialog(IDCANCEL);
        return FALSE;
    }


    return TRUE;  // return TRUE  unless you set the focus to a control
}
```

4. Select the IDC_BUTTON1 object in the object list and select BN_CLICKED from the message list. Enter OnProcessList for the name of the function and enter the following code into the OnProcessList member function:

```
void CTaskDialog::OnProcessList()
{
    // Get a snapshot of the thread li
    HANDLE hSnapshot = pCreateToolhelp32Snapshot( TH32CS_SNAPPROCESS, 0 );
    PROCESSENTRY32 pe;

    if ( !hSnapshot )
        return;

    CListBox *list = (CListBox *)GetDlgItem(IDC_LIST1);

    // Clear out the list box

    list->ResetContent();

        // Initialize size in structure

    pe.dwSize = sizeof(pe);
    for ( int i = pProcess32First( hSnapshot, &pe ); i; i =
        pProcess32Next( hSnapshot, &pe ) )
    {

        HANDLE          hModuleSnap = NULL;
        MODULEENTRY32 me;
```

```
        // Take a snapshot of all modules in the specified process
        hModuleSnap = pCreateToolhelp32Snapshot(TH32CS_SNAPMODULE,
                                        pe.th32ProcessID );
        if (hModuleSnap == (HANDLE)-1)
          return;

        // Fill the size of the structure before using it
        me.dwSize = sizeof(MODULEENTRY32);


        // Walk the module list of the process, and find the module of
        // interest. Then copy the information to the buffer pointed
        // to by lpMe32 so that it can be returned to the caller
        if (pModule32First(hModuleSnap, &me)) {
            do {
                if (me.th32ModuleID == pe.th32ModuleID) {
                            list->AddString ( me.szExePath );
                            break;
                }
            }
                while (pModule32Next(hModuleSnap, &me));
            }

    }

        CloseHandle( hSnapshot );    // Done with this snapshot. Free it

}
```

5. Select the IDC_BUTTON2 object in the object list and select BN_CLICKED from the message list. Enter OnWindowList for the name of the function and enter the following code into the OnWindowList member function:

```
void CTaskDialog::OnWindowList()
{
    // Get the list box from the dialog

    CListBox *list = (CListBox *)GetDlgItem(IDC_LIST1);

    // Clear out the list box

    list->ResetContent();

    // Make a callback procedure for Windows to use to iterate through
    // the Window list.

    FARPROC EnumProcInstance = MakeProcInstance( (FARPROC)EnumWindowsProc,
                                        AfxGetInstanceHandle() );

    // Call the EnumWindows function to start the iteration

    EnumWindows ( (WNDENUMPROC)EnumProcInstance, (LPARAM)list );

    // Don't forget to free up the allocated memory handle

    FreeProcInstance ( EnumProcInstance );
```

continued on next page

continued from previous page

```
    // Make sure the dialog gets updated

    UpdateData();
}
```

6. Next, add the following code just above the OnWindowList member function:

```
BOOL CALLBACK EnumWindowsProc(HWND hwnd, LPARAM lParam)
{
    // Get the list box

    CListBox *list = (CListBox *)lParam;

    // Get the window text to insert

    char buffer[256];
    GetWindowText(hwnd, buffer, 256);

    // Insert it into the list box

    if ( strlen(buffer) ) {
        list->AddString ( buffer );
    }

    return TRUE;
}
```

7. Select the IDC_BUTTON3 object in the object list and select BN_CLICKED from the message list. Enter OnModuleList for the name of the function and enter the following code into the OnModuleList member function:

```
void CTaskDialog::OnModuleList()
{
    MODULEENTRY32 me;

    // Get the list box from the dialog

    CListBox *list = (CListBox *)GetDlgItem(IDC_LIST1);

    // Clear out the list box

    list->ResetContent();

    // Initialize the MODULEENTRY structure to 0 and set the
    // size of the structure in the dwSize element.

    memset ( &me, 0, sizeof(me) );
    me.dwSize = sizeof(MODULEENTRY32);

    HANDLE hSnapshot = pCreateToolhelp32Snapshot( TH32CS_SNAPPROCESS, 0 );

    if ( !hSnapshot )
        return;

    // Clear out the list box
```

```
    list->ResetContent();

    for ( int i = pModule32First( hSnapshot, &me ); i; i =
pModule32Next( hSnapshot, &me ) )
    {
        list->AddString ( me.szExePath );

    }

    CloseHandle( hSnapshot );    // Done with this snapshot.  Free it


}
```

8. Add the following declarations and code to the top of the TASKDIAL.CPP file:

```
// Type definitions for pointers to call tool help functions.
typedef BOOL (WINAPI *MODULEWALK)(HANDLE hSnapshot,
    LPMODULEENTRY32 lpme);
typedef BOOL (WINAPI *THREADWALK)(HANDLE hSnapshot,
    LPTHREADENTRY32 lpte);
typedef BOOL (WINAPI *PROCESSWALK)(HANDLE hSnapshot,
    LPPROCESSENTRY32 lppe);
typedef HANDLE (WINAPI *CREATESNAPSHOT)(DWORD dwFlags,
    DWORD th32ProcessID);

// File scope globals. These pointers are declared because of the need
// to dynamically link to the functions.  They are exported only by
// the Windows 95 kernel. Explicitly linking to them will make this
// application unloadable in Microsoft(R) Windows NT(TM) and will
// produce an ugly system dialog box.
static CREATESNAPSHOT pCreateToolhelp32Snapshot = NULL;
static MODULEWALK   pModule32First   = NULL;
static MODULEWALK   pModule32Next    = NULL;
static PROCESSWALK  pProcess32First  = NULL;
static PROCESSWALK  pProcess32Next   = NULL;
static THREADWALK   pThread32First   = NULL;
static THREADWALK   pThread32Next    = NULL;

// Function that initializes tool help functions.
BOOL InitToolhelp32 (void)
{
    BOOL   bRet  = FALSE;
    HINSTANCE hKernel = NULL;

    // Obtain the module handle of the kernel to retrieve addresses of
    // the tool helper functions.
    hKernel = GetModuleHandle("KERNEL32.DLL");

    if (hKernel){
        pCreateToolhelp32Snapshot =
            (CREATESNAPSHOT)GetProcAddress(hKernel,
            "CreateToolhelp32Snapshot");

        pModule32First  = (MODULEWALK)GetProcAddress(hKernel,
            "Module32First");
```

continued on next page

continued from previous page

```
            pModule32Next   = (MODULEWALK)GetProcAddress(hKernel,
                "Module32Next");

            pProcess32First = (PROCESSWALK)GetProcAddress(hKernel,
                            "Process32First");
            pProcess32Next  = (PROCESSWALK)GetProcAddress(hKernel,
                            "Process32Next");

            pThread32First  = (THREADWALK)GetProcAddress(hKernel,
                            "Thread32First");
            pThread32Next   = (THREADWALK)GetProcAddress(hKernel,
                            "Thread32Next");

            // All addresses must be non-NULL to be successful.
            // If one of these addresses is NULL, one of
            // the needed lists cannot be walked.
            bRet =  pModule32First && pModule32Next  && pProcess32First &&
                    pProcess32Next && pThread32First && pThread32Next &&
                    pCreateToolhelp32Snapshot;
    }
    else
        bRet = FALSE; // could not even get the module handle of
                        // kernel

    return bRet;
}
```

9. Finally, add the following include file line to the TASKDIAL.CPP file:

```
#include <tlhelp32.h>
```

10. Return to AppStudio and add a new menu to the main menu called Tasks. Add a new menu item to the menu called View Tasks. Give this menu item the identifier of ID_VIEW_TASKS.

11. Go into ClassWizard and select the CMainFrame object from the drop-down list. Select the ID_VIEW_TASKS object from the object list and the COMMAND message from the message list. Click on the Add Function button and enter OnViewTasks as the name of the function.

12. Enter the following code into the OnViewTasks member function for CMainFrame:

```
void CMainFrame::OnViewTasks()
{
    CTaskDialog dlg;
    dlg.DoModal();
}
```

13. Now, go to the top of the CMainFrame object file (MAINFRM.CPP) and enter the following line after the "#include "mainfrm.h" line:

```
#include "taskdial.h"
```

14. Compile and run the application.

How It Works

This How-To shows the primary methods of listing tasks, windows, and DLLs in the Windows system and also uses three different Windows API function sets.

The first method, listing processes, makes use of the new Windows 95 API functions Process32First and Process32Next. To use these functions, the programmer must first initialize the Toolhelp functionality by loading the functions from the kernel32 DLL. This is accomplished using the InitToolhelp32 function defined above in step 8. These functions will "walk" the process list, returning process identifiers for each running process. From these identifiers, the Module functions (Module32First and Module32Next) are used to walk through the modules to find the corresponding names for the processes.

The second method, listing windows, uses a more advanced and slightly less intuitive set of Windows API functions, the MakeProcInstance and EnumWindows functions. MakeProcInstance takes the address of a function in your program and converts it into something called a FARPROC. This FARPROC is then passed to Windows 95 to iterate through all of the open windows on the desktop. Note that only main-level windows are listed by this function. The function that is called is called EnumWindowsProc and accepts two arguments. The first will be the handle of the window that is currently being examined, and the second is a user-defined argument that is passed to the EnumWindows function. In our case, the argument passed is the CListBox member that we would like data stored in. In the EnumWindowsProc function (also known as a callback function, since it is called back by Windows 95), the title of the window is stored in the list box for the user to view.

COMPLEXITY
MODERATE

3.2   How do I...
Activate another task?

Problem

I would like to be able to list the current running tasks for users and allow them to select one to activate. I would prefer to let them only activate tasks that have visible windows associated with them, as these are really the only ones that they can use. How can I use the Windows 95 API functions to accomplish this task?

Technique

The previous How-To showed you how to accomplish half of your task—the problem of listing all of the active windows on the screen. In this How-To, we will examine the problem of activating, or bringing to the front, a window that does not belong to your own application.

The technique used for this How-To is quite similar to the previous How-To. You enumerate the windows on the desktop, allowing the user to select from the list to activate one. The difference lies in what is done after the enumeration. In this case, we will allow the user to select one of the windows on the desktop and then "activate" that window by using the Windows 95 API function BringWindowToTop. This function will put the window at the top of the Z order and allow the user to send all keystrokes and mouse events to that window.

Steps

Open and run the CH32.MAK make file in Visual C++. Select the Tasks main menu item and then the Activate Task drop-down menu selection. A dialog will display a list of windows that are currently running on the system, as shown in Figure 3-2. Select one of the windows and click on the Activate button. The dialog box will close, and the window you selected will be placed in front of the CH3 application.

To duplicate the functionality of this example, follow this procedure:

1. Create a new project using AppWizard. Give the project the name CH32.MAK. Enter AppStudio and create a new dialog.

2. Add a list box to the dialog. Delete the Cancel button and rename the Ok button to Close. Give the dialog the title Activate Task.

3. Add a new button to the dialog labeled Activate.

4. Start ClassWizard and create a new dialog class for the dialog template you have just created. Call the new dialog class CTaskActivateDlg. Select the CTaskActivateDlg from the object list in ClassWizard and the WM_INITDIALOG

Figure 3-2 Activate Task dialog

message from the message list. Click on the Add Function button. Enter the following code into the OnInitDialog member function of CTaskActivateDlg:

```
BOOL CTaskActivateDlg::OnInitDialog()
{
    CDialog::OnInitDialog();

    // Get the list box from the dialog

    CListBox *list = (CListBox *)GetDlgItem(IDC_LIST1);

    // Clear out the list box

    list->ResetContent();

    // Make a callback procedure for Windows to use to iterate through
    // the Window list.

    FARPROC EnumProcInstance = MakeProcInstance( (FARPROC)EnumWindowsProc,
                                                 AfxGetInstanceHandle() );

    // Call the EnumWindows function to start the iteration

    EnumWindows ( (WNDENUMPROC)EnumProcInstance, (LPARAM)list );

    // Don't forget to free up the allocated memory handle

    FreeProcInstance ( EnumProcInstance );

        return TRUE;   // return TRUE  unless you set the focus to a
                       // control
}
```

5. Add the following function to the TASKACTI.CPP file immediately before the OnInitDialog member function:

```
static BOOL CALLBACK EnumWindowsProc(HWND hwnd, LPARAM lParam)
{
    // Get the list box

    CListBox *list = (CListBox *)lParam;

    // Get the window text to insert

    char buffer[256];
    GetWindowText(hwnd, buffer, 256);

    // Insert it into the list box

    if ( strlen(buffer) ) {
        int idx = list->AddString ( buffer );
        list->SetItemData ( idx, (DWORD)hwnd );
    }

    return TRUE;
}
```

6. Add a member function handler for the button by selecting the IDC_BUTTON1
object from the object list and the BN_CLICKED message from the message
list. Click on the Add Function button and enter OnActivateTask for the
name of the function. Add the following code to the OnActivateTask member
function:

```
void CTaskActivateDlg::OnActivateTask()
{
    // Get the list box from the dialog

    CListBox *list = (CListBox *)GetDlgItem(IDC_LIST1);

    // Get the selected window number

    int idx  = list->GetCurSel();

    // See if there was a selection

    if ( idx == LB_ERR ) {
        MessageBox("You must select a window to activate!", "Error",
                MB_APPLMODAL | MB_OK );
        return;
    }

    // Get the handle of the window to activate

    HWND hWnd = (HWND)list->GetItemData ( idx );

    ::BringWindowToTop (hWnd);

    // Close the dialog

    EndDialog ( IDOK );
}
```

7. Add a new menu item under the Tasks main menu title called Activate Task.
Give the menu item the identifier ID_ACTIVATE_TASK.

8. Select the CMainFrame object from the drop-down list in ClassWizard. Select
the ID_ACTIVATE_TASK object and the COMMAND message. Click on the
Add Function button. Add the following code to the OnActivateTask member
function of CMainFrame:

```
void CMainFrame::OnActivateTask()
{
    CTaskActivateDlg dlg;
    dlg.DoModal();
}
```

9. At the same time, add the following line to the top of the MAINFRM.CPP file
below the "#include "mainfrm.h" line:

```
#include "taskacti.h"
```

10. Compile and run the application.

How It Works

Similarly to the previous How-To, this How-To builds on the idea of enumerating windows using the EnumWindows API function along with the callback function EnumWindowsProc. In this case, however, we store the window handle that is passed to the EnumWindowsProc function in the item data associated with the list item for the window title. This window handle is then retrieved when the user makes a selection.

The actual process is as follows: The user selects a window title from the list box and clicks on the Activate Task button. The OnActivateTask member function of CTaskActivateDlg is called, which retrieves the stored windows handle. This windows handle is then passed to the Windows 95 API function BringWindowToTop (the :: scope operator is necessary because all Cwnd-derived objects have a BringWindowToTop member function as well). This API function then brings the window to the top of the Z order, making it the window that appears on top of all others.

> Note: The SetWindowPos function can also be used to set a window to be on top of all other windows. We will discuss this function later in the book.

Comments

You can accomplish the same task performed in this How-To using Visual Basic. Visual Basic lacks the ability to create true Windows callback functions, so we will need to use a different method to create the window list to call back from. Here is the procedure:

1. Create a new project or add a new form to an existing project. Add a list box object with the name list1 and two buttons with the captions Activate and Close.

2. Add the following code to the FormLoad method of the new form:

```
Sub Form_Load
CurrWnd = GetWindow(Form1.hWnd, GW_HWNDFIRST)
    While CurrWnd <> 0
        Length = GetWindowTextLength(CurrWnd)
        Item$ = Space$(Length + 1)
        Length = GetWindowText(CurrWnd, Item$, Length + 1)
        If Length > 0 Then
            List1.AddItem Item$
        End If
        CurrWnd = GetWindow(CurrWnd, GW_HWNDNEXT)
        x = DoEvents()
    Wend
End Sub
```

3. Next, add the following code to the "general" section of the form:

```
DefInt A-Z
Const GW_HWNDFIRST = 0
```

continued on next page

continued from previous page

```
Const GW_HWNDNEXT = 2
DefInt A-Z
Const GW_HWNDFIRST = 0
Const GW_HWNDNEXT = 2
Private Declare Function GetWindow Lib "user32" (ByVal hwnd%, ByVal
cmd%) As Integer
Private Declare Function GetWindowText Lib "user32" Alias
"GetWindowTextA" (ByVal hwnd As Long, ByVal lpString As String, ByVal
cch As Long) As Long
Private Declare Function GetWindowTextLength Lib "user32" Alias
"GetWindowTextLengthA" (ByVal hwnd As Long) As Long
```

4. Add this code to the first Activate button Click event handler:

```
Sub Command1_Click
If List1.ListIndex <> -1 Then
      Item$ = List1.List(List1.ListIndex)
      On Local Error Resume Next
      AppActivate Item$
   Else
      MsgBox "No item selected to activate"
   End If
End Sub
```

5. Finally, add this code to the Close button Click event handler:

```
Sub Command2_Click ()
   End
End Sub
```

6. Run the application. You will see a form that looks like the one in Figure 3-3.

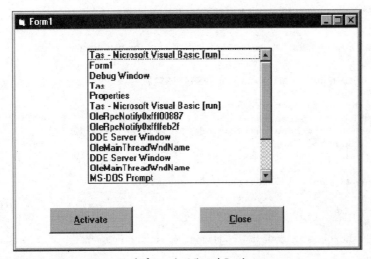

Figure 3-3 Activate Task form in Visual Basic

COMPLEXITY
MODERATE

3.3   How do I...
Shut down another application?

Problem

I would like to be able to allow users to run another application from mine and then shut it down when they are finished. For example, it would be wonderful if they could launch Windows Write from my application, write a note or memo, and then shut it down. I would also like to bypass the Write message box asking users whether they want to save the changes to the current file.

How can I use the Windows 95 API to accomplish these two tasks with a minimum of work?

Technique

How-To 3.2 dealt with the problem of allowing the user to view a list of tasks running and how to activate one of those tasks. This task is similar, but in this case, we know what task we would like to activate and which one we would like to shut down. For the purposes of this How-To, however, we will make the process more general and once again allow the user to select which application to shut down and the method they would like for shutting it down.

To accomplish this job, we will make use of the PostMessage Windows API function.

Steps

Open and run the CH33.MAK file in Visual C++. Select the Tasks main menu item and then the Terminate Task drop-down menu selection. A dialog displays a list of windows that are currently running on the system, as shown in Figure 3-4. Select one of the windows and click on either the Close App or Quit App button. The dialog box will close and the window you selected will be closed as well.

Experiment with the two buttons by starting an instance of Windows WordPad and placing text into the window. You will notice that in some cases the WordPad program will ask you whether to save the changed text and in some it will not.

To duplicate the functionality of this example, follow this procedure:

1. Create a new project in Visual C++ using AppWizard. Give this project the name CH33.MAK. Enter AppStudio and create a new dialog.

2. Add a list box to the dialog. Delete the Cancel button and rename the Ok button to Close. Give the dialog the title Terminate Task.

3. Add two new buttons to the dialog labeled Close App and Quit App.

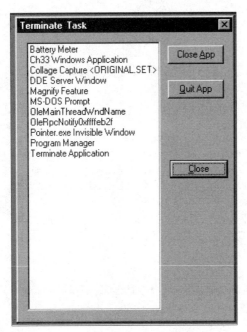

Figure 3-4 Terminate Task dialog

4. Start ClassWizard and create a new dialog class for the dialog template you have just created. Call the new dialog class CTerminateTaskDlg. Select the CTerminateTaskDlg from the object list in ClassWizard and the WM_INITDIALOG message from the message list. Click on the Add Function button. Enter the following code into the OnInitDialog member function of CTerminateTaskDlg:

```
BOOL CTerminateTaskDlg::OnInitDialog()
{
    CDialog::OnInitDialog();

    // Get the list box from the dialog

    CListBox *list = (CListBox *)GetDlgItem(IDC_LIST1);

    // Clear out the list box

    list->ResetContent();

    // Make a callback procedure for Windows to use to iterate through
    // the Window list.

    FARPROC EnumProcInstance = MakeProcInstance( (FARPROC)EnumWindowsProc,
                                        AfxGetInstanceHandle() );
```

```
    // Call the EnumWindows function to start the iteration

    EnumWindows ( (WNDENUMPROC)EnumProcInstance, (LPARAM)list );

    // Don't forget to free up the allocated memory handle

    FreeProcInstance ( EnumProcInstance );

    CenterWindow();

    return TRUE;  // return TRUE  unless you set the focus to a control
}
```

5. Add the following function to the TASKACTI.CPP file immediately before the OnInitDialog member function:

```
static BOOL CALLBACK EnumWindowsProc(HWND hwnd, LPARAM lParam)
{
    // Get the list box

    CListBox *list = (CListBox *)lParam;

    // Get the window text to insert

    char buffer[256];
    GetWindowText(hwnd, buffer, 256);

    // Insert it into the list box

    if ( strlen(buffer) ) {
        int idx = list->AddString ( buffer );
        list->SetItemData ( idx, (DWORD)hwnd );
    }

    return TRUE;
}
```

6. Add a member function handler for the button by selecting the IDC_BUT-TON1 object from the object list and the BN_CLICKED message from the message list. Click on the Add Function button and enter OnCloseApp for the name of the function. Add the following code to the OnCloseApp member function:

```
void CTerminateTaskDlg::OnCloseApp()
{
    // Get the list box from the dialog

    CListBox *list = (CListBox *)GetDlgItem(IDC_LIST1);

    // Get the selected window number

    int idx  = list->GetCurSel();

    // See if there was a selection

    if ( idx == LB_ERR ) {
```

continued on next page

continued from previous page

```
        MessageBox("You must select a window to close!", "Error",
                MB_APPLMODAL | MB_OK );
        return;
    }

    // Get the handle of the window to close

    HWND hWnd = (HWND)list->GetItemData ( idx );

    ::PostMessage( hWnd, WM_CLOSE, 0, 0L );

}
```

7. Add a member function handler for the button by selecting the IDC_BUT-TON2 object from the object list and the BN_CLICKED message from the message list. Click on the Add Function button and enter OnQuitApp for the name of the function. Add the following code to the OnQuitApp member function:

```
void CTerminateTaskDlg::OnQuitApp()
{
    // Get the list box from the dialog

    CListBox *list = (CListBox *)GetDlgItem(IDC_LIST1);

    // Get the selected window number

    int idx  = list->GetCurSel();

    // See if there was a selection

    if ( idx == LB_ERR ) {
        MessageBox("You must select a window to quit!", "Error",
                MB_APPLMODAL | MB_OK );
        return;
    }

    // Get the handle of the window to quit

    HWND hWnd = (HWND)list->GetItemData ( idx );

    ::PostMessage( hWnd, WM_QUIT, 0, 0L );

}
```

8. Add a new menu item under the Tasks main menu title called Terminate Task. Give the menu item the identifier ID_TERMINATE_TASK.

9. Select the CMainFrame object from the drop-down list in ClassWizard. Select the ID_TERMINATE_TASK object and the COMMAND message. Click on the Add Function button. Add the following code to the OnTerminateTask member function of CMainFrame:

```
void CMainFrame::OnTerminateTask()
{
```

```
CTerminateTaskDlg dlg;
    dlg.DoModal();
}
```

10. At the same time, add the following line to the top of the MAINFRM.CPP file below the "#include "mainfrm.h" line:

```
#include "terminat.h"
```

11. Compile and run the application.

How It Works

As in the previous How-To's, this one builds on the idea of enumerating the window list by using the EnumWindows API function along with a callback function called EnumWindowsProc. Also, like the previous How-To, this one stores the handle of the window in the extra data portion of the list box.

When the user selects the Close App button from the dialog, the selected list box entry is retrieved, and the window handle that accompanies it is also retrieved. This handle is then used to post a message to the window with the message identifier of WM_CLOSE. This indicates to the window that it should close. Closing a window via the WM_CLOSE message will not prompt the user to save changes to the text.

When the user selects the Quit App button from the dialog, the selected list box entry and the window handle that accompanies it is retrieved. This handle is then used to post a message to the window with the message identifier of WM_QUIT. This indicates to the window that it should close. Closing a window via the WM_QUIT message prompts users to save changes to the text and allows them to cancel the request if they choose.

COMPLEXITY

EASY

3.4 How do I...
Find out the executable file name of my application?

Problem

My application is often run using different names for different customers. I would like the ability to know what the actual file name is so that I can find the directory where it is running and write copyright information to the actual executable file. How can I accomplish this?

Technique

The Windows 95 API contains many functions that were designed specifically for the application developer. The problem at hand—finding the executable file name—is a common one for Windows developers, and the Windows 95 design team kept that in mind during the API design.

The Windows API function GetModuleFileName will return the name of the executable file that is associated with the instance handle of your application. It can also be used for other running applications, as we have seen using the previous How-To's in this section. For this How-To, we will simply display the file name of the currently running executable, rather than any others running on the system.

Steps

Open and run the CH34.MAK file in Visual C++. Select the Application main menu item and then Executable File Name from the drop-down menu list. You will see a message box appear, as in Figure 3-5, showing you the full path name of the executable that is currently running.

To duplicate this functionality, use the following procedure:

1. Create a new project using AppWizard. Give the project the name CH34.MAK.

2. In AppStudio, add a new item to the main-level menu called Applications. Add a new menu item to the Applications main-level menu. Give it the string Executable File Name and the identifier ID_EXE_FILE_NAME.

3. Go into ClassWizard and select the CMainFrame class from the drop-down list. Select ID_EXE_FILE_NAME from the object list and COMMAND from the message list. Click on the Add Function button and accept the name OnExeFileName.

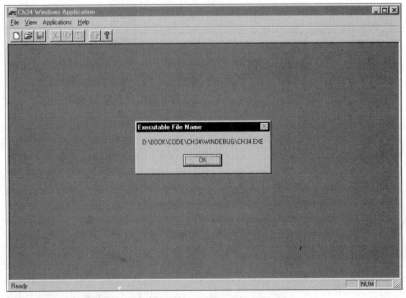

Figure 3-5 Executable File Name message box display

4. Enter the following code into the CMainFrame method OnExeFileName in the MAINFRM.CPP file:

```
void CMainFrame::OnExeFileName()
{
    char fileName[_MAX_PATH];

    GetModuleFileName ( AfxGetInstanceHandle(), fileName, _MAX_PATH );
    MessageBox ( fileName, "Executable File Name", MB_APPLMODAL | MB_OK );
}
```

5. Compile and run the application.

How It Works

When the user selects the menu item Executable File Name from the menu in Visual C++, or clicks on the Get Name button in Delphi, the program calls the Windows API function GetModuleFileName. This function takes three parameters. The first parameter is the instance handle of the executable you want the file name for. In Visual C++, the instance handle of the application is retrieved using the AfxGetInstanceHandle() function call. In Delphi, the Hinstance global variable holds this information. The second and third parameters specify the buffer in which to place the returned string and the size of the buffer you are passing (in bytes).

Once the function has returned, a message box is displayed showing you the returned buffer contents. Note that long file names can be returned by Windows 95 applications running on long file name systems. You should check to see if a file system has long file names before using the buffer containing the file name.

Comments

To accomplish the task performed in this How-To in Delphi, do the following:

1. Start Delphi and create a new form or add a new form to an existing application.

2. Add two buttons to the form, labeled Get Name and Close. Change the title of the form's caption to Get Executable File Name. Give the Get Name button the name of GetName.

3. Double-click on the Get Name button and add the following code to the TForm1.GetNameClick method that is generated:

```
procedure TForm1.GetNameClick(Sender: TObject);
var
    fileName : PChar;
    ret      : Integer;
begin
    fileName := StrAlloc(251);
    GetModuleFileName(HInstance, fileName, 250);
    ret := Application.MessageBox(fileName, 'Executable File Name',
                                  mb_OK);
    StrDispose(fileName);
end;
```

4. Double-click on the Close button and add the following code to the TForm1.Button1Click method that is generated:

```
procedure TForm1.Button1Click(Sender: TObject);
begin
    Close;
end;
```

5. Compile and run the executable. When you click on the Get Name button, you will see the dialog displayed in Figure 3-6.

COMPLEXITY
EASY

3.5 How do I...
Allow only one copy of my executable to run at a time?

Problem

I would like to restrict the user from starting multiple instances of my application. In the old Windows 3.x days, I could simply check the hPrevInstance data field in my WinMain function, but I understand that procedure will no longer work in Windows 95. Why is this, and how do I get around this problem?

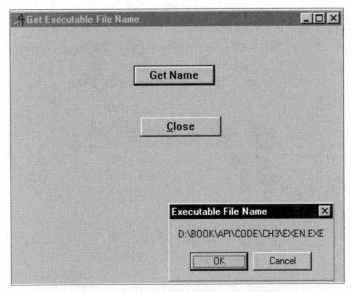

Figure 3-6 Executable File Name display in Delphi

Technique

You're right, the hPrevInstance variable is no longer of use to you in Windows 95. In the new version of Windows, the hPrevInstance argument passed to WinMain is there simply for compatibility with older programs that ran under Windows 3.x. This variable will always be NULL in Windows 95.

This How-To gives you the "officially sanctioned" method of how to find out if a previous instance of your application is running and go back to that instance if the user requests the program to be run a second time. Since it is especially easy to "lose" applications under Windows 95, with all of the space available to them, this How-To is particularly useful.

Steps

Open and run the CH35.MAK file in Visual C++. Minimize the application and rerun the executable (either with the Project | Execute command or using Explorer/File Manager). When the second instance of the application is run, a message box will be displayed, indicating that you may not run more than one instance of the executable (see Figure 3-7). Once this message box is closed, the previous instance of the executable will be shown, restored to its normal size.

To duplicate this functionality, use the following procedure:

1. Create a new project in Visual C++ using AppWizard. Give the new project the name CH35.MAK.

2. Go into the CH35.CPP file and locate the method InitInstance. Make the following modifications to the InitInstance method of CCh35App. Note that the code to be added is marked in bold print.

```
BOOL CCh35App::InitInstance()
{
    HWND FirsthWnd, FirstChildhWnd;
    static char *title = "Ch35 Windows Application";

    if (FirsthWnd = FindWindow(NULL, title)) {

        MessageBox ( NULL, "You may only run a single instance of this",;
                    program! "Error", MB_APPLMODAL | MB_OK );
        FirstChildhWnd = GetLastActivePopup(FirsthWnd);
        BringWindowToTop(FirsthWnd);        // Bring main window to top.

        if (FirsthWnd != FirstChildhWnd)
            BringWindowToTop(FirstChildhWnd);

        // Don't forget to restore the state to normal

        ShowWindow(FirsthWnd, SW_SHOWNORMAL);

        return (FALSE);                     // Do not run second
                                            // instance.
    }
```

continued on next page

continued from previous page

```
// Standard initialization
// If you are not using these features and wish to reduce the size
//  of your final executable, you should remove from the following
//  the specific initialization routines you do not need.

SetDialogBkColor();          // Set dialog background color to gray
LoadStdProfileSettings();    // Load standard INI file options
                             // (including MRU)

// Register the application's document templates. Document templates
//  serve as the connection between documents, frame windows and
//  views.

CMultiDocTemplate* pDocTemplate;
pDocTemplate = new CMultiDocTemplate(
    IDR_CH35TYPE,
    RUNTIME_CLASS(CCh35Doc),
    RUNTIME_CLASS(CMDIChildWnd),          // standard MDI child frame
    RUNTIME_CLASS(CCh35View));
AddDocTemplate(pDocTemplate);

// create main MDI Frame window
CMainFrame* pMainFrame = new CMainFrame;
if (!pMainFrame->LoadFrame(IDR_MAINFRAME))
    return FALSE;
m_pMainWnd = pMainFrame;


if (m_lpCmdLine[0] != '\0')
{
    // TODO: add command line processing here
}

// The main window has been initialized, so show and update it.
pMainFrame->ShowWindow(m_nCmdShow);
pMainFrame->UpdateWindow();

return TRUE;
}
```

3. Compile and run the application. You will see the dialog displayed whenever you attempt to run a second instance of the application.

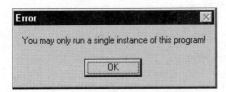

Figure 3-7 Second instance dialog box

How It Works

When the user attempts to run a second instance of the application, the Microsoft Foundation Classes (MFC) will create an instance of the application object CCh35App. One of the first things that the MFC will then do is to call the InitInstance handler of the application object. This happens before any windows are created on the screen.

The program then uses the FindWindow API function to locate any existing applications that have the same title as yours. This title is stored in the resource file for the application. If a matching window title is found, the program displays the message box indicating that a single instance is all that is allowed for this application. The window handle is then used to find any pop-up windows for that application, and both the original instance and the pop-up children of that instance are brought to the top of the Z order chain. The window is made active and restored to its normal size by the ShowWindow call. Finally, the function returns FALSE to the MFC, indicating that the instance should not be created.

One final note. The Windows 95 API has a new 32-bit function called FindWindowEx. It works almost exactly the same way as FindWindow but allows you to specify two additional parameters: the main-level window to search from (or NULL for the desktop) and the child window to begin searching after (or NULL for all).

COMPLEXITY
DIFFICULT

3.6 How do I... Perform other tasks in the background?

Problem

I would like to be able to perform some tasks in the background of Windows, while allowing the user to continue doing other things. Some of the things I might want to do include printing, copying files, and displaying animated bitmaps in a window. How can I do this and still allow Windows to continue its standard processing of user requests?

Technique

The ability to do background processing is the hallmark of any multitasking operating system, and Windows 95 is no exception. There are two methods to doing background processing. The first, a preemptive message loop, is portable between Windows 3.x, Windows 95, and Windows NT. This is the method we will focus on in this How-To. A preemptive loop is simply a way to receive messages from the underlying operating system and pass them on to the windows they are intended for. Rather than using the main application loop to accomplish this, our program will create its own message loop to pass messages. The second method, which will only be mentioned briefly, will work in Windows 95 or Windows NT only. This method uses the 32-bit API function CreateThread to actually start a new process under the existing one. See the "Comments" section for a discussion of how threads work and how to use them to provide "true" background processing.

The important API functions used in this How-To are PeekMessage, TranslateMessage, DispatchMessage, and PostQuitMessage. These functions form the kernel for the Windows 95 message system and also form the center of our background processing module. Not surprisingly, the module we will write will neatly lay itself over the Windows messaging system and will take over the job of determining when the application should do things. This process is straightforward, but should be undertaken with care in order to maintain the ability of Windows to multitask smoothly.

Steps

Open and run the CH36.MAK file in Visual C++. Open a new window either by clicking on the new window icon in the toolbar (the first icon from the left) or by selecting the File | New menu. Select the second document template in the list and click on OK. You will see a blank window appear in your application window (as shown in Figure 3-8).

Next, select the Graphics menu and click on the Start Graphics menu item in the drop-down menu list. The window will begin to display random rectangles of color in its client area. Notice that you can switch applications, bring up help, or do other tasks, and the rectangles will continue to be drawn and painted. Select Stop Graphics from the Graphics menu, and the rectangles will stop being drawn. The screen

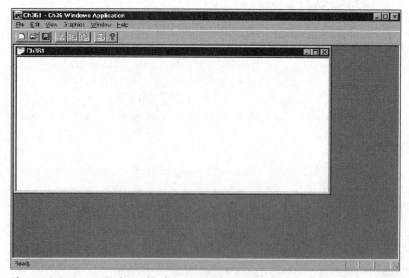

Figure 3-8 New window displayed with no graphics

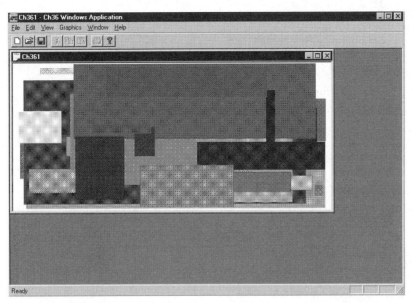

Figure 3-9 New Window displayed with graphics after ceasing background processing

should look something like that in Figure 3-9. You can replicate this functionality with the following procedure:

1. Create a new project in Visual C++ using AppWizard. Give the project the name CH36.MAK. Enter ClassWizard and click on the Add Class button. Use CGfxView for the name of the class and select CView for the base class of the class. Allow the default values for all other entries in the dialog.

2. Select the GFXVIEW.CPP class source file and add the following code to the constructor and destructor for the class:

```
CGfxView::CGfxView()
{
    bProcessing = 0;
}

CGfxView::~CGfxView()
{
    bProcessing = 0;
}
```

3. Add the following function to the GFXVIEW.CPP source file:

```
void CGfxView::DoIdleProcess()
{
    // Loop until we are finished or the user tells us to
    MSG msg;
```

continued on next page

continued from previous page

```
while (bProcessing)
{
    while (::PeekMessage(&msg, NULL, 0, 0, PM_REMOVE))
    {
        if (msg.message == WM_QUIT)
        {
            bProcessing = FALSE;
            ::PostQuitMessage(0);
            break;
        }
        if (!AfxGetApp()->PreTranslateMessage(&msg))
        {
            ::TranslateMessage(&msg);
            ::DispatchMessage(&msg);
        }
    }
    AfxGetApp()->OnIdle(0);    // updates user interface
    AfxGetApp()->OnIdle(1);    // frees temporary objects

    CDC *dc = GetDC();
    CPen pen;

    int red = rand() % 256;
    int green = rand() % 256;
    int blue = rand() % 256;

    pen.CreatePen ( PS_SOLID, 1, RGB(red, green, blue) );
    CBrush brush;

    brush.CreateSolidBrush ( RGB(red,green,blue) );

    dc->SelectObject ( &pen );
    dc->SelectObject ( &brush );

    CRect r;
    GetClientRect(&r);

    int height = r.bottom - r.top + 1;
    int width  = r.right - r.left + 1;

    int st_x = (rand() % width) + 1;
    int st_y = (rand() % height) + 1;
    int end_x = (rand() % width) + 1;
    int end_y = (rand() % height) + 1;

    if ( st_x > end_x ) {
        int temp = st_x;
        st_x = end_x;
        end_x = temp;
    }
    if ( st_y > end_y ) {
        int temp = st_y;
        st_y = end_y;
        end_y = temp;
    }
```

```
        dc->Rectangle ( st_x,st_y,end_x,end_y );

        ReleaseDC(dc);
    }
}
```

4. Next, modify the class definition in the GFXVIEW.H header file as follows (modifications are shown in bold print):

```
// gfxview.h : header file
//


/////////////////////////////////////////////////////////////////////////
// CGfxView view

class CGfxView : public CView
{
private:
    BOOL bProcessing;
    DECLARE_DYNCREATE(CGfxView)
protected:
    CGfxView();          // protected constructor used by dynamic creation
    void DoIdleProcess();

// Attributes
public:

// Operations
public:

// Implementation
protected:
    virtual ~CGfxView();
    virtual void OnDraw(CDC* pDC);        // overridden to draw this view

    // Generated message map functions
protected:
    //{{AFX_MSG(CGfxView)
    afx_msg void OnGfxStart();
    afx_msg void OnGfxStop();
    //}}AFX_MSG
    DECLARE_MESSAGE_MAP()
};


/////////////////////////////////////////////////////////////////////////
```

5. Enter AppStudio and add a new menu to the main menu with the caption Graphics. Add two menu items to the Graphics menu with the captions Start Graphics and Stop Graphics. Give these two menu items the identifiers ID_GFX_START and ID_GFX_STOP, respectively.

6. Go into ClassWizard and select the CGfxView class from the drop-down list. Select the ID_GFX_START object from the object list and the COMMAND message from the message list. Accept OnGfxStart as the name of the new function and enter the following code into the OnGfxStart method:

```
void CGfxView::OnGfxStart()
{
    bProcessing = 1;
    DoIdleProcess();
}
```

7. Go into ClassWizard and select the CGfxView class from the drop-down list.
Select the ID_GFX_STOP object from the object list and the COMMAND
message from the message list. Accept OnGfxStop as the name of the new
function and enter the following code into the OnGfxStop method:

```
void CGfxView::OnGfxStop()
{
    bProcessing = 0;
}
```

8. Select the CH36.CPP source file and make the following modifications to the
InitIntance method of the CCh36App object (modifications are shown in bold
print):

```
BOOL CCh36App::InitInstance()
{
    // Standard initialization
    // If you are not using these features and wish to reduce the size
    //  of your final executable, you should remove from the following
    //  the specific initialization routines you do not need.

    SetDialogBkColor();              // Set dialog background color to gray
    LoadStdProfileSettings();        // Load standard INI file options
                                     // (including MRU)

    // Register the application's document templates. Document
    //  templates serve as the connection between documents, frame
    //  windows and views.

    CMultiDocTemplate* pDocTemplate;
    pDocTemplate = new CMultiDocTemplate(
        IDR_CH36TYPE,
        RUNTIME_CLASS(CCh36Doc),
        RUNTIME_CLASS(CMDIChildWnd),          // standard MDI child frame
        RUNTIME_CLASS(CGfxView));
    AddDocTemplate(pDocTemplate);

    // create main MDI Frame window
    CMainFrame* pMainFrame = new CMainFrame;
    if (!pMainFrame->LoadFrame(IDR_MAINFRAME))
        return FALSE;
    m_pMainWnd = pMainFrame;

    // create a new (empty) document
    OnFileNew();

    if (m_lpCmdLine[0] != '\0')
    {
        // TODO: add command line processing here
    }
```

```
    // The main window has been initialized, so show and update it.
    pMainFrame->ShowWindow(m_nCmdShow);
    pMainFrame->UpdateWindow();

    return TRUE;
}
```

9. Compile and run the application.

How It Works

When the user opens a new view, the GfxView is created. It then sits around waiting for a message to start the graphics. Selecting the ID_START_GFX message from the menu by clicking on Start Graphics starts the procedure. When the message is received, the view then sits in an infinite loop displaying random rectangles in random colors and checking the message queue while it is at it. The process terminates when the user selects the Stop Graphics menu item, sending the ID_STOP_GFX message to the view. This message will set the global flag and terminate the "infinite" loop.

Comments

As mentioned at the beginning of the chapter, Windows NT and Windows 95 allow you to create actual threads to execute pieces of code. The following code snippet will show you how to create a thread to execute some code:

```
DWORD ThreadFunc(LPDWORD param)
{
    MessageBox(NULL, "Got an argument of %ld\n", *param);
    return 0;
}
// Inside of your function...
DWORD id, param = 12345;
HANDLE hThread = CreateThread(NULL, 0,
(LPTHREAD_START_ROUTINE)ThreadFunc, &param, 0, &id );
// More code below.
```

COMPLEXITY
MODERATE

3.7 How do I...
Run another program and wait for it to finish?

Problem

I would like to be able to run another Windows application and then wait for it to finish before doing anything else in my application. How can I start the other application and be sure that it has finished before I continue with my own application?

Technique

The job of starting another Windows application is quite trivial under Windows. The WinExec function of the API will do the job, as will the ShellExecute function of Visual Basic. Knowing when the other program has stopped running, however, is a whole other task. In this How-To, we will combine the things we have learned in this chapter with the new function WinExec to form a method for determining whether an application has completed. There is another way to do this as well, once again, using the TOOL-HELP.DLL functionality. That other method will be discussed in the "Comments" section.

Steps

Open and run the CH37.MAK file in Visual C++. Select the main menu item Application and the drop-down menu item Terminate and Wait. The Windows Notepad program will be launched, as shown in Figure 3-10. Terminate the Notepad program by selecting File | Exit from the menu, and the CH3 application program will once again be displayed. A message box will pop up in front of the application, displaying the message "Application is done!" as shown in Figure 3-11.

To duplicate this functionality, follow this procedure:

1. Create a new project in Visual C++ using AppWizard. Give this project the name CH37.MAK. Enter AppStudio and edit the IDR_MAINFRAME menu and add a new drop-down menu item to the Application main-level menu. Give the new menu item the caption Terminate and Wait and the identifier ID_TERM_WAIT.

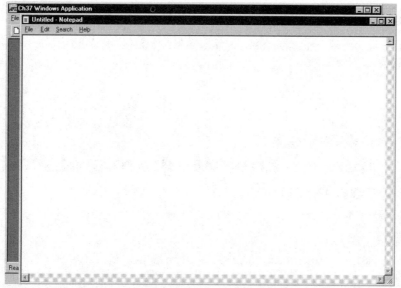

Figure 3-10 Notepad running with CH3 application

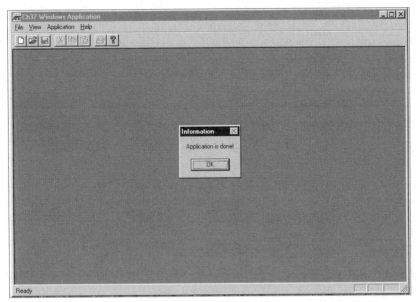

Figure 3-11 Application with message box displayed after Notepad exits

2. Enter ClassWizard and select the CMainFrame object from the drop-down list. Select the ID_TERM_WAIT object from the object list and the COMMAND message from the message list. Click on the Add Function button.

3. Select OnTermWait for the name of the new function and click on the Edit Code button. Enter the following code into the OnTermWait method of CMainFrame:

```
void CMainFrame::OnTermWait()
{

    STARTUPINFO StartupInfo = {0};
    PROCESS_INFORMATION ProcessInfo;

    StartupInfo.cb = sizeof(STARTUPINFO);
    if (CreateProcess(NULL, "notepad.exe", NULL, NULL, FALSE,
                       0, NULL, NULL, &StartupInfo, &ProcessInfo))
    {
        WaitForSingleObject(ProcessInfo.hProcess, INFINITE);
        MessageBox ( "Application is done!", "Information", MB_OK );
    }
    else
    {
        MessageBox ( "Unable to run application!", "Error", MB_OK );
    }

}
```

4. Compile and run the application.

How It Works

When the user selects the Terminate and Wait menu selection from the Application menu, the OnTermWait method is called for the CMainFrame object. This method then launches the Notepad executable applet from Windows as a separate process and checks to make sure it has been successfully started. This is accomplished by using the CreateProcess function of the Windows 95 API.

If the Notepad application is successfully started, the OnTermWait method "waits" for the application/process to complete by calling the new Windows 95 API function WaitForSingleObject. This function will simply check the thread that is running the process and not return until that process has completed. This is considerably easier than the methods needed in Windows 3.x, which involved either looping around and checking for the window name or using the TOOLHELP functions (as shown next) to wait for a callback notification of the window closing.

Comments

As noted, there is another way to determine whether an application has finished. This method uses the TOOLHELP.DLL functionality to install a callback function that is notified whenever an application starts or finishes. The following Delphi example shows how such a procedure works.

1. Delphi requires that TOOLHELP callbacks reside within a DLL. Create a new project and replace the project source with the following:

```
Library Hook;


uses HookForm;

exports
    HookProc,
    InstallHook,
    UnInstallHook;

begin
    targetHWnd:= 0;
end.
```

2. Next, add the following file to your project:

```
Unit HookForm;

interface

{$F+}
{$K+}

Uses WinTypes, Messages, WinProcs, Toolhelp;

Const
    WM_NOTIFY = WM_USER+$100;
```

```
Procedure UnInstallHook; export;
Procedure InstallHook( notifyWindow: HWnd ); export;
Function HookProc( wID: Word; dwData: LongInt ): Bool; export;

Var
  targetHWnd: HWnd;

implementation

Function HookProc( wID: Word; dwData: LongInt ): Bool;
  Begin
    PostMessage( targetHWnd, WM_NOTIFY, wID, dwData );
    Result := False
  End;

Procedure InstallHook( notifyWindow: HWnd );
  Begin
    If targetHWnd = 0 Then Begin
      If not NotifyRegister( 0, HookProc, NF_NORMAL )
      Then Begin
        MessageBox( notifyWindow, 'NotifyRegister failed!',
                    'Error!', MB_OK+MB_ICONSTOP );
      End
      Else Begin
        targetHWnd:= notifyWindow;
        PostMessage( notifyWindow, WM_USER+1, $8976, 0 );
      End;
    End;
  End;

Procedure UnInstallHook;
  Begin
    If targetHWnd <> 0 Then Begin
      NotifyUnregister( 0 );
      targetHWnd := 0;
    End;
  End;

end;

end.
```

3. Now, compile the resulting project. You will create a DLL that exports two functions: InstallHook and UnInstallHook. These two functions can be used in your own projects to capture the messages from TOOLHELP.DLL. The function HookProc will post a message to your application containing the message ID of WM_USER+$100, with the wParam field filled in with the identifier of the notification. Possible notifications are NFY_EXITTASK, indicating that a task has exited, and NFY_STARTTASK, indicating a task has begun.

4. To test this program, create a new form with a single button on it labeled Run. Double-click on the Run button and enter the following code into the editor window:

```
Procedure UnInstallHook; far; external 'HOOK';
Procedure InstallHook( notifyWindow: HWnd ); far; external 'Hook';

procedure TForm1.Button1Click(Sender: TObject);
begin
    InstallHook(Handle);
    Application.OnMessage := AppMessage;
    WinExec('notepad.exe', SW_SHOW);
end;

procedure TForm1.AppMessage(var Msg: TMsg; var Handled: Boolean);
begin
    if ( Msg.message = WM_USER+$100 ) then
        begin
            case Msg.wparam of
                NFY_EXITTASK:
                    begin
                        MessageBox(0, 'Task Ended', 'Info', MB_OK );
                        UnInstallHook;
                    end;
            end;
        end;
end;
```

5. Compile and run the application.

3.8 How do I...
Terminate and restart Windows from within my application?

COMPLEXITY
EASY

Problem

I would like to be able to restart Windows from my application. When my application is installed, it makes certain modifications to the Windows operating system and I need to ensure that the operating system is closed down and restarted before the application is run for the first time. I would prefer that users not have to stop the operating system and shut it down by themselves, as this could lead to application crashes when they fail to do so. How can I use the Windows 95 API to help me accomplish this goal?

Technique

It is so useful to be able to restart Windows from your application that Microsoft developers provided not one, but two methods to do so. You can either restart Windows from scratch or, if you are so inclined, restart the entire machine by doing a "soft boot." The latter approach has certain advantages in knowing that device drivers and the like are cleared out of memory. Also, if you were to modify the AUTOEXEC.BAT file, the latter method would force it to be reloaded at restart time.

Microsoft provides the ExitWindowsEx function to complete this task. The ExitWindowsEx function takes two parameters. The first parameter indicates the mode in which you wish to restart Windows. This first parameter can be either EWX_SHUT-DOWN, which simply restarts the operating system, or EWX_REBOOT, which will do a warm start of the entire machine. In either case, you will want to OR the parameter with the value EWX_FORCE, which will not allow other programs to interfere in your API call.

Steps

Open and run the CH38.MAK file in Visual C++. Select the main menu item Application and the menu selection Exit Windows. This menu item will then display a dialog box asking you to confirm your selection. It is usually best to confirm a user's request to restart or reboot Windows, since the changes can be irrevocable. The dialog box is shown in Figure 3-12.

Alternatively, you can select the Application main menu item and the drop-down selection Exit Windows and Reboot. This selection will reboot the machine using a warm boot. It also displays a dialog to confirm the user's selection, as shown in Figure 3-13. Select the Yes button and the machine will reboot itself.

To duplicate the functionality of these procedures, follow this plan:

1. Create a new project in Visual C++ using AppWizard. Give the new project the name CH38.MAK. Enter AppStudio, edit the IDR_MAINFRAME menu, and add a new drop-down menu item to the Application main-level menu. Give the new menu item the caption Exit Windows and the identifier ID_EXIT_WINDOWS.

2. Create a new dialog in AppStudio. Add a static text field with the caption "Are you sure you want to Exit Windows and Restart?" Enter ClassWizard and add a new class based on the dialog template. Give the class the name CConfirmDlg. Click

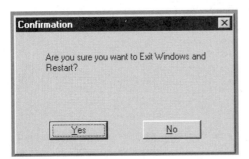

Figure 3-12 Dialog requesting that user confirm Windows restart

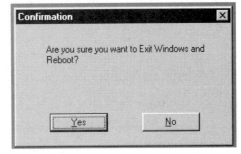

Figure 3-13 Dialog requesting that user confirm Windows reboot

on the CConfirmDlg in the object list and the WM_INITDIALOG in the message list. Add the following code to the OnInitDialog method of the CConfirmDlg:

```
BOOL CConfirmDlg::OnInitDialog()
{
   CDialog::OnInitDialog();

   CenterWindow();

   return TRUE;  // return TRUE  unless you set the focus to a control
}
```

3. Enter ClassWizard and select the CMainFrame object from the drop-down list. Select ID_EXIT_WINDOWS from the object list and COMMAND from the message list. Click on the Add Function button and accept the OnExitWindows name for the new function. Enter the following code into the OnExitWindows function of CMainFrame:

```
void CMainFrame::OnExitWindows()
{
   CConfirmDlg dlg;

   if ( dlg.DoModal() == IDOK ) {
      ExitWindowsEx(EWX_FORCE | EWX_SHUTDOWN, 0);
   }
}
```

4. At the top of the CMainFrame class source file, add the following include file line:

```
#include "confirmd.h"
```

5. Enter AppStudio, edit the IDR_MAINFRAME menu, and add a new drop-down menu item to the Application main-level menu. Give the new menu item the caption Exit Windows and Reboot and the identifier ID_EXIT_REBOOT.

6. Create a new dialog in AppStudio. Add a static text field with the caption "Are you sure you want to Exit Windows and Reboot?" Enter ClassWizard and add a new class based on the dialog template. Give the class the name CRebootDlg. Click on the CRebootDlg in the object list and the WM_INITDIALOG in the message list. Add the following code to the OnInitDialog method of the CRebootDlg:

```
BOOL CRebootDlg::OnInitDialog()
{
   CDialog::OnInitDialog();

   CenterWindow();

   return TRUE;  // return TRUE  unless you set the focus to a control
}
```

7. Enter ClassWizard and select the CMainFrame object from the drop-down list. Select ID_EXIT_REBOOT from the object list and COMMAND from the message list. Click on the Add Function button and accept the OnExitReboot name for the new function. Enter the following code into the OnExitReboot function of CMainFrame:

```
void CMainFrame::OnExitReboot()
{
    CRebootDlg dlg;

    if ( dlg.DoModal() == IDOK ) {
        ExitWindowsEx(EWX_FORCE | EWX_REBOOT, 0);
    }

}
```

8. At the top of the CMainFrame class source file, add the following include file line:

```
#include "rebootdl.h"
```

9. Compile and run the application.

How It Works

When the Exit Windows menu item is selected, the CMainFrame method OnExitWindows is called. This method will call the Windows API function ExitWindowsEx, passing it the exit code values of EWX_FORCE and EWX_SHUTDOWN, which tells Windows to simply restart itself without rebooting the machine, ignoring any requests from other applications not to restart.

When the Exit Windows and Reboot menu item is selected, the CMainFrame method OnExitReboot is called. This method calls the Windows API function ExitWindowsEx, passing it the exit code value of EWX_REBOOT, which tells the operating system not only to restart itself but to do a warm boot of the entire computer.

Comments

The ExitWindowsEx API function is easy to call and can be implemented in any language. Here is a procedure for doing an ExitWindowsEx call in Visual Basic:

1. First, create a new project or add a new form to a project. Add the following declarations to the general section of the form:

```
Const EWX_LOGOFF = 0
Const EWX_SHUTDOWN = 1
Const EWX_REBOOT = 2
Const EWX_FORCE = 4

Private Declare Function ExitWindowsEx Lib "user32" (ByVal uFlags As
Long, ByVal dwReserved As Long) As Long
```

2. Next, add two buttons to the form labeled Exit Windows and Exit and Reboot.

3. Double-click on the Exit Windows button. Add the following code to the Command1_Click function:

```
Private Sub Command1_Click()
    x% = ExitWindowsEx(EWX_FORCE Or EWX_SHUTDOWN, 0)
End Sub
```

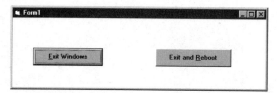

Figure 3-14 Visual Basic form for exiting
Windows and exiting with reboot

4. Double-click on the Exit and Reboot button. Add the following code to the
Command2_Click function:

```
Private Sub Command2_Click()
    x% = ExitWindowsEx(EWX_FORCE Or EWX_REBOOT, 0)
End Sub
```

5. Save your project and run it. You should see a dialog displayed similar to that
in Figure 3-14. Click on the Exit Windows button. Windows will restart itself.
Rerun the application and click on the Exit and Reboot button. Windows will
exit and the system should reboot.

CHAPTER 4

DRAWING AND THE GRAPHICS DEVICE INTERFACE

DRAWING AND THE GRAPHICS DEVICE INTERFACE

How do I...

The graphics device interface, or GDI, is a library of routines that makes up a major part of the Windows interface. GDI routines are used for virtually all screen output and output to other devices such as printers and plotters. This chapter covers common questions raised by programmers using the GDI and provides a number of recipes that will make your application's graphics stand out from the crowd.

Table 4-1 lists the Windows APIs covered in this chapter.

LoadBitmap	CreatePalette	SelectPalette
RealizePalette	SetDIBits	FindResource
LoadResource	LockResource	BitBlt
SetROP2	GetWindowRect	GetClientRect
ClientToScreen	ClipCursor	GetDesktopWindow
GetForegroundWindow	StretchBlt	timeBeginPeriod
timeSetEvent	timeKillEvent	timeEndPeriod

 Table 4-1 Windows APIs covered in Chapter 4

4.1   Display 256-Color Bitmaps

Many programmers design a glorious splash screen, backdrop, or other bitmap to be displayed in their applications. Unfortunately, creating the picture is only part of the problem. Getting your 256-color masterpiece to display is not as easy as it sounds. This How-To helps you master the art of loading and displaying device-independent bitmaps.

4.2   Change the Colors in a Bitmap

This How-To introduces the second important component of working with a bitmap–manipulating the palette. It discusses the different ways you can use palettes in a bitmap and demonstrates a simple method to change the colors displayed in your bitmap.

4.3   Rotate a Bitmap

This How-To demonstrates a simple method of rotating a bitmap by 90-degree increments. This will also give you insight into how you can access the internal data of a device-independent bitmap without using the GDI functions.

4.4   Draw a "Rubber Band" as the Mouse Is Moved

Whether you are writing the definitive drawing application or the next hot word proces- sor, it is frequently necessary to allow the user to draw an object by dragging the mouse. Rubber-banding is the act of drawing a rectangle or sample shape that moves and changes shape as the user moves the mouse. Use rubber-banding to give the user feedback as he or she draws. This section shows how to use the Windows API functions to draw a simple and quick rubber band.

4.5   Capture a Window or Part of the Screen

This How-To shows you how you can use the GDI to capture a bitmap image of the screen or any window. You can now capture images from other applications for use in your own.

4.6   Perform Animation

This How-To shows you how you can use the Windows 95 API to produce simple bitmap animations. It builds on the bitmap operations from the previous exercises and introduces methods of simulating transparency in bitmaps.

4.7   Allow a Bitmap to Be Dragged on Screen

Windows 95 makes extensive use of drag-and-drop in its Object Linking and Embedding (OLE). Even without OLE, other parts of the Windows interface and applications use the drag-and-drop principle to simplify tasks. In this How-To you will learn a technique that allows a bitmap to be picked up and dragged to a new location.

COMPLEXITY
MODERATE

4.1   How do I...
Display 256-color bitmaps?

Problem

I have just added a great looking bitmap to my application's resources. In my application I use LoadBitmap to load this bitmap, then select it into a device context and BitBlt it to the screen. It all seems simple enough, but the bitmap only displays a few colors. How can I get my bitmaps to display in 256 colors?

Technique

To understand what is happening to your bitmap, you need to understand a little about how bitmaps work in Windows 95. There are basically two varieties of bitmaps. Traditional device-dependent bitmaps (DDBs) contain size information and the bitmap data itself. No information is included about the resolution of the device from which the bitmap was recorded, nor is there information about the colors to be displayed in the bitmap.

When Microsoft introduced Windows 3.0, they designed a new bitmap format: the device-independent bitmap (DIB). This form of bitmap contains information about the resolution and colors in which the bitmap should be displayed. It is this bitmap format that is commonly stored in .BMP files and produced by resource editors. Figure 4-1 illustrates the differences between device-independent bitmaps and device-dependent bitmaps.

When you build an application, your development environment binds resource data onto the end of the application. The bitmaps used in your application are bound as device-independent bitmaps, containing full-color palette information. However, the bitmaps that are referenced by bitmap handles (HBITMAP) within the Windows API are device-dependent bitmaps. These bitmaps can only be manipulated once they have been selected into a compatible device context, which supplies color, size, and resolution information to the bitmap.

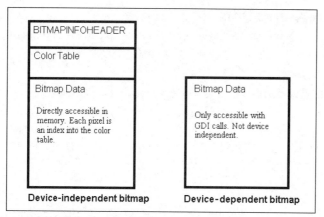

Figure 4-1 Different structures of device-independent bitmaps and device-dependent bitmaps

When you call the LoadBitmap API function, Windows reads your device-independent bitmap resource and loads it into memory, converting it automatically into a 4-bit (16-color) device-dependent bitmap, with a loss of color information. The example application discussed in this section demonstrates how you can use lower-level API functions to load the resource manually into memory, then lock it so your application can access it, and use the GDI functions to convert the device-independent bitmap to a device-dependent bitmap for display. By using this technique, you retain the desired color information.

Steps

Open and run the application 256COLOR.EXE from the CHAPTER4\256COLOR directory on the CD that comes with this book. This application opens a simple window with a menu. When you choose the LoadBitmap menu item from the File menu, the application uses the LoadBitmap API function to load a bitmap resource, which is then selected into a device context and transferred into the window.

Now compare the effect when you choose the LoadResource menu item. This option loads the same bitmap, but uses lower-level Windows API functions to load the resource and convert it to a device-dependent bitmap. The difference in the two bitmaps should be highly visible on 256-color and higher displays. Figure 4-2 shows the main window of the application after the LoadResource menu item has been selected.

Note: If you run this application on a system that has a monochrome display, or a display driver that only supplies 16 colors, you will not be able to see any difference between the two options.

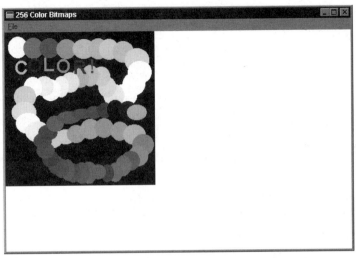

Figure 4-2 The 256COLOR application using LoadResource

Follow these steps to create this example application:

1. Create a new directory and name it 256COLOR. You will create all the files for this project in this directory.

2. Now you need to create a bitmap to be incorporated into the application and displayed at runtime. If you choose, you may use a resource editor or paint application to create a 256-by-256-pixel bitmap that can be displayed by the application. If you do this, make sure that the bitmap is a 256-color (8-bit) bitmap and that you save it as a standard Windows bitmap file. Call it SAMPLE.BMP. Don't use RLE (run length encoding) compression when you save this file, as not all display drivers support this compression.

If you prefer, you may find it simpler to copy the sample bitmap from the CD that accompanies the book. The file is called SAMPLE.BMP, and you will find it in the CHAPTER4\256COLOR directory on the CD.

3. You will need an icon for this application as well. Again, you may choose to create it yourself using a resource editor, but you will probably find it quicker and simpler to copy the icon file from the CD. The file is 256COLOR.ICO, and it is in the CHAPTER4\256COLOR directory on the CD.

4. Now create a resource script containing the menu, the application icon, and the bitmap. These resources will be added to your finished application. You are probably accustomed to creating resource scripts using your resource editor. In this case however, use a text editor to enter the following lines of text. Save the file as 256COLOR.RC.

```
/* ------------------------------------------------------------------ */
/*                                                                    */
/* MODULE: 256COLOR.RC                                                */
/* PURPOSE: This resource script defines the menu and application     */
/*          icon associated with this application, and also           */
/*          includes a bitmap to be loaded and displayed.             */
/*                                                                    */
/* ------------------------------------------------------------------ */

#include "256color.rh"

IDM_BITMAPMENU MENU
{
    POPUP "&File"
    {
        MENUITEM "Use &LoadBitmap", CM_USELOADBITMAP
        MENUITEM "Use &DIB Functions", CM_USEDIBFUNCS
        MENUITEM SEPARATOR
        MENUITEM "E&xit", CM_EXIT
    }
}


IDI_APPICON ICON "256color.ico"

IDBM_SAMPLEBITMAP BITMAP "sample.bmp"
```

5. The resource file that you just created defines the resources for the application. However, it includes another file that we have not yet created. The resource include file, 256COLOR.RH, will define the constants that give unique numbers to the menu items, icon, and bitmap. The identifiers defined in this file will also be used within the program to refer to those resources. Create a new file and save it as 256COLOR.RH. Type the following lines of code into this file:

```
#ifndef __256COLOR_RH
/* ------------------------------------------------------------------ */
/*                                                                    */
/* MODULE: 256COLOR.RH                                                */
/* PURPOSE: Defines identifiers used to address resources.            */
/*                                                                    */
/* ------------------------------------------------------------------ */
#define __256COLOR_RH

#define IDM_BITMAPMENU       301
#define CM_USELOADBITMAP     101
#define CM_USEDIBFUNCS       102
#define CM_EXIT              103

#define IDI_APPICON            1
#define IDBM_SAMPLEBITMAP   3567

#endif
```

6. At last you can start on the application code itself. The code for this How-To is written in straight C, without the use of an application framework at all. For this reason, you will be able to run it on any C compiler. To start creating the program, create a new file in a text editor. Add the following code to the file and save it as 256COLOR.C. The code includes the necessary Windows include files and the 256COLOR.RH file that contains the resource identifiers for this project. In addition, it defines the preprocessor symbol STRICT, which ensures that proper type safety rules are followed with the many different window, menu, and bitmap handles used in Windows applications.

```
/* ------------------------------------------------------------- */
/*                                                               */
/* MODULE: 256COLOR.C                                            */
/* PURPOSE: This C program loads and displays a 256 color bitmap */
/*          using the Windows 95 API routines. If you use the API */
/*          LoadBitmap to load a bitmap from a resource, a DDB    */
/*          (device dependent bitmap) is created with only 16 colors.*/
/*          By loading the bitmap ourselves and converting it from */
/*          a DIB (device independent bitmap) to a DDB, we retain  */
/*          the correct colors.                                    */
/*                                                               */
/* ------------------------------------------------------------- */
#define STRICT

#include <windows.h>
#include <windowsx.h>
#include "256color.rh"
```

7. Add the few declarations shown next to the same source file. MainWindowClassName defines the name of the window class that will be used for this application. The other handles and pointers are global variables. They will be filled in and referred to during the application. Here, they are initialized to zero or NULL to avoid errors arising later.

```
char             *MainWindowClassName = "256ColorTest";
HBITMAP          hDDBitmap = NULL;
HPALETTE         hPalette = NULL;
BITMAPINFOHEADER *pInfoHeader = NULL;
HINSTANCE        hInstance = NULL;
```

8. Add the following function to the source file. Function CreateDIBPalette extracts the color table information from the device-independent bitmap structure and creates a logical palette that will be used in creating and displaying a device-dependent bitmap. The BITMAPINFOHEADER structure that is passed in is a pointer to the memory of the device-independent bitmap resource. The function returns a handle for the logical palette that was created. If the function fails, this handle will be NULL.

```
/* ------------------------------------------------------------- */
/* This function creates a logical palette structure from the color */
/* table supplied with our device independent bitmap.            */
/* ------------------------------------------------------------- */
HPALETTE CreateDIBPalette(BITMAPINFOHEADER *info)
{
```

continued on next page

continued from previous page

```
LOGPALETTE    *palPtr;
RGBQUAD       *colorTable;
WORD          i;
DWORD         numEntries;
HPALETTE      hPal;

/* Allocate space for a LOGPALETTE structure and array of
   entries. Using LocalAlloc with the LMEM_FIXED argument
   gives us a pointer without having to lock and unlock it. */
if (info->biClrUsed != 0)
    numEntries = info->biClrUsed;
else
    numEntries = 1 << info->biBitCount;

palPtr = (NPLOGPALETTE)LocalAlloc(LMEM_FIXED,sizeof(LOGPALETTE) +
                            numEntries * sizeof(PALETTEENTRY));
if (!palPtr)
    return NULL;

palPtr->palVersion = 0x300;
palPtr->palNumEntries = (WORD)numEntries;

// Now fill in the array of palette entries from the color table.
colorTable = (RGBQUAD *)((LPSTR)info + (WORD)info->biSize);
for (i = 0; i < numEntries; i++)
{
    palPtr->palPalEntry[i].peRed = colorTable[i].rgbRed;
    palPtr->palPalEntry[i].peGreen = colorTable[i].rgbGreen;
    palPtr->palPalEntry[i].peBlue = colorTable[i].rgbBlue;
    palPtr->palPalEntry[i].peFlags = 0;
}

hPal = CreatePalette(palPtr);
LocalFree((HLOCAL)palPtr);
return hPal;
}
```

9. Now add the following code to the source file. The ConvertDIBToDDB function performs the actual legwork of converting a device-independent bitmap into a device-dependent bitmap that can be quickly displayed on the screen.

The basic technique is this: First, create a memory device context that is compatible with the screen where the image will eventually be displayed. Next, create a bitmap in that device context, making sure that it is the same size as the device-independent bitmap that you have. This bitmap will be the device-dependent bitmap. Now select the palette that you created previously into the device context and realize it. Finally, use SetDIBits to copy the bitmap bits from one bitmap to another, converting the colors as required. The DIB_RGB_COLORS argument to this call specifies that the colors in the color table of the device-independent bitmap are actual RGB color values, rather than indices into the system palette.

```
/* ---------------------------------------------------------------- */
/* This function converts a DIB to a DDB created for a specific DC   */
/* and palette. Note that we use the screen DC as we are going to    */
/* place the image in a window. If we were going to use another      */
/* device we should create a compatible DC for that device. Usually  */
/* when printing to a printer device, time constraints are not so     */
/* important, so conversion from DIB to DDB and the actual painting   */
/* can be done in one step.                                          */
/* ---------------------------------------------------------------- */
HBITMAP ConvertDIBToDDB(HWND hWnd, BITMAPINFOHEADER *info,
                        HPALETTE *hPalette)
{
    HDC              hDC, hMemDC;
    HPALETTE         hOldPalette;
    HBITMAP          hOldBitmap, hDDBitmap;
    DWORD            numEntries;

    hDC = GetDC(hWnd); // Get a handle to our device context
    if ((*hPalette = CreateDIBPalette(info)) != NULL)
    {
        hMemDC = CreateCompatibleDC(hDC);
        hOldPalette = SelectPalette(hMemDC,*hPalette,FALSE);
        RealizePalette(hMemDC);
        hDDBitmap = CreateCompatibleBitmap(hDC,
                                           info->biWidth,
                                           info->biHeight);
        hOldBitmap = SelectObject(hMemDC,hDDBitmap);
        if (info->biClrUsed != 0)
            numEntries = info->biClrUsed;
        else
            numEntries = 1 << info->biBitCount;
        /* Use SetDIBits to place the device independent bitmap data
           into the new bitmap that we have created, hDDBitmap. */
        SetDIBits(hMemDC,hDDBitmap,
                  0,info->biHeight,
                  (LPSTR)info + (info->biSize +
                                 (numEntries * sizeof(RGBQUAD))),
                  (BITMAPINFO *)info, DIB_RGB_COLORS);
        SelectObject(hMemDC,hOldBitmap);
        SelectPalette(hMemDC,hOldPalette,FALSE);
        DeleteDC(hMemDC);
    }
    ReleaseDC(hWnd,hDC);

    return hDDBitmap;
}
```

10. Add the function LoadBitmapResource to the same source file, 256COLOR.C. This function uses a combination of FindResource, LoadResource, and LockResource to load the requested bitmap resource into memory. The function returns a pointer to a BITMAPINFOHEADER, which is the start of the device-independent bitmap resource in memory.

There are two things to note about using these functions. First, resources are read-only. Although LockResource returns a pointer to the resource in memory, attempting to modify this memory will cause a protection fault. If you want to modify a bitmap (as some of the later How-To's in this chapter do), you will need to take a copy of it first, and only modify the copy.

The second thing to note is that Windows 95 and Windows NT both track the use of resources by the application. You do not have to explicitly free the resource if you do not want to—Windows will free it automatically when your application terminates.

```
/* ------------------------------------------------------------------ */
/* This function opens a bitmap resource attached to our executable  */
/* file and loads it into memory as a device independent bitmap.     */
/* The function returns a pointer to the resource data, or NULL if   */
/* it fails.                                                          */
/* ------------------------------------------------------------------ */
BITMAPINFOHEADER *LoadBitmapResource(HINSTANCE hInstance, WORD resId)
{
    HRSRC   hResource;
    HGLOBAL hDib;

    if (((hResource = FindResource(hInstance,
                        MAKEINTRESOURCE(resId),
                        RT_BITMAP)) != NULL) &&
        ((hDib = LoadResource(hInstance,hResource)) != NULL))
        return (BITMAPINFOHEADER *)LockResource(hDib);
    return NULL;
}
```

11. Now add the Paint function to the source file. This function will be called whenever the Windows operating system sends a WM_PAINT message to the application window. Now that the bitmap is stored in memory as a device-dependent bitmap and a palette, displaying on the screen is a comparatively quick and simple matter. Selecting the palette into the on-screen device context and realizing it ensures that the colors of the image are those that were intended. The image is then selected into a memory device context, and the BitBlt API function is called to transfer the data to the screen.

```
/* ------------------------------------------------------------------ */
/* This is the actual drawing function called when WM_PAINT is       */
/* received. Because the conversion from DIB to DBB is done once     */
/* when the bitmap is loaded, this routine is a small and QUICK      */
/* Realization of the palette and BitBlt into the device context.    */
/* ------------------------------------------------------------------ */
void Paint(HWND hWnd, HPALETTE hPalette, HBITMAP hBitmap,
           int BitmapWidth, int BitmapHeight)
{
    PAINTSTRUCT         ps;
    HDC                 hDC, hMemDC;
    HPALETTE            hOldPalette;
    HBITMAP             hOldBitmap;
```

```
hDC = BeginPaint(hWnd, &ps);

// Realize the palette so that the colors are correct.
if (hPalette)
{
    hOldPalette = SelectPalette(hDC, hPalette, FALSE);
    RealizePalette(hDC);
}

// Select the bitmap into a memory DC then Blit it to the screen.
if ((hMemDC = CreateCompatibleDC(hDC)) != NULL)
{
    hOldBitmap = SelectObject(hMemDC,hBitmap);
    BitBlt(hDC, 0, 0, BitmapWidth, BitmapHeight,
            hMemDC, 0, 0,SRCCOPY);
    SelectBitmap(hMemDC,hOldBitmap);
    DeleteDC(hMemDC);
}

if (hPalette)
   SelectPalette(hDC,hOldPalette,FALSE);
EndPaint(hWnd, &ps);
}
```

12. You have now entered most of the code that makes this application work. In
the next few steps you will add the "worker" functions that provide the framework for all the applications in this chapter. The function immediately
following, MainWndProc, is the callback function that processes all the messages coming to the application window. In this application, it needs to
respond to the three menu options, CM_USELOADBITMAP for the
LoadBitmap menu item, CM_USEDIBFUNCS for the LoadResource menu
item, and CM_EXIT for the Exit menu item. When the user selects the
LoadResource menu item, this code uses the functions that you have already
written–loading the bitmap from the resource, creating a palette, and converting the device-independent bitmap to a device-dependent bitmap. The
window is then invalidated by calling InvalidateRect, causing the newly
loaded bitmap to be displayed.

When the user selects the LoadBitmap menu item from the menu, the application
discards the previously loaded bitmap and loads the bitmap from the resource
using the LoadBitmap API function. In this case, Windows performs the color
conversions, producing a 16-color device-dependent bitmap.

```
/* ---------------------------------------------------------------- */
/* This function is the main window callback function which will be */
/* called by Windows to process messages for our window.            */
/* ---------------------------------------------------------------- */
LPARAM CALLBACK MainWndProc(HWND hWnd, UINT message,
                    WPARAM wParam, LPARAM lParam)
{

    switch (message)
    {
```

continued on next page

continued from previous page

```
                    case WM_COMMAND:
                        switch(wParam)
                        {
                            /* Usually the first method tried - load the resource
                                directly into a DDB - Windows does the color
                                conversion */
                            case CM_USELOADBITMAP:
                                /* Don't bother with anything if a DDB is already
                                    loaded but no DIB */
                                if ((hDDBitmap) && (!pInfoHeader))
                                    break;

                                // If the DIB stuff is around, remove it.
                                if (pInfoHeader)
                                    pInfoHeader = NULL;
                                if (hDDBitmap)
                                {
                                    DeleteObject(hDDBitmap);
                                    hDDBitmap = NULL;
                                }
                                if (hPalette)
                                {
                                    DeleteObject(hPalette);
                                    hPalette = NULL;
                                }

                                if ((hDDBitmap = LoadBitmap(hInstance,
                                    MAKEINTRESOURCE(IDBM_SAMPLEBITMAP))) != NULL)
                                InvalidateRect(hWnd,NULL,FALSE);
                                break;

                            /* The user would like to load the resource as a DIB and
                                have it converted to a DDB to display, retaining color
                                information */
                            case CM_USEDIBFUNCS:
                                // Don't bother to reload if already exists.
                                if (pInfoHeader)
                                    break;
                                // Remove the old Bitmap.
                                if (hDDBitmap)
                                {
                                    DeleteObject(hDDBitmap);
                                    hDDBitmap = NULL;
                                }
                                /* Now load a DIB, convert it to DDB (creating a
                                    palette along the way */
                                if ((pInfoHeader = LoadBitmapResource(hInstance,
                                                IDBM_SAMPLEBITMAP)) != NULL)
                                {
                                    if ((hDDBitmap = ConvertDIBToDDB(hWnd,
                                            pInfoHeader,&hPalette)) != NULL)
                                        InvalidateRect(hWnd,NULL,FALSE);
                                    else
                                        MessageBox(hWnd,"Unable to create DDB",
                                                NULL,MB_ICONSTOP | MB_OK);
```

```
                        }
                        else
                           MessageBox(hWnd,"Unable to load DIB",
                                        NULL,MB_ICONSTOP | MB_OK);
                        break;

                   case CM_EXIT:
                        DestroyWindow(hWnd);
                        break;
                   default:
                        return (DefWindowProc(hWnd,message,wParam,lParam));
            }
            break;
       case WM_PALETTECHANGED:
            // Force a repaint.
            if (((HWND)wParam != hWnd) && (hDDBitmap != NULL))
                InvalidateRect(hWnd,NULL,TRUE);
            break;
       case WM_PAINT:
            if (hDDBitmap != NULL)
            {
                if (pInfoHeader)
                    Paint(hWnd,hPalette,hDDBitmap,
                             pInfoHeader->biWidth,pInfoHeader->biHeight);
                else
                    Paint(hWnd,hPalette,hDDBitmap,256,256);
            }
            else
                return (DefWindowProc(hWnd, message, wParam, lParam));
            break;
       case WM_DESTROY:
            if (hDDBitmap)
                DeleteObject(hDDBitmap);
            if (hPalette)
                DeleteObject(hPalette);
            PostQuitMessage(0);
            break;
       default:
            return DefWindowProc(hWnd, message, wParam, lParam);
   }
   return 0;
}
```

13. Add the InitApplication function to the source file. This function is called once when the application is first run, and then only if the window class for this window does not already exist. It initializes and registers a window class for the main window of the application.

```
/* ------------------------------------------------------------------ */
/* This function initializes a WNDCLASS structure and uses it to      */
/* register a class for our main window.                              */
/* ------------------------------------------------------------------ */
BOOL InitApplication(HINSTANCE hInstance)
{
    WNDCLASS  wc;
```

continued on next page

continued from previous page

```
        wc.style = 0;
        wc.lpfnWndProc = MainWndProc;
        wc.cbClsExtra = 0;
        wc.cbWndExtra = 0;
        wc.hInstance = hInstance;
        wc.hIcon = LoadIcon(NULL, IDI_APPLICATION);
        wc.hCursor = LoadCursor(NULL, IDC_ARROW);
        wc.hbrBackground = (HBRUSH)(COLOR_WINDOW + 1);
        wc.lpszMenuName =  MAKEINTRESOURCE(IDM_BITMAPMENU);
        wc.lpszClassName = MainWindowClassName;

        return RegisterClass(&wc);
}
```

14. Now add the InitInstance function. This function is called every time the application is run. It creates and displays the main window of the application.

```
/* ------------------------------------------------------------- */
/* This function creates an instance of our main window. The window */
/* is given a class name and a title, and told to display anywhere. */
/* The nCmdShow argument passed to the program determines how the   */
/* window will be displayed.                                        */
/* ------------------------------------------------------------- */
BOOL InitInstance(HINSTANCE hInst, int nCmdShow)
{
    HWND hWnd;

    hInstance = hInst; // Store in global variable.

    hWnd = CreateWindow(MainWindowClassName,"256 Color Bitmaps",
                 WS_OVERLAPPEDWINDOW,CW_USEDEFAULT,
                 CW_USEDEFAULT,CW_USEDEFAULT,CW_USEDEFAULT,
                 NULL,NULL,hInstance,NULL);
    if (!hWnd)
        return FALSE;

    ShowWindow(hWnd, nCmdShow);
    UpdateWindow(hWnd);         // Send a WM_PAINT message
    return TRUE;
}
```

15. The final piece of code for this application is the WinMain function. This is the main entry point for an application for the Windows operating system. This function initializes the window class and the window, then processes messages in a loop until the application is closed.

```
/* ------------------------------------------------------------- */
/* The main entry point for Windows applications. Check to see if */
/* the main window class name has already been registered; if it has */
/* not, call InitApplication to register it. Call InitInstance to  */
/* create an instance of our main window, then pump messages until */
/* the application is closed.                                      */
/* ------------------------------------------------------------- */
int PASCAL WinMain(HINSTANCE hInstance, HINSTANCE hPrevInstance,
              LPSTR lpCmdLine, int nCmdShow)
{
```

```
        MSG msg;

        if (!FindWindow(MainWindowClassName,NULL))
            if (!InitApplication(hInstance))
                return FALSE;

        if (!InitInstance(hInstance, nCmdShow))
            return FALSE;

        while (GetMessage(&msg,NULL,0,0))
        {
            TranslateMessage(&msg);
            DispatchMessage(&msg);
        }
        return (msg.wParam);
    }
```

16. Compile and run the application.

Comments

Displaying a 256-color bitmap in Windows is by no means a simple task. The example discussed here is suitable for static display of a bitmap but would not be practical for an animation application. The time taken to realize logical palettes into the physical palette, and to convert device-independent bitmap RGB values into palette entries in a device-dependent bitmap and then into the physical palette, would make the process too slow. Other methods for dealing with palettes are discussed in the next How-To and in How-To 4.5.

COMPLEXITY
MODERATE

4.2   How do I...
Change the colors in a bitmap?

Problem

I would like my application to change some of the colors in my bitmap. How do I achieve this?

Technique

Each byte in an 8-bit device-independent bitmap is an index into a palette of some sort. The palette may be the color table that follows the BITMAPINFOHEADER structure for the bitmap. Alternatively, it may be the currently realized logical palette, or the physical palette of the device. For a bitmap that is interpreted using the color table (type DIB_RGB_COLORS), you can change any color in the image by changing the entry in the color table for that color. If you know the index within the color table for each color that you wish to change, you can directly modify that value in the color table. If you know the RGB value of the color to be changed, but not the index, it is possible to iterate through the color table, comparing the RGB values and replacing any entries that match. This latter method is the approach used by the example program in this How-To.

The most important thing to remember when modifying the color table is that the resource cannot be modified directly. In 32-bit Windows software, resources are read-only. To change the color table, the example application makes a copy of the resource, or at least the part to be modified— the BITMAPINFOHEADER and the color table. In order to save time and space, the actual bits of the DIB are not copied—the application keeps a pointer to this data and uses it along with the copies of the header and color table to create a device-dependent bitmap and palette. If you are going to be changing the actual bitmap itself, you will have to copy this as well.

Steps

Open and run the sample application CHANGE.EXE. You will find it in the CHAPTER4\CHANGE directory on the CD that accompanies this book. When this application opens, it displays a very simple 256-color bitmap. If you choose the Change Colors item from the File menu, the bitmap appears to change. Some words disappear, and others change color. The actual bitmap itself has not changed, only the palette that is used to interpret it. Choosing the Change Colors item again restores the image to its original state. Figure 4-3 shows the application before the colors have been changed.

Follow these steps to implement this application:

Figure 4-3 CHANGE application before changing the colors

1. Create a new directory for this application, calling it CHGCOLOR. This directory will hold all the files that you use to create this project.

2. You will need a 256-color bitmap for this project. The example application is going to selectively change colors in the bitmap, so we recommend that you copy the bitmap off the CD that accompanies this book. The bitmap is called SAMPLE.BMP and is in the CHAPTER4\CHGCOLOR directory on the CD.

If you don't have access to a CD drive, you will have to create your own. Use a resource editor to create a 256-color bitmap (around 256-by-256 pixels in size, although this is not critical). Make sure that you have some red (RGB value 0xFF0000 or 255,0,0), some blue (RGB value 0x0000FF or 0,0,255), and some green (RGB value 0x00FF00 or 0,255,0) in the bitmap, as these are the colors that this sample application will manipulate. If you don't have those colors in the bitmap, the application will still work, but you won't be able to see anything happening.

3. In order to include the bitmap in the application as a resource, you will need to create a resource script. This script will also define the menus and application icon. Create a new text file and call it CHANGE.RC. Type in the following resource script:

```
/* --------------------------------------------------------------- */
/*                                                                  */
/* MODULE: CHANGE.RC                                                */
/* PURPOSE: This resource script defines the menu and application   */
/*          icon associated with this application, and also         */
/*          includes a bitmap to be loaded and displayed.           */
/*                                                                  */
/* --------------------------------------------------------------- */

#include "change.rh"

IDM_BITMAPMENU MENU
{
    POPUP "&File"
    {
        MENUITEM "Change Color", CM_CHANGE
        MENUITEM SEPARATOR
        MENUITEM "E&xit", CM_EXIT
    }
}


IDI_APPICON ICON "change.ico"

IDBM_SAMPLEBITMAP BITMAP "sample.bmp"
```

4. The resource script that you just entered needs an include file called CHANGE.RH. This file defines the identifiers used to reference the different resources, and it is used in both the resource script and in the application itself. Create a new file and enter the following code. Save it as CHANGE.RH.

```
#ifndef __CHANGE_RH
/* ------------------------------------------------------------------ */
/*                                                                     */
/* MODULE: CHANGE.RH                                                   */
/* PURPOSE: Defines identifiers used to address resources.            */
/*                                                                     */
/* ------------------------------------------------------------------ */
#define __CHANGE_RH

#define IDM_BITMAPMENU          301
#define CM_CHANGE               101
#define CM_EXIT                 102

#define IDI_APPICON               1
#define IDBM_SAMPLEBITMAP       3567

#endif
```

5. The other thing that the resource script needs before it compiles is the application icon. Again, copy the file from the CD, using the file CHANGE.ICO from the CHAPTER4\CHGCOLOR directory on the CD. If you need to, you can create a 32-by-32-pixel, 16-color icon, and save it as CHANGE.ICO.

6. Now you can start creating the main source file for the application. Using a text editor, create a new file, and save it as CHANGE.C. Add the following lines of code to the top of the file. This code includes the header files required for this application. It also defines the preprocessor symbol, STRICT, which ensures that proper type checking is carried out between the many different types and handles that are used in programs for the Windows operating system.

In addition, the code defines some constants and global variables. The MainWindowClassName is used to search for and register a class for the window of the application. The four RGBQUAD values define the colors to be manipulated in this palette demonstration. All the global variables are initialized to default values.

```
/* ------------------------------------------------------------------ */
/*                                                                     */
/* MODULE: CHANGE.C                                                    */
/* PURPOSE: Demonstrates how you can change the colors in the         */
/*          palette of a device independent bitmap.                    */
/*                                                                     */
/* ------------------------------------------------------------------ */
#define STRICT

#include <windows.h>
#include <windowsx.h>
#include "change.rh"

// Constants.
char        *MainWindowClassName = "ColorChangeTest";

RGBQUAD     colorRed = { 0x00, 0x00, 0xFF, 0 };
RGBQUAD     colorGreen = { 0x00, 0xFF, 0x00, 0 };
```

```
RGBQUAD       colorBlue = { 0xFF, 0x00, 0x00, 0 };
RGBQUAD       colorBlack = { 0x00, 0x00, 0x00, 0 };

// Global variables.
HBITMAP       hDDBitmap = NULL;
HPALETTE      hPalette = NULL;
BITMAPINFO    *pResourceDIB = NULL;
BITMAPINFO    *pActiveDIB = NULL;
VOID          *pResourceBits = NULL;
HINSTANCE     hInstance = NULL;
BOOL          isOriginal = TRUE;
```

7. Add the function CreateDIBPalette to the same source file. The code immediately following lists this function, which creates a logical palette using the
supplied color table information. The function returns a handle to the created
palette if successful or NULL if it fails.

```
/* ------------------------------------------------------------------ */
/* This function creates a logical palette structure from the color  */
/* table supplied with our device independent bitmap.                */
/* ------------------------------------------------------------------ */
HPALETTE CreateDIBPalette(BITMAPINFO *info)
{
    LOGPALETTE   *palPtr;
    DWORD        i, numEntries;
    HPALETTE     hPal;

    /* Allocate space for a LOGPALETTE structure and array of
       entries. Using LocalAlloc with the LMEM_FIXED argument
       gives us a pointer without having to lock and unlock it. */
    if ((numEntries = info->bmiHeader.biClrUsed) == 0)
        numEntries = 1L << info->bmiHeader.biBitCount;

    palPtr = (LOGPALETTE *)LocalAlloc(LMEM_FIXED,sizeof(LOGPALETTE) +
                                   numEntries * sizeof(PALETTEENTRY));
    if (!palPtr)
        return NULL;

    palPtr->palVersion = 0x300;
    palPtr->palNumEntries = (WORD)numEntries;

    // Now fill in the array of palette entries from the color table.
    for (i = 0; i < numEntries; i++)
    {
        palPtr->palPalEntry[i].peRed = info->bmiColors[i].rgbRed;
        palPtr->palPalEntry[i].peGreen = info->bmiColors[i].rgbGreen;
        palPtr->palPalEntry[i].peBlue = info->bmiColors[i].rgbBlue;
        palPtr->palPalEntry[i].peFlags = 0;
    }

    hPal = CreatePalette(palPtr);
    LocalFree((HLOCAL)palPtr);
    return hPal;
}
```

8. Next, add the function ConvertDIBToDDB. This function creates a new device-dependent bitmap and copies the bitmap data from the supplied device-independent bitmap, performing the necessary transformations along the way. The function calls CreateDIBPalette to create a logical palette; then it ensures that this palette is used when converting the bitmaps, by selecting and realizing the palette in the memory device context being used.

```
/* ---------------------------------------------------------------- */
/* This function converts the DIB supplied as the info argument into */
/* a DDB ready for display in the given window. Along the way it     */
/* modifies the global variables hPalette and hDDBitmap. Returns     */
/* TRUE if successful, otherwise FALSE.                              */
/* ---------------------------------------------------------------- */
BOOL ConvertDIBToDDB(HWND hWnd, BITMAPINFO *info, VOID *bits)
{
    HDC                   hDC, hMemDC;
    HPALETTE              hOldPalette;
    HBITMAP               hOldBitmap;

    // Release the old palette.
    if (hPalette != NULL)
    {
        DeleteObject(hPalette);
        hPalette = NULL;
    }

    // Release the old bitmap.
    if (hDDBitmap != NULL)
    {
        DeleteObject(hDDBitmap);
        hDDBitmap = NULL;
    }

    /* Create a new palette with CreateDIBPalette (above), then
        create a bitmap in the device context with CreateCompatibleBitmap
        and SetDIBits. By selecting the palette into the device
        context, we ensure that the colors are correct. */
    hDC = GetDC(hWnd);
    if ((hPalette = CreateDIBPalette(info)) != NULL)
    {
        if ((hMemDC = CreateCompatibleDC(hDC)) != NULL)
        {
            hOldPalette = SelectPalette(hMemDC,hPalette,FALSE);
            RealizePalette(hMemDC);
            if ((hDDBitmap = CreateCompatibleBitmap(hDC,
                                    info->bmiHeader.biWidth,
                                    info->bmiHeader.biHeight)) != NULL)
            {
                hOldBitmap = SelectObject(hMemDC,hDDBitmap);

                // Copy the bitmap data to the new bitmap (hDDBitmap).
                SetDIBits(hMemDC,hDDBitmap,0,
                        info->bmiHeader.biHeight,
                        bits,info,DIB_RGB_COLORS);
```

```
            SelectObject(hMemDC,hOldBitmap);
        }
        SelectPalette(hMemDC,hOldPalette,FALSE);
        DeleteDC(hMemDC);
    }
    ReleaseDC(hWnd,hDC);

    // If bitmap creation failed, free the palette also.
    if (!hDDBitmap)
    {
        DeleteObject(hPalette);
        hPalette = NULL;
    }
    }

    return (hDDBitmap != NULL);
}
```

9. Add the following code to the same source file, CHANGE.C. This function uses
FindResource and LoadResource to retrieve a handle to the bitmap resource. It
then uses LockResource to get a pointer to the resource in memory. Because this
application will modify the color table of the bitmap, and resources are read-only,
the code calculates the size of the color table and bitmap header and allocates
memory for a copy of this information. The application can now modify the copy
rather than the resource itself.

```
/* ------------------------------------------------------------- */
/* This function opens a bitmap resource attached to our executable */
/* file and loads it into memory as a device independent bitmap (DIB)*/
/* The function then locks the resource and makes a copy of it using */
/* a global memory block of the same size. The function modifies the */
/* global pointers pResourceDIB and pActiveDIB. It returns TRUE if   */
/* successful, or FALSE if not.                                      */
/* ------------------------------------------------------------- */
BOOL LoadBitmapResource(HINSTANCE hInstance, WORD resId)
{
    HRSRC    hResource;
    HGLOBAL  hDib;
    DWORD    nSize, numEntries;

    if (((hResource = FindResource(hInstance,
                                   MAKEINTRESOURCE(resId),
                                   RT_BITMAP)) != NULL) &&
        ((hDib = LoadResource(hInstance,hResource)) != NULL))
    {
        pResourceDIB = (BITMAPINFO *)LockResource(hDib);
        if ((numEntries = pResourceDIB->bmiHeader.biClrUsed) == 0)
            numEntries = 1L << pResourceDIB->bmiHeader.biBitCount;
        nSize = pResourceDIB->bmiHeader.biSize +
                (numEntries * sizeof(RGBQUAD));
        pActiveDIB = (BITMAPINFO *)LocalAlloc(LMEM_FIXED,nSize);
        if (pActiveDIB != NULL)
        {
            CopyMemory(pActiveDIB,pResourceDIB,nSize);
            pResourceBits = (LPSTR)pResourceDIB + nSize;
```

continued on next page

continued from previous page

```
                return TRUE;
        }
    }
    return FALSE;
}
```

10. Now add the main drawing function. The Paint function will be called when
the window requires painting. It selects the current palette into the device
context for the window and realizes the palette so that those colors will be
used for drawing. The code then calls the Windows API BitBlt function to display the bitmap image on screen.

```
/* ------------------------------------------------------------------ */
/* This is the actual drawing function called when WM_PAINT is        */
/* received. Because the conversion from DIB to DBB is done once       */
/* when the bitmap is loaded, this routine is a small and QUICK        */
/* realization of the palette and BitBlt into the device context.      */
/* ------------------------------------------------------------------ */
void Paint(HWND hWnd, HPALETTE hPalette, HBITMAP hBitmap,
           int BitmapWidth, int BitmapHeight)
{
    PAINTSTRUCT         ps;
    HDC                 hDC, hMemDC;
    HPALETTE            hOldPalette;
    HBITMAP             hOldBitmap;

    hDC = BeginPaint(hWnd, &ps);

    if ((hMemDC = CreateCompatibleDC(hDC)) != NULL)
    {
        hOldPalette = SelectPalette(hDC, hPalette, FALSE);
        RealizePalette(hDC);
        hOldBitmap = SelectObject(hMemDC,hBitmap);
        BitBlt(hDC, 0, 0, BitmapWidth, BitmapHeight,
               hMemDC, 0, 0,SRCCOPY);
        SelectBitmap(hMemDC,hOldBitmap);
        SelectPalette(hDC,hOldPalette,FALSE);
        DeleteDC(hMemDC);
    }
    EndPaint(hWnd, &ps);
}
```

11. Add the ChangeColor function, listed next. This function scans through the
color table that is supplied in the BITMAPINFO structure and replaces all
occurrences of the specified fromColor RGB value with the specified toColor
RGB value.

```
/* ------------------------------------------------------------------ */
/* This function works on the color table for a DIB. It changes all   */
/* the entries in the table for fromColor to toColor. Do not use      */
/* this function on the DIB in the resource itself, as resources are  */
/* read-only. Use a copy of the resource DIB.                         */
/* ------------------------------------------------------------------ */
void ChangeColor(BITMAPINFO *info, RGBQUAD fromColor,
                 RGBQUAD toColor)
```

```
{
    DWORD i, numEntries;

    if ((numEntries = info->bmiHeader.biClrUsed) == 0)
        numEntries = 1L << info->bmiHeader.biBitCount;

    for (i = 0; i < numEntries; i++)
        if ((info->bmiColors[i].rgbRed == fromColor.rgbRed) &&
            (info->bmiColors[i].rgbGreen == fromColor.rgbGreen) &&
            (info->bmiColors[i].rgbBlue == fromColor.rgbBlue))
        {
            info->bmiColors[i].rgbRed = toColor.rgbRed;
            info->bmiColors[i].rgbGreen = toColor.rgbGreen;
            info->bmiColors[i].rgbBlue = toColor.rgbBlue;
        }
}
```

12. The next function to add to this source file is the HandleChange function. HandleChange will be called when the user selects the Change Colors menu item from the File menu. If the original bitmap from the file is currently visible (with the blue and green colors), the code calls ChangeColor to change the green palette entries to black and the blue palette entries to red. If the altered bitmap is visible, the isOriginal variable will be FALSE. If this is the case, the code simply copies the color table back from the resource, restoring the original color combinations. In either case, the code must call ConvertDIBToDDB to re-create the logical palette and the device-dependent bitmap, then call InvalidateRect to update the screen display.

```
/* ---------------------------------------------------------------- */
/* This function responds to the CM_CHANGE message. If the flag     */
/* isOriginal is TRUE, the bitmap is the same as the resource. Two  */
/* colors are changed and the DDB re-created from the DIB. If the   */
/* flag is FALSE, this has already been done, so the original color */
/* information is copied from the resource to restore the colors.   */
/* In either case the DDB is then re-created.                       */
/* ---------------------------------------------------------------- */
void HandleChange(HWND hWnd, BOOL isOriginal)
{
    DWORD numEntries;

    if (isOriginal)
    {
        ChangeColor(pActiveDIB,colorBlue,colorRed);
        ChangeColor(pActiveDIB,colorGreen,colorBlack);
    }
    else
    {
        if ((numEntries = pResourceDIB->bmiHeader.biClrUsed) == 0)
            numEntries = 1L << pResourceDIB->bmiHeader.biBitCount;
        CopyMemory(pActiveDIB,pResourceDIB,
                pResourceDIB->bmiHeader.biSize +
                (numEntries * sizeof(RGBQUAD)));
    }
    ConvertDIBToDDB(hWnd,pActiveDIB,pResourceBits);
```

continued on next page

continued from previous page

```
        InvalidateRect(hWnd,NULL,FALSE);
}
```

13. Add the following code to the source file CHANGE.C. This is function MainWndProc, a callback function that responds to the messages sent to the application window. In particular, this function responds to the WM_CREATE message, which is sent when the window is first created. It loads the original bitmap and prepares it for display. In response to the CM_CHANGE command message, this code calls the HandleChange function to modify the color table of the bitmap and redisplay it. It toggles the value of the isOriginal flag, so selecting this action again undoes the previous changes.

```
/* ------------------------------------------------------------------ */
/* This function is the main window callback function which will be   */
/* called by Windows to process messages for our window.              */
/* ------------------------------------------------------------------ */
LPARAM CALLBACK MainWndProc(HWND hWnd, UINT message,
                            WPARAM wParam, LPARAM lParam)
{

    switch (message)
    {
        case WM_CREATE:
            if (LoadBitmapResource(hInstance,IDBM_SAMPLEBITMAP))
            {
                ConvertDIBToDDB(hWnd,pActiveDIB,pResourceBits);
                InvalidateRect(hWnd,NULL,FALSE);
                isOriginal = TRUE;
            }
            break;
        case WM_COMMAND:
            switch(wParam)
            {
                case CM_CHANGE:
                    HandleChange(hWnd,isOriginal);
                    isOriginal = !isOriginal;
                    break;
                case CM_EXIT:
                    DestroyWindow(hWnd);
                    break;
                default:
                    return (DefWindowProc(hWnd,message,wParam,lParam));
            }
            break;
        case WM_PALETTECHANGED:
            if (((HWND)wParam != hWnd) && (hDDBitmap != NULL))
                InvalidateRect(hWnd,NULL,TRUE); /* force a repaint */
            break;
        case WM_PAINT:
            if (hDDBitmap != NULL)
            {
                Paint(hWnd,hPalette,hDDBitmap,
                    pActiveDIB->bmiHeader.biWidth,
                    pActiveDIB->bmiHeader.biHeight);
            }
            else
```

```
                    return (DefWindowProc(hWnd, message, wParam, lParam));
                break;
            case WM_DESTROY:
                if (hPalette)
                    DeleteObject(hPalette);
                if (hDDBitmap)
                    DeleteObject(hDDBitmap);
                if (pActiveDIB)
                    LocalFree((HLOCAL)pActiveDIB);
                PostQuitMessage(0);
                break;
            default:
                return DefWindowProc(hWnd, message, wParam, lParam);
    }
    return 0;
}
```

14. Add the InitApplication function to the source file. This function is called
once when the application is first run, and then only if the window class for
this window does not already exist. It initializes and registers a window class
for the main window of the application.

```
/* ------------------------------------------------------------- */
/* This function initializes a WNDCLASS structure and uses it to  */
/* register a class for our main window.                          */
/* ------------------------------------------------------------- */
BOOL InitApplication(HINSTANCE hInstance)
{
    WNDCLASS  wc;

    wc.style = 0;
    wc.lpfnWndProc = MainWndProc;
    wc.cbClsExtra = 0;
    wc.cbWndExtra = 0;
    wc.hInstance = hInstance;
    wc.hIcon = LoadIcon(NULL, IDI_APPLICATION);
    wc.hCursor = LoadCursor(NULL, IDC_ARROW);
    wc.hbrBackground = (HBRUSH)(COLOR_WINDOW + 1);
    wc.lpszMenuName =  MAKEINTRESOURCE(IDM_BITMAPMENU);
    wc.lpszClassName = MainWindowClassName;

    return RegisterClass(&wc);
}
```

15. Now add the InitInstance function. This function is called every time the
application is run. It creates and displays the main window of the application.

```
/* ------------------------------------------------------------- */
/* This function creates an instance of our main window. The window */
/* is given a class name and a title, and told to display anywhere. */
/* The nCmdShow argument passed to the program determines how the   */
/* window will be displayed.                                        */
/* ------------------------------------------------------------- */
BOOL InitInstance(HINSTANCE hInst, int nCmdShow)
{
    HWND hWnd;
```

continued on next page

continued from previous page

```
        hInstance = hInst; /* Store in global variable */

        hWnd = CreateWindow(MainWindowClassName,"Changing the Palette",
                        WS_OVERLAPPEDWINDOW,CW_USEDEFAULT,
                        CW_USEDEFAULT,CW_USEDEFAULT,CW_USEDEFAULT,
                        NULL,NULL,hInstance,NULL);
        if (!hWnd)
            return FALSE;

        ShowWindow(hWnd, nCmdShow);
        UpdateWindow(hWnd);            /* Send a WM_PAINT message */
        return TRUE;
    }
```

16. The final piece of code for this application is the WinMain function. This is the main entry point for an application for the Windows operating system. This function initializes the window class and the window, then processes messages in a loop until the application is closed.

```
/* ----------------------------------------------------------------- */
/* The main entry point for Windows applications. Check to see if    */
/* the main window class name has already been registered, if it has */
/* not, call InitApplication to register it. Call InitInstance to    */
/* create an instance of our main window, then pump messages until   */
/* the application is closed.                                        */
/* ----------------------------------------------------------------- */
int PASCAL WinMain(HINSTANCE hInstance, HINSTANCE hPrevInstance,
                LPSTR lpCmdLine, int nCmdShow)
{
    MSG msg;

    if (!FindWindow(MainWindowClassName,NULL))
        if (!InitApplication(hInstance))
            return (FALSE);

    if (!InitInstance(hInstance, nCmdShow))
        return (FALSE);

    while (GetMessage(&msg,NULL,0,0))
    {
        TranslateMessage(&msg);
        DispatchMessage(&msg);
    }
    return (msg.wParam);
}
```

17. Compile and run the applicaton.

Comments

This example searches through the color table to find all entries that match the color to be changed. If the actual positions of each color in the table are known, you can index directly into the color table to change the colors. Note that a new device-dependent bitmap is created each time the color table of the device-independent bitmap is modified.

COMPLEXITY
DIFFICULT

4.3   How do I...
Rotate a bitmap?

Problem

I want my application to rotate the bitmap that it displays. Is there any way to do this without having lots of different bitmap files or resources?

Technique

While there is no Windows API function to rotate an image for you, rotating a bitmap by a multiple of 90 degrees can be easily achieved by modifying the actual bitmap component of a device-independent bitmap. In addition, this is a good example of how you can directly manipulate a DIB.

When you are called upon to rotate a bitmap, you must take a copy of the DIB resource (remember that resources are read-only) and manipulate the bits. When operating on an 8-bits per pixel bitmap (256 colors), you can simply progress through the bitmap row by row, copying one byte at a time from a position in the source to the destination. There are several important tricks to remember:

- Every line in a DIB must be padded to a DWORD boundary–32 bits. You can check the biWidth member of the bitmap header to determine whether the width is an even multiple of 32 bits. If not, you will need to add an extra offset for padding when calculating source and destination byte offsets.

- When you rotate a bitmap by 90 or 270 degrees, the bitmap's height member becomes its width, and vice versa. While the actual allocated size of the bitmap need not change, you will need to calculate a padding factor to pad the height to DWORD boundaries as it becomes the width in the new bitmap.

- Device-independent bitmaps are stored with the scan lines running from left to right as expected, but with the lines stored from bottom to top in memory. Thus the scan line displayed at the top of the image on screen is actually stored last in memory. Figure 4-4 illustrates this point. You need to consider this when writing algorithms that manipulate bitmaps directly. The classic code for rotating data 90 degrees clockwise will rotate DIBs 90 degrees counterclockwise, or 270 degrees clockwise because of this inversion.

Steps

Open and run the ROTATE.EXE example application. You can find this application in the CHAPTER4\ROTATE directory of the CD that comes with this book. The

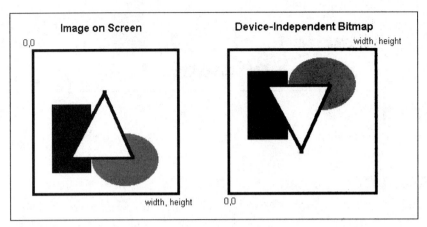

Figure 4-4 DIB scan lines are stored from bottom to top in memory

application opens a window and displays a small bitmap. Choosing the Normal menu item from the Rotate menu duplicates this effect–it uses the bitmap from the resource to create and display the bitmap on screen. When you choose the Rotate 90 menu item from the Rotate menu, the image displayed is rotated by 90 degrees in the clockwise direction. You can see an example of this effect in Figure 4-5. Choosing Rotate 180 turns the bitmap so that it is displayed upside down, and choosing Rotate 270 turns the bitmap a further 90 degrees so that it is rotated 270 degrees clockwise, or 90 degrees counterclockwise.

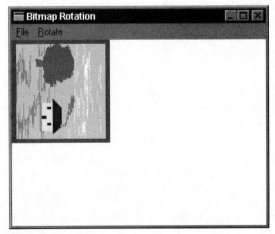

Figure 4-5 ROTATE application with a 90 degree rotation

The sample application uses three separate functions to achieve the rotation, although most of the code for each rotation follows the same pattern. The following steps show you how to build this sample application.

1. Create a new directory called ROTATE, which will be the place where you store all the files for this project.

2. You will need a bitmap to rotate. You can find a sample bitmap in the CHAPTER4\ROTATE directory of the CD that accompanies this book. It is a 256-color bitmap called SAMPLE.BMP. If you don't have a CD-ROM drive, you can use a resource editor to create the sample bitmap. Create a 256-color bitmap (this is important, because the application assumes an 8-bit bitmap), approximately 128-by-128 pixels in size. Save the bitmap as SAMPLE.BMP in your working directory. When you save the bitmap, make sure that you save it as uncompressed–the run length encoding (RLE) compression used by some paint packages is not compatible with all display drivers.

3. You will also need an application icon. Copy the file ROTATE.ICO from the CHAPTER4\ROTATE directory on the CD, or create your own 32-by-32, 16-color bitmap using a resource editor, and save it as ROTATE.ICO.

4. Now you can create the resource file to combine these resources so that they become part of the completed application. Create a new file using a text editor and call it ROTATE.RC. Add the following lines of resource script. These lines define the menus for the application and reference the bitmap and the application icon.

```
/* ---------------------------------------------------------------- */
/*                                                                   */
/* MODULE: ROTATE.RC                                                 */
/* PURPOSE: This resource script defines the menu and application    */
/*          icon associated with this application, and also          */
/*          includes a bitmap to be loaded and displayed.            */
/*                                                                   */
/* ---------------------------------------------------------------- */

#include "rotate.rh"

IDM_BITMAPMENU MENU
{
    POPUP "&File"
    {
        MENUITEM "E&xit", CM_EXIT
    }
    POPUP "&Rotate"
    {
        MENUITEM "&Normal" CM_NORMAL CHECKED
        MENUITEM "Rotate &90" CM_90DEG
        MENUITEM "Rotate &180" CM_180DEG
        MENUITEM "Rotate &270" CM_270DEG
    }
}
```

continued on next page

continued from previous page

```
IDBM_SAMPLEBITMAP BITMAP "sample.bmp"

IDI_APPICON ICON "rotate.ico"
```

5. The resource script in step 4 references an include file, ROTATE.RH, which is also included by the main application source code. This file defines the identifiers for the resources. Using a text editor, create a new file and save it as ROTATE.RH. Place the following definitions in this file:

```
#ifndef __ROTATE_RH
/* ------------------------------------------------------------- */
/*                                                               */
/* MODULE: ROTATE.RH                                             */
/* PURPOSE: Defines identifiers used to address resources.       */
/*                                                               */
/* ------------------------------------------------------------- */
#define __ROTATE_RH

#define IDM_BITMAPMENU          301
#define CM_NORMAL               111
#define CM_90DEG                112
#define CM_180DEG               113
#define CM_270DEG               114
#define CM_EXIT                 101

#define IDI_APPICON               1
#define IDBM_SAMPLEBITMAP       3567

#endif
```

6. Create the source file for the application. Using a text editor, create a file and call it ROTATE.C. Type the following code fragment in at the top of the file. The code includes the various files needed to get the application to compile. In addition, it defines the preprocessor symbol STRICT, which turns on strict type checking of the various handles and other types used by the Windows operating system.

Below the include files is the name of the class for this application's main window and the global variables used by the application. Each of the variables is initialized to a default value, to avoid possible errors later in the program code.

```
/* ------------------------------------------------------------- */
/*                                                               */
/* MODULE: ROTATE.C                                             */
/* PURPOSE: This small application demonstrates how to manipulate */
/*          a device independent bitmap to rotate or flip an image. */
/*                                                               */
/* ------------------------------------------------------------- */
#define STRICT

#include <windows.h>
#include <windowsx.h>
#include "rotate.rh"

// Constants.
```

```
char *MainWindowClassName = "RotateDemoWindow";

// Instance variables.
HBITMAP        hDDBitmap = NULL;
HPALETTE       hPalette = NULL;
BITMAPINFO     *pResourceDIB = NULL;
WPARAM         currentRotation = CM_NORMAL;
HINSTANCE      hInstance = NULL;
DWORD          nResourceSize = 0;
```

7. If you have created one of the other example applications in this chapter, you
will recognize the next piece of code. The CreateDIBPalette function uses the
color table contained in a device-independent bitmap to create a logical
palette. This palette can then be realized into a device context to define the
colors to be used for further operations. This function ensures that the bitmap
that is displayed has the colors that you intended when you designed the
image. The function takes a pointer to the header part of the device-independent bitmap, a BITMAPINFO structure, and returns a handle to the palette if
successful or NULL if it fails.

```
/* ---------------------------------------------------------------- */
/* This function creates a logical palette structure from the color */
/* table supplied with our device independent bitmap. The palette is*/
/* saved into the global hPalette variable for use when converting   */
/* and displaying the image.                                         */
/* ---------------------------------------------------------------- */
HPALETTE CreateDIBPalette(BITMAPINFO *info)
{
    LOGPALETTE    *palPtr;
    DWORD         i, numEntries;
    HPALETTE      hPal;

    /* Allocate space for a LOGPALETTE structure and array of
       entries. Using LocalAlloc with the LMEM_FIXED argument
       gives us a pointer without having to lock and unlock it. */
    if ((numEntries = info->bmiHeader.biClrUsed) == 0)
        numEntries = 1L << info->bmiHeader.biBitCount;

    palPtr = (NPLOGPALETTE)LocalAlloc(LMEM_FIXED,sizeof(LOGPALETTE) +
                                    numEntries * sizeof(PALETTEENTRY));
    if (!palPtr)
        return NULL;

    palPtr->palVersion = 0x300;
    palPtr->palNumEntries = (WORD)numEntries;

    // Now fill in the array of palette entries from the color table.
    for (i = 0; i < numEntries; i++)
    {
        palPtr->palPalEntry[i].peRed = info->bmiColors[i].rgbRed;
        palPtr->palPalEntry[i].peGreen = info->bmiColors[i].rgbGreen;
        palPtr->palPalEntry[i].peBlue = info->bmiColors[i].rgbBlue;
        palPtr->palPalEntry[i].peFlags = 0;
    }
}
```

continued on next page

continued from previous page

```
            hPal = CreatePalette(palPtr);
            LocalFree((HLOCAL)palPtr);
            return hPal;
}
```

8. Now add the function ConvertDIBToDDB to the source file. This function creates the palette using the preceding code, then selects it into a memory device
context and realizes it. The code then creates a new (device-dependent)
bitmap in the device context and performs SetDIBits to copy data from the
device-independent bitmap into the new device-dependent bitmap.

```
/* ------------------------------------------------------------------- */
/* This function converts the DIB supplied as the info argument into */
/* a DDB ready for display in the given window. Along the way it      */
/* modifies the global variables hPalette and hDDBitmap. Returns      */
/* TRUE if successful, otherwise FALSE.                               */
/* ------------------------------------------------------------------- */
BOOL ConvertDIBToDDB(HWND hWnd, BITMAPINFO *info)
{
        HDC                  hDC, hMemDC;
        HPALETTE             hOldPalette;
        HBITMAP              hOldBitmap;
        DWORD                numEntries, nSize;
        VOID                 *bits;

        // Free the old palette and bitmap.
        if (hPalette != NULL)
        {
            DeleteObject(hPalette);
            hPalette = NULL;
        }
        if (hDDBitmap != NULL)
        {
            DeleteObject(hDDBitmap);
            hDDBitmap = NULL;
        }

        /* Create a new palette, then create a temporary device context
            and select the palette into it. Create a bitmap in the device
            context, and use SetDIBits to convert the DIB into this DDB. */
        hDC = GetDC(hWnd);
        if ((hPalette = CreateDIBPalette(info)) != NULL)
        {
            if ((hMemDC = CreateCompatibleDC(hDC)) != NULL)
            {
                hOldPalette = SelectPalette(hMemDC,hPalette,FALSE);
                RealizePalette(hMemDC);
                if ((hDDBitmap = CreateCompatibleBitmap(hDC,
                                  info->bmiHeader.biWidth,
                                  info->bmiHeader.biHeight)) != NULL)
                {
                    if ((numEntries = info->bmiHeader.biClrUsed) == 0)
                        numEntries = 1 << info->bmiHeader.biBitCount;
                    nSize = info->bmiHeader.biSize + (numEntries
                                          * sizeof(RGBQUAD));
```

```
            bits = (LPSTR)info + nSize;
            hOldBitmap = SelectObject(hMemDC,hDDBitmap);

            // Copy the data into the new bitmap (hDDBitmap).
            SetDIBits(hMemDC,hDDBitmap,0,
                    info->bmiHeader.biHeight,
                    bits,info,DIB_RGB_COLORS);
            SelectObject(hMemDC,hOldBitmap);
        }
        SelectPalette(hMemDC,hOldPalette,FALSE);
        DeleteDC(hMemDC);
    }
    ReleaseDC(hWnd,hDC);

    // If bitmap creation failed, free the palette.
    if (!hDDBitmap)
    {
        DeleteObject(hPalette);
        hPalette = NULL;
    }
    }
    return (hDDBitmap != NULL);
}
```

9. You will need to load the bitmap into memory before it can be manipulated, so add this next function. The LoadBitmapResource function uses the API functions FindResource, LoadResource, and LockResource to obtain a pointer to the bitmap in memory. It sets two global variables. The nResourceSize variable will hold the size of the allocated bitmap, and pResourceDIB is a pointer to the bitmap in memory.

```
/* ---------------------------------------------------------------- */
/* This function opens a bitmap resource attached to our executable */
/* file and loads it into memory as a device independent bitmap (DIB).*/
/* ---------------------------------------------------------------- */
BOOL LoadBitmapResource(HINSTANCE hInstance, WORD resId)
{
    HRSRC   hResource;
    HGLOBAL hDib;

    if (((hResource = FindResource(hInstance,
                            MAKEINTRESOURCE(resId),
                            RT_BITMAP)) != NULL) &&
        ((hDib = LoadResource(hInstance,hResource)) != NULL))
    {
        nResourceSize = SizeofResource(hInstance,hResource);
        pResourceDIB = (LPBITMAPINFO)LockResource(hDib);
        return (pResourceDIB != NULL);
    }
    return FALSE;
}
```

10. Type the following function into the same source file. The Paint function will be called whenever the window has to be redisplayed. The function gets a handle to the device context, selects the palette into it, and realizes the palette.

It then uses the BitBlt API function to copy the bitmap from a memory device context onto the screen.

```
/* ---------------------------------------------------------------- */
/* This is the actual drawing function called when WM_PAINT is      */
/* received. It creates a compatible DC, and selects the Device     */
/* Dependent bitmap into it. It then uses BitBlt to copy this to the*/
/* device context.                                                  */
/* ---------------------------------------------------------------- */
void Paint(HWND hWnd, HPALETTE hPalette, HBITMAP hBitmap,
           BITMAPINFO *info)
{
    PAINTSTRUCT         ps;
    HDC                 hDC, hMemDC;
    HPALETTE            hOldPalette;
    HBITMAP             hOldBitmap;

    hDC = BeginPaint(hWnd, &ps);
    if ((hMemDC = CreateCompatibleDC(hDC)) != NULL)
    {
        hOldPalette = SelectPalette(hDC, hPalette, FALSE);
        RealizePalette(hDC);
        hOldBitmap = SelectObject(hMemDC,hBitmap);
        BitBlt(hDC, 0, 0, info->bmiHeader.biWidth,
                info->bmiHeader.biHeight, hMemDC, 0, 0,SRCCOPY);
        SelectBitmap(hMemDC,hOldBitmap);
        SelectPalette(hDC,hOldPalette,FALSE);
        DeleteDC(hMemDC);
    }
    EndPaint(hWnd, &ps);
}
```

11. Finally, after all the preliminaries, here is some manipulation of the device-independent bitmap. The first thing that function Rotate90Degrees does is allocate a block of memory to make a copy of the bitmap resource. Remember that you cannot directly modify a resource, as they are read-only. Attempting to modify a resource will cause a protection fault, and your application will fail.

Having obtained memory for the new bitmap, the code copies the bitmap header and color table from the resource into the new bitmap. The width and height members of the bitmap header are swapped as the bitmap is being turned on its side. The next step is to calculate the padding factor, which is the number of unused bits at the end of each scan line in the bitmap. Scan lines must start on a 32-bit boundary, so you need to know the difference between the width of one row and the starting point of the next row. The Rotate90Degrees function calculates two values: padWidth is the number of bytes to add to the end of a scan line in the resource bitmap to get to the next scan line, and padHeight is the number of bytes to add to the end of a scan line in the destination bitmap to achieve the same result. In a square bitmap, the number of bytes will be the same in both cases. The values will be different in a rectangular bitmap.

The final step is to iterate through the scan lines (rows) in the resource bitmap and transform each pixel in the row to its new position in the destination bitmap. The formula for a 90 degree transformation is as follows:

```
(NewBitmapHeight x SourceColumn) + SourceRow =
(OldBitmapWidth x SourceRow) + SourceColumn
```

Each pixel in a 256-color bitmap is 8 bits, or 1 byte in size.

```c
/* ---------------------------------------------------------------- */
/* Create a copy of a device dependent bitmap, and copy the header  */
/* Then copy bits from the source to the destination. Finally,      */
/* use CreateDDBitmap to convert the DIB to a DDB to display.       */
/* Remember that scanlines in a DIB are stored bottom to top. The   */
/* top line of the displayed image is the bottom line of the bitmap */
/* ---------------------------------------------------------------- */
void Rotate90Degrees(HWND hWnd, BITMAPINFO *srcInfo)
{
    HGLOBAL            hGlobal;
    BITMAPINFOHEADER   *destBitmap, *srcBitmap;
    DWORD              row, col, padHeight, padWidth;
    DWORD              numEntries, nSize;
    LPSTR              srcBits, destBits;

    srcBitmap = &srcInfo->bmiHeader;
    if ((hGlobal = GlobalAlloc(GMEM_FIXED,nResourceSize)) != NULL)
    {
        if ((destBitmap = (BITMAPINFOHEADER *)GlobalLock(hGlobal)) !=
                          NULL)
        {
            // Work out how many entries there are in the color table.
            if ((numEntries = srcBitmap->biClrUsed) == 0)
                numEntries = 1L << srcBitmap->biBitCount;

            /* Now work out the size the color table and header take up,
               and copy from the resource into our memory block.   */
            nSize = srcBitmap->biSize + (numEntries * sizeof(RGBQUAD));
            CopyMemory(destBitmap,srcBitmap,nSize);

            // Swap the width and height members in our destination.
            destBitmap->biHeight = srcBitmap->biWidth;
            destBitmap->biWidth = srcBitmap->biHeight;

            // Calculate offsets to the actual bitmap data.
            srcBits = (LPSTR)srcBitmap + nSize;
            destBits = (LPSTR)destBitmap + nSize;

            /* Work out the extra number of bytes to pad each line to a
               DWORD boundary. For a copy we would only need padWidth,
               but as we rotate, our height will be the new width */
            if ((padHeight = (srcBitmap->biHeight % sizeof(DWORD))) != 0)
                padHeight = sizeof(DWORD) - padHeight;
            if ((padWidth = (srcBitmap->biWidth % sizeof(DWORD))) != 0)
                padWidth = sizeof(DWORD) - padWidth;
```

continued on next page

continued from previous page

```
                    // Now do the actual byte by byte transformation.
                    for (row = 0; row < srcBitmap->biHeight; row++)
                        for (col = 0; col < srcBitmap->biWidth; col++)
                            destBits[((srcBitmap->biHeight + padHeight) *
                                    col) + row]
                              = srcBits[((srcBitmap->biWidth + padWidth) *
                                    row) + col];

                    // Finally create a DDB and tell Windows to update the
                    // display.
                    ConvertDIBToDDB(hWnd,(BITMAPINFO *)destBitmap);
                    InvalidateRect(hWnd,NULL,TRUE);

                    GlobalUnlock(hGlobal);
                }
                GlobalFree(hGlobal);
            }
    }
```

12. The next function to add is the Rotate270Degrees function. As its name suggests, this function rotates the resource bitmap 270 degrees clockwise (or 90 degrees counterclockwise) to produce a new bitmap. The procedure followed is exactly the same as the 90 degree rotation just given, except for the formula used to calculate the new position for each pixel. Here is the formula for the 270 degree rotation:

```
((NewBitmapHeight * SourceColumn) + (OldBitmapHeight - SourceRow - 1)
= (OldBitmapWidth * SourceRow) + SourceColumn
```

Here is the code to add to the source file:

```
/* ------------------------------------------------------------------ */
/* Create a copy of a device dependent bitmap, and copy the header     */
/* Then copy bits from the source to the destination. Finally,         */
/* use CreateDDBitmap to convert the DIB to a DDB to display.          */
/* Remember that scanlines in a DIB are stored bottom to top. The      */
/* top line of the displayed image is the bottom line of the bitmap    */
/* ------------------------------------------------------------------ */
void Rotate270Degrees(HWND hWnd, BITMAPINFO *srcInfo)
{
    HGLOBAL             hGlobal;
    BITMAPINFOHEADER    *destBitmap, *srcBitmap;
    DWORD               row, col, padHeight, padWidth;
    DWORD               numEntries, nSize;
    LPSTR               srcBits, destBits;

    srcBitmap = &srcInfo->bmiHeader;
    if ((hGlobal = GlobalAlloc(GMEM_FIXED,nResourceSize)) != NULL)
    {
        if ((destBitmap = (BITMAPINFOHEADER *)GlobalLock(hGlobal)) !=
            NULL)
        {
            // Work out how many entries there are in the color table.
            if ((numEntries = srcBitmap->biClrUsed) == 0)
                numEntries = 1L << srcBitmap->biBitCount;
```

```
      /* Now work out the size the color table and header take up,
         and copy from the resource into our memory block.   */
      nSize = srcBitmap->biSize + (numEntries * sizeof(RGBQUAD));
      CopyMemory(destBitmap,srcBitmap,nSize);

      // Swap the width and height members in our destination.
      destBitmap->biHeight = srcBitmap->biWidth;
      destBitmap->biWidth = srcBitmap->biHeight;

      // Calculate offsets to the actual bitmap data.
      srcBits = (LPSTR)srcBitmap + nSize;
      destBits = (LPSTR)destBitmap + nSize;

      /* Work out the extra number of bytes to pad each line to a
         DWORD boundary. For a copy we would only need padWidth,
         but as we rotate, our height will be the new width */
      if ((padHeight = (srcBitmap->biHeight % sizeof(DWORD))) != 0)
          padHeight = sizeof(DWORD) - padHeight;
      if ((padWidth = (srcBitmap->biWidth % sizeof(DWORD))) != 0)
          padWidth = sizeof(DWORD) - padWidth;

      // Now do the actual byte by byte transformation.
      for (row = 0; row < srcBitmap->biHeight; row++)
          for (col = 0; col < srcBitmap->biWidth; col++)
              destBits[((srcBitmap->biHeight + padHeight) * col) +
                       ((srcBitmap->biHeight + padHeight) -
                        row - 1)] =
                  srcBits[((srcBitmap->biWidth + padWidth) * row) +
                      col];

      // Finally create a DDB and tell Windows to update the
      // display.
      ConvertDIBToDDB(hWnd,(BITMAPINFO *)destBitmap);
      InvalidateRect(hWnd,NULL,TRUE);

      GlobalUnlock(hGlobal);
    }
    GlobalFree(hGlobal);
  }
}
```

13. The third rotation follows a similar principle, but there are some slight differences. Because the bitmap is being rotated 180 degrees, there is no need to swap the width and height fields in the new bitmap header. Similarly, only one padding factor, padWidth, needs to be calculated. The padding factor will be the same for both bitmaps. Let's have a look at the formula for this transformation:

```
(OldBitmapWidth x (OldBitmapHeight - SourceRow - 1) + (OldBitmapWidth
- SourceColumn - 1) = (OldBitmapWidth * SourceRow) + SourceColumn
```

The pixel is copied from its position in the source bitmap to the opposite position on the opposite row of the destination bitmap. As an example, consider a pixel at position (3,5) in a 100-by-200-pixel bitmap. It would be copied to position (95,195) in the destination bitmap.

```
/* ------------------------------------------------------------------ */
/* Create a copy of a device dependent bitmap, and copy the header    */
/* Then copy bits from the source to the destination. Finally,        */
/* use CreateDDBitmap to convert the DIB to a DDB to display.         */
/* Remember that scanlines in a DIB are stored bottom to top. The     */
/* top line of the displayed image is the bottom line of the bitmap   */
/* ------------------------------------------------------------------ */
void Rotate180Degrees(HWND hWnd, BITMAPINFO *srcInfo)
{
    HGLOBAL           hGlobal;
    BITMAPINFOHEADER  *destBitmap, *srcBitmap;
    DWORD             row, col, padWidth;
    DWORD             numEntries, nSize;
    LPSTR             srcBits, destBits;

    srcBitmap = &srcInfo->bmiHeader;
    if ((hGlobal = GlobalAlloc(GMEM_FIXED,nResourceSize)) != NULL)
    {
        if ((destBitmap = (BITMAPINFOHEADER *)GlobalLock(hGlobal)) !=
            NULL)
        {
            // Work out how many entries there are in the color table.
            if ((numEntries = srcBitmap->biClrUsed) == 0)
                numEntries = 1L << srcBitmap->biBitCount;

            /* Now work out the size the color table and header take up,
               and copy from the resource into our memory block.  */
            nSize = srcBitmap->biSize + (numEntries * sizeof(RGBQUAD));
            CopyMemory(destBitmap,srcBitmap,nSize);

            // Swap the width and height members in our destination.
            destBitmap->biHeight = srcBitmap->biWidth;
            destBitmap->biWidth = srcBitmap->biHeight;

            // Calculate offsets to the actual bitmap data.
            srcBits = (LPSTR)srcBitmap + nSize;
            destBits = (LPSTR)destBitmap + nSize;

            /* Work out the extra number of bytes to pad each line to a
               DWORD boundary.  */
            if ((padWidth = (srcBitmap->biWidth % sizeof(DWORD))) != 0)
                padWidth = sizeof(DWORD) - padWidth;

            // Now do the actual byte by byte transformation.
            for (row = 0; row < srcBitmap->biHeight; row++)
                for (col = 0; col < srcBitmap->biWidth; col++)
                    destBits[((srcBitmap->biWidth + padWidth) *
                             (srcBitmap->biHeight - row - 1)) +
                             (srcBitmap->biWidth - col - 1)] =
                        srcBits[((srcBitmap->biWidth + padWidth) * row) +
                                col];

            // Finally create a DDB and tell Windows to update the
            // display.
            ConvertDIBToDDB(hWnd,(BITMAPINFO *)destBitmap);
            InvalidateRect(hWnd,NULL,TRUE);
```

```
        GlobalUnlock(hGlobal);
    }
    GlobalFree(hGlobal);
}
}
```

14. The MainWndProc function is the callback function that processes messages
for the application window. In particular, it responds to the WM_CREATE
message by loading the bitmap resource from the file, initializing the current
rotation position (to the Normal position), and displaying the bitmap. In addition, the function responds to WM_COMMAND messages received from the
menu. In response to the CM_90DEG, CM_180DEG, and CM_270DEG messages, it calls the appropriate functions to rotate the bitmap and force a redraw
of the window. In response to the CM_NORMAL message, the function simply calls ConvertDIBToDDB using the bitmap in the resource–essentially just
restoring the original bitmap once again.

```
/* --------------------------------------------------------------- */
/* This function is the main window callback function which will be */
/* called by Windows to process messages for our window.           */
/* --------------------------------------------------------------- */
LPARAM CALLBACK MainWndProc(HWND hWnd, UINT message,
                            WPARAM wParam, LPARAM lParam)
{

    switch (message)
    {
        case WM_CREATE:
            if (LoadBitmapResource(hInstance,IDBM_SAMPLEBITMAP))
            {
                currentRotation = CM_NORMAL;
                ConvertDIBToDDB(hWnd,pResourceDIB);
                InvalidateRect(hWnd,NULL,TRUE);
            }
            break;
        case WM_COMMAND:
            switch (wParam)
            {
                case CM_EXIT:
                    DestroyWindow(hWnd);
                    break;
                case CM_NORMAL:
                case CM_90DEG:
                case CM_180DEG:
                case CM_270DEG:
                    if (currentRotation != wParam)
                    {
                        CheckMenuItem(GetMenu(hWnd),currentRotation,
                                MF_BYCOMMAND | MF_UNCHECKED);
                        CheckMenuItem(GetMenu(hWnd),wParam,
                                MF_BYCOMMAND | MF_CHECKED);
                        currentRotation = wParam;
                        switch (wParam)
```

continued on next page

continued from previous page

```
                                {
                                        case CM_NORMAL:
                                                ConvertDIBToDDB(hWnd,pResourceDIB);
                                                InvalidateRect(hWnd,NULL,TRUE);
                                                break;
                                        case CM_90DEG:
                                                Rotate90Degrees(hWnd,pResourceDIB);
                                                break;
                                        case CM_180DEG:
                                                Rotate180Degrees(hWnd,pResourceDIB);
                                                break;
                                        case CM_270DEG:
                                                Rotate270Degrees(hWnd,pResourceDIB);
                                                break;
                                }
                        }
                        break;
                default:
                        return (DefWindowProc(hWnd,message,wParam,lParam));
                }
                break;
        case WM_PALETTECHANGED:
                // Force a repaint.
                if (((HWND)wParam != hWnd) && (hDDBitmap != NULL))
                        InvalidateRect(hWnd,NULL,TRUE);
                break;
        case WM_PAINT:
                if (hDDBitmap != NULL)
                        Paint(hWnd,hPalette,hDDBitmap,pResourceDIB);
                else
                        return (DefWindowProc(hWnd, message, wParam, lParam));
                break;
        case WM_DESTROY:
                if (hPalette)
                        DeleteObject(hPalette);
                if (hDDBitmap)
                        DeleteObject(hDDBitmap);
                PostQuitMessage(0);
                break;
        default:
                return DefWindowProc(hWnd, message, wParam, lParam);
        }
        return 0;
}
```

15. The application is just about complete. Add the two helper functions listed
here to the same source file, ROTATE.C. The InitApplication function registers
a window class for use when creating the window for this application. This
function will only be called if the window class does not already exist. In contrast, the InitInstance function is called each time this application is run, even
if an instance of the application is already running. It creates the main window
for the application and displays it on the screen.

```
/* ------------------------------------------------------------------ */
/* This function initializes a WNDCLASS structure and uses it to      */
/* register a class for our main window.                              */
/* ------------------------------------------------------------------ */
BOOL InitApplication(HINSTANCE hInstance)
{
    WNDCLASS  wc;

    wc.style = 0;
    wc.lpfnWndProc = MainWndProc;
    wc.cbClsExtra = 0;
    wc.cbWndExtra = 0;
    wc.hInstance = hInstance;
    wc.hIcon = LoadIcon(NULL, IDI_APPLICATION);
    wc.hCursor = LoadCursor(NULL, IDC_ARROW);
    wc.hbrBackground = (HBRUSH)(COLOR_WINDOW + 1);
    wc.lpszMenuName =  MAKEINTRESOURCE(IDM_BITMAPMENU);
    wc.lpszClassName = MainWindowClassName;

    return RegisterClass(&wc);
}


/* ------------------------------------------------------------------ */
/* This function creates an instance of our main window. The window   */
/* is given a class name and a title, and told to display anywhere.   */
/* The nCmdShow argument passed to the program determines how the     */
/* window will be displayed.                                          */
/* ------------------------------------------------------------------ */
BOOL InitInstance(HINSTANCE hInst, int nCmdShow)
{
    HWND hWnd;

    hInstance = hInst;     // Store in global variable.

    hWnd = CreateWindow(MainWindowClassName,"Bitmap Rotation",
                        WS_OVERLAPPEDWINDOW,CW_USEDEFAULT,
                        CW_USEDEFAULT,CW_USEDEFAULT,CW_USEDEFAULT,
                        NULL,NULL,hInstance,NULL);
    if (!hWnd)
        return FALSE;

    ShowWindow(hWnd, nCmdShow);
    UpdateWindow(hWnd);    // Send a WM_PAINT message/
    return TRUE;
}
```

16. The final piece of code to add is the WinMain function, the entry point for all Windows applications. This function initializes the window class and the main window by calling InitApplication and InitInstance. It then processes messages until the application completes.

```
/* ---------------------------------------------------------------- */
/* The main entry point for Windows applications. Check to see if    */
/* the main window class name has already been registered; if it has*/
/* not, call InitApplication to register it. Call InitInstance to    */
/* create an instance of our main window, then pump messages until   */
/* the application is closed.                                        */
/* ---------------------------------------------------------------- */
int PASCAL WinMain(HINSTANCE hInstance, HINSTANCE hPrevInstance,
                   LPSTR lpCmdLine, int nCmdShow)
{
    MSG msg;

    if (!FindWindow(MainWindowClassName,NULL))
        if (!InitApplication(hInstance))
            return FALSE;

    if (!InitInstance(hInstance, nCmdShow))
        return FALSE;

    while (GetMessage(&msg,NULL,0,0))
    {
        TranslateMessage(&msg);
        DispatchMessage(&msg);
    }
    return (msg.wParam);
}
```

17. Compile and run the application.

Comments

This sample application demonstrates how you can rotate a device-independent bitmap by 90 degree increments. You can extend this basic technique to a wide range of possible applications. If you are writing a drawing program, you can use this method to rotate the entire bitmap, or possibly just a selected area. By changing the formula that calculates the new pixel position, you can change the amount by which the bitmap is rotated.

This How-To has also demonstrated how easy it is to directly manipulate a device-independent bitmap. Using this knowledge, you will be able to write your own drawing routines that render directly into the device-independent bitmap, rather than having to use the GDI.

COMPLEXITY

EASY

4.4 How do I...
Draw a "rubber band" as the mouse is moved?

Problem

I would like my application to respond, as the user clicks and drags the mouse, by drawing a box or shape, and changing the shape as the user moves the mouse.

Technique

The effect you want to achieve, called rubber-banding, is a practical means of providing feedback to users as they move or resize objects or draw. It's not difficult to implement the technique in your applications. The key to using this technique is the small function SetROP2. This API function controls the raster operator (ROP) used when drawing into a device context. The raster operator defines how colors are combined into each pixel in the bitmap.

Table 4-2 lists the commonly used raster operators. C programmers will recognize many of these operators as being analogous to the C bitwise operators, such as ~ (the bitwise NOT operator), & (the bitwise AND operator), and | (the bitwise OR operator).

OPERATOR	MNEMONIC VALUE	RESULTING PIXEL
R2_BLACK	1	Always 0
R2_WHITE	16	Always 1
R2_NOP	11	Remains unchanged
R2_NOT	6	Inverse of the screen color
R2_COPYPEN	13	Pen color
R2_NOTCOPYPEN	4	Inverse of the pen color
R2_MERGEPENNOT	14	Pen color merged with the inverse of the screen color
R2_MASKPENNOT	5	Colors common to both pen and the inverse of the screen
R2_MERGENOTPEN	12	Screen color merged with the inverse of pen color
R2_MASKNOTPEN	3	Colors common to both screen and the inverse of the pen
R2_MERGEPEN	15	A combination of pen color and screen color
R2_NOTMERGEPEN	2	Inverse of the R2_MERGEPEN color
R2_MASKPEN	9	Colors common to both the pen and the screen
R2_NOTMASKPEN	8	Inverse of the R2_MASKPEN color
R2_XORPEN	7	Combination of the colors in pen and in the screen, but not in both
R2_NOTXORPEN	10	Inverse of the R2_XORPEN color

Table 4-2 Raster operators for the SetROP2 function

The most useful operators for rubber-banding are the R2_XORPEN and R2_NOTXORPEN operators. These operators cause drawing functions to perform a logical XOR operation between each bit of the pen and the screen color. The R2_XORPEN operator causes the resulting pixel to be a combination of all the bits in the pen and the screen, except where the bits are set in both. The R2_NOTXORPEN performs the same operation, then inverts the result by setting all the one bits to zero and the zero bits to one. The main advantage in using the XOR operators is that you can repeat a drawing operation with the same pen and coordinates, and the background will be restored without the application having to store it at all.

The other technique needed to produce a rubber-banding application is that of tracking mouse actions. In the sample application discussed in this How-To, the application receives a WM_LBUTTONDOWN message when it should start dragging. The application can then track the mouse movement by handling the WM_MOUSEMOVE message, and it can stop rubber-banding when it receives the WM_LBUTTONUP message.

Steps

Open and run the sample application DRAWDEMO.EXE. This application is in the CHAPTER4\RBRBAND directory on the CD that accompanies this book. DRAWDEMO is a very simple drawing application. It allows the user to draw filled rectangles and ellipses in a number of colors. While the user is drawing a shape, the application draws a rubber band so that the user can tell what the final shape will look like.

To try this, choose the Rectangle or Ellipse option from the Tools menu, and draw a rectangle. You can use the Colors menu item on the Tools menu to choose the color to be used for drawing. Click the left mouse button on the window, and drag the mouse with the button held down. As you drag the mouse, you will observe a rectangle or ellipse following the mouse, changing size and shape as you move the mouse. When you release the left mouse button, the rubber band is replaced with the filled, colored shape. Figure 4-6 shows the application in action, with the user dragging to produce a rectangle.

The following steps will guide you in reproducing this example application. Along the way, you will learn about drawing using the XOR raster operators and about tracking the current position of the mouse.

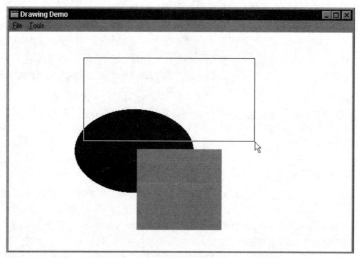

Figure 4-6 Dragging to produce a rectangle in the
DRAWDEMO application

DRAW A "RUBBER BAND" AS THE MOUSE IS MOVED?

1. Create a directory and call it RBRBAND. This directory will serve as the working directory for this project. Each time you are instructed to create or copy a file, place it in this directory.

2. You will need an icon for the application. Copy the file DRAWDEMO.ICO from the CHAPTER4\RBRBAND directory on the CD. Alternatively, you can create your own 32-by-32-pixel, 16-color icon using a resource editor. In this case, save the completed icon as DRAWDEMO.ICO.

3. Using a text editor, create a new file and call it DRAWDEMO.RC. You will place the resource script for the application in this file. Enter the following text for the resource script. This text defines the menus for the application and includes the application icon.

```
/* ------------------------------------------------------------------ */
/*                                                                    */
/* MODULE: DRAWDEMO.RC                                                */
/* PURPOSE: This resource script defines the menus and application    */
/*          icon associated with this application.                    */
/*                                                                    */
/* ------------------------------------------------------------------ */

#include "drawdemo.rh"

IDM_DRAWMENU MENU
{
    POPUP "&File"
    {
        MENUITEM "E&xit", CM_EXIT
    }
    POPUP "&Tools"
    {
        MENUITEM "&Rectangle", CM_RECTANGLE, CHECKED
        MENUITEM "&Ellipse", CM_ELIPSE
        MENUITEM SEPARATOR
        MENUITEM "&Colors...", CM_COLORS
    }
}

IDI_APPICON ICON "drawdemo.ico"
```

4. You also need to define the resource identifiers to be used in the resource script and the application. Create a new file and save it as DRAWDEMO.RH. Add the following definitions to this file:

```
#ifndef __DRAWDEMO_RH
/* ------------------------------------------------------------------ */
/*                                                                    */
/* MODULE: DRAWDEMO.RH                                                */
/* PURPOSE: Defines identifiers used to address resources.            */
/*                                                                    */
/* ------------------------------------------------------------------ */
#define __DRAWDEMO_RH
```

continued on next page

continued from previous page

```
#define IDM_DRAWMENU            2
#define CM_EXIT               101
#define CM_RECTANGLE          201
#define CM_ELIPSE             202
#define CM_COLORS             203

#define IDI_APPICON          1000

#endif
```

5. Now you are ready to start writing the source code for this application. Using a text editor, create a new file and call it DRAWDEMO.C. Add the following code fragment at the top of the file. The code defines the STRICT preprocessor symbol so that strict type checking is enforced across the many handles and other types defined in the Windows include files. The code then includes the files necessary for compilation. It also declares the global variables to be used by this application and initializes them so they are ready for use.

```
/* ------------------------------------------------------------- */
/*                                                               */
/* MODULE: DRAWDEMO.                                             */
/* PURPOSE: This demonstration program uses the SetROP2 API function */
/*          in combination with a number of rectangle and drawing */
/*          functions to demonstrate rubber-banding.             */
/*                                                               */
/* ------------------------------------------------------------- */
#define STRICT

#include <windows.h>
#include <commdlg.h>
#include <stdlib.h>
#include "drawdemo.rh"


// Constants.
char *MainWindowClassName = "DrawDemoWindow";

// Instance variables.
HINSTANCE       hInstance = NULL;
COLORREF        customColors[16];
COLORREF        currentColor = 0;
BOOL            elipseOn = FALSE;
BOOL            isDrawing = FALSE;
RECT            currentRect;
POINT           startingPoint;
```

6. Add the first function to the source file. The following code defines the ChangeCurrentColor function. This function displays a Choose Color common dialog and lets the user select the color to be used for future drawing operations. The function initializes a CHOOSECOLOR structure, then calls the ChangeColor API function. The resulting color selection is stored in the global variable currentColor, while the customColors array stores up to 16 colors that the user may define during the course of the application.

```
/* ------------------------------------------------------------- */
/* This function uses the ChooseColor common dialog box to let the */
/* user select the drawing color. The currentColor variable is    */
/* modified if the user selects OK. The customColors array is     */
/* modified if the user defines any custom colors.                */
/* ------------------------------------------------------------- */
void ChangeCurrentColor(HWND hWnd)
{
    CHOOSECOLOR cc;

    cc.lStructSize = sizeof(CHOOSECOLOR);
    cc.hwndOwner = hWnd;
    cc.hInstance = NULL; // No template specified, so unused.
    cc.rgbResult = currentColor;
    cc.lpCustColors = customColors;
    cc.Flags = CC_RGBINIT;
    if (ChooseColor(&cc))
        currentColor = cc. rgbResult;
}
```

7. The function that you will add next is the MouseMove function. It will be called whenever a WM_MOUSEMOVE message is processed and will receive the current mouse coordinates as parameters. It is this function that does the rubber-banding, so let's have a closer look at how it works.

The first thing that this code does is obtain a handle to the device context for the window. It is necessary to use the GetDC function because you will be drawing straight into the window without using a paint function. Note that a DC obtained with GetDC has to be released with a call to ReleaseDC. This is done at the end of the function.

The next step is set the raster operation code that controls how drawing will be done. The function calls SetROP2 with the R2_NOTXORPEN argument, setting the drawing mode to XOR. Future GDI drawing routines will use this mode. The code also stores the return code from SetROP2 in a variable, oldROPCode. Another call to SetROP2 at the end of this function will restore the old raster operation mode.

Finally, the code generates a rectangle using the starting mouse point and the current mouse coordinates. The bottom right corner of a rectangle must always have higher coordinates than the top left corner, so the coordinates are swapped if they are the wrong way around. By doing this, you ensure that the code will still work, even if the user drags the mouse above or to the left of his or her original starting point. When the rectangle has been calculated, the Rectangle or Ellipse GDI functions are called to draw the shape in the window. Because the R2_NOTXORPEN mode is set, the outline of the shape will be shown on screen as the classic inverted rubber-band effect.

```
/* ------------------------------------------------------------------ */
/* This function does the rubber banding. It tracks the current       */
/* position and the original position using currentRect. The key to   */
/* drawing the rubber band is the XOR operator set with SetROP2.       */
/* This operator lets us restore the background by simply              */
/* redrawing the shape at the same position.                          */
/* ------------------------------------------------------------------ */
void MouseMove(HWND hWnd, LONG mouseX, LONG mouseY)
{
    int oldROPCode;
    HDC hdc;

    // Draw straight into the device context.
    hdc = GetDC(hWnd);

    // Set the XOR operator to draw or erase.
    oldROPCode = SetROP2(hdc, R2_NOTXORPEN);

    // Erase any old shape from the last move.
    if (!IsRectEmpty(&currentRect))
        if (elipseOn)
            Ellipse(hdc,currentRect.left,currentRect.top,
                    currentRect.right,currentRect.bottom);
        else
            Rectangle(hdc,currentRect.left,currentRect.top,
                    currentRect.right,currentRect.bottom);
    /* Assign the new coordinates to the rectangle. Note that we
       need to swap coordinates if the user moves the mouse to the
       left of or above the original starting position. */
    if (mouseX < startingPoint.x)
    {
        currentRect.left = mouseX;
        currentRect.right = startingPoint.x;
    }
    else
    {
        currentRect.left = startingPoint.x;
        currentRect.right = mouseX;
    }
    if (mouseY < startingPoint.y)
    {
        currentRect.top = mouseY;
        currentRect.bottom = startingPoint.y;
    }
    else
    {
        currentRect.top = startingPoint.y;
        currentRect.bottom = mouseY;
    }

    // Now draw the new rectangle or ellipse.
    if (elipseOn)
        Ellipse(hdc,currentRect.left,currentRect.top,
                currentRect.right,currentRect.bottom);
    else
        Rectangle(hdc,currentRect.left,currentRect.top,
```

```
                        currentRect.right,currentRect.bottom);

    SetROP2(hdc, oldROPCode);
    ReleaseDC(hWnd, hdc);
}
```

8. Now add the StartDrawing function to the same source file. This function will be called when the user presses the left mouse button inside the client area of the window. The first thing that this function does is use the ClipCursor API function to trap the mouse cursor inside the client area of the window. This simplifies the management of the mouse and drawing routines. In a commercial application, you may not want to trap the user in one part of the screen. If you choose not to use ClipCursor, you will have to handle activation and deactivation of your window, pausing or canceling the current drawing while the application is inactive.

Using the code that you will enter next, the cursor is only contained within the client area of the window while the user holds down the mouse button. The moment the button is released, the user is free to move the mouse once more. The code before the ClipCursor call uses GetClientRect to retrieve the coordinates of the client area, then uses the ClientToScreen function to convert those coordinates to the screen-relative values needed by the ClipCursor function. The code also saves the initial X and Y positions of the mouse pointer for use when rubber-banding and resets the rectangle used to draw the rubber band.

```
/* --------------------------------------------------------------- */
/* This function stores the starting point and starts drawing.      */
/* --------------------------------------------------------------- */
void StartDrawing(HWND hWnd, LONG mouseX, LONG mouseY)
{
    RECT   clientRectangle;
    POINT point;

    /* Get the client rectangle, and convert it to screen
       coordinates. Convert top and left, then bottom and right. */
    GetClientRect(hWnd,&clientRectangle);
    point.x = clientRectangle.left;
    point.y = clientRectangle.top;
    ClientToScreen(hWnd,&point);
    clientRectangle.left = point.x;
    clientRectangle.top = point.y;
    point.x = clientRectangle.right;
    point.y = clientRectangle.bottom;
    ClientToScreen(hWnd,&point);
    clientRectangle.right = point.x;
    clientRectangle.bottom = point.y;

    // Keep the mouse inside the client area.
    ClipCursor(&clientRectangle);

    /* Save the coordinates of the mouse cursor. Because the
       rectangle is initially empty, set the right and bottom
       to be the same as left and top. */
```

continued on next page

continued from previous page

```
        startingPoint.x = mouseX;
        startingPoint.y = mouseY;
        SetRectEmpty(&currentRect);
}
```

9. If the previous function was called in response to the mouse button being
pressed, the FinishDrawing function, shown next, will be called when the user
releases the mouse button. When this function is called, the currentRect global variable will contain the coordinates of the rectangle or ellipse that the user
has selected. This function creates a solid brush of the selected color and
draws a filled ellipse or rectangle into the device context for the window. It
also calls ClipCursor with a NULL pointer argument. This removes the previous clipping of the mouse cursor, allowing the user freedom of movement
over the entire screen once more.

```
/* ----------------------------------------------------------------- */
/* This function ends the drawing operation by drawing an ellipse     */
/* or a rectangle, stopping the rubber-banding, and releasing the     */
/* cursor to move outside the window.                                 */
/* ----------------------------------------------------------------- */
void FinishDrawing(HWND hWnd)
{
    HDC     hdc;
    HBRUSH  colorBrush, oldBrush;

    // Draw straight into the device context.
    hdc = GetDC(hWnd);
    colorBrush = CreateSolidBrush(currentColor);
    oldBrush = SelectObject(hdc,colorBrush);
    if (elipseOn)
        Ellipse(hdc,currentRect.left,currentRect.top,
                currentRect.right,currentRect.bottom);
    else
        FillRect(hdc,&currentRect,colorBrush);
    SelectObject(hdc,oldBrush);
    DeleteObject(colorBrush);
    ClipCursor(NULL);
}
```

10. The next function that you will add to the source file is MainWndProc, the
callback function that receives messages sent to the application window. Three
of the messages that the code responds to in this part of the application are
critical for the rubber-banding and dragging effects. The WM_LBUTTON-
DOWN message is sent to the application when the user presses the left
mouse button (or the right mouse button if the buttons have been swapped)
while the cursor is over the window. The WM_LBUTTONUP message is sent
when the cursor is released. In response to these two messages, the code calls
StartDrawing and FinishDrawing, respectively. The third message is the
WM_MOUSEMOVE message, which is sent to the window when the mouse is
moved over it. If the user is currently drawing a shape (the isDrawing flag is
TRUE), then the MouseMove function will be called to draw the rubber band.

DRAW A "RUBBER BAND" AS THE MOUSE IS MOVED?

```
/* ------------------------------------------------------------- */
/* This function is the main window callback function which will be */
/* called by Windows to process messages for our window.          */
/* ------------------------------------------------------------- */
LPARAM CALLBACK MainWndProc(HWND hWnd, UINT message,
                            WPARAM wParam, LPARAM lParam)
{
    HMENU hMenu;

    hMenu = GetMenu(hWnd);
    switch (message)
    {
        case WM_LBUTTONDOWN:
            StartDrawing(hWnd,(LONG)LOWORD(lParam),(LONG)HIWORD(lParam));
            isDrawing = TRUE;
            break;
        case WM_MOUSEMOVE:
            if (isDrawing)
            {
            MouseMove(hWnd,(LONG)LOWORD(lParam),(LONG)HIWORD(lParam));
            break;
            }
        case WM_LBUTTONUP:
            if (isDrawing)
            {
            FinishDrawing(hWnd);
            isDrawing = FALSE;
            break;
            }
        case WM_COMMAND:
            switch (wParam)
            {
                case CM_EXIT:
                    DestroyWindow(hWnd);
                    break;
                case CM_RECTANGLE:
                    CheckMenuItem(hMenu,CM_ELIPSE,MF_BYCOMMAND |
                    MF_UNCHECKED);
                    CheckMenuItem(hMenu,CM_RECTANGLE,MF_BYCOMMAND |
                    MF_CHECKED);
                    elipseOn = FALSE;
                    break;
                case CM_ELIPSE:
                    CheckMenuItem(hMenu,CM_RECTANGLE,MF_BYCOMMAND |
                    MF_UNCHECKED);
                    CheckMenuItem(hMenu,CM_ELIPSE,
                            MF_BYCOMMAND | MF_CHECKED);
                        elipseOn = TRUE;
                        break;
                case CM_COLORS:
                    ChangeCurrentColor(hWnd);
                    break;
            }
            break;
```

continued on next page

continued from previous page

```
            case WM_DESTROY:
                    PostQuitMessage(0);
                    break;
            default:
                    return DefWindowProc(hWnd, message, wParam, lParam);
        }
        return 0;
}
```

11. Add the next two functions to the same source file, DRAWDEMO.C. The
InitApplication function is responsible for registering the window class that
the application window will use. This function will only be called if an
instance of this window class does not already exist. The InitInstance function
will be called when the application begins. It creates and displays the main
window of the application.

```
/* ------------------------------------------------------------------ */
/* This function initializes a WNDCLASS structure and uses it to       */
/* register a class for our main window.                               */
/* ------------------------------------------------------------------ */
BOOL InitApplication(HINSTANCE hInstance)
{
    WNDCLASS   wc;

    wc.style = 0;
    wc.lpfnWndProc = MainWndProc;
    wc.cbClsExtra = 0;
    wc.cbWndExtra = 0;
    wc.hInstance = hInstance;
    wc.hIcon = LoadIcon(NULL, IDI_APPLICATION);
    wc.hCursor = LoadCursor(NULL, IDC_ARROW);
    wc.hbrBackground = (HBRUSH)(COLOR_WINDOW + 1);
    wc.lpszMenuName =  MAKEINTRESOURCE(IDM_DRAWMENU);
    wc.lpszClassName = MainWindowClassName;

    return RegisterClass(&wc);
}


/* ------------------------------------------------------------------ */
/* This function creates an instance of our main window. The window    */
/* is given a class name and a title, and told to display anywhere.    */
/* The nCmdShow argument passed to the program determines how the      */
/* window will be displayed.                                           */
/* ------------------------------------------------------------------ */
BOOL InitInstance(HINSTANCE hInst, int nCmdShow)
{
    HWND hWnd;

    hInstance = hInst;     // Store in global variable.

    hWnd = CreateWindow(MainWindowClassName,"Drawing Demo",
                    WS_OVERLAPPEDWINDOW,CW_USEDEFAULT,
                    CW_USEDEFAULT,CW_USEDEFAULT,CW_USEDEFAULT,
                    NULL,NULL,hInstance,NULL);
```

```
    if (!hWnd)
        return FALSE;

    ShowWindow(hWnd, nCmdShow);
    UpdateWindow(hWnd);    // Send a WM_PAINT message.
    return TRUE;
}
```

12. There is one more function to add before you can compile and test this project. Add the WinMain function to the end of the same source file. The WinMain function is the entry point for the application and is responsible for setting up the application, then processing messages until the user closes the application.

```
/* -------------------------------------------------------------- */
/* The main entry point for Windows applications. Check to see if  */
/* the main window class name has already been registered, if it has*/
/* not, call InitApplication to register it. Call InitInstance to   */
/* create an instance of our main window, then pump messages until  */
/* the application is closed.                                       */
/* -------------------------------------------------------------- */
int PASCAL WinMain(HINSTANCE hInstance, HINSTANCE hPrevInstance,
                   LPSTR lpCmdLine, int nCmdShow)
{
    MSG msg;

    if (!FindWindow(MainWindowClassName,NULL))
        if (!InitApplication(hInstance))
            return FALSE;

    if (!InitInstance(hInstance, nCmdShow))
        return FALSE;

    while (GetMessage(&msg,NULL,0,0))
    {
        TranslateMessage(&msg);
        DispatchMessage(&msg);
    }
    return (msg.wParam);
}
```

Comments

It is important to understand how to track the mouse effectively, as demonstrated in this How-To. This will be expanded upon in How-To 4.7, where you will learn how to drag and drop a bitmap. So how can you build on this example to produce a useful application? A good first step would be to store the shapes that the user has created. At present the application does not respond to the WM_PAINT message, nor does it store information about the shapes that have been drawn. If you move the window of another application over this window, and then remove it again, all your previous drawing will have disappeared. To save this information, either save a copy of the client area as a bitmap, or save a record of the shapes that have been drawn, along with their size and color. When the application receives a WM_PAINT message, you can respond by redrawing the display.

4.5 How do I...
Capture a window or part of the screen?

Problem

Some Windows applications allow the user to capture part of the screen and store the result in the clipboard or paste it into a paint application. How can I reproduce this behavior in my application?

Technique

The GetDC, ReleaseDC, CreateDC, and DeleteDC functions allow the application programmer to access the device context associated with any window, provided that the application can get a handle to the window. There are a number of Windows API functions that let an application find the active window, the topmost window, and the window that has just received a mouse click or similar action. An application can then create a compatible bitmap and select it into a memory device context. You can use the BitBlt function to copy from the screen DC to the device context in memory, and hence the bitmap.

When capturing a bitmap image from the screen, you will also need to store the current logical palette, so that your application will have palette information when saving the bitmap to disk or displaying it.

Steps

Open and run the CAPDEMO application. You will find this application in the CHAPTER4\CAPTURE directory on the CD that accompanies this book. Drop down the Capture menu and examine the options. The Entire Screen menu item is checked by default, indicating that a capture will make a copy of the entire screen. The other capture options are Active Window, which will capture the entire image of the foreground window (including its title, scroll bars, maximize and minimize buttons), and Active Client Area, which will capture the same window but without the title, scroll bar, or other non-client area imagery.

Select the Start Capture menu item from the Capture menu. A message box will display, informing you that the capture will take place five seconds after you click the OK button. When you do click the OK button, the CAPDEMO application minimizes itself for five seconds and sets the focus to the previous application in the Z order. At the end of the time, it captures the area that you selected, then restores its main window. Figure 4-7 shows the CAPDEMO application after capturing an image of the entire screen. As you can see, the image that was captured is scaled to fit in the main window of the CAPDEMO application.

The following instructions will show you how to reproduce this application.

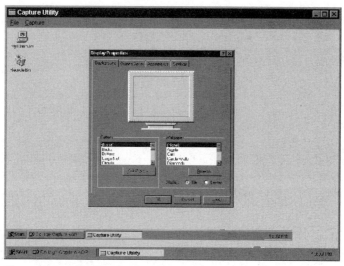

Figure 4-7 CAPDEMO application after capturing the entire screen

1. Create a working directory for this project and name it CAPTURE. You will create all your working files for the project in this directory.

2. You will need an icon for this application. The CHAPTER4\CAPTURE directory on the CD contains an icon called CAPDEMO.ICO, or if you don't have a CD-ROM drive, you can create your own using a resource editor. Create a 32-by-32-pixel icon with 16 colors, and save it as CAPDEMO.ICO.

3. The next step is to create a resource script to include the application icon and define the menus for the application. Usually, resource scripts are created by using a resource editor. However, use a text editor to create this script, and enter the following lines. Save the file as CAPDEMO.RC.

```
/* ----------------------------------------------------------------- */
/*                                                                    */
/* MODULE: CAPDEMO.RC                                                 */
/* PURPOSE: This resource script defines the menus and application    */
/*          icon associated with this application.                    */
/*                                                                    */
/* ----------------------------------------------------------------- */

#include "capdemo.rh"

IDM_CAPTUREMENU MENU
{
    POPUP "&File"
    {
        MENUITEM "E&xit", CM_EXIT
    }
    POPUP "&Capture"
```

continued on next page

continued from previous page

```
    {
        MENUITEM "&Entire Screen", CM_ENTIRESCREEN, CHECKED
        MENUITEM "&Active Window", CM_ACTIVEWINDOW
        MENUITEM "Active &Client Area", CM_ACTIVECLIENT
        MENUITEM SEPARATOR
        MENUITEM "&Start Capture", CM_CAPTURE
    }
}

IDI_APPICON ICON "capdemo.ico"
```

4. You will also need to create an include file to define the resource identifiers. These identifiers are shared between both the resource script that you have just entered and the main source file that you will begin next. Create a new file called CAPDEMO.RH and add the following definitions:

```
#ifndef __CAPDEMO_RH
/* ------------------------------------------------------------------ */
/*                                                                    */
/* MODULE: CAPDEMO.RH                                                 */
/* PURPOSE: Defines identifiers used to address resources.           */
/*                                                                    */
/* ------------------------------------------------------------------ */
#define __CAPDEMO_RH

#define IDM_CAPTUREMENU         2
#define CM_EXIT                 101
#define CM_ENTIRESCREEN         201
#define CM_ACTIVEWINDOW         202
#define CM_ACTIVECLIENT         203
#define CM_CAPTURE              204

#define IDI_APPICON             1000

#endif
```

5. Now you can start on the main part of the application. Using a text editor, create a source file called CAPDEMO.C. Type the following code fragment in at the start of the file. This code includes the Windows include files that are required for compilation. Before including these files, the code defines a pre-processor symbol, STRICT. This symbol ensures that type checking will be enforced across the different handle types that are used in programming for the Windows operating system. The code also defines the class name for the application window and declares some global variables for this application. The global variables are all initialized to default values to avoid errors later.

```
/* ------------------------------------------------------------------ */
/*                                                                    */
/* MODULE: CAPDEMO.                                                   */
/* PURPOSE: This small application demonstrates how to capture a      */
/*          bitmap image from the screen, the active window, or the   */
/*          client area of the active window. The captured bitmap is  */
/*          scaled and displayed in the application's window.         */
/*                                                                    */
/* ------------------------------------------------------------------ */
```

```
#define STRICT

#include <windows.h>
#include "capdemo.rh"


// Constants.
char *MainWindowClassName = "CaptureWindow";

// Instance variables.
HINSTANCE      hInstance = NULL;
HBITMAP        hBitmap = NULL;
HPALETTE       hPalette = NULL;
WORD           tickCounter = 0;
int            captureOptions = CM_ENTIRESCREEN;
```

6. Add the CaptureImage function to the source file. This function is responsible for finding what area of the display is to be captured and creating a bitmap and palette with the captured data. Let's have a look at the operation of this code in a little more detail.

The first switch statement retrieves the screen coordinates of the area to be captured. To capture the entire screen, you can use GetDesktopWindow to obtain a handle to the desktop, then use GetWindowRect to retrieve the rectangle that defines the desktop. In order to capture the active window, the process is similar. Use GetForegroundWindow to retrieve a handle to the window (notice that you don't use GetActiveWindow, which just returns the active window of your own application), then use GetWindowRect to retrieve the coordinates.

Retrieving the coordinates of the client area is a more complex task. First use GetForegroundWindow to retrieve the window handle, then call GetClientRect to get the coordinates. However, the rectangle returned by GetClientRect is relative to the client area itself–the coordinates of the top left corner are (0,0). To convert these to screen coordinates, you must call ClientToScreen, which converts a point to screen coordinates. The function must be called twice–once to convert the top left corner and once for the bottom right corner.

Having obtained the coordinates, you now need a device context to copy the bitmap from. Calling CreateDC with the driver string "DISPLAY" and all other parameters set to NULL returns a handle to the device context of the screen. You can then create a memory device context and a bitmap and use BitBlt to copy data from the screen to the bitmap in memory.

Taking a copy of the palette is also reasonably simple. Call the GetSystemPaletteEntries function to copy the color table for the device context into a buffer in memory. Your buffer must be large enough to contain the number of entries required; however, you can find out the number of palette entries supported by calling GetDeviceCaps with the SIZEPALETTE parameter.

```
/* ------------------------------------------------------------- */
/* This function captures an area of the display into a bitmap and a*/
/* logical palette. It modifies the bitmap handle and palette handle */
/* passed as arguments. Depending upon the value of option, it       */
/* captures the entire screen (CM_ENTIRESCREEN), the active window    */
/* (CM_ACTIVEWINDOW), or the client area of the active window         */
/* (CM_ACTIVECLIENT).                                                 */
/* ------------------------------------------------------------- */
void CaptureImage(int options, HBITMAP *bmPtr, HPALETTE *palPtr)
{
    HDC         hScreenDC, hMemoryDC;
    HWND        hTopWnd;
    LONG        xRes, yRes, width, height;
    RECT        capRect;
    POINT       point;
    HBITMAP     hOldBitmap;
    int         nColors;
    HGLOBAL     hGlobal;
    LOGPALETTE  *pPalette;

    *bmPtr = NULL;
    *palPtr = NULL;

    // Use a different rectangle depending upon options.
    switch (options)
    {
        case CM_ENTIRESCREEN:
            GetWindowRect(GetDesktopWindow(),&capRect);
            break;
        case CM_ACTIVEWINDOW:
            hTopWnd = GetForegroundWindow();
            GetWindowRect(hTopWnd,&capRect);
            break;
        case CM_ACTIVECLIENT:
            hTopWnd = GetForegroundWindow();
            /* Work out the client area. */
            GetClientRect(hTopWnd,&capRect);
            point.x = capRect.left;
            point.y = capRect.top;
            ClientToScreen(hTopWnd,&point);
            capRect.left = point.x;
            capRect.top = point.y;
            point.x = capRect.right;
            point.y = capRect.bottom;
            ClientToScreen(hTopWnd,&point);
            capRect.right = point.x;
            capRect.bottom = point.y;
            break;
    }

    hScreenDC = CreateDC("DISPLAY",NULL,NULL,NULL);
    hMemoryDC = CreateCompatibleDC(hScreenDC);

    // Make sure that the capture area is visible.
    xRes = GetDeviceCaps(hScreenDC,HORZRES);
```

```
    yRes = GetDeviceCaps(hScreenDC,VERTRES);
    if (capRect.top < 0)
        capRect.top = 0;
    if (capRect.left < 0)
        capRect.left = 0;
    if (capRect.bottom > yRes)
        capRect.bottom = yRes;
    if (capRect.right > xRes)
        capRect.right = xRes;
    width = capRect.right - capRect.left;
    height = capRect.bottom - capRect.top;

    // Create a bitmap and store the image into it.
    *bmPtr = CreateCompatibleBitmap(hScreenDC,width,height);
    holdBitmap = SelectObject(hMemoryDC,*bmPtr);
    BitBlt(hMemoryDC,0,0,width,height,hScreenDC,capRect.left,
            capRect.top,SRCCOPY);
    SelectObject(hMemoryDC,holdBitmap);
    DeleteDC(hMemoryDC);

    // Allocate space for a LOGPALETTE structure.
    nColors = GetDeviceCaps(hScreenDC,SIZEPALETTE);
    if (nColors == 0)
        nColors = GetDeviceCaps(hScreenDC,NUMCOLORS);
    hGlobal = GlobalAlloc(GHND,sizeof(LOGPALETTE) +
                        (nColors * sizeof(PALETTEENTRY)));
    pPalette = (LOGPALETTE *)GlobalLock(hGlobal);

    // Fill in the structure from the system palette.
    pPalette->palVersion = 0x300;
    pPalette->palNumEntries = (WORD)nColors;
    GetSystemPaletteEntries(hScreenDC,0,nColors,
                        pPalette->palPalEntry);

    // Create a logical palette, and delete the LOGPALETTE structure.
    *palPtr = CreatePalette(pPalette);
    GlobalUnlock(hGlobal);
    GlobalFree(hGlobal);

    // Delete the DC as well.
    DeleteDC(hScreenDC);
}
```

7. Next add the Paint function. This function will display the bitmap once it has been captured, scaling it to fit in the window. The GetObject function is used to fill in information about the width and height of the bitmap in a BITMAP structure. These values are then used with the StretchBlt function to display the bitmap in the window.

```
/* ---------------------------------------------------------------- */
/* This function displays the captured bitmap in the window. It     */
/* uses the palette of the captured bitmap so that the colors are   */
/* correct.                                                         */
/* ---------------------------------------------------------------- */
void Paint(HWND hWnd, HPALETTE hPalette, HBITMAP hBitmap)
```

continued on next page

continued from previous page

```
{
    PAINTSTRUCT         ps;
    HDC                 hDC, hMemDC;
    HPALETTE            holdPalette;
    HBITMAP             holdBitmap;
    BITMAP              bmInfo;

    hDC = BeginPaint(hWnd, &ps);

    GetObject(hBitmap,sizeof(BITMAP),&bmInfo);
    if ((hMemDC = CreateCompatibleDC(hDC)) != NULL)
    {
        holdPalette = SelectPalette(hDC, hPalette, FALSE);
        RealizePalette(hDC);
        holdBitmap = SelectObject(hMemDC,hBitmap);
        StretchBlt(hDC, ps.rcPaint.left, ps.rcPaint.top,
                    (ps.rcPaint.right - ps.rcPaint.left),
                    (ps.rcPaint.bottom - ps.rcPaint.top),
                    hMemDC, 0, 0, bmInfo.bmWidth,
                    bmInfo.bmHeight, SRCCOPY);
        SelectObject(hMemDC,holdBitmap);
        SelectPalette(hDC,holdPalette,FALSE);
        DeleteDC(hMemDC);
    }
    EndPaint(hWnd, &ps);
}
```

8. Now type the following code into the source file. The MainWndProc function
is a callback function that will receive messages sent to the application window.
The interesting messages processed by this function are the CM_CAPTURE
command message, which is sent when the Start Capture menu item is selected, and the WM_TIMER message, which indicates a timer tick.

The code responds to the CM_CAPTURE message by displaying the warning
message that capturing will start in five seconds. It then calls the SetTimer API
function to set up a timer that will tick every second. The ShowWindow API
function is used to minimize the application window, and SetActiveWindow is
used to select the previously active top-level window. This removes the focus
from the icon for the application and avoids capturing an image of the icon.

The code responds to the WM_TIMER message by incrementing a counter,
tickCounter. When the counter reaches five, the Capture function that you
defined earlier is called to capture the entire screen, active window, or active
client area to a bitmap. The application window is then restored so that the
results may be displayed. Restoring the window will cause it to receive a
WM_PAINT message, so the results of the screen capture will be displayed.

```
/* ------------------------------------------------------------------ */
/* This function is the main window callback function which will be   */
/* called by Windows to process messages for our window.              */
/* ------------------------------------------------------------------ */
LPARAM CALLBACK MainWndProc(HWND hWnd, UINT message,
                            WPARAM wParam, LPARAM lParam)
{
```

```
switch (message)
{
    case WM_COMMAND:
        switch (wParam)
        {
            case CM_EXIT:
                DestroyWindow(hWnd);
                break;
            case CM_ENTIRESCREEN:
            case CM_ACTIVEWINDOW:
            case CM_ACTIVECLIENT:
                CheckMenuItem(GetMenu(hWnd),captureOptions,
                            MF_BYCOMMAND | MF_UNCHECKED);
                captureOptions = (int)wParam;
                CheckMenuItem(GetMenu(hWnd),captureOptions,
                            MF_BYCOMMAND | MF_CHECKED);
                break;
            case CM_CAPTURE:
                MessageBox(hWnd,"The area that you have chosen\n"
                            "will be captured 5 seconds after\n"
                            "you click the OK button.",
                            "Capture", MB_ICONINFORMATION | MB_OK);
                if (hPalette)
                    DeleteObject(hPalette);
                hPalette = NULL;
                if (hBitmap)
                    DeleteObject(hBitmap);
                hBitmap = NULL;
                tickCounter = 0;
                if (SetTimer(hWnd,1,1000,NULL) != NULL)
                {
                    EnableMenuItem(GetMenu(hWnd),CM_CAPTURE,
                                MF_BYCOMMAND | MF_GRAYED);
                    /* Minimize this application, and select
                        another window on the desktop. */
                    ShowWindow(hWnd,SW_MINIMIZE);
                    SetActiveWindow(GetWindow(hWnd,GW_HWNDPREV));
                }
                break;
            default:
                return DefWindowProc(hWnd,message,wParam,lParam);
        }
        break;
    case WM_TIMER:
        tickCounter = tickCounter + 1;
        if (tickCounter == 5)
        {
            KillTimer(hWnd,1);
            CaptureImage(captureOptions,&hBitmap,&hPalette);
            ShowWindow(hWnd,SW_RESTORE);
            EnableMenuItem(GetMenu(hWnd),CM_CAPTURE,
                        MF_BYCOMMAND | MF_ENABLED);
        }
        break;
    case WM_PAINT:
        if ((hBitmap) && (hPalette))
```

continued on next page

continued from previous page

```
                                Paint(hWnd,hPalette,hBitmap);
                    else
                            return DefWindowProc(hWnd,message,wParam,lParam);
                    break;
            case WM_SIZE:
                    if ((wParam == SIZE_RESTORED) || (wParam == SIZE_MAXIMIZED))
                        InvalidateRect(hWnd,NULL,TRUE);
                    break;
            case WM_DESTROY:
                    if (hPalette)
                        DeleteObject(hPalette);
                    if (hBitmap)
                        DeleteObject(hBitmap);
                    KillTimer(hWnd,1);
                    PostQuitMessage(0);
                    break;
            default:
                    return DefWindowProc(hWnd, message, wParam, lParam);
    }
    return 0;
}
```

9. Add the following two functions to the source file. The InitApplication function will only be called if the window class name is not already in use by a
window. It registers the window class that will be used for the main window.
The InitInstance function creates the main window and displays it.

```
/* ----------------------------------------------------------------- */
/* This function initializes a WNDCLASS structure and uses it to     */
/* register a class for our main window.                             */
/* ----------------------------------------------------------------- */
BOOL InitApplication(HINSTANCE hInstance)
{
    WNDCLASS  wc;

    wc.style = 0;
    wc.lpfnWndProc = MainWndProc;
    wc.cbClsExtra = 0;
    wc.cbWndExtra = 0;
    wc.hInstance = hInstance;
    wc.hIcon = LoadIcon(NULL, IDI_APPLICATION);
    wc.hCursor = LoadCursor(NULL, IDC_ARROW);
    wc.hbrBackground = (HBRUSH)(COLOR_WINDOW + 1);
    wc.lpszMenuName =  MAKEINTRESOURCE(IDM_CAPTUREMENU);
    wc.lpszClassName = MainWindowClassName;

    return RegisterClass(&wc);
}


/* ----------------------------------------------------------------- */
/* This function creates an instance of our main window. The window  */
/* is given a class name and a title, and told to display anywhere.  */
/* The nCmdShow argument passed to the program determines how the    */
/* window will be displayed.                                         */
/* ----------------------------------------------------------------- */
```

```
BOOL InitInstance(HINSTANCE hInst, int nCmdShow)
{
    HWND hWnd;

    hInstance = hInst;    // Store in global variable.

    hWnd = CreateWindow(MainWindowClassName,"Capture Utility",
                    WS_OVERLAPPEDWINDOW,CW_USEDEFAULT,
                    CW_USEDEFAULT,CW_USEDEFAULT,CW_USEDEFAULT,
                    NULL,NULL,hInstance,NULL);
    if (!hWnd)
        return FALSE;

    ShowWindow(hWnd, nCmdShow);
    UpdateWindow(hWnd);  // Send a WM_PAINT message.
    return TRUE;
}
```

10. The final component that you need in the source file is the WinMain function. This function will be called by Windows 95 when the application starts. It registers the window class if no other window with that class exists, then creates and displays the main window using InitInstance. Finally, it processes messages until the application exits.

```
/* ------------------------------------------------------------ */
/* The main entry point for Windows applications. Check to see if   */
/* the main window class name has already been registered, if it has */
/* not, call InitApplication to register it. Call InitInstance to   */
/* create an instance of our main window, then pump messages until  */
/* the application is closed.                                       */
/* ------------------------------------------------------------ */
int PASCAL WinMain(HINSTANCE hInstance, HINSTANCE hPrevInstance,
                LPSTR lpCmdLine, int nCmdShow)
{
    MSG msg;

    if (!FindWindow(MainWindowClassName,NULL))
        if (!InitApplication(hInstance))
            return FALSE;

    if (!InitInstance(hInstance, nCmdShow))
        return FALSE;

    while (GetMessage(&msg,NULL,0,0))
    {
        TranslateMessage(&msg);
        DispatchMessage(&msg);
    }
    return (msg.wParam);
}
```

11. Compile and run the application.

Comments

This sample application neither prints nor saves the bitmap to a file. A genuine screen capture application could be readily assembled from this framework, however. The print function would operate very similarly to the paint function, and saving to a file would involve the conversion from device-dependent bitmap and palette into a device-independent bitmap, using functions such as GetDIBits.

COMPLEXITY
DIFFICULT

4.6   How do I...
Perform animation?

Problem

I would like to bring my application to life by adding some animation. I know that there is third-party software available to do this, but can I use the Windows API to do animation?

Technique

You can use the Windows API to perform simple animation. As long as the images are not large, and the overall animation is not too complicated, you will have relatively little flicker or speed problems. This has been greatly aided in Windows 95 because much of the graphics device interface has been rewritten using 32-bit code. In earlier versions of Windows, this was 16-bit code with an associated reduction in performance.

When animating a bitmap, there are a number of things to bear in mind. First, as an object moves across the background, you will want the background to be restored to its previous state. The easiest way to accomplish this is by capturing the background into an off-screen bitmap before the image is displayed on it. When the image moves off that area, the background will need to be restored.

The second thing to consider is how to implement animation of images that are not of a regular square or rectangular shape. Windows supports the use of the API function SetBkMode to set the drawing mode to transparent or opaque, but this mode is not used for bitmap operations. The only way to produce bitmaps with transparent parts is to perform multiple BitBlt operations with a mask bitmap.

The final thing to consider when performing animation is how the animation should be timed. Calling the animation functions in a simple loop is not generally useful; it tends to inundate the processor, and the animation will often occur faster than desired. A better technique is to use a timer. The system timer, initialized with SetTimer, sends WM_TIMER messages that your application can respond to. However, this method suffers from two problems. Timer messages are low priority, so they only occur after all other messages except WM_PAINT messages have been processed. The second, and more pressing problem with the system timer, is that it has a maximum resolution of 55 milliseconds, meaning that your application will only receive about 18 messages per second. The example application in this How-To uses the multimedia timer service's timeSetEvent function with a callback function to achieve a rate of around 25 events per second–enough to perform smooth animation.

Steps

Open and run the ANIMATE.EXE sample application. You will find this application in the CHAPTER4\ANIMATE directory on the CD that comes with this book. This application opens a window with a green background. A multicolored ball bounces around the window, changing direction when it comes in contact with an edge of the client area. When you size the application, the ball starts again in the top left corner of the window and bounces off the new sides of the window. You can close the application by clicking on the close button in the top right corner of the window. Figure 4-8 shows the ANIMATE application in action.

The following steps will guide you in reproducing this application.

1. Start by creating a directory called ANIMATE to hold this application.

2. You will need a bitmap for the bouncing ball in this application. Copy the file BALL.BMP from the CHAPTER4\ANIMATE directory on the CD into your working directory. If you don't have access to a CD-ROM drive, you can create your own bitmap. Use a resource editor or paint program to create a 32-by-32-pixel bitmap with up to 16 colors (4 bits per pixel). Save the file as BALL.BMP.

3. You will also require an icon for this application. Copy the file ANIMATE.ICO from the CD. You will find the file in the CHAPTER4\ANIMATE directory. Again, you can create the icon using a resource editor if you do not have a CD-ROM drive. Create a 32-by-32-pixel, 16-color icon and save it as ANIMATE.ICO.

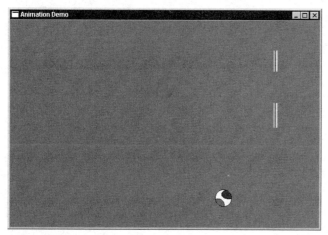

Figure 4-8 ANIMATE application

4. The next step is to create the resource script for the application. Using a text editor, create a new file called ANIMATE.RC and enter this text:

```
/* ------------------------------------------------------------------ */
/*                                                                    */
/* MODULE: ANIMATE.RC                                                 */
/* PURPOSE: This resource script defines the bitmap and application   */
/*          icon associated with this application.                    */
/*                                                                    */
/* ------------------------------------------------------------------ */

#include "animate.rh"

IDBM_BALL BITMAP "ball.bmp"

IDI_APPICON ICON "app.ico"
```

5. The resource script references an include file, ANIMATE.RH. This file will define the resource identifiers used for the bitmap and the application icon; it is used by both the resource script and the application source code. Create a new file with the following definitions. Save the file as ANIMATE.RH.

```
#ifndef __ANIMATE_RH
/* ------------------------------------------------------------------ */
/*                                                                    */
/* MODULE: ANIMATE.RH                                                 */
/* PURPOSE: Defines identifiers used to address resources.            */
/*                                                                    */
/* ------------------------------------------------------------------ */
#define __ANIMATE_RH

#define IDI_APPICON        1
#define IDBM_BALL       1000

#endif
```

6. You are now ready to create the main source file for the application. Use a text editor to create a new file, and name it ANIMATE.C. Add the following code fragment to the top of the file. Notice that this code defines the preprocessor symbol STRICT, which ensures that strict type checking is carried out on the handles used in your program. It also defines some constants for use in the application. Besides the name of the window class for the application, the code defines a user-defined message to be sent to the application window when a multimedia timer event occurs (more about that later) and three RGB values to be used in transparently blitting the bitmap onto the screen.

```
/* ------------------------------------------------------------------ */
/*                                                                    */
/* MODULE: ANIMATE.C                                                  */
/* PURPOSE: This application demonstrates simple bitmap animation     */
/*          using a timer.                                            */
/*                                                                    */
/* ------------------------------------------------------------------ */
```

```
#define STRICT
#include <windows.h>
#include <mmsystem.h>
#include "animate.rh"
// Constants.
char *MainWindowClassName = "AnimateWindow";
#define MYMSG_TIMER   (WM_USER + 50)
#define RGBBLACK RGB(0,0,0)
#define RGBWHITE RGB(255,255,255)
#define RGBTRANSPARENT RGBWHITE


// Instance variables.
HINSTANCE     hInstance = NULL;
HBITMAP       hBitmap = NULL;
HBITMAP       hMask = NULL;
HBITMAP       hBackground = NULL;
LONG          left, top;
LONG          width, height;
LONG          xincrement, yincrement;
UINT          timerId = 0;
BOOL          firstPaint = TRUE;
```

7. Now add the first function to the file. The CaptureBackground function is used to get a bitmap of the background where you are about to place the image. The background is stored so that it can be replaced when the image is moved. This function creates a bitmap the size of the object or reuses the existing bitmap once it has been created. Using a memory device context, the code performs a BitBlt to copy the data from the window into the bitmap.

```
/* ---------------------------------------------------------------- */
/* This function captures the background at a given location into    */
/* the bitmap hBackground. If the bitmap handle is NULL, a bitmap    */
/* is created to contain the image. If the bitmap is not NULL, just  */
/* use the existing bitmap.                                          */
/* ---------------------------------------------------------------- */
HBITMAP CaptureBackground(HWND hWnd, LONG left, LONG top,
                          LONG width, LONG height,
                          HBITMAP hBackground)
{
    HDC          hDC, hMemoryDC;
    HBITMAP      hOldBitmap;

    hDC = GetDC(hWnd);

    if (!hBackground)
        hBackground = CreateCompatibleBitmap(hDC,width,height);

    hMemoryDC = CreateCompatibleDC(hDC);
    hOldBitmap = SelectObject(hMemoryDC,hBackground);
    BitBlt(hMemoryDC,0,0,width,height,hDC,left,top,SRCCOPY);
    SelectObject(hMemoryDC,hOldBitmap);
    DeleteDC(hMemoryDC);
    ReleaseDC(hWnd,hDC);
    return hBackground;
}
```

8. Here is the function for placing a bitmap on the screen with transparency. Unless you are animating a solid rectangle, you will need to have the background showing through any transparent parts of the object. Windows does not provide a transparent BitBlt function or operator, but you can produce a transparent blit with just two BitBlt calls, provided that you have a monochrome mask bitmap already produced. The mask bitmap will be the same size as your image, and it will have white pixels (1) where the background should show through and black pixels (0) where the image is opaque. The image bitmap must have black (palette index 0) pixels where the background is to show through, although it may also have black in other areas. Let's have a look at the two BitBlt operations.

The first call copies the mask onto the background of the window. It uses the SRCAND raster operator to merge the images with a logical AND operator. The call sets the parts of the destination to black where the image will be placed. The other parts of the bitmap are untouched.

The second BitBlt call uses the SRCPAINT raster operator to blit the image onto the destination. The operation merges the two images with the logical OR operator. Where the background was black in the destination, the image will appear, while the black pixels in the image will leave the destination untouched. In blitting large bitmaps on slower PCs, you may find that there will be a visible flicker between the two BitBlt calls. You can resolve this by adding two more BitBlt calls. The first call copies the background to a device context and bitmap in memory. The next two calls are the same as the two calls already discussed. A final BitBlt call copies the modified bitmap back to the screen. This removes flicker by avoiding modification of the screen until the operation is complete–however, it also adds two BitBlt function calls, with the resulting performance hit. For small bitmaps, this two-call approach should work well:

```
/* -------------------------------------------------------------- */
/* This function performs a transparent BitBlt of the bitmap into  */
/* the chosen device context. It does this by using two BitBlt     */
/* operations with different operators.                            */
/* -------------------------------------------------------------- */
void TransparentBlt(HDC hDestDC, LONG left, LONG top,
                    LONG width, LONG height,
                    HDC hSrcDC, LONG srcleft, LONG srctop,
                    HBITMAP hMask)
{
    HDC       hMaskDC;
    HBITMAP   oldBitmap;

    hMaskDC = CreateCompatibleDC(hDestDC);
    oldBitmap = SelectObject(hMaskDC,hMask);
    /* Use SRCAND so that all but the transparent
       bits of the destination are set to black. */
    BitBlt(hDestDC,left,top,width,height,
           hMaskDC,srcleft,srctop,SRCAND);
```

```
    /* Use SRCPAINT so that all but the black bits
       of the source are placed into the destination */
    BitBlt(hDestDC,left,top,width,height,
          hSrcDC,srcleft,srctop,SRCPAINT);
    SelectObject(hMaskDC,oldBitmap);
    DeleteDC(hMaskDC);
}
```

9. Add the DoAnimation function to the same source file, ANIMATE.C. This function does the actual animation. It restores the previous background bitmap using a BitBlt call, then calculates the new image position by adding *xincrement* and *yincrement* to the top and left coordinates. The CaptureBackground function is used to take a copy of the background before the image is placed on it, then a call to the TransparentBlt function is used to place the image onto the background.

```
/* ---------------------------------------------------------------- */
/*  This function performs the actual display of the animated bitmap.*/
/*  It follows these steps:         1. Put back the saved background  */
/*                                  2. Calculate new top/left positions */
/*                                  3. Save the background            */
/*                                  4. Blit the bitmap                */
/* ---------------------------------------------------------------- */
void DoAnimation(HWND hWnd)
{
    HDC       hDC, hMemoryDC;
    HBITMAP   hOldBitmap;

    hDC = GetDC(hWnd);
    hMemoryDC = CreateCompatibleDC(hDC);

    // If the background was saved, restore it.
    if (hBackground)
    {
        hOldBitmap = SelectObject(hMemoryDC,hBackground);
        BitBlt(hDC,left,top,width,height,hMemoryDC,0,0,SRCCOPY);
        SelectObject(hMemoryDC,hOldBitmap);
    }

    // Calculate the new top and left coordinates.
    top += yincrement;
    left += xincrement;

    // Now capture the background at the new location.
    hBackground = CaptureBackground(hWnd,left,top,width,
                                    height,hBackground);

    // Finally, display the object at that location.
    if (hBitmap)
    {
        hOldBitmap = SelectObject(hMemoryDC,hBitmap);
        TransparentBlt(hDC,left,top,width,height,
                       hMemoryDC,0,0,hMask);
        SelectObject(hMemoryDC,hOldBitmap);
    }
```

continued on next page

continued from previous page

```
        DeleteDC(hMemoryDC);
        ReleaseDC(hWnd,hDC);
}
```

10. The TestForCollision routine uses GetClientRect to get the current dimensions
of the window. It then tests to see if the image has collided with any of the
sides of the window. If the image has collided with the top or bottom of the
window, the code inverts the value of the *yinc* variable. If the image has collided with the sides of the window, the code inverts the value of the *xinc* variable.
A collision with a corner will result in both *xinc* and *yinc* variables being
reversed.

```
/* ----------------------------------------------------------------- */
/* This function tests to see if our object has collided with any of */
/* the sides of the window's client area. If it has, the xincrement  */
/* and yincrement variables are changed.                             */
/* ----------------------------------------------------------------- */
void TestForCollision(HWND hWnd, LONG top, LONG left,
                      LONG width, LONG height,
                      LONG *xinc, LONG *yinc)
{
    RECT rcClient;

    GetClientRect(hWnd,&rcClient);
    if ((top <= rcClient.top) ||
        ((top + height) >= rcClient.bottom))
        *yinc *= -1;
    if ((left <= rcClient.left) ||
        ((left + width) >= rcClient.right))
        *xinc *= -1;
}
```

11. Now add the following function. The CreateBitmaps function does just what
its name indicates. It uses the API function LoadBitmap to load a 16-color
bitmap to be animated and uses it to create the two bitmaps required by the
TransparentBlt function. The function expects a monochrome mask bitmap
that has white (1) pixels where the background is to show through and black
(0) pixels where the image is to be opaque. It also expects a color bitmap that
will have black pixels wherever the mask bitmap had white pixels.

A monochrome bitmap is created in a memory device context using
CreateCompatibleBitmap. This works because device contexts created using
CreateCompatibleDC have by default a 1 pixel-by-1 pixel monochrome
bitmap. The bitmap that the code creates is compatible with that, and thus is
monochrome also. We perform a BitBlt from a DC containing the original
bitmap into the DC containing the monochrome bitmap. The BitBlt function
automatically converts all those pixels that match the background color in the
source DC into white in the destination. All other pixels are converted to
black. Using this technique, you can quickly create a mask. The code then
performs a normal BitBlt to make a copy of the original bitmap into hBitmap.
A third BitBlt operation with the SRCAND raster operator is used to perform a

logical AND between the bits of the hMask bitmap and the hBitmap bitmap. The result is that those areas that are to be transparent are set to black in the hBitmap bitmap.

```
/* ---------------------------------------------------------------- */
/* This function creates the bitmaps and assigns them to the bitmap */
/* handles for this instance - hBitmap and hMask. When complete,    */
/* hMask is a mask bitmap and hBitmap is a copy of the resource,     */
/* modified to work with the mask.                                   */
/* ---------------------------------------------------------------- */
void CreateBitmaps(HWND hWnd)
{
    BITMAP    bmInfo;
    HBITMAP   hResBitmap, hOldSrc, hOldDest;
    HDC       hSrcDC, hDestDC, hDC;
    COLORREF  oldColor, oldText;

    hResBitmap = LoadBitmap(hInstance,
                         MAKEINTRESOURCE(IDBM_BALL));
    GetObject(hResBitmap,sizeof(BITMAP),&bmInfo);
    width = bmInfo.bmWidth;
    height = bmInfo.bmHeight;
    hDC = GetDC(hWnd);

    hSrcDC = CreateCompatibleDC(hDC);
    hDestDC = CreateCompatibleDC(hDC);
    /* Creates a bitmap compatible with the default bitmap
       in hMaskDC. This is a monochrome bitmap.
       Select the resource bitmap into hSrcDC and use
       BitBlt to make a mask bitmap. */
    hMask = CreateCompatibleBitmap(hDestDC,width,height);
    hOldDest = SelectObject(hDestDC,hMask);
    hOldSrc = SelectObject(hSrcDC,hResBitmap);
    oldColor = SetBkColor(hSrcDC,RGBTRANSPARENT);
    BitBlt(hDestDC,0,0,width,height,hSrcDC,0,0,SRCCOPY);
    SetBkColor(hSrcDC,oldColor);

    /* Create a Color bitmap to hold the image. Note we create
       the bitmap compatible with the screen to get a color one.
       Make a copy of the hResBitmap into hBitmap. */
    hBitmap = CreateCompatibleBitmap(hDC,width,height);
    SelectObject(hDestDC,hBitmap);
    BitBlt(hDestDC,0,0,width,height,hSrcDC,0,0,SRCCOPY);

    /*  Now combine hMask with hBitmap to black out the white
        bits in hBitmap. */
    SelectObject(hSrcDC,hMask);
    SelectObject(hDestDC,hBitmap);
    oldColor = SetBkColor(hDestDC,RGBBLACK);
    oldText = SetTextColor(hDestDC,RGBWHITE);
    BitBlt(hDestDC,0,0,width,height,hSrcDC,0,0,SRCAND);
    SetTextColor(hDestDC,oldText);
    SetBkColor(hDestDC,oldColor);

    // Restore the old bitmaps and delete DCs.
```

continued on next page

continued from previous page

```
            SelectObject(hDestDC,hOldDest);
            SelectObject(hSrcDC,hOldSrc);
            DeleteDC(hDestDC);
            DeleteDC(hSrcDC);
            ReleaseDC(hWnd,hDC);
            DeleteObject(hResBitmap);
}
```

12. Add the following code to the example. The CatchMMTimer function is used as a callback function to receive notification of multimedia timer events. The function simply posts a user-defined message (WM_USER + 50 in this case) to the window queue. The handle of the window is supplied as user data when the function is set up.

You might think that it would make sense to do the animation inside this function—after all, that was the whole point of the timer. However, code in a timer callback function should be kept as brief as possible. Time-consuming operations such as bitmap manipulation should not be carried out in such a function. Instead, this function posts a message to the window. After the callback has completed, when the system allocates time to the application once more, the message can be processed and the animation performed. You can read more about responding to timer events in the box—"Responding to Multimedia Timer Events."

```
/* ------------------------------------------------------------- */
/* This callback function receives multimedia timer events.      */
/* Because you should not do tasks which may take a while (like   */
/* blitting a bitmap) in a timer callback, post an application    */
/* message to the window.                                        */
/* ------------------------------------------------------------- */
void CALLBACK CatchMMTimer(UINT IDEvent,         /* event Id */
                           UINT uReserved,       /* unused    */
                           DWORD dwUser,         /* our hWnd  */
                           DWORD dwReserved1,    /* unused    */
                           DWORD dwReserved2)    /* unused    */
{
    PostMessage((HWND)dwUser,MYMSG_TIMER,0,0);
}
```

Responding to Multimedia Timer Events

Although multimedia timers are not interrupt events as they were in earlier versions of Windows, they still can affect system performance. You should not perform any operations within a timer callback function that might take a long time to process (for instance, BitBlt operations). In fact, Microsoft suggests that only the following API functions should be used while inside a timer callback:

EnterCriticalSection	PostThreadMessage
LeaveCriticalSection	SetEvent
midiOutLongMsg	timeGetTime
midiOutShortMsg	timeGetSystemTime
OutputDebugString	timeKillEvent
PostMessage	timeSetEvent

13. Add the SetupAnimation function to the source file. The following code sets the initial position of the ball using the left and top variables, and its initial direction using the *xincrement* and *yincrement* variables. It also initializes the multimedia timer. The call to timeBeginPeriod sets the minimum timer resolution that the application will use–in this case 40 milliseconds. The next call, timeSetEvent, starts a periodic timer to be called every 40 milliseconds. When a timer event occurs, the system will call the CatchMMTimer routine that you entered previously.

```
/* ----------------------------------------------------------------- */
/* Use the paint function to set up the animation. At this stage you*/
/* know that the background has been painted for the first time, so */
/* you can safely start displaying the image.                       */
/* ----------------------------------------------------------------- */
void SetupAnimation(HWND hWnd)
{
    /* Now set up the animation increments. */
    left = 1;
    top = 1;
    xincrement = 4;
    yincrement = 4;

    /* Set up the animation timer. */
    if (timeBeginPeriod(40) == 0)
        timerId = timeSetEvent(40,40,CatchMMTimer,
                               (DWORD)hWnd,TIME_PERIODIC);
}
```

14. The MainWndProc function that you will add next is the callback function that receives messages sent to the application window. This function only processes a subset of these messages, with all unprocessed messages being handed on to the DefWindowProc API function. There are some messages that are worth examining in detail.

The function responds to the user-defined message that you defined at the top of the file–MYMSG_TIMER. This message will be sent whenever the timer callback function, CatchMMTimer, is called. In response to this message, the code calls TestForCollision to test for collision with the window edges and change direction, then calls the DoAnimation function to perform the animation itself.

The function also responds to the WM_PAINT message, although only the first WM_PAINT message is used. The code calls CreateBitmaps and SetupAnimation to start the animation, then clears the firstPaint flag so that the initialization will not be performed again. This initialization is performed in response to the WM_PAINT message rather than the WM_CREATE message, because you know that the background color has been filled in by the time the application receives its first WM_PAINT message.

The other message of interest is the WM_SIZE message. Windows sends this message to the window when it is minimized, maximized, restored, or resized in any way. This code responds by restarting the animation from the top left corner of the window. It also forces a complete redraw of the window.

```
/* ----------------------------------------------------------------- */
/* This function is the main window callback function which will be   */
/* called by Windows to process messages for our window.             */
/* ----------------------------------------------------------------- */
LPARAM CALLBACK MainWndProc(HWND hWnd, UINT message,
                            WPARAM wParam, LPARAM lParam)
{
    switch (message)
    {
        case MYMSG_TIMER:
            TestForCollision(hWnd,top,left,width,height,
                                &xincrement,&yincrement);
            DoAnimation(hWnd);
            break;
        case WM_PAINT:
            if (firstPaint)
            {
                firstPaint = FALSE;
                CreateBitmaps(hWnd);
                SetupAnimation(hWnd);
            }
            return DefWindowProc(hWnd, message, lParam, wParam);
        case WM_SIZE:
            /* Make sure that the bitmap is visible */
            DeleteObject(hBackground);
            hBackground = NULL;
            top = 1; left = 1;
            InvalidateRect(hWnd,NULL,TRUE);
            break;
        case WM_DESTROY:
            if (hBitmap)
                DeleteObject(hBitmap);
            if (hMask)
                DeleteObject(hMask);
            if (hBackground)
                DeleteObject(hBackground);
            if (timerId)
                timeKillEvent(timerId);
            timeEndPeriod(40);
            PostQuitMessage(0);
            break;
        default:
            return DefWindowProc(hWnd, message, wParam, lParam);
    }
    return 0;
}
```

15. Add the next two functions to the end of the same source file. These two functions are both helper functions—they are used to set up the application. The InitApplication function registers a new window class for use by the application window. Because a class is shared by all the windows that use it, this function will only be called when no other windows with the class exist. In contrast, the InitInstance function will be called each time this application is run. This function is responsible for creating the main window of the application and displaying it on screen.

```c
/* ------------------------------------------------------------------ */
/* This function initializes a WNDCLASS structure and uses it to      */
/* register a class for our main window.                              */
/* ------------------------------------------------------------------ */
BOOL InitApplication(HINSTANCE hInstance)
{
    WNDCLASS   wc;
    LOGBRUSH   lb;

    wc.style = 0;
    wc.lpfnWndProc = MainWndProc;
    wc.cbClsExtra = 0;
    wc.cbWndExtra = 0;
    wc.hInstance = hInstance;
    wc.hIcon = LoadIcon(NULL, IDI_APPLICATION);
    wc.hCursor = LoadCursor(NULL, IDC_ARROW);
    wc.lpszMenuName =  NULL;
    wc.lpszClassName = MainWindowClassName;
    lb.lbStyle = BS_SOLID;
    lb.lbColor = RGB(0,128,64); // Blue-Green brush.
    wc.hbrBackground = CreateBrushIndirect(&lb);

    return RegisterClass(&wc);
}


/* ------------------------------------------------------------------ */
/* This function creates an instance of our main window. The window   */
/* is given a class name and a title, and told to display anywhere.   */
/* The nCmdShow argument passed to the program determines how the     */
/* window will be displayed.                                          */
/* ------------------------------------------------------------------ */
BOOL InitInstance(HINSTANCE hInst, int nCmdShow)
{
    HWND hWnd;

    hInstance = hInst;        // Store in global variable.

    hWnd = CreateWindow(MainWindowClassName,"Animation Demo",
                    WS_OVERLAPPEDWINDOW,CW_USEDEFAULT,
                    CW_USEDEFAULT,CW_USEDEFAULT,CW_USEDEFAULT,
                    NULL,NULL,hInstance,NULL);
    if (!hWnd)
        return FALSE;

    ShowWindow(hWnd, nCmdShow);
    UpdateWindow(hWnd);        // Send a WM_PAINT message.
    return TRUE;
}
```

16. The final function that you will need is the WinMain function. Add this function at the end of the source file. The WinMain function is the entry point for a Windows application. The following code registers the window class by calling InitApplication, then creates and displays the main window by calling InitInstance. Finally, it processes messages until the application is closed.

```
/* ---------------------------------------------------------------- */
/* The main entry point for Windows applications. Check to see if   */
/* the main window class name has already been registered; if it has*/
/* not, call InitApplication to register it. Call InitInstance to   */
/* create an instance of our main window, then pump messages until  */
/* the application is closed.                                       */
/* ---------------------------------------------------------------- */
int PASCAL WinMain(HINSTANCE hInstance, HINSTANCE hPrevInstance,
                   LPSTR lpCmdLine, int nCmdShow)
{
    MSG msg;

    if (!FindWindow(MainWindowClassName,NULL))
        if (!InitApplication(hInstance))
            return FALSE;

    if (!InitInstance(hInstance, nCmdShow))
        return FALSE;

    while (GetMessage(&msg,NULL,0,0))
    {
        TranslateMessage(&msg);
        DispatchMessage(&msg);
    }
    return (msg.wParam);
}
```

17. Compile and run the application.

Comments

This example can form the basis of more complex animation using the Windows API routines. If the animations that you are attempting to perform are reasonably large, or the code to perform each animation is very processor intensive, you may find that performance is suffering. You will notice that the image flickers unacceptably, or that the animation is not smooth enough. If this occurs, you should first check that you are minimizing the use of processor-intensive calls such as BitBlt, and particularly StretchBlt, GetDIBits, SetDIBits, and StretchDIBits. If this does not result in a performance improvement, the animation that you are attempting may be beyond the basic capabilities of the functions shown here. The DirectX API, part of the Microsoft Game software development kit, will allow you to perform swift and smooth animation and other drawing operations.

COMPLEXITY

DIFFICULT

4.7 How do I...
Allow a bitmap to be dragged on screen?

Problem

I would like the users of my application to be able to move a bitmap image by selecting it with the mouse and dragging. How can I do this?

Technique

Windows 95 makes extensive use of the drag-and-drop approach to manipulating objects—be they files, folders, documents, or even a few lines of text. In addition, paint applications and word processors allow the user to fine-tune the position of objects by dragging them to a new location. Dragging between windows is usually performed by changing the mouse cursor to a new shape that reflects the objects being dragged. Dragging objects within a window, however, often involves the movement of an entire bitmap. This How-To provides a recipe that you can use to implement this type of dragging in your applications.

Dragging a bitmap combines two techniques that have been discussed earlier in this chapter–tracking the movement of the mouse and animation of a bitmap. The basic technique is to respond to a WM_LBUTTONDOWN message in order to start dragging. Your application must then respond to WM_MOUSEMOVE messages by restoring the background at the previous bitmap position, capturing the background at the new mouse position, and then displaying the bitmap at that position. Finally, the application must handle the WM_LBUTTONUP message and stop the dragging, leaving the bitmap at the new position.

Steps

Open the DRAG.EXE application that is in the CHAPTER4\DRAGBMP directory of the CD. This small application displays a tile in the top left corner of a yellow window. Click on the tile with the left mouse button and drag it around the window. When you release the tile, it stays where you left it. When you push the tile past the edge of the window, only a portion of the tile is displayed. Finally, you will notice that while you are dragging the tile, you cannot move the mouse outside the client area of the window. The application has restricted the mouse movement to this window. Figure 4-9 is a screen shot of the tile being dragged in this application.

Follow these steps to reproduce this application:

1. Create a working directory to use when developing this application. Call the directory DRAGBMP. You will place all the source files in this directory.

Figure 4-9 Dragging the tile in the DRAG application

2. You will need a bitmap image of a tile to be dragged, which you will find in the CHAPTER4\DRAGBMP directory of the CD. Copy the IMAGE.BMP file into your working directory. Alternatively, you can use a resource editor or paint application to create a 64-by-64-pixel, 16-color bitmap. Save this bitmap to a file called IMAGE.BMP.

3. The application will also require an icon. Copy the file DRAG.ICO from the CHAPTER4\DRAGBMP directory on the CD. If you don't have access to a CD-ROM drive, you can create an icon using a resource editor. Create a 32-by-32-pixel, 16-color icon, and save it as DRAG.ICO.

4. Now create the resource script for the application. When the resource script is compiled, the bitmap and icon will be linked into the executable file of the application. Use a text editor to create a new file and save it as DRAG.RC. Type the following resource script into the file:

```
/* ------------------------------------------------------------------ */
/*                                                                    */
/* MODULE: DRAG.RC                                                    */
/* PURPOSE: This resource script defines the bitmap and application   */
/*          icon associated with this application.                    */
/*                                                                    */
/* ------------------------------------------------------------------ */

#include "drag.rh"

IDBM_IMAGE BITMAP "image.bmp"

IDI_APPICON ICON "app.ico"
```

5. The resource script includes another file, DRAG.RH, which defines the resource identifier values for the bitmap and the application icon. The resource identifiers are kept in a separate file so they can also be used in the main source file. Create a new file and add the following definitions. Save the file as DRAG.RH.

```
#ifndef __DRAG_RH
/* ------------------------------------------------------------------- */
/*                                                                     */
/* MODULE: DRAG.RH                                                     */
/* PURPOSE: Defines identifiers used to address resources.             */
/*                                                                     */
/* ------------------------------------------------------------------- */
#define __DRAG_RH

#define IDI_APPICON        1
#define IDBM_IMAGE       1000

#endif
```

6. You are now ready to create the C source file. Create a new file and call it DRAG.C. Add the following code to the top of the file. Here are a few things to note while you are typing this in: The code defines a preprocessor symbol, STRICT, which causes the Windows include files to force each different handle type to be a different type, enabling better type checking of your application code. The code also defines the window class name for the main window and declares and initializes the global variables that will be used by this small example application.

```
/* ------------------------------------------------------------------- */
/*                                                                     */
/* MODULE: DRAG.C                                                      */
/* PURPOSE: This application demonstrates simple bitmap dragging.      */
/*                                                                     */
/* ------------------------------------------------------------------- */
#define STRICT

#include <windows.h>
#include "drag.rh"

// Constants.
char *MainWindowClassName = "DragDemoWindow";

// Instance variables.
HINSTANCE     hInstance = NULL;
HBITMAP       hBitmap = NULL;
HBITMAP       hBackground = NULL;
LONG          left, top, width, height;
LONG          xOffset, yOffset;
LONG          saveLeft, saveTop, saveWidth, saveHeight;
BOOL          dragging = FALSE;
BOOL          firstPaint = TRUE;
```

7. Now add the first function to the source file. If you have worked through the example for How-To 4.8, you might recognize this piece of code. The CaptureBackground function copies a section of the window into a bitmap, using CreateCompatibleBitmap to create a bitmap of the appropriate size if one does not exist. The function uses the BitBlt function to copy from the window bitmap into a memory device context containing the bitmap.

```
/* ------------------------------------------------------------------ */
/* This function captures the background at a given location into    */
/* the bitmap hBackground. If the bitmap handle is NULL, a bitmap is*/
/* created to contain the image. If the bitmap is not NULL, just use*/
/* the existing bitmap.                                              */
/* ------------------------------------------------------------------ */
HBITMAP CaptureBackground(HWND hWnd, LONG left, LONG top,
                          LONG width, LONG height,
                          HBITMAP hBackground)
{
    HDC         hDC, hMemoryDC;
    HBITMAP     hOldBitmap;

    hDC = GetDC(hWnd);

    if (!hBackground)
        hBackground = CreateCompatibleBitmap(hDC,width,height);

    hMemoryDC = CreateCompatibleDC(hDC);
    hOldBitmap = SelectObject(hMemoryDC,hBackground);
    BitBlt(hMemoryDC,0,0,width,height,hDC,left,top,SRCCOPY);
    SelectObject(hMemoryDC,hOldBitmap);
    DeleteDC(hMemoryDC);
    ReleaseDC(hWnd,hDC);
    return hBackground;
}
```

8. Add the following function to the source file. This is the HandleMouseMove function, and it is modeled on the DoAnimate function from How-To 4.8. If you haven't worked through that section, don't be too concerned–you can pause here and examine how this function works.

The first major thing that this function does is look to see if the background has previously been stored in a bitmap. If it has, the function uses BitBlt with the SRCCOPY raster argument to restore the old background. If you were to stop the application at this stage, you would see that the tile has disappeared from the screen. Next, the function calculates the new position of the tile. The top and left coordinates of the tile are adjusted for the new mouse position. The xoffset and yoffset variables are used to remember where the mouse sits within the tile, while the mouseX and mouseY positions give the mouse position within the window. The saveTop, saveLeft, saveWidth, and saveHeight variables are then adjusted to account for the new tile position, including the possibility that part of the tile will be outside the window and therefore not visible.

Now the code calls the CaptureBackground function to take a copy of the background where the image is about to be drawn. Finally, the BitBlt API function is used to copy the image into the window. Note that the saveTop, saveLeft, saveWidth, and saveHeight coordinates are used when storing the background and drawing the image.

There is one more thing that is worth noting while you are examining this code. The code assumes that the image is an opaque rectangular shape. If the image has holes in it, or is a circular or elliptical shape, you will need to do a transparent blit to retain the background image under the bitmap. If you must do this, read How-To 4.8 and work through the example in that section, where you will find a useful TransparentBlt function.

```
/* ---------------------------------------------------------------- */
/*  This function performs the actual display of the tile bitmap.   */
/*  It follows these steps:        1. Put back the saved background  */
/*                                 2. Update the top/left positions  */
/*                                 3. Save the background            */
/*                                 4. Blit the bitmap                */
/* ---------------------------------------------------------------- */
void HandleMouseMove(HWND hWnd, LONG mouseX, LONG mouseY)
{
    HDC       hDC, hMemoryDC;
    HBITMAP   hOldBitmap;
    RECT      rcClient;

    hDC = GetDC(hWnd);
    hMemoryDC = CreateCompatibleDC(hDC);

    // If the background was saved, restore it.
    if (hBackground)
    {
        hOldBitmap = SelectObject(hMemoryDC,hBackground);
        BitBlt(hDC,saveLeft,saveTop,saveWidth,saveHeight,
            hMemoryDC,0,0,SRCCOPY);
        SelectObject(hMemoryDC,hOldBitmap);
    }

    /* Calculate the new top and left coordinates.
       Adjust for where the mouse pointer is on the bitmap.
       Deal with the possibility that the bitmap extends
       outside the window client area.*/
    left = mouseX - xOffset;
    top = mouseY - yOffset;
    GetClientRect(hWnd,&rcClient);
    saveTop = max(top,rcClient.top);
    saveLeft = max(left,rcClient.left);
    if (top >= rcClient.top)
       saveHeight = min(height,rcClient.bottom - saveTop);
    else
       saveHeight = height + top;
    if (left >= rcClient.left)
       saveWidth = min(width,rcClient.right - saveLeft);
    else
```

continued on next page

continued from previous page

```
        saveWidth = width + left;

        // Now capture the background at the new location.
        hBackground = CaptureBackground(hWnd,saveLeft,saveTop,
                                        saveWidth,saveHeight,
                                        hBackground);

        // Finally, display the object at that location.
        hOldBitmap = SelectObject(hMemoryDC,hBitmap);
        BitBlt(hDC,saveLeft,saveTop,saveWidth,saveHeight,
               hMemoryDC,saveLeft - left,saveTop - top,SRCCOPY);
        SelectObject(hMemoryDC,hOldBitmap);

        DeleteDC(hMemoryDC);
        ReleaseDC(hWnd,hDC);
}
```

9. The next function will be called when the user presses the left mouse button
in the client area of the window. If the cursor is over the image, dragging can
begin. The following code tests the mouse position (contained in the mouseX
and mouseY arguments) against the position of the image bitmap and returns
FALSE if the mouse was clicked outside the image. If the mouse was inside the
image, dragging can begin. The xoffset and yoffset variables are initialized to
hold the offset of the mouse cursor within the image.

The ClipCursor function is called to contain the cursor inside the window,
because the dragging code only handles movement within the window.
ClipCursor needs a rectangle in screen coordinates, so the GetClientRect function is called to retrieve the interior coordinates of the window, and then
ClientToScreen is called to convert those client coordinates to screen coordinates. Because ClientToScreen only converts a point, the function has to be
called twice, to process the top left and bottom right points of the rectangle.

```
/* ------------------------------------------------------------------ */
/* This function checks to see if the mouse has been clicked on the   */
/* bitmap. If it has, it limits the mouse to movement within the      */
/* client area of the window, ensuring that the user does not drag    */
/* the bitmap outside the window. In a commercial application you     */
/* could allow the user to move outside, but test on each MouseMove   */
/* message and display a different pointer when the cursor is not     */
/* inside the window.                                                 */
/* ------------------------------------------------------------------ */
BOOL StartDragging(HWND hWnd, LONG mouseX, LONG mouseY)
{
    RECT   clientRectangle;
    POINT point;

    // First check to see if the mouse was clicked in the image.
    if ((mouseX < saveLeft) ||
        (mouseX > (saveLeft + saveWidth)) ||
        (mouseY < saveTop) ||
        (mouseY > (saveTop + saveHeight)))
        return FALSE;
```

```
xOffset = mouseX - left;
yOffset = mouseY - top;

/* Get the client rectangle, and convert it to screen
   coordinates. Convert top and left, then bottom and right. */
GetClientRect(hWnd,&clientRectangle);
point.x = clientRectangle.left;
point.y = clientRectangle.top;
ClientToScreen(hWnd,&point);
clientRectangle.left = point.x;
clientRectangle.top = point.y;
point.x = clientRectangle.right;
point.y = clientRectangle.bottom;
ClientToScreen(hWnd,&point);
clientRectangle.right = point.x;
clientRectangle.bottom = point.y;

// Keep the mouse inside the client area.
ClipCursor(&clientRectangle);

return TRUE;
}
```

10. Now add the Paint function. This function will be called when the window should be painted. If a window is resized, maximized, or restored, or another window is removed from on top of it, Windows 95 will send a WM_PAINT message to the window. This function is called in response to this event. It draws the tile onto the window background using the BitBlt function. In addition, on the first WM_PAINT message, this function captures the background bitmap before drawing the tile image. This ensures that the background is properly restored when the tile is first moved.

```
/* ---------------------------------------------------------------- */
/* This function performs painting. It is done when not dragging.   */
/* ---------------------------------------------------------------- */
void Paint(HWND hWnd)
{
    HDC          hDC, hMemoryDC;
    PAINTSTRUCT  ps;
    RECT         rcClient;
    HBITMAP      hOldBitmap;

    BeginPaint(hWnd,&ps);

    // If necessary, update the saveWidth and saveHeight.
    GetClientRect(hWnd,&rcClient);
    if (top >= rcClient.top)
      saveHeight = min(height,rcClient.bottom - saveTop);
    else
      saveHeight = height + top;
    if (left >= rcClient.left)
      saveWidth = min(width,rcClient.right - saveLeft);
    else
      saveWidth = width + left;
```

continued on next page

continued from previous page

```
        // If it is the first paint, store the background.
        if (firstPaint)
        {
            hBackground = CaptureBackground(hWnd,left,top,
                                       width,height,hBackground);
            firstPaint = FALSE;
        }

        // Get a DC and draw the bitmap.
        hDC = GetDC(hWnd);
        hMemoryDC = CreateCompatibleDC(hDC);
        hOldBitmap = SelectObject(hMemoryDC,hBitmap);
        BitBlt(hDC,saveLeft,saveTop,saveWidth,saveHeight,
               hMemoryDC,saveLeft - left,saveTop - top,SRCCOPY);
        SelectObject(hMemoryDC,hOldBitmap);
        DeleteDC(hMemoryDC);
        ReleaseDC(hWnd,hDC);

        EndPaint(hWnd,&ps);
}
```

11. The MainWndProc function that you will add next is a callback function that
processes messages sent to the application window. In particular, it processes
the WM_CREATE message to load the bitmap. It uses the API LoadBitmap
function to load the 16-color bitmap from the resource, and then uses
GetObject to retrieve width and height information in a BITMAP structure.
The width and height are stored in global variables to be used for storing the
background, testing that the mouse cursor is inside the image and drawing the
image on screen.

The code responds to the WM_LBUTTONDOWN message that is sent when
the user depresses the left mouse button. This message causes the code to call
the StartDragging function, containing the cursor within the client area of the
window. In comparison, the WM_LBUTTONUP message is handled by setting
the isDragging flag to FALSE and calling ClipCursor with a NULL rectangle,
allowing the cursor to move freely over the desktop once more. In the
WM_DESTROY response, the bitmaps allocated to hold the image and the
background are released.

```
/* ---------------------------------------------------------------- */
/* This function is the main window callback function which will be  */
/* called by Windows to process messages for our window.            */
/* ---------------------------------------------------------------- */
LPARAM CALLBACK MainWndProc(HWND hWnd, UINT message,
                            WPARAM wParam, LPARAM lParam)
{
    BITMAP bmInfo;

    switch (message)
    {
        case WM_CREATE:
                hBitmap = LoadBitmap(hInstance,
                                MAKEINTRESOURCE(IDBM_IMAGE));
```

```
                GetObject(hBitmap,sizeof(BITMAP),&bmInfo);
                saveWidth = width = bmInfo.bmWidth;
                saveHeight = height = bmInfo.bmHeight;
                saveLeft = left = 0;
                saveTop = top = 0;
                InvalidateRect(hWnd,NULL,TRUE);
                break;
        case WM_LBUTTONDOWN:
                if (!dragging)
                        dragging = StartDragging(hWnd,(LONG)LOWORD(lParam),
                                                (LONG)HIWORD(lParam));
                break;
        case WM_LBUTTONUP:
                if (dragging)
                {
                        // Set the mouse free.
                        ClipCursor(NULL);
                        dragging = FALSE;
                }
                break;
        case WM_MOUSEMOVE:
                if (dragging)
                        HandleMouseMove(hWnd,(LONG)LOWORD(lParam),
                                        (LONG)HIWORD(lParam));
                break;
        case WM_PAINT:
                if (!dragging)
                {
                        Paint(hWnd);
                        break;
                }
                else
                        return DefWindowProc(hWnd,message,wParam,lParam);
        case WM_DESTROY:
                if (hBitmap)
                        DeleteObject(hBitmap);
                if (hBackground)
                        DeleteObject(hBackground);
                PostQuitMessage(0);
                break;
        default:
                return DefWindowProc(hWnd, message, wParam, lParam);
    }
    return 0;
}
```

12. Add the next two helper functions to the source file DRAG.C. The InitApplication function registers the window class for the application's main window. It is only called when no other windows with that window class exist. Notice particularly the call to CreateBrushIndirect to create a light yellow brush. The function takes a LOGBRUSH structure as an argument, which is initialized with the style BS_SOLID and the RGB values for the yellow color. The brush created by CreateBrushIndirect will be freed by Windows when the last window of this class is closed.

The InitInstance function is called each time the application is run. It creates the
main window of the application and calls ShowWindow and UpdateWindow so
that it is displayed.

```
/* -------------------------------------------------------------- */
/* This function initializes a WNDCLASS structure and uses it to  */
/* register a class for our main window.                          */
/* -------------------------------------------------------------- */
BOOL InitApplication(HINSTANCE hInstance)
{
    WNDCLASS  wc;
    LOGBRUSH  lb;

    wc.style = 0;
    wc.lpfnWndProc = MainWndProc;
    wc.cbClsExtra = 0;
    wc.cbWndExtra = 0;
    wc.hInstance = hInstance;
    wc.hIcon = LoadIcon(NULL, IDI_APPLICATION);
    wc.hCursor = LoadCursor(NULL, IDC_ARROW);
    wc.lpszMenuName =   NULL;
    wc.lpszClassName = MainWindowClassName;
    lb.lbStyle = BS_SOLID;
    lb.lbColor = RGB(255,255,128); // Light Yellow brush.
    wc.hbrBackground = CreateBrushIndirect(&lb);

    return RegisterClass(&wc);
}


/* -------------------------------------------------------------- */
/* This function creates an instance of our main window. The window */
/* is given a class name and a title, and told to display anywhere. */
/* The nCmdShow argument passed to the program determines how the */
/* window will be displayed.                                      */
/* -------------------------------------------------------------- */
BOOL InitInstance(HINSTANCE hInst, int nCmdShow)
{
    HWND hWnd;

    hInstance = hInst;     // Store in global variable.

    hWnd = CreateWindow(MainWindowClassName,"Drag the tile!",
                WS_OVERLAPPEDWINDOW,CW_USEDEFAULT,
                CW_USEDEFAULT,CW_USEDEFAULT,CW_USEDEFAULT,
                NULL,NULL,hInstance,NULL);
    if (!hWnd)
        return FALSE;

    ShowWindow(hWnd, nCmdShow);
    UpdateWindow(hWnd);    // Send a WM_PAINT message.
    return TRUE;
}
```

13. The final code in this application is the WinMain function. Add the following
code to the end of the source file. The WinMain function is called by

Windows to run this application. It uses FindWindow to see if any windows of this class exist, and if no windows do, it calls the InitApplication function to register the window class. The code then calls the InitInstance function to create the window and processes messages until the application is closed.

```
/* ---------------------------------------------------------------- */
/* The main entry point for Windows applications. Check to see if   */
/* the main window class name has already been registered; if it has*/
/* not, call InitApplication to register it. Call InitInstance to   */
/* create an instance of our main window, then pump messages until  */
/* the application is closed.                                       */
/* ---------------------------------------------------------------- */
int PASCAL WinMain(HINSTANCE hInstance, HINSTANCE hPrevInstance,
                   LPSTR lpCmdLine, int nCmdShow)
{
    MSG msg;

    if (!FindWindow(MainWindowClassName,NULL))
        if (!InitApplication(hInstance))
            return FALSE;

    if (!InitInstance(hInstance, nCmdShow))
        return FALSE;

    while (GetMessage(&msg,NULL,0,0))
    {
        TranslateMessage(&msg);
        DispatchMessage(&msg);
    }
    return (msg.wParam);
}
```

14. Compile and run the application.

Comments

The code in this How-To demonstrates a fairly bulletproof way to drag a bitmap. Two possibilities that were not covered are dragging the bitmap out of the window (presumably into another window) and dragging a bitmap in a scrolling window. The two possibilities are really mutually exclusive—how do you tell whether users are moving the mouse outside the window because they want to drag the bitmap elsewhere, or because they expect the window to scroll to a new position? In either case, you will not want to use ClipCursor to contain the cursor within the client area. Instead, you should use the SetCapture API function, so that your application receives mouse movement messages regardless of what window the mouse is over.

CHAPTER 5
DIALOG BOXES: WINDOWS ON THE WORLD

5

DIALOG BOXES: WINDOWS ON THE WORLD

How do I...

By far the most visible aspect of Windows 95 programming is the dialog boxes. Programmers consider dialog boxes to be simple ways to retrieve data from the user so that the programs can go on to more complex processing and "the fun stuff" of graphical presentation. To the user, however, the dialog box is the forefront of the application. Nothing will affect the user more than the ease with which he or she can manipulate input through dialogs, and nothing will make a program more difficult to use than badly designed or implemented dialog boxes.

With this in mind, we dedicate this chapter of How-To's to the mighty dialog box. With the power of Windows 95 at your fingertips, there is no longer any reason to turn out dialogs that are anything short of stunning. Custom fonts, colors, and a three-dimensional look are almost required in today's sophisticated user interfaces. *Property sheets* form the very basis of Windows 95 and are a simple addition that adds considerable value to a dialog. Property sheets are the "tabbed" dialogs that present multiple screens of information to the user in a single dialog frame. In this chapter, you will learn how to conquer the dialog and bend its powers to your will.

5.1   Use a Dialog Box as the Main Window of an Application

Quite often, when writing simple utilities, it is overkill to supply a complete program with menus, multiple document interfaces, About boxes, and so forth. For the user, it is confusing to face an array of menu choices for a utility that only performs a single task. This How-To examines how to use the power of Visual C++ to create an application consisting solely of a dialog box as its window. The functionality of the application is unchanged; only the user interface differs from the standard Windows 95 application. Copy utilities, database lookups, and Wizards are some of the applications that can be created with this technique.

5.2   Change the Font in a Dialog

It is a simple fact that different users have different preferences. One of the most basic differences comes in the area of fonts. Some users prefer a simple typewriter font for their displays and dialogs, while others prefer to spice up their dialogs with esoteric and exotic (or at least interesting) fonts. This How-To will show you how to satisfy even the most picky of users and allow them to set the fonts for their dialogs by themselves.

5.3   Change the Font in a Control of a Dialog

Once How-To 5.2 is accomplished, the text that is displayed in a dialog box is completely changed to match a user's preference. What can you do to change a single static text or edit control so that the font stands out from other controls in the dialog? In this How-To, you find out how to set a single control in a dialog to a given font.

5.4   Change the Background Color of a Dialog

The metal gray background of dialogs is all the rage today. The incised edges and gray colors are standard in Windows 95 applications. Suppose, though, that you would prefer to color your dialogs a different shade. Perhaps a nice fuchsia or a purple with pink bands? Or perhaps not. In any case, this How-To looks at how you can set the color of your dialog box to be whatever you would like it to be, from a single color to a rainbow of colors. You decide what you want the background to look like, and this How-To will show you how it is accomplished.

5.5 Enable and Disable Controls in a Dialog

Users want to do a minimum of work with dialogs, and they don't want to fill in a lot of edit boxes. Nothing is more annoying than to find out that you entered data in 20 or more edit fields and only 3 of those fields were required because of other options you had chosen. Even more disconcerting to the user is being presented with options that appear contradictory to other options available on the same dialog.

This How-To examines how you, as the application programmer, can use the Windows 95 API to selectively enable and disable controls in a dialog based on selections that a user makes within the dialog. Such internal logic for dialogs makes the program seem more complete and professional to the user and eliminates the need for a multitude of checking at commit time as to the validity of the information gathered in the dialog.

5.6 Change the Controls Shown in a Dialog

Today's professional programs display dialogs that can add or delete controls based on selections made by the user. For example, a novice user might only want to see the simple options for a dialog, while a power user might want to see all available options. This How-To will examine the methods necessary to display only those controls that you want to show in a dialog while hiding the controls that are not needed at that point.

5.7 Use Property Sheets in a Dialog

One of the core additions to Windows 95 over Windows 3.x is the property sheet or tabbed dialog. Property sheets make it possible to have many more controls on a single dialog without the clutter that arises by putting them all on the same screen at the same time. Property sheets also make it possible to segregate data into logical units that allow the user to consider only small sections at a time. This leads to less frustration on the part of the user and thus less support requirements for the developer.

5.8 Draw a Picture on a Button in a Dialog

Most modern Windows 95 applications display an About box that contains the icon for the minimized application. How can this be accomplished when there is no discrete icon control in either Windows 3.x or Windows 95? This How-To will show you how you can accomplish this task in your own applications.

5.9 Display a "Progress" Dialog While Another Activity Takes Place

It is particulary frustrating to a user when the application goes off to do something that is not visible on the screen. Tasks such as copying files, printing documents, querying databases, and the like, require the attention of the program but do not necessarily provide any feedback for the user. Users can grow fidgety waiting for an application to return to the screen and may even attempt to terminate the application, thinking it has hung. This How-To shows how you can provide users with some feedback while you are running a long task in a way that will keep them happy and stop them from murdering your application.

Table 5-1 lists the Windows 95 API functions used in this chapter.

Post Message	PostQuitMessage	GetObject
CreateFontIndirect	MakeProcInstance	FreeProcInstance
EnumChildWindows	SendMessage	FillRect
SetBkMode	CreateSolidBrush	SetCheck
EnableWindow	IsWindowVisible	ShowWindow
SetWindowText	GetWindowLong	SetWindowLong
CreateWindowEx	PeekMessage	TranslateMessage
DispatchMessage		

 Table 5-1 Windows 95 API functions used in Chapter 5

5.1 How do I...
Use a dialog box as the main window of an application?

COMPLEXITY
MODERATE

Problem

I have a simple application that performs a utility for the user. I do not want the user to have to open my application, choose a drop-down menu item from the menu, run the dialog, and then have to close down the application as well. Isn't there an easier way to allow the user to use my dialog box? I would prefer not to give up the power of Visual C++ and the MFC, but I really don't want all of the extras that go along with them.

Technique

Although most people are aware of the power of Visual C++ in either Windows 3.x or Windows 95, many are not aware that Visual C++ does not require you to use the AppWizard or ClassWizard applets to generate your application. It is perfectly feasible to create a new project in Visual C++ without the AppWizard and then paste in the code you would like to use.

For many years before there were program generators, programmers used templates of their own. These templates were skeleton applications that they had developed to solve a specific problem. When problems similar to the one for which the template was designed cropped up, the programmer simply cloned the template into a new application, adding the code necessary to solve the new problem.

Figure 5-1 Dialog as main window in action

In this How-To, we will examine how to use this template approach to create a program whose main window is a dialog. Further, we will see how the MFC interacts with the Windows 95 API to do things behind the scenes.

Steps

Open and run the Visual C++ application CH51.MAK from the CHAPT5\SAMPLES\CH51 directory on the CD that comes with this book. You will see a main dialog on the screen and no frame window or menu associated with it. The dialog itself is shown in Figure 5-1. When you have finished looking at the dialog, click on the Close button and the dialog and program will terminate.

To duplicate the functionality of this program, follow this procedure:

1. Create a new project in Visual C++ by selecting File | New. Select Project from the dialog box and click OK. Give the project the name CH51.MAK. Click on the OK button and then the cancel button for selecting files to add to the project.

2. Create a new file by clicking on the New File icon or selecting File | New from the main menu and then selecting Code/Text from the dialog box. Enter the following code into the file:

```
#ifndef __CH51_H__
#define __CH51_H__

// The dialog window class derived from CDialog.

class CDlgWin : public CDialog
{
private:
public:
    // Constructor for class
    CDlgWin();
    // Overrides for the button handlers
    void OnOK();
    void OnHelp();
```

continued on next page

continued from previous page

```
            // When the dialog window is closed, free the memory for
            // it since it is not the child of anything.
            void OnClose() {
                delete this;
            }
            DECLARE_MESSAGE_MAP()
    };
    // The application object class
    class CTheApp : public CWinApp
    {
    public:
        BOOL InitInstance();
    };
    #endif
```

3. Save this file as CH51.H.

4. Once again, select the New File icon or the File | New menu item. Enter the following code into the code editor window:

```
#include "afxwin.h"
#include "resource.h"
#include "ch51.h"   // Contains class definitions

// Constructor for dialog window. Simply calls the modeless create
// method to create the window based on the MAINDLG template in the
// resource file.

CDlgWin::CDlgWin()
{
    Create("MAINDLG");
}

// User clicked OK. Close the window and quit the application.

void CDlgWin::OnOK() {
    PostMessage(WM_CLOSE);
    PostQuitMessage(0);
}

// User clicked Help. Show a message box with help text.

void CDlgWin::OnHelp()
{
    MessageBox("You can display message boxes or anything else!",
"Help", MB_OK );
}

BEGIN_MESSAGE_MAP(CDlgWin, CDialog)
    ON_WM_CLOSE()
    ON_COMMAND(IDC_HELP, OnHelp)
    ON_COMMAND(IDOK, OnOK)
END_MESSAGE_MAP()

CTheApp theApp;

// This is the entry point for the application.
```

```
BOOL CTheApp::InitInstance()
{
    // Create a new modeless dialog box and assign
    // it to the main window pointer in the application
    // object.

    m_pMainWnd = new CDlgWin();

    // Make sure it is visible.
    m_pMainWnd->ShowWindow(m_nCmdShow);

    // And fully updated.

    m_pMainWnd->UpdateWindow();
    return TRUE;
}
```

5. Save this file as CH51.CPP.

6. Create a new file and enter the following lines into it. Save this file as RESOURCE.H:

```
#ifndef _RESOURCE_H_
#define _RESOURCE_H_

#define IDC_HELP 110

#endif
```

7. Create another new file to hold the resource script for this application. Enter the following code into the resource file:

```
//Microsoft App Studio generated resource script.
//
#define APSTUDIO_READONLY_SYMBOLS
/////////////////////////////////////////////////////////////////////////////
//
// Generated from the TEXTINCLUDE 2 resource.
//
#define APSTUDIO_HIDDEN_SYMBOLS
#include "windows.h"
#undef APSTUDIO_HIDDEN_SYMBOLS
#include "afxres.h"
#include "resource.h"


/////////////////////////////////////////////////////////////////////////////
///////
#undef APSTUDIO_READONLY_SYMBOLS


/////////////////////////////////////////////////////////////////////////////
//
// Dialog
//

MAINDLG DIALOG DISCARDABLE  44, 32, 219, 122
STYLE WS_MINIMIZEBOX | WS_CAPTION | WS_SYSMENU
CAPTION "Dialog as main window"
FONT 8, "MS Sans Serif"
```

continued on next page

continued from previous page

```
BEGIN
    PUSHBUTTON       "&OK",IDOK,26,92,62,17
    PUSHBUTTON       "&Help",IDC_HELP,136,90,63,22
    LTEXT            "This is a static text field in the dialog",
                     IDC_STATIC, 54,14,125,15
END


#ifdef APSTUDIO_INVOKED
/////////////////////////////////////////////////////////////////////////////
///////
//
// TEXTINCLUDE
//

1 TEXTINCLUDE DISCARDABLE
BEGIN
    "resrc1.h\0"
END

2 TEXTINCLUDE DISCARDABLE
BEGIN
    "#define APSTUDIO_HIDDEN_SYMBOLS\r\n"
    "#include ""windows.h""\r\n"
    "#undef APSTUDIO_HIDDEN_SYMBOLS\r\n"
    "#include ""afxres.h""\r\n"
    "#include ""resource.h""\r\n"
    "\0"
END

3 TEXTINCLUDE DISCARDABLE
BEGIN
    "\r\n"
    "\0"
END


/////////////////////////////////////////////////////////////////////////////
//////////////
#endif      // APSTUDIO_INVOKED

#ifndef APSTUDIO_INVOKED
/////////////////////////////////////////////////////////////////////////////
/////////
//
// Generated from the TEXTINCLUDE 3 resource.
//


/////////////////////////////////////////////////////////////////////////////
//////////////
#endif      // not APSTUDIO_INVOKED
```

8. Save this file as CH51.RC. Add the three files, CH51.CPP, CH51.H, and
CH51.RC, to the project and compile the executable. Run it, and you should
see the dialog displayed in Figure 5-1, which we looked at previously.

How It Works

When the Microsoft Foundation Class (MFC) library starts up in an application, the first object that is instantiated is the Application object. This object (theApp in our sample program) is then constructed and the InitInstance method called. In our sample program, the InitInstance method creates a new instance of the CDlgWin class and assigns it to the main window pointer of the application object. The object is then shown on the screen and updated.

In the constructor for the CWinDlg class, the dialog Create method is called to create a new modeless dialog on the screen (using the CreateDialog Windows API function). The CreateDialog function to instantiate a Microsoft Windows modeless dialog box looks like this:

```
HWND CreateDialog(HINSTANCE hinst, LPSTR lpszDlgTemp, HWND hwndOwner,
FARPROC dlgprc);
```

The MFC takes care of the hinst parameter by calling the AfxGetInstance function, which is set up when the application starts. The lpszDlgTemp parameter is the name of the dialog template found in the resource file (in our case, MAINDLG). Nobody owns this dialog since it exists outside a main window. The dlgprc is the callback function that is used for all processing by the dialog. This procedure is part of the base Cdialog class in the MFC.

Comments

This dialog class can be the basis for utility programs that interact with the user to provide a simple method to do one task. It can also be used as the basis for a stand-alone pop-up dialog such as the Find/Replace dialog or a floating toolbar.

COMPLEXITY
MODERATE

5.2   How do I...
Change the font in a dialog?

Problem

I would like to be able to change the font associated with my dialog box in order to suit user preferences. I need to be able to make all of the controls on my dialog, the edit boxes, static text fields, buttons, and combo boxes work with the font, regardless of what font the dialog was initially defined with. How can I use the Windows 95 API functions to help me accomplish this goal?

Technique

If you are like most programmers, your first thought was to look in the manual for a function to set the font in the dialog box. Imagine your surprise when you discovered that the SetFont method was clearly documented in the Foundation Class library doc-umentation. Further imagine how shocked you were when you gleefully implemented the SetFont call in your dialog initialization function and found that it made not the slightest bit of difference!

The MFC uses its own method for setting the font in the dialog box. All controls are defined using either the font declared in the FONT resource statement or the default system font under Windows 95. The controls are all based around this font as well. How then can you work around these MFC limitations to make the controls use your own font? The answer lies within the power of several different Windows 95 API func-tions working together.

You will first learn to create a font by displaying the common dialog box for fonts to the user. This common dialog will give you the information you need to create fonts using GDI functions. Next, you will find out how to use the EnumChildWindows func-tion to loop through all of the controls for a dialog. Finally, you will see how the SendMessage function can be used to change the font a window uses to display itself.

Steps

Open and run the Visual C++ application CH52.MAK from the CHAPT5\SAM-PLES\CH52 directory on the CD that comes with this book. Select the Change Current Font drop-down menu item under the Fonts main menu item. The common Font dialog box will be displayed, as shown in Figure 5-2. Select a font family name, a style (regular, bold, italic), and a point size. Click on the OK button. Select the Display

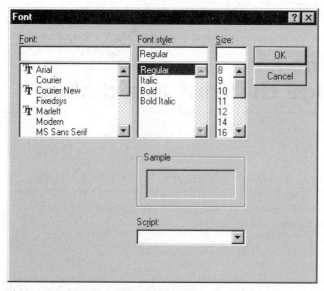

Figure 5-2 Font common dialog box

Dialog drop-down menu under the Font dialog, and you will see the dialog displayed with that font. Figure 5-3 shows the dialog displayed with the Roman, Regular, 10-point font selected.

To duplicate this functionality, follow this procedure:

1. Create a new project in Visual C++ using AppWizard. Give the new project the name CH52.MAK.

2. Select the application object header file, CH52.H. Add the following lines to the header file, marked in bold print:

```
class CCh52App : public CWinApp
{
private:

CFont *current_font;  // Font used for dialogs

public:
  CCh52App();
  virtual ~CCh52App();

  CFont *GetCurrentFont(void) { return current_font; };

// Overrides
  virtual BOOL InitInstance();
```

3. Enter AppStudio and select the main menu from the menu list. Add a new main-level menu called Fonts with two drop-down menus named Change Current Font and Display Dialog. Give the two drop-down menus the identifiers ID_CHANGE_FONT and ID_FONT_DLG, respectively.

4. Enter ClassWizard and select the CCh52App object from the drop-down list. Select the ID_CHANGE_FONT identifier from the object list and select COMMAND from the message list. Click on the Add Function button. Accept the OnChangeFont method name and add the following code to this method:

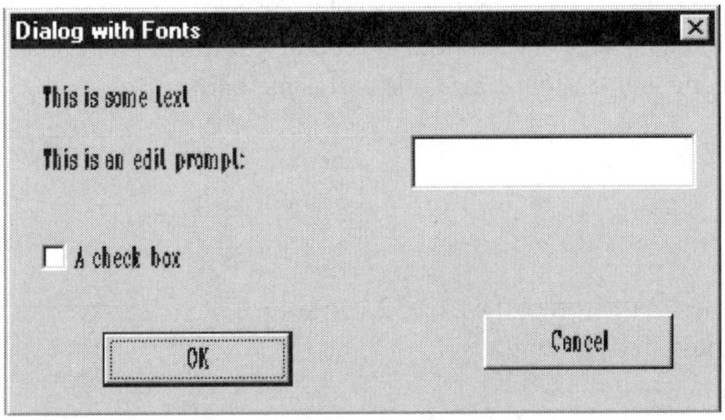

Figure 5-3 Dialog displayed using 10-point Roman font

```
void CCh52App::OnChangeFont()
{
    // Get the information from the existing font.

    CFont* pFont = current_font;

    // Initialize font structure

    LOGFONT lf;
    memset ( &lf, 0, sizeof(lf) );

    // Get the font structure information out of the font object.

    if ( pFont )
        pFont->GetObject(sizeof(LOGFONT), &lf);

    // Display a common dialog box for fonts with this default
    // information.

    CFontDialog dlg(&lf, CF_SCREENFONTS|CF_INITTOLOGFONTSTRUCT);
    if (dlg.DoModal() != IDOK)
        return;

    // Create a new font based on the user request.

    CFont *tempFont = new CFont;
    if ( !tempFont->CreateFontIndirect ( &lf ) ) {
        delete tempFont;
     MessageBox(NULL, "Unable to create font!", "Error", MB_OK );
        return;
    }

    // If there is an existing font, delete it and replace it.

    if ( current_font )
        delete current_font;
    current_font = tempFont;

}
```

5. In ClassWizard, select the CCh52App object in the drop-down list once again, and then select the ID_FONT_DLG from the object list. Select COMMAND from the message list and click on the Add Function button. Accept OnFontDlg as the method name and add the following code to this method:

```
void CCh52App::OnFontDlg()
{
    CDlgFont dlg;
    dlg.DoModal();
}
```

6. Add the following lines to the top of the CCh52App source file (CH52.CPP). Lines to add are marked in bold print.

```
#include "ch52view.h"
```

```
#include "dlgfont.h"

#ifdef _DEBUG
#undef THIS_FILE
static char BASED_CODE THIS_FILE[] = __FILE__;
#endif

///////////////////////////////////////////////////////////////////////
//////
// CCh52App

BEGIN_MESSAGE_MAP(CCh52App, CWinApp)
  //{{AFX_MSG_MAP(CCh52App)
  ON_COMMAND(ID_APP_ABOUT, OnAppAbout)
  ON_COMMAND(ID_CHANGE_FONT, OnChangeFont)
  ON_COMMAND(ID_FONT_DLG, OnFontDlg)
  //}}AFX_MSG_MAP
  // Standard file based document commands
  ON_COMMAND(ID_FILE_NEW, CWinApp::OnFileNew)
  ON_COMMAND(ID_FILE_OPEN, CWinApp::OnFileOpen)
  // Standard print setup command
  ON_COMMAND(ID_FILE_PRINT_SETUP, CWinApp::OnFilePrintSetup)
END_MESSAGE_MAP()

///////////////////////////////////////////////////////////////////////
// CCh52App construction

CCh52App::CCh52App()
{
    current_font = NULL;
}

CCh52App::~CCh52App()
{
    if ( current_font )
        delete current_font;
}
```

7. Enter AppStudio and create a new dialog. Add any fields you wish, working from the template shown in Figure 5-3. When you are finished with the dialog, save it and select ClassWizard. Generate a new dialog class for the dialog template. Give the dialog class the name CDlgFont.

8. Select the CDlgFont object from the drop-down list in ClassWizard. Select CDlgFont from the object list and the WM_INITDIALOG from the message list. Click on Add Function. Add the following code to the OnInitDialog method of CDlgFont:

```
BOOL CDlgFont::OnInitDialog()
{
  CDialog::OnInitDialog();

  // Make sure the window is centered on our application window.
```

continued on next page

continued from previous page

```
        CenterWindow();

        // Get the current defined font..

        CCh52App *app = (CCh52App *)AfxGetApp();
        CFont *font = app->GetCurrentFont();

        // If there was no font defined, just get out of here..

        if ( font == NULL )
          return TRUE;

        // Make the callback function.

        FARPROC proc = MakeProcInstance((FARPROC)SetFontProc,
   AfxGetInstanceHandle());

        // Loop through the child windows, setting the fonts as we go.

        EnumChildWindows(m_hWnd, (WNDENUMPROC)proc, (LPARAM)font->m_hObject );

        // Free the callback function memory.

        FreeProcInstance ( proc );

        return TRUE;   // Return TRUE  unless you set the focus to a control.
      }
```

9. Add the following function immediately preceding the OnInitDialog method
of CDlgFont:

```
BOOL CALLBACK SetFontProc(HWND hwnd, LPARAM lParam)
{
    // Get the font handle from the lParam.

    HFONT font = (HFONT)lParam;

    // Set the window font.

    SendMessage ( hwnd, WM_SETFONT, (WPARAM)font, (LPARAM)
MAKELONG((WORD) TRUE, 0) );

    return TRUE;
}
```

10. Compile and run the application.

How It Works

When the user selects the Change Current Font menu item, the program will display
a Font dialog that contains the currently selected font (if there is one). Once the user
makes his or her choices from the Font dialog, the currently selected font data is used
to create a new CFont object. All of this takes place in the CCh52App::OnChangeFont
member function.

When the user selects the Display Dialog menu item, the program will create a new instance of the CFontDlg class. This object will then request the current font from the application object, and the current font will be used to update each control, using the EnumChildWindows function. This function loops through each child window of a given parent window. In this case, the parent window is the dialog box, and all of the child windows are the controls that have been created on that dialog box. The EnumChildWindows function takes a window handle, indicating the parent window to traverse, a callback procedure, and a parameter to pass to the callback procedure. In this case, we use the font handle to send as the parameter.

As each window is passed to the callback function (SetFontProc), the font handle is sent to the child window via a SendMessage call. The command for this call is WM_SET-FONT, and the information passed is a font handle and a flag indicating that the control should redraw itself immediately.

Once all of the controls have been updated with the proper font, the procedure passes control to Windows, which draws the dialog box on the screen using the new fonts.

COMPLEXITY
MODERATE

5.3   How do I...
Change the font in a control of a dialog?

Problem

I would like to be able to do on-the-fly changes to the font of a control in a dialog box. Specifically, I would like to show the user different fonts using a single static text string in a dialog. The previous How-To dealt only with static initialization of an entire dialog box and all of the controls. How can I do the same task, only dynamically and at user-defined times?

Technique

One of the normal ways to select a font for something in your application is to show the user what the font would look like with a sample of text from your own application. For various reasons it is not always feasible to rely on the common Font dialog to do this for the user. Instead, users may want to see the font with a combination of other styles, or next to other fonts, to see what they look like together. To accomplish this task, you do indeed need the ability to set a single static text field (or multiple static text fields) to a given font without disturbing other fields on the dialog. This How-To will show you how it is done.

Steps

Open and run the Visual C++ application CH53.MAK from the CHAPT5\SAM-PLES\CH53 directory on the CD that comes with this book. Select the Fonts main menu and the menu item Change Control Fonts. A dialog will appear (as shown in Figure 5-4). Click on any of the Font buttons and change the font shown in the common dialog box. The corresponding text field next to the button will change the font to reflect the new font selection.

To reproduce this functionality, do the following:

1. Create a new project inVisual C++ using AppWizard. Give the project the name CH53.MAK. Enter AppStudio and add a new dialog. Add to the dialog three static text fields with the captions Text Field 1, Text Field 2, and Text Field 3. Add three buttons aligned horizontally with the text fields and give each button the label Font.

2. Enter ClassWizard and generate a dialog class for the dialog template you have just created. Give the dialog class the name CControlFontDlg. Select the IDC_BUTTON1 object and the COMMAND message and click on the Add Function button. Enter OnTextField1 as the name of the method and add the following code to the OnTextField1 method handler:

```
void CControlFontDlg::OnTextField1()
{
    DoFont(1);
}
```

3. Select the IDC_BUTTON2 object and the COMMAND message in ClassWizard. Click on the Add Function button. Enter OnTextField2 as the name of the method and add the following code to the OnTextField2 method handler:

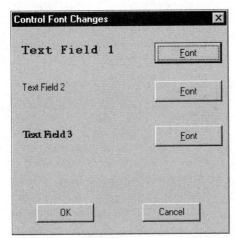

Figure 5-4 Dialog to change fonts for specific controls in a dialog

```
void CControlFontDlg::OnTextField2()
{
    DoFont(2);
}
```

4. Select the IDC_BUTTON3 object and the COMMAND message in ClassWizard.
Click on the Add Function button. Name the method OnTextField3 and add
the following code to the OnTextField3 method handler:

```
void CControlFontDlg::OnTextField3()
{
    DoFont(3);
}
```

5. Select the CControlFontDlg object and the WM_INITDIALOG message in
ClassWizard. Click on the Add Function button. Enter the following code to
the OnInitDialog method:

```
BOOL CControlFontDlg::OnInitDialog()
{
   CDialog::OnInitDialog();

   CenterWindow();

   return TRUE;  // Return TRUE  unless you set the focus to a control.
}
```

6. Finally, add the following method definition to the CControlFontDlg source
file (CONTROLF.CPP):

```
void CControlFontDlg::DoFont ( int whichField )
{
    CFont *font = NULL;

    switch ( whichField ) {
        case 1:
            font = font1;
            break;
        case 2:
            font = font2;
            break;
        case 3:
            font = font3;
            break;
    }

    // Initialize font structure.

    LOGFONT lf;
    memset ( &lf, 0, sizeof(lf) );

    // Get the font structure information out of the font object.

    if ( font )
        font->GetObject(sizeof(LOGFONT), &lf);

    // Display a common dialog box for fonts with this default information.
```

continued on next page

continued from previous page

```
    CFontDialog dlg(&lf, CF_SCREENFONTS|CF_INITTOLOGFONTSTRUCT);
    if (dlg.DoModal() != IDOK)
        return;

    // Build the new font from this information.

    CFont *tempFont = new CFont;
    if ( !tempFont->CreateFontIndirect ( &lf ) ) {
        delete tempFont;
        MessageBox("Unable to create font!", "Error", MB_OK );
        return;
    }

    // If there is an existing font, delete it and replace it.

    if ( font )
        delete font;

    switch ( whichField ) {
        case 1:
            font1 = tempFont;
            break;
        case 2:
            font2 = tempFont;
            break;
        case 3:
            font3 = tempFont;
            break;
    }

    // Now, update the text control..

    GetDlgItem(IDC_TXT_FLD1+whichField-1)->SendMessage ( WM_SETFONT,
(WPARAM)tempFont->m_hObject, (LPARAM) MAKELONG((WORD) TRUE, 0) );

}
```

7. Make the following modifications (shown in bold print) to the constructor for the dialog class, CFontControlDlg::CFontControlDlg:

```
CControlFontDlg::CControlFontDlg(CWnd* pParent /*=NULL*/)
    : CDialog(CControlFontDlg::IDD, pParent)
{
    font1 = NULL;
    font2 = NULL;
    font3 = NULL;
    //{{AFX_DATA_INIT(CControlFontDlg)
    // NOTE: the ClassWizard will add member initialization here.
    //}}AFX_DATA_INIT
}
```

8. In the CONTROL.H header file, add the following declarations to the class definition:

```
private:
    CFont *font1;
    CFont *font2;
```

```
    CFont *font3;
protected:
void DoFont ( int whichField );
```

9. In AppStudio, add a new drop-down menu item to the main-level Fonts menu. Give the menu the caption Change Control Fonts and the identifier ID_FONTS_CHANGECONTROLFONTS. Enter ClassWizard and select the application object, CCh53App. Click on the ID_FONTS_CHANGECON-TROLFONTS object identifier and the COMMAND message. Click on the Add Function button and enter OnChangeControlFont as the name of the function. Enter the following code into the OnChangeControlFont method:

```
void CCh53App::OnChangeControlFont()
{
    CControlFontDlg dlg;
    dlg.DoModal();
}
```

10. Add the following line to the top of the CH53.CPP file after the include lines for CH53DOC.H and CH53VIEW.H:

```
#include "controlf.h"
```

11. Compile and run the application.

How It Works

When the user selects one of the font buttons from the dialog box, the dialog box class handler instantiates a font dialog, using the font that is currently defined for that position in the dialog box (if there is one). The font dialog then returns to the program a font structure that can be used to construct a new font object. The program uses this font handle exactly as it did in the previous How-To, sending a message containing the identifier of WM_SETFONT with the font handle to the control in question.

Comments

This methodology can be used to change the font of any windowed object on a dialog. You can accomplish the same thing in Delphi with considerably less code. Here is an example of how to do it:

1. Create a new project in Delphi or add a new form to an existing project. Add to this form three static text fields and three buttons. Label the text fields Text Field 1, Text Field 2, and Text Field 3. Label the buttons Font. Add a Font Dialog object to the form as well. Finally, add a button at the bottom of the form labeled Close.

2. Double-click on the first Font button and add the following code to the handler:

```
procedure TForm1.Button1Click(Sender: TObject);
begin
    FontDialog1.Execute;
    Label1.Font.Assign(FontDialog1.Font);
end;
```

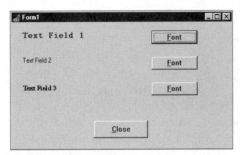

Figure 5-5 Delphi form to change fonts for specific controls in a dialog

3. Double-click on the second Font button and add the following code to the handler:

```
procedure TForm1.Button2Click(Sender: TObject);
begin
    FontDialog1.Execute;
    Label2.Font.Assign(FontDialog1.Font);
end;
```

4. Double-click on the third Font button and add the following code to the handler:

```
procedure TForm1.Button3Click(Sender: TObject);
begin
    FontDialog1.Execute;
    Label3.Font.Assign(FontDialog1.Font);
end;
```

5. Finally, double-click on the Close button and add the following code to the handler:

```
procedure TForm1.Button4Click(Sender: TObject);
begin
    Close;
end;
```

6. Compile and run the dialog. Click on the Font buttons and change the various fonts to whatever you like. You should end up with a dialog that looks like the one shown in Figure 5-5.

COMPLEXITY
MODERATE

5.4 How do I...
Change the background color of a dialog?

Problem

While the colors provided by Visual C++ and Windows 95 are quite nice and pretty, my users cannot easily distinguish the grays that make up the background of dialogs.

Is there any way that I can change the dialog box background to something like a nice bright green?

Technique

A nice bright green would certainly liven up any application, although it might drive many users completely out of their minds! In this How-To, we will show you how to set the background color of a dialog to anything you would like it to be.

It happens that this technique can also be modified to allow you to display a bitmap of your choosing in the background of the dialog box. When Windows 95 wants a dialog box to display the background of the window, it sends the dialog a message of WM_ERASEBKGND. This message indicates to you, the programmer, that it is time to show the background of the window. You can elect to do pretty much anything you would like with the background of the dialog. How do you accomplish this? With the Windows 95 API, of course!

One of the things we will discover in this How-To is that the code generated by Visual C++ is not quite so sacred after all. You can do quite a bit with message maps and over-ridden functions without using ClassWizard, and in this case, you will need to, as ClassWizard does not allow access to all windows messages.

Steps

Open and run the Visual C++ application CH54.MAK from the CHAPT5\SAM-PLES\CH54 directory on the CD that comes with this book. Select the Colors main menu and the menu item Dialog Background. A dialog will be displayed for an address book-style dialog like the one shown in Figure 5-6. The background of the dialog will be a rather stunning light green.

To duplicate this functionality, do the following:

1. Create a new project in Visual C++ using AppWizard. Give the project the name CH54.MAK. Go into AppStudio and add a new dialog. Add the phone

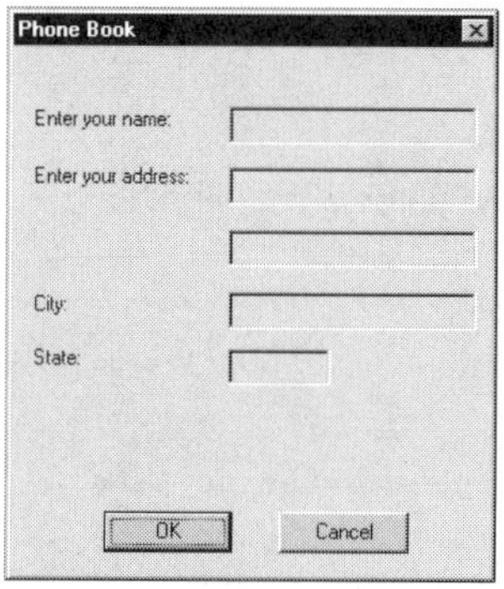

Figure 5-6 Dialog with green background

book-style text fields along with corresponding edit fields. In this case, the field titles are Enter your name:, Enter your address:, City:, and State:. Add five edit fields for the name, two for the address, and one each for the city and state.

2. Select ClassWizard and generate a dialog class for this template. Give the class the name CPhoneDlg. Close both AppStudio and ClassWizard.

3. Select the PHONEDLG.CPP source file from the project list. Add the following functions to the file:

```
BOOL CPhoneDlg::OnEraseBkgnd(CDC* pDC)
{
    // Get the window rectangle to fill...

    CRect r;
    GetClientRect ( &r );

    // Fill in the background with the correct color.

    pDC->FillRect ( &r, &color_brush );

    return TRUE;      // No more background painting needed.
}


HBRUSH CPhoneDlg::OnCtlColor(CDC* pDC, CWnd* pWnd, UINT nCtlColor)
{
    pDC->SetBkMode( TRANSPARENT );
    return m_brush;
}
```

4. Make the following modifications (shown in bold print) to the constructor for the class (CPhoneDlg::CPhoneDlg):

```
CPhoneDlg::CPhoneDlg(CWnd* pParent /*=NULL*/)
    : CDialog(CPhoneDlg::IDD, pParent)
{
    m_brush = (HBRUSH)GetStockObject( HOLLOW_BRUSH );
    color_brush.CreateSolidBrush( RGB(0,255,0) );
    //{{AFX_DATA_INIT(CPhoneDlg)
        // NOTE: the ClassWizard will add member initialization here.
    //}}AFX_DATA_INIT
}
```

5. Modify the message map entry for this class by adding the lines marked in bold print to the code.

```
BEGIN_MESSAGE_MAP(CPhoneDlg, CDialog)
    //{{AFX_MSG_MAP(CPhoneDlg)
        ON_WM_ERASEBKGND()
        ON_WM_CTLCOLOR()
        // NOTE: the ClassWizard will add message map macros here.
    //}}AFX_MSG_MAP
END_MESSAGE_MAP()
```

6. Next, open the PHONEDLG.H include file from the project list. Add the following lines to the file (marked in bold print):

```
class CPhoneDlg : public CDialog
{
private:

   CBrush color_brush;
   HBRUSH m_brush;          // Handle of background brush

// Construction
public:
   CPhoneDlg(CWnd* pParent = NULL);  // standard constructor

// Dialog Data
   //{{AFX_DATA(CPhoneDlg)
   enum { IDD = IDD_DIALOG3 };
      // NOTE: the ClassWizard will add data members here.
   //}}AFX_DATA

// Implementation
protected:
   virtual void DoDataExchange(CDataExchange* pDX);  // DDX/DDV support

   // Generated message map functions
   //{{AFX_MSG(CPhoneDlg)
      // NOTE: the ClassWizard will add member functions here
      afx_msg BOOL    OnEraseBkgnd(CDC* pDC);
      afx_msg HBRUSH OnCtlColor(CDC* pDC, CWnd* pWnd, UINT nCtlColor);
   //}}AFX_MSG
   DECLARE_MESSAGE_MAP()
};
```

7. Reenter AppStudio and add a new main-level menu with the caption Colors. Add a new drop-down menu item to the menu with the caption Dialog Background. Give this drop-down menu item the identifier ID_DLG_BKGD.

8. Start ClassWizard and select the application object, Ch54App. Select the ID_DLG_BKGD object from the object list and COMMAND from the message list. Click on the Add Function button and give the function the name OnDlgBkgd. Add the following code to the OnDlgBkgd function:

```
void CCh54App::OnDlgBkgd()
{
   CPhoneDlg dlg;
   dlg.DoModal();
}
```

9. Add the following include file to the CH54.CPP file below all other "#include" lines:

```
#include "phonedlg.h"
```

10. Compile and run the application.

How It Works

When Windows 95 initializes a window and displays it on the screen, it sends a message to the window (or dialog box) to paint its background. If you do not override this message, the normal behavior of the background is to use the brush defined when the window class was created. For dialog boxes, this default box is normally gray but can be customized for different window classes.

This dialog box simply overrides the handling of the message sent to erase the background, called, appropriately enough, WM_ERASEBKGND. This message expects to receive as its return value a flag indicating whether the message was handled, so we return TRUE to the operating system.

COMPLEXITY
EASY

5.5 How do I... Enable and disable controls in a dialog?

Problem

I would like to be able to selectively enable or disable controls in my dialog based on user input. For example, if the user selects one of two mutually exclusive options, I would like to disable all of the other options that go along with the second choice. On the other hand, I also need the ability to enable all of those options and disable the first set if the user changes his or her mind.

How can I use the power of the Windows 95 API to accomplish these goals with minimum fuss and time?

Technique

The ability to selectively enable and disable controls in a dialog box is one that separates well-written, well-thought-out programs from those that simply accept user input to do a job. Users may or may not be aware of what constitutes "mutually exclusive choices." It is your job as the programmer to decide which options are compatible and which cannot coexist. It is also your job to protect the user from making choices that cannot be combined.

When faced with a dialog full of contradictory elements, the programmer can use two basic approaches to control the resulting logic of the dialog box. The first is to display an error when the user attempts to save his or her choices after the contradictory elements have been discovered. This has two problems. First, the user may be unaware of why the choices are bad and may have problems discovering a set of options that do work together. Second, the frustrated user will quite rightly wonder, "Why did it let me do that if it knew I couldn't?"

The second approach to protecting against incompatible options is to disable all incompatible options once an option is selected. Of course, if the option is deselected, or another option chosen, the controls must be updated to reflect this.

Steps

Open and run the Visual C++ application CH55.MAK from the CHAPT5\SAM-PLES\CH55 directory on the CD that comes with this book. Select the Controls main menu and the drop-down menu item Enable and Disable. A dialog box will be displayed, as shown in Figure 5-7. The check boxes at the top of the dialog are the keys to the entire dialog. If a check box is selected, the corresponding control set (edit fields, combo boxes, and check boxes) will be enabled for the user to input into them. If the check box is not selected, the corresponding control set will be disabled and will not allow the user to input into them. Play with the dialog for a while until you are satisfied with the way it works.

To duplicate this functionality in your own program, do the following:

1. Create a new project in Visual C++ using AppWizard. Give this project the name CH55.MAK. Enter AppStudio and create a new dialog. In this dialog, you should first add three check boxes at the top. Label the check boxes Enable All Check Boxes, Enable All Edit Fields, and Enable All Combo Boxes. Give the check boxes the identifiers IDC_CHECKBOX1, IDC_CHECKBOX2, and IDC_CHECKBOX3. For the styles, select the Group and Tab Stop check boxes and deselect the Auto check box.

2. Next, add a group box with the caption Check Boxes to the dialog. Within this group box, add three check box buttons to the dialog. Give the check boxes

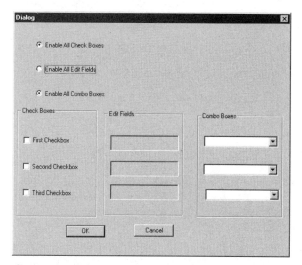

Figure 5-7 Dialog with built-in enabling and disabling of controls

the labels First Checkbox, Second Checkbox and Third Checkbox. Accept the
default identifiers ID_CHECK1, ID_CHECK2, and ID_CHECK3.

3. Add a group box with the caption Edit Fields to the dialog. Within this group
box, add three edit fields to the dialog. Accept the identifiers ID_EDIT1,
ID_EDIT2, and ID_EDIT3.

4. Finally, add a group box with the caption Combo Boxes. Add three combo
boxes to the group box and accept the identifiers ID_COMBO1, ID_COMBO2,
and ID_COMBO3. Select the ID_COMBO1 combo box and click on the "Enter
list choices" box to the right of the pop-up dialog. Enter the following strings
into the edit box, each terminated by pressing (CTRL)-(ENTER): "Choice A1,"
"Choice A2," "Choice A3," and "Choice A4."

5. Select the second combo box, ID_COMBO2, and click on the "Enter list
choices" box. Enter the following strings into the edit box, each terminated by
pressing (CTRL)-(ENTER): "Choice B1," "Choice B2," and "Choice B3."

6. Select the third combo box, ID_COMBO3, and click on the "Enter list choices" box. Enter the following strings into the edit box, each terminated by
pressing (CTRL)-(ENTER): "Choice C1" and "Choice C2."

7. Select the ClassWizard and generate a new dialog class for this template. Give
the dialog class the name CEnableDlg. Select the CEnableDlg from the drop-
down list in ClassWizard and select it in the object list. Select
WM_INITDIALOG in the message list and click on the Add Function button.
Enter the following code into the OnInitDialog method of CEnableDlg:

```
BOOL CEnableDlg::OnInitDialog()
{
    CDialog::OnInitDialog();

    CenterWindow();

    CButton *b1 = (CButton *)GetDlgItem(IDC_CHECKBOX1);
    b1->SetCheck(1);
    CButton *b2 = (CButton *)GetDlgItem(IDC_CHECKBOX2);
    b2->SetCheck(1);
    CButton *b3 = (CButton *)GetDlgItem(IDC_CHECKBOX3);
    b3->SetCheck(1);

    Return TRUE;   // Return TRUE  unless you set the focus to a
                   // control.
}
```

8. Select the IDC_CHECKBOX1 object from the object list in ClassWizard and
select BN_CLICKED from the message list. Click on the Add Function button
and name the method OnButton1. Enter the following code into the
OnButton1 method of CEnableDlg:

```
void CEnableDlg::OnButton1()
{
    // Flip the button state.
```

```
    if ( button1_flag )
       button1_flag = 0;
    else
       button1_flag = 1;

    // Reset the control to this state.

    CButton *b1 = (CButton *)GetDlgItem(IDC_CHECKBOX1);
    b1->SetCheck(button1_flag);

    BOOL enable_flag;

    // See if we should enable or disable the edit fields.

    if ( button1_flag == 1 ) // Button is set
       enable_flag = TRUE;
    else
       enable_flag = FALSE;

    GetDlgItem(IDC_CHECK1)->EnableWindow(enable_flag);
    GetDlgItem(IDC_CHECK2)->EnableWindow(enable_flag);
    GetDlgItem(IDC_CHECK3)->EnableWindow(enable_flag);
}
```

9. Select the IDC_CHECKBOX2 object from the object list in ClassWizard and select BN_CLICKED from the message list. Click on the Add Function button and name the method OnButton2. Enter the following code into the OnButton2 method of CEnableDlg:

```
void CEnableDlg::OnButton2()
{
    // Flip the button state.

    if ( button2_flag )
       button2_flag = 0;
    else
       button2_flag = 1;

    // Reset the control to this state.

    CButton *b2 = (CButton *)GetDlgItem(IDC_CHECKBOX2);
    b2->SetCheck(button2_flag);

    BOOL enable_flag;

    // See if we should enable or disable the edit fields.

    if ( button2_flag == 1 ) // Button is set
       enable_flag = TRUE;
    else
       enable_flag = FALSE;

    GetDlgItem(IDC_EDIT1)->EnableWindow(enable_flag);
    GetDlgItem(IDC_EDIT2)->EnableWindow(enable_flag);
    GetDlgItem(IDC_EDIT3)->EnableWindow(enable_flag);
}
```

10. Select the IDC_CHECKBOX3 object from the object list in ClassWizard and select BN_CLICKED from the message list. Click on the Add Function button and name the method OnButton3. Enter the following code into the OnButton3 method of CEnableDlg:

```
void CEnableDlg::OnButton3()
{
    // Flip the button state.

    if ( button3_flag )
        button3_flag = 0;
    else
        button3_flag = 1;

    // Reset the control to this state.

    CButton *b3 = (CButton *)GetDlgItem(IDC_CHECKBOX3);
    b3->SetCheck(button3_flag);

    BOOL enable_flag;

    // See if we should enable or disable the combo boxes.

    if ( button3_flag == 1 ) // Button is set
        enable_flag = TRUE;
    else
        enable_flag = FALSE;

    GetDlgItem(IDC_COMBO1)->EnableWindow(enable_flag);
    GetDlgItem(IDC_COMBO2)->EnableWindow(enable_flag);
    GetDlgItem(IDC_COMBO3)->EnableWindow(enable_flag);
}
```

11. Add the following code to the constructor for the class CEnableDlg::CEnableDlg:

```
button1_flag = 1;
button2_flag = 1;
button3_flag = 1;
```

12. Add the following declarations to the header file for the CEnableDlg class (ENABLEDL.H):

```
private:
    int button1_flag;
    int button2_flag;
    int button3_flag;
```

13. Go back to AppStudio and select the menu for the main menu. Add a new main menu with the caption Controls and add a new menu item with the caption Enable and Disable. Give the drop-down menu item the identifier ID_CTRL_ENABLE.

14. Entering ClassWizard, select the CCh55App class from the drop-down list. Select the ID_CTRL_ENABLE object from the object list and the COMMAND message from the message list. Click on the Add Function button and accept the OnCtrlEnable name for the method. Add the following code to the OnCtrlEnable method of CCh55App:

```
void CCh55App::OnCtrlEnable()
{
    CEnableDlg dlg;
    dlg.DoModal();
}
```

15. Add the following include file to the top of the CH55.CPP file:

```
#include "enabledl.h"
```

16. Compile and run the application.

How It Works

When the user selects the dialog from the menu, the OnInitDialog method of the class is invoked. This method sets the initial state of the three check boxes to "on" by sending a SetCheck message with the flag set to TRUE. The internal program state variables for controlling the check boxes are also set to TRUE.

When the user selects one of the check boxes from the dialog, the program calls the appropriate handler for that check box (OnButton1, OnButton2, or OnButton3). This handler then responds by checking its internal state flag to see whether the check box was previously on or off. If it was on, it is flipped to off, and vice versa. The current state is then used to either Enable (on) or Disable (off) the set of controls associated with that check box.

To enable a control, the Enable method is called for that window. What is actually happening here is that the EnableWindow of the Windows 95 API is being called for the window handle of the control in question. EnableWindow takes two parameters—the handle of the window and a flag indicating whether the window is to be enabled (TRUE) or disabled (FALSE). The MFC method Enable is a call-through to this API function.

Comments

This powerful technique in Visual C++ is quite simple to duplicate in Delphi. To accomplish this, do the following:

1. Create a new project with the name ENDIS.DPR. To this form add three check boxes labeled Enable All Check Boxes, Enable All Edit Controls, and Enable All Combo Boxes. Also add to the form three group boxes with the labels Check Boxes, Edit Controls, and Combo Boxes.

2. To the group box labeled Check Boxes, add three check boxes. Allow the default labels CheckBox 1, CheckBox 2, and CheckBox 3.

3. To the group labeled Edit Controls, add three edit fields. Accept the default values.

4. To the group labeled Combo Boxes, add three combo boxes. For each one, click on the Items property and add several strings. This is to make the enabling/disabling obvious for combo boxes.

5. Double-click on the Enable All Check Boxes check box and add the following code to the TForm1.Checkbox1Click method :

```
procedure TForm1.CheckBox1Click(Sender: TObject);
begin
    if CheckBox1.Checked = False Then
        begin
            CheckBox4.Enabled := False;
            CheckBox5.Enabled := False;
            CheckBox6.Enabled := False;
        end
    else
        begin
            CheckBox4.Enabled :- True;
            CheckBox5.Enabled := True;
            CheckBox6.Enabled := True;
        end

end;
```

6. Double-click on the Enable All Edit Controls check box and add the following code to the TForm1.Checkbox2Click method:

```
procedure TForm1.CheckBox2Click(Sender: TObject);
begin
    if CheckBox2.Checked = False Then
        begin
            Edit1.Enabled := False;
            Edit2.Enabled := False;
            Edit3.Enabled := False;
        end
    else
        begin
            Edit1.Enabled := True;
            Edit2.Enabled := True;
            Edit3.Enabled := True;
        end

end;
```

7. Double-click on the Enable All Combo Boxes check box and add the following code to the TForm1.Checkbox3Click method:

```
procedure TForm1.CheckBox2Click(Sender: TObject);
begin
    if CheckBox2.Checked = False Then
        begin
            Edit1.Enabled := False;
            Edit2.Enabled := False;
            Edit3.Enabled := False;
        end
    else
        begin
            Edit1.Enabled := True;
            Edit2.Enabled := True;
            Edit3.Enabled := True;
        end

end;
```

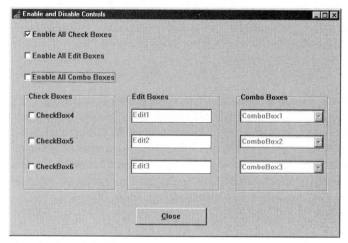

Figure 5-8 Delphi form showing enabling and disabling controls

8. Compile and run the application. You should see the dialog displayed in Figure 5-8.

COMPLEXITY
MODERATE

5.6 How do I...
Change the controls shown in a dialog?

Problem

I want to be able to show some controls in my dialog at certain times but hide them at other times. For example, users might only need to see "advanced" options after they have progressed through the preliminaries. Is there a way I can avoid destroying and re-creating the controls each time I would like to temporarily get rid of them, using the Windows 95 API?

Technique

The ability to selectively hide or show windows or controls is built into the Windows API and does not require destroying and re-creating the windows at runtime. The ShowWindow function of the API lets you do this. The ShowWindow function accepts two parameters—the handle of the window and a flag indicating whether the window is to be shown or hidden. The function "hides" a window by removing it from the screen, but it does not affect any of its internal state.

In this How-To, we will examine how you can selectively hide and show windows in your dialog box and, in the process, look at two important functions of the Windows 95 API, ShowWindow and SetWindowText.

Steps

Open and run the Visual C++ application CH56.MAK from the CHAPT5\SAM-PLES\CH56 directory on the CD that comes with this book. Select the Controls main menu and the menu item Show and Hide. A dialog box will be displayed, as shown in Figure 5-9. If the buttons on the dialog are clicked, the dialog will show or hide the text fields that are currently displayed. The buttons act as a toggle between hiding and showing the text fields, and each button controls a single text field.

To duplicate this functionality in your own program, do the following:

1. Create a new project in Visual C++ using AppWizard. Give the project the name CH56.MAK. Enter AppStudio and create a new dialog. In this dialog add three text fields at the top. Label the first text field "This is the first line of text in the dialog" and give it the identifier IDC_LINE1. Label the second text field "This is the second line of text in the dialog" and give it the identifier IDC_LINE2. Label the third text field "This is the third line of text in the dialog" and give it the identifier IDC_LINE3. Add three buttons to the dialog and give them the captions Hide Line 1, Hide Line 2, and Hide Line 3.

2. Enter ClassWizard and generate a new dialog class for this dialog template. Give the dialog class the name CShowControlDlg. Select the CShowControlDlg class from the drop-down list in ClassWizard and select it

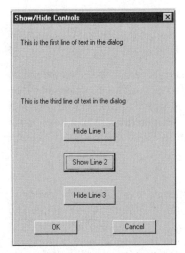

Figure 5-9 Dialog with built-in showing and hiding of controls

in the object list. Select WM_INITDIALOG from the message list and click on the Add Function button. Enter the following code into the OnInitDialog method of CShowControlDlg:

```
BOOL CShowControlDlg::OnInitDialog()
{
    CDialog::OnInitDialog();

    CenterWindow();

    return TRUE;  // Return TRUE  unless you set the focus to a control.
}
```

3. Select the IDC_BUTTON1 object from the object list in ClassWizard and select COMMAND from the message list. Click on the Add Function button. Accept the name OnButton1 for the name of the method and enter the following code into the OnButton1 method of CShowControlDlg:

```
void CShowControlDlg::OnButton1()
{
    CStatic *text = (CStatic *)GetDlgItem(IDC_LINE1);
    CButton *b1   = (CButton *)GetDlgItem(IDC_BUTTON1);

    if ( text->IsWindowVisible() ) {
        text->ShowWindow(SW_HIDE);
        b1->SetWindowText ( "Show Line 1");
    }
    else {
        text->ShowWindow(SW_SHOW);
        b1->SetWindowText ( "Hide Line 1");
    }
}
```

4. Select the IDC_BUTTON2 object from the object list in ClassWizard and select COMMAND from the message list. Click on the Add Function button. Accept the name OnButton2 for the name of the method and enter the following code into the OnButton2 method of CShowControlDlg:

```
void CShowControlDlg::OnButton2()
{
    CStatic *text = (CStatic *)GetDlgItem(IDC_LINE2);
    CButton *b1   = (CButton *)GetDlgItem(IDC_BUTTON2);

    if ( text->IsWindowVisible() ) {
        text->ShowWindow(SW_HIDE);
        b1->SetWindowText ( "Show Line 2");
    }
    else {
        text->ShowWindow(SW_SHOW);
        b1->SetWindowText ( "Hide Line 2");
    }
}
```

5. Select the IDC_BUTTON3 object from the object list in ClassWizard and select COMMAND from the message list. Click on the Add Function button. Accept the name OnButton3 for the name of the method and enter the following code into the OnButton3 method of CShowControlDlg:

```
void CShowControlDlg::OnButton3()
{
    CStatic *text = (CStatic *)GetDlgItem(IDC_LINE3);
    CButton *b1    = (CButton *)GetDlgItem(IDC_BUTTON3);

    if ( text->IsWindowVisible() ) {
        text->ShowWindow(SW_HIDE);
        b1->SetWindowText ( "Show Line 3");
    }
    else {
        text->ShowWindow(SW_SHOW);
        b1->SetWindowText ( "Hide Line 3");
    }
}
```

6. Next, enter AppStudio and add a new main menu with the caption Controls. Add a new menu item to the Controls menu called Show and Hide, and give it the identifier ID_CONTROLS_SHOWANDHIDE.

7. Enter ClassWizard and select the CCh56App object from the drop-down list. Select ID_CONTROLS_SHOWANDHIDE from the object list and COMMAND from the message list. Click on the Add Function button and accept the OnControlsShowandhide name. Enter the following code into the OnControlsShowandhide method of CCh56App:

```
void CCh56App::OnControlsShowandhide()
{
    CShowControlDlg    dlg;
    dlg.DoModal();
}
```

8. Enter the following include file line at the top of the CH56.CPP file:

```
#include "showcont.h"
```

9. Compile and run the application.

How It Works

When the dialog is created, it is first centered in the parent window by the CenterWindow call in OnInitDialog. When any of the buttons is pressed in the dialog, the method for that button is called and the following procedure is enacted: First, the handler checks to see if the text field associated with that button is currently visible. This is accomplished using the IsWindowVisible method of the MFC, which corresponds to the IsVisibleWindow function of the Windows API.

After the window visibility is checked, the button handler will then call ShowWindow, passing it either TRUE, if the text field was not currently visible, or FALSE, if the text field was visible. The ShowWindow call will "flip" the visibility state of the text field, either making it visible to the user or hiding it on the dialog.

Following the visibility check and set, the dialog handler will then update the text that appears on the button itself by using the SetWindowText function. This function will change the window text for a window on any screen—dialog or not. The window text for a button, for example, is the actual button caption. For text fields, the window text is the text that appears in a static text control. For "normal" windows with caption bars, the window text is the title of the caption bar.

That's all there is to it. Everything else is handled directly by the Windows 95 API layer.

COMPLEXITY
MODERATE

5.7 How do I... Use property sheets in a dialog?

Problem

The new Windows 95 interface seems to be built solely on the property sheet motif. I would like to emulate that motif in my own Windows applications. How can I use property sheets in my own application that look like the ones that Windows 95 uses in the desktop?

Technique

The property sheet (or tabbed dialog as it was once called) is an excellent way to allow the programmer to group dialogs without using up valuable screen real estate. In addition, property sheets avoid the clutter of too many controls in a single dialog box without requiring the user to call up multiple dialog boxes to accomplish a single task. Data for the program can be collected into categories (called property pages) and then set up as separate dialog templates, which are then grouped together through a property sheet.

Visual C++ offers an excellent interface to property sheets via the CPropertySheet and CPropertyPage classes. Unfortunately, if you are using the 16-bit development tools (MSVC 1.5x), the tools are not quite up to the task of automatically generating the classes for you. In this How-To, we will take the approach of the 16-bit application in order to better explain what is going on and to provide a simple template that you can use in either 16-bit or 32-bit applications for Windows 95.

Steps

Open and run the Visual C++ application CH57.MAK from the CHAPT5\SAMPLES\CH57 directory on the CD that comes with this book. Select the Controls main menu and the drop-down menu item Property Sheet. You will see the property sheet dialog displayed in Figure 5-10. Click on the second tab of the property sheet (labeled Page Two), and you will see a second property page displayed, as shown in Figure 5-11.

247

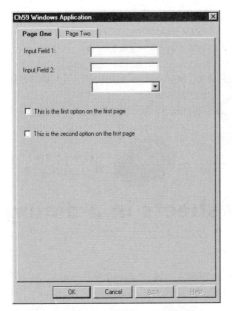

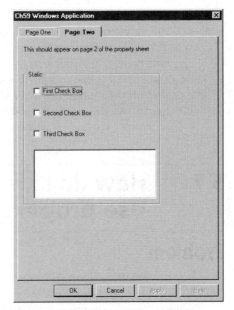

Figure 5-10 Property sheet with Page One displayed

Figure 5-11 Property sheet with Page Two displayed

To duplicate this functionality in your own application, do the following:

1. Create a new project in Visual C++ using AppWizard. Give this project the name CH57.MAK. Enter AppStudio and create two new dialogs. Note the identifiers of the dialogs as you create them. Although it does not matter for this example, try to add as many types of controls as you can. Be sure to make both dialogs the same size.

2. In AppStudio, select the first dialog and bring up the properties for it by double-clicking anywhere in the dialog itself without being on a control. Select the Style drop-down from the combo box and select Child from the style combo box on that page. Select the Thin border from the border combo box and make sure the check boxes for Disabled and Titlebar are checked. In the General drop-down box, set the caption to Page One for the first dialog and Page Two for the second dialog. These are the captions that will appear in the tabs on the property sheet.

3. Save the dialogs. Select the main menu from the Menus list and add a main menu with the caption Controls. Add a new drop-down menu to the Controls main menu. Give the menu the caption Property Sheet and the identifier ID_CONTROLSPROPERTYSHEET. Save the menu and exit AppStudio.

4. In Visual C++, create a new file by clicking on the New File icon or selecting New from the File menu. Enter the following code into the file and save the file as PROPPGE.CPP:

```
// proppge.cpp : implementation file
//

#include "stdafx.h"
#include "proppge.h"


#ifdef _DEBUG
#undef THIS_FILE
static char BASED_CODE THIS_FILE[] = __FILE__;
#endif

/////////////////////////////////////////////////////////////////
// CPropPage dialog


CPropPage::CPropPage(int id) : CPropertyPage(id)
{
  //{{AFX_DATA_INIT(CPropPage)
  //}}AFX_DATA_INIT
}

void CPropPage::DoDataExchange(CDataExchange* pDX)
{
  CPropertyPage::DoDataExchange(pDX);
  //{{AFX_DATA_MAP(CPropPage)
  //}}AFX_DATA_MAP
}


BEGIN_MESSAGE_MAP(CPropPage, CPropertyPage)
  //{{AFX_MSG_MAP(CPropPage)
    // NOTE: the ClassWizard will add message map macros here
  //}}AFX_MSG_MAP
END_MESSAGE_MAP()

/////////////////////////////////////////////////////////////////
// CPropPage message handlers
```

5. Next, create another new file in Visual C++. Enter the following code into the file and save it as PROPPGE.H:

```
// proppge.h : header file
//


/////////////////////////////////////////////////////////////////
// CPropPage dialog

class CPropPage : public CPropertyPage
{
// Construction
public:
  CPropPage(int id);

// Dialog Data
  //{{AFX_DATA(CPropPage)
```

continued on next page

continued from previous page
```
    //}}AFX_DATA


// Overrides
    // ClassWizard generates virtual function overrides.
    //{{AFX_VIRTUAL(CPropPage)
    protected:
    virtual void DoDataExchange(CDataExchange* pDX);      // DDX/DDV support
    //}}AFX_VIRTUAL

// Implementation
protected:
    // Generated message map functions
    //{{AFX_MSG(CPropPage)
      // NOTE: the ClassWizard will add member functions here.
    //}}AFX_MSG
    DECLARE_MESSAGE_MAP()
};
```

6. The PROPPGE.CPP and PROPPGE.H files are the skeleton templates you will use for your property sheet pages. In this step you will create the actual property sheet dialog and pages.

Enter ClassWizard and select the CCh57App from the drop-down list. Select the ID_CONTROLSPROPERTYSHEET from the object list and COMMAND from the message list. Click on the Add Function button and give the new method the name OnPropertySheet. Enter the following code into the OnPropertySheet method of CCh57App:

```
void CCh57App::OnPropertySheet()
{
    CPropertySheet prop(AFX_IDS_APP_TITLE, AfxGetMainWnd());
    CPropPage *page1 = new CPropPage(IDD_DIALOG11);
    CPropPage *page2 = new CPropPage(IDD_DIALOG12);

    prop.AddPage ( page1 );
    prop.AddPage ( page2 );
    prop.DoModal();
    delete page1;
    delete page2;
}
```

7. Add the following include file line to the top of the CH57.CPP file:

```
#include "proppge.h"
```

8. Compile and run the application.

How It Works

The property sheet dialogs of Windows 95 are encapsulated by the CPropertySheet class of the MFC. Each property sheet "tab" is a dialog in your application that is encapsulated by the CPropertyPage class. When you want to add a new property sheet to your application, you simply use a CPropertySheet object (or derive your own class from CPropertySheet to do special processing) and add individual pages to the dialog. The pages are simply CPropertyPage derivatives, which we have created via the CPropPage class. This class accepts a new dialog identifier as the dialog "page" to use when displaying that tab.

The skeleton class CPropPage can be reused in your applications. To add member variable processing to the page, simply derive a class from CPropPage and use the data exchange properties of the MFC to get and set data in the property sheet.

Once the property sheet and pages have been created, use the AddPage method of CPropertySheet to associate each page with the property sheet. The tabs will use the caption of the dialog as the tab title and will be displayed in the order they were added to the property sheet. Once all of the property pages have been added to the property sheet, call the DoModal method of CPropertySheet to display the dialog and allow the user to enter data into the various pages.

When you are done with the property sheet, remember to delete the individual pages that were created for it to free up memory for Windows 95 to run with. Don't forget to do this or your application may eventually run out of memory while it is running.

Comments

The property sheet motif is an excellent method for getting discrete pieces of information that are somehow related from the user. For example, you could use property sheets to set properties for your views. One tab might contain foreground (text) colors, background colors, and fonts, while another might contain options for displaying all or partial data. Still another tab could deal with printing options or file saving options.

The property sheet is integral to the workings of Windows 95. Adding them to your application will not only simplify the work for your users but will also make them more comfortable with your application.

COMPLEXITY
MODERATE

5.8   How do I...
Draw a picture on a button in a dialog?

Problem

The newer interfaces for Windows 95 applications all seem to have buttons that display graphical images rather than simple text. Some of these buttons seem animated, in that they change as you click on them to indicate something is happening. I would like the ability to add a button to my own dialogs that contains an image, but I don't know how to go about it. How can the API help me out with this problem?

Technique

In order to display an image on a button in either Windows 3.x or Windows 95 (or for that matter Windows NT), it is necessary to create what is known as an *owner-drawn* button. This indicates to Windows that the programmer will take responsibility for handling the display and interface for the button, while Windows will simply be responsible for passing along messages to tell the programmer which state he or she is in.

Visual C++ allows the creation of a CBitmapButton class that encapsulates the functionality of owner-drawn buttons and allows you to create buttons by drawing the images (or bitmaps) that you want displayed on the button and then instantiating a copy of the CBitmapButton class for that set of images. In this How-To, we examine the steps necessary to create a button that displays an image as well as how to animate that button as the user clicks on it.

Steps

Open and run the Visual C++ application CH58.MAK from the CHAPT5\SAMPLES\CH58 directory on the CD that comes with this book. Select the Controls main menu and the menu item Picture Dialog. A dialog box will be displayed, as shown in Figure 5-12. Click and hold the left mouse button on the displayed "house" button and you will see the button figure change to that shown in Figure 5-13.

To duplicate this functionality, perform the following procedure:

1. Create a new project in Visual C++ using AppWizard. Give the project the name CH58.MAK. Enter AppStudio and create a new dialog. In this dialog, add a static text field and a button.

2. Label the static text field with the caption "Here is a picture button:". Leave the identifier as the default IDC_STATIC.

3. Give the button the caption DOORBUTTON and the identifier the caption IDC_DOORBUTTON. Set the properties for the button to be Visible, Owner Draw, and TabStop.

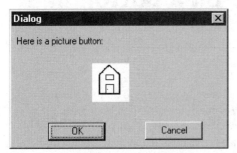

Figure 5-12 Picture dialog with button in "up" position

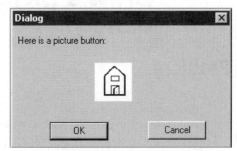

Figure 5-13 Picture dialog with button in "down" position

4. Enter the bitmap area of AppStudio and create two new bitmaps. Give the first bitmap the identifier "DOORBUTTONU" and the second bitmap the identifier "DOORBUTTOND". Include the quotation marks in both identifiers so that Visual C++ does not generate identifier #defines for them. Save the bitmaps and the resource file.

5. Select the dialog you have just created in AppStudio and select ClassWizard. Create a new dialog class for the template and give the new class the name CPictureDlg. Select the CPictureDlg object from the object list in ClassWizard and select the message WM_INITDIALOG. Enter the following code into the OnInitDialog of the CPictureDlg class:

```
BOOL CPictureDlg::OnInitDialog()
{
   CDialog::OnInitDialog();

   VERIFY(m_Button.SubclassDlgItem(IDC_DOORBUTTON, this));
   m_Button.SizeToContent();

   return TRUE;   // Return TRUE  unless you set the focus to a control.
}
```

6. Enter the following code into the constructor for the class, CPictureDlg:: CPictureDlg:

```
if (!m_Button.LoadBitmaps("DOORBUTTONU", "DOORBUTTOND") )
   {
     TRACE("Failed to load bitmaps for buttons\n");
     AfxThrowResourceException();
   }
```

7. Finally, add the following entries into the header file for the class, PICTURED.H:

```
private:
   CBitmapButton m_Button;
```

8. Next, reenter AppStudio and add a new main-level menu labeled Controls. To this menu, add a menu item with the caption Picture Dialog. Give the menu item the identifier ID_PICTURE_DLG.

9. Select ClassWizard and select the CCh58App object from the drop-down list. Select the ID_PICTURE_DLG object from the object list and the COMMAND message from the message list. Click on the Add Function button and give the new method the name OnPictureDlg. Enter the following code into the OnPictureDlg method of CCh58App:

```
void CCh58App::OnPictureDlg()
{
   CPictureDlg dlg;

   dlg.DoModal();
}
```

10. Enter the following include file line at the top of the CH58.CPP file:

```
#include "pictured.h"
```

11. Compile and run the application.

How It Works

When the user selects the picture dialog box menu option, the dialog object is constructed in the application object. When the dialog is first instantiated, two things occur. First, the object is created. This calls the constructor for the object, which uses its member variable, m_Button, to load the bitmaps associated with the button. The CBitmapButton class contains an array of up to four bitmaps to associate with the images to display for the Up, Down, GetFocus, and Disabled states of the button. These four images are stored within the class and used as the messages come in that make them necessary.

Next, the OnInitDialog method of the CPictureDlg class is called. This method occurs just after the actual window is instantiated, but before the window is displayed on the screen. This method calls the SubclassDlgItem of the button to "subclass" the item on the dialog. Subclassing is a powerful technique that uses the SetWindowLong function of the API.

Subclassing a control in a dialog involves getting the window procedure or callback function via the GetWindowLong function of the API. The SetWindowLong function is then used to reset the window callback procedure (for message handling) to a procedure that is specified by the programmer. The process itself looks something like this:

```
// Get the existing window procedure.

FARPROC old_proc = (FARPROC)GetWindowLong(hWnd, GWL_WNDPROC);

// Reset the window procedure to be our callback function.

FARPROC new_proc = (FARPROC)MakeProcInstance((FARPROC)MyWindowHandler,
                    hInst);

// This would be the callback function.

SetWindowLong ( hWnd, GWL_WNDPROC, new_proc );
```

Once the window procedure has been replaced, all messages come to the new window message callback function (new_proc in the preceding example). The SubclassDlgItem method of CBitmapButton does all of this for you. Once it has been called, the CBitmapButton member functions are called for Paint, Left Button Down, and so forth.

It is not necessary to "un-subclass" the button, as the button class will do that automatically.

Once the button has been subclassed, the paint function displays the image associated with the "up" position of the button automatically. Pressing the left mouse button and holding it down on the button will cause the "down" position of the button to be displayed, and releasing the button will once again cause the "up" position to be displayed.

COMPLEXITY
MODERATE

5.9 How do I...
Display a "progress" dialog while another activity takes place?

Problem

I would like to display a "progress" dialog like many of the newer applications do when something is happening that the user cannot see on the screen. If, for example, the program is copying one file to another file, I would like to display a message indicating what percentage of the operation is complete and allow the user to cancel the procedure if he or she is not happy with it.

How can I use the Windows API to display such a dialog and allow the user to cancel an operation in the middle? The copy process is fairly "tight," being in a small loop. How can users indicate that they would like to cancel that loop?

Technique

The problem of displaying a dialog that allows users to cancel a tight loop has always been an ugly one in Windows. Status dialogs have become quite common, and users are accustomed to being able to cancel an operation that they have started at any point. In this How-To, we examine how the Windows messaging system works and how we can take advantage of that messaging system for our own purposes.

The basic premise of this idea is that you display a modal dialog box on the screen that contains a status indicator of some kind and a Cancel button. The status indicator keeps users informed as to how far along the process is, and the Cancel button allows them to cancel the operation before its completion. In this case, our status indicator will be a progress bar that is one of the common controls added to Win32.

Steps

Open and run the Visual C++ application CH59.MAK from the CHAPT5\SAMPLES\CH59 directory on the CD that comes with this book. Select the main-level menu option for Controls and the drop-down menu item for Copy File. You will see the dialog displayed in Figure 5-14. Enter a valid file name to copy from and a name for the file you wish to create. Click on the OK button. Try to choose a large file or you will be unable to cancel the request.

When the progress dialog appears (Figure 5-15), click on the Close button. The dialog will go away and the copy will be aborted. In the meantime, up until you click on Close, the dialog will continue to update itself with the progress of the copy operation.

To duplicate this functionality, do the following:

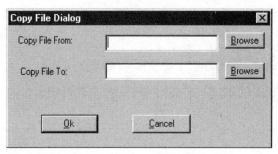

Figure 5-14 Dialog for copying files

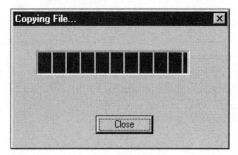

Figure 5-15 Progress dialog for copying
files

1. Create a new project in Visual C++ using AppWizard. Give the new project the name CH59.MAK. Enter AppStudio and create a new dialog. In this new dialog add two static fields labeled Copy File From: and Copy File To:. Add two edit fields to the dialog, aligned horizontally with the static text fields. Add two buttons aligned horizontally with the edit fields. Give the two buttons the caption &Browse.

2. Select ClassWizard and generate a new dialog class for this dialog template. Give the class the name CCopyDlg. Click on the member variables tab of ClassWizard and add two new member variables for the IDC_EDIT1 and IDC_EDIT2 control identifiers. Give the IDC_EDIT1 variable the name m_CopyFrom and the IDC_EDIT2 variable the name m_CopyTo.

3. Reenter ClassWizard and select the IDC_BUTTON1 button for the CCopyDlg class and the BN_CLICKED message from the message list. Select the Add Function button. Enter the name OnBrowseOpen for the name of the new function. Enter the following code for the OnBrowseOpen method of CCopyDlg:

```
void CCopyDlg::OnBrowseOpen()
{
    // Put up a file open dialog.
```

```
    static char szFilter[] = "Text Files (*.txt) | *.TXT | All Files
(*.*) | *.* ||";
    CFileDialog dlg ( TRUE, "DLL", NULL, OFN_HIDEREADONLY, szFilter,
this );

    if ( dlg.DoModal() == IDOK ) {
        GetDlgItem(IDC_EDIT1)->SetWindowText ( dlg.GetPathName() );
    }
}
```

4. Select the IDC_BUTTON2 object from the object list and the BN_CLICKED
message from the message list. Select Add Function and give the new function
the name OnBrowseSave. Enter the following code for the OnBrowseSave
function of CCopyDlg:

```
void CCopyDlg::OnBrowseSave()
{
    // Put up a file open dialog.

    static char szFilter[] = "Text Files (*.txt) | *.TXT | All Files
(*.*) | *.* ||";
    CFileDialog dlg ( FALSE, "DLL", NULL, OFN_HIDEREADONLY | OFN_OVER-
WRITEPROMPT, szFilter, this );

    if ( dlg.DoModal() == IDOK ) {
        GetDlgItem(IDC_EDIT2)->SetWindowText ( dlg.GetPathName() );
    }
}
```

5. Create another new dialog in AppStudio. Delete the OK button from the dialog and center the Cancel button within the dialog.

6. Select ClassWizard and generate a new dialog class for this dialog template.
Give the class the name CProgressDlg. Select the CProgressDlg in the
ClassWizard drop-down combo box and select it as well in the object ID list.
Click on the WM_INITDIALOG message and then click the Add Function
button. Enter the following code into OnInitDialog for CProgressDlg:

```
BOOL CProgressDlg::OnInitDialog()
{
  CDialog::OnInitDialog();

  // Create a progress bar.

  hWndPB = CreateWindowEx ( 0, PROGRESS_CLASS, NULL, WS_CHILD |
          WS_VISIBLE, 30, 30, 200, 30, m_hWnd, 0,
          AfxGetInstanceHandle(),
       NULL );
  ::SendMessage( hWndPB, PBM_SETRANGE, 0, MAKELPARAM(0,100) );

  CenterWindow();
  PostMessage(WM_COMMAND, CM_DO_COPY);

  return TRUE;  // Return TRUE  unless you set the focus to a control.
}
```

7. Next, add the following method immediately below the OnInitDialog method of CProgressDlg:

```
void CProgressDlg::DoCopy(void)
{
    char buffer[256];

    // Open the files.

    FILE *fp = fopen ( copyFrom, "r" );
    if ( fp == (FILE *)NULL ) {
        MessageBox("Unable to open input file!", "Error", MB_OK |
                  MB_APPLMODAL | MB_ICONEXCLAMATION );
        return;
    }

    // Get File size of input file.

    fseek ( fp, OL, SEEK_END );
    long tot_bytes = ftell( fp );
    fseek ( fp, OL, SEEK_SET );

    FILE *ofp = fopen ( copyTo, "w" );
    if ( ofp == (FILE *)NULL ) {
        fclose(fp);
        MessageBox("Unable to open output file!", "Error", MB_OK |
                  MB_APPLMODAL | MB_ICONEXCLAMATION );
        return;
    }

    // Loop through and copy the files.

    long bytes = 0;
    aborted   = 0;

    while ( !feof(fp) && !aborted ) {

        // Get a line from the input file.

        fgets ( buffer, 256, fp );

        // Write it to the output file.

        fprintf(ofp, "%s", buffer );

        // Update progress bar.

        bytes += strlen(buffer);
        int pct = (int) (100.0 * (double(bytes)/(double)tot_bytes));
        ::SendMessage( hWndPB, PBM_SETPOS, pct, 0 );

        // Check for other messages.

        MSG msg;
```

```
        if( PeekMessage( (LPMSG)&msg, (HWND)NULL, (WORD)NULL,
          (WORD)NULL, TRUE ) )
        {
            TranslateMessage( (LPMSG)&msg );
            DispatchMessage( (LPMSG)&msg );
        }

    }

    fclose(fp);
    fclose(ofp);
    GetDlgItem(IDCANCEL)->SetWindowText ( "Close" );
    ::SendMessage( hWndPB, PBM_SETPOS, 100, 0 );

}
```

8. In ClassWizard, click on the IDCANCEL object in the object list and the
COMMAND message in the message list. Click on the Add Function button
and add the following code to the OnCancel method of CProgressDlg:

```
void CProgressDlg::OnCancel()
{
  aborted = 1;

  CDialog::OnCancel();
}
```

9. Make the following changes to the constructor for CProgressDlg, the method
CProgressDlg::CProgressDlg:

```
CProgressDlg::CProgressDlg(CString& file1, CString& file2, CWnd*
pParent /*=NULL*/)
  : CDialog(CProgressDlg::IDD, pParent)
{
  copyFrom = file1;
  copyTo   = file2;
  aborted  = 0;

  //{{AFX_DATA_INIT(CProgressDlg)
    // NOTE: the ClassWizard will add member initialization here.
  //}}AFX_DATA_INIT
}
```

10. Make the following changes to the include file for the class, PROGRESS.H.
Note that the lines to modify or add in the header file are marked with bold
print.

```
const int CM_DO_COPY = 101;

class CProgressDlg : public CDialog
{
private:
  CString copyFrom;
  CString copyTo;
  int     aborted;
  HWND    hWndPB;
```

continued on next page

continued from previous page

```
// Construction
public:
    CProgressDlg(CString& file1, CString& file2, CWnd* pParent = NULL);
// standard constructor

// Dialog Data
    //{{AFX_DATA(CProgressDlg)
    enum { IDD = IDD_DIALOG10 };
        // NOTE: the ClassWizard will add data members here.
    //}}AFX_DATA

// Implementation
protected:
    virtual void DoDataExchange(CDataExchange* pDX);   // DDX/DDV support

    // Generated message map functions
    //{{AFX_MSG(CProgressDlg)
    virtual BOOL OnInitDialog();
    afx_msg void DoCopy(void);
    virtual void OnCancel();
    //}}AFX_MSG
    DECLARE_MESSAGE_MAP()
};
```

11. Modify the message map in PROGRESS.CPP to read as follows. Changes are marked in bold print.

```
BEGIN_MESSAGE_MAP(CProgressDlg, CDialog)
    //{{AFX_MSG_MAP(CProgressDlg)
    ON_COMMAND(CM_DO_COPY, DoCopy)
    //}}AFX_MSG_MAP
END_MESSAGE_MAP()
```

12. Reenter AppStudio and add a new menu with the caption Controls. Add a new menu item to the Controls menu with the identifier ID_COPY_FILE and the caption Copy File.

13. Select the CCh59App object from the drop-down list in ClassWizard. Click on the ID_COPY_FILE object in the object list and the COMMAND message in the message list. Click on the Add Function button and accept the name of OnCopyFile for the new method. Add the following code to the OnCopyFile method of CCh59App:

```
void CCh59App::OnCopyFile()
{
    CCopyDlg dlg;

    if ( dlg.DoModal() == IDOK ) {
        CProgressDlg pdlg(dlg.m_CopyFrom, dlg.m_CopyTo);
        pdlg.DoModal();
    }

}
```

14. Add the following include file line to the top of the source file CH59.CPP:

```
#include "copydlg.h"
#include "progress.h"
```

15. Compile and run the application.

How It Works

When the Copy File dialog is displayed, the user enters a file name to copy from and a destination file name to copy to. These file names are passed to the CProgressDialog, which uses them to set up the files to copy.

When the progress dialog is initially displayed, the OnInitDialog method of the dialog is called. The first thing that is done is to call the base class method. Next, a progress bar is created using the CreateWindowEx API function and the PROGRESS_CLASS class name. The method then centers the dialog on the screen using the CenterWindow function and then posts a message to itself using the PostMessage function of the API. This message is then "caught" by the DoCopy method of the CProgressDlg class and does the real work.

In the DoCopy method, the function first opens the first file for input and the second file for output. The routine then loops through the file one line at a time, copying the input file to the output file. The interesting work in DoCopy is done at the bottom of the method where the PeekMessage, TranslateMessage, and DispatchMessage API functions are called. This is called a preemptive loop because it temporarily takes control away from the dialog and passes it back to Windows. This is what the Yield function of the API should do, but doesn't.

In addition to copying the file, the function also shows how to update the progress bar control by sending a PBM_SETPOS message to the control.

Finally, the function closes the output file and is done. How does it handle users canceling the operation? Simple. The OnCancel method of the dialog catches any user Cancel event (clicking on the Cancel button or pressing [ESC]) and sets an internal flag in the dialog indicating that the user has aborted the process. This flag is checked each time through the loop, and if it is set, the process quits.

CHAPTER 6
EDIT
CONTROLS

6

EDIT CONTROLS

How do I...

Edit controls are one of the most commonly applied parts of the Windows user interface. Windows 95 provides a wide range of functionality that application developers can choose to add to their Windows applications. Unfortunately, many applications still look and feel as if they were developed for Windows 2.0 rather than a later version! In this chapter you will learn how to use the enhanced facilities of edit controls to make your application look and feel more professional.

6.1   Make an Edit Control Read-Only

Have you ever seen an application that lets you edit data on screen, then decides afterwards that the data is not editable, and lets you know with a message box? Learn how you can protect the data from the start, so that the user realizes that they can look, but not touch. Learn too, how you can make data editable or read-only on the fly, depending upon the state of a database or other data source.

6.2   Use an Edit Control to Get a Password

Make your secure applications even more secure, by not displaying the password as the user enters it. This How-To explains how you can implement a password protection dialog box that displays asterisks as the user enters his or her password.

6.3   Change the Background Color of an Edit Control

This How-To will teach you how you can make your important edit controls stand out from the crowd by changing the background and text colors of the control. Learn the right way to change colors to produce a consistent user interface that works properly and looks good.

6.4   Replace Text within an Edit Control

Learn how word processors replace the selected text in an edit control without having to retrieve and modify the entire contents of the control. This How-To shows how you can quickly and easily replace just the text that the user has selected.

6.5   Add an Undo Function to an Edit Control

Implement quick-and-easy undo in your application using the built-in functions of the Windows edit control. The simple undo provided by Windows may not be enough if you are writing the next great word processor or programmers' editor, but will be a great help to the user who accidentally pressed DEL while the entire contents of the edit control were selected.

6.6   Validate Input into an Edit Control

Windows applications generally do not validate user input until the user clicks the OK button in a dialog. This is for good reason, as the Windows API does not make validation of edit controls particularly easy. This section provides some practical demonstrations of how you can implement field validation in your application.

6.7   Cut and Paste Using the Clipboard

If you are going to implement a user-friendly application, you will want to allow the user to cut, copy, and paste text between your edit controls and the clipboard. In this How-To you will learn how you can quickly and simply add this functionality to your applications.

Table 6-1 lists the Windows APIs covered in this chapter.

ES_READONLY	EM_SETREADONLY	GetWindowLong	GetDlgItem
SendMessage	ES_PASSWORD	WM_CTLCOLOREDIT	SetTextColor
SetBkColor	CreateSolidBrush	EM_REPLACESEL	SendDlgItemMessage
EM_GETSEL	EN_CHANGE	EM_CANUNDO	EM_UNDO
SetWindowText	EnableWindow	CreateWindow	SetWindowLong
WM_CHAR	MessageBeep	CallWindowProc	EM_LIMITTEXT
WM_CUT	WM_COPY	WM_PASTE	WM_CLEAR
EnableMenuItem	IsClipboardFormatAvailable	WM_SIZE	MoveWindow

 Table 6-1 Windows APIs covered in Chapter 6

COMPLEXITY
EASY

6.1 How do I...
Make an edit control read-only?

Problem

At times in my application, I don't want the user to be able to change the information that I am displaying in an edit control. How can I make the edit control read-only, so that it can be scrolled if necessary but not modified?

Technique

Beginning with Windows 3.1, the ES_READONLY style was made available for edit controls. You can make an edit control read-only by adding this style to the resource script for an edit control, or you can add it to or remove it from an edit control at run-time by using the EM_SETREADONLY message.

Windows also provides a mechanism for you to test the state of an edit control, by looking at the control style to see if the ES_READONLY bit is set.

Steps

Open and run the sample application, READONLY.EXE. You will find this application in the CHAPTER6\READONLY directory on the CD that accompanies this book. Running this application opens a window with a menu. Select the Test menu item from the File menu to see the application work.

The application opens a small dialog with an edit control, a close button, and a button that can be used to toggle the edit control between read-only and editable. If the edit control is already read-only, the button will be titled Allow Edit. Clicking the button allows the edit control to be modified and changes the button text to Read-Only. You can toggle the edit control between the two states. Figure 6-1 shows the dialog box from this application.

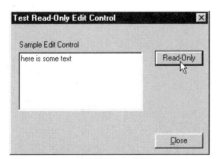

Figure 6-1 Changing the state of the read-only edit control

The following steps will guide you in reproducing this application.

1. Create a working directory for this application called READONLY. You will place all the source files for the application in this directory.

2. You will need a resource script for this application. The resource script will define the dialog, its controls, and buttons. The ES_READONLY style is applied to the edit control to make it initially read-only. If you would like the edit control to be initially modifiable, remove the ES_READONLY style. The application will detect which style is set when the dialog box is displayed. Create a new file using a text editor and name it READONLY.RC. Add the following resource script:

```
/* ------------------------------------------------------------------ */
/*                                                                    */
/* MODULE: READONLY.RC                                                */
/* PURPOSE: This resource script defines the menu and test dialog     */
/*          for the sample application.                               */
/*                                                                    */
/* ------------------------------------------------------------------ */

#include <windows.h>
#include "readonly.rh"

IDD_EDITTEST DIALOG 6, 15, 202, 119
STYLE DS_MODALFRAME | DS_3DLOOK | WS_POPUP | WS_VISIBLE |
      WS_CAPTION | WS_SYSMENU
CAPTION "Test Read-Only Edit Control"
FONT 8, "MS Sans Serif"
{
    PUSHBUTTON "&Close", IDCLOSE, 147, 100, 50, 14
    LTEXT "Sample Edit Control", -1, 8, 14, 74, 8
    EDITTEXT IDC_SAMPLEEDIT, 7, 25, 127, 54, ES_MULTILINE | ES_READONLY |
             ES_WANTRETURN | WS_BORDER | WS_TABSTOP
    DEFPUSHBUTTON "Read-Only", IDTOGGLE, 147, 24, 50, 14
}

IDM_TESTMENU MENU
{
    POPUP "&File"
    {
        MENUITEM "&Test", CM_TEST
        MENUITEM SEPARATOR
        MENUITEM "E&xit", CM_EXIT
    }
}

IDI_APPICON ICON "readonly.ico"
```

3. The resource script includes an icon for the application. Copy the icon from the CHAPTER6\READONLY directory on the CD-ROM. The file is called READONLY.ICO. If you don't have a CD drive, you can use a resource editor to create an icon for the application. Create a 32-by-32-pixel icon with up to 16 colors, and save it as READONLY.ICO.

4. The resource script that you created also includes a header file, READONLY.RH, which will define the resource identifiers for the application. Defining these values as constants in a separate file allows the application code to reference them. Create a file called READONLY.RH and add the following definitions:

```
#ifndef __READONLY_RH
/* ------------------------------------------------------------------ */
/*                                                                    */
/* MODULE: READONLY.RH                                                */
/* PURPOSE: This include file defines the resource identifiers used.  */
/*                                                                    */
/* ------------------------------------------------------------------ */
#define __READONLY_RH

#define IDM_TESTMENU    200
#define CM_TEST         101
#define CM_EXIT         102

#define IDD_EDITTEST    201
#define IDC_SAMPLEEDIT  101
#define IDTOGGLE        102
#define IDCLOSE         103

#define IDI_APPICON     201

#endif
```

5. Now create a new source file called READONLY.C. This is the main C source file for the application. Add the following lines to the top of the file. These lines include the Windows files necessary for compilation. They also define the preprocessor symbol STRICT, which allows strict type checking of Windows handles to be enforced in the C environment.

```
/* ------------------------------------------------------------------ */
/*                                                                    */
/* MODULE: READONLY.C                                                 */
/* PURPOSE: This sample application demonstrates how to make an edit */
/*          control read-only within your application, how to test    */
/*          to see if an edit control is read-only, and how to make  */
/*          a read-only edit control editable again.                  */
/*                                                                    */
/* ------------------------------------------------------------------ */

#define STRICT
#include <windows.h>
#include <winnt.h>
#include "readonly.rh"

static char *MainWindowClassName = "ReadonlyTestWindow";
HINSTANCE hInstance = NULL;
```

6. Add the IsReadOnly function to the same source file. This function returns
TRUE if the edit control has the ES_READONLY bit set in the style. The
GetWindowLong function is used to retrieve the style word for the control.
GWL_STYLE is a value defined in WINDOWS.H, which provides the offset
from the window handle to the style word.

```
/* ---------------------------------------------------------------- */
/* This function tests to see if an edit control is read-only. It    */
/* returns TRUE if it is, or false if it is not.                     */
/* ---------------------------------------------------------------- */
BOOL IsReadOnly(HWND hWnd)
{
    return (GetWindowLong(hWnd,GWL_STYLE) & ES_READONLY);
}
```

7. Next, add the following code. The ToggleReadonlyState function calls
IsReadOnly to get the current state of the edit control. It then uses SendMessage
to send the EM_SETREADONLY message to the edit control. The WPARAM
argument to SendMessage is TRUE (non-zero) if the ES_READONLY bit is to be
set and FALSE if the bit should be cleared. The function also toggles the text of
the button depending on the new state of the edit control.

```
/* ---------------------------------------------------------------- */
/* This function toggles the read-only state of the edit control.   */
/* If the edit control is read-only, it makes it editable; if it     */
/* can be edited, it makes it read-only.                             */
/* ---------------------------------------------------------------- */
void ToggleReadonlyState(HWND hWnd)
{
    HWND hChild;
    BOOL newStatus;

    if ((hChild = GetDlgItem(hWnd,IDC_SAMPLEEDIT)) != NULL)
    {
        newStatus = !IsReadOnly(hChild);
        SendMessage(hChild,EM_SETREADONLY,newStatus,0);
        if (newStatus)
            SetDlgItemText(hWnd,IDTOGGLE,"Allow Edit");
        else
            SetDlgItemText(hWnd,IDTOGGLE,"Read-Only");
    }
}
```

8. The next function to add is the callback procedure for the dialog. The
TestDialogProc function receives messages sent to the dialog. In response to
the WM_INITDIALOG message, the code tests to see the initial state of the
edit control. It does this by calling IsReadOnly, which you entered. The code
sets the text on the button depending on whether the control is read-only or
not. The function also responds to WM_COMMAND messages, closing the
dialog if the IDCLOSE message is received and toggling the edit control state
(and button text) when the IDTOGGLE message is received.

```
/* ---------------------------------------------------------------- */
/* This is the dialog function for the dialog. It handles clicks to  */
/* the read-only toggle button, and to the close button. It also     */
/* sets the initial text of the toggle button based upon the initial */
/* state of the edit control.                                        */
/* ---------------------------------------------------------------- */
BOOL CALLBACK TestDialogProc(HWND hWnd, UINT message,
                              WPARAM wParam, LPARAM lParam)
{
    HWND hChild;

    switch (message)
    {
        case WM_INITDIALOG:
            if ((hChild = GetDlgItem(hWnd,IDC_SAMPLEEDIT)) != NULL)
            {
                if (IsReadOnly(hChild))
                    SetDlgItemText(hWnd,IDTOGGLE,"Allow Edit");
                else
                    SetDlgItemText(hWnd,IDTOGGLE,"Read-Only");
            }
            break;
        case WM_COMMAND:
            if (wParam == IDTOGGLE)
                ToggleReadonlyState(hWnd);
            else
                if (wParam == IDCLOSE)
                    EndDialog(hWnd,1);
            break;
        default:
            return FALSE;
    }
    return TRUE;
}
```

9. The MainWndProc function that you will add next is the callback procedure
for the application window. This function responds to the menu and creates
the testing dialog when the Test menu item is selected. Add this function to
the same source file as the previous functions, READONLY.C.

```
/* ---------------------------------------------------------------- */
/* This function is the main window callback function which will be  */
/* called by Windows to process messages for our window.             */
/* ---------------------------------------------------------------- */
LPARAM CALLBACK MainWndProc(HWND hWnd, UINT message,
                             WPARAM wParam, LPARAM lParam)
{
    switch (message)
    {
        case WM_COMMAND:
            if (wParam == CM_TEST)
                DialogBox(hInstance,MAKEINTRESOURCE(IDD_EDITTEST),
                          hWnd,TestDialogProc);
            else
```

```
                              if (wParam == CM_EXIT)
                                   DestroyWindow(hWnd);
                         break;
                case WM_DESTROY:
                         PostQuitMessage(0);
                         break;
                default:
                         return DefWindowProc(hWnd, message, wParam, lParam);
        }
        return 0;
}
```

10. Now add the following three functions to the end of the same source file. These functions form the framework of the example applications used throughout this chapter. The InitApplication function registers the window class to be used by the application window. The InitInstance function creates the main window and makes sure that it is displayed.

The final function, WinMain, is the entry point for the application. This function calls InitApplication and InitInstance to set up the application, then processes messages until the program is closed. When you have added these three functions, you can compile and test the sample application.

```
/* --------------------------------------------------------------------- */
/* This function initializes a WNDCLASS structure and uses it to          */
/* register a class for our main window.                                  */
/* --------------------------------------------------------------------- */
BOOL InitApplication(HINSTANCE hInstance)
{
        WNDCLASS   wc;

        wc.style = 0;
        wc.lpfnWndProc = MainWndProc;
        wc.cbClsExtra = 0;
        wc.cbWndExtra = 0;
        wc.hInstance = hInstance;
        wc.hIcon = LoadIcon(NULL,MAKEINTRESOURCE(IDI_APPICON));
        wc.hCursor = LoadCursor(NULL, IDC_ARROW);
        wc.hbrBackground = (HBRUSH)(COLOR_WINDOW + 1);
        wc.lpszMenuName =  MAKEINTRESOURCE(IDM_TESTMENU);
        wc.lpszClassName = MainWindowClassName;

        return RegisterClass(&wc);
}


/* --------------------------------------------------------------------- */
/* This function creates an instance of our main window. The window       */
/* is given a class name and a title, and told to display anywhere.       */
/* The nCmdShow argument passed to the program determines how the         */
/* window will be displayed.                                              */
/* --------------------------------------------------------------------- */
BOOL InitInstance(HINSTANCE hInst, int nCmdShow)
{
```

```
    HWND hWnd;

    hInstance = hInst;      // Store in global variable.

    hWnd = CreateWindow(MainWindowClassName,"Edit Read-only demo",
                  WS_OVERLAPPEDWINDOW,CW_USEDEFAULT,
                  CW_USEDEFAULT,CW_USEDEFAULT,CW_USEDEFAULT,
                  NULL,NULL,hInstance,NULL);
    if (!hWnd)
        return FALSE;

    ShowWindow(hWnd, nCmdShow);
    UpdateWindow(hWnd);     // Send a WM_PAINT message.
    return TRUE;
}


/* ------------------------------------------------------------------ */
/* The main entry point for Windows applications. Check to see if     */
/* the main window class name has already been registered; if it has */
/* not, call InitApplication to register it. Call InitInstance to     */
/* create an instance of our main window, then pump messages until    */
/* the application is closed.                                         */
/* ------------------------------------------------------------------ */
int PASCAL WinMain(HINSTANCE hInstance, HINSTANCE hPrevInstance,
               LPSTR lpCmdLine, int nCmdShow)
{
    MSG msg;

    if (!FindWindow(MainWindowClassName,NULL))
        if (!InitApplication(hInstance))
            return (FALSE);

    if (!InitInstance(hInstance, nCmdShow))
        return (FALSE);

    while (GetMessage(&msg,NULL,NULL,NULL))
    {
        TranslateMessage(&msg);
        DispatchMessage(&msg);
    }
    return (msg.wParam);
}
```

11. Compile and run the application.

Comments

Try removing or adding the ES_READONLY style in the resource script, as described in step 2. You will notice that the dialog always opens with the correct button state, as the code tests the style of the edit control each time the dialog opens.

Using a read-only edit control lets users know that the text is unmodifiable the moment they attempt to change it. This avoids the frustration of modifying text, then finding that the changes won't be saved.

COMPLEXITY
EASY

6.2 How do I...
Use an edit control to get a password?

Problem

I need to get a password in my application. How do I retrieve the password without other people seeing what the user is entering?

Technique

The Windows API provides the facility to make an edit control into a password edit control. A password edit control replaces the characters the user enters with asterisks (*) so that other people cannot see what the password is. Figure 6-2 shows how a password control looks. The ES_PASSWORD style is usually applied to an edit control in a resource script. It specifies that the edit control is to behave as a password edit control.

Steps

Open and run the PASSWORD.EXE sample application. You will find this application in the CHAPTER6\PASSWORD directory on the CD that accompanies this book. When you select the Test menu item from the File menu of this application, a small dialog prompts you for a password. You can enter a sample password in the edit control and observe that only asterisks are displayed.

The sample application is not very secure. When you press the OK button, the password that you entered is displayed to prove that it was really stored. Don't use your system passwords when testing this application!

1. To start creating this application, make a new directory in which the source files you create will be stored. Call the directory PASSWORD.

2. Now create a resource file for the application. The key to this application is the ES_PASSWORD style, which is applied to the edit control in the following script. Use a text editor to enter this script and save the file as PASSWORD.RC.

Figure 6-2 Using an edit control with the ES_PASSWORD style

```
/* ----------------------------------------------------------- */
/*                                                             */
/* MODULE: PASSWORD.RC                                         */
/* PURPOSE: This resource script defines the menu and test dialog */
/*          for the sample application.                        */
/*                                                             */
/* ----------------------------------------------------------- */

#include <windows.h>
#include "password.rh"

IDD_EDITTEST DIALOG 6, 15, 202, 63
STYLE DS_MODALFRAME | DS_3DLOOK | WS_POPUP | WS_VISIBLE |
      WS_CAPTION | WS_SYSMENU
CAPTION "Test Password Edit Control"
FONT 8, "MS Sans Serif"
{
    LTEXT "Enter Password:", -1, 5, 12, 55, 8
    EDITTEXT IDC_SAMPLEEDIT, 72, 10, 109, 12, ES_PASSWORD |
             WS_BORDER | WS_TABSTOP
    DEFPUSHBUTTON "OK", IDOK, 27, 32, 50, 14
    PUSHBUTTON "Cancel", IDCANCEL, 125, 32, 50, 14
}

IDM_TESTMENU MENU
{
    POPUP "&File"
    {
        MENUITEM "&Test", CM_TEST
        MENUITEM SEPARATOR
        MENUITEM "E&xit", CM_EXIT
    }
}

IDI_APPICON ICON "password.ico"
```

3. You will need an icon for this application. If you have a CD-ROM drive, copy the file PASSWORD.ICO from the CHAPTER6\PASSWORD directory of the CD that comes with this book. If you don't have a CD-ROM drive, you can use a resource editor to create an icon. Create a 32-by-32-pixel, 16-color icon, and save it as PASSWORD.ICO.

4. The resource file also makes use of an include file to define the resource identifiers for the application. Using a text editor, create the file PASSWORD.RH and add the following definitions to the file. The identifiers declared in this file are used in the resource script, and they are also used to access the resources from within the application.

```
#ifndef __PASSWORD_RH
/* ----------------------------------------------------------- */
/*                                                             */
/* MODULE: PASSWORD.RH                                         */
/* PURPOSE: This include file defines the resource identifiers used. */
/*                                                             */
/* ----------------------------------------------------------- */
```

```
#define __PASSWORD_RH

#define IDM_TESTMENU     200
#define CM_TEST          101
#define CM_EXIT          102

#define IDD_EDITTEST     201
#define IDC_SAMPLEEDIT   101

#define IDI_APPICON      203

#endif
```

5. Now you are ready to create the main source file for the application. Create a new file and save it as PASSWORD.C. Add the following code fragment at the top of the file. The code includes the Windows header files and the resource identifier include file. It also defines the window class name for the main window.

```
/* ------------------------------------------------------------- */
/*                                                               */
/* MODULE: PASSWORD.C                                            */
/* PURPOSE: This small application demonstrates the use of the   */
/*          ES_PASSWORD style to hide edit control input for entry */
/*          of a password.                                       */
/*                                                               */
/* ------------------------------------------------------------- */

#define STRICT
#include <windows.h>
#include <winnt.h>
#include "password.rh"

static char *MainWindowClassName = "PasswordTestWindow";
HINSTANCE hInstance = NULL;
```

6. The next step is to add the TestDialogProc callback function. This function responds to the IDOK and IDCANCEL command messages that are sent when the user clicks a button in the dialog. When the user clicks the OK button, the code uses GetDlgItemText to retrieve the password from the edit control. In this sample application, the password is then displayed in a message box—not something that you will want to do in your production applications!

```
/* ------------------------------------------------------------- */
/* This dialog function handles the WM_COMMAND messages, responding */
/* to IDOK by displaying the password entered, then closing the  */
/* dialog.                                                       */
/* ------------------------------------------------------------- */
BOOL CALLBACK TestDialogProc(HWND hWnd, UINT message,
                             WPARAM wParam, LPARAM lParam)
{
    char buf[100];

    switch (message)
    {
        case WM_INITDIALOG:
```

```
                    return TRUE;
            case WM_COMMAND:
                    if ((wParam == IDOK) || (wParam == IDCANCEL))
                    {
                            if (wParam == IDOK)
                            {
                                    GetDlgItemText(hWnd,IDC_SAMPLEEDIT,buf,100);
                                    MessageBox(hWnd,buf,"Your Password",
                                            MB_ICONINFORMATION | MB_OK);
                            }
                            EndDialog(hWnd,wParam);
                    }
                    break;
            default:
                    return FALSE;
    }
    return TRUE;
}
```

7. Now add the MainWndProc function to the source file. This function
responds to messages sent to the main window of the application. In particular, it responds to the WM_COMMAND message IDTEST, creating and
displaying the dialog.

```
/* ---------------------------------------------------------------- */
/* This function is the main window callback function which will be  */
/* called by Windows to process messages for our window.             */
/* ---------------------------------------------------------------- */
LPARAM CALLBACK MainWndProc(HWND hWnd, UINT message,
                            WPARAM wParam, LPARAM lParam)
{
    switch (message)
    {
        case WM_COMMAND:
                if (wParam == CM_TEST)
                    DialogBox(hInstance,MAKEINTRESOURCE(IDD_EDITTEST),
                            hWnd,TestDialogProc);
                else
                        if (wParam == CM_EXIT)
                            DestroyWindow(hWnd);
                break;
        case WM_DESTROY:
                PostQuitMessage(0);
                break;
        default:
                return DefWindowProc(hWnd, message, wParam, lParam);
    }
    return 0;
}
```

8. The following three functions form the framework of the application. Add the
functions at the end of the same source file. The InitApplication function registers the window class of the application window. This function will only be
called if another window with the same class does not already exist. The
InitInstance function creates and displays the main window of the application

and also stores the instance handle so that it can be used when creating the dialog.

The final function, WinMain, is called by the Windows operating system to run the application. The function uses InitApplication and InitInstance to create the application. It then processes messages until the application completes.

```
/* ---------------------------------------------------------------- */
/* This function initializes a WNDCLASS structure and uses it to    */
/* register a class for our main window.                            */
/* ---------------------------------------------------------------- */
BOOL InitApplication(HINSTANCE hInstance)
{
    WNDCLASS   wc;

    wc.style = 0;
    wc.lpfnWndProc = MainWndProc;
    wc.cbClsExtra = 0;
    wc.cbWndExtra = 0;
    wc.hInstance = hInstance;
    wc.hIcon = LoadIcon(NULL,MAKEINTRESOURCE(IDI_APPICON));
    wc.hCursor = LoadCursor(NULL, IDC_ARROW);
    wc.hbrBackground = (HBRUSH)(COLOR_WINDOW + 1);
    wc.lpszMenuName =  MAKEINTRESOURCE(IDM_TESTMENU);
    wc.lpszClassName = MainWindowClassName;

    return RegisterClass(&wc);
}


/* ---------------------------------------------------------------- */
/* This function creates an instance of our main window. The window */
/* is given a class name and a title, and told to display anywhere. */
/* The nCmdShow argument passed to the program determines how the   */
/* window will be displayed.                                        */
/* ---------------------------------------------------------------- */
BOOL InitInstance(HINSTANCE hInst, int nCmdShow)
{
    HWND hWnd;

    hInstance = hInst;      // Store in global variable.

    hWnd = CreateWindow(MainWindowClassName,"Password Demo",
                  WS_OVERLAPPEDWINDOW,CW_USEDEFAULT,
                  CW_USEDEFAULT,CW_USEDEFAULT,CW_USEDEFAULT,
                  NULL,NULL,hInstance,NULL);
    if (!hWnd)
        return FALSE;

    ShowWindow(hWnd, nCmdShow);
    UpdateWindow(hWnd);     // Send a WM_PAINT message.
    return TRUE;
}
```

```
/* ------------------------------------------------------------- */
/* The main entry point for Windows applications. Check to see if   */
/* the main window class name has already been registered; if it has */
/* not, call InitApplication to register it. Call InitInstance to    */
/* create an instance of our main window, then pump messages until    */
/* the application is closed.                                         */
/* ------------------------------------------------------------- */
int PASCAL WinMain(HINSTANCE hInstance, HINSTANCE hPrevInstance,
                   LPSTR lpCmdLine, int nCmdShow)
{
    MSG msg;

    if (!FindWindow(MainWindowClassName,NULL))
        if (!InitApplication(hInstance))
            return (FALSE);

    if (!InitInstance(hInstance, nCmdShow))
        return (FALSE);

    while (GetMessage(&msg,NULL,NULL,NULL))
    {
        TranslateMessage(&msg);
        DispatchMessage(&msg);
    }
    return (msg.wParam);
}
```

9. Compile and run the application.

Comments

Use a password edit control to restrict access to important parts of your multiuser application or to retrieve the passwords necessary to access client-server databases.

COMPLEXITY
MODERATE

6.3 How do I...
Change the background color of an edit control?

Problem

I would like my edit control to stand out, so I want to change the background color of the control. I have tried using the SetBkColor function with the handle of the control, but it doesn't work as I expected. How can I change the color in a way that works?

Technique

You can change the colors of an edit control by processing the WM_CTLCOL-OREDIT message. Windows sends this message to your application when it is time to redraw the edit control. When your application receives this message, it can select the text and background color of the control and also return the handle of a brush that Windows will use when painting the control.

Changing Edit Control Colors

Usually when you use colors for elements of the Windows interface, you are urged to use the standard Windows colors that the user has selected from the Appearance tab of the Display property sheet. These colors have identifier values such as COLOR_WINDOW and COLOR_BTNTEXT, and you can get their RGB values by calling GetSysColor.

When you are changing edit control colors, you usually don't want to use the system colors—instead you are defining your own. However, do make sure that you set both the text and background colors of the control. If you change the background color of a control to green and leave the text color as the default, all may look fine on your computer. However, a user who has set up his or her system with green text will not be impressed when the text is invisible. Similarly, changing only the text color to gray will not work well if the user has selected a gray background for windows.

Steps

Open and run the CTLCOLOR application from the CHAPTER6\CTLCOLOR directory on the CD that accompanies this book. When you select the Test menu item from the File menu, a sample dialog like that shown in Figure 6-3 is displayed. The important field, Customer No., is highlighted using black text on a yellow background.

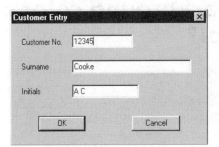

Figure 6-3 Changing the colors of an edit control

CHANGE THE BACKGROUND COLOR OF AN EDIT CONTROL?

The other edit controls are displayed using the standard colors that you have selected for your system.

Follow these steps to re-create this application. Along the way you will learn how to change the colors used in an edit control.

1. Create a new directory and call it CTLCOLOR. You will use this directory to hold the source files for this application. When you are prompted to create or copy a file, place it in this directory.

2. You will need an icon for this application. Copy the file CTLCOLOR.ICO from the CHAPTER6\CTLCOLOR directory on the CD into your working directory. If you don't have a CD-ROM drive, you can create an icon yourself, using a resource editor. Create a 32-by-32-pixel icon, with up to 16 colors. Save the icon as CTLCOLOR.ICO.

3. Now create a resource script for the application. The resource script defines the menu for the application, includes the application icon, and defines the dialog that is displayed. Use a text editor to create a new file and call it CTL-COLOR.RC. Type the following text into the file:

```
/* ------------------------------------------------------------- */
/*                                                                */
/* MODULE: CTLCOLOR.RC                                            */
/* PURPOSE: This resource script defines the menu and test dialog */
/*          for the sample application.                           */
/*                                                                */
/* ------------------------------------------------------------- */

#include <windows.h>
#include "ctlcolor.rh"

IDD_EDITTEST DIALOG 6, 15, 202, 111
STYLE DS_MODALFRAME | DS_3DLOOK | WS_POPUP | WS_VISIBLE |
      WS_CAPTION | WS_SYSMENU
CAPTION "Customer Entry"
FONT 8, "MS Sans Serif"
{
    LTEXT "Customer No.", -1, 10, 12, 45, 8
    LTEXT "Surname", -1, 10, 35, 32, 8
    LTEXT "Initials", -1, 10, 58, 22, 8
    EDITTEXT IDC_CUSTNO, 63, 10, 63, 12, WS_BORDER | WS_TABSTOP
    EDITTEXT IDC_SURNAME, 63, 33, 123, 12
    EDITTEXT IDC_INITIALS, 63, 56, 69, 12
    DEFPUSHBUTTON "OK", IDOK, 27, 85, 50, 14
    PUSHBUTTON "Cancel", IDCANCEL, 125, 85, 50, 14
}

IDM_TESTMENU MENU
{
    POPUP "&File"
    {
        MENUITEM "&Test", CM_TEST
        MENUITEM SEPARATOR
        MENUITEM "E&xit", CM_EXIT
```

continued on next page

continued from previous page

```
            }
    }

    IDI_APPICON ICON "ctlcolor.ico"
```

4. The next file that you will need is the include file that defines the resource
   identifiers. This file is used by both the resource script and the main C source
   file. Create a new file and add the following text. Save the file as
   CTLCOLOR.RH.

```
#ifndef __CTLCOLOR_RH
/* ------------------------------------------------------------------ */
/*                                                                    */
/* MODULE: CTLCOLOR.RH                                                */
/* PURPOSE: This include file defines the resource identifiers used.  */
/*                                                                    */
/* ------------------------------------------------------------------ */
#define __CTLCOLOR_RH

#define IDM_TESTMENU    200
#define CM_TEST         101
#define CM_EXIT         102

#define IDD_EDITTEST    201
#define IDC_CUSTNO      101
#define IDC_SURNAME     102
#define IDC_INITIALS    103

#define IDI_APPICON     203

#endif
```

5. Create the main source file for the application and call it CTLCOLOR.C. Type
   the following code in at the start of the file. Notice the global variable hBrush.
   This variable will be used to hold a brush for painting the background of the
   edit control.

```
/* ------------------------------------------------------------------ */
/*                                                                    */
/* MODULE: CTLCOLOR.C                                                 */
/* PURPOSE: This application demonstrates how to handle the           */
/*          WM_CTLCOLOREDIT message to change the colors of an edit   */
/*          control.                                                  */
/*                                                                    */
/* ------------------------------------------------------------------ */

#define STRICT
#include <windows.h>
#include <winnt.h>
#include "ctlcolor.rh"

static char *MainWindowClassName = "ColorTestWindow";
HBRUSH      hBrush = NULL;
HINSTANCE   hInstance = NULL;
```

6. Now add the SetEditColor function. This function will be called whenever Windows sends a WM_CTLCOLOREDIT message to the window. The code compares the handle of the edit control that Windows supplies (in the LPARAM argument of the message) to that of the edit control. If this is the edit control that you want a different background color for, then the code does three things. First it uses SetTextColor to set the text color of the control. It then calls SetBkColor to set the RGB values of the background. Finally, it returns the handle of the brush that Windows can use when painting the control.

```
/* --------------------------------------------------------------- */
/* Set the colors to be used in the edit control. Returns NULL if  */
/* the control is not the right one.                               */
/* --------------------------------------------------------------- */
HBRUSH SetEditColor(HWND hWndOwner, HDC hDCEdit, HWND hWndEdit)
{
    if (hWndEdit == GetDlgItem(hWndOwner,IDC_CUSTNO))
    {
        SetTextColor(hDCEdit,RGB(0,0,0));    // black text.
        SetBkColor(hDCEdit,RGB(255,255,0)); // yellow background.
        return hBrush;
    }
    else
        return NULL;
}
```

7. The next function to add to the file is the TestDialogProc function that is listed next. This callback function is called by Windows whenever a message is sent to the dialog. It responds to the WM_INITDIALOG message by creating the brush to use when painting the control. The code uses the CreateSolidBrush API function to create a brush with the solid color closest to the requested RGB values.

The following code uses the RGB macro to specify a bright yellow brush. The brush is released by calling DeleteObject when the window is destroyed. In response to the WM_CTLCOLOREDIT message, the code calls the SetEditColor function that you wrote previously. The LPARAM argument specifies the handle of the edit control, and the WPARAM argument provides a handle to the device context.

```
/* --------------------------------------------------------------- */
/* The dialog function for the dialog handles all the messages.    */
/* It creates a brush when it receives WM_INITDIALOG, and deletes  */
/* the brush on WM_DESTROY. It returns the brush in WM_CTLCOLOREDIT. */
/* --------------------------------------------------------------- */
BOOL CALLBACK TestDialogProc(HWND hWnd, UINT message,
                             WPARAM wParam, LPARAM lParam)
{
    HDC       hDCEdit;
    HWND      hWndEdit;

    switch (message)
    {
```

```
          case WM_INITDIALOG:
                  hBrush = CreateSolidBrush(RGB(255,255,0));
                  return TRUE;
          case WM_COMMAND:
                  if ((wParam == IDOK) || (wParam == IDCANCEL))
                      EndDialog(hWnd,wParam);
                  break;
          case WM_CTLCOLOREDIT:
                  hWndEdit = (HWND)lParam;
                  hDCEdit = (HDC)wParam;
                  return (BOOL)SetEditColor(hWnd,hDCEdit,hWndEdit);
          case WM_DESTROY:
                  DeleteObject(hBrush);
                  break;
          default:
                  return FALSE;
      }
      return TRUE;
}
```

8. Finally, add the following four functions to the source code file. These functions provide the framework of the application. The MainWndProc function responds to messages sent to the main window. The code in this function displays the dialog when the user selects the Test menu item, and it closes the window and application when the user selects the Exit menu item. The InitApplication function registers the window class that is used for the main window of the application, and the InitInstance function creates and displays the main window.

The last function is the WinMain function, which is the main entry point of the application. This code initializes the application, then processes messages until the application is closed.

```
/* ---------------------------------------------------------------- */
/* This function is the main window callback function which will be  */
/* called by Windows to process messages for our window.            */
/* ---------------------------------------------------------------- */
LPARAM CALLBACK MainWndProc(HWND hWnd, UINT message,
                             WPARAM wParam, LPARAM lParam)
{
    switch (message)
    {
        case WM_COMMAND:
                if (wParam == CM_TEST)
                    DialogBox(hInstance,MAKEINTRESOURCE(IDD_EDITTEST),
                              hWnd,TestDialogProc);
                else
                    if (wParam == CM_EXIT)
                        DestroyWindow(hWnd);
                break;
        case WM_DESTROY:
                PostQuitMessage(0);
                break;
```

```
        default:
                return DefWindowProc(hWnd, message, wParam, lParam);
    }
    return 0;
}


/* ---------------------------------------------------------------- */
/* This function initializes a WNDCLASS structure and uses it to    */
/* register a class for our main window.                            */
/* ---------------------------------------------------------------- */
BOOL InitApplication(HINSTANCE hInstance)
{
    WNDCLASS   wc;

    wc.style = 0;
    wc.lpfnWndProc = MainWndProc;
    wc.cbClsExtra = 0;
    wc.cbWndExtra = 0;
    wc.hInstance = hInstance;
    wc.hIcon = LoadIcon(NULL,MAKEINTRESOURCE(IDI_APPICON));
    wc.hCursor = LoadCursor(NULL, IDC_ARROW);
    wc.hbrBackground = (HBRUSH)(COLOR_WINDOW + 1);
    wc.lpszMenuName =  MAKEINTRESOURCE(IDM_TESTMENU);
    wc.lpszClassName = MainWindowClassName;

    return RegisterClass(&wc);
}


/* ---------------------------------------------------------------- */
/* This function creates an instance of our main window. The window */
/* is given a class name and a title, and told to display anywhere. */
/* The nCmdShow argument passed to the program determines how the   */
/* window will be displayed.                                        */
/* ---------------------------------------------------------------- */
BOOL InitInstance(HINSTANCE hInst, int nCmdShow)
{
    HWND hWnd;

    hInstance = hInst;           // Store in global variable.

    hWnd = CreateWindow(MainWindowClassName,"Edit Color Demo",
                    WS_OVERLAPPEDWINDOW,CW_USEDEFAULT,
                    CW_USEDEFAULT,CW_USEDEFAULT,CW_USEDEFAULT,
                    NULL,NULL,hInstance,NULL);
    if (!hWnd)
        return FALSE;

    ShowWindow(hWnd, nCmdShow);
    UpdateWindow(hWnd);          // Send a WM_PAINT message.
    return TRUE;
}
```

continued on next page

continued from previous page

```
/* ----------------------------------------------------------------- */
/* The main entry point for Windows applications. Check to see if    */
/* the main window class name has already been registered; if it has*/
/* not, call InitApplication to register it. Call InitInstance to    */
/* create an instance of our main window, then pump messages until   */
/* the application is closed.                                        */
/* ----------------------------------------------------------------- */
int PASCAL WinMain(HINSTANCE hInstance, HINSTANCE hPrevInstance,
                   LPSTR lpCmdLine, int nCmdShow)
{
    MSG msg;

    if (!FindWindow(MainWindowClassName,NULL))
        if (!InitApplication(hInstance))
            return (FALSE);

    if (!InitInstance(hInstance, nCmdShow))
        return (FALSE);

    while (GetMessage(&msg,NULL,NULL,NULL))
    {
        TranslateMessage(&msg);
        DispatchMessage(&msg);
    }
    return (msg.wParam);
}
```

9. Compile and run the application.

Comments

Responding to WM_CTLCOLOREDIT to change the colors of an edit control can be useful to highlight important controls. Try to keep your use of unusual colored controls to a minimum, however. Having a few colored controls is more effective than an entire collection, and also honors the user's preferences.

COMPLEXITY
EASY

6.4   How do I...
Replace text within an edit control?

Problem

How can I replace the selected text in the edit control with other text (for instance, if I implement a replace function in my application)?

Technique

The Windows API provides the EM_REPLACESEL message, which lets you replace areas of selected text with other text. The message assumes that an area of text is already selected. If nothing is selected, then your replacement text will be inserted at the current caret position.

Steps

Open and run the REPLACE.EXE application from the CHAPTER6\REPLACE directory on the CD that accompanies this book. When you select the Test menu item from the File menu, a dialog like that shown in Figure 6-4 will appear.

The dialog contains two edit controls, the second of which will already contain some sample text. You can type into the first edit control, then select some text in the second control and click the Replace button. The selected text in the second control will be replaced with the contents of the first edit control. If you click the Replace button with no text selected, the replacement text will simply be inserted at the current position of the caret.

The following steps will guide you through production of this example application.

1. Create a directory, and call it REPLACE. Use this directory as your working directory throughout this exercise.

2. Now you will need an icon for the application. Copy the file REPLACE.ICO from the CHAPTER6\REPLACE directory on the CD into your working directory. If you don't have a CD-ROM drive, you can use a resource editor to create an icon. Create a 32-by-32-pixel icon with 16 colors. Save the icon as REPLACE.ICO.

3. The next step is to create a resource script for use by the application. The resource script will define the dialog shown in Figure 6-4 and will also ensure that the application icon is bound to the application. Use a text editor to create a file and enter the following lines. Save the file as REPLACE.RC.

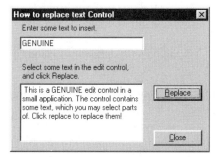

Figure 6-4 Replacing text in an edit control

```
/* ------------------------------------------------------------------ */
/*                                                                    */
/* MODULE: REPLACE.RC                                                 */
/* PURPOSE: This resource script defines the menu and test dialog     */
/*          for the sample application.                               */
/*                                                                    */
/* ------------------------------------------------------------------ */

#include <windows.h>
#include "replace.rh"

IDD_EDITTEST DIALOG 6, 15, 202, 119
STYLE DS_MODALFRAME | DS_3DLOOK | WS_POPUP | WS_VISIBLE |
      WS_CAPTION | WS_SYSMENU
CAPTION "How to replace text Control"
FONT 8, "MS Sans Serif"
{
    LTEXT "Enter some text to insert.", -1, 10, 2, 79, 8
    LTEXT "Select some text in the edit control, and click Replace.",
          -1, 10, 38, 112, 16
    EDITTEXT IDC_REPLACE, 8, 14, 128, 12
    EDITTEXT IDC_SAMPLEEDIT, 8, 57, 127, 54, ES_MULTILINE | ES_WANTRETURN |
             WS_BORDER | WS_TABSTOP
    PUSHBUTTON "&Replace", IDREPLACE, 146, 59, 50, 14
    PUSHBUTTON "&Close", IDCLOSE, 146, 100, 50, 14
}


IDM_TESTMENU MENU
{
    POPUP "&File"
    {
        MENUITEM "&Test", CM_TEST
        MENUITEM SEPARATOR
        MENUITEM "E&xit", CM_EXIT
    }
}


IDI_APPICON ICON "replace.ico"
```

4. The resource script you just entered requires an include file, REPLACE.RH.
This file defines the identifiers used for the dialog and icon, so they can be
accessed by both the resource script and the application code. Create a new
file and call it REPLACE.RH. Type the following definitions into the file:

```
#ifndef __REPLACE_RH
/* ------------------------------------------------------------------ */
/*                                                                    */
/* MODULE: REPLACE.RH                                                 */
/* PURPOSE: This include file defines the resource identifiers used.  */
/*                                                                    */
/* ------------------------------------------------------------------ */
#define __REPLACE_RH

#define IDM_TESTMENU    200
#define CM_TEST         101
#define CM_EXIT         102
```

```
#define IDD_EDITTEST    201
#define IDC_REPLACE     101
#define IDC_SAMPLEEDIT  102
#define IDREPLACE       103
#define IDCLOSE         104

#define IDI_APPICON     202

#endif
```

5. You are now ready to start entering the source code for the file. The example application is written in standard C, but the messages that are sent to the edit controls can be sent from any programming language. Use a text editor to create a new file, and save it as REPLACE.C. Type the following lines in at the top of the file:

```
/* ------------------------------------------------------------ */
/*                                                              */
/* MODULE: REPLACE.C                                            */
/* PURPOSE: This sample application demonstrates how to replace */
/*          selected text from within your application with other */
/*          text. This application gets text from the control   */
/*          IDC_REPLACE, and uses it to replace whatever text    */
/*          is selected in the IDC_SAMPLEEDIT control.           */
/*                                                              */
/* ------------------------------------------------------------ */

#define STRICT
#include <windows.h>
#include <winnt.h>
#include "replace.rh"

static char *MainWindowClassName = "ReplaceTestWindow";
HINSTANCE hInstance = NULL;
```

6. Now add the TestDialogProc function, which is listed next. This callback function will be called by Windows when there is a message to be processed by the dialog. The function handles the WM_INITDIALOG message, inserting some sample text into the lower edit control. The function also responds to the WM_COMMAND messages generated when the user clicks on a button in the dialog. In response to the IDREPLACE command, the code uses GetDlgItemText to retrieve the text in the upper edit control, then sends an EM_REPLACESEL message to the lower edit control. This message causes the edit control to replace any selected text with the string. If no text is selected, it inserts the string at the current caret position.

```
/* ------------------------------------------------------------ */
/* This is the dialog function for the dialog. It returns TRUE to */
/* the WM_INITDIALOG message to accept the default focused control. */
/* It handles the IDREPLACE button by using EM_REPLACESEL to replace */
/* the selected text in one edit control with the contents of the */
/* other. It handles IDCLOSE by calling EndDialog.             */
/* ------------------------------------------------------------ */
```

continued on next page

continued from previous page

```
BOOL CALLBACK TestDialogProc(HWND hWnd, UINT message,
                             WPARAM wParam, LPARAM lParam)
{
    char buf[100];

    switch (message)
    {
        case WM_INITDIALOG:
            SetDlgItemText(hWnd,IDC_SAMPLEEDIT,
                             " This is a sample edit control"
                             " in a small application. The"
                             " control contains some text,"
                             " which you may select parts of."
                             " Click replace to replace them!");
            return TRUE;
        case WM_COMMAND:
            if (wParam == IDREPLACE)
            {
                GetDlgItemText(hWnd,IDC_REPLACE,buf,100);
                SendDlgItemMessage(hWnd,IDC_SAMPLEEDIT,
                             EM_REPLACESEL,0,(LPARAM)buf);
            }
            else
                if (wParam == IDCLOSE)
                    EndDialog(hWnd,1);
            break;
        default:
            return FALSE;
    }
    return TRUE;
}
```

7. Now add the callback function for the application window. The MainWndProc function handles the messages sent to the application window. It responds to the menu selections that the user makes. When the user selects the Test item from the File menu, the application receives a CM_TEST command message. The following code responds by displaying the demonstration dialog.

```
/* ---------------------------------------------------------------- */
/* This function is the main window callback function which will be  */
/* called by Windows to process messages for our window.            */
/* ---------------------------------------------------------------- */
LPARAM CALLBACK MainWndProc(HWND hWnd, UINT message,
                            WPARAM wParam, LPARAM lParam)
{
    switch (message)
    {
        case WM_COMMAND:
            if (wParam == CM_TEST)
                DialogBox(hInstance,MAKEINTRESOURCE(IDD_EDITTEST),
                        hWnd,TestDialogProc);
            else
                if (wParam == CM_EXIT)
```

```
                    DestroyWindow(hWnd);
                break;
        case WM_DESTROY:
                PostQuitMessage(0);
                break;
        default:
                return DefWindowProc(hWnd, message, wParam, lParam);
    }
    return 0;
}
```

8. Add the final three functions to the same source file, REPLACE.C. When you have added this code, you will be ready to compile and test the project. These three functions form the basic framework of the sample application. The WinMain function receives control when the application is started. This function calls InitApplication to create a class for the main window. It then calls InitInstance to create and display the main window of the application. The function processes messages until the application is closed.

```
/* ------------------------------------------------------------------ */
/* This function initializes a WNDCLASS structure and uses it to      */
/* register a class for our main window.                              */
/* ------------------------------------------------------------------ */
BOOL InitApplication(HINSTANCE hInstance)
{
    WNDCLASS   wc;

    wc.style = 0;
    wc.lpfnWndProc = MainWndProc;
    wc.cbClsExtra = 0;
    wc.cbWndExtra = 0;
    wc.hInstance = hInstance;
    wc.hIcon = LoadIcon(NULL,MAKEINTRESOURCE(IDI_APPICON));
    wc.hCursor = LoadCursor(NULL, IDC_ARROW);
    wc.hbrBackground = (HBRUSH)(COLOR_WINDOW + 1);
    wc.lpszMenuName =  MAKEINTRESOURCE(IDM_TESTMENU);
    wc.lpszClassName = MainWindowClassName;

    return RegisterClass(&wc);
}


/* ------------------------------------------------------------------ */
/* This function creates an instance of our main window. The window   */
/* is given a class name and a title, and told to display anywhere.   */
/* The nCmdShow argument passed to the program determines how the     */
/* window will be displayed.                                          */
/* ------------------------------------------------------------------ */
BOOL InitInstance(HINSTANCE hInst, int nCmdShow)
{
    HWND hWnd;

    hInstance = hInst;       // Store in global variable.
```

continued on next page

continued from previous page

```
        hWnd = CreateWindow(MainWindowClassName,"Edit replace demo",
                        WS_OVERLAPPEDWINDOW,CW_USEDEFAULT,
                        CW_USEDEFAULT,CW_USEDEFAULT,CW_USEDEFAULT,
                        NULL,NULL,hInstance,NULL);
        if (!hWnd)
            return FALSE;

        ShowWindow(hWnd, nCmdShow);
        UpdateWindow(hWnd);        // Send a WM_PAINT message.
        return TRUE;
    }


    /* ------------------------------------------------------------- */
    /* The main entry point for Windows applications. Check to see if */
    /* the main window class name has already been registered; if it has */
    /* not, call InitApplication to register it. Call InitInstance to */
    /* create an instance of our main window, then pump messages until */
    /* the application is closed.                                    */
    /* ------------------------------------------------------------- */
    int PASCAL WinMain(HINSTANCE hInstance, HINSTANCE hPrevInstance,
                    LPSTR lpCmdLine, int nCmdShow)
    {
        MSG msg;

        if (!FindWindow(MainWindowClassName,NULL))
            if (!InitApplication(hInstance))
                return (FALSE);

        if (!InitInstance(hInstance, nCmdShow))
            return (FALSE);

        while (GetMessage(&msg,NULL,NULL,NULL))
        {
            TranslateMessage(&msg);
            DispatchMessage(&msg);
        }
        return (msg.wParam);
    }
```

9. Compile and run the application.

Comments

You might decide that the replace function will only be available if the user has some text selected. To determine if this is the case, you can use the EM_GETSEL message to find out the start and end character positions of the selection in the edit control. If the two values are different, then some text is selected. If the two positions are the same, then there is no selection, and you can disable the replace function. You can learn more about the EM_GETSEL message in How-To 6.7.

COMPLEXITY
MODERATE

6.5   How do I...
Add an undo function to an edit control?

Problem

I would like to add an undo function to my application's edit control. How can I accomplish this?

Technique

The Windows API implements a single-level undo buffer for edit controls. Implementing single-level undo, then, is simply a matter of sending the right messages to the controls to get it to work.

There are three important messages that you need to know about to implement single-level undo in your application. The first of these, EN_CHANGE, is a notification message that the edit control sends to the owning dialog or window when the text of the edit control has changed. The sample application uses this message as the ideal opportunity to check the status of the undo function.

The next important message is the EM_CANUNDO message. An application can send this message to an edit control to see if the undo function will have any effect if it is used. SendMessage will return FALSE if the EM_CANUNDO message is sent to an edit control that has nothing to undo, or immediately after the text is set using SetWindowText. This allows the application program to disable the undo function where it doesn't make any sense to undo.

The third message is the EM_UNDO message. When your application sends this message to an edit control, the edit control will undo the last change that the user made. This may be as small as removing a single letter, or as large as undoing the deletion of the entire contents of the control.

Steps

Open the UNDO.EXE sample application that is in the CHAPTER6\UNDO directory on the CD. When you run this application, you will see a window with a menu. Select the Test item from the File menu to display a dialog. The edit control in the dialog initially contains text, and the Undo button is initially disabled. You can type text into the edit control and delete parts or all of the text. After each operation, try using the Undo button to restore the contents of the edit control to what they were after the last operation. Figure 6-5 shows this application in operation, with the Undo button enabled.

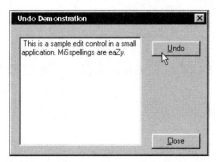

Figure 6-5 Using the Undo sample
application

The Undo button stays enabled after you have used it to undo an action. If you try clicking it again, you will see that it undoes the undo action—it functions as a Redo button.
The following steps will guide you in implementing this application.

1. Create a new directory and call it UNDO. You will use this as your working
directory for this application, placing all the source code files in this directory.

2. Use a text editor to create a new file and save it as UNDO.RC. Type the following resource script into the file. This script defines the menu for the main
window and also defines the test dialog for the application. You can see the
definition of the multiline edit control and the Undo button.

```
/* ------------------------------------------------------------------- */
/*                                                                     */
/* MODULE: UNDO.RC                                                     */
/* PURPOSE: This resource script defines the menu and test dialog      */
/*          for the sample application.                                */
/*                                                                     */
/* ------------------------------------------------------------------- */

#include <windows.h>
#include "undo.rh"

IDD_EDITTEST DIALOG 6, 15, 202, 119
STYLE DS_MODALFRAME | DS_3DLOOK | WS_POPUP | WS_VISIBLE |
      WS_CAPTION | WS_SYSMENU
CAPTION "Undo Demonstration"
FONT 8, "MS Sans Serif"
{
    EDITTEXT IDC_SAMPLEEDIT, 8, 11, 127, 100, ES_MULTILINE | ES_WANTRETURN |
             WS_BORDER | WS_TABSTOP
    PUSHBUTTON "&Undo", IDUNDO, 146, 15, 50, 14, WS_DISABLED | WS_TABSTOP
    PUSHBUTTON "&Close", IDCLOSE, 146, 100, 50, 14
}

IDM_TESTMENU MENU
{
```

ADD AN UNDO FUNCTION TO AN EDIT CONTROL?

```
    POPUP "&File"
    {
        MENUITEM "&Test", CM_TEST
        MENUITEM SEPARATOR
        MENUITEM "E&xit", CM_EXIT
    }
}

IDI_APPICON ICON "undo.ico"
```

3. You will need an icon for the application. Copy the file UNDO.ICO from the CHAPTER6\UNDO directory of the CD into your working directory. If you don't have access to a CD-ROM drive, use a resource editor to create a 32-by-32-pixel icon in 16 colors. Save the icon as UNDO.ICO.

4. You will also need the file included by the resource script, UNDO.RH. This file defines the resource identifiers needed to compile the script. While these values could be hard-coded in the resource script, having them in a separate file allows them to be accessed by the application source code. It also reduces the effort of changing two sets of code should you ever need to add or remove resources. Create a new file called UNDO.RH and add the following definitions.

```
#ifndef __UNDO_RH
/* ---------------------------------------------------------------- */
/*                                                                  */
/* MODULE: UNDO.RH                                                  */
/* PURPOSE: This include file defines the resource identifiers used. */
/*                                                                  */
/* ---------------------------------------------------------------- */
#define __UNDO_RH

#define IDM_TESTMENU      200
#define CM_TEST           101
#define CM_EXIT           102

#define IDD_EDITTEST      201
#define IDC_SAMPLEEDIT    102
#define IDUNDO            103
#define IDCLOSE           104

#define IDI_APPICON       202

#endif
```

5. Now you can create the main C source file for the project. This example is coded in straight C, but the use of the EM_UNDO and EM_CANUNDO messages applies to all programming environments. Use a text editor to create a new source file and call it UNDO.C. Type the following statements at the top of the file. This code declares the global variables used by the application and also includes the files necessary to compile the project. In addition, the STRICT preprocessor symbol is defined, allowing more stringent type checking of the Windows types used in the application.

```
/* ------------------------------------------------------------------ */
/*                                                                    */
/* MODULE: UNDO.C                                                     */
/* PURPOSE: This sample application demonstrates how to use the       */
/*          edit control messages, EM_CANUNDO and EM_UNDO.            */
/*                                                                    */
/* ------------------------------------------------------------------ */

#include <windows.h>
#include <winnt.h>

#include "undo.rh"

static char *MainWindowClassName = "UndoTestWindow";
HINSTANCE hInstance = NULL;
```

6. Add the following code to the same source file. The ProcessChangeMessage
function will be called when a EN_CHANGE notification message is received
from the edit control, signaling that the user has changed the contents of the
edit control in some way. This function sends the EM_CANUNDO message to
the edit control. This message returns non-zero (TRUE) if the last change can
be undone and a zero (FALSE) value if the change cannot be undone. The
code then calls EnableWindow to enable or disable the Undo button depending upon the result.

```
/* ------------------------------------------------------------------ */
/* In response to an EN_CHANGE message from the edit control, this    */
/* function queries the edit control to see if the changes can be     */
/* undone. If the changes can be undone, it enables the Undo button;  */
/* otherwise it disables the Undo button.                             */
/* ------------------------------------------------------------------ */
void ProcessChangeMessage(HWND hWnd)
{
    BOOL canUndo;
    HWND hChild;

    // Find if the edit control can undo the change.
    canUndo = (BOOL)SendDlgItemMessage(hWnd,IDC_SAMPLEEDIT,
                                    EM_CANUNDO,0,0);

    // Get a handle to the button, and enable or disable it.
    hChild = GetDlgItem(hWnd,IDUNDO);
    if (canUndo)
        EnableWindow(hChild,TRUE);
    else
        EnableWindow(hChild,FALSE);
}
```

7. The next function to add is the TestDialogProc function. This callback function
handles messages sent to the dialog. In particular, it handles WM_INITDIALOG
to set the initial text in the edit control. It also responds to WM_COMMAND
messages to process the edit control notifications and the user clicking the buttons.
In response to the IDUNDO command generated when the Undo button is
clicked, the following code sends the EM_UNDO message to the edit control.

This example uses SendDlgItemMessage to send the message, specifying the dialog handle and the control ID of the edit control. Alternatively, you can use GetDlgItem to retrieve the handle of the edit control and call SendMessage to send the EM_UNDO message.

```
/* ---------------------------------------------------------------- */
/* This is the dialog function for the dialog. It returns TRUE to   */
/* the WM_INITDIALOG message to accept the default focused control. */
/* The function handles the EN_CHANGE notification by using the     */
/* EM_CANUNDO message to see if the edit control can undo changes.  */
/* If it can, the Undo button is enabled; otherwise it is grayed.   */
/* If the Undo button is clicked, the EM_UNDO message is used to    */
/* undo the changes.                                                */
/* ---------------------------------------------------------------- */
BOOL CALLBACK TestDialogProc(HWND hWnd, UINT message,
                             WPARAM wParam, LPARAM lParam)
{
    switch (message)
    {
        case WM_INITDIALOG:
            SetDlgItemText(hWnd,IDC_SAMPLEEDIT,
                              " This is a sample edit control"
                              " in a small application. Make"
                              " some changes, and click Undo.");
            return TRUE;
        case WM_COMMAND:
            if (HIWORD(wParam) == EN_CHANGE)
                ProcessChangeMessage(hWnd);
            else
                if (wParam == IDUNDO)
                    SendDlgItemMessage(hWnd,IDC_SAMPLEEDIT,EM_UNDO,0,0);
                else
                    if (wParam == IDCLOSE)
                        EndDialog(hWnd,1);
            break;
        default:
            return FALSE;
    }
    return TRUE;
}
```

8. You can now add the remaining functions used in this example. Add the following code to the same source file, UNDO.C. When you have added this code, you can compile and run the example application. The MainWndProc function is a callback function that responds to messages sent to the application's main window. It responds to the Test and Exit menu items, displaying the test dialog and closing the application, respectively.

The InitApplication function is used to initialize and register the window class used for the main application window. It will only be called if the class is not already registered. The InitInstance function is used to create and display the main window, using the CreateWindow and ShowWindow functions. Finally, WinMain forms the entry point for the application, setting up the application and processing messages until it is complete.

```
/* ------------------------------------------------------------------ */
/* This function is the main window callback function which will be   */
/* called by Windows to process messages for our window.             */
/* ------------------------------------------------------------------ */
LPARAM CALLBACK MainWndProc(HWND hWnd, UINT message,
                            WPARAM wParam, LPARAM lParam)
{
    switch (message)
    {
        case WM_COMMAND:
            if (wParam == CM_TEST)
                DialogBox(hInstance,MAKEINTRESOURCE(IDD_EDITTEST),
                          hWnd,TestDialogProc);
            else
                if (wParam == CM_EXIT)
                    DestroyWindow(hWnd);
            break;
        case WM_DESTROY:
            PostQuitMessage(0);
            break;
        default:
            return DefWindowProc(hWnd, message, wParam, lParam);
    }
    return 0;
}


/* ------------------------------------------------------------------ */
/* This function initializes a WNDCLASS structure and uses it to      */
/* register a class for our main window.                             */
/* ------------------------------------------------------------------ */
BOOL InitApplication(HINSTANCE hInstance)
{
    WNDCLASS  wc;

    wc.style = 0;
    wc.lpfnWndProc = MainWndProc;
    wc.cbClsExtra = 0;
    wc.cbWndExtra = 0;
    wc.hInstance = hInstance;
    wc.hIcon = LoadIcon(NULL,MAKEINTRESOURCE(IDI_APPICON));
    wc.hCursor = LoadCursor(NULL, IDC_ARROW);
    wc.hbrBackground = (HBRUSH)(COLOR_WINDOW + 1);
    wc.lpszMenuName =  MAKEINTRESOURCE(IDM_TESTMENU);
    wc.lpszClassName = MainWindowClassName;

    return RegisterClass(&wc);
}


/* ------------------------------------------------------------------ */
/* This function creates an instance of our main window. The window   */
/* is given a class name and a title, and told to display anywhere.   */
/* The nCmdShow argument passed to the program determines how the     */
/* window will be displayed.                                         */
/* ------------------------------------------------------------------ */
```

```
BOOL InitInstance(HINSTANCE hInst, int nCmdShow)
{
    HWND hWnd;

    hInstance = hInst;              // Store in global variable.

    hWnd = CreateWindow(MainWindowClassName,"Edit Undo Demo",
                    WS_OVERLAPPEDWINDOW,CW_USEDEFAULT,
                    CW_USEDEFAULT,CW_USEDEFAULT,CW_USEDEFAULT,
                    NULL,NULL,hInstance,NULL);
    if (!hWnd)
        return FALSE;

    ShowWindow(hWnd, nCmdShow);
    UpdateWindow(hWnd);             // Send a WM_PAINT message.
    return TRUE;
}


/* ---------------------------------------------------------------- */
/* The main entry point for Windows applications. Check to see if   */
/* the main window class name has already been registered; if it    */
/* has not, call InitApplication to register it. Call InitInstance  */
/* to create an instance of our main window, then pump messages     */
/* until the application is closed.                                 */
/* ---------------------------------------------------------------- */
int PASCAL WinMain(HINSTANCE hInstance, HINSTANCE hPrevInstance,
                LPSTR lpCmdLine, int nCmdShow)
{
    MSG msg;

    if (!FindWindow(MainWindowClassName,NULL))
        if (!InitApplication(hInstance))
            return (FALSE);

    if (!InitInstance(hInstance, nCmdShow))
        return (FALSE);

    while (GetMessage(&msg,NULL,NULL,NULL))
    {
        TranslateMessage(&msg);
        DispatchMessage(&msg);
    }
    return (msg.wParam);
}
```

9. Compile and run the application.

Comments

Implementing single-level undo in an edit control is a relatively simple, if little known, technique. Use it to raise your application out of the ordinary. To make your application really professional, you may want to implement a multiple-level undo scheme. Such a scheme will allow the user to undo a series of changes. How you choose to implement this will really depend on your application—a word processor will implement this very differently than a text editor, and a painting application might do it differently again. Here are some tips for implementing multiple-level undo in your application:

- Find out where the changes are occurring. In a simple project, handling the EN_CHANGE notification message might be sufficient. In a more complex application, you will want to handle all the extra functions independently—cut, copy, paste, and delete. In a word processor, you will need to handle formatting as well.

- Quantify the changes. In a large document you will want to store only the deleted or changed text. Storing several copies of the entire document is not practical.

- Maintain a FIFO (first in-first out) list or array of modifications, dropping old modifications off the list as new ones are added.

COMPLEXITY
MODERATE

6.6   How do I...
Validate input into an edit control?

Problem

How can I validate the keys that a user is typing into an edit control, so that only the correct data is entered?

Technique

Validation of data is not as simple a matter for Windows application programmers as it once was for programmers using MS-DOS. DOS applications typically had control of the system and would not allow the user to add text unless it was valid. In the Windows model, the operating system itself facilitates user input, and the application program is typically not involved until input is complete, usually as a result of the user clicking the OK button.

It is, however, possible to implement some checks on an edit control while the user is entering data. It is also possible to change the format of the data if required. There are a number of window and edit control messages that you can use to monitor the state of the edit control, and act appropriately.

In the example application for this How-To, you will learn how you can control what characters are entered in an edit control through the use of a technique called subclassing.

What is Subclassing?

Typically, all the messages for a class of Windows control (such as the EDIT or BUTTON classes) are sent to a single window procedure for that class. This procedure responds to the messages by implementing the behavior that we expect of the control.

You can change the behavior of an individual control by subclassing it. When you do this, you stop Windows from calling the normal procedure for the class, and have it call a procedure that you define instead. In this procedure, you can then handle the messages for the control and implement the type of behavior that you require.

You will probably only want to change the control's response to a few of the messages that it receives. You can handle the other messages by calling the original class procedure for those messages.

The GetWindowLong function is used with the GWL_WNDPROC argument to retrieve the address of the original class procedure, and the SetWindowLong function is used to store your new function. To call the old procedure, use the CallWindowProc function. Note that you must restore the old window procedure before the control is destroyed.

Steps

Open and run the VALIDATE.EXE sample application. You will find this application in the CHAPTER6\VALIDATE directory on the CD that comes with this book. Select the Text menu item from the File menu. You will see the dialog that is shown in Figure 6-6.

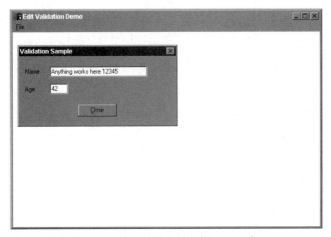

Figure 6-6 Dialog with validated edit controls

The dialog has two controls. The Name edit control lets you enter a 30-character name containing any combination of characters. The Age edit control is a validated field. It will only let you enter numeric characters into the control. When you try to insert a character such as a letter, the control just beeps. This is a very simple form of validation, and because the contents of the edit control are always valid (either blank or numeric), the application does not need to validate the contents of the control as the user moves off it. Performing validation as the user moves off the control is discussed at the end of this How-To.

Follow these steps to reproduce this example application.

1. Create a directory to contain your working files for this project. Call this directory VALIDATE.

2. You will need an icon for your application. You can copy the file VALIDATE.ICO from the CHAPTER6\VALIDATE directory on the CD that accompanies this book. If you don't have a CD drive, use a resource editor to create a 32-by-32-pixel icon with 16 colors or less. Save the icon as VALIDATE.ICO.

3. Now create the resource script for the application. Use a text editor to create a new file and save it as VALIDATE.RC. Type the following lines into the file. This script defines the dialog for the application, the menu, and the application icon.

```
/* ------------------------------------------------------------------ */
/*                                                                    */
/* MODULE: VALIDATE.RC                                                */
/* PURPOSE: This resource script defines the menu and test dialog     */
/*          for the sample application.                               */
/*                                                                    */
/* ------------------------------------------------------------------ */

#include <windows.h>
#include "validate.rh"

IDD_EDITTEST DIALOG 6, 15, 202, 79
STYLE DS_MODALFRAME | DS_3DLOOK | WS_POPUP | WS_VISIBLE |
      WS_CAPTION | WS_SYSMENU
CAPTION "Validation Sample"
FONT 8, "MS Sans Serif"
{
    LTEXT "Name", -1, 7, 13, 23, 8
    LTEXT "Age", -1, 7, 33, 18, 8
    EDITTEXT IDC_NAME, 39, 11, 126, 12
    EDITTEXT IDC_AGE, 39, 31, 24, 12
    PUSHBUTTON "&Close", IDCLOSE, 76, 55, 50, 14
}

IDM_TESTMENU MENU
{
    POPUP "&File"
    {
        MENUITEM "&Test", CM_TEST
```

```
        MENUITEM SEPARATOR
        MENUITEM "E&xit", CM_EXIT
    }
}


IDI_APPICON ICON "validate.ico"
```

4. In order to compile the resource script, you will also need the VALIDATE.RH include file that is referenced in the script. This file defines the resource identifiers and is also included by the main source code that you will write shortly. Create a new file and call it VALIDATE.RH. Add the identifiers listed here:

```
#ifndef __VALIDATE_RH
/* ------------------------------------------------------------- */
/*                                                               */
/* MODULE: VALIDATE.RH                                           */
/* PURPOSE: This include file defines the resource identifiers used. */
/*                                                               */
/* ------------------------------------------------------------- */
#define __VALIDATE_RH

#define IDM_TESTMENU      200
#define CM_TEST           101
#define CM_EXIT           102

#define IDD_EDITTEST      201
#define IDC_NAME          101
#define IDC_AGE           102
#define IDCLOSE           104

#define IDI_APPICON       202

#endif
```

5. Now you are ready to create the main C source file for this application. This example uses straight C and the API so you can see clearly how to use the API functions. You could reproduce the effect of this code in virtually any development environment. Create a new file and call it VALIDATE.C. Type the following code in at the top of the file. This code fragment includes the files needed to compile this program and also defines some global variables. Of interest among these variables is oldAgeProc, which will be used to store the address of the original edit control class procedure.

```
/* ------------------------------------------------------------- */
/*                                                               */
/* MODULE: VALIDATE.C                                            */
/* PURPOSE: This application demonstrates how to subclass an edit */
/*          control to perform validation of user input.         */
/*                                                               */
/* ------------------------------------------------------------- */

#define STRICT
#include <windows.h>
#include <winnt.h>
```

```
#include "validate.rh"

static char *MainWindowClassName = "ValidateTestWindow";
HINSTANCE hInstance = NULL;
LONG        oldAgeProc = 0;
```

6. Now add the following function to the source file. The AgeWndProc is a call-back procedure that will replace the default class window procedure for the Age edit control. This procedure handles each WM_CHAR message that is sent to the edit control. It only allows characters in the range 0 to 9 and the BACKSPACE key (VK_BACK). All other characters cause the application to beep using MessageBeep. The WM_CHAR messages that are allowed through, along with any other messages, are sent to the original edit control procedure by calling CallWindowProc and passing the arguments and the address of the procedure.

```
/* ---------------------------------------------------------------- */
/* This window procedure is used to handle messages from an edit    */
/* control which is to be validated.                                */
/* ---------------------------------------------------------------- */
LPARAM CALLBACK AgeWndProc(HWND hWnd, UINT message,
                           WPARAM wParam, LPARAM lParam)
{
    // Validate character input.
    if ((message == WM_CHAR) && (wParam != VK_BACK) &&
        ((wParam < '0') || (wParam > '9')))
    {
        MessageBeep(-1);
        return 0;
    }

    // For other events, call the original edit control procedure.
    return CallWindowProc((WNDPROC)oldAgeProc,
                          hWnd,message,wParam,lParam);
}
```

7. The next function to add is the TestDialogProc function. This callback function will process the messages sent to the dialog. In particular, the code processes the WM_INITDIALOG and WM_DESTROY messages, as well as the IDCLOSE command message generated when the close button is pressed.

In response to the WM_INITDIALOG message, the following code sends the EM_LIMITTEXT message to both the name and age edit controls, limiting the number of characters that can be entered to 30 and 3 characters, respectively. It then uses SetWindowLong with the GWL_WNDPROC argument to replace the edit control's window procedure with the AgeWndProc function that you entered earlier. This function returns the old window procedure, which is then stored in the oldAgeProc variable. Farther down the function is the response to the WM_DESTROY message. In response to this message, SetWindowLong is used again, this time restoring the old window procedure before the edit control is destroyed.

```
/* ------------------------------------------------------------ */
/* This is the dialog function for the dialog. It returns TRUE to   */
/* the WM_INITDIALOG message to accept the default focused control. */
/* In addition, it subclasses the age edit control, so that messages*/
/* for that control go to AgeWndProc rather than the default class  */
/* procedure. This function responds to WM_DESTROY by removing the  */
/* subclassing, restoring the original window procedure.            */
/* ------------------------------------------------------------ */
BOOL CALLBACK TestDialogProc(HWND hWnd, UINT message,
                             WPARAM wParam, LPARAM lParam)
{
    HWND hChild;

    switch (message)
    {
        case WM_INITDIALOG:
            // Set the maximum name length.
            SendDlgItemMessage(hWnd,IDC_NAME,EM_LIMITTEXT,30,0);

            /* Subclass the edit control - replace the default
             procedure with your own - for this control only. */
            hChild = GetDlgItem(hWnd,IDC_AGE);
            if (hChild)
            {
                SendMessage(hChild,EM_LIMITTEXT,3,0);
                oldAgeProc = SetWindowLong(hChild,
                                    GWL_WNDPROC,
                                    (LONG)AgeWndProc);
            }
            return TRUE;
        case WM_COMMAND:
            if (wParam == IDCLOSE)
                EndDialog(hWnd,TRUE);
            return TRUE;
        case WM_DESTROY:
            // Remove the subclassing.
            hChild = GetDlgItem(hWnd,IDC_AGE);
            SetWindowLong(hChild,GWL_WNDPROC,
                        oldAgeProc);
            return TRUE;
    }
    return FALSE;
}
```

8. Add the following code to the same source file, VALIDATE.C. The next four functions are all considered together, as they form a simple framework for your application. The MainWndProc function handles the messages sent to the main window of the application, activating the test dialog when the user selects the Test menu item and closing the application when the user selects the Exit menu item from the File menu. The InitApplication function is used to register the window class that is used by the main window. It is called only if a window of this class does not already exist. The InitInstance function is used to create and display the main window of the application using CreateWindow and ShowWindow.

Finally, the WinMain function receives control from Windows when the application is started. It is this function that calls the earlier functions to set up and run the application.

```
/* ---------------------------------------------------------------- */
/* This function is the main window callback function which will be  */
/* called by Windows to process messages for our window.            */
/* ---------------------------------------------------------------- */
LPARAM CALLBACK MainWndProc(HWND hWnd, UINT message,
                            WPARAM wParam, LPARAM lParam)
{
    switch (message)
    {
        case WM_COMMAND:
            if (wParam == CM_TEST)
                DialogBox(hInstance,MAKEINTRESOURCE(IDD_EDITTEST),
                        hWnd,TestDialogProc);
            else
                if (wParam == CM_EXIT)
                    DestroyWindow(hWnd);
            break;
        case WM_DESTROY:
            PostQuitMessage(0);
            break;
        default:
            return DefWindowProc(hWnd, message, wParam, lParam);
    }
    return 0;
}


/* ---------------------------------------------------------------- */
/* This function initializes a WNDCLASS structure and uses it to    */
/* register a class for our main window.                            */
/* ---------------------------------------------------------------- */
BOOL InitApplication(HINSTANCE hInstance)
{
    WNDCLASS  wc;

    wc.style = 0;
    wc.lpfnWndProc = MainWndProc;
    wc.cbClsExtra = 0;
    wc.cbWndExtra = 0;
    wc.hInstance = hInstance;
    wc.hIcon = LoadIcon(NULL,MAKEINTRESOURCE(IDI_APPICON));
    wc.hCursor = LoadCursor(NULL, IDC_ARROW);
    wc.hbrBackground = (HBRUSH)(COLOR_WINDOW + 1);
    wc.lpszMenuName =  MAKEINTRESOURCE(IDM_TESTMENU);
    wc.lpszClassName = MainWindowClassName;

    return RegisterClass(&wc);
}
```

```
/* ------------------------------------------------------------- */
/* This function creates an instance of our main window. The window */
/* is given a class name and a title, and told to display anywhere. */
/* The nCmdShow argument passed to the program determines how the */
/* window will be displayed.                                     */
/* ------------------------------------------------------------- */
BOOL InitInstance(HINSTANCE hInst, int nCmdShow)
{
    HWND hWnd;

    hInstance = hInst;      // Store in global variable.

    hWnd = CreateWindow(MainWindowClassName,"Edit Validation Demo",
                   WS_OVERLAPPEDWINDOW,CW_USEDEFAULT,
                   CW_USEDEFAULT,CW_USEDEFAULT,CW_USEDEFAULT,
                   NULL,NULL,hInstance,NULL);
    if (!hWnd)
        return FALSE;

    ShowWindow(hWnd, nCmdShow);
    UpdateWindow(hWnd);      // Send a WM_PAINT message.
    return TRUE;
}


/* ------------------------------------------------------------- */
/* The main entry point for Windows applications. Check to see if */
/* the main window class name has already been registered; if it */
/* has not, call InitApplication to register it. Call InitInstance */
/* to create an instance of our main window, then pump messages */
/* until the application is closed.                              */
/* ------------------------------------------------------------- */
int PASCAL WinMain(HINSTANCE hInstance, HINSTANCE hPrevInstance,
                LPSTR lpCmdLine, int nCmdShow)
{
    MSG msg;

    if (!FindWindow(MainWindowClassName,NULL))
        if (!InitApplication(hInstance))
            return (FALSE);

    if (!InitInstance(hInstance, nCmdShow))
        return (FALSE);

    while (GetMessage(&msg,NULL,NULL,NULL))
    {
        TranslateMessage(&msg);
        DispatchMessage(&msg);
    }
    return (msg.wParam);
}
```

9. Compile and run the application.

Comments

This example shows in a very simple way how you can use subclassing to alter the behavior of a control and provide field-level validation. The same technique can be effectively applied to implement more complex field validation techniques, including those that actually retrieve and reformat the text buffer of the edit control. If your application modifies the edit control buffer on the fly using SetWindowText or the WM_SETTEXT message, you should also send the EM_SETMODIFY message to the control to maintain its state correctly.

A particular concern of many people is how to validate the field when the user tries to move off the field. In general, this is not recommended in Windows applications, as it is contrary to the nature of the interface. A user may start entering data in a field and then decide "I'll just check this box too...", and this is quite acceptable in the Windows paradigm. The data is not considered complete until the user clicks the OK button or an equivalent. Most field validation routines force the user to remain on that field until it is complete, and this is not compatible with the Windows user interface.

If you are implementing a traditional data entry application using Windows, you may be able to justify field-level validation. The WM_KILLFOCUS message, which is sent to a control immediately before it loses the keyboard focus, is suitable for use in validation. However, an application must not display a message box or other window, or attempt to change the focus back to the control while processing this message. Instead, use PostMessage to send a user-defined message to your window procedure. When it receives this user-defined message, your application is safe to display an error, if required, and return the focus to the edit control.

6.7 How do I... Cut and paste using the clipboard?

Problem

I know that the user can press CTRL-C to copy, CTRL-V to paste, and CTRL-X to cut text, but I would like to make my application a little more intuitive to use. How can I put these functions on the menu and have the edit control in the window respond to them?

Technique

You can very readily get an edit control to cut, copy, and paste data, and also remove text from the control without putting it in the clipboard (often called clear or delete). You can accomplish this by sending the messages WM_CUT, WM_COPY, WM_PASTE, and WM_CLEAR, respectively, to the end of the edit control. The cut, copy, and clear messages work on any selected text in the control, and the paste message inserts any text in the clipboard into the current position in the edit control, replacing any selected text. Thus an application that implements an edit menu need only respond to the menu commands by sending the appropriate message to the control—a trivial task.

What if the user has not selected any text in the control? It doesn't make sense to have the cut, copy, and clear options available if there is nothing selected, as they will have no effect. Similarly, it is not really appropriate to have the paste option available if there is no text in the clipboard to be inserted.

The steps in this How-To serve two purposes. They show you how to send the cut, copy, clear, and paste messages to an edit control, and they also teach you how to respond to the WM_INITMENU message in order to enable and disable menu items appropriately. You will find more about enabling and disabling menu items in How-To 8.1.

Steps

Open and run the PASTE.EXE sample application from the CHAPTER6\CUTPASTE directory on the CD that accompanies this book. The application opens a window that contains a multiline edit control. The control lets you type in up to 32K of text, and it operates very similarly to the Notepad application that comes with Windows 95. In addition to a simple File menu, there is an Edit menu containing the items Cut, Copy, Delete, and Paste. The Delete menu item implements the WM_CLEAR behavior discussed earlier. Type some text into the edit control and select the items from the menu to see how they behave. When you have selected some text in the control, the Cut, Copy, and Delete menu items are enabled; otherwise they are grayed. Similarly, the Paste menu item is only enabled when there is text in the clipboard. Figure 6-7 shows this application in action.

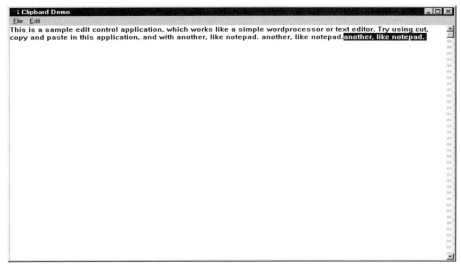

Figure 6-7 Using cut, copy, and paste in an edit control

The following steps explain how this application is implemented.

1. Create a new directory and name it CUTPASTE. This directory will be your
working directory while you create this application. Place all the source files in
this directory.

2. Now use a text editor to create a new file, and save it as PASTE.RC. Type the
following resource script into the file. This resource script defines the File and
Edit menus used in the application and also includes the application icon.

```
/* ------------------------------------------------------------------ */
/*                                                                    */
/* MODULE: PASTE.RC                                                   */
/* PURPOSE: This resource script defines the menu and test dialog     */
/*          for the sample application.                               */
/*                                                                    */
/* ------------------------------------------------------------------ */

#include <windows.h>
#include "paste.rh"

IDM_TESTMENU MENU
{
    POPUP "&File"
    {
        MENUITEM "E&xit", CM_EXIT
    }
    POPUP "&Edit"
    {
        MENUITEM "Cu&t", CM_CUT
        MENUITEM "&Copy", CM_COPY
        MENUITEM "&Delete", CM_CLEAR
        MENUITEM "&Paste", CM_PASTE
    }
}


IDI_APPICON ICON "paste.ico"
```

3. You will need an icon file for this application. If you have a CD drive, copy the
file PASTE.ICO from the CHAPTER6\CUTPASTE directory on the CD and
place it in your working directory. If you don't have a CD drive, you can use a
resource editor to create a 32-by-32-pixel icon, with 16 colors or less. Save the
icon as PASTE.ICO.

4. The resource script also includes a file called PASTE.RH. This file will define
the identifier names given to the resources, so they can be referenced from
within the C program source. Create a new file with a text editor and call it
PASTE.RH. Put the following definitions into this file:

```
#ifndef __PASTE_RH
/* ------------------------------------------------------------------ */
/*                                                                    */
/* MODULE: PASTE.RH                                                   */
/* PURPOSE: This include file defines the resource identifiers used.  */
/*                                                                    */
/* ------------------------------------------------------------------ */
```

```
#define __PASTE_RH

#define IDM_TESTMENU    200
#define CM_EXIT         101
#define CM_CUT          102
#define CM_COPY         103
#define CM_CLEAR        104
#define CM_PASTE        105

#define IDC_SAMPLEEDIT  201

#define IDI_APPICON     202

#endif
```

5. You are now ready to start writing the C source code for this application. Like many other examples in this book, this application is written in C. You can implement the same functionality just as easily in most other application development environments, using the same API calls and messages.

Create a new file and call it PASTE.C. Type the following code fragment in at the start of the file. This code includes the files necessary for compilation and defines the STRICT preprocessor symbol so that window and menu handle errors are caught at compile time, rather than causing problems later. The code also declares several global variables, including hEdit, which will hold the handle of the multiline edit control.

```
/* ------------------------------------------------------------------- */
/*                                                                      */
/* MODULE: PASTE.C                                                      */
/* PURPOSE: This sample application demonstrates how to use the         */
/*          Windows messages, WM_CUT, WM_COPY and WM_PASTE to           */
/*          implement clipboard cut copy and paste from an edit         */
/*          control.                                                    */
/*                                                                      */
/* ------------------------------------------------------------------- */

#define STRICT
#include <windows.h>
#include <winnt.h>
#include "paste.rh"

static char *MainWindowClassName = "PasteTestWindow";
HINSTANCE hInstance = NULL;
HWND      hEdit = NULL;
```

6. Add the CreateEditControl function to the same source file. This function uses CreateWindow to create a new window with the class name EDIT—an edit control. The size of the window is not set in this function, as later code will respond to WM_SIZE messages to ensure that the edit control fills the entire client area of the window.

```
/* ------------------------------------------------------------- */
/* This function uses CreateWindow to create an edit control within */
/* the main window. It adds some sample text to the edit control.   */
/* ------------------------------------------------------------- */
HWND CreateEditControl(HWND hWndParent)
{
        HWND hChild;

        // Create the edit control using CreateWindow.
        hChild = CreateWindow("EDIT",NULL,
                              WS_CHILD | WS_VISIBLE | WS_VSCROLL |
                              ES_LEFT | ES_MULTILINE | ES_AUTOVSCROLL,
                              0,0,0,0, // size will be set by WM_SIZE.
                              hWndParent,(HMENU)IDC_SAMPLEEDIT,
                              hInstance,NULL);

        // Place some sample text in the control.
        SetWindowText(hChild,"This is a sample edit control "
                              "application, which works like "
                              "a simple wordprocessor or text "
                              "editor. Try using cut, copy "
                              "and paste in this application, "
                              "and with another, like notepad. ");
        return hChild;
}
```

7. The next function to add is the SetupEditMenu function. This function will be called whenever the application receives a WM_INITMENU message. This message is sent when the user clicks or otherwise attempts to pull down a menu. The message is sent to the application window before any menus are displayed, so it is an ideal opportunity to enable or disable menu items depending upon the application state.

The following code checks to see if any text is selected by sending the EM_GETSEL message to the edit control. The edit control responds to this message by returning the current start and end positions of the text selection, with the start position in the low word of the return value and the end position in the high word. If the two values are the same, no text is selected, and the menu items are disabled by calling EnableMenuItem with the MF_GRAYED flag. If some text is selected, the menu items are enabled by calling the same function with the MF_ENABLED flag. See How-To 8.1 for a discussion of the various menu item flags.

A second test is made to determine whether the Paste menu item should be enabled. The IsClipboardFormatAvailable function is called with the CF_TEXT parameter. This function will return TRUE if some data of the requested format is available on the clipboard; it will return FALSE if no data is available, or if it is in the wrong format.

```
/* ---------------------------------------------------------------- */
/* This function checks to see if any text is selected in the edit   */
/* control. If it is, then cut, copy and delete are enabled in the   */
/* menu; otherwise they are grayed. It also checks to see if there   */
/* is any compatible text in the clipboard. If there is, then the    */
/* paste option is enabled; otherwise it is grayed.                  */
/* ---------------------------------------------------------------- */
void SetupEditMenu(HMENU hMenu, HWND hEdit)
{
    DWORD selection;
    int   selStart, selEnd;

    // See if any text is selected.
    selection = SendMessage(hEdit,EM_GETSEL,0,0);
    selStart = LOWORD(selection);
    selEnd = HIWORD(selection);
    if (selStart != selEnd)
    {
        // Text is selected - enable menu items.
        EnableMenuItem(hMenu,CM_CUT,MF_BYCOMMAND | MF_ENABLED);
        EnableMenuItem(hMenu,CM_COPY,MF_BYCOMMAND | MF_ENABLED);
        EnableMenuItem(hMenu,CM_CLEAR,MF_BYCOMMAND | MF_ENABLED);
    }
    else
    {
        // No text selected - disable items.
        EnableMenuItem(hMenu,CM_CUT,MF_BYCOMMAND | MF_GRAYED);
        EnableMenuItem(hMenu,CM_COPY,MF_BYCOMMAND | MF_GRAYED);
        EnableMenuItem(hMenu,CM_CLEAR,MF_BYCOMMAND | MF_GRAYED);
    }

    // Now see if there is any text in the clipboard.
    if (IsClipboardFormatAvailable(CF_TEXT))
        EnableMenuItem(hMenu,CM_PASTE,MF_BYCOMMAND | MF_ENABLED);
    else
        EnableMenuItem(hMenu,CM_PASTE,MF_BYCOMMAND | MF_GRAYED);
}
```

8. Now add the callback function to process the messages sent to the window. The MainWndProc function responds to a number of messages and calls DefWindowProc for those messages that it does not handle. In particular, the function responds to WM_CREATE by calling CreateEditControl and to WM_INITMENU by calling SetupEditMenu. The function also handles WM_SIZE messages sent to the window. In response to these messages, the code calls the MoveWindow API function, resizing the edit control to take the entire area of the window.

In response to the WM_COMMAND messages sent when the user selects a menu option, the code sends the appropriate messages to the edit control. WM_PASTE is sent for the Paste menu item and WM_CUT for the Cut menu item. The Copy menu item causes WM_COPY to be sent, and the Delete menu item causes WM_CLEAR to be sent. None of these messages requires any parameters, so the LPARAM and WPARAM arguments to SendMessage are left as zeros.

```
/* ------------------------------------------------------------------ */
/* This function is the main window callback function which will be   */
/* called by Windows to process messages for our window.              */
/* ------------------------------------------------------------------ */
LPARAM CALLBACK MainWndProc(HWND hWnd, UINT message,
                            WPARAM wParam, LPARAM lParam)
{
    switch (message)
    {
        case WM_CREATE:
            hEdit = CreateEditControl(hWnd);
            return 0;
        case WM_INITMENU:
            SetupEditMenu((HMENU)wParam,hEdit);
        case WM_COMMAND:
            switch (wParam)
            {
                case CM_CUT:
                    SendMessage(hEdit,WM_CUT,0,0);
                    return 0;
                case CM_COPY:
                    SendMessage(hEdit,WM_COPY,0,0);
                    return 0;
                case CM_CLEAR:
                    SendMessage(hEdit,WM_CLEAR,0,0);
                    return 0;
                case CM_PASTE:
                    SendMessage(hEdit,WM_PASTE,0,0);
                    return 0;
                case CM_EXIT:
                    DestroyWindow(hWnd);
                    return 0;
            }
            break;
        case WM_DESTROY:
            PostQuitMessage(0);
            return 0;
        case WM_SETFOCUS:
            SetFocus(hEdit);
            return 0;
        case WM_SIZE:
            MoveWindow(hEdit,0,0,LOWORD(lParam),
                    HIWORD(lParam),TRUE);
            return 0;
    }
    return DefWindowProc(hWnd, message, wParam, lParam);
}
```

9. Now add the following three functions to the same source file. These three functions provide the framework for the application, setting up the window and processing messages until the application completes. The InitApplication function is used to register the window class for the main window, and the InitInstance function creates and displays an instance of the main window. The WinMain function serves as the entry point for the application and also uses GetMessage and DispatchMessage to service the message queue.

```c
/* ---------------------------------------------------------------- */
/* This function initializes a WNDCLASS structure and uses it to    */
/* register a class for our main window.                            */
/* ---------------------------------------------------------------- */
BOOL InitApplication(HINSTANCE hInstance)
{
    WNDCLASS  wc;

    wc.style = 0;
    wc.lpfnWndProc = MainWndProc;
    wc.cbClsExtra = 0;
    wc.cbWndExtra = 0;
    wc.hInstance = hInstance;
    wc.hIcon = LoadIcon(NULL,MAKEINTRESOURCE(IDI_APPICON));
    wc.hCursor = LoadCursor(NULL, IDC_ARROW);
    wc.hbrBackground = (HBRUSH)(COLOR_WINDOW + 1);
    wc.lpszMenuName =  MAKEINTRESOURCE(IDM_TESTMENU);
    wc.lpszClassName = MainWindowClassName;

    return RegisterClass(&wc);
}


/* ---------------------------------------------------------------- */
/* This function creates an instance of our main window. The window */
/* is given a class name and a title, and told to display anywhere. */
/* The nCmdShow argument passed to the program determines how the   */
/* window will be displayed.                                        */
/* ---------------------------------------------------------------- */
BOOL InitInstance(HINSTANCE hInst, int nCmdShow)
{
    HWND hWnd;

    hInstance = hInst;         // Store in global variable.

    hWnd = CreateWindow(MainWindowClassName,"Clipbard Demo",
                  WS_OVERLAPPEDWINDOW,CW_USEDEFAULT,
                  CW_USEDEFAULT,CW_USEDEFAULT,CW_USEDEFAULT,
                  NULL,NULL,hInstance,NULL);
    if (!hWnd)
        return FALSE;

    ShowWindow(hWnd, nCmdShow);
    UpdateWindow(hWnd);          // Send a WM_PAINT message.
    return TRUE;
}
```

continued on next page

continued from previous page

```
/* ------------------------------------------------------------------- */
/* The main entry point for Windows applications. Check to see if       */
/* the main window class name has already been registered; if it        */
/* has not, call InitApplication to register it. Call InitInstance      */
/* to create an instance of our main window, then pump messages         */
/* until the application is closed.                                     */
/* ------------------------------------------------------------------- */
int PASCAL WinMain(HINSTANCE hInstance, HINSTANCE hPrevInstance,
                   LPSTR lpCmdLine, int nCmdShow)
{
    MSG msg;

    if (!FindWindow(MainWindowClassName,NULL))
        if (!InitApplication(hInstance))
            return (FALSE);

    if (!InitInstance(hInstance, nCmdShow))
        return (FALSE);

    while (GetMessage(&msg,NULL,NULL,NULL))
    {
        TranslateMessage(&msg);
        DispatchMessage(&msg);
    }
    return (msg.wParam);
}
```

10. Compile and run the application.

Comments

Simple implementation of the cut and paste family of functions in your applications
can be augmented with an enabling/disabling technique such as that described in this
How-To to give your application a better honed, more professional feel.

LIST BOXES

LIST BOXES

How do I...

List boxes are one of the most natural and prevalent methods for allowing a user to choose from a specific set of options. Windows 95 uses list boxes in a wide variety of places and a wide variety of ways for user input. From simple single option selections such as which printer driver to install, to complex "tree" lists for directories, the list box is central to the workings of the Windows 95 user interface.

Your program also requires the same sorts of user inputs. From selecting which report to run, to selecting specific options for the application, the list box is certain to appear in your programs. This chapter will show you how you can use the power of the Windows 95 API to enhance your list boxes and make them easier for the user to understand and manipulate.

7.1   Store Information Along with List Box Items

The majority of list boxes that appear in programs today are really used to select from a list of identifiers that tie in to other data. For example, you might use a list box filled with the last names of people to tie to a database of contact information. In this How-To, we show you how you can more easily tie together the two bits of information—the name and the contact data—so that you have less work to do!

7.2   Catch Double-Clicks in a List Box

One of the more annoying aspects of list boxes is that there is no predefined behavior for a user double-clicking in the list box. Many times a dialog box will consist solely of a list box and an OK (and optionally, a Cancel) button. The user must click on the item he or she wants from the list and then select the OK button to continue. How much more intuitive and straightforward it would be to let them simply double-click on the list item they want in order to both select the item and close the dialog. This How-To will show you the technique used to accomplish this task.

7.3   Move an Item in a List Box by Drag-and-Drop

List boxes are often used to select items to copy, print, or otherwise operate on an application. Many times the order of the items is as important to the user as the data behind those items. While several techniques exist for selecting and moving items in a list box, by far the easiest is simply to select the one you want in the list and drag it to a new location. This How-To will show you a quick and easy way to accomplish this with a minimum of coding, using the Windows 95 API power to help you along.

7.4   Scroll a List Box

We have all seen applications that seem to scroll through a list box as a user types in an edit box at the top. This autoscrolling behavior exists to a certain point in normal list boxes. When you press a character in a list box, it automatically moves to the first item that matches that key. Unfortunately, this behavior stops at the first key. Pressing a second key will move the list box to the first element with that key as the first letter. This How-To will show you how you can automatically scroll or position a list box to a given entry by syncing up the list box entries with user entries in an edit box above it.

7.5   Allow Wide Lists to Scroll Horizontally

Certainly nothing is more annoying to the user than to have a list box that displays information wider than the list box window. It is impossible to see the additional data, which often is most crucial to the user. If you have looked at the MFC for list boxes, you know that there is no direct way to scroll a list box horizontally, even if there is a horizontal scrollbar. In this How-To, we show you how to use the power of the Windows 95 API to provide that horizontal scrolling capability to your own list boxes.

7.6   Right-Justify Numbers in a List Box

List boxes, by their very nature, do not allow entries to be displayed in anything but a left-justified manner. This can be irritating when the data involved is more suited to a right-justified system, such as currency amounts. Many people would prefer to see the currency amounts to the right of the box, rather than the left. This How-To will show you how you can do this in your own list boxes.

7.7 Draw My Own List Box

There is no reason that list boxes need to be restricted to displaying textual data. Colors, images, and other data can also be displayed in a list box. This powerful technique, known as "owner-drawing" can be used simply and effectively in your application to make lists simpler to select from and more informative to the user. In this How-To, we will show you how you can create owner-drawn list boxes and present a simple skeleton control that will do most of the work for you!

7.8 Store More Items in a List Box

List boxes can only hold a specific number of items (64K for total text or number of items). This number, while quite large for most purposes, can be rather small for large database applications. This How-To will show you how you can use the power of the Windows 95 API, along with the owner-draw concept shown in the previous How-To, to extend greatly the number of items that can be displayed in a given list box at one time.

7.9 Make a Hierarchical List or Tree

Windows 95 contains many new types of controls specifically geared toward the programmer. One of these controls, the tree-list or tree-view, allows you to set up a hierarchical tree of entries with expandable and contractable nodes. This How-To, which is Windows 95 and Windows NT specific, will show you how you can simply and easily encapsulate the power of the tree-list in your own application for whatever purpose you desire. Whether it be displaying a directory tree, as Windows does, or displaying a program structure diagram, the tree-list can be invaluable for saving you time and effort in writing your application.

Table 7-1 lists the Windows 95 API functions used in this chapter.

GetDlgItem	GetWindowText	SetWindowText	SetFocus
SendMessage	PostMessage	SelectObject	SetROP2
MoveTo	LineTo	SetTimer	SetCapture
KillTimer	ReleaseCapture	GetTextExtent	EnableWindow
InvalidateRect	DrawFocusRect	InvertRect	DrawText
FillRect	SetTextColor	PatBlt	SetBkColor
SetBkMode	SetCursor		

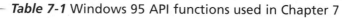
Table 7-1 Windows 95 API functions used in Chapter 7

7.1 How do I...
Store information along with list box items?

Problem

I have a list box on one of my dialogs that contains names of contacts for a salesperson. This list corresponds to an internal database of other information about those people. For example, my internal list might have the last name, first name, address, city, state, and zip code information for the person, while the list might contain the first and last names of the individual.

Presently, I need to scan that entire internal list each time the user makes a selection from the list box in order to find the record that corresponds to the names in the list box. This is made more difficult by the fact that the list box contains the names in a more formatted way than the internal list. The list box has the last name, a comma, and the first name. I then need to parse this into the format that I use internally and scan for a match.

Is there a better way to do this using the Windows 95 API?

Technique

As a matter of fact, there is a considerably better way to do this using the Windows 95 API. List boxes in Windows can store information along with the visible content of the list. In other words, you can save a pointer to your own information in addition to the string that you place in a list box. This pointer will be automatically shuffled around as the list box is reorganized by, for example, inserting a new string into a sorted list.

In addition to the benefits of having the list automatically in sync with the pointer, this method provides the advantage that Windows itself is holding onto your pointers, and you need not carry them around in your program.

In this How-To, we will examine the methodology involved in creating additional data for list box items and storing that information internally in the Windows list box itself.

Steps

Open and run the Visual C++ application CH71.MAK from the CHAPT7\SAM-PLES\CH71 directory on the CD that comes with this book. Select the main menu item Dialogs and the menu item Contact Dialog. You will see a dialog like the one shown in Figure 7-1. Enter some data into the edit fields on the left-hand side of the dialog and click on the Add Entry button. The last and first names of the entry will be shown in the list box on the right-hand side of the dialog. Enter a few more contact names

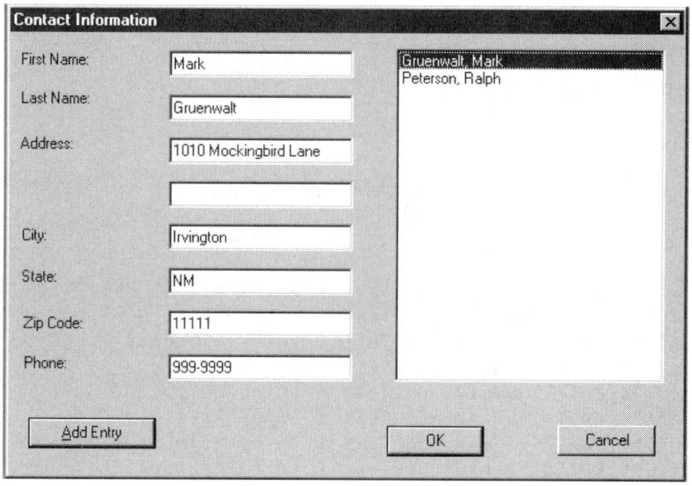

Figure 7-1 Contact dialog with sample entries

and addresses. Now, click on one of the contact names in the list box. You will see the edit fields filled with the information you entered originally for that person.

To duplicate this functionality in your own application, do the following:

1. Create a new project in Visual C++ using AppWizard. Give the application the name CH71.MAK. Enter AppStudio and add a new dialog. To this new dialog add the following static text fields:

```
First Name:
Last Name:
Address:
City:
State:
Zip Code:
Phone:
```

2. Add edit boxes for each of the static text fields, adding one additional edit box for the second address line between Address: and City:. Accept the default names (IDC_EDIT) for the edit fields. Clear out any text in the edit field within AppStudio.

3. Add a new button to the bottom of the dialog and give it the caption Add New Entry. Accept the default name (IDC_BUTTON1) for the new button.

4. Add a list box to the right-hand side of the dialog. Accept the name IDC_LIST1 for the identifier of the list box. Finally, change the caption of the dialog to read Contact Information.

5. Select ClassWizard and generate a new dialog class for the template you have just created. Give the dialog class the name CContactDlg. Select the IDC_BUTTON1 object from the object list and the BN_CLICKED message from the message list. Click on the Add Function button and enter the name

OnAddEntry as the name of the new function. Enter the following code into the OnAddEntry method of CContactDlg:

```
void CContactDlg::OnAddEntry()
{
    // Create a new structure.

    ContactEntry *entry = new ContactEntry;

    // Load it from the dialog box

    GetDlgItem(IDC_EDIT1)->GetWindowText ( entry->first_name, 80 );
    GetDlgItem(IDC_EDIT2)->GetWindowText ( entry->last_name, 80 );
    GetDlgItem(IDC_EDIT3)->GetWindowText ( entry->address_1, 80 );
    GetDlgItem(IDC_EDIT4)->GetWindowText ( entry->address_2, 80 );
    GetDlgItem(IDC_EDIT5)->GetWindowText ( entry->city, 80 );
    GetDlgItem(IDC_EDIT6)->GetWindowText ( entry->state, 10 );
    GetDlgItem(IDC_EDIT7)->GetWindowText ( entry->zip_code, 15 );
    GetDlgItem(IDC_EDIT8)->GetWindowText ( entry->phone, 20 );

    // Add the last name + the first name to the list box

    CListBox *list = (CListBox *)GetDlgItem(IDC_LIST1);

    char buffer[256];
    sprintf(buffer, "%s, %s", entry->last_name, entry->first_name );

    int idx = list->AddString ( buffer );

    // Now, add the data for the list entry

    list->SetItemData ( idx, (DWORD)entry );

    // Clear the input fields

    // Set the fields

    GetDlgItem(IDC_EDIT1)->SetWindowText ( "" );
    GetDlgItem(IDC_EDIT2)->SetWindowText ( "" );
    GetDlgItem(IDC_EDIT3)->SetWindowText ( "" );
    GetDlgItem(IDC_EDIT4)->SetWindowText ( "" );
    GetDlgItem(IDC_EDIT5)->SetWindowText ( "" );
    GetDlgItem(IDC_EDIT6)->SetWindowText ( "" );
    GetDlgItem(IDC_EDIT7)->SetWindowText ( "" );
    GetDlgItem(IDC_EDIT8)->SetWindowText ( "" );

    // Reset the input focus to the first edit field

    GetDlgItem(IDC_EDIT1)->SetFocus();

}
```

6. Select the IDC_LIST1 object from the object list and select the LBN_SELCHANGE message from the message list. Click on the Add Function button and use the name OnListChange for the name of the new function. Enter the following code into the OnListChange method of CContactDlg:

```
void CContactDlg::OnListChange()
{
    // Get the current selection

    CListBox *list = (CListBox *)GetDlgItem(IDC_LIST1);
    int idx = list->GetCurSel();

    // Get the data associated with this item

    ContactEntry *entry = (ContactEntry *)list->GetItemData(idx);

    // Set the fields

    GetDlgItem(IDC_EDIT1)->SetWindowText ( entry->first_name );
    GetDlgItem(IDC_EDIT2)->SetWindowText ( entry->last_name );
    GetDlgItem(IDC_EDIT3)->SetWindowText ( entry->address_1 );
    GetDlgItem(IDC_EDIT4)->SetWindowText ( entry->address_2 );
    GetDlgItem(IDC_EDIT5)->SetWindowText ( entry->city );
    GetDlgItem(IDC_EDIT6)->SetWindowText ( entry->state );
    GetDlgItem(IDC_EDIT7)->SetWindowText ( entry->zip_code );
    GetDlgItem(IDC_EDIT8)->SetWindowText ( entry->phone );

}
```

7. Now select the IDOK object from the object list and the BN_CLICKED message from the message list. Click on the Add Function button and accept the OnOK name for the function. Enter the following code into the OnOK method of CContactDlg:

```
void CContactDlg::OnOK()
{
    CListBox *list = (CListBox *)GetDlgItem(IDC_LIST1);
    for ( int i=0; i<list->GetCount(); ++i ) {
        ContactEntry *entry = (ContactEntry *)list->GetItemData(i);
        delete entry;
    }

    CDialog::OnOK();
}
```

8. Select the CONTACTD.H file in Visual C++ and add the following structure definition to the top of the file:

```
typedef struct {
    char first_name[80];
    char last_name[80];
    char address_1[80];
    char address_2[80];
    char city[80];
    char state[10];
    char zip_code[15];
    char phone[20];
} ContactEntry;
```

9. In AppStudio, add a new main-level menu entry with the caption Dialogs. Add a menu item called Contact Dialog. Give this drop-down menu item the identifier ID_CONTACT_DLG.

10. In ClassWizard, select the application object CCh71App from the drop-down list. Select the ID_CONTACT_DLG identifier from the object list and the COMMAND message in the message list. Click on the Add Function button. Accept the name OnContactDlg as the name of the new function and enter the following code into the OnContactDlg method of CCh71App:

```
void CCh71App::OnContactDlg()
{
    CContactDlg dlg;
    dlg.DoModal();
}
```

11. Finally, add the following line to the top of the CH71.CPP file:

```
#include "contactd.h"
```

12. Compile and run the application.

How It Works

When the user selects the contact dialog and adds a new entry, the program allocates space for a new ContactEntry structure. This structure is then filled in with the information from the edit fields and added to the ItemData portion of the list box using the MFC method SetItemData for CListBox. The list box then maintains a pointer to this item data for the specified index in the list. The index is found via the AddString method of CListBox, which adds a new string to the list and returns its position to the program.

When the user selects an item from the list, the OnListChange method of CContactDlg is called. This method simply retrieves the index of the currently selected list item and retrieves the pointer stored with that item via the GetItemData function call. Note that the return needs to be cast to the proper value since it is returned as a DWORD (or long integer) value. The data from the pointer is then stored in the edit fields from this structure.

Finally, when the user selects the OK button, each of the items stored is retrieved from the list box in an identical manner to the OnListChange method, and the pointer is then deleted, freeing up the memory allocated initially.

Comments

This How-To is incredibly valuable in showing you how to store and retrieve information from list boxes. This could be the basis for the contact information sheet shown here or any other application that requires a "lookup" value via list entries. To show you the actual underlying Windows API functionality called, we present the same application in Delphi (which has no corresponding SetItemData and GetItemData functions).

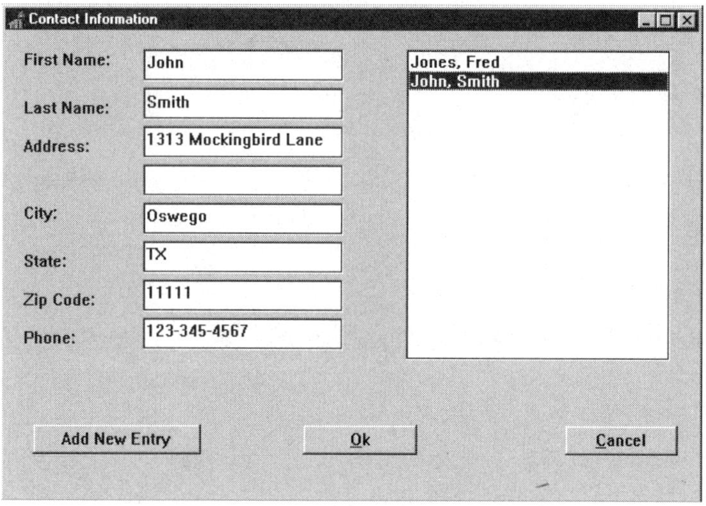

Figure 7-2 Delphi contact form with sample entries

Open the LIST.DPR project file in Delphi and run the application. You will see the form displayed in Figure 7-2. Enter some contact information as before in the edit fields and click on the Add New Entry button. As in Visual C++, you will see the entry displayed in the list box. Enter a few more data values and select one from the list box. You will see the edit fields refreshed with the data from the list.

To create this same functionality in your own Delphi application, do the following:

1. Create a new project file or add a new form to an existing Delphi project. To this form, add the following static text fields:

```
First Name:
Last Name:
Address:
City:
State:
Zip Code:
Phone:
```

2. Add edit boxes that correspond to the static text fields in the order of the text fields, with one additional edit box between Address: and City:. This additional edit box will hold the second line of the address.

3. Add three buttons to the form: Add New Entry, OK, and Cancel.

4. Double-click on the Add New Entry button. Add the following code to the TForm1.Button1Click method:

```
procedure TForm1.Button1Click(Sender: TObject);
var
    entry : ^ContactEntry;
    temp  : String;
    idx   : Integer;
```

continued on next page

continued from previous page

```
begin
  { Create a new entry variable }

  New(entry);

  { Assign the pieces of the entry variable }

  entry^.FirstName := Edit1.Text;
  entry^.LastName  := Edit2.Text;
  entry^.Address1  := Edit3.Text;
  entry^.Address2  := Edit4.Text;
  entry^.City      := Edit5.Text;
  entry^.State     := Edit6.Text;
  entry^.ZipCode   := Edit7.Text;
  entry^.Phone     := Edit8.Text;

  { Put it into the list }

  temp := entry^.LastName + ', ' + entry^.FirstName;
  idx := ListBox1.Items.Add( temp );

  { Send a message to store this information }

  SendMessage( ListBox1.handle, LB_SETITEMDATA, idx, LongInt(entry) );

  { Clear the edit fields }

  Edit1.Text := '';
  Edit2.Text := '';
  Edit3.Text := '';
  Edit4.Text := '';
  Edit5.Text := '';
  Edit6.Text := '';
  Edit7.Text := '';
  Edit8.Text := '';

  { Set the focus to the first edit field }

  Edit1.SetFocus;
end;
```

5. Double-click on the list box and add the following code into the
TForm1.ListBox1Click method:

```
procedure TForm1.ListBox1Click(Sender: TObject);
var
    idx : Integer;   { Selected index in list }
    entry : ^ContactEntry; { Entry from data }
begin
    idx := ListBox1.ItemIndex;

    entry := Pointer(SendMessage( ListBox1.handle, LB_GETITEMDATA, idx, 0 ));
    Edit1.Text := entry^.FirstName;
    Edit2.Text := entry^.LastName;
    Edit3.Text := entry^.Address1;
    Edit4.Text := entry^.Address2;
```

```
    Edit5.Text := entry^.City;
    Edit6.Text := entry^.State;
    Edit7.Text := entry^.ZipCode;
    Edit8.Text := entry^.Phone;

end;
```

6. Double-click on the OK button and enter the following code into the TForm1.Button2Click method:

```
procedure TForm1.Button2Click(Sender: TObject);
begin
    Close;
end;
```

7. Double-click on the Cancel button and enter the following code into the TForm1.Button3Click method:

```
procedure TForm1.Button3Click(Sender: TObject);
begin
    Close;
end;
```

8. Finally, enter the following code into the form's Type section, above the Tform1 declaration:

```
ContactEntry = Record
    FirstName  : String;
    LastName   : String;
    Address1   : String;
    Address2   : String;
    City       : String;
    State      : String;
    ZipCode    : String;
    Phone      : String;
end;
```

9. Compile and run the application.

COMPLEXITY
EASY

7.2 How do I...
Catch double-clicks in a list box?

Problem

I would like to let the user double-click in my list box and then be able to detect that double-click in my application. This will permit me to close a dialog that contains only a list box and an OK button when the user double-clicks on a single item in the list box. I would, of course, like the double-click to select the item that is double-clicked before closing the dialog.

Technique

This seems like a reasonable request. So reasonable, in fact, that it is rather surprising that the designers of Windows never allowed this functionality for the programmer! The ability to extend an existing control in Windows is one of the things that makes little oversights like this tolerable to the Windows programmer. If you use a method known as "subclassing," you will find that you are able to do things with standard controls that the original programmers of the operating system never even considered. It is this power that we will examine in this How-To.

When the user double-clicks with the mouse in a window, a specific Windows message (WM_LBUTTONDBLCLK) is sent to that window. In this How-To, we will look at how you can create your own control handling class in Visual C++ and how to use that class to intercept the WM_LBUTTONDBLCLK message and use it in your own application.

Steps

Open and run the Visual C++ application CH72.MAK from the CHAPT7\SAM-PLES\CH72 directory on the CD that comes with this book. Select the Dialog main menu item, and then select the Double Click Dialog menu item from the drop-down list. You will see the dialog displayed in Figure 7-3. Double-click the mouse on one of the entries. The dialog box should display a message box with the item selected and then close the dialog box.

To duplicate this functionality in your own application, follow this procedure:

1. Create a new project in Visual C++ using AppWizard. Go into AppStudio and create a new dialog. On this dialog, add a list box.

Figure 7-3 Double-click dialog
displayed

2. Start ClassWizard and generate a new dialog class for this template. Call the dialog class CDblClickDlg. Click on the CDblClickDlg object in the object list of ClassWizard and the WM_INITDIALOG message in the message list. Click on the Add Function button. Enter the following code into the OnInitDialog method of CDblClickDlg:

```
BOOL CDblClickDlg::OnInitDialog()
{
  CDialog::OnInitDialog();

  m_list.SubclassDlgItem(IDC_LIST1, this );

  // Add items to the list

  m_list.AddString ( "Item 1" );
  m_list.AddString ( "Item 2" );
  m_list.AddString ( "Item 3" );
  m_list.AddString ( "Item 4" );
  m_list.AddString ( "Item 5" );
  m_list.AddString ( "Item 6" );
  m_list.AddString ( "Item 7" );
  m_list.AddString ( "Item 8" );
  m_list.AddString ( "Item 9" );
  m_list.AddString ( "Item 10" );

  return TRUE;  // return TRUE  unless you set the focus to a control
}
```

3. Next, add the following line to the message map of CDblClickDlg:

```
ON_MESSAGE ( WM_DBLCLICK, OnListDblClick )
```

4. Now, add the following method to the CDblClickDlg class:

```
LRESULT CDblClickDlg::OnListDblClick(WPARAM wParam, LPARAM lParam)
{
    int idx = wParam;

    char buffer[80];
    sprintf(buffer, "Item %d Selected", idx );
    MessageBox(buffer, "Info", MB_OK );
    EndDialog(IDOK);
    return 0;
}
```

5. Add the following line to the top of your dialog class source file:

```
#define WM_DBLCLICK (WM_USER+1)
```

6. Next, add the following lines to your header file for the dialog class:

```
private:
    CDblClkList m_list;
```

7. And add the following line (the line marked with bold print) to the message map entries in the header file for your dialog class.

```
// Generated message map functions
 //{{AFX_MSG(CDblClickDlg)
 virtual BOOL OnInitDialog();
 afx_msg LRESULT OnListDblClick(WPARAM, LPARAM);
 //}}AFX_MSG
 DECLARE_MESSAGE_MAP()
```

8. You are now ready to create a new list box class. Unfortunately, Visual C++ provides no simple mechanism for deriving classes from base classes outside of the list that is given to you initially. Here's how you create a list-box derived class. First, go into ClassWizard and select the Add Class button. For the name of the class, use CDblClkList. Select generic CWnd for the class from which to derive this class. Allow all other defaults to remain unchanged.

9. Select the DBLCLKLI.H file from the project list (you may need to scan all dependencies to get this file into the list). Change all occurrences of the string CWnd to CListBox. Go into the source file, DBLCLKLI.CPP and do the same thing. Your class will now be recognized by ClassWizard as a valid CListBox, rather than a CWnd.

10. Enter ClassWizard and select the CDblClkList class from the drop-down combo box. Select the CDblClkList object from the object list and the WM_LBUTTONDBLCLK message from the message list. Click on the Add Function button. Add the following code into the OnLButtonDblClk method of CDblClkList:

```
void CDblClkList::OnLButtonDblClk(UINT nFlags, CPoint point)
{
  // Get the size of a line in the list box.

  int height = GetItemHeight(0);

  // Figure out if this point is on a valid item.

  int num_items = GetCount() - GetTopIndex();  // Number of items displayed.
  if ( point.y < 0 || point.y > height * num_items )
     return;

  CListBox::OnLButtonDown(nFlags, point);

  int idx = GetCurSel();

  GetParent()->PostMessage(WM_USER+1, idx, 0 );
}
```

11. Enter AppStudio and select the main menu. Add a main menu entry for Dialogs (if one is not already present), and add a menu item to the Dialogs menu called Double Click ListBox. Give this drop-down menu the identifier ID_DOUBLE_CLICK.

12. Enter ClassWizard and select the CCh72App object from the drop-down combo box. Select the ID_DOUBLE_CLICK object and the COMMAND message. Click on the Add Function button and accept the name OnDoubleClick as the name of the new function. Add the following code into the OnDoubleClick method of CCh72App:

```
void CCh72App::OnDoubleClick()
{
    CDblClickDlg dlg;
    dlg.DoModal();
}
```

13. Add the following line to the include file list at the top of the CH7.CPP file:

```
#include "dblclick.h"
```

14. Compile and run the application.

How It Works

When the user selects the Double Click ListBox menu option from the Dialogs main menu entry, the CDblClickDlg object is created in the OnDoubleClick method of the application object, CCh7App. The first thing that happens is that the OnInitDialog method of the CDblClickDlg is called in response to Windows issuing a WM_INITDIALOG message to the window. This message subclasses the list box item in the dialog (IDC_LIST1) by calling the SubclassDlgItem method of the list box. This makes the list box handler call our window procedure rather than the one built into the default list box within Windows.

Once our list box handler is called, it defaults all operations with the exception of the double-click message. This message is handled in the OnLButtonDblClick method of our list box class, CDblClkList. This message handler simply creates a message called WM_USER+1, which is referred to as a "user-defined message." This message is then passed back up to the parent of the list box, which is the dialog box. The dialog box receives this message via the ON_MESSAGE handler defined in its message map. The handler for this message, OnListDblClick, simply displays a message box indicating that the dialog received that message and the item that was selected. Then the method shuts down the dialog box by calling the EndDialog method.

Comments

The CDblClkList object presented here is an excellent starting point for your own investigations into the handling of list boxes. We will use this same technique later in the chapter to show how you can implement drag-and-drop within your list boxes, as well as for painting the items yourself.

The new list class could be used for presenting information to the user in a dialog with a single list control. Alternatively, you could intercept the message passed by the control in order to supply other controls with information. You could, for example, use the list box to hold font names and pass those names to a static text control to display. Perhaps the list box might hold directory information and could be used to update a file listing in another list box on the control. The choices are up to you.

COMPLEXITY
DIFFICULT

7.3 How do I...
Move an item in a list box by drag-and-drop?

Problem

My application requires that I be able to allow users to select not only the options that they would like to display but the order in which they would like them displayed. I would very much like to do both at the same time by allowing them to drag and drop the items they have selected in a list box into the order in which they would like them to appear. Unfortunately, I cannot find any way to enable drag-and-drop in a list box using either the MFC or the Windows 95 API. How can I accomplish this task with a minimum of time and effort?

Technique

The idea of a drag-and-drop list box has always been quite appealing. Unfortunately, as you have pointed out, the MFC does not provide this functionality to you. It is up to you to extend the MFC by using the power of the Windows 95 API functions to do the job for yourself.

In this How-To, we will look at the problem of dragging and dropping items within a single list box. To do this, it is necessary to use the concept of subclassing, which involves replacing selected portions of the existing procedures for a Windows control. A list box will be subclassed to capture certain Windows messages and processing put in place to make those messages handle the work of dragging an item to a given location.

The technique used follows this procedure. First, the user will select an item that he or she would like to drag to a new location. The item number and text associated with that item are stored off in your application program. Next, the user will move the item to a new location. The process of moving will allow the program to mark the path the user takes and note when he or she has reached a new location. Finally, the user will release the mouse button, indicating that the item is in the correct position. This is our cue to do the actual move of the item from one location in the list to another.

For this example, we will note the movement of the item through the list by drawing a dashed line at the position where the new item would be inserted if the user were to release the mouse button at that time. The item itself will remain where it started until the user commits to the move by releasing the mouse button.

Steps

Open and run the Visual C++ application CH73.MAK from the CHAPT7\SAM-PLES\CH73 directory on the CD that comes with this book. Select the Dialogs main menu item and the menu item Drag List Dialog. You will see a dialog displayed like

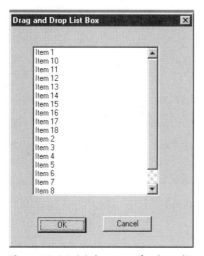

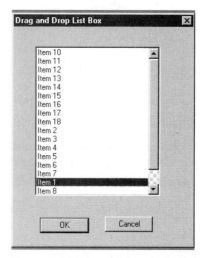

Figure 7-4 Initial state of "drag list" dialog

Figure 7-5 State of "drag list" dialog after drag-and-drop operation

the one in Figure 7-4. Select an item such as Item 1 and drag the mouse down until the dashed line is directly below the item labeled Item 7. You will now see the display in Figure 7-5.

To duplicate this functionality in your own application, do the following:

1. Create a new project in Visual C++ using AppWizard. Give the new project the name CH73.MAK. Enter AppStudio and create a new dialog. Move the OK and Cancel buttons to the bottom of the dialog and add a single list box to the dialog.

2. Enter ClassWizard and generate a new dialog class for this template. Call the dialog CDragDlg and accept all other defaults. Click on the CDragDlg object in the object list in ClassWizard and select the WM_INITDIALOG message from the message list. Enter the following code into the OnInitDialog method of CDragDlg:

```
BOOL CDragDlg::OnInitDialog()
{
  CDialog::OnInitDialog();

    m_DragList.SubclassDlgItem(IDC_LIST1, this);
    m_DragList.AddString ( "Item 1" );
    m_DragList.AddString ( "Item 2" );
    m_DragList.AddString ( "Item 3" );
    m_DragList.AddString ( "Item 4" );
    m_DragList.AddString ( "Item 5" );
    m_DragList.AddString ( "Item 6" );
    m_DragList.AddString ( "Item 7" );
    m_DragList.AddString ( "Item 8" );
    m_DragList.AddString ( "Item 9" );
    m_DragList.AddString ( "Item 10" );
    m_DragList.AddString ( "Item 11" );
```

continued on next page

continued from previous page

```
        m_DragList.AddString ( "Item 12" );
        m_DragList.AddString ( "Item 13" );
        m_DragList.AddString ( "Item 14" );
        m_DragList.AddString ( "Item 15" );
        m_DragList.AddString ( "Item 16" );
        m_DragList.AddString ( "Item 17" );
        m_DragList.AddString ( "Item 18" );

    return TRUE;  // return TRUE  unless you set the focus to a control
}
```

3. Add the following lines that are marked with bold print to the top of the header file for the dialog (DRAGDLG.H):

```
#include "dragdrop.h"

class CDragDlg : public CDialog
{
private:
  CDragDropList m_DragList;
```

4. Next, go back to ClassWizard and select the Add Class button. Enter CDragDropList as the name of the class and select generic CWnd as the base type for the class. Accept the other defaults and click on the Create Class button.

5. In the new class source file and header file, change all occurrences of the string "CWnd" to "CListBox". Enter ClassWizard again and select the new class (CDragDropList). Click on the CDragDropList object in the object list and the WM_MOUSEMOVE message from the message list. Click on the Add Function button and add the following code to the OnMouseMove method of CDragDropList:

```
void CDragDropList::OnMouseMove(UINT nFlags, CPoint point)
{
    CRect r, wr;
    GetClientRect(&r);
    // How tall is one item?

    int height = GetItemHeight(0);

    // Figure out which one this is

    int idx = point.y / height;
    int num_items = (wr.bottom-wr.top) / height;

    CDC *dc = GetDC();

    if ( is_tracking && idx < 0 || idx + GetTopIndex() > GetCount() ) {

        // Erase previous selection

      CPen pen(PS_DASH, 1, RGB(0,0,0));
      dc->SelectObject(&pen);
      dc->SetROP2(R2_XORPEN);
```

```
   if ( last_idx != -1 ) {
       dc->MoveTo(0,((last_idx+1) * height));
       dc->LineTo(r.right, ((last_idx+1) * height));
   }

   ReleaseDC(dc);

   return;
}


   // If we are "dragging" don't do the normal move

if ( !is_tracking )
   CListBox::OnMouseMove(nFlags, point);
else {
   CPen pen(PS_DASH, 1, RGB(0,0,0));
   dc->SelectObject(&pen);
   dc->SetROP2(R2_XORPEN);
   if ( last_idx != -1 ) {
       dc->MoveTo(0,((last_idx+1) * height));
       dc->LineTo(r.right, ((last_idx+1) * height));
   }
   dc->MoveTo(0,((idx+1) * height));
   dc->LineTo(r.right, ((idx+1) * height));
   last_idx = idx;
   }

   ReleaseDC(dc);
}
```

6. Click on the CDragDropList object in the object list and the WM_LBUTTON-DOWN message from the message list. Click on the Add Function button and add the following code to the OnLButtonDown method of CDragDropList:

```
void CDragDropList::OnLButtonDown(UINT nFlags, CPoint point)
{
   CListBox::OnLButtonDown(nFlags, point);

   cur_sel = GetCurSel();
   GetText(cur_sel, cur_text);
   is_tracking = TRUE;
   SetTimer( ID_TIMER, 100, NULL );
   SetCapture();

}
```

7. Click on the CDragDropList object in the object list and the WM_LBUTTONUP message from the message list. Click on the Add Function button and add the following code to the OnLButtonUp method of CDragDropList:

```
void CDragDropList::OnLButtonUp(UINT nFlags, CPoint point)
{
    if ( is_tracking ) {

        // How tall is one item?
```

continued on next page

continued from previous page

```
            int height = GetItemHeight(0);

            // Figure out which one this is

            int idx = GetTopIndex() + point.y / height;

            // Make sure this one is in list

            if ( idx < 0 || idx > GetCount() )
                return;

            // Delete current item

            DeleteString( cur_sel );

            // Insert this one.

            InsertString ( idx, cur_text );

            // Clear the tracking flag

            is_tracking = FALSE;

            // And select this item...

            SetCurSel(idx);

            last_idx = -1;

            KillTimer( ID_TIMER );

            ReleaseCapture();
        }

    CListBox::OnLButtonUp(nFlags, point);
}
```

8. Click on the CDragDropList object in the object list and the WM_TIMER message from the message list. Click on the Add Function button and add the following code to the OnTimer method of CDragDropList:

```
void CDragDropList::OnTimer(UINT nIDEvent)
{
    POINT pt;
    GetCursorPos(&pt);

    CRect rect;
        GetClientRect( &rect );
    ClientToScreen( &rect );

    int TopIndex = GetTopIndex();

    if( pt.y < rect.top )
    {
        if( TopIndex > 0 )
```

```
      SetTopIndex( --TopIndex );
   }
   else if( pt.y > rect.bottom )
   {
     if( TopIndex < GetCount() )
       SetTopIndex( ++TopIndex );
   }
}
```

9. Add the following lines to the constructor for the CDragDropList object (CDragDropList::CDragDropList):

```
is_tracking = FALSE;
last_idx = -1;
```

10. Next, select the header file for the CDragDropList class, DRAGDROP.H. Add the following lines to the header file:

```
private:
    int cur_sel;        // Currently selected item
    int is_tracking;    // flag for dragging and dropping
    int last_idx;
    CString cur_text; // string for selected item.
```

11. Go back into AppStudio and select the main menu. Add a main-level menu entry with the caption Dialogs. To the Dialogs main menu item, add a new menu item with the caption Drag List Dialog. Give this new menu item the identifier ID_DRAG_LIST_DLG.

12. In ClassWizard, select the application object, CCh73App. Click on the ID_DRAG_LIST_DLG object from the object list and the message COMMAND. Click on the Add Function button and accept OnDragListDlg as the name of the new method. Add the following code to the OnDragListDlg method of CCh73App:

```
void CCh73App::OnDragListDlg()
{
    CDragDlg dlg;
    dlg.DoModal();
}
```

13. Add the following line to the include file list at the top of CH7.CPP:

```
#include "dragdlg.h"
```

14. Compile and run the application.

How It Works

The principle of drag-and-drop is reasonably straightforward. You wait until the user clicks the left mouse button while on top of something. You then capture mouse input so that all mouse moves and clicks go to your application. While the mouse is moving, you track the user's movements and indicate that a drag is in progress by displaying some sort of indicator or icon. Finally, when the user releases the mouse button, you drop the item to the new position desired.

The details of the implementation are of more interest. When the user clicks the left mouse button on an item in the list, the OnLButtonDown method of CDragDropList is called. This method does three things. First, it saves off the index and string of the item that the user selected. Next, it creates a timer object in Windows. Timer objects simply send a WM_TIMER message to the window that creates them each time a specified interval has passed. In this case, the interval used is 100 milliseconds. This timer will be used to scroll the list if the user moves the mouse outside the list box while holding the left button down. Finally, the SetCapture method of the API is called to reroute all mouse events to the window. This means that even if the mouse is moved outside of the list box, the list box will receive messages.

Once the user begins to move the mouse while holding down the left mouse button, the OnMouseMove method is called. This method simply draws a dashed line at the bottom of the item that the mouse is currently over. This provides visual feedback to the user that the drag is actually taking place. This routine performs quite a bit of checking to be sure that the mouse is still within the bounds of the list box. If the mouse is outside of the list box, no drawing of lines is done.

Next, the OnTimer method of the list box class is called each 100 milliseconds by Windows. This method will simply check to see if the mouse is within the bounds of the list box window. If it is not, it checks to see if the mouse is above the list box. If the mouse is above the list box, it is autoscrolled upward. If the mouse is below the list box window, it is autoscrolled downward. This gives the appearance that the list box is responding to the user's request to move.

Finally, the OnLButtonUp method is called when the user releases the mouse button. If the mouse cursor is within the list box, it simply figures out which item is currently under the cursor. The old item is then deleted and reinserted at the new position.

Comments

The CDragDropList is a good starting point for dragging and dropping items within a list box, but it is certainly not perfect. Changes could be made to allow multiple selections to be made and dragged. In addition, the OnLButtonUp routine could make sure that the list box selected is, in fact, the correct one. A simple change could be made to allow multiple list boxes to "share" items and drag and drop them between several lists.

Dragging and dropping is not the most intuitive method for user interaction and should be carefully considered before implementing in your application. Many novice Windows 95 users are leery of using this method, so you should always provide an alternate way of accomplishing the same thing.

COMPLEXITY
MODERATE

7.4   How do I...
Scroll a list box?

Problem

I would like to add the ability to "quick search" my list boxes by allowing the user to type portions of a search string into an edit box and have the list box automatically reposition itself in response to these keystrokes. I know that Windows 95 list boxes have the ability to go to the first character typed, but how can I look for multiple characters and scroll the list box accordingly?

Technique

The "quick search" method you mention has become quite popular in recent applications. Many Windows 95 common controls use this method (OpenFile dialog and Font Dialog), and numerous applications also use it. To accomplish this job, you need to know a little bit about the way Windows 95 messages work with respect to controls on the screen. Several messages can be trapped to indicate that controls are changing their values. In addition, there are messages you can send to Windows controls that allow you to change the behavior of the controls as if the user had performed some action on the controls.

In this How-To, we will look at two specific sets of control messages. Notification messages are sent by a control to the "parent" of that control when the user does something to change the state of the control. Manipulation messages allow you to change the state of a Windows control as though the user had done something in that control.

The two messages we will look at specifically are EN_CHANGE and LB_SELECTSTRING. The EN_CHANGE message is sent by an edit control to the parent dialog of the edit control when the user makes a change to the edit string. This change can be typing characters, deleting characters, or pasting in selections. The LB_SELECTSTRING message is a manipulation message that you can send to a list box to "find" a string in the list box that matches certain criteria.

Steps

Open and run the Visual C++ application CH74.MAK from the CHAPT7\SAMPLES\CH74 directory on the CD that comes with this book. Run the application and select the Dialogs main menu item. From the drop-down menu, select the Search List menu item. You should see the dialog displayed in Figure 7-6. Type several characters into the edit box that match one of the entries in the list. You will see the highlight in the list box move in accordance with your typing.

Figure 7-6 Search list dialog
displayed

ters into the edit box that match one of the entries in the list. You will see the highlight in the list box move in accordance with your typing.

To accomplish this same functionality in your own application, do the following:

1. Create a new project in Visual C++ using AppWizard. Give the new project the
name CH74.MAK. Enter AppStudio and create a new dialog. Move the OK
and Cancel buttons to the bottom of the dialog and add a single edit box and
list box to the dialog.

2. Select ClassWizard and generate a new dialog class for the template you have
just created. Give the new dialog class the name CSearchDlg. Accept all other
defaults for the dialog class.

3. Select the CSearchDlg object from the object list in ClassWizard and select the
WM_INITDIALOG message from the message list. Click on the Add Function
button. Enter the following code into the OnInitDialog method of
CSearchDlg:

```
BOOL CSearchDlg::OnInitDialog()
{
    CDialog::OnInitDialog();

    // Add some terms that we can search on

    CListBox *list = (CListBox *)GetDlgItem(IDC_LIST1);
```

```
list->AddString ( "Alphabet" );
list->AddString ( "BetaZoid" );
list->AddString ( "Carnival" );
list->AddString ( "Caramel" );
list->AddString ( "Country" );
list->AddString ( "Diamond" );
list->AddString ( "Elephant" );
list->AddString ( "Eeyore" );
list->AddString ( "Eyesight" );
list->AddString ( "Animal" );
list->AddString ( "Copper" );
list->AddString ( "Gold" );
list->AddString ( "Farley" );
list->AddString ( "Borrow" );
list->AddString ( "Candy" );
list->AddString ( "Ginger" );
list->AddString ( "Flint" );
list->AddString ( "New York" );
list->AddString ( "Idaho" );
list->AddString ( "Irving" );
list->AddString ( "Jenny" );
list->AddString ( "Rachel" );
list->AddString ( "Dawnna" );
list->AddString ( "Matt" );

CenterWindow();

return TRUE;  // return TRUE  unless you set the focus to a control
}
```

4. Select the IDC_EDIT1 object from the object list and the EN_CHANGE notification message from the message list. Click on the Add Function button and enter the name OnEditChange for the new message handler method. Enter the following code into the OnEditChange method of CSearchDlg:

```
void CSearchDlg::OnEditChange()
{
    // Get the string from the edit box

    char buffer[256];
    GetDlgItem(IDC_EDIT1)->GetWindowText(buffer, 256);

    // Search for the string in the list box

    CListBox *list = (CListBox *)GetDlgItem(IDC_LIST1);
    list->SendMessage( LB_SELECTSTRING, -1, (LPARAM)(LPCSTR)buffer );
}
```

5. Enter AppStudio and select the main menu from the menu list. Add a new main menu item with the caption Dialogs if there is not already one. Add a menu item to the Dialogs main menu with the caption Search List. Give this new menu item the identifier ID_SEARCH_LIST.

6. Enter ClassWizard and select the CCh74App application object from the drop-down combo list. Select the ID_SEARCH_LIST object from the object list and the COMMAND message from the message list. Click on the Add

Function button and name the new function OnSearchList. Enter the following code into the OnSearchList method of CCh74App:

```
void CCh74App::OnSearchList()
{
    CSearchDlg dlg;
    dlg.DoModal();
}
```

7. Add the following line to the include list at the top of CH74.CPP:

```
#include "searchdl.h"
```

8. Compile and run the application.

How It Works

When the dialog is displayed, the edit box is initially empty. As the user types into the edit box, Windows sends EN_CHANGE messages for each keystroke to the dialog class. This class simply calls the API function GetWindowText to extract the current text string from the edit box and then sends that string to the list box with a LB_SELECTSTRING message.

The LB_SELECTSTRING message tries to match the number of characters in the string with one of the entries in the list. It begins at the index of the string passed as the second parameter of the SendMessage call. If this parameter is equal to -1, the entire list is searched from the top item; otherwise the searching begins at the list entry following this parameter value. The string that is passed into the message is then matched against each entry. When a match is found, the list is repositioned to that location, scrolling the top of the list if necessary.

Comments

This particular technique is not restricted to Visual C++. As a matter of fact, it is so useful that we will present an alternative way of doing it in Visual Basic. The Visual Basic form to search for strings in a list is shown in Figure 7-7.

To duplicate this functionality, do the following:

1. Open or create a new project in Visual Basic. Add a new form to the project.

2. To this form add a static text control with the caption Search String. Next to the static text control add an edit field. Finally, add a list box to the form.

3. Add the following code to the "general" section of the form:

```
DefInt A-Z
Private Declare Function SendMessage Lib "user32" Alias "SendMessageA"
(ByVal hwnd As Long, ByVal wMsg As Long, ByVal wParam As Long, ByVal
Lp As Any) As Long
Const WM_USER = &H400
Const LB_SELECTSTRING = &H18C
Const LB_SETTOPINDEX = (WM_USER + 24)
```

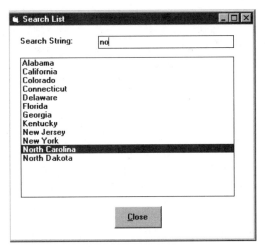

Figure 7-7 The search list program in Visual Basic

4. Next, double-click on the edit box and add the following code to the "Change" method of the edit box:

```
Private Sub Text1_Change()
    S$ = Text1.Text
    Index = SendMessage(List1.hwnd, LB_SELECTSTRING, -1, S$)
    Err = SendMessage(List1.hwnd, LB_SETTOPINDEX, Index, 0&)
End Sub
```

5. Finally, add a command button with the caption &Close. Add the following code to the "Click" method of the Close button:

```
Private Sub Command1_Click ()
    End
End Sub
```

COMPLEXITY
MODERATE

7.5   How do I...
Allow wide lists to scroll horizontally?

Problem

I have several list boxes in my application that display user information. Quite often, the user information to be displayed is much larger than the width that I would like to use for displaying the list box. Although I could make the list box wider, it might not fit on several of the older monitors in use around the company.

Is there any way that I can use the Windows API to allow me to scroll the list boxes horizontally? I have tried turning on the horizontal scrolling flag in AppStudio for the dialog template, but it doesn't seem to work at runtime. How do I make the list box scroll to the width of the widest string in the list box?

Technique

It seems like a major oversight that Microsoft chose not to make list boxes automatically scroll themselves in response to clicks on the horizontal scroll bar. This capability seems quite useful in many applications. As you have noticed, simply adding a list box horizontal scroll bar will not make the list box scroll horizontally.

The key to horizontal scrolling for list boxes lies in the Windows API function SendMessage. The list box API contains a manipulation message known as LB_SETHO-RIZONTALEXTENT. This message allows you to set the horizontal range of the horizontal scroll bar, which permits the list box to scroll the text in it sideways as you click on that scroll bar.

In this How-To, we show you how to find the largest string in a list box and how to set the horizontal scrolling factor for the list box so that the largest string is displayed correctly.

Steps

Open and run the Visual C++ application CH75.MAK from the CHAPT7\SAM-PLES\CH75 directory on the CD that comes with this book. Run the application and select the Dialogs main menu item. From the drop-down menu select the Horizontal Scroll List menu item. You should see the dialog displayed in Figure 7-8. Notice that no horizontal scroll bar appears in the list box. Click on the Set Horizontal Scrolling On button and the horizontal scroll bar will appear at the bottom of the list box. You can then use this scroll bar to scroll through the list sideways and view the really really long string in the list.

To reproduce this functionality in your own application, do the following:

1. Create a new project in Visual C++ using AppWizard. Give the new project the name CH75.MAK. Enter AppStudio and create a new dialog. Move the OK and Cancel buttons to the bottom of the dialog and add a single list box to the dialog. Double-click on the list box and set the horizontal scroll bar check box to checked. Add a single button to the list box above the list box and give it the caption Set Horizontal Scrolling On.

2. Select ClassWizard and generate a new dialog class for the template you have just created. Give the new dialog class the name CHScrollList. Accept all other defaults for the dialog class.

3. In ClassWizard, select the CHScrollList class from the drop-down list. Select the CHScrollList object from the object list and the WM_INITDIALOG

Figure 7-8 Horizontal scroll list
dialog with no scroll bar displayed

message from the message list. Click on the Add Function button and enter
the following code into the OnInitDialog method of CHScrollList:

```
BOOL CHScrollList::OnInitDialog()
{
  CDialog::OnInitDialog();

  CListBox *list = (CListBox *)GetDlgItem(IDC_LIST1);
  list->AddString ( "This is a really really really really really
                    really long string" );
  list->AddString ( "This is a shorter string" );
  list->AddString ( "short string" );
  list->AddString ( "Another longer string" );
  list->AddString ( "The final String - A Very long String" );


  return TRUE;  // return TRUE  unless you set the focus to a control
}
```

4. Again in ClassWizard, select the IDC_BUTTON1 object from the object list
and the COMMAND message from the message list. Click on the Add
Function button. Enter the name OnDoHScroll as the name of the new
method and add the following code to the OnDoHScroll method of
CHScrollList:

```
void CHScrollList::OnDoHScroll()
{
   CListBox *list = (CListBox *)GetDlgItem(IDC_LIST1);

   // Get the length of the longest string.

   CDC *dc = list->GetDC();
   char string[256];
   int   max_len = 0;

   // Loop through all strings in the list box

   for ( int i=0; i<list->GetCount(); ++i ) {

      // Get the text associated with this item

      list->GetText ( i, string );

      // Get the length in pixels of this string.

      CSize size = dc->GetTextExtent(string, strlen(string));

      // If it is bigger than the biggest, reset the biggest

      if ( size.cx > max_len )
         max_len = size.cx;
   }

   ReleaseDC(dc);

   list->SendMessage(LB_SETHORIZONTALEXTENT, max_len, 0 );

   // Disable the button so it can't be pressed again

   GetDlgItem(IDC_BUTTON1)->EnableWindow(FALSE);
}
```

5. Enter AppStudio and select the main menu from the menu list. Add a new main menu item with the caption Dialogs. Add a menu item to the Dialogs menu with the caption Horizontal Scroll List. Give this menu the identifier ID_HSCROLL_LIST.

6. Reenter ClassWizard and select the application object, CCh75App. Select the ID_HSCROLL_LIST identifier from the object list and the COMMAND message from the message list. Click on the Add Function button. Accept the name OnHscrollList and enter the following code into this new method of CCh75App:

```
void CCh75App::OnHscrollList()
{
   CHScrollList dlg;
   dlg.DoModal();
}
```

7. Add the following include line to the include list at the top of CH75.CPP:

```
#include "hscrolll.h"
```

8. Compile and run the application.

How It Works

Clicking on the button in the dialog is the key to the whole application. When the button is pressed, the OnDoHScroll method of the dialog class is called. This method first gets the device context (DC) for the list box, which allows it to use the same text characteristics as the list box. Then, the method gets each string from the dialog and calls the GetTextExtent API function to get the length (in pixels) of the string. This is compared to the largest string so far, and if it is greater, the largest is reset.

Once the loop is completed, the method then calls the SendMessage function to send a LB_SETHORIZONTALEXTENT message to the list box with the longest string length as its parameter. Finally, the button is disabled by calling the EnableWindow API function to reset it so that it cannot be used again.

The GetTextExtent function basically "draws" the string in memory and returns the size of the area required to display it given the current settings of that device context. It is a handy and convenient way to find out how big something is going to be before you draw it. This procedure can be used to determine whether a given string will fit in a given area for something such as word-wrapping, for example.

Comments

The example given is a good start toward a new component for your applications. By extracting the code for determining the string length, for example, you could create a new list box class that automatically sets the horizontal extent for the list box based on the strings added.

You might try creating a new list class and overriding the AddString method to check this length. Once you have the length, you can keep it in an internal member data variable and use this variable to set the horizontal text extent to a new value each time. This will allow you to forget all about horizontal scrolling and always have it available when needed.

COMPLEXITY

DIFFICULT

7.6 How do I... Right-justify numbers in a list box?

Problem

I would like to be able to display numbers in my list boxes that are right-justified. These numbers are to be displayed for accounting people, who are accustomed to looking at money numbers from the right side of the screen. I cannot seem to find a simple way to tell list boxes to justify text to the right. A method exists for static text to be displayed right, left, or centered—why is there no such method for list boxes? How can I solve this problem without getting the accountants mad at me?

Technique

It is quite true that there is no direct way of putting text into list boxes right-justified. I am sure that you tried all of the obvious things: setting the DT_RIGHT bit in the style flags, using sprintf to try to right-justify the values, and so forth. Unfortunately, as you have discovered, these methods simply don't line things up properly.

There is a method that will work to justify text in a list box, though. This will be our first example of owner-drawn list boxes. These list boxes rely on the programmer to write a display function to show the text on the screen. Owner-drawn controls are an extremely powerful use of the Windows API and are responsible for many of the really cool effects you find in Windows applications.

In this How-To, we will barely scratch the surface of the whole owner-draw concept. In later How-To's in this chapter, we will make more extensive uses of the concept, including putting graphics and bitmaps into list box entries.

Steps

Open and run the Visual C++ application CH76.MAK from the CHAPT7\SAMPLES\CH76 directory on the CD that comes with this book. Select the Dialogs main menu item and select the Justify List menu item. You should see the dialog displayed in Figure 7-9. Click on the three justification buttons and watch the text in the list box change position. When you are done, click on the OK or Cancel buttons to end the dialog.

To reproduce this functionality in your own application, do the following:

1. Create a new project in Visual C++ using AppWizard. Give the new project the name CH76.MAK. Enter AppStudio and create a new dialog. Move the OK and Cancel buttons to the bottom of the dialog and add three buttons to the top of the dialog. Add a list box below the buttons.

2. Double-click on the list box and make sure the following Owner Draw combo box is set to Variable.

3. Select ClassWizard and generate a new dialog class for the template you have just created. Give the new dialog class the name CJustifyList. Accept all other defaults for the dialog class.

4. In ClassWizard, select the CJustifyList and click on the CJustifyList item in the object list. Click on the WM_INITDIALOG message in the message list. Finally, click on the Add Function button and enter the following code into the OnInitDialog method of CJustifyList:

```
BOOL CJustifyList::OnInitDialog()
{
  CDialog::OnInitDialog();
```

```
m_List.SubclassDlgItem(IDC_LIST1, this );

// Add items to the List

m_List.AddString ( "Item 1" );
m_List.AddString ( "Item 2" );
m_List.AddString ( "Item 3" );
m_List.AddString ( "Item 4" );
m_List.AddString ( "Item 5" );
m_List.AddString ( "Item 6" );
m_List.AddString ( "Item 7" );
m_List.AddString ( "Item 8" );
m_List.AddString ( "Item 9" );
m_List.AddString ( "Item 10" );


   return TRUE;  // return TRUE  unless you set the focus to a control
}
```

5. Next, click on the IDC_BUTTON1 object in the object list and the COMMAND message in the message list. Click on the Add Function button and select OnRightJustify for the name of the new method. Add the following code to the OnRightJustify method of CJustifyList:

```
void CJustifyList::OnRightJustify()
{
   m_List.SetJustification ( RightJustifyList );
}
```

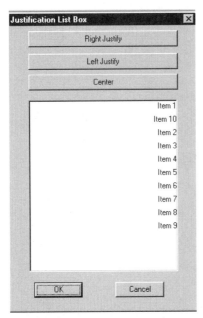

Figure 7-9 List box justification dialog

6. Click on the IDC_BUTTON2 object in the object list and the COMMAND message in the message list. Click on the Add Function button and select OnLeftJustify for the name of the new method. Add the following code to the OnLeftJustify method of CJustifyList:

```
void CJustifyList::OnLeftJustify()
{
    m_list.SetJustification ( LeftJustifyList );
}
```

7. Click on the IDC_BUTTON3 object in the object list and the COMMAND message in the message list. Click on the Add Function button and select OnCenterJustify for the name of the new method. Add the following code to the OnCenterJustify method of CJustifyList:

```
void CJustifyList::OnCenterJustify()
{
    m_list.SetJustification ( CenterJustifyList );
}
```

8. Select ClassWizard once again and click on the Add Class button. Give the new class the name CRightList. Select generic CWnd for the name of the base class and accept all other defaults.

9. Go into the RIGHTLIS.CPP file and change all occurrences of the string "CWnd" to the string "CListBox". Next, select the RIGHTLIS.H header file and make the same change. Save both files.

10. Add the following code that is marked in bold print to the RIGHTLIS.CPP source file:

```
CRightList::CRightList()
{
    mode = RightJustifyList;
}


CRightList::~CRightList()
{
}

void CRightList::SetJustification(int just)
{
    mode = just;
    InvalidateRect(NULL);
}

BEGIN_MESSAGE_MAP(CRightList, CListBox)
  //{{AFX_MSG_MAP(CRightList)
  //}}AFX_MSG_MAP
END_MESSAGE_MAP()


/////////////////////////////////////////////////////////////////////////////
// CRightList message handlers
```

```
void CRightList::DrawItem(LPDRAWITEMSTRUCT lpdi)
{
    // Losing focus?

    if (lpdi->itemID == -1) {
        DrawFocusRect(lpdi->hDC, &lpdi->rcItem);
    return;
    }

    // Draw the whole item

    if (lpdi->itemAction & ODA_DRAWENTIRE) {

        CDC dc;
        dc.m_hDC = lpdi->hDC;
        char *text = (char *)lpdi->itemData;

        int justification = DT_RIGHT;
        switch ( mode ) {
            case RightJustifyList:
                justification = DT_RIGHT;
                break;
            case LeftJustifyList:
                justification = DT_LEFT;
                break;
            case CenterJustifyList:
                justification = DT_CENTER;
                break;

        }

        dc.DrawText(text, strlen(text), &(lpdi->rcItem), justification);

        if (lpdi->itemState & ODS_SELECTED)
            InvertRect(lpdi->hDC, &lpdi->rcItem);

        if (lpdi->itemState & ODS_FOCUS)
            DrawFocusRect(lpdi->hDC, &lpdi->rcItem);

        dc.m_hDC = NULL;
    return;
    }

    // Selection made?

    if (lpdi->itemAction & ODA_SELECT) {
        InvertRect(lpdi->hDC, &lpdi->rcItem);
    return;
    }

    // Getting focus?

    if (lpdi->itemAction & ODA_FOCUS) {
        DrawFocusRect(lpdi->hDC, &lpdi->rcItem);
        return;
```

continued on next page

continued from previous page

```
        }
    }

    int CRightList::CompareItem(LPCOMPAREITEMSTRUCT lpCompareItemStruct)
    {
        char *text1 = (char *)lpCompareItemStruct->itemData1;
        char *text2 = (char *)lpCompareItemStruct->itemData2;
        return strcmp(text1,text2);
    }

    void CRightList::MeasureItem(LPMEASUREITEMSTRUCT lpMeasureItemStruct)
    {
        // Get the default list height

        lpMeasureItemStruct->itemHeight = 20;
    }
```

11. Add the following code to the RIGHLIST.H header file. Once again, the lines to add are marked in bold print.

```
const RightJustifyList = 0;
const LeftJustifyList  = 1;
const CenterJustifyList= 2;

class CRightList : public CListBox
{
private:
    int mode;

// Construction
public:
    CRightList();

// Attributes
public:

// Operations
public:

// Implementation
public:
    virtual ~CRightList();
    void  SetJustification(int just);

protected:
    virtual void MeasureItem(LPMEASUREITEMSTRUCT lpMIS);
    virtual void DrawItem(LPDRAWITEMSTRUCT lpDIS);
    virtual int CompareItem(LPCOMPAREITEMSTRUCT lpCIS);

    // Generated message map functions
    //{{AFX_MSG(CRightList)
    //}}AFX_MSG
    DECLARE_MESSAGE_MAP()
};
```

12. Select the JUSTIFYL.H header file and make the following additions. Add only those lines marked with bold print.

```
#include "rightlis.h"

class CJustifyList : public CDialog
{
    CRightList m_list;
```

13. Next, reenter AppStudio and select the main menu. Add a main menu with the caption Dialogs. Add a new menu item with the caption Justify List to the Dialogs menu. Give this menu item the identifier ID_JUSTIFY_LIST.

14. In ClassWizard, select the application object, CCh76App. Select the ID_JUSTIFY_LIST identifier from the object list and the COMMAND message from the message list. Click on the Add Function button and accept the name OnJustifyList. Enter the following code into the OnJustifyList method of CCh76App:

```
void CCh76App::OnJustifyList()
{
    CJustifyList dlg;
    dlg.DoModal();
}
```

15. Add the following include file line to the include list at the top of CH76.CPP:

```
#include "justifyl.h"
```

16. Compile and run the application.

How It Works

When the dialog box is initially displayed, the OnInitDialog method of the dialog class subclasses the list box with the new list box class CRightList. This class is an owner-drawn list box class and does the work of displaying the text in the proper way.

There are three functions necessary to make an owner-drawn list box (or any other owner-drawn control). First, you need a function to tell the list box how tall a given item is. This is the MeasureItem method of CRightList. This method will simply set all of the items in the list to the same size (in this case 20 pixels). As the list box needs to draw each item, it will call this method to determine the size of the bounding box to use to display the item.

Next, the list box manager requires that you have a compare function. This method is used to determine where an item in a sorted list belongs. In our case, since the list box items are simply text values, we can just return the value of the function call strcmp, which compares two strings and returns a value that is compatible with the compare function. This function is called CompareItem.

Finally, the meat of the list box functionality occurs in the DrawItem method. This method is responsible for actually rendering each list box entry onto the screen within the confines of that item's bounding box in the list box. The function is called with a single parameter, which is of type LPDRAWITEMSTRUCT. Although there are quite a few fields in this structure, the ones that are important to us are the focus setting, the item data, and the bounding rectangle for the item. The focus setting is stored in the itemAction member of the structure and can have one of the following values: ODA_DRAWENTIRE, ODA_SELECTED, ODA_SELECT, and ODA_FOCUS. These settings determine whether or not we draw the item and whether or not we draw the focus rectangle around the item.

The DrawItem method is most important for the ODA_DRAWENTIRE setting of the itemAction parameter. If this setting is in effect, the list box is asking the function to actually render the item onto the list box "canvas." This is where the justification setting comes into play. When the user selects a justification setting by clicking on one of the buttons in the dialog, the list box setting is updated with the proper value. This value (DT_RIGHT, DT_LEFT, or DT_CENTER) is then passed to the API function DrawText, which does the work of actually putting the string in the proper position. DrawText also accepts a bounding rectangle, which we supply as the rectangle passed to the DrawItem method of CRightList.

The final piece of the puzzle is the InvalidateRect call in SetJustification. This function "invalidates" the window, indicating that Windows should redraw it. When Windows does redraw the window, our DrawItem call is called for each item. This allows us to redisplay the text in the new justification.

Comments

The owner-draw concept is extremely powerful in all versions of Windows. The important things to remember in handling owner-drawing of controls is that you are not in charge. You must respond to messages in the order Windows wants you to respond and no other.

This How-To could easily be the basis for many other types of controls. This list box could be used for displaying money values (right-justified), string values (left-justified), or other data that requires centering, such as headers and footers for documents.

With the power of owner-drawing, you can also render colors, graphics, icons, or bitmaps into your list boxes. Jazz those lists up with eye-catching graphics! In our next How-To selection, we will examine how you would go about putting in graphics.

COMPLEXITY
DIFFICULT

7.7   How do I...
Draw my own list box?

Problem

I would like to be able to display items in a list box that contains other attributes than those allowed in "normal" list boxes. For example, it would be nice to display a color box along with the color name and display the color name in the color that was selected. List boxes supplied with Windows and Windows 95 do not allow this functionality by themselves.

How can I "draw" my own list box to do this sort of thing without having to write all of the other functionality that is supported by the normal list boxes? I really don't want to write sorting routines, keyboard entry routines, drag-and-drop routines, and so forth.

Technique

As discussed in the previous How-To, the owner-drawn list box is an extremely powerful weapon in the Windows programmer's arsenal. The technique for drawing your own list boxes is straightforward. First, you need to be able to measure the height of the items in the list. Next, you need to be able to compare two items in a list. Finally, you need to draw the item on the list box.

In this How-To, we look at how you can use the power of subclassing and owner-drawing to create a list box that contains text, colors, and graphics.

Steps

Open and run the Visual C++ application CH77.MAK from the CHAPT7\SAM-PLES\CH77 directory on the CD that comes with this book. Select the Dialogs main menu item and select the Owner Draw Dialog drop-down menu item. You should see the dialog displayed in Figure 7-10. You can select one of the color items in the list box and watch how the cursor moves. When you are done, click on the OK or Cancel buttons to end the dialog.

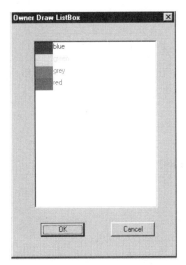

Figure 7-10 Owner-drawn list box example

To reproduce this functionality in your own application, do the following:

1. Create a new project in Visual C++ using AppWizard. Give the new project the name CH77.MAK. Enter AppStudio and create a new dialog. Move the OK and Cancel buttons to the bottom of the dialog and add three buttons to the top of the dialog. Add a list box below the buttons.

2. Double-click on the list box and make sure the following Owner Draw combo box is set to Variable.

3. Select ClassWizard and generate a new dialog class for the template you have just created. Give the new dialog class the name COwnerDrawDlg. Accept all other defaults for the dialog class.

4. In ClassWizard, select the COwnerDrawDlg and click on the CJustifyList item in the object list. Click on the WM_INITDIALOG message in the message list. Finally, click on the Add Function button and enter the following code into the OnInitDialog method of COwnerDragDlg:

```
BOOL COwnerDrawDlg::OnInitDialog()
{
  CDialog::OnInitDialog();

  m_list.SubclassDlgItem(IDC_LIST1, this );

  // Add a bunch of items to the list

  m_list.AddString ( RGB(255,0,0), "red" );
  m_list.AddString ( RGB(0,255,0), "green" );
  m_list.AddString ( RGB(0,0,255), "blue" );
  m_list.AddString ( RGB(128,128,128), "grey" );

  return TRUE;  // return TRUE  unless you set the focus to a control
}
```

5. Add the following lines shown in bold print to the header file for the COwnerDrawDlg class (OWNERDRA.H):

```
#include "ownlis.h"

class COwnerDrawDlg : public CDialog
{
private:
   COwnerDrawList m_list;
```

6. Create a new file in Visual C++ and enter the following code into the file:

```
// ownlis.cpp : implementation file
//

#include "stdafx.h"
#include "ch77.h"
#include "ownlis.h"

#ifdef _DEBUG
#undef THIS_FILE
```

```
static char BASED_CODE THIS_FILE[] = __FILE__;
#endif

///////////////////////////////////////////////////////////////////////////
// COwnerDrawList

COwnerDrawList::COwnerDrawList()
{
}

COwnerDrawList::~COwnerDrawList()
{
}

COwnerDrawList::AddString ( COLORREF color, char *string )
{
    ColorStruct *s = new ColorStruct;
    s->string = new char[strlen(string)+1];
    strcpy ( s->string, string );
    s->color = color;

    // Add the string to the list box

    int idx = CListBox::AddString ( (char *)s );

    // Save the pointer as item data so we can delete it later

    SetItemData( idx, (DWORD)s );

    return idx;
}

BEGIN_MESSAGE_MAP(COwnerDrawList, CListBox)
  //{{AFX_MSG_MAP(COwnerDrawList)
  //}}AFX_MSG_MAP
END_MESSAGE_MAP()

///////////////////////////////////////////////////////////////////////////
// COwnerDrawList message handlers

void COwnerDrawList::DrawItem(LPDRAWITEMSTRUCT lpdi)
{
    ColorStruct *s = (ColorStruct *)lpdi->itemData;

    // Losing focus?

    if (lpdi->itemID == -1) {
        DrawFocusRect(lpdi->hDC, &lpdi->rcItem);
        return;
    }

    // Draw the whole item

    if (lpdi->itemAction & ODA_DRAWENTIRE) {
```

continued on next page

continued from previous page

```
            CDC dc;
            dc.m_hDC = lpdi->hDC;
            char *text = s->string;

            // First, draw the color

            COLORREF color = s->color;

            RECT r;
            r.top = lpdi->rcItem.top;
            r.bottom = lpdi->rcItem.bottom;
            r.left = lpdi->rcItem.left;
            r.right = r.left + 30;

            CBrush brush( color );
            dc.FillRect ( &r, &brush );

            r = lpdi->rcItem;
            r.left += 30;

            dc.SetTextColor ( color );
            dc.DrawText(text, strlen(text), &r, DT_LEFT);

            if (lpdi->itemState & ODS_SELECTED)
                InvertRect(lpdi->hDC, &lpdi->rcItem);

            if (lpdi->itemState & ODS_FOCUS)
                DrawFocusRect(lpdi->hDC, &lpdi->rcItem);

            dc.m_hDC = NULL;
        return;
        }

        // Selection made?

        if (lpdi->itemAction & ODA_SELECT) {
            InvertRect(lpdi->hDC, &lpdi->rcItem);
        return;
    }

        // Getting focus?

        if (lpdi->itemAction & ODA_FOCUS) {
            DrawFocusRect(lpdi->hDC, &lpdi->rcItem);
            return;
        }
    }

    int COwnerDrawList::CompareItem(LPCOMPAREITEMSTRUCT
    lpCompareItemStruct)
    {
        ColorStruct *s1 = (ColorStruct *)lpCompareItemStruct->itemData1;
        ColorStruct *s2 = (ColorStruct *)lpCompareItemStruct->itemData2;
        return strcmp(s1->string,s2->string);
    }
```

```
void COwnerDrawList::MeasureItem(LPMEASUREITEMSTRUCT
lpMeasureItemStruct)
{
    // Get the default list height

    lpMeasureItemStruct->itemHeight = 20;
}
```

7. Save the file as OWNLIST.CPP. Next, create another new file in Visual C++ and enter the following into the new file window:

```
// ownlist.h : header file
//


/////////////////////////////////////////////////////////////////////
// COwnerDrawList window

class COwnerDrawList : public CListBox
{
typedef struct {
    char *string;
    COLORREF color;
} ColorStruct;

// Construction
public:
  COwnerDrawList();

// Attributes
public:

// Operations
public:
    int AddString ( COLORREF color, char *string );

// Implementation
public:
  virtual ~COwnerDrawList();

protected:
    virtual void MeasureItem(LPMEASUREITEMSTRUCT lpMIS);
    virtual void DrawItem(LPDRAWITEMSTRUCT lpDIS);
    virtual int CompareItem(LPCOMPAREITEMSTRUCT lpCIS);

  // Generated message map functions
  //{{AFX_MSG(COwnerDrawList)
  //}}AFX_MSG
  DECLARE_MESSAGE_MAP()
};


/////////////////////////////////////////////////////////////////////
```

8. Save this file as OWNLIS.H.

9. Enter AppStudio and select the main menu. Add a new main menu with the caption Dialogs. Add a new menu item to the Dialogs menu and give this new menu item the identifier of ID_OWNER_DRAW_DLG. Give the new item the caption Owner Draw Dialog.

10. Enter ClassWizard and select the application object, CCh77App. Click on the ID_OWNER_DRAW_DLG object in the object list and the COMMAND message from the message list. Click on the Add Function button. Accept the name OnOwnerDrawDlg for the new function name. Enter the following code into the OnOwnerDragDlg method of CCh77App:

```
void CCh77App::OnOwnerDrawDlg()
{
    COwnerDrawDlg dlg;
    dlg.DoModal();

}
```

11. Add the following include file line to the top of the CH77.CPP source file:

```
#include "ownerdra.h"
```

12. Compile and run the application.

How It Works

In the previous How-To, we discussed how owner-drawn list boxes work in general, so refer to that section to understand the basics of the owner-draw process. In this How-To, we are more concerned with the logistics and techniques used to actually render the item onto the list box background.

When the dialog is displayed and the list box begins to paint itself, the list box function calls our DrawItem method to render the item onto the dialog list box. The DrawItem function casts the input data value for the list box to a ColorStruct structure pointer and uses the color and text members of the ColorStruct structure to render the item.

First, the color is used to "paint" a rectangle in the list box item area that contains the color selected. Next, the color is used to set the text color for displaying text in the list box item area. Finally, the text is drawn to the list box immediately following color box for that item.

How, then, does this ColorStruct get into the item data for this list box item? The answer lies in the overloading of the AddString method for our owner-drawn list box. If you examine the code for the overloaded AddString, you will see that the method is called with a color reference (RGB) value and a string to display. The method then creates a new instance of the ColorStruct structure and assigns these values to the individual structure elements of the structure. This structure is then stored as the "string" in the list box. Since the list box will only look at the data when it passes it to our handler functions, this is quite all right. Notice that the compare function first casts both inputs to ColorStructs before it manipulates that data.

Finally, in the destructor for our owner-drawn list box, we retrieve each element from the list box and delete the memory that was allocated to store the element and the string associated with that element.

Comments

This is the kind of component that can remain in your toolbox of routines to use in many different applications. It can be extended to handle much more than the simple case of color. In addition, you could manage fonts, numbers, or any other information that you would like to store along with the list box.

If you were to combine the techniques of this How-To with the techniques of storing item data with the list items, you could build a mini-database within your list boxes to store all of the information necessary for your application.

In addition to the Visual C++ example, there is an example on disk of how to create an owner-drawn list box using Delphi. Lack of space prohibits us from listing it here, but you will find it in the code section under the project name OWNDRAW.DPR.

COMPLEXITY
MODERATE

7.8   How do I...
Store more items in a list box?

Problem

In my application I have a list box that needs to hold a large number of items. Unfortunately, this application needs to run in 16-bit mode due to the need to run on Windows 3.x as well as Windows 95. Under Windows 95 the application runs fine, but the program crashes under Windows 3.x when it runs out of space inserting items into the list box in the application.

What I would like is a single list box that will work in either the 16-bit or 32-bit world that doesn't have the limitations of the normal 16-bit list boxes. Ideally, I would be able to customize the list box in ways that I can't in Windows 3.1, such as setting the background color, the text color, and so forth. How can this be accomplished?

Technique

Although it is possible to accomplish the things you want by using a list box control, it is more difficult than the previous examples. It would require rewriting most of the internals of the list box control and would return at best marginal improvements. List boxes in 16-bit environments are limited to 32,767 bytes of data, which equates to several thousand entries at best. To modify this limit you would need to change each and every routine that referenced the items, since they refer to an integer value rather than a long value.

Instead, in this How-To we will examine another of the capabilities of the Windows operating system—creating custom controls. We will use the API to create a new Windows class that will be used to display virtual list boxes on a screen. As a bonus, this class can be used to display columnar lists and allow horizontal scrolling. All this will be built into the control. Surprisingly, all of the code to accomplish this will be smaller than what would have been required to subclass a list box and allow an arbitrary number of elements to be added.

The "virtual" aspect of the control will come from the fact that it will not store actual items. Instead, we will create a "provider" object that "feeds" the virtual list box with the information it needs to display items on the screen. This has two advantages. One is that we can change the way we enter data into the system without modifying the list box display object. The second advantage is that it does not rely on any capabilities of the Windows list box and therefore will run unchanged on either Windows 3.x, Windows 95, or Windows NT.

Steps

Open and run the Visual C++ application CH78.MAK from the CHAPT7\SAMPLES\CH78 directory on the CD that comes with this book. Click on the New File button or select File | New from the main menu. A dialog box will be displayed listing two document types. Select the second document type and click on the OK button. You should see the screen displayed in Figure 7-11. You can scroll through the items for as long as you want, horizontally and vertically. When you are done, click on the close button or double-click on the system menu in Windows 3.x.

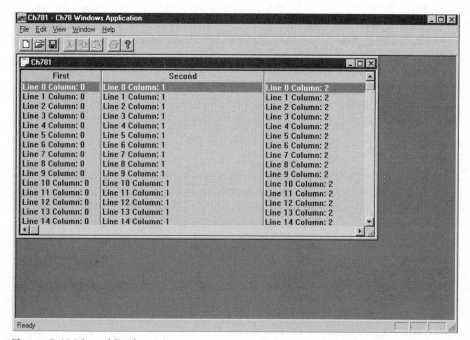

Figure 7-11 Virtual list box view

To reproduce this functionality in your own application, follow this procedure:

1. Create a new project in Visual C++ using AppWizard. Give this new project the name CH78.MAK. Create a new file in the environment by selecting the File main menu and clicking on the New drop-down menu. Enter the following code into the new file:

```
#include "stdafx.h"
#include "listconf.h"

ListConfiguration::ListConfiguration(long totalItems)
{
    totalNumberOfItems = totalItems;
    currentItem        = 0L;
}


ListConfiguration::~ListConfiguration(void)
{
}

// Access methods

int ListConfiguration::AddColumn(int width, const CString&
headerString)
{
    positions.Add ( width );
    headers.Add ( headerString );
    return 0;
}

int ListConfiguration::SetColumnWidth(int which, int width)
{
    int status = 0;

    // See if this item already exists...

    if ( positions.GetSize() > which )
        positions[which] = width;
    else
        status = -1;

    return status;
}

int ListConfiguration::GetColumnWidth(int which)
{
    if ( positions.GetSize() > which )
        return positions.GetAt(which);
    return -1;
}

int ListConfiguration::SetColumnHeader(
int which, const CString& headerString)
{
```

continued on next page

continued from previous page

```
        int status = 0;

        // See if this item already exists...

        if ( headers.GetSize() > which )
            headers[which] = headerString;
        else
            status = -1;

        return status;
    }

    int ListConfiguration::GetColumnHeader(int which, CString& s)
    {
        if ( headers.GetSize() > which ) {
            s = headers.GetAt(which);
            return 0;
        }
        return -1;
    }

    // Actual list text provider methods

    int ListConfiguration::SetCurrentItemNumber(long item)
    {
        int status = 0;
        if ( item >= 0 && item < totalNumberOfItems )
            currentItem = item;
        else
            status = -1;
        return status;
    }

    long ListConfiguration::GetCurrentItemNumber(void)
    {
        return currentItem;
    }

    char *ListConfiguration::GetColumn(int which)
    {
        static char buffer[80];
        sprintf(buffer, "Line %ld Column: %d", currentItem, which );
        return buffer;
    }

    int ListConfiguration::NumberOfColumns()
    {
        return positions.GetSize();
    }
```

2. Save the file as LISTCONF.CPP and create another new file. Add this code to the new file you have created:

```
#ifndef _LCONFIG_H_
#define _LCONFIG_H_
```

```
class ListConfiguration {

private:
    CUIntArray    positions;
    CStringArray headers;
    long          totalNumberOfItems;
    long          currentItem;

public:
    ListConfiguration(long totalItems);
    virtual ~ListConfiguration(void);

// Access methods

    int NumberOfColumns();
    int AddColumn(int width, const CString& headerString);
    int SetColumnWidth(int which, int width);
    int GetColumnWidth(int which);
    int SetColumnHeader(int which, const CString& headerString);
    int GetColumnHeader(int which, CString& s);

// Actual list text provider methods

    long NumberOfItems(void) { return totalNumberOfItems; };
    int  SetCurrentItemNumber(long item);
    long GetCurrentItemNumber(void);
    char *GetColumn(int which);

};

#endif
```

3. Save the file as LISTCONF.H. Next, create a new file and save it as VLIST-WND.CPP. Add the following code to the VLISTWND.CPP file:

```
// vlistwnd.cpp : implementation file
//

#include "stdafx.h"
#include "ch7.h"
#include "vlistwnd.h"


#ifdef _DEBUG
#undef THIS_FILE
static char BASED_CODE THIS_FILE[] = __FILE__;
#endif

/////////////////////////////////////////////////////////////////////////
// CVListWnd

CVListWnd::CVListWnd(ListConfiguration *config)
{
    xoffset = 0;
    cur_row = 0;
    top_row = 0;
```

continued on next page

continued from previous page

```
        last_screen_row = 8;
        top_of_list_area = 20;
        conf = config;
    }


    CVListWnd::~CVListWnd()
    {
    }


    BEGIN_MESSAGE_MAP(CVListWnd, CWnd)
      //{{AFX_MSG_MAP(CVListWnd)
      ON_WM_ERASEBKGND()
      ON_WM_PAINT()
      ON_WM_HSCROLL()
      ON_WM_CREATE()
      ON_WM_VSCROLL()
      ON_WM_KEYDOWN()
      ON_WM_LBUTTONDOWN()
      //}}AFX_MSG_MAP
    END_MESSAGE_MAP()


    //////////////////////////////////////////////////////////////////////
    // CVListWnd message handlers


    BOOL CVListWnd::OnEraseBkgnd(CDC* pDC)
    {
        COLORREF rgbBkColor = GetSysColor(COLOR_BTNFACE);
        //
        // Erase only the area needed
        //
        CRect rect;
        GetClientRect(&rect) ;

        //
        // Make a brush to erase the background.
        //
        CBrush NewBrush(rgbBkColor);

        pDC->SetBrushOrg(0,0) ;

        CBrush* pOldBrush = (CBrush*)pDC->SelectObject(&NewBrush);

        //
        // Paint the Background....
        //
        pDC->PatBlt(rect.left, rect.top, rect.Width(), rect.Height(),PATCOPY);
        pDC->SelectObject(pOldBrush);
        return TRUE;
    }


    void CVListWnd::OnPaint()
    {
      CPaintDC dc(this); // device context for painting

        CPen text_pen(PS_SOLID, 1, GetSysColor(COLOR_GRAYTEXT));
```

```
CPen dark_pen(PS_SOLID, 1, GetSysColor(COLOR_BTNSHADOW));
CPen shadow_pen(PS_SOLID, 1, GetSysColor(COLOR_BTNHIGHLIGHT));
CRect r;
GetClientRect(&r);
TEXTMETRIC tm;
dc.GetTextMetrics( &tm );

// Next, draw the lines for the column boundaries

int x = 0;
int totalColumns = 0;

for ( int i=0; i<conf->NumberOfColumns(); ++i ) {
    dc.SelectObject(&text_pen);

    int offset = (conf->GetColumnWidth(i) - xoffset) * tm.tmMaxCharWidth;

    // Do the header...

    CRect r1(x+1, 1, offset-1, top_of_list_area-1 );
    CRect tRect = r1;

    CString s;
    conf->GetColumnHeader(i, s);

    DoColumnHeader ( dc, s, r1 );


    dc.MoveTo(offset,0);
    dc.LineTo(offset,r.bottom);

    dc.SelectObject(&dark_pen);
    dc.MoveTo(offset-1,0);
    dc.LineTo(offset-1,r.bottom);

    dc.SelectObject(&shadow_pen);
    dc.MoveTo(offset+1,0);
    dc.LineTo(offset+1,r.bottom);

    x = offset + 2;
    if ( totalColumns < conf->GetColumnWidth(i) )
        totalColumns = conf->GetColumnWidth(i);
}

SetScrollRange ( SB_HORZ, 0, totalColumns+conf->NumberOfColumns() );

// Draw a line for the top of the list area

dc.SelectObject ( &dark_pen );
dc.MoveTo ( 0, top_of_list_area-1 );
dc.LineTo ( r.right, top_of_list_area-1 );

int y = top_of_list_area;
long line = top_row;
while ( y < dc.m_ps.rcPaint.bottom && line < conf->NumberOfItems() ) {
    y = DisplayLine ( &dc, line );
```

continued on next page

continued from previous page

```
            if ( y < dc.m_ps.rcPaint.bottom )
                last_line = line;
            line++;
        }

        ShowCursor(&dc, cur_row);
    }

void CVListWnd::OnHScroll(UINT nSBCode, UINT nPos, CScrollBar* pScrollBar)
{
    int xInc = 0;
    int min, max;

    GetScrollRange ( SB_HORZ, &min, &max );

    switch(nSBCode)
    {
      case SB_PAGEUP:
        if ( xoffset > 8 )
            xInc = -8;
        else
            xInc = -xoffset;
        break;

      case SB_PAGEDOWN:
        xInc = 8;
        break;

      case SB_LINEUP:
        if ( xoffset )
            xInc = -1;
        break;

      case SB_LINEDOWN:
        if ( xoffset < max )
            xInc = 1;
        break;

      default:
        return;

    }
    xoffset += xInc;
    SetScrollPos(SB_HORZ,xoffset,TRUE);

    CWnd::OnHScroll(nSBCode, nPos, pScrollBar);
    if ( xInc )
        InvalidateRect ( NULL );
}

int CVListWnd::OnCreate(LPCREATESTRUCT lpCreateStruct)
{
    if (CWnd::OnCreate(lpCreateStruct) == -1)
        return -1;
```

```
      return 0;
}

void CVListWnd::ShowCursor(CDC *dc, long row)
{
    // Determine the start of this row on the screen

      TEXTMETRIC tm;
      dc->GetTextMetrics( &tm );
      int y = top_of_list_area + tm.tmHeight * (int)(row-top_row);

      // For each "field", hilight the rectangle

      int st_x = 3;
      CRect r;

      for ( int i=0; i<conf->NumberOfColumns(); ++i ) {

          int end_x = (conf->GetColumnWidth(i)-xoffset) *
                        tm.tmMaxCharWidth;
          r.top = y;
          r.bottom = y + tm.tmHeight;
          r.left = st_x;
          if ( r.left < 3 )
              r.left = 3;
          r.right = end_x - 3;
          if ( r.right < 3 )
              r.right = 3;

          dc->InvertRect ( &r );

          st_x = end_x + 3;
      }
}

int CVListWnd::DisplayLine ( CDC *dc, long row )
{
    // Determine the start of this row on the screen

      TEXTMETRIC tm;
      dc->GetTextMetrics( &tm );
      int y = top_of_list_area + tm.tmHeight * (int)(row-top_row);

      // For each "field", hilight the rectangle

      int st_x = 3;
      CRect r;
      dc->SetTextColor ( GetSysColor(COLOR_BTNTEXT) );
      dc->SetBkColor ( GetSysColor( COLOR_BTNFACE) );

      int offset = xoffset;

      for ( int i=0; i<conf->NumberOfColumns(); ++i ) {
```

continued on next page

continued from previous page

```
          int end_x = (conf->GetColumnWidth(i)-xoffset) * tm.tmMaxCharWidth;

          r.top = y;
          r.bottom = y + tm.tmHeight;

          r.left = st_x;
          r.right = end_x - 3;

          conf->SetCurrentItemNumber(row);

          char *text = conf->GetColumn(i);
          if ( offset < (int)strlen(text) )
              text += offset;
          else
              text= NULL;

          if ( text )
              dc->DrawText ( text, strlen(text),
                          &r, DT_LEFT | DT_SINGLELINE );

          offset = xoffset-conf->GetColumnWidth(i);
          if ( offset < 0 )
              offset = 0;


          st_x = end_x + 3;
          if ( st_x < 3 )
              st_x = 3;
      }

      return y + tm.tmHeight;
}

void CVListWnd::OnVScroll(UINT nSBCode, UINT nPos, CScrollBar* pScrollBar)
{
   double dpct;

   CDC *dc = GetDC();

   // Get the text metrics used for this screen.

   TEXTMETRIC tm;
   dc->GetTextMetrics( &tm );


   // Calculate total lines per page

   CRect r;
   GetClientRect(&r);

   int num_lines = (r.bottom - top_of_list_area) / tm.tmHeight;

   switch(nSBCode)
   {
     case SB_PAGEUP:
```

```
// First case:  Not enough lines to "page"

if ( top_row < num_lines ) {

    // Silly case -- top line is already first line

    if ( top_row == 0 ) {
        ReleaseDC(dc);
        return;
    }

    // Otherwise make first line top line

    top_row = 0;
    cur_row = top_row;
    InvalidateRect(NULL);
}
else {  // Next case, just reset top line to be the old top
        // line - "page"
    top_row = top_row - num_lines + 1;
    cur_row = top_row;
    InvalidateRect(NULL);
}

break;

case SB_PAGEDOWN:
    // Are we already at the end?

    if ( last_line == conf->NumberOfItems() -1 ) {
        ReleaseDC(dc);
        return;
    }

    // No. Make the last line the first line

    top_row = last_line;
    cur_row = last_line;
    InvalidateRect(NULL);

    break;

case SB_LINEUP:
    if ( cur_row > top_row ) {
        ShowCursor(dc, cur_row);
        cur_row--;
        ShowCursor(dc, cur_row);
    }
    else
        if ( top_row ) {
            top_row--;
            cur_row--;
            InvalidateRect(NULL);
        }
    break;
```

continued on next page

continued from previous page

```
      case SB_LINEDOWN:
        if ( cur_row < last_line) {
            ShowCursor(dc, cur_row);
            cur_row++;
            ShowCursor(dc, cur_row);
        }
        else {
            if ( cur_row < conf->NumberOfItems()-1 ) {
                top_row ++;
                cur_row ++;
                InvalidateRect(NULL);
            }
        }
        break;


      case SB_THUMBPOSITION:

        // The position of the thumb indicates what percentage of the
        // items we are at.
        // Use it to determine where we are.

        dpct = (double)nPos / 100.0;
        top_row = (long)((double)conf->NumberOfItems() * dpct);
        cur_row = top_row;
        InvalidateRect(NULL);
        break;


    default:
        ReleaseDC(dc);
        return;

    }
    SetScrollRange(SB_VERT, 0, 100);
    // Determine where we are in the list
    if ( cur_row != 0 ) {
        int pct = (int)(((double)(cur_row+1) / (double)
                conf->NumberOfItems()) * 100.0);
        SetScrollPos(SB_VERT, pct, TRUE );
    }
    else
        SetScrollPos(SB_VERT, 0, TRUE);
    ReleaseDC(dc);
    CWnd::OnVScroll(nSBCode, nPos, pScrollBar);
}

void CVListWnd::OnKeyDown(UINT nChar, UINT nRepCnt, UINT nFlags)
{
    WORD mScrollNotify = -1;
    WORD mScrollType = -1;
    switch (nChar)
    {
    case VK_RIGHT:
        mScrollType    = WM_HSCROLL;
```

```
        mScrollNotify = SB_LINEDOWN;
        break;

    case VK_LEFT:
      mScrollType   = WM_HSCROLL;
      mScrollNotify = SB_LINEUP;
      break;

    case VK_UP:
      mScrollType   = WM_VSCROLL;
      mScrollNotify = SB_LINEUP;
      break;

    case VK_PRIOR:
      mScrollType   = WM_VSCROLL;
      mScrollNotify = SB_PAGEUP;
      break;

    case VK_NEXT:
      mScrollType   = WM_VSCROLL;
      mScrollNotify = SB_PAGEDOWN;
      break;

    case VK_DOWN:
      mScrollType   = WM_VSCROLL;
      mScrollNotify = SB_LINEDOWN;
      break;

    case VK_HOME:
      mScrollType   = WM_VSCROLL;
      mScrollNotify = SB_TOP;
      break;

    case VK_END:
      mScrollType   = WM_VSCROLL;
      mScrollNotify = SB_BOTTOM;
      break;

    case VK_RETURN:
        return;
    default:
      break;
    }

  if (mScrollNotify != -1)
    PostMessage(mScrollType,mScrollNotify);


  CWnd::OnKeyDown(nChar, nRepCnt, nFlags);
}

void CVListWnd::OnLButtonDown(UINT nFlags, CPoint point)
{
  TEXTMETRIC tm;
  CDC *dc = GetDC();
  dc->GetTextMetrics( &tm );
```

continued on next page

continued from previous page

```
        // Figure out which one it is...

        long which_row = top_row + ( (point.y-top_of_list_area) / tm.tmHeight);

        // If the line selected is within the current range of items,
        // select it.

        if ( which_row < conf->NumberOfItems() ) {
           ShowCursor(dc, cur_row);
           cur_row = which_row;
           ShowCursor(dc, cur_row);
        }

         ReleaseDC(dc);

        // Life is good. Do the default processing.

        CWnd::OnLButtonDown(nFlags, point);
    }



    void CVListWnd::DoColumnHeader ( CDC&dc, CString& s, CRect r )
    {
        CBrush b(GetSysColor(COLOR_BTNFACE));
        dc.FillRect ( &r, &b );
        int mode = dc.GetBkMode();

        dc.SetBkMode(TRANSPARENT);
        dc.SetBkColor ( GetSysColor(COLOR_BTNFACE) );
        dc.DrawText( s, strlen(s), &r, DT_CENTER );

        dc.SetBkMode(mode);
    }
```

4. Create a new file and save it as VLISTWND.H. Enter the following code into the VLISTWND.H file:

```
// vlistwnd.h : header file
//

/////////////////////////////////////////////////////////////////////
// CVListWnd window

// Include files for this object

#include "listconf.h"

class CVListWnd : public CWnd
{
private:
    int xoffset;
    int header_mode;
    int last_screen_row;
    long cur_row;
    long top_row;
```

```
        CRect draw_rect;
        int current_select_line;
        int top_of_list_area;
        long last_line;
        ListConfiguration *conf;

// Construction
public:
    CVListWnd(ListConfiguration *conf);

// Attributes
public:

// Operations
public:

// Implementation
public:
    virtual ~CVListWnd();
    virtual void DoColumnHeader ( CDC&dc, CString& s, CRect r );

protected:
        void ShowCursor(CDC *dc, long row);
        int  DisplayLine ( CDC *dc, long row );

    // Generated message map functions
    //{{AFX_MSG(CVListWnd)
    afx_msg BOOL OnEraseBkgnd(CDC* pDC);
    afx_msg void OnPaint();
    afx_msg void OnHScroll(UINT nSBCode, UINT nPos, CScrollBar* pScrollBar);
    afx_msg int OnCreate(LPCREATESTRUCT lpCreateStruct);
    afx_msg void OnVScroll(UINT nSBCode, UINT nPos, CScrollBar* pScrollBar);
    afx_msg void OnKeyDown(UINT nChar, UINT nRepCnt, UINT nFlags);
    afx_msg void OnLButtonDown(UINT nFlags, CPoint point);
    //}}AFX_MSG
    DECLARE_MESSAGE_MAP()
};
```

//

5. Select the application object source file, CH78.CPP, and add the following
code to the source file in the InitInstance method just below the creation of
the pDocTemplate object:

```
pDocTemplate = new CMultiDocTemplate(
    IDR_CH7TYPE,
    RUNTIME_CLASS(CNewDoc),
    RUNTIME_CLASS(CMDIChildWnd),           // standard MDI child frame
    RUNTIME_CLASS(CNewView));
  AddDocTemplate(pDocTemplate);
```

6. Finally, add these two include files to the include file list at the top of CH78.CPP:

```
#include "newview.h"
#include "newdoc.h"
```

7. Enter ClassWizard and click on the Add Class button. Name the new class CNewView, and select the CView class as the base class for the new class. In ClassWizard, click on the CNewView object in the object list and the WM_CREATE message in the message list. Add the following code to the OnCreate method of CNewView:

```
int CNewView::OnCreate(LPCREATESTRUCT lpCreateStruct)
{
  if (CView::OnCreate(lpCreateStruct) == -1)
    return -1;

    conf = new ListConfiguration(50);

    conf->AddColumn(10, "First");
    conf->AddColumn(30, "Second" );
    conf->AddColumn(60, "Third" );

    wnd = new CVListWnd(conf);

    CRect r1;
    GetClientRect(&r1);

    BOOL what= wnd->Create(NULL,
                      "",
                      WS_CHILD |WS_VISIBLE |WS_VSCROLL|WS_BORDER|WS_HSCROLL,
                      r1,
                      this,
                      NULL);
  return 0;
}
```

8. Click on the CNewView object in the object list in ClassWizard and the WM_SIZE message in the message list. Add the following code to the OnSize method of CNewView:

```
void CNewView::OnSize(UINT nType, int cx, int cy)
{
    CView::OnSize(nType, cx, cy);

    CRect r;
    GetClientRect(&r);
    wnd->MoveWindow ( &r );
}
```

9. Add the following lines shown in bold print to the constructor and destructor for the CNewView class:

```
CNewView::CNewView()
{
    wnd = NULL;
    conf = NULL;
}

CNewView::~CNewView()
{
```

```
   if ( wnd )
      delete wnd;
   if ( conf )
      delete conf;
}
```

10. Add the following lines to the NEWVIEW.H header file. Once again, add only the lines marked with bold print.

```
class CVListWnd;
class ListConfiguration;

class CNewView : public CView
{
 private:
     CVListWnd *wnd;
     ListConfiguration *conf;
```

11. Go back into ClassWizard and again click on the Add Class button. Enter the name CNewDoc for the name of the new class and select CDocument for the base class for this new class. Click on the Generate Class button.

12. Compile and run the application.

How It Works

The document/view architecture of the MFC allows us to simply "drop in" new view types and have the foundation class library system do all of the background processing in order to get the views into our application when it is running. The Windows API, on the other hand, allows us the flexibility to create new window types and base them on existing MFC classes. The combination of the two is extremely powerful, as this example shows.

When the view is created by the MFC in response to the user's File | New request, the CNewView object is instantiated. This, in turn, calls the OnCreate method of the view, which creates a new basic window type within the confines of the view window. As far as the view is concerned, that area of the screen is now no longer its responsibility. All messages, keystrokes, and paint actions occur in our own pseudo-list box class. You will notice that we call the Create method of the CVListWnd object. This Create method exactly maps onto the Windows API CreateWindow function. The window has a name "", which is simply an empty string, and horizontal and vertical scroll bars.

Once the window is created, the CVListWnd methods come into play. They are really quite in sync with the owner-drawn list boxes we saw earlier in this chapter. The OnPaint method of CVListWnd responds to the WM_PAINT message from Windows. This method then retrieves data from the provider object and displays that data in orderly columns on the window.

The real work of the system is done in the provider class. This is the class that makes it possible to write truly unlimited size lists and have the user select from them. The provider class in our example simply builds strings to display based on the line number and the column number of the requested item.

Several important things to notice in this example are the uses of the Windows API functions and their results. In the DoColumnHeader method of CVListWnd we see three good examples of calling Windows API functions (in this case, indirectly through the MFC objects). First, the SetBkMode function is called with the TRANSPARENT parameter. This function indicates to Windows how the background should be treated when rendering text or graphics on the screen. In this case, TRANSPARENT indicates that the background should not be modified when drawing text. Next, the SetBkColor function is called. This method sets the background color for text drawing. Finally, the DrawText method is called to actually render the text onto the screen. A similar method is used to show the text in the columns of the list box.

Comments

The virtual list box shown is an excellent start toward a fully functional virtual columnar list box. With very little work, it could be made into a generalized component that could be dropped into an application. Further, with a little investigation into the SetCapture and WM_MOUSEMOVE API functions, you could make it a fully functional grid tool.

The best use for this sort of component is in a database or text retrieval application. The items in the virtual list can represent records in a database or files in a text retrieval. The columns would then be fields or attributes of the file search.

COMPLEXITY
MODERATE

7.9 How do I...
Make a hierarchical list or tree?

Problem

I would like the ability to use the "tree" view that is shown to some extent in File Manager in Windows 3.1 and to a greater extent in Windows 95. Is it very difficult to create such a control? How would I go about it?

Technique

It is somewhat difficult to say how complex a job it would be to write a tree control such as you see in the Windows 95 Explorer. It is even more difficult to estimate how long it would take to write, since no one in their right minds would consider writing one for Windows 95. After all, the control already exists, doesn't it? Why should you go about reinventing the wheel if you can just pick one up at your local store (to mix metaphors a bit)?

In this How-To, we will examine how you go about creating a new view in the MFC using a tree control as the basis for the view. As you will see in the example, it is really rather simple to create a tree control for your application. It is slightly more complex to respond to the messages from the tree control, but the capability to use the existing functionality far overrides the problems involved in using the built-in control.

> Note: Most of the examples in this book will compile equally well in either Visual C++ 1.52 or Visual C++ 2.1. However, this particular example, because it takes advantage of a 32-bit control built into Windows 95, will only work in Visual C++ 2.1 or higher.

Steps

Open and run the Visual C++ 2.1 application TREE.MAK from the CHAPT7\SAM-PLES\CH79 directory on the CD that comes with this book. You should see the tree view displayed in Figure 7-12. Click on the plus and minus boxed symbols on the left-hand side of the view. The tree will expand and contract in response. When you have finished playing with the tree control, select File | Exit to end the program.

To reproduce this functionality in your own application, do the following:

1. Create a new project in Visual C++ 2.1 using AppWizard. Give the new project the name TREE.MAK. Create a new view class by selecting ClassWizard and clicking on the Add Class button. Give the new class the name CTreeView and the base class CView.

2. Select the CTreeView object from the object list in ClassWizard and select the WM_MOUSEMOVE message from the message list. Click on the Add

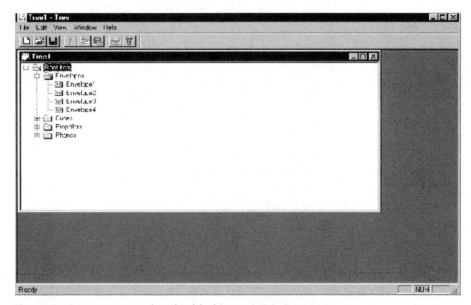

Figure 7-12 A tree control embedded in an MFC view

Function button. Enter the following code into the OnMouseMove method of
CTreeView:

```
void CTreeView::OnMouseMove(UINT nFlags, CPoint point)
{
    if (m_pDragImage)
    {
        TV_HITTESTINFO tvht;

        // Fill out hit test struct with mouse pos
        tvht.pt.x = point.x;
        tvht.pt.y = point.y;

        // Check to see if an item lives under the mouse
        HTREEITEM hTarget;
        if (NULL != (hTarget = GetTreeCtrl().HitTest(&tvht)))
        {
            // find out what kind of item we are looking at
            TV_ITEM tvi;              // Temporary Item
            tvi.mask = TVIF_PARAM;
            tvi.hItem = hTarget;
            GetTreeCtrl().GetItem(&tvi);

            // If item can be dropped on...
            if (0 != tvi.lParam) // can't put anything in the root
                                 //   except the root
            {
                SetCursor(LoadCursor(NULL, IDC_ARROW));
            }
            else
            {
                SetCursor(LoadCursor(NULL, IDC_NO));
            }
            if ( hTarget != GetTreeCtrl().GetDropHilightItem() )
            {
                // Hide the drag image
                ImageList_DragShowNolock(FALSE);
                // Select the item
                GetTreeCtrl().SelectDropTarget(hTarget);
                // Show the drag image
                ImageList_DragShowNolock(TRUE);
            }
        }
        // Do standard drag drop movement
        m_pDragImage->DragMove(point);
    }

    CView::OnMouseMove(nFlags, point);
}
```

3. Next, click on the WM_LBUTTONUP message and the CTreeView object in
ClassWizard. Click on the Add Function button and enter the following code
into the OnLButtonUp function of CTreeView:

```
void CTreeView::OnLButtonUp(UINT nFlags, CPoint point)
{
```

```
if (NULL != m_pDragImage)
{
    TV_ITEM          tvi;              // Temporary Item
    TV_HITTESTINFO tvht;

    // Fill out hit test struct with mouse pos
    tvht.pt.x = point.x;
    tvht.pt.y = point.y;
    // Check to see if an item lives under the mouse
    HTREEITEM hTarget = GetTreeCtrl().HitTest(&tvht);

    ImageList_EndDrag();
    ImageList_DragLeave(m_hWnd);
    ShowCursor ( TRUE );
    SetCursor(LoadCursor(NULL, IDC_ARROW));
    ReleaseCapture();
    m_pDragImage->DeleteImageList();
    m_pDragImage = NULL;

    GetTreeCtrl().SelectDropTarget(NULL);

    if (NULL != hTarget && m_hDragItem != hTarget)
        // Can't drop on nothing or itself
    {
        TV_INSERTSTRUCT tvis;
        tvi.mask = TVIF_PARAM;
        tvi.hItem = hTarget;
        GetTreeCtrl().GetItem(&tvi);
        if (0 != tvi.lParam && tvi.hItem != m_hDragItem)
        {
            // First, get the data from the object we dragged
            //  and delete it from the tree
            char buf[1024];
            tvis.item.mask = TVIF_TEXT | TVIF_IMAGE |
                             TVIF_SELECTEDIMAGE | TVIF_PARAM;
            tvis.item.hItem = m_hDragItem;
            tvis.item.pszText = buf;
            tvis.item.cchTextMax = 1024;
            GetTreeCtrl().GetItem(&(tvis.item));
            GetTreeCtrl().DeleteItem(m_hDragItem);
            if (1 == tvi.lParam) // it's a folder, add it to
                                 //   that folder
            {
                tvis.hParent = hTarget;
                tvis.hInsertAfter = TVI_LAST;
                GetTreeCtrl().InsertItem(&tvis);
            }
            else // put it after the object that's the target
            {
                tvis.hParent = GetTreeCtrl().GetParentItem(hTarget);
                tvis.hInsertAfter = hTarget;
                GetTreeCtrl().InsertItem(&tvis);
            }
        }
    }
}
```

continued on next page

continued from previous page

```
            m_hDragItem = NULL;
    }


    CView::OnLButtonUp(nFlags, point);
}
```

4. The following functions need to be added to respond to messages from the Tree control. First, add a new method to the class called OnChildNotify. This method is called in response to messages from child controls in the view. In this case, the method is called for any messages that are posted from the Tree control to its parent, the view:

```
BOOL CTreeView::OnChildNotify(UINT message, WPARAM wParam, LPARAM
                             lParam, LRESULT* pLResult)
{
    // Let this window handle its own notifications
    if (WM_NOTIFY == message)
    {
        switch ( ((NMHDR*)lParam)->code )
        {
            case TVN_GETDISPINFO:
                OnGetDispInfo((NMHDR*)lParam);
            return TRUE;

            case TVN_ENDLABELEDIT:
                OnEndLabelEdit((NMHDR*)lParam);
            return TRUE;

            case TVN_BEGINLABELEDIT:
                *pLResult = OnBeginLabelEdit((NMHDR*)lParam);
            return TRUE;

            case TVN_BEGINDRAG:
                OnBeginDrag((NMHDR*)lParam);
            return TRUE;
        }
    }

    return CView::OnChildNotify(message, wParam, lParam, pLResult);
}
```

5. Next, add the OnGetDispInfo method. This method is called to get the display information for a given node entry in the tree. Here, we are simply checking which image to display in the tree, depending on whether the node is expanded or contracted.

```
void CTreeView::OnGetDispInfo(NMHDR* pNotifyStruct)
{
    ASSERT(m_hWnd == pNotifyStruct->hwndFrom);
    TV_DISPINFO* pDispInfo = (TV_DISPINFO*)pNotifyStruct;

    if ( pDispInfo->item.state & TVIS_EXPANDED )
        pDispInfo->item.iSelectedImage = pDispInfo->item.iImage
                                       = imageFolderOpen;
    else
```

```
                    pDispInfo->item.iSelectedImage = pDispInfo->item.iImage
                                                   = imageFolder;
}
```

6. Next, we add a method to allow the user to edit the labels in the tree. This method is called in OnChildNotify in response to a TVN_ENDLABELEDIT message from the Tree control:

```
void CTreeView::OnEndLabelEdit(NMHDR* pNotifyStruct)
{
    ASSERT(m_hWnd == pNotifyStruct->hwndFrom);

    TV_DISPINFO* pDispInfo = (TV_DISPINFO*)pNotifyStruct;

    // don't do anything if the mask isn't valid or if the user
    //   pressed escape
    if (NULL == pDispInfo->item.pszText) return;
    TV_ITEM tvi;
    tvi.mask = TVIF_TEXT;
    tvi.pszText = pDispInfo->item.pszText;
    tvi.cchTextMax = lstrlen(tvi.pszText);
    tvi.hItem      = pDispInfo->item.hItem;

    GetTreeCtrl().SetItem(&tvi);
}
```

7. Add a method for the begin label edit message. The only purpose of this method is to check whether the item being edited is a valid item—that is, a leaf-level node:

```
LRESULT CTreeView::OnBeginLabelEdit(NMHDR* pNotifyStruct)
{
    ASSERT(m_hWnd == pNotifyStruct->hwndFrom);

    if (((TV_DISPINFO*)pNotifyStruct)->item.lParam > 1) return 0;
// Can't edit folder titles or root
    else return 1;
}
```

8. The final notification message to handle from the tree is the begin drag message. Here, we need to make sure they are only dragging leaf-level items and not a root- or folder-level item. Assuming this is true, we need to set the capture to this window so we can find out where the item gets dropped (this happens in OnLButtonUp):

```
void CTreeView::OnBeginDrag(NMHDR* pNotifyStruct)
{
    ASSERT(m_hWnd == pNotifyStruct->hwndFrom);

    NM_TREEVIEW* pNMTreeView = (NM_TREEVIEW*)pNotifyStruct;

    // First, determine if this object is drag-and-droppable
    if (pNMTreeView->itemNew.lParam > 1)
// 0 is root, 1 is a folder, they can't be dragged
    {
        // create the drag image
```

continued on next page

continued from previous page

```
            m_hDragItem = pNMTreeView->itemNew.hItem;
            m_pDragImage = GetTreeCtrl().CreateDragImage(m_hDragItem);

            // Get the location of the item rectangle's text
            CRect rc;
            GetTreeCtrl().GetItemRect(m_hDragItem, &rc, TRUE);
            int cx,cy;
            ImageList_GetIconSize(m_pDragImage->m_hImageList, &cx, &cy);
            CPoint ptHotSpot(8, 8);    // center it
            CPoint ptDragSpot(pNMTreeView->ptDrag.x, pNMTreeView->ptDrag.y);
            m_pDragImage->BeginDrag(0, ptHotSpot);
            m_pDragImage->DragEnter(&GetTreeCtrl(), ptDragSpot);

            ShowCursor(TRUE);
            SetCapture();
        }
    }
```

9. Another method that is overridden is the PreCreateWindow method. Here, we will set the class name for the window to be the tree control class. This will force the MFC to create a tree control within our view rather than a standard window:

```
BOOL CTreeView::PreCreateWindow(CREATESTRUCT& cs)
{
    // Force class to be a tree control..

    cs.lpszClass = WC_TREEVIEW;

    // map default CView style to default CEditView style
    cs.style |= TVS_HASLINES | TVS_EDITLABELS | TVS_HASBUTTONS |
TVS_LINESATROOT;

    return CView::PreCreateWindow(cs);
}
```

10. Next, modify the OnInitialUpdate method of the view class to insert the nodes we want to see when the view is displayed. OnInitialUpdate is called once when the view is created in order to allow the program to set the initial state of the display and initialize any structures:

```
void CTreeView::OnInitialUpdate()
{
    CRect rectClient;
    GetClientRect(&rectClient);

    // Create the image list and set it in the tree control
    m_imageList.Create(IDB_BITMAP1, 16, 1, RGB(255,255,255));
    GetTreeCtrl().SetImageList(TVSIL_NORMAL, &m_imageList);

    // Build the starting tree
    HTREEITEM hRootItem, hFolderItem;

    hRootItem = CreateTree("Root item");
    hFolderItem = InsertTreeItem("Envelopes", 1, hRootItem, I_IMAGECALLBACK);
    InsertTreeItem("Envelope1", 2, hFolderItem, imageEnvelope);
```

```
InsertTreeItem("Envelope2", 2, hFolderItem, imageEnvelope);
InsertTreeItem("Envelope3", 2, hFolderItem, imageEnvelope);
InsertTreeItem("Envelope4", 2, hFolderItem, imageEnvelope);

hFolderItem = InsertTreeItem("Cubes", 1, hRootItem, I_IMAGECALLBACK);
InsertTreeItem("Cube1", 3, hFolderItem, imageCube);
InsertTreeItem("Cube2", 3, hFolderItem, imageCube);
InsertTreeItem("Cube3", 3, hFolderItem, imageCube);
InsertTreeItem("Cube4", 3, hFolderItem, imageCube);

hFolderItem = InsertTreeItem("Propellers", 1, hRootItem, I_IMAGECALLBACK);
InsertTreeItem("Propeller1", 4, hFolderItem, imagePropeller);
InsertTreeItem("Propeller2", 4, hFolderItem, imagePropeller);
InsertTreeItem("Propeller3", 4, hFolderItem, imagePropeller);
InsertTreeItem("Propeller4", 4, hFolderItem, imagePropeller);

hFolderItem = InsertTreeItem("Phones", 1, hRootItem, I_IMAGECALLBACK);
InsertTreeItem("Phone1", 5, hFolderItem, imagePhone);
InsertTreeItem("Phone2", 5, hFolderItem, imagePhone);
InsertTreeItem("Phone3", 5, hFolderItem, imagePhone);
InsertTreeItem("Phone4", 5, hFolderItem, imagePhone);

// Expand the tree

GetTreeCtrl().Expand(GetTreeCtrl().GetRootItem(), TVE_EXPAND);
}
```

11. Add the following utility functions to the class source file. These two functions
are simply wrappers around the tree control functionality to make the remainder of the application code more compact:

```
HTREEITEM CTreeView::CreateTree(char *text)
{
    // Initialize tree structure

    TV_INSERTSTRUCT tvInsertStruct;
    tvInsertStruct.item.mask = TVIF_TEXT | TVIF_IMAGE |
TVIF_SELECTEDIMAGE | TVIF_PARAM;
    tvInsertStruct.item.stateMask = 0;

    // Set the text for the root item

    tvInsertStruct.item.pszText = text;
    tvInsertStruct.item.iSelectedImage = tvInsertStruct.item.iImage =
I_IMAGECALLBACK;
    tvInsertStruct.item.cchTextMax = lstrlen(tvInsertStruct.item.pszText);
    tvInsertStruct.item.lParam = 0;
    tvInsertStruct.hParent = NULL;
    tvInsertStruct.hInsertAfter = (HTREEITEM)TVI_ROOT;
    return GetTreeCtrl().InsertItem(&tvInsertStruct);
}

HTREEITEM CTreeView::InsertTreeItem(char *text, int idx,
                                    HTREEITEM parent, int image)
{
```

continued on next page

continued from previous page

```
        TV_INSERTSTRUCT tvInsertStruct;
        tvInsertStruct.item.mask = TVIF_TEXT | TVIF_IMAGE | TVIF_SELECTED-
IMAGE | TVIF_PARAM;
        tvInsertStruct.item.stateMask = 0;
        tvInsertStruct.item.pszText = text;
        tvInsertStruct.item.iSelectedImage = tvInsertStruct.item.iImage = image;
        tvInsertStruct.item.cchTextMax = lstrlen(tvInsertStruct.item.pszText);
        tvInsertStruct.item.lParam = idx;
        tvInsertStruct.hParent = parent;
        tvInsertStruct.hInsertAfter = TVI_LAST;
        return GetTreeCtrl().InsertItem(&tvInsertStruct);
}
```

12. Finally, you will need to update the header file for the CTreeView class. The
following is a listing of the CTreeView class with the additional methods to
add marked with bold print.

```
// Treeview.h : interface of the CTreeView class
//
/////////////////////////////////////////////////////////////////////////////

enum { imageEnvelope, imageCube, imagePropeller, imagePhone,
imageFolder,  imageFolderOpen };

class CTreeView : public CView
{
protected: // create from serialization only
  CTreeView();
  DECLARE_DYNCREATE(CTreeView)

// Attributes
public:
  CTreeDoc* GetDocument();
  CTreeCtrl &GetTreeCtrl()  { return *(CTreeCtrl*)this; }
  HTREEITEM CreateTree(char *text);
  HTREEITEM InsertTreeItem(char *text, int idx, HTREEITEM parent, int image);

// Operations
public:

// Overrides
  // ClassWizard generated virtual function overrides
  //{{AFX_VIRTUAL(CTreeView)
  public:
  virtual void OnDraw(CDC* pDC);  // overridden to draw this view
  virtual void OnInitialUpdate();
  virtual BOOL OnChildNotify(UINT message, WPARAM wParam, LPARAM lParam,
  LRESULT* pLResult);
  protected:
  virtual BOOL PreCreateWindow(CREATESTRUCT& cs);
  //}}AFX_VIRTUAL

// Implementation
public:
  virtual ~CTreeView();
```

```
#ifdef _DEBUG
  virtual void AssertValid() const;
  virtual void Dump(CDumpContext& dc) const;
#endif

 protected:
  HTREEITEM m_hDragItem;
  CImageList m_imageList;
  CImageList *m_pDragImage;

// Generated message map functions
protected:
  //{{AFX_MSG(CTreeView)
  afx_msg void OnPaint();
  afx_msg void OnMouseMove(UINT nFlags, CPoint point);
  afx_msg void OnLButtonUp(UINT nFlags, CPoint point);
  //}}AFX_MSG
  DECLARE_MESSAGE_MAP()

  // Notifications from the tree control, processed in OnChildNotify
  void OnBeginDrag(NMHDR* pNotifyStruct);
  void OnGetDispInfo(NMHDR* pNotifyStruct);
  void OnEndLabelEdit(NMHDR* pNotifyStruct);
  LRESULT OnBeginLabelEdit(NMHDR* pNotifyStruct);
};

#ifndef _DEBUG  // debug version in Treeview.cpp
inline CTreeDoc* CTreeView::GetDocument()
   { return (CTreeDoc*)m_pDocument; }
#endif
```

///

13. Compile and run the application.

How It Works

The important API functions in this example are generally related to the tree control itself. First, in the OnInitialUpdate method of the view, you will notice that a call to the Create method of the CImageList object m_imageList is called. This method will initialize an image list to contain a given number of images (or bitmaps) and associate them with a specific bitmap in the MFC resource file. In this case, the bitmap used is IDB_BITMAP1. Next, the image list is associated with the tree control by calling the API function TreeView_SetImageList, which is called indirectly through the MFC member function SetImageList of the CTreeCtrl object. This call associates the image list with the tree control, allowing it access to the bitmaps to draw in the view.

After the bitmaps have been associated, a series of calls to the CreateTree and InsertTreeItem functions are called. CreateTree simply initializes the structure to create a root entry in the tree and then calls the InsertItem method of the CTreeCtrl class to insert the root item into the tree. The returned handle can be used to further insert items below the root in the tree.

If you create the tree with the TVS_EDITLABELS style flag, as we have done in the PreCreateWindow call, you can edit the labels on the tree in place. This is what the OnBeginLabelEdit and OnEndLabelEdit functions do. The OnGetDispInfo function simply tells the tree control which image to display for a given item. The OnBeginDrag method is called by the Tree control when the user attempts to drag and drop a tree item from one place in the tree to another. The dragging stops when the user releases the mouse button, which is indicated by a call to the OnLButtonUp method in CTreeView.

That's really all there is to creating trees in MFC views. The same methodology can be used to create trees in dialog boxes as well.

Comments

This example is a good starting point for understanding and using the tree control in Windows 95. Because of the prevalence of the tree control, it behooves you as a programmer to learn as much as you can about this control.

While the tree control cannot be used directly at this point for Delphi and Visual Basic users (since it is a 32-bit control and Delphi and Visual Basic only work with 16-bit types), there are many existing custom controls that mimic the capabilities and functionality of the Windows 95 tree control. You might consider using these controls in your application as soon as possible in order to accustom users to the look and feel of this control.

MENUS

MENUS

How do I...

In this chapter you will learn a number of techniques that operate on your application's menus. The menu is an ubiquitous Windows interface element—all but the most trivial applications need a menu. Before you say, "No, my application will just use tool-bar buttons," consider the user who cannot or does not use a mouse. Menus can be pulled down using the keyboard or the mouse, and should certainly be used. If you have a button on a toolbar, make sure that you have the same option on a menu as well.

The functions covered in this chapter, which are listed in Table 8-1, show how you can change the menus programmatically—showing different options depending upon the active window or application component, and graying out menu options that cannot be used at a given time. By using these tips, you will give feedback to the user, making the user interface of your application more intuitive.

GetMenu	EnableMenuItem
WM_INITMENU	DrawMenuBar
GetMenuState	GetSubMenu
AppendMenu	InsertMenu
DeleteMenu	RemoveMenu
CheckMenuItem	SetMenuItemBitmaps
GetSystemMetrics	GetSysColor
GetSystemMenu	ExitWindowsEx
CreatePopupMenu	LoadMenu
TrackPopupMenu	MYMSG_CONTEXTMENU

 Table 8-1 Windows 95 APIs covered in Chapter 8

8.1   Enable and Disable Menu Items

This How-To shows you how you can enable and disable menu items, depending on conditions in your application. It demonstrates two techniques for managing this process.

8.2   Add and Remove Menu Items

This How-To discusses methods of adding new items to the end of existing menus or to specific positions within a menu. It shows you how to check for the existence of menu items and how to remove menu items when they are no longer required.

8.3   Add a Check Mark to a Menu Item

You can provide feedback to the user by using check marks beside menu items to indicate whether an item is currently active or not. You can even emulate the behavior of radio buttons, checking one button in a group and unchecking others. This How-To shows you how you can use both methods in your application.

8.4   Use My Own Check Mark

This How-To builds on How-To 8.3 and shows you how you can replace the standard Windows check mark with something more appropriate to your application—a color or a symbol for example.

8.5   Add Options to the System Menu

In addition to modifying your application's own menus, you can apply the same modifications to the system menu of your application, or even of other windows in your application. This How-To demonstrates how to add a Shutdown System menu item to the system menu of your application's main window.

8.6   Make a Menu That Pops Up on Right Mouse Button Clicks

One of the latest user interface tools to appear in Windows 95 is the context-sensitive pop-up menu. Pressing the right mouse button in the client area of just about any application will provide a floating pop-up menu with options that apply to the current state of the application, or the part of the application in which you clicked. This How-To shows how you can incorporate this behavior in your application.

COMPLEXITY
EASY

8.1 How do I...
Enable and disable menu items?

Problem

I would like my application's menus to reflect more accurately the current state of the application. For example, there is no point having the Cut or Copy menu item enabled if there is no text selected to cut or copy. I would also like to be able to enable or disable entire menus. How can I do this?

Technique

You can easily disable a menu item at design time by adding the GRAYED style to a menu item in the resource script, or by checking the appropriate box in your resource editor. Changing the state of a menu item or menu at runtime is also not a great problem.

Before you can change anything about a menu, you need to have a handle to the menu. The API function GetMenu takes as its argument a handle to a window and returns an HWND, a handle to the menu for that window. Note that calling GetMenu for a child window will never return a valid menu—child windows cannot have menus.

Having retrieved a handle to the menu, you can then call the API function EnableMenuItem. Despite its name, EnableMenuItem is used to both enable and gray menu items. (We use "grayed" to speak of disabled menu items—see the box "Grayed vs. Disabled" for more information.) When you call EnableMenuItem, you pass it the handle to the menu to modify. You also pass it the ID of the item to be changed, or the position of the item in the menu. Finally, you pass it some flags. MF_BYCOMMAND tells Windows to search for the item by its ID, or MF_BYPOSITION tells Windows to search for the item by position. The MF_ENABLED flag is used to enable the item, and MF_GRAYED grays and disables the menu item.

While you can enable and gray menu items explicitly in response to an event occurring, you can also utilize the WM_INITMENU message that Windows sends before a menu is pulled down. When your application receives this message, you can enable or gray menu items depending on the current state of the application. This second method often makes for simpler, more robust and extensible applications, because the enabling and graying code is kept in one place.

Grayed vs. Disabled

In early versions of Windows, applications did not gray unselectable menu items. Instead, the item looked and performed normally—the application just did not respond to it. In fact, the menu items were disabled using the MF_DISABLED flag. This flag stops Windows from sending the WM_COMMAND message to your application for that menu item, but does not change the appearance of the item.

Modern applications use the MF_GRAYED flag instead, so that the user can see that the item cannot be selected and doesn't have to puzzle out why a function does not work.

So, although it would be simpler to refer to menu items as Enabled and Disabled, this book uses the terms Enabled and Grayed to avoid any confusion over what flags your application should set.

Steps

Open and run the sample application ENABLE.EXE from the directory CHAPTER8\ENABLE on the CD that comes with this book. You will see a window such as that displayed in Figure 8-1. The application has two menus: a File menu and an Options menu. The figure shows the Options menu enabled, but it can be enabled and grayed by selecting the Enable Menu and Disable Menu items from the File menu. In the example shown, the Disable Menu command is enabled, but the Enable Menu command is grayed, because the Options menu is already enabled.

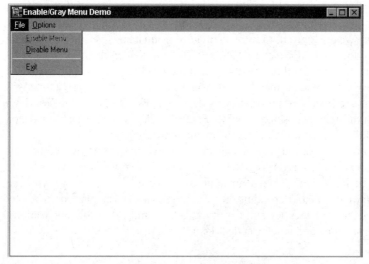

Figure 8-1 Running the ENABLE sample application

The following steps will guide you through reproducing this application.

1. Start by creating a working directory where you will store the source files for the application. To do this, create a new directory and call it ENABLE.

2. Now create a resource file for the application. This file will define the menus used in the application and will include the application icon. Use a text editor to create a new file, and call it ENABLE.RC. Type the following resource script into the file:

```
/* ------------------------------------------------------------------ */
/*                                                                     */
/*                                                                     */
/* MODULE: ENABLE.RC                                                   */
/* PURPOSE: This resource script defines the base menu for this        */
/*          example application.                                       */
/*                                                                     */
/* ------------------------------------------------------------------ */

#include <windows.h>
#include "enable.rh"

IDM_TESTMENU MENU
{
    POPUP "&File"
    {
        MENUITEM "&Enable Menu", CM_ENABLE
        MENUITEM "&Disable Menu", CM_DISABLE
        MENUITEM SEPARATOR
        MENUITEM "E&xit", CM_EXIT
    }
    POPUP "&Options"
    {
        MENUITEM "&Configure...", CM_CONFIGURE
        MENUITEM "&Directories...", CM_DIRECTORIES
        MENUITEM "&Save Options", CM_SAVEOPTIONS
    }
}


IDI_APPICON ICON "app.ico"
```

3. Now create another new file and insert the following code. Save this file as ENABLE.RH. This file will define the resource identifiers for the menu and menu items and will be referenced by both the resource script and the C source code.

```
#ifndef __ENABLE_RH
/* ------------------------------------------------------------------ */
/*                                                                     */
/* MODULE: ENABLE.RH                                                   */
/* PURPOSE: This include file defines the resource identifiers used.   */
/*                                                                     */
/* ------------------------------------------------------------------ */
#define __ENABLE_RH

#define IDM_TESTMENU    200
```

continued on next page

continued from previous page

```
#define CM_ENABLE        102
#define CM_DISABLE       101
#define CM_EXIT          103
#define CM_CONFIGURE     111
#define CM_DIRECTORIES   112
#define CM_SAVEOPTIONS   113

#define IDI_APPICON      202

#endif
```

4. The resource script also references an icon file, APP.ICO. You can copy this file from the CHAPTER8\ENABLE directory on the CD. Alternatively, if you don't have access to a CD drive, you can use a resource editor to create a standard 32-by-32-pixel icon with 16 colors or less. Save the icon as APP.ICO in your working directory.

5. Now create a new file that will contain the C source code for the application. Name this file ENABLE.C. Add the following comments and global variables to the source. The code includes the Windows header files and the resource header file that you already added. It also defines the name of the window class for this application.

```
/* ------------------------------------------------------------ */
/*                                                              */
/* MODULE: ENABLE.C                                             */
/* PURPOSE: This sample application demonstrates how to use the */
/*          EnableMenuItem function to enable and disable menu items */
/*          and Menus. It also demonstrates how to respond to the */
/*          WM_INITMENU message, which signals that the menu is  */
/*          about to be displayed. This is a good time to change */
/*          menu state depending upon some condition.           */
/*                                                              */
/* ------------------------------------------------------------ */

#define STRICT
#include <windows.h>
#include <winnt.h>
#include "enable.rh"

static char *MainWindowClassName = "EnableMenuWindow";
```

6. Add the following function to the same source file. Function ChangeOptionsMenuState is used to explicitly enable or disable the Options menu. It uses GetMenu to get a handle to the menu and EnableMenuItem to change the state of the menu. Notice that you have to use the MF_BYPOSITION flag and supply the position of the menu across the menu bar. This is because pop-up menus do not have ID values as menu items do. Menu positions are 0 based, so the Options menu has a position of 1—the second menu across the menu bar.

```
/* ---------------------------------------------------------------- */
/* This function gets the handle of the main menu from the window,  */
/* and uses EnableMenuItem to change the state of the Options menu.  */
/* If the command is CM_ENABLE then the menu will be enabled; if it  */
/* is CM_DISABLE, then it will be grayed.                            */
/* ---------------------------------------------------------------- */
void ChangeOptionsMenuState(HWND hWnd, UINT command)
{
    HMENU hMenu;

    // Get a handle to the main menu.
    hMenu = GetMenu(hWnd);
    if (!hMenu)
        return;

    /* Test the value of the command and enable or disable
        the Options menu. Note that we use the position of the
        menu (1) as a popup menu does not have an ID. */
    if (command == CM_ENABLE)
        EnableMenuItem(hMenu,1,MF_BYPOSITION | MF_ENABLED);
    else
        EnableMenuItem(hMenu,1,MF_BYPOSITION | MF_GRAYED);

    // Refresh the menu bar.
    DrawMenuBar(hWnd);
}
```

7. Now add the function that enables and grays the items on the File menu. This function will be called in response to the WM_INITMENU message. Windows sends this message to a window when the user starts to pull down one of the menus. The message affects all the menus because it is only sent once—the user can move between the menus along the menu bar without generating more messages. It is only when the menus have been closed and the user selects the menu bar again that another WM_INITMENU message is generated.

The code uses GetMenuState to return the state of the Options menu. Based on this state, it enables and grays the Enable Menu and Disable Menu items on the File menu. GetMenuState returns a set of flags. If the MF_GRAYED flag is set within the return value, the code uses EnableMenuItem to enable the Enable Menu option and gray the Disable Menu option. If the bit is not set, the actions are reversed.

```
/* ---------------------------------------------------------------- */
/* This function uses GetMenuState to test whether the Options menu  */
/* is enabled or grayed. If the menu is enabled, then the Enable    */
/* Menu item needs to be grayed, and the Disable Menu item needs to  */
/* be enabled. If the menu is grayed, then the item states are      */
/* reversed.                                                         */
/* ---------------------------------------------------------------- */
void MenuPulledDown(HWND hWnd)
{
    HMENU hMenu;
```

continued on next page

continued from previous page

```
        // Get a handle to the main menu.
        hMenu = GetMenu(hWnd);
        if (!hMenu)
            return;

        // Get the Options menu state, and see if it is grayed.
        if (GetMenuState(hMenu,1,MF_BYPOSITION) & MF_GRAYED)
        {
            EnableMenuItem(hMenu,CM_ENABLE,
                        MF_BYCOMMAND | MF_ENABLED);
            EnableMenuItem(hMenu,CM_DISABLE,
                        MF_BYCOMMAND | MF_GRAYED);
        }
        else
        {
            EnableMenuItem(hMenu,CM_ENABLE,
                        MF_BYCOMMAND | MF_GRAYED);
            EnableMenuItem(hMenu,CM_DISABLE,
                        MF_BYCOMMAND | MF_ENABLED);
        }
}
```

8. The preceding functions add the functionality to the application. Now you need a window procedure to handle messages from Windows and call those functions. Add the following code to the source file. Notice that this code responds to the WM_INITMENU message sent by Windows. It calls the MenuPulledDown function to enable or gray the items on the File menu before the menu is displayed. The window procedure also handles the WM_COMMAND messages generated by the menu. CM_EXIT causes the window to be closed and the application to exit. The CM_ENABLE and CM_DISABLE messages call the ChangeOptionsMenuState function that you added previously.

```
/* ---------------------------------------------------------------- */
/* This function is the main window callback function which will be  */
/* called by Windows to process messages for the window.            */
/* ---------------------------------------------------------------- */
LPARAM CALLBACK MainWndProc(HWND hWnd, UINT message,
                            WPARAM wParam, LPARAM lParam)
{
    switch (message)
    {
        case WM_COMMAND:
            switch (wParam)
            {
                case CM_EXIT:
                    DestroyWindow(hWnd);
                    return 0;
                case CM_ENABLE:
                case CM_DISABLE:
                    ChangeOptionsMenuState(hWnd,(UINT)wParam);
                    return 0;
            }
```

400

```
        break;
    case WM_INITMENU:
        MenuPulledDown(hWnd);
        return 0;
    case WM_DESTROY:
        PostQuitMessage(0);
        return 0;
    }
    return DefWindowProc(hWnd, message, wParam, lParam);
}
```

9. The next three functions are listed as a block for you to add to the same source file, ENABLE.C. These three functions, InitApplication, InitInstance, and WinMain, provide the framework for the application. WinMain is the interface routine called by Windows when your application starts. It checks to see if the window class name for this application has been registered, and if not, calls InitApplication to create and register the window class, including setting up the menu and icon for the application. WinMain also calls InitInstance, which creates the main window and thus sets the application running. WinMain then loops, retrieving messages from the message queue and sending them to the window procedure for processing until the application is finished.

```
/* -------------------------------------------------------------- */
/* This function initializes a WNDCLASS structure and uses it to  */
/* register a class for our main window.                          */
/* -------------------------------------------------------------- */
BOOL InitApplication(HINSTANCE hInstance)
{
    WNDCLASS   wc;

    wc.style = 0;
    wc.lpfnWndProc = MainWndProc;
    wc.cbClsExtra = 0;
    wc.cbWndExtra = 0;
    wc.hInstance = hInstance;
    wc.hIcon = LoadIcon(hInstance,MAKEINTRESOURCE(IDI_APPICON));
    wc.hCursor = LoadCursor(NULL, IDC_ARROW);
    wc.hbrBackground = (HBRUSH)(COLOR_WINDOW + 1);
    wc.lpszMenuName =  MAKEINTRESOURCE(IDM_TESTMENU);
    wc.lpszClassName = MainWindowClassName;

    return RegisterClass(&wc);
}


/* -------------------------------------------------------------- */
/* This function creates an instance of our main window. The window */
/* is given a class name and a title, and told to display anywhere. */
/* The nCmdShow argument passed to the program determines how the   */
/* window will be displayed.                                        */
/* -------------------------------------------------------------- */
BOOL InitInstance(HANDLE hInst, int nCmdShow)
{
```

continued on next page

continued from previous page

```
        HWND hWnd;

        hWnd = CreateWindow(MainWindowClassName,"Enable/Gray Menu Demo",
                        WS_OVERLAPPEDWINDOW,CW_USEDEFAULT,
                        CW_USEDEFAULT,CW_USEDEFAULT,CW_USEDEFAULT,
                        NULL,NULL,hInst,NULL);
        if (!hWnd)
            return FALSE;

        ShowWindow(hWnd, nCmdShow);
        UpdateWindow(hWnd);            // Send a WM_PAINT message.
        return TRUE;
    }


    /* ------------------------------------------------------------------ */
    /* The main entry point for Windows applications. Check to see if     */
    /* the main window class name has already been registered; if it      */
    /* has not, call InitApplication to register it. Call InitInstance     */
    /* to create an instance of our main window, then pump messages        */
    /* until the application is closed.                                    */
    /* ------------------------------------------------------------------ */
    int PASCAL WinMain(HINSTANCE hInstance, HINSTANCE hPrevInstance,
                    LPSTR lpCmdLine, int nCmdShow)
    {
        MSG msg;

        if (!FindWindow(MainWindowClassName,NULL))
            if (!InitApplication(hInstance))
                return FALSE;

        if (!InitInstance(hInstance, nCmdShow))
            return FALSE;

        while (GetMessage(&msg,NULL,0,0))
        {
            TranslateMessage(&msg);
            DispatchMessage(&msg);
        }
        return msg.wParam;
    }
```

10. Compile and run the application.

Comments

As the example code demonstrates, you can use EnableMenuItem to enable and gray menu items and submenus. A special case arises in which you want to gray a submenu below the main menu. In this case, asking for menu 0 or 1 by position using the code shown in the How-To would gray out the top-level menu instead of the intended submenu. You will need to use GetSubMenu to get the handle of the menu that contains the submenu to be grayed, then call EnableMenuItem using that handle rather than the handle of the main menu.

COMPLEXITY
EASY

8.2 How do I...
Add and remove menu items?

Problem

I would like to be able to add and remove items on the menu of my application, for instance, when the user wants to customize the menu options. How can I add items to a menu and delete items from a menu?

Technique

The Windows API provides a number of functions for manipulating menus in different ways. This How-To shows how you can use the AppendMenu, InsertMenu, and DeleteMenu functions to add items to the end of menus, insert items anywhere in a menu, and remove items from a menu.

The AppendMenu function is used to add a menu item or submenu to the end of an existing menu. It requires the handle of the menu to which the item is to be added. Adding an item to the menu handle returned from GetMenu adds another menu or item to the menu bar. To add an item to one of the pull-down menus, you need to get the handle of that menu first, by calling the GetSubMenu function.

The InsertMenu function works in the same way, but also takes the ID or position of an existing item. The new item will be added in front of or above this item.

Finally, the DeleteMenu function can be used to remove an item or submenu from a menu and destroy it. If you want to reuse a submenu at a later stage, you should remove the item using RemoveMenu instead, as this removes the item or menu from its parent, but does not destroy it.

Steps

Run the sample application ADDITEM.EXE. You will find this application in the CHAPTER8\ADDITEM directory on the CD. This application has two menus: a File menu and a Test menu. The Test menu initially contains only a single item called Empty. This item remains grayed throughout the application; its only purpose being to let you pull down the Test menu to look for other items. The File menu contains two items that let you add to the menu: a submenu that allows you to delete items from the menu, and of course, an Exit item.

Select Append Item from the File menu, and then go back and pull down the Test menu. You will notice that an item called Appended has been added to the end of the Test menu. If you select the Append Item menu item again, you will see a message box, as the application tests to see if an item has already been appended. Look at the File menu again and highlight the Remove Item menu option. This opens a submenu with two options—Appended Item and Inserted Item. If you select Appended Item, the item labeled Append will be removed from the Test menu.

Now select Insert Item from the File menu. Check the Test menu again, and you will see that a new item has been added at the top of the menu, above the Empty menu item. This item is called Inserted. You can use the Remove Item menu item on the File menu to remove the Inserted item. Figure 8-2 shows the ADDITEM application with both the Appended and Inserted items.

The following steps will lead you through the construction of this sample application.

1. Create a new directory for this application and call it ADDITEM. Place all the source files for this application in this directory as you work.

2. Use a text editor to create the resource script for this application. Name the file ADDITEM.RC and insert the following resource script code. Aside from including the icon to be used by the application, this code defines the initial menus that will appear when the application is tested. Note that this code does not initially gray any menu items except a dummy Empty item on the Test menu—graying the Remove Item submenu items is handled by the application itself.

```
/* --------------------------------------------------------------- */
/*                                                                  */
/* MODULE: ADDITEM.RC                                               */
/* PURPOSE: This resource script defines the base menu for this     */
/*          example application.                                    */
/*                                                                  */
/* --------------------------------------------------------------- */

#include <windows.h>
#include "additem.rh"

IDM_TESTMENU MENU
{
    POPUP "&File"
    {
        MENUITEM "&Insert Item", CM_INSERTITEM
        MENUITEM "&Append Item", CM_APPENDITEM
        POPUP "&Remove Item"
        {
            MENUITEM "Inserted Item", CM_DELINSERTED
            MENUITEM "Appended Item", CM_DELAPPENDED
        }
        MENUITEM SEPARATOR
        MENUITEM "E&xit", CM_EXIT
    }
    POPUP "&Test"
    {
        MENUITEM "Empty", CM_DONOTHING, GRAYED
    }
}


IDI_APPICON ICON "app.ico"
```

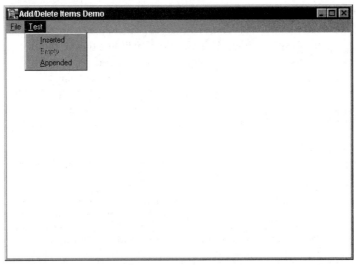

Figure 8-2 Appended and Inserted items in the ADDITEM application

3. Now create the include file that defines the identifiers used in the resource file. The include file will also be used by the C source code to reference the menu items. Create a file and insert the following definitions. Save the file as ADDITEM.RH.

```
#ifndef __ADDITEM_RH
/* ------------------------------------------------------------------ */
/*                                                                    */
/* MODULE: ADDITEM.RH                                                 */
/* PURPOSE: This include file defines the resource identifiers used.  */
/*                                                                    */
/* ------------------------------------------------------------------ */
#define __ADDITEM_RH

#define IDM_TESTMENU    200
#define CM_INSERTITEM   101
#define CM_APPENDITEM   102
#define CM_DELINSERTED  103
#define CM_DELAPPENDED  104
#define CM_EXIT         105

#define CM_DONOTHING    110

#define CM_APPENDED     120
#define CM_INSERTED     121

#define IDI_APPICON     202

#endif
```

4. The next step is to create a file for the C source code and name it
ADDITEM.C. Add the following comments and code to the top of the file. By
defining the preprocessor symbol STRICT before including the windows
include files, you ensure that proper type checks of all handles occur. This
protects you from accidentally passing a window handle where a menu handle
is required, for instance. This code also defines an identifier, ITEMINVALID,
which will be used later in the application to see if menu items exist. A call to
GetMenuState returns -1 or 0xFFFFFFFF if the menu or item referred to does
not exist.

```
/* ------------------------------------------------------------------ */
/*                                                                    */
/* MODULE: ADDITEM.C                                                  */
/* PURPOSE: This sample application demonstrates how to use the       */
/*          InsertMenu and AppendMenu API functions to append items   */
/*          to and insert into existing menus. It also shows how to   */
/*          use the DeleteMenu API function to delete items, and how  */
/*          you can use GetSubMenu to get submenu handles and         */
/*          GetMenuState to find out if an item exists.               */
/*                                                                    */
/* ------------------------------------------------------------------ */

#define STRICT
#include <windows.h>
#include <winnt.h>
#include "additem.rh"

#define ITEMINVALID 0xFFFFFFFF

static char *MainWindowClassName = "AddItemWindow";
HINSTANCE hInstance = NULL;
```

5. Add the function AppendMenuItem, listed next. This function contains the
code to get a handle to the Test menu and uses the AppendMenu API function
to add an item to the end of the menu. The AppendMenu function takes four
arguments. The first argument is the handle to the menu or submenu to add
the item to. If you wanted to add a new menu to the menu bar, you would use
the menu handle returned from GetMenu in this argument. In this case, you
want to add an item to the Test menu, so you need to obtain the handle of that
menu by using GetSubMenu.

The next argument specifies flags for the new item. The MF_STRING flag is
used to specify that the information supplied is a string to be displayed. While
MF_STRING is the default, you can also specify MF_BITMAP (for an image)
or MF_POPUP (for a submenu). The third argument is the ID value to be
assigned to that menu item. This argument is ignored if the flag specifies
MF_POPUP, as pop-up menus do not have ID values. The final argument is
the string or bitmap to display. In this case, you specify the string for the
inserted item, using an ampersand (&) character to produce the underlined
accelerator key for that menu item.

```
/* ---------------------------------------------------------------- */
/* This function uses AppendMenu to add a new item to the second    */
/* menu (the Test menu). The item is called "Appended".             */
/* ---------------------------------------------------------------- */
void AppendMenuItem(HWND hWnd)
{
    HMENU hMenu, hTestMenu;

    /* Get a handle to the main menu. Leave the
       function if the main menu does not exist. */
    hMenu = GetMenu(hWnd);
    if (!hMenu)
        return;

    /* Get a handle to the test menu. Leave the
       function if the test menu does not exist. */
    hTestMenu = GetSubMenu(hMenu,1);
    if (!hTestMenu)
        return;

    /* Add an item to the END of the test menu.
       Give it the ID CM_APPENDED, and the name "Appended". */
    AppendMenu(hTestMenu,MF_STRING,CM_APPENDED,"&Appended");

    /* Refresh the menu bar. */
    DrawMenuBar(hWnd);
}
```

6. Now add the following code for the InsertMenuItem function. This function demonstrates the use of a second menu modification function, InsertMenu. You can use InsertMenu to place submenus or menu items at any location in a menu, provided that you have a handle to that menu and you know the position in which you want to insert the item, or the ID value of an item to insert in front of. In this example, a new menu item called Inserted is added in front of the existing item at position 0 in the Test menu. The 0 argument specifies the position, and the MF_BYPOSITION flag tells windows that the 0 is a position rather than an item ID. CM_INSERTED is the ID value for the new menu item, and the final argument is the string for the menu item.

```
/* ---------------------------------------------------------------- */
/* This function uses InsertMenu to add a new item into the second  */
/* menu (the Test menu). The item is called "Inserted".             */
/* ---------------------------------------------------------------- */
void InsertMenuItem(HWND hWnd)
{
    HMENU hMenu, hTestMenu;

    /* Get a handle to the main menu. Leave the
       function if the main menu does not exist. */
    hMenu = GetMenu(hWnd);
    if (!hMenu)
        return;
```

continued on next page

continued from previous page

```
      /* Get a handle to the test menu. Leave the
         function if the test menu does not exist. */
      hTestMenu = GetSubMenu(hMenu,1);
      if (!hTestMenu)
         return;

      /* Add an item to the START of the test menu (in front
         of item number 0 by position).
         Give it the ID CM_INSERTED, and the name "Inserted". */
      InsertMenu(hTestMenu,0,MF_BYPOSITION | MF_STRING,
                 CM_INSERTED,"&Inserted");

      /* Refresh the menu bar. */
      DrawMenuBar(hWnd);
}
```

7. Add the code listed next. Function DeleteMenuItem demonstrates how you
can use a call to the DeleteMenu API function to remove a menu item. The
following code also uses the GetMenuState function to determine whether
the requested menu item exists. The result from GetMenuState is usually a
combination of flags that describes the specified menu item (MF_GRAYED,
MF_ENABLED, MF_CHECKED, and so on). If the item does not exist, however, the function will return -1, which is represented by the identifier
ITEMINVALID in this application.

Note: GetMenuState and DeleteMenu are both able to operate on the item
using the main menu. This is because searches for an existing item automatically search all submenus of the specified menu. You only need to specify
an exact menu handle if you are inserting or appending new items, or are
working with submenus that do not have an item ID. In this case, the exact
menu handle must be specified and the position of the item passed rather
than its ID.

```
/* --------------------------------------------------------------- */
/* This function deletes the menu item specified from the test menu */
/* --------------------------------------------------------------- */
void DeleteMenuItem(HWND hWnd, UINT command)
{
    HMENU hMenu;

    /* Get a handle to the main menu. Leave the
       function if the main menu does not exist. */
    hMenu = GetMenu(hWnd);
    if (!hMenu)
        return;

    /* See if the Edit menu exists - return if it doesn't. */
    if (GetMenuState(hMenu,command,MF_BYCOMMAND) == ITEMINVALID)
        return;

    /* Delete the menu item */
    DeleteMenu(hMenu,command,MF_BYCOMMAND);
```

```
    /* Refresh the menu bar. */
    DrawMenuBar(hWnd);
}
```

8. Add the following function to the source file. The EnableMenuItems is called in response to the WM_INITMENU message, which Windows sends before displaying the menu. Each time the user accesses the pull-down menus, this message is processed, which provides a convenient time to test conditions and set the state of menu items as checked, unchecked, enabled, or grayed. In this example, GetMenuState is used to determine whether the Appended and Inserted menu items exist in the Test menu. If either of these items exists, the corresponding Remove Item submenu item is enabled; otherwise it is grayed. The actual graying or enabling of the items is performed by calling the EnableMenuItem API function. See How-To 8.1 for a discussion about enabling and graying menu items.

```
/* ------------------------------------------------------------- */
/* This function uses GetMenuState to see if the appended and/or  */
/* inserted menu items exist. If one or other exists, the         */
/* corresponding Remove item is enabled; otherwise it is grayed.  */
/* ------------------------------------------------------------- */
void EnableMenuItems(HWND hWnd)
{
    HMENU hMenu;

    hMenu = GetMenu(hWnd);
    if (!hMenu)
        return;

    /* Test to see if the "Appended" menu item exists.
       If it does, enable the Remove function for it. */
    if (GetMenuState(hMenu,CM_APPENDED,
                    MF_BYCOMMAND) != ITEMINVALID)
        EnableMenuItem(hMenu,CM_DELAPPENDED,
                        MF_BYCOMMAND | MF_ENABLED);
    else
        EnableMenuItem(hMenu,CM_DELAPPENDED,
                        MF_BYCOMMAND | MF_GRAYED);

    /* Test to see if the "Inserted" menu item exists.
       If it does, enable the Remove function for it. */
    if (GetMenuState(hMenu,CM_INSERTED,
                    MF_BYCOMMAND) != ITEMINVALID)
        EnableMenuItem(hMenu,CM_DELINSERTED,
                        MF_BYCOMMAND | MF_ENABLED);
    else
        EnableMenuItem(hMenu,CM_DELINSERTED,
                        MF_BYCOMMAND | MF_GRAYED);
}
```

9. Function MainWndProc, listed next, is the main window procedure for the application. It is registered with Windows as a callback function when the window class for the application is registered. All window messages (such as WM_INITMENU, WM_CREATE, and WM_DESTROY) are sent to this function, as are all command messages from the menu (WM_COMMAND messages such as CM_EXIT and CM_APPENDITEM). The function calls the AppendMenuItem, InsertMenuItem, and DeleteMenuItem functions in response to user actions, and it makes sure that the appropriate menu items are enabled by calling EnableMenuItems when it receives the WM_INITMENU message.

```
/* ------------------------------------------------------------------ */
/* This function is the main window callback function which will be   */
/* called by Windows to process messages for the window.              */
/* ------------------------------------------------------------------ */
LPARAM CALLBACK MainWndProc(HWND hWnd, UINT message,
                                 WPARAM wParam, LPARAM lParam)
{
    switch (message)
    {
        case WM_COMMAND:
            switch (wParam)
            {
                case CM_EXIT:
                    DestroyWindow(hWnd);
                    return 0;
                case CM_APPENDITEM:
                    AppendMenuItem(hWnd);
                    return 0;
                case CM_INSERTITEM:
                    InsertMenuItem(hWnd);
                    return 0;
                case CM_DELAPPENDED:
                    DeleteMenuItem(hWnd,CM_APPENDED);
                    return 0;
                case CM_DELINSERTED:
                    DeleteMenuItem(hWnd,CM_INSERTED);
                    return 0;
            }
            break;
        case WM_INITMENU:
            EnableMenuItems(hWnd);
            return 0;
        case WM_DESTROY:
            PostQuitMessage(0);
            return 0;
    }
    return DefWindowProc(hWnd, message, wParam, lParam);
}
```

10. Now add the following three functions, which together make up the remainder of the source file. These three functions are the framework of the sample application, and the same functions are used almost without modification in all the examples for this chapter. The InitApplication function registers a window class for the main window of the application. The class name is specified by the identifier MainWindowClassName, which you defined at the top of the source file. This function is only called if the window class with that name has not already been registered. In contrast, the InitInstance function is called

once for each instance of the main window being created. So, if you have
more than one copy of this application running at a time, InitApplication will
only be called once, but InitInstance will be called each time. InitInstance is
used to create and display the main window.

Finally, the WinMain function is called by Windows when the application
instance begins. This function tests to see if the window class has been registered and calls InitApplication and InitInstance. The function also pumps
messages, which allows the application to receive and process messages.

```c
/* ------------------------------------------------------------ */
/* This function initializes a WNDCLASS structure and uses it to */
/* register a class for our main window.                          */
/* ------------------------------------------------------------ */
BOOL InitApplication(HINSTANCE hInstance)
{
    WNDCLASS   wc;

    wc.style = 0;
    wc.lpfnWndProc = MainWndProc;
    wc.cbClsExtra = 0;
    wc.cbWndExtra = 0;
    wc.hInstance = hInstance;
    wc.hIcon = LoadIcon(hInstance,MAKEINTRESOURCE(IDI_APPICON));
    wc.hCursor = LoadCursor(NULL, IDC_ARROW);
    wc.hbrBackground = (HBRUSH)(COLOR_WINDOW + 1);
    wc.lpszMenuName =  MAKEINTRESOURCE(IDM_TESTMENU);
    wc.lpszClassName = MainWindowClassName;

    return RegisterClass(&wc);
}


/* ------------------------------------------------------------ */
/* This function creates an instance of our main window. The window */
/* is given a class name and a title, and told to display anywhere. */
/* The nCmdShow argument passed to the program determines how the */
/* window will be displayed.                                        */
/* ------------------------------------------------------------ */
BOOL InitInstance(HINSTANCE hInst, int nCmdShow)
{
    HWND hWnd;

    hInstance = hInst;        // Store in global variable.

    hWnd = CreateWindow(MainWindowClassName,"Add/Delete Items Demo",
                WS_OVERLAPPEDWINDOW,CW_USEDEFAULT,
                CW_USEDEFAULT,CW_USEDEFAULT,CW_USEDEFAULT,
                NULL,NULL,hInstance,NULL);
    if (!hWnd)
        return FALSE;

    ShowWindow(hWnd, nCmdShow);
    UpdateWindow(hWnd);       // Send a WM_PAINT message.
    return TRUE;
```

continued on next page

continued from previous page

```
    }


    /* ------------------------------------------------------------------ */
    /* The main entry point for Windows applications. Check to see if      */
    /* the main window class name has already been registered; if it       */
    /* has not, call InitApplication to register it. Call InitInstance     */
    /* to create an instance of our main window, then pump messages         */
    /* until the application is closed.                                     */
    /* ------------------------------------------------------------------ */
    int PASCAL WinMain(HINSTANCE hInstance, HINSTANCE hPrevInstance,
                       LPSTR lpCmdLine, int nCmdShow)
    {
        MSG msg;

        if (!FindWindow(MainWindowClassName,NULL))
            if (!InitApplication(hInstance))
                return FALSE;

        if (!InitInstance(hInstance, nCmdShow))
            return FALSE;

        while (GetMessage(&msg,NULL,0,0))
        {
            TranslateMessage(&msg);
            DispatchMessage(&msg);
        }
        return msg.wParam;
    }
```

11. Compile and run the application.

Comments

The same techniques that you have used here to add, insert, and delete menu items can be applied to entire menus and submenus. You can apply both of these approaches to place items on the menus, depending on what windows are open in your application, or the menu configuration of your application.

COMPLEXITY
EASY

8.3   How do I...
Add a check mark to a menu item?

Problem

I would like to let the user know that a menu selection is currently "turned on" by adding a check mark to the menu item. How do I accomplish this?

Technique

You can check and uncheck any items in a menu using the CheckMenuItem API function. In addition, you can test to see if a menu item is checked using the GetMenuState function. The example application discussed in this How-To will show you how you can use these two functions together to toggle the check mark beside a menu item.

The example application will also teach you how you can use a set of menu items in a way that is similar to using a group of radio buttons, with only one item selected from the group at all times. With a little planning, the work can be left to Windows, with only a single variable required to maintain the currently selected item for the group.

Steps

Run the example application for this How-To. You will find the program in the CHAPTER8\CHECK directory on the CD, called CHECK.EXE. When you run the application, you will see that it has two menus. The File menu only contains an Exit item, while the Options menu contains three text colors (black, red, and green) and an Allow Undo option. The options don't actually affect the functioning of this application as they would a real application. Instead, this application concerns itself with demonstrating how you can check and uncheck the menu items.

When you initially start the application, there is a check mark beside the Black Text item. Select another color from the menu, for instance, the Red Text item. You will see that the check mark is removed from the Black Text item and that the Red Text item is checked instead. This is an example of using a check mark with a group of menu items like a set of radio buttons—only one item in the group can be selected at a time.

Now move down the menu and select the Allow Undo item. You will see a check mark appear beside this item, which does not affect the check mark beside the Red Text item. Select the Allow Undo item again. This time the check mark disappears. This is an example of toggling a check mark. Try different combinations of the color items with the Allow Undo item to convince yourself that the two do operate totally independently. Figure 8-3 shows how the application looks with Red Text and Allow Undo both checked.

The following steps will guide you in implementing the example application that you have just examined.

1. Create a new directory and name it CHECK. You will use this directory as your working directory while building this application. Place all the source files in this directory.

2. Next you need to create the menu resource that will be used by this application. Create a text file and enter the following resource script code. Save the file as CHECK.RC. Look carefully at the second menu, the Options menu. You will notice that the Black Text item has an extra style that the other menu items do not have. The CHECKED style means that the Black Text item will initially appear with a check mark.

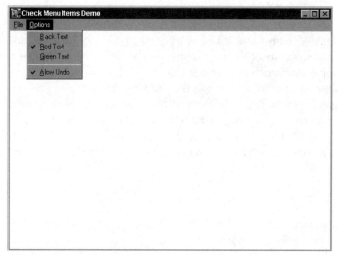

Figure 8-3 Using check marks in a menu

```
/* ------------------------------------------------------------------ */
/*                                                                    */
/* MODULE: CHECK.RC                                                   */
/* PURPOSE: This resource script defines the base menu for this       */
/*          example application.                                      */
/*                                                                    */
/* ------------------------------------------------------------------ */

#include <windows.h>
#include "check.rh"

IDM_TESTMENU MENU
{
    POPUP "&File"
    {
        MENUITEM "E&xit", CM_EXIT
    }
    POPUP "&Options"
    {
        MENUITEM "&Black Text", CM_TEXTBLACK, CHECKED
        MENUITEM "&Red Text", CM_TEXTRED
        MENUITEM "&Green Text", CM_TEXTGREEN
        MENUITEM SEPARATOR
        MENUITEM "&Allow Undo", CM_ALLOWUNDO
    }
}

IDI_APPICON ICON "app.ico"
```

3. Now create an include file that will define the identifiers used in the menu. This include file will be used by both the resource script from step 2 and the C source code, ensuring that the menu items that are defined in the resource script have the same values as those that the application responds to in the code. Create a new file for the following definitions, and save it as CHECK.RH.

```
#ifndef __CHECK_RH
/* ------------------------------------------------------------------ */
/*                                                                    */
/* MODULE: CHECK.RH                                                   */
/* PURPOSE: This include file defines the resource identifiers used.  */
/*                                                                    */
/* ------------------------------------------------------------------ */
#define __CHECK_RH

#define IDM_TESTMENU     200
#define CM_EXIT          101

#define CM_TEXTBLACK     111
#define CM_TEXTRED       112
#define CM_TEXTGREEN     113
#define CM_ALLOWUNDO     114

#define IDI_APPICON      202

#endif
```

4. Now create a C source file and call it CHECK.C. Into this file you will place all the code to run the application and control the menus. Insert the following comments and declarations at the top of the source file. Note the use of the STRICT identifier before including the Windows files. This identifier causes the windows code to use distinct types for different handles, so that your C compiler can easily warn you if you try to pass a HMENU where a HWND is required.

An important variable being declared in the following code is colorGroup. This UINT value will be used to store the currently selected menu item. This code initializes it to CM_TEXTBLACK, because the Black Text item is initially checked.

```
/* ------------------------------------------------------------------ */
/*                                                                    */
/* MODULE: CHECK.C                                                    */
/* PURPOSE: This sample application demonstrates how to use the       */
/*          CheckMenuItem API function to check and uncheck menu      */
/*          items, and also demonstrates how you can use a set of     */
/*          menu items like a set of radio buttons, with only one     */
/*          member of the set being checked at any one time.         */
/*                                                                    */
/* ------------------------------------------------------------------ */

#define STRICT
#include <windows.h>
#include <winnt.h>
#include "check.rh"
```

continued on next page

continued from previous page

```
static char *MainWindowClassName = "CheckItemWindow";
HINSTANCE     hInstance = NULL;

// colorGroup stores the menu ID which has the checkmark.
UINT          colorGroup = CM_TEXTBLACK;
```

5. Add the ToggleState function listed next. This function changes the check mark on the Allow Undo item. It uses GetMenuState to return the current state of the item, and it uses the logical AND operator (&) to test whether the MF_CHECKED flag is set for the item. It then calls the CheckMenuItem API function to change the check state of the item.

CheckMenuItem takes three arguments. The first argument is the handle of the menu to be modified. The second argument is the ID of the menu item to be modified, or the zero-based position of that item within the menu. Finally, the flags argument is used to indicate whether the second argument is an ID (MF_BYCOMMAND) or position (MF_BYPOSITION), and whether the menu item should be checked (MF_CHECKED) or unchecked (MF_UNCHECKED).

```
/* ---------------------------------------------------------------- */
/* This function can be used to turn a checkmark on or off for any   */
/* single menu item, based on its previous state.                    */
/* ---------------------------------------------------------------- */
void ToggleState(HWND hWnd, UINT command)
{
    HMENU hMenu;

    // Get a handle to the main menu.
    hMenu = GetMenu(hWnd);
    if (!hMenu)
        return;

    /* Look at the state of the menu item. If it is already
       checked, uncheck it, otherwise check it. */
    if (GetMenuState(hMenu,command,MF_BYCOMMAND) & MF_CHECKED)
        CheckMenuItem(hMenu,command,MF_BYCOMMAND | MF_UNCHECKED);
    else
        CheckMenuItem(hMenu,command,MF_BYCOMMAND | MF_CHECKED);
}
```

6. Add the following function to the source file. The CheckGroupItem function is called by the window procedure in response to the user's selecting one of the menu items, which are being handled like radio buttons. The function takes the item being selected in the command and a pointer to the variable that contains the currently checked item ID. The function uses CheckMenuItem with the MF_UNCHECKED flag to remove the check mark from beside the existing menu item. Then it calls CheckMenuItem with the MF_CHECKED flag to place a check mark beside the newly selected item. Finally, it stores the ID of the new item into the variable.

```
/* ----------------------------------------------------------------- */
/* This function checks one menu item in a group, and unchecks the   */
/* other items in the group. The function uses a single variable to  */
/* store the ID of the currently checked menu item. You determine    */
/* which items belong to the group programmatically; by calling this */
/* function for any item which you want to participate.              */
/* ----------------------------------------------------------------- */
void CheckGroupItem(HWND hWnd, UINT command, UINT *variable)
{
    HMENU hMenu;

    // Nothing to do if this is the same item.
    if (command == *variable)
        return;

    // Get a handle to the main menu.
    hMenu = GetMenu(hWnd);
    if (!hMenu)
        return;

    // Uncheck the previous command.
    CheckMenuItem(hMenu,*variable,MF_BYCOMMAND | MF_UNCHECKED);

    // Check the new command, and store the result.
    CheckMenuItem(hMenu,command,MF_BYCOMMAND | MF_CHECKED);
    *variable = command;
}
```

7. The following code implements the callback function, which is called by
Windows whenever there is a message to process. This code responds to the
WM_COMMAND message to process the menu selections, and to the
WM_DESTROY message to close down the application when the window is
closed. In response to the selection of the Allow Undo menu item
(CM_ALLOWUNDO), the function calls the ToggleState function that you
entered earlier. In response to any of the text color items (CM_TEXTBLACK,
CM_TEXTRED, or CM_TEXTGREEN), the function calls the
CheckGroupItem function to handle moving the check mark from one item to
another.

```
/* ----------------------------------------------------------------- */
/* This function is the main window callback function which will be  */
/* called by Windows to process messages for the window.             */
/* ----------------------------------------------------------------- */
LPARAM CALLBACK MainWndProc(HWND hWnd, UINT message,
                            WPARAM wParam, LPARAM lParam)
{
    switch (message)
    {
        case WM_COMMAND:
            switch (wParam)
            {
                case CM_EXIT:
```

continued on next page

continued from previous page

```
                                 DestroyWindow(hWnd);
                                 return 0;
                      case CM_TEXTBLACK:
                      case CM_TEXTRED:
                      case CM_TEXTGREEN:
                                 CheckGroupItem(hWnd,(UINT)wParam,&colorGroup);
                                 return 0;
                      case CM_ALLOWUNDO:
                                 ToggleState(hWnd,(UINT)wParam);
                                 return 0;
                 }
                 break;
          case WM_DESTROY:
                 PostQuitMessage(0);
                 return 0;
          }
          return DefWindowProc(hWnd, message, wParam, lParam);
}
```

8. Finally, add the three functions in the following code to the source file. The
InitApplication function is used to register the window class if the class has
not been registered already. A different window class is used for each of the
sample applications, as they all use different menus and window procedures.
The InitInstance function is called when it is time to create and display the
main window of the application. The WinMain function calls both of these
functions, and it is the main entry point for the application. In addition to calling the other functions to set up the application, WinMain also performs the
GetMessage, TranslateMessage, and DispatchMessage processing that allows
the application to receive and process messages.

```
/* ------------------------------------------------------------- */
/* This function initializes a WNDCLASS structure and uses it to */
/* register a class for our main window.                         */
/* ------------------------------------------------------------- */
BOOL InitApplication(HINSTANCE hInstance)
{
     WNDCLASS  wc;

     wc.style = 0;
     wc.lpfnWndProc = MainWndProc;
     wc.cbClsExtra = 0;
     wc.cbWndExtra = 0;
     wc.hInstance = hInstance;
     wc.hIcon = LoadIcon(hInstance,MAKEINTRESOURCE(IDI_APPICON));
     wc.hCursor = LoadCursor(NULL, IDC_ARROW);
     wc.hbrBackground = (HBRUSH)(COLOR_WINDOW + 1);
     wc.lpszMenuName =  MAKEINTRESOURCE(IDM_TESTMENU);
     wc.lpszClassName = MainWindowClassName;

     return RegisterClass(&wc);
}
```

```
/* ---------------------------------------------------------------- */
/* This function creates an instance of our main window. The window  */
/* is given a class name and a title, and told to display anywhere.  */
/* The nCmdShow argument passed to the program determines how the    */
/* window will be displayed.                                         */
/* ---------------------------------------------------------------- */
BOOL InitInstance(HINSTANCE hInst, int nCmdShow)
{
    HWND hWnd;

    hInstance = hInst;      // Store in global variable.

    hWnd = CreateWindow(MainWindowClassName,"Check Menu Items Demo",
                    WS_OVERLAPPEDWINDOW,CW_USEDEFAULT,
                    CW_USEDEFAULT,CW_USEDEFAULT,CW_USEDEFAULT,
                    NULL,NULL,hInstance,NULL);
    if (!hWnd)
        return FALSE;

    ShowWindow(hWnd, nCmdShow);
    UpdateWindow(hWnd);     // Send a WM_PAINT message.
    return TRUE;
}


/* ---------------------------------------------------------------- */
/* The main entry point for Windows applications. Check to see if    */
/* the main window class name has already been registered; if it     */
/* has not, call InitApplication to register it. Call InitInstance   */
/* to create an instance of our main window, then pump messages      */
/* until the application is closed.                                  */
/* ---------------------------------------------------------------- */
int PASCAL WinMain(HINSTANCE hInstance, HINSTANCE hPrevInstance,
                LPSTR lpCmdLine, int nCmdShow)
{
    MSG msg;

    if (!FindWindow(MainWindowClassName,NULL))
        if (!InitApplication(hInstance))
            return FALSE;

    if (!InitInstance(hInstance, nCmdShow))
        return FALSE;

    while (GetMessage(&msg,NULL,0,0))
    {
        TranslateMessage(&msg);
        DispatchMessage(&msg);
    }
    return msg.wParam;
}
```

9. Before you compile and run the application, you will need to add the application icon that is referenced in the resource script. Copy the file APP.ICO from the CHAPTER8\CHECK directory on the CD, or create your own 32-by-32-pixel icon with the same name using a resource editor.

Comments

Using check marks beside menu items is a widely accepted method of providing feedback to users about the current state of menu selections. Obviously, check marks are not appropriate beside menu commands that are strong verbs, such as Open, Close, Save, and Print. However, they should be used wherever possible beside menu items that are options or have states, such as Ruler, Show Toolbars, Allow Undo, and other option settings.

COMPLEXITY
DIFFICULT

8.4 How do I...
Use my own check mark?

Problem

I would like to place a small graphic beside the items on the menu so the user can tell the state of an option, in a way that suits the option. For instance, I would like to display colors beside color items, or different symbols beside other menu items when they are turned on. How do I change the check mark that appears by menu items when they are selected, so that I can use my own graphic rather than the default check?

Technique

How-To 8.3 shows you how you can use the default check marks in the menu. You can use check marks to indicate if an option is turned on or off, or use a single check mark within a group of options rather like a set of radio buttons. Windows actually uses two check mark bitmaps for each menu item in the menu. One of these bitmaps is displayed when the MF_CHECKED state is set for the item (the standard check mark), and the other is shown when the item is unchecked. By default, the unchecked image is blank.

You can change either or both of the check mark images for any item in the menu by calling the SetMenuItemBitmaps function. This function takes two handles to bitmaps (HBITMAP) to use when displaying the item. If you set either of these handles to NULL, you will get the default Windows bitmaps (a blank image for unchecked and the standard check mark if the item is checked). Before you change the bitmaps used to draw a menu item, you need to consider a few other problems.

The first question is how large should the bitmap be? The Windows API documentation doesn't make this clear, and the reason is that you don't know until you draw the menu how large the bitmap should be. The size of menu items is determined by the screen resolution that the system is using and the font that the user has selected for the menus. You can find out the size that your bitmaps should be by calling the API function GetSystemMetrics and passing SM_CXMENUCHECK to retrieve the width, and SM_CYMENUCHECK to return the height.

The second problem is what color the image should be. Obviously, the foreground colors of the check mark are up to you, the application designer, but the menu background can be changed by the user, using the screen property sheet. Some users may stick to the white used in Windows 3.1, and others will prefer the gray of the default Windows 95 colors. Still other users will have their own color settings, using any color combination possible. You can't be certain that the color scheme that you select for your custom check mark will look good with the user's color choices, but you can at least ensure that the background color of your image is the same as that of the menu. You can do this by using the GetSysColor function with the COLOR_MENU argument to get the RGB values for the menu background. You can then alter the color table of your bitmap before it is displayed, making sure that the background matches. The example application for this How-To uses device-independent bitmaps so that it can directly access the color table of the bitmap. You can learn more tricks about altering the color table of bitmaps in How-To 4.2.

The sample application discussed in this How-To performs all of the operations just described.

Steps

Run the CHECKBMP.EXE application found in the CHAPTER8\CHECKBMP directory on the CD-ROM accompanying this book. If you have read How-To 8.3, which describes how to add check marks to a menu item, you will recognize that this is the same application discussed in that section. There are two menus: a File menu that contains only an Exit item and an Options menu that contains three text color options (Black Text, Red Text, and Green Text) and an Allow Undo option. In the previous application, the Black Text item was initially checked, and all the other items were unchecked. In this application, there is a small black box to the right of the Black Text item. There are no marks beside the other colors, but there is a circle with a slash across it beside the Allow Undo item—the international symbol for "No." You can see an illustration of this menu in Figure 8-4.

Select another color from the Options menu. If you select the Red Text item, a red box appears beside that item, and the black box disappears. Similarly, selecting the Green Text item places a green box beside the Green Text item and removes the red box.

Now select the Allow Undo menu item. The circular "No" symbol disappears and is replaced by a green check mark.

1. Start by creating a directory and naming it CHECKBMP. Use this directory as your working directory for this project.

2. Create a file called CHECKBMP.RC and enter the following resource script. If you have been through the steps for How-To 8.3, you will recognize that this

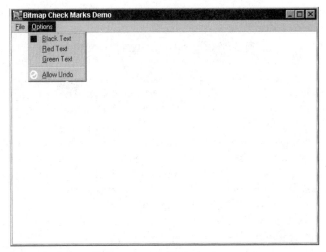

Figure 8-4 Using custom check marks in a menu

is almost the same resource script. The menu structure is identical; the only addition is the bitmaps that will be used to generate the check marks. There are five bitmaps—three colored boxes for the text color options and a red "No" symbol and green check mark for the Allow Undo menu item.

```
/* -------------------------------------------------------------- */
/*                                                                */
/* MODULE: CHECKBMP.RC                                            */
/* PURPOSE: This resource script defines the base menu for this   */
/*          example application.                                  */
/*                                                                */
/* -------------------------------------------------------------- */

#include <windows.h>
#include "checkbmp.rh"

IDM_TESTMENU MENU
{
    POPUP "&File"
    {
        MENUITEM "E&xit", CM_EXIT
    }
    POPUP "&Options"
    {
        MENUITEM "&Black Text", CM_TEXTBLACK, CHECKED
        MENUITEM "&Red Text", CM_TEXTRED
        MENUITEM "&Green Text", CM_TEXTGREEN
        MENUITEM SEPARATOR
        MENUITEM "&Allow Undo", CM_ALLOWUNDO
    }
}
```

```
/* Application Icon */
IDI_APPICON ICON "app.ico"

/* Menu Checkmark Bitmaps */
IDBM_BLACKBOX BITMAP "black.bmp"
IDBM_REDBOX BITMAP "red.bmp"
IDBM_GREENBOX BITMAP "green.bmp"
IDBM_CHECK BITMAP "check.bmp"
IDBM_UNCHECK BITMAP "uncheck.bmp"
```

3. Before any of this resource script will compile, you will need the five bitmaps and the application icon. If you wish, you can create the 24-by-24-pixel, 16-color bitmaps and the application icon, using a resource editor, and save them to the file names listed in Table 8-2. A quicker method will be to copy the bitmap and icon files from the directory on the CD-ROM: CHAPTER8\CHECKBMP.

FILE NAME	CONTENTS
APP.ICO	Application icon
BLACK.BMP	The black box bitmap
RED.BMP	The red box bitmap
GREEN.BMP	The green box bitmap
CHECK.BMP	The green check mark
UNCHECK.BMP	The red "No" symbol

Table 8-2 Bitmap and icon file names for the project

4. Now create an include file that will define the identifiers used to load the bitmaps and reference the menu items. Save the include file as CHECKBMP.RH. This file will be shared between both the resource script and the C source file. The contents of CHECKBMP.RH are listed here:

```
#ifndef __CHECKBMP_RH
/* ---------------------------------------------------------------- */
/*                                                                  */
/* MODULE: CHECKBMP.RH                                              */
/* PURPOSE: This include file defines the resource identifiers used. */
/*                                                                  */
/* ---------------------------------------------------------------- */
#define __CHECKBMP_RH

#define IDM_TESTMENU    200
#define CM_EXIT         101

#define CM_TEXTBLACK    111
#define CM_TEXTRED      112
#define CM_TEXTGREEN    113
#define CM_ALLOWUNDO    114
```

continued on next page

continued from previous page

```
#define IDBM_BLACKBOX      301
#define IDBM_REDBOX        302
#define IDBM_GREENBOX      303
#define IDBM_CHECK         304
#define IDBM_UNCHECK       305

#define IDI_APPICON        202

#endif
```

5. Now you can create the C source file and start learning how to replace check marks. Create a file called CHECKBMP.C and add the following comments and declarations. The definition of the STRICT preprocessor symbol is used so that the C compiler warns you if you try to mix handles and other types. For instance, it warns you if you try to pass a Windows function a HWND where a HMENU is expected. RGBLIGHTGRAY is defined to hold the RGB values for light gray, and it will be used to replace the background color of the check mark bitmaps with that of the menu bar. The colorGroup variable is used to store the ID of the currently selected text color menu item (initially Black Text), and the various bitmap handles are used to load and delete the check mark bitmaps.

```
/* ----------------------------------------------------------------- */
/*                                                                   */
/* MODULE: CHECKBMP.C                                                */
/* PURPOSE: This example application demonstrates the use of the     */
/*          GetMenuCheckMarkDimensions and SetMenuItemBitmaps API    */
/*          functions to set the checked and unchecked bitmaps for   */
/*          selected menu items. It also demonstrates how to load    */
/*          bitmaps as device independent bitmaps, and change the    */
/*          colors of the bitmap to match the background before      */
/*          display.                                                 */
/*                                                                   */
/* ----------------------------------------------------------------- */

#define STRICT
#include <windows.h>
#include <winnt.h>
#include "checkbmp.rh"

static char    *MainWindowClassName = "BitmapCheckWindow";
HINSTANCE       hInstance = NULL;

// colorGroup stores the menu ID which has the checkmark.
UINT            colorGroup = CM_TEXTBLACK;
static RGBQUAD  RGBLIGHTGRAY = { 192, 192, 192, 0 };

// The following bitmap handles store the checkmarks.
HBITMAP         blackBox = NULL;
HBITMAP         redBox = NULL;
HBITMAP         greenBox = NULL;
HBITMAP         checkOn = NULL;
HBITMAP         checkOff = NULL;
```

6. Add the following code to the source file that you have created. The LoadBitmapResource function is used instead of the LoadBitmap API function to retrieve bitmaps from resources. This function has been stolen from the examples used in Chapter 4. It is used to load the bitmaps as device-independent bitmaps rather than the device-dependent bitmaps that you get with LoadBitmap. These bitmaps will contain a color table that you can alter to modify the background color of the bitmap.

```
/* ------------------------------------------------------------- */
/* This function uses LoadResource to get a bitmap resource as a  */
/* DIB; it takes a copy of the DIB and returns a pointer to the   */
/* copy. Free the pointer with LocalFree((HLOCAL)pointer) when done. */
/* ------------------------------------------------------------- */
BITMAPINFO *LoadBitmapResource(HINSTANCE hInstance, WORD resId)
{
    HRSRC        hResource;
    HGLOBAL      hDib;
    int          nSize, numEntries;
    BITMAPINFO *pResourceDIB, *pCopyDIB;

    if (((hResource = FindResource(hInstance,
                                MAKEINTRESOURCE(resId),
                                RT_BITMAP)) != NULL) &&
        ((hDib = LoadResource(hInstance,hResource)) != NULL))
    {
        pResourceDIB = (LPBITMAPINFO)LockResource(hDib);
        if ((numEntries = pResourceDIB->bmiHeader.biClrUsed) == 0)
            numEntries = 1L << pResourceDIB->bmiHeader.biBitCount;
        nSize = pResourceDIB->bmiHeader.biSize +
                (numEntries * sizeof(RGBQUAD)) +
                pResourceDIB->bmiHeader.biSizeImage;
        if ((pCopyDIB = (BITMAPINFO NEAR *)LocalAlloc(LMEM_FIXED,
                                                nSize)) != NULL)
        {
            CopyMemory(pCopyDIB,pResourceDIB,nSize);
            return pCopyDIB;
        }
    }
    return NULL;
}
```

7. The following code is also taken from the color example in How-To 4.2. It is used to scan through the color table of a device-independent bitmap (such as the ones loaded with LoadBitmapResource, just given) and change all occurrences of one color to another color. Put this code in the same source file.

```
/* ------------------------------------------------------------- */
/* This function works on the color table for a DIB. It changes all */
/* the entries in the table for fromColor to toColor. Do not use   */
/* this function on the DIB in the resource itself, as resources   */
/* are read-only. Use a copy of the resource DIB.                  */
/* ------------------------------------------------------------- */
```

continued on next page

continued from previous page

```
void ChangeColor(BITMAPINFO *info, RGBQUAD fromColor,
                 RGBQUAD toColor)
{
    int i, numEntries;

    if ((numEntries = info->bmiHeader.biClrUsed) == 0)
        numEntries = 1L << info->bmiHeader.biBitCount;

    for (i = 0; i < numEntries; i++)
        if ((info->bmiColors[i].rgbRed == fromColor.rgbRed) &&
            (info->bmiColors[i].rgbGreen == fromColor.rgbGreen) &&
            (info->bmiColors[i].rgbBlue == fromColor.rgbBlue))
        {
            info->bmiColors[i].rgbRed = toColor.rgbRed;
            info->bmiColors[i].rgbGreen = toColor.rgbGreen;
            info->bmiColors[i].rgbBlue = toColor.rgbBlue;
        }
}
```

8. A third routine taken from How-To 4.2 converts a device-independent bitmap
into a device-dependent bitmap. The original routine in that section realized a
logical palette, matching the bitmap into the device context (DC) before conversion. This ensured that the right bits were placed into the bitmap for use
with that palette, allowing display of 256-color bitmaps. In this function, the
palette code has been removed. This is because you will not be drawing the
bitmaps—Windows will display the check marks in the menu using the
default system palette.

Add the following code to the source file. This code creates a memory DC that
is compatible with the window DC and then creates a bitmap of the right size
and selects it into the DC. Finally, the function uses StretchDIBits to copy from
the DIB into the DC (and thus the new bitmap), scaling the image as required.

```
/* --------------------------------------------------------------- */
/* This function converts the DIB supplied as the info argument into */
/* a DDB ready for display in the given window. It returns the       */
/* HBITMAP handle of the bitmap.                                     */
/* --------------------------------------------------------------- */
HBITMAP ConvertDIBToDDB(HWND hWnd, BITMAPINFO *info,
                        int width, int height)
{
    HDC       hDC, hMemDC;
    HBITMAP   hBitmap, hOldBitmap;
    int       numEntries, bytesToSkip;
    void      *bits;

    /* Work out where the bitmap data itself starts. Point
       bits to this location. */
    if ((numEntries = info->bmiHeader.biClrUsed) == 0)
        numEntries = 1L << info->bmiHeader.biBitCount;
    bytesToSkip = info->bmiHeader.biSize +
                        (numEntries * sizeof(RGBQUAD));
    bits = (LPCSTR)info + bytesToSkip;
```

```
        /* Get a handle to a device context */
        hDC = GetDC(hWnd);

        /* Create a memory DC and a bitmap of the right size.
           Select the bitmap into the DC, then use
           StretchDIBits to convert the DIB into the bitmap. */
        if ((hMemDC = CreateCompatibleDC(hDC)) != NULL)
        {
            if ((hBitmap = CreateCompatibleBitmap(hDC,
                                        width,height)) != NULL)
            {
                hOldBitmap = SelectObject(hMemDC,hBitmap);
                StretchDIBits(hMemDC,
                              0,0,width,height,
                              0,0,info->bmiHeader.biHeight,
                              info->bmiHeader.biWidth,
                              bits,info,DIB_RGB_COLORS,SRCCOPY);
                SelectObject(hMemDC,hOldBitmap);
            }
            DeleteDC(hMemDC);
        }
        ReleaseDC(hWnd,hDC);

        return hBitmap;
}
```

9. Add the next function to the source file. Function LoadCheckMark performs
the steps required to load a bitmap from a resource, change the background
color to match the menu, and then scale the image to the correct size, converting it to a device-dependent bitmap for display. The code calls the API
function GetSystemMetrics to find the required width (using the
SM_CXMENUCHECK) and height (using SM_CYMENUCHECK) of the
menu item, and GetSysColor(COLOR_MENU) to return the RGB value of the
menu background. The bitmap resource is then loaded, and the light gray
color from the resource is converted to the menu color by calling
ChangeColor. Finally, the ConvertDIBToDDB function that you added earlier
is called to convert the bitmap and scale it to the correct size. The function
returns a handle to the completed check mark bitmap.

```
/* ------------------------------------------------------------ */
/* This function loads a single bitmap from the resource file, for */
/* use as a menu checkmark. The bitmap is loaded as a Device       */
/* Independent bitmap (DIB) and the light gray color replaced with */
/* the menu background color (COLOR_MENU) before conversion to a   */
/* bitmap and stretching to the correct dimensions.                */
/* ------------------------------------------------------------ */
HBITMAP LoadCheckMark(HINSTANCE hInstance, HWND hWnd,
                      WORD resourceId)
{
    BITMAPINFO *pDIB;
    HBITMAP    hBitmap;
    int        width, height;
    LONG       dimensions;
```

continued on next page

continued from previous page

```
            RGBQUAD        menuColor;
            DWORD          mColor;

            // Find out the correct size for menu checkmarks.
            dimensions = GetMenuCheckMarkDimensions();
            width = LOWORD(dimensions);
            height = HIWORD(dimensions);

            // Load a DIB from the resource.
            if ((pDIB = LoadBitmapResource(hInstance,resourceId)) != NULL)
            {
                // Get the menu color, and convert to a RGBQUAD.
                mColor = GetSysColor(COLOR_MENU);
                menuColor.rgbRed = LOBYTE(LOWORD(mColor));
                menuColor.rgbGreen = HIBYTE(LOWORD(mColor));
                menuColor.rgbBlue = LOBYTE(HIWORD(mColor));
                menuColor.rgbReserved = 0;
                // Change the background to menu color.
                ChangeColor(pDIB,RGBLIGHTGRAY,menuColor);

                // Convert to a DDB and scale to the correct size.
                hBitmap = ConvertDIBToDDB(hWnd,pDIB,width,height);
                LocalFree((HLOCAL)pDIB);
                return hBitmap;
            }
            return NULL;
        }
```

10. The SetupCheckMarks function, shown next, loads each of the check marks
for this application by calling LoadCheckMark. The LoadCheckMark function
sizes and recolors each bitmap as required, so all that is required for this function is to store the handle returned and use the SetMenuItemBitmaps function
to set the bitmaps for each item. Check mark bitmaps are set on a per-item
basis—you can't just assign a single check mark for use by an entire submenu.

The calls in this function set the item check marks using the ID value of each
item, hence the reason for specifying MF_BYCOMMAND in the flags for each
call. Note that in the first three calls, there is a NULL before the handle of the
bitmap. This NULL is the handle of the bitmap to use when the item is
unchecked. Using NULL as the handle tells Windows to use the default
imagery—in this case, a blank space. The last call to SetMenuItemBitmaps
passes two bitmap handles: a "No" symbol for when the item is unchecked,
and a green check mark for when it is checked.

```
/* ---------------------------------------------------------------- */
/* This function loads the bitmaps for each checkmark. The bitmap    */
/* handles are stored in variables global to this instance, because  */
/* you need to free them before the window closes.                   */
/* ---------------------------------------------------------------- */
void SetupCheckMarks(HINSTANCE hInstance, HWND hWnd)
{
    HMENU hMenu;
```

```
    // Get a handle to the main menu.
    hMenu = GetMenu(hWnd);
    if (!hMenu)
        return;

    // Load the bitmap for the black text.
    blackBox = LoadCheckMark(hInstance,hWnd,IDBM_BLACKBOX);
    if (blackBox)
        SetMenuItemBitmaps(hMenu,CM_TEXTBLACK,MF_BYCOMMAND,
                           NULL,blackBox);

    // Load the bitmap for the red text.
    redBox = LoadCheckMark(hInstance,hWnd,IDBM_REDBOX);
    if (redBox)
        SetMenuItemBitmaps(hMenu,CM_TEXTRED,MF_BYCOMMAND,
                           NULL,redBox);

    // Load the bitmap for the green text.
    greenBox = LoadCheckMark(hInstance,hWnd,IDBM_GREENBOX);
    if (greenBox)
        SetMenuItemBitmaps(hMenu,CM_TEXTGREEN,MF_BYCOMMAND,
                           NULL,greenBox);

    // Load the two bitmaps for the Allow Undo checkmarks.
    checkOn = LoadCheckMark(hInstance,hWnd,IDBM_CHECK);
    checkOff = LoadCheckMark(hInstance,hWnd,IDBM_UNCHECK);
    if ((checkOn) && (checkOff))
        SetMenuItemBitmaps(hMenu,CM_ALLOWUNDO,MF_BYCOMMAND,
                           checkOff,checkOn);
}
```

11. Add the following code to the source file. The RemoveCheckMarks function is
used to change the menu item check marks back to the system defaults and
then release the memory occupied by the bitmaps. This function will be called
when it is time to close the application and also when the user changes the
screen properties, because the menu background color or font size may have
changed. RemoveCheckMarks calls SetMenuItemBitmaps for each menu item
that was modified, passing a NULL value for each bitmap handle. This returns
the check marks to the default system check marks. The code then releases
each bitmap by calling DeleteObject, and sets the handle to NULL.

```
/* ------------------------------------------------------------- */
/* This function removes the user-defined checkmarks by setting  */
/* the menus back to the Windows defaults. It then destroys the  */
/* bitmaps and sets the handles to NULL.                         */
/* ------------------------------------------------------------- */
void RemoveCheckMarks(HWND hWnd)
{
    HMENU hMenu;

    // Get a handle to the main menu.
    hMenu = GetMenu(hWnd);
```

continued on next page

continued from previous page

```
         if (!hMenu)
             return;

         // Release the bitmap for the black text.
         if (blackBox)
         {
             SetMenuItemBitmaps(hMenu,CM_TEXTBLACK,MF_BYCOMMAND,
                                NULL,NULL);
             DeleteObject(blackBox);
             blackBox = NULL;
         }

         // Release the bitmap for the red text.
         if (redBox)
         {
             SetMenuItemBitmaps(hMenu,CM_TEXTRED,MF_BYCOMMAND,
                                NULL,NULL);
             DeleteObject(redBox);
             redBox = NULL;
         }

         // Release the bitmap for the green text.
         if (greenBox)
         {
             SetMenuItemBitmaps(hMenu,CM_TEXTGREEN,MF_BYCOMMAND,
                                NULL,NULL);
             DeleteObject(greenBox);
             greenBox = NULL;
         }

         if ((checkOn) || (checkOff))
         {
             SetMenuItemBitmaps(hMenu,CM_ALLOWUNDO,MF_BYCOMMAND,
                                NULL,NULL);
             if (checkOn)
                 DeleteObject(checkOn);
             if (checkOff)
                 DeleteObject(checkOn);
             checkOn = checkOff = NULL;
         }
     }
```

12. Now it's time to add the functions that actually turn the check marks on and off. If you have worked through How-To 8.3, you will find that these functions are exactly the same as the functions used in that How-To, to toggle check marks on and off in response to the user's actions. The functions do not specifically deal with the custom check marks—once the check marks are set up with SetMenuItemBitmaps, Windows handles them completely. Add the two functions listed in the following code to the source code. Function ToggleState is used to toggle the check mark for the Allow Undo item on and off, as required. Function CheckGroupItem is used to check one item from the text color menu items and remove the check mark from the previously selected item, causing the group of menu items to function as though they were radio buttons.

```
/* ----------------------------------------------------------------- */
/* This function can be used to turn a checkmark on or off for any    */
/* single menu item, based on its previous state.                     */
/* ----------------------------------------------------------------- */
void ToggleState(HWND hWnd, UINT command)
{
    HMENU hMenu;

    // Get a handle to the main menu.
    hMenu = GetMenu(hWnd);
    if (!hMenu)
        return;

    /* Look at the state of the menu item. If it is already
       checked, uncheck it, otherwise check it. */
    if (GetMenuState(hMenu,command,MF_BYCOMMAND) & MF_CHECKED)
        CheckMenuItem(hMenu,command,MF_BYCOMMAND | MF_UNCHECKED);
    else
        CheckMenuItem(hMenu,command,MF_BYCOMMAND | MF_CHECKED);
}


/* ----------------------------------------------------------------- */
/* This function checks one menu item in a group, and unchecks the    */
/* other items in the group. The function uses a single variable to   */
/* store the ID of the currently checked menu item. You determine     */
/* which items belong to the group programmatically; by calling this  */
/* function for any item which you want to participate.               */
/* ----------------------------------------------------------------- */
void CheckGroupItem(HWND hWnd, UINT command, UINT *variable)
{
    HMENU hMenu;

    // Nothing to do if this is the same item.
    if (command == *variable)
        return;

    // Get a handle to the main menu.
    hMenu = GetMenu(hWnd);
    if (!hMenu)
        return;

    // Uncheck the previous command.
    CheckMenuItem(hMenu,*variable,MF_BYCOMMAND | MF_UNCHECKED);

    // Check the new command, and store the result.
    CheckMenuItem(hMenu,command,MF_BYCOMMAND | MF_CHECKED);
    *variable = command;
}
```

13. The following function is the main window procedure for the application. It is called whenever a message is to be processed for the main window. The function responds to a number of window messages, and also to the WM_COMMAND messages caused by the user selecting menu items. In response to the WM_CREATE message, issued when the window is created,

the code calls the SetupCheckMarks function. In response to the
WM_DESTROY message, the code calls the RemoveCheckMarks function.

A special case occurs when the application receives the WM_SYSCOLORCHANGE
message. This message indicates that the user has changed the screen properties.
This may be a change in resolution, in color, or in the font used to draw the menu.
To make sure that the menu behaves consistently, the code uses RemoveCheckMarks
to remove the check marks, then calls SetupCheckMarks to create the check mark
bitmaps again with the new settings. Add the following code to the same source
file, CHECKBMP.C.

```
/* ------------------------------------------------------------------ */
/* This function is the main window callback function which will be  */
/* called by Windows to process messages for the window.            */
/* ------------------------------------------------------------------ */
LPARAM CALLBACK MainWndProc(HWND hWnd, UINT message,
                            WPARAM wParam, LPARAM lParam)
{
    switch (message)
    {
        case WM_CREATE:
            SetupCheckMarks(hInstance,hWnd);
            return 0;
        case WM_SYSCOLORCHANGE:
            RemoveCheckMarks(hWnd);
            SetupCheckMarks(hInstance,hWnd);
            return 0;
        case WM_COMMAND:
            switch (wParam)
            {
                case CM_EXIT:
                    DestroyWindow(hWnd);
                    return 0;
                case CM_TEXTBLACK:
                case CM_TEXTRED:
                case CM_TEXTGREEN:
                    CheckGroupItem(hWnd,(UINT)wParam,&colorGroup);
                    return 0;
                case CM_ALLOWUNDO:
                    ToggleState(hWnd,(UINT)wParam);
                    return 0;
            }
            break;
        case WM_DESTROY:
            RemoveCheckMarks(hWnd);
            PostQuitMessage(0);
            return 0;
    }
    return DefWindowProc(hWnd, message, wParam, lParam);
}
```

14. Finally, add the following three functions to the source file. These three functions provide the framework for the application. Function InitApplication

registers the window class with a unique name for this application. The function will be called only if the window class does not already exist. Function InitInstance creates and displays the main window for the application. Finally, WinMain executes the two functions and pumps messages so that the application can operate.

```
/* ---------------------------------------------------------------- */
/* This function initializes a WNDCLASS structure and uses it to    */
/* register a class for our main window.                            */
/* ---------------------------------------------------------------- */
BOOL InitApplication(HINSTANCE hInstance)
{
    WNDCLASS  wc;

    wc.style = 0;
    wc.lpfnWndProc = MainWndProc;
    wc.cbClsExtra = 0;
    wc.cbWndExtra = 0;
    wc.hInstance = hInstance;
    wc.hIcon = LoadIcon(hInstance,MAKEINTRESOURCE(IDI_APPICON));
    wc.hCursor = LoadCursor(NULL, IDC_ARROW);
    wc.hbrBackground = (HBRUSH)(COLOR_WINDOW + 1);
    wc.lpszMenuName = MAKEINTRESOURCE(IDM_TESTMENU);
    wc.lpszClassName = MainWindowClassName;

    return RegisterClass(&wc);
}


/* ---------------------------------------------------------------- */
/* This function creates an instance of our main window. The window */
/* is given a class name and a title, and told to display anywhere. */
/* The nCmdShow argument passed to the program determines how the   */
/* window will be displayed.                                        */
/* ---------------------------------------------------------------- */
BOOL InitInstance(HINSTANCE hInst, int nCmdShow)
{
    HWND hWnd;

    hInstance = hInst;      // Store in global variable.

    hWnd = CreateWindow(MainWindowClassName,"Bitmap Check Marks Demo",
                   WS_OVERLAPPEDWINDOW,CW_USEDEFAULT,
                   CW_USEDEFAULT,CW_USEDEFAULT,CW_USEDEFAULT,
                   NULL,NULL,hInstance,NULL);
    if (!hWnd)
        return FALSE;

    ShowWindow(hWnd, nCmdShow);
    UpdateWindow(hWnd);     // Send a WM_PAINT message.
    return TRUE;
}
```

```
/* ------------------------------------------------------------ */
/* The main entry point for Windows applications. Check to see if   */
/* the main window class name has already been registered; if it has*/
/* not, call InitApplication to register it. Call InitInstance to    */
/* create an instance of our main window, then pump messages until   */
/* the application is closed.                                         */
/* ------------------------------------------------------------ */
int PASCAL WinMain(HINSTANCE hInstance, HINSTANCE hPrevInstance,
                   LPSTR lpCmdLine, int nCmdShow)
{
    MSG msg;

    if (!FindWindow(MainWindowClassName,NULL))
        if (!InitApplication(hInstance))
            return FALSE;

    if (!InitInstance(hInstance, nCmdShow))
        return FALSE;

    while (GetMessage(&msg,NULL,0,0))
    {
        TranslateMessage(&msg);
        DispatchMessage(&msg);
    }
    return msg.wParam;
}
```

15. Compile and run the application.

Comments

The example in this How-To is more complex than the other sample applications in this chapter. Most of this extra complexity is not associated directly with the SetMenuItemBitmaps and GetSystemMetrics functions, but with the preparations that must be made to the bitmaps before SetMenuItemBitmaps can be used. It is important to make these preparations however, because an application that looks great on your 800-by-600 screen must also work on a user's 640-by-400 screen with a totally different color scheme and font.

COMPLEXITY
EASY

8.5 How do I...
Add options to the system menu?

Problem

I would like to add an option to the system menu on the windows of my application. Can I do this, or is the system menu read-only?

Technique

The system menu both is and is not read-only. When you first create a window with the WS_SYSMENU style, it uses the default system menu provided by Windows. In return, Windows looks after the items on the menu—graying the Restore menu item until the window has been maximized or minimized, graying the Minimize item when the window is iconic, and more. You cannot alter this default system menu (or at least you shouldn't) because it is used by Windows for many applications.

However, Windows does allow you to modify the system menu for your window in an easy way. When you call GetSystemMenu, Windows will create a copy of the system menu for your application's window and return a handle to that menu. You can modify this menu in any way. On subsequent calls to GetSystemMenu, you can request that the system use the existing copy of the menu for this window, or that the system discard any changes that you may have made and give you a handle to a new copy of the system menu.

The example application that you will build for this exercise will show you how easy it is to add items to the system menu.

Steps

Run the sample application for this How-To, which is on the CD-ROM as CHAPTER8\ADDSYS\ADDSYS.EXE. The sample application opens a simple window with no menus except the system menu in the top left corner of the title bar.

When you pull down the system menu, you will notice that an extra menu item has been added below the Close menu item. The Shutdown System menu item will cause Windows to shut down, as though you had selected the Shutdown item from the Start menu. This is one example of adding an item to the system menu of an application. Figure 8-5 shows how the application looks with the item added to the system menu.

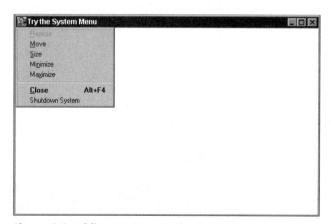

Figure 8-5 Adding an item to the system menu

You can close the application by choosing Close from the system menu or by clicking the close icon on the far right of the title bar. The following steps will guide you through implementing this small example application.

1. Create a working directory for this application and call it ADDSYS. Place all the source files for this project into this directory.

2. Next, create a resource script for this application. Create a text file called ADDSYS.RC and add the following code. This is a very simple resource file, as the application only has an icon.

```
/* ------------------------------------------------------------------ */
/*                                                                    */
/* MODULE: ADDSYS.RC                                                  */
/* PURPOSE: This resource script defines the application icon for     */
/*          this application.                                         */
/*                                                                    */
/* ------------------------------------------------------------------ */

#include "addsys.rh"

IDI_APPICON ICON "app.ico"
```

3. Before this resource script will compile, you will need to add the icon to the directory that you are working in. Copy the file CHAPTER8\ADDSYS\APP.ICO from the CD-ROM to your working directory.

4. You will also need the include file mentioned in the source in step 2. Create a file called ADDSYS.RH. This file will contain the definitions that link the resource IDs mentioned in the C source code with the resources in the resource script—in this case, just the application icon.

```
#ifndef __ADDSYS_RH
/* ------------------------------------------------------------------ */
/*                                                                    */
/* MODULE: ADDSYS.RH                                                  */
/* PURPOSE: This include file defines the resource identifiers used.  */
/*                                                                    */
/* ------------------------------------------------------------------ */
#define __ADDSYS_RH

#define IDI_APPICON      202

#endif
```

5. Now it is time to create the C source file for the application. The code in this file will handle creating the application and inserting a Shutdown System item on the system menu of the application. It will also handle the messages for that item, shutting down the system if the user requires. Create a new file and call it ADDSYS.C. Add the following code to the beginning of the file. This code includes the Windows files and defines STRICT, so that the compiler will better enforce your use of Windows types such as HWND and HMENU. Notice that the code defines an identifier too, SC_SHUTDOWN will be the ID for the Shutdown System menu item.

```
/* ---------------------------------------------------------------- */
/*                                                                  */
/* MODULE: ADDSYS.C                                                 */
/* PURPOSE: This sample application demonstrates how you can use    */
/*          GetSystemMenu to get a handle to a copy of the system   */
/*          menu for a Window, and then modify that menu using the  */
/*          AppendMenu API function.                                */
/*                                                                  */
/* ---------------------------------------------------------------- */

#define STRICT
#include <windows.h>
#include <winnt.h>
#include "addsys.rh"

#define SC_SHUTDOWN    1000

static char *MainWindowClassName = "AddSystemWindow";
```

6. Now add the following function. This is the key function for understanding
how to modify the system menu. The function uses GetSystemMenu to get an
HMENU handle to the system menu for the window. Now if the window has
just opened, chances are that it will be using the default system menu provided by Windows. If this is the case, Windows will now create a copy of this
menu and return a handle to it. If you call this function later in an application,
some other code may have already modified the menu. At this stage, you have
two choices—you can further modify the existing menu, or you can get a
clean copy from Windows and start over. The second argument to
GetSystemMenu lets you select which option to use. A value of FALSE says,
"Use what's there," and a value of TRUE says, "Get me a clean copy." In this
example, you will use FALSE, because it makes sense not to destroy any existing changes to the menu when you add a new item. Once you have the handle
to the menu, you can modify it in any way that you can modify a traditional
menu. This function uses AppendMenu to add a new item to the end of the
menu, with an ID value of SC_SHUTDOWN and the text Shutdown System.

```
/* ---------------------------------------------------------------- */
/* This function gets a handle to a copy of the system menu for     */
/* this window. It then uses AppendMenu to add the "Shutdown System" */
/* item to the menu.                                                */
/* ---------------------------------------------------------------- */
void AddSystemShutdownItem(HWND hWnd)
{
    HMENU hMenu;

    /* Get a handle to the system menu for this window. If
       this Window's menu is no different from the default
       system menu, Windows will make a copy of the system
       menu first, and give us the handle to that. */
    hMenu = GetSystemMenu(hWnd,FALSE);
    if (!hMenu)
        return;
```

continued on next page

continued from previous page

```
        /* Add an item to the end of the system menu.
           Give it the ID SC_SHUTDOWN. */
        AppendMenu(hMenu,MF_STRING,SC_SHUTDOWN,"Shutdown System");
}
```

7. Add the following code to the source file. Function StartSystemShutdown will be called when the user selects the Shutdown System item from the system menu of the application. The function uses a message box to confirm that the user really does want to shut down the system. If he or she says okay, the system will be closed with a call to ExitWindowsEx. The system is closed with the EWX_SHUTDOWN argument, which causes the system to be shut down and ready to be turned off. A smarter version of this code might give the user the option of restarting the system, or restarting in MS-DOS mode, similar to the dialog that runs when you select the Shutdown item from the Start menu.

```
/* ------------------------------------------------------------------ */
/* This function calls ExitWindowsEx with the EWX_SHUTDOWN argument    */
/* to shutdown the system in preparation for turning off the PC.       */
/* ------------------------------------------------------------------ */
void StartSystemShutdown(HWND hWnd)
{
    if (MessageBox(hWnd,"Shutdown the system?",
                "Confirm Shutdown",
                MB_OKCANCEL | MB_ICONQUESTION) == IDOK)
    {
        ExitWindowsEx(EWX_SHUTDOWN,0);
    }
}
```

8. The function listed next is the main callback procedure for the application. All messages for the window of the application are processed through this procedure. The application processes the WM_CREATE message that is sent after the window is created but before it is displayed. In response to this message, the code calls the function written earlier, AddSystemShutdownItem. This will add the Shutdown System item to the system menu. When the user selects the item from the menu, a message will be sent to this window procedure. Unlike normal menu messages, which send a WM_COMMAND message, with the message ID in the WPARAM, system menu items send a WM_SYSCOMMAND message, with the message ID also in the WPARAM argument. The following code handles this event and calls the StartSystemShutdown function that you entered previously.

```
/* ------------------------------------------------------------------ */
/* This function is the main window callback function which will be    */
/* called by Windows to process messages for the window.               */
/* ------------------------------------------------------------------ */
LPARAM CALLBACK MainWndProc(HWND hWnd, UINT message,
                            WPARAM wParam, LPARAM lParam)
{
    switch (message)
    {
        case WM_CREATE:
```

```
                    AddSystemShutdownItem(hWnd);
                    return 0;
            case WM_SYSCOMMAND:
                    if (wParam == SC_SHUTDOWN)
                    {
                            StartSystemShutdown(hWnd);
                            return 0;
                    }
                    break;
            case WM_DESTROY:
                    PostQuitMessage(0);
                    return 0;
        }
        return DefWindowProc(hWnd, message, wParam, lParam);
}
```

9. The next three functions form the framework of this application and, indeed, all the applications in this chapter. Add the following code to the end of the source file. The InitApplication function registers the window class used by this application. It is only called if the class is not already registered. The InitInstance function creates and displays the main window of the application. Finally, the WinMain function serves as the entry point for the application. It registers the window and creates it, then uses GetMessage, TranslateMessage, and DispatchMessage to pump messages so that the application can operate.

```
/* ------------------------------------------------------------- */
/* This function initializes a WNDCLASS structure and uses it to */
/* register a class for our main window.                         */
/* ------------------------------------------------------------- */
BOOL InitApplication(HINSTANCE hInstance)
{
    WNDCLASS   wc;

    wc.style = 0;
    wc.lpfnWndProc = MainWndProc;
    wc.cbClsExtra = 0;
    wc.cbWndExtra = 0;
    wc.hInstance = hInstance;
    wc.hIcon = LoadIcon(hInstance,MAKEINTRESOURCE(IDI_APPICON));
    wc.hCursor = LoadCursor(NULL, IDC_ARROW);
    wc.hbrBackground = (HBRUSH)(COLOR_WINDOW + 1);
    wc.lpszMenuName = NULL;
    wc.lpszClassName = MainWindowClassName;

    return RegisterClass(&wc);
}


/* ------------------------------------------------------------- */
/* This function creates an instance of our main window. The window */
/* is given a class name and a title, and told to display anywhere. */
/* The nCmdShow argument passed to the program determines how the   */
/* window will be displayed.                                        */
/* ------------------------------------------------------------- */
```

continued on next page

continued from previous page

```
BOOL InitInstance(HINSTANCE hInst, int nCmdShow)
{
    HWND hWnd;

    hWnd = CreateWindow(MainWindowClassName,"Try the System Menu",
                WS_OVERLAPPEDWINDOW,CW_USEDEFAULT,
                CW_USEDEFAULT,CW_USEDEFAULT,CW_USEDEFAULT,
                NULL,NULL,hInst,NULL);
    if (!hWnd)
        return FALSE;

    ShowWindow(hWnd, nCmdShow);
    UpdateWindow(hWnd);          // Send a WM_PAINT message.
    return TRUE;
}


/* ------------------------------------------------------------------- */
/* The main entry point for Windows applications. Check to see if      */
/* the main window class name has already been registered; if it       */
/* has not, call InitApplication to register it. Call InitInstance      */
/* to create an instance of our main window, then pump messages        */
/* until the application is closed.                                     */
/* ------------------------------------------------------------------- */
int PASCAL WinMain(HINSTANCE hInstance, HINSTANCE hPrevInstance,
                LPSTR lpCmdLine, int nCmdShow)
{
    MSG msg;

    if (!FindWindow(MainWindowClassName,NULL))
        if (!InitApplication(hInstance))
            return FALSE;

    if (!InitInstance(hInstance, nCmdShow))
        return FALSE;

    while (GetMessage(&msg,NULL,0,0))
    {
        TranslateMessage(&msg);
        DispatchMessage(&msg);
    }
    return msg.wParam;
}
```

10. Compile and run the application.

Comments

Adding items to the system menu is a fairly straightforward matter once you have a handle to the system menu. Be careful when adding items to the system menu. Most users do not use the system menu; they use the application menus. In fact, because Windows 95 has a separate close button on the right of the title bar, a user may never access the system menu. Apart from utility functions such as shutting down the system, most of your menu operations should be done using the normal application menus.

COMPLEXITY
MODERATE

8.6   How do I...
Make a menu that pops up on right mouse button clicks?

Problem

I would like to implement a context-sensitive menu that the user can pop up by pressing the right mouse button over a region of my application. How do I go about this?

Technique

There are two parts to displaying a floating pop-up menu. The first question is when to display the menu. The example application used in this How-To will respond to right mouse button clicks. However, right mouse button clicks are not sent to the dialog or window, but are instead sent to the control that the cursor is positioned over. To catch these messages, you have to subclass the control, replacing the message-handling function defined by the class with your own message-handling function. Within this function, you can look for WM_RBUTTONDOWN messages and notify the parent window when they occur. All other messages can be passed on to the original handler for the control.

The next part to the problem is how to display the pop-up menu. You can create the menu by copying an existing application menu, by creating a menu on the fly with CreatePopupMenu, or by loading a menu from a resource using LoadMenu. When you have a handle to the menu to display, you can call TrackPopupMenu to display the menu and track the user's selection. The actual selection message will be sent to your application's window after TrackPopupMenu has returned.

Steps

Run the POPUP.EXE application from the CHAPTER8\POPUP directory of the CD-ROM. The sample application appears with a standard window and a File menu. The File menu only contains the option Exit. If this application was a word processor, the File menu would contain other options, such as New, Open, Save, and Save As. In addition, a word processor would probably have an Edit menu with Cut, Copy, and Paste options, a Format menu, and a Help menu.

All these menus are great, but it means that users must remember what menu the commands are on that they want to use. Now position the mouse pointer somewhere inside the window, and click the right mouse button. A context-sensitive menu pops up, as you might expect to find in a word processor. Now users do not have to search through the menus to find the command they want—at least, not so often. The frequently used commands that are applicable to what the user is doing at the moment are all available on the pop-up menu. Figure 8-6 shows you how the application looks when the pop-up menu is displayed.

The menu displayed in this example contains Cut, Copy, and Paste items such as you might find in a word processor or a text editor. In addition, it contains a Help item like those you often find in modern programming environments. You can move the mouse over the menu and select any of the items on it. The Help item simply displays a message dialog, but the other items work. In addition, the Cut and Copy options will only be enabled if some text is selected, and the Paste item will only be enabled if there is text in the clipboard that can be pasted. If you click somewhere other than on the menu, it disappears without making any selection.

The following steps guide you through implementing this simple demonstration. Along the way, you'll learn how to load a menu from a resource and display it as a pop-up menu. For more ideas about using this sort of menu, read the comments section at the end of this How-To.

1. Before you start cutting code for this application, create a working directory to store the source code in. Call the directory POPUP.

2. A good place to start this example application is by creating a resource file to hold the menus. Create the following resource script in a text editor, and save the file as POPUP.RC. Note that two separate menus are defined: IDM_TESTMENU for the main menu and IDM_POPUPMENU for the pop-up menu.

```
/* ---------------------------------------------------------------- */
/*                                                                   */
/* MODULE: POPUP.RC                                                  */
/* PURPOSE: This resource script defines the base menu for this      */
/*          example application.                                     */
/*                                                                   */
/* ---------------------------------------------------------------- */
```

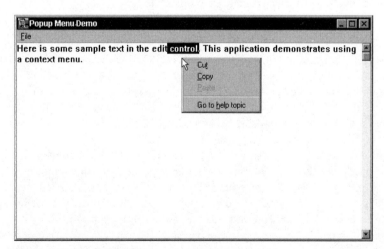

Figure 8-6 Displaying a pop-up menu

```
#include <windows.h>
#include "popup.rh"

IDM_TESTMENU MENU
{
    POPUP "&File"
    {
        MENUITEM "E&xit", CM_EXIT
    }
}

IDM_POPUPMENU MENU
{
    POPUP "&Not used"
    {
        MENUITEM "Cu&t", CM_EDITCUT
        MENUITEM "&Copy", CM_EDITCOPY
        MENUITEM "&Paste", CM_EDITPASTE
        MENUITEM SEPARATOR
        MENUITEM "Go to &help topic", CM_GOTOHELP
    }
}

IDI_APPICON ICON "app.ico"
```

3. Now create the include file, which will be used by both the resource script and the C source code. The following code defines the resource identifiers used in the application. Save this new file as POPUP.RH.

```
#ifndef __POPUP_RH
/* ---------------------------------------------------------------- */
/*                                                                  */
/* MODULE: POPUP.RH                                                 */
/* PURPOSE: This include file defines the resource identifiers used. */
/*                                                                  */
/* ---------------------------------------------------------------- */
#define __POPUP_RH

#define IDM_TESTMENU    200
#define CM_EXIT         103

#define IDM_POPUPMENU   203
#define CM_EDITCUT      111
#define CM_EDITCOPY     112
#define CM_EDITPASTE    113
#define CM_GOTOHELP     115

#define IDI_APPICON     202

#endif
```

4. Before the resources can be compiled, you will need the file containing the application icon. Copy this file from the CD-ROM. It is called CHAPTER8\POPUP\APP.ICO. Alternatively, create a 16-color, 32-by-32-pixel icon using a resource editor, and save it as APP.ICO.

5. Now you can create the source code for the sample application. Create a new
file, POPUP.C, and add the following comments and definitions. Notice that
you are declaring a handle to an edit control that will be shown in the application window and also a LONG value to hold the address to the default handler
for messages sent to the edit control. The code also defines a custom message,
MYMSG_CONTEXTMENU, to be sent to the callback procedure for the main
window when the user right-clicks on the edit control. The window procedure will respond to this message by displaying the menu.

```
/* ----------------------------------------------------------------- */
/*                                                                    */
/* MODULE: POPUP.C                                                    */
/* PURPOSE: This example application demonstrates how you can catch   */
/*          the right mouse button click over an area of your window  */
/*          and use TrackPopupMenu to display a context-sensitive     */
/*          popup menu.                                               */
/*                                                                    */
/* ----------------------------------------------------------------- */

#define STRICT
#include <windows.h>
#include <winnt.h>
#include "popup.rh"

static char *MainWindowClassName = "PopupMenuWindow";
HINSTANCE hInstance = NULL;
HWND      hEdit = NULL;
LONG      oldEditProc = 0;

#define MYMSG_CONTEXTMENU (WM_USER + 400)
```

6. Now add the following function. The EditWndProc function is a replacement
window procedure for the edit control. It responds to right mouse clicks
(WM_RBUTTONDOWN messages) by sending the MYMSG_CONTEXTMENU
message to the parent window. All other messages are processed by using
CallWindowProc to call the original window procedure, stored in oldEditProc.

```
/* ----------------------------------------------------------------- */
/* This window procedure is used to handle messages from an edit     */
/* control. It catches right mouse clicks and creates context menu   */
/* messages to be sent to the owner.                                 */
/* ----------------------------------------------------------------- */
LPARAM CALLBACK EditWndProc(HWND hWnd, UINT message,
                            WPARAM wParam, LPARAM lParam)
{
    HWND hOwner;

    // Grab right mouse button clicks, send a MYMSG_CONTEXTMENU message.
    if (message == WM_RBUTTONDOWN)
    {
        hOwner = GetParent(hWnd);
        PostMessage(hOwner,MYMSG_CONTEXTMENU,(WPARAM)hWnd,lParam);
        return 0;
```

```
    }

    // For other events, call the original edit control procedure.
    return CallWindowProc((WNDPROC)oldEditProc,
                         hWnd,message,wParam,lParam);
}
```

7. Add the next function to the same source file. The CreateEditControl function uses CreateWindow to create a new window with the class "EDIT"—in short, an edit control. It does not set the size and position of the edit control within the application window, as this will be done in response to a WM_SIZE message before the control is displayed. The code also calls SetWindowLong to modify the GWL_WNDPROC long integer associated with the edit control. It replaces the class window handler with the EditWndProc handler that you defined earlier. The old value is returned by SetWindowLong and will be stored in the oldEditProc variable. This handler must be restored before the edit control is destroyed.

```
/* ---------------------------------------------------------------- */
/* This function uses CreateWindow to create an edit contol within  */
/* the main window. It adds some sample text to the edit control.   */
/* ---------------------------------------------------------------- */
HWND CreateEditControl(HWND hWndParent)
{
    HWND hChild;

    // Create the edit control using CreateWindow.
    hChild = CreateWindow("EDIT",NULL,
                    WS_CHILD | WS_VISIBLE | WS_VSCROLL |
                    ES_LEFT | ES_MULTILINE | ES_AUTOVSCROLL,
                    0,0,0,0, // size will be set be WM_SIZE.
                    hWndParent,NULL,hInstance,NULL);

    // Subclass the control - set up a handler for messages.
    oldEditProc = SetWindowLong(hChild,GWL_WNDPROC,(LONG)EditWndProc);

    return hChild;
}
```

8. The SetupEditMenu function that you will now add takes care of enabling and graying the Cut, Copy, and Paste items on the pop-up menu. In a complete application, you could use the same piece of code here and on the main Edit menu, simply passing in the appropriate menu handle to operate on. The code uses EM_GETSEL to retrieve the start and finish positions of the current selection within the edit control. If the start and finish values retrieved from the DWORD are the same, then no text is selected, so the Cut and Copy commands can be grayed.

A slightly different technique is used to determine whether the Paste item should be enabled. The code calls IsClipboardFormatAvailable to determine whether anything with the standard CF_TEXT format is available in the

clipboard. If there is something with the right format, the code uses
EnableMenuItem to enable the Paste item; otherwise, it disables it.

```
/* ------------------------------------------------------------------ */
/* This function checks to see if any text is selected in the edit    */
/* control. If it is, then cut and copy are enabled in the menu;      */
/* otherwise they are grayed. It also checks to see if there is any   */
/* compatible text in the clipboard. If there is, then the paste      */
/* option is enabled; otherwise it is grayed.                         */
/* ------------------------------------------------------------------ */
void SetupEditMenu(HMENU hMenu, HWND hEdit)
{
    DWORD selection;
    int   selStart, selEnd;

    // See if any text is selected.
    selection = SendMessage(hEdit,EM_GETSEL,0,0);
    selStart = LOWORD(selection);
    selEnd = HIWORD(selection);
    if (selStart != selEnd)
    {
        // Text is selected - enable menu items.
        EnableMenuItem(hMenu,CM_EDITCUT,MF_BYCOMMAND | MF_ENABLED);
        EnableMenuItem(hMenu,CM_EDITCOPY,MF_BYCOMMAND | MF_ENABLED);
    }
    else
    {
        // No text selected - disable items.
        EnableMenuItem(hMenu,CM_EDITCUT,MF_BYCOMMAND | MF_GRAYED);
        EnableMenuItem(hMenu,CM_EDITCOPY,MF_BYCOMMAND | MF_GRAYED);
    }

    // Now see if there is any text in the clipboard.
    if (IsClipboardFormatAvailable(CF_TEXT))
        EnableMenuItem(hMenu,CM_EDITPASTE,MF_BYCOMMAND | MF_ENABLED);
    else
        EnableMenuItem(hMenu,CM_EDITPASTE,MF_BYCOMMAND | MF_GRAYED);
}
```

9. Add the following function. This function takes care of loading the pop-up
menu from the resource script, using the LoadMenu API function, and displaying it, using the TrackPopupMenu function. Look at the steps that the
function takes to display the menu.

First the function loads the resource using LoadMenu. The MAKEINTRESOURCE
macro is used because the resource identifiers for this application are integer
values. If you use strings to identify your resources, you don't have to use the
MAKEINTRESOURCE macro, because LoadMenu expects a string. However,
using integers tends to make your applications smaller and faster. The handle
returned from LoadMenu is a HMENU, but not quite the one that is required.
The code uses GetSubMenu to retrieve a handle to the submenu that is to be
displayed. By using this method, you can have the pop-up menus in one

menu resource and use GetSubMenu to retrieve a handle to the appropriate menu to be displayed.

Finally, the mouse coordinates are converted to screen coordinates and used to position the menu at the mouse position. TrackPopupMenu will return once the user has selected an item from the menu, or clicked off the menu to cancel the menu selection.

```c
/* ----------------------------------------------------------------- */
/* This function uses LoadMenu to load the resource of the popup      */
/* menu. It then decides where to place the menu, and uses the        */
/* TrackPopupMenu function to display the menu. It destroys the       */
/* menu when done, using DestroyMenu to release resources.            */
/* This function returns TRUE if the menu was displayed.              */
/* ----------------------------------------------------------------- */
BOOL HandlePopupMenu(HINSTANCE hInstance, HWND hWnd,
                     LONG mouseX, LONG mouseY, HWND hEdit)
{
    HMENU hResourceMenu, hPopupMenu;
    POINT mousePos;
    RECT  rcClient;

    /* Get the bounds of the client area, and make sure
       that the mouse was inside it when the button was
       clicked. If it wasn't, return straight away. */
    GetClientRect(hWnd,&rcClient);
    mousePos.x = mouseX;
    mousePos.y = mouseY;
    if (!PtInRect(&rcClient,mousePos))
        return FALSE;

    // Load the Popup menu from the resource.
    hResourceMenu = LoadMenu(hInstance,
                      MAKEINTRESOURCE(IDM_POPUPMENU));
    if (!hResourceMenu)
        return FALSE;

    // Get the popup menu from the resource menu.
    hPopupMenu = GetSubMenu(hResourceMenu,0);

    // Enable or disable menu items.
    SetupEditMenu(hPopupMenu,hEdit);

    /* Convert the mouse coordinates to screen coordinates
       for use by TrackPopupMenu. */
    ClientToScreen(hWnd,&mousePos);

    /* Track the context-sensitive popup menu. Destroy
       it when done. Use TPM_LEFTALIGN so that the menu
       pops up to the right of the mouse, and use
       TPM_RIGHTBUTTON so the user can use the right mouse
       button to select items from the menu. */
    TrackPopupMenu(hPopupMenu,TPM_LEFTALIGN | TPM_RIGHTBUTTON,
                   mousePos.x,mousePos.y,0,hWnd,NULL);
```

continued on next page

continued from previous page

```
        DestroyMenu(hResourceMenu);

        return TRUE;
}
```

10. Add the following code to the source file. MainWndProc is the message-handling function for the window. This function receives messages from Windows and processes them. The code demonstrates how you can trap the right mouse button event for a window and display the menu. When the user presses the right mouse button, the application will receive a MYMSG_CONTEXTMENU message from your edit control procedure. In response to this message, the following code calls the HandlePopupMenu function that you just entered, to load and display the menu. Because the LPARAM argument contains the mouse coordinates (copied from the original WM_RBUTTONDOWN message), the function uses LOWORD(lParam) to retrieve the x position of the mouse, and HIWORD(lParam) to get the y position of the mouse down the screen.

While you are entering the code, notice that the edit control is created by calling CreateEditControl when a WM_CREATE message is received. The WM_DESTROY function is used as your cue to replace the old window procedure in the edit control, before the window and control are destroyed. Finally, the code responds to any WM_SIZE message, always ensuring that the edit control takes up the entire client area of the window.

```
/* ------------------------------------------------------------------- */
/* This is the main window procedure for the application. This         */
/* procedure responds to the WM_RBUTTONDOWN message by displaying      */
/* the popup menu.                                                     */
/* ------------------------------------------------------------------- */
LPARAM CALLBACK MainWndProc(HWND hWnd, UINT message,
                            WPARAM wParam, LPARAM lParam)
{
    switch (message)
    {
        case WM_CREATE:
            hEdit = CreateEditControl(hWnd);
            return 0;
        case WM_COMMAND:
            switch (wParam)
            {
                case CM_EDITCUT:
                    SendMessage(hEdit,WM_CUT,0,0);
                    return 0;
                case CM_EDITCOPY:
                    SendMessage(hEdit,WM_COPY,0,0);
                    return 0;
                case CM_EDITPASTE:
                    SendMessage(hEdit,WM_PASTE,0,0);
                    return 0;
                case CM_GOTOHELP:
                    MessageBox(hWnd,"Help item selected.",
                            "Popup Response",
                            MB_ICONINFORMATION | MB_OK);
```

```
                              return 0;
                  case CM_EXIT:
                          DestroyWindow(hWnd);
                          return 0;
              }
              break;
          case MYMSG_CONTEXTMENU:
              // Handle right clicks.
              HandlePopupMenu(hInstance,hWnd,LOWORD(lParam),
                          HIWORD(lParam),hEdit);
              return 0;
          case WM_SIZE:
              // Resize the edit control to the entire window.
              MoveWindow(hEdit,0,0,LOWORD(lParam),
                          HIWORD(lParam),TRUE);
              return 0;
          case WM_SETFOCUS:
              // Set the focus to the edit control.
              SetFocus(hEdit);
              return 0;
          case WM_DESTROY:
              SetWindowLong(hEdit,GWL_WNDPROC,oldEditProc);
              PostQuitMessage(0);
              return 0;
      }
      return DefWindowProc(hWnd, message, wParam, lParam);
}
```

11. The three functions shown next form the framework for the application. Add
the functions to the POPUP.C source file and save the file. The InitApplication
function, shown first, is responsible for registering the window class for the
application with Windows. This function will only be called by the main routine if the window class name has not already been registered.

The InitInstance function creates the main window of the application and uses
ShowWindow to make sure that it is displayed. Finally, the WinMain function
forms the entry point to the application. This routine calls the other two functions and also pumps messages in a loop so that the application can operate.

```
/* ------------------------------------------------------------- */
/* This function initializes a WNDCLASS structure and uses it to  */
/* register a class for our main window.                          */
/* ------------------------------------------------------------- */
BOOL InitApplication(HINSTANCE hInstance)
{
    WNDCLASS  wc;

    wc.style = 0;
    wc.lpfnWndProc = MainWndProc;
    wc.cbClsExtra = 0;
    wc.cbWndExtra = 0;
    wc.hInstance = hInstance;
    wc.hIcon = LoadIcon(hInstance,MAKEINTRESOURCE(IDI_APPICON));
    wc.hCursor = LoadCursor(NULL, IDC_ARROW);
    wc.hbrBackground = (HBRUSH)(COLOR_WINDOW + 1);
```

continued on next page

continued from previous page

```
        wc.lpszMenuName =  MAKEINTRESOURCE(IDM_TESTMENU);
        wc.lpszClassName = MainWindowClassName;

        return RegisterClass(&wc);
    }


    /* ------------------------------------------------------------------- */
    /* This function creates an instance of our main window. The window    */
    /* is given a class name and a title, and told to display anywhere.    */
    /* The nCmdShow argument passed to the program determines how the       */
    /* window will be displayed.                                            */
    /* ------------------------------------------------------------------- */
    BOOL InitInstance(HINSTANCE hInst, int nCmdShow)
    {
        HWND hWnd;

        hInstance = hInst;      // Store in global variable.

        hWnd = CreateWindow(MainWindowClassName,"Popup Menu Demo",
                       WS_OVERLAPPEDWINDOW,CW_USEDEFAULT,
                       CW_USEDEFAULT,CW_USEDEFAULT,CW_USEDEFAULT,
                       NULL,NULL,hInstance,NULL);
        if (!hWnd)
            return FALSE;

        ShowWindow(hWnd, nCmdShow);
        UpdateWindow(hWnd);       // Send a WM_PAINT message.
        return TRUE;
    }


    /* ------------------------------------------------------------------- */
    /* The main entry point for Windows applications. Check to see if       */
    /* the main window class name has already been registered; if it        */
    /* has not, call InitApplication to register it. Call InitInstance      */
    /* to create an instance of our main window, then pump messages         */
    /* until the application is closed.                                      */
    /* ------------------------------------------------------------------- */
    int PASCAL WinMain(HINSTANCE hInstance, HINSTANCE hPrevInstance,
                   LPSTR lpCmdLine, int nCmdShow)
    {
        MSG msg;

        if (!FindWindow(MainWindowClassName,NULL))
            if (!InitApplication(hInstance))
                return FALSE;

        if (!InitInstance(hInstance, nCmdShow))
            return FALSE;

        while (GetMessage(&msg,NULL,0,0))
        {
            TranslateMessage(&msg);
            DispatchMessage(&msg);
```

```
    }
    return msg.wParam;
}
```

12. Compile and run the application.

Comments

The example application discussed in this How-To shows you the basics that you need to know to display a pop-up menu in your application. To make your application stand out from the crowd, you can change what appears in the context-sensitive menu, depending on what the user is working on at the moment. Does it make sense to spell-check the document at this stage? If it does, add the item to the menu. Change the pop-up menu that is displayed if the user right-clicks over a different window or control—the user can perform different actions with each component of your application, so the pop-up menu should reflect this.

While you can modify the menu items directly using the handle of the menu, you might find it more convenient to have more than one possible pop-up menu in the resource. You can load different menus by using different resource IDs with LoadMenu, or you can load one menu that contains all your options as submenus. In that case, you can use GetSubMenu to retrieve the appropriate submenu by its position. Both of these methods are quite valid.

CHAPTER 9
DOCUMENTS AND EDITORS

DOCUMENTS AND EDITORS

How do I...

Computers have certainly changed the way the business world works. Where once documents were typed on typewriters and copied with copiers, there are now word processors and laser printers. Databases have replaced filing cabinets in many offices. The "paperless" office hasn't come around quite yet, but we inch ever closer with each passing year. Some things, however, remain constant in this ever changing world of technological breakthroughs. People still need to enter data into forms, letters, and other documents. Programmers still need to view physical source code listings in addition to their graphical representations. Secretaries still use typing skills to generate documents.

Documents and editors are at the center of most computer applications. Whether you are simply viewing data in a textual representation or entering data through a complex form application, there is certain to be some amount of editing involved. In this chapter, we take aim at the document editor and look at ways to use the Windows API to improve your applications for the user doing the editing. We will examine displaying text, accepting data for forms, and other niceties such as making the blinking cursor blink the way you would like it to, rather than the way it was designed.

In addition to the standard Windows controls, Windows 95 introduces new controls for your use and edification. In this chapter we examine another new Windows 95 control, the Rich Text Edit control. This control replaces the standard Windows edit control and allows you considerably more control over the size and display attributes of your textual information.

Finally, we will examine how to use the standard Windows controls to extend the functionality of your own documents and editors. You can use the Windows API to search for and replace text in a document that is displayed on the screen. You can quickly and easily display files in a window in your application. Finally, you can use the form functionality built into dialog boxes in non-modal windows in your application. This chapter will show you how to do all of this and more.

9.1   Open an MDI Child Window Automatically

This How-To will show you a method you can use to create MDI child windows automatically in an MDI frame. All Visual C++ programmers know that within the application object you can call OnFileOpen, but few are aware that there are alternatives. In this How-To, we examine one of those alternatives.

9.2   Use a Non-Modal Dialog Box in an MDI Window

When you are displaying MDI child windows on the screen, it is often nice to allow the user to be presented with a dialog box-like appearance without restricting the user to that window. This How-To will show you how you can use an MDI child window as a form window and display non-modal dialogs to the user.

9.3   Resize a List Box or Edit Control with an MDI Child Window

A common usage of MDI windows is to present the user with a full-screen editor or list selection box. One of the problems with using a window that contains a Windows control such as a list box or edit control is that the edit control or list box is not resized when the parent MDI window frame is changed. This How-To will show you the Windows messages and notifications that you need to know about to deal with this problem and automatically resize the controls for the user. We will also look at the problem from the perspective of Visual Basic and present a VB form that automatically resizes its controls as well.

9.4   Make a Simple File Viewer

From time to time every programmer needs to be able to display a small file for the user to view. This might be a "readme" file, or perhaps a report output file. In any case, neither Visual C++ nor Delphi presents you with a simple method to display a file for the user to look at without modifying. In this How-To, we will show you how to accomplish this necessary task.

9.5   Find and Replace Text

Wouldn't it be nice if you could automatically search for and replace all occurrences of a simple text string in your document without adding any overhead code to your application? This particular task has been approached in many different ways, but none so easy as this one. By simply calling several Windows API functions, you can implement a complete Find and Replace dialog, find the text in the document, and then replace the text in the document.

9.6   Display Files Larger Than 64K

Windows 95 offers a new control for displaying large amounts of text, called the Rich Text Edit control. We will examine how to use this control to display files that are greater than 64K bytes in size. (The normal Windows edit control, as you might remember from Windows 3.1, is limited in size to between 32 and 64K of data). Along the way, we will also see how you can use the new Rich Text control to display text with formatting and different fonts.

9.7   Change the Caret Type in an Edit Control

It is a simple fact that not everyone likes the same things. The thing that many programmers prefer in an editor is a different sort of caret or edit cursor than the standard cursor. We will look at how you can change the size and shape of the caret in your application in this How-To.

9.8   Change the Speed at Which the Caret Blinks

Some people simply cannot stand working with a caret that blinks in their editors. Others prefer it to blink more rapidly so they can more easily find it. The important thing is that Windows users should be allowed to get what they want out of their applications. In this How-To, we examine how to change the speed of a blinking caret.

Table 9-1 lists the Windows 95 API functions used in this chapter.

CreateDialog	MoveWindow	GetClientRect
GetDlgItem	SetWindowText	GetWindowText
SendMessage	RegisterWindowMessage	CreateCaret
ShowCaret	DestroyCaret	SetCaretBlinkTime

Table 9-1 Windows 95 API functions used in Chapter 9

COMPLEXITY
MODERATE

9.1   How do I...
Open an MDI child window automatically?

Problem

I am using Visual C++ to create my application and would like to be able to open new document windows on the screen. The Visual C++ documentation tells me to call OnFileNew for new windows and OnFileOpen for windows with files associated with them. Unfortunately, I have multiple kinds of windows that I would like to display. If I use the OnFileNew or OnFileOpen methods, the MFC displays a rather garish dialog asking the user which kind of document they want to open.

How can I use the underlying power built into the MFC by the Windows API to open the document window I want to open directly, rather than relying on Visual C++? What is really going on here?

Technique

When you are opening a new MDI (Multiple Document Interface) window on the parent MDI frame window, you are really sending a simple Windows message to the parent frame window. This message is the WM_MDICREATE message. It would be fairly simple to implement a function in your program that calls the SendMessage function of the Windows API with the WM_MDICREATE message and set up the proper parameters to send to the parent frame window.

Unfortunately, the Microsoft Foundation Classes don't like you to go "around" the normal method of creating windows. None of the message mapping functions work correctly, the window's menu is not updated correctly, and in general, things do not work the way you would like them to. That is the bad news.

The good news is that it is quite possible to bypass the OnFileNew and OnFileOpen functions of the MFC and go directly to the code that creates the windows. If you use this method, the MFC will continue to work properly and all other functionality will remain intact. In this How-To, we will show you how to use this base functionality.

Steps

Open and run the Visual C++ application CH91.MAK from the CHAPT9\SAMPLES\CH91 directory on the CD that comes with this book. Select the main menu item Dialog and the drop-down menu item Create New MDI Window. You will see a new MDI child window displayed, as shown in Figure 9-1.

To reproduce this functionality in your own application, follow these steps:

1. Create a new project in Visual C++ using AppWizard. Give the application the name CH91.MAK. Enter AppStudio and select the main menu from the menu

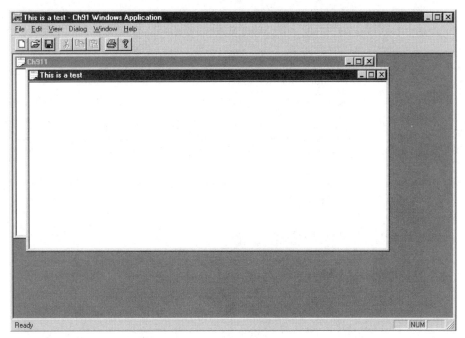

Figure 9-1 New MDI child window

list. Add a new main-level menu with the caption Dialog. To the Dialog main
menu add a new drop-down menu with the caption Create New MDI
Window. Give this drop-down menu item the identifier ID_NEW_MDI_WIN-
DOW. Save the resource file and exit AppStudio.

2. In the application object header file, add the following lines marked with bold
print to the top of the class definition:

```
class CCh91App : public CWinApp
{
private:
  CMultiDocTemplate* pDocTemplate;
```

3. Select the CH91.CPP file from the project list and edit it. Make the following
change to the InitInstance method of CCh91App:

```
// Register the application's document templates. Document templates
  //  serve as the connection between documents, frame windows and views.

  // *** Remove the declaration of pDocTemplate here ***
  pDocTemplate = new CMultiDocTemplate(
    IDR_CH9TYPE,
    RUNTIME_CLASS(CCh91Doc),
    RUNTIME_CLASS(CMDIChildWnd),          // standard MDI child frame
    RUNTIME_CLASS(CCh91View));
  AddDocTemplate(pDocTemplate);
```

4. Enter ClassWizard and select the CCh91App object from the drop-down list. Select the ID_NEW_MDI_WINDOW from the object list and the COMMAND message from the message list. Accept the name OnNewMdiWindow as the name of the new function and add the following code to the OnNewMdiWindow method of CCh91App:

```
void CCh91App::OnNewMdiWindow()
{
    CCh91Doc *doc = new CCh91Doc("This is a test");
    CFrameWnd *wnd = pDocTemplate->CreateNewFrame(doc, NULL);
    pDocTemplate->InitialUpdateFrame(wnd, doc, TRUE);
}
```

5. Enter the CCh91Doc object class definition in CH91DOC.H. Add the following declaration to the header file:

```
public:
    CCh91Doc(char *title);
```

6. Next, add the following code to the CH91DOC.CPP source file:

```
CCh91Doc::CCh91Doc(char *title)
{
    SetTitle(title);
}
```

7. Compile and run the application.

How It Works

The document template system for Visual C++ creates a single binding that allows the MFC to implement a complete MDI window from the template definition. Within the template object (CMultiDocTemplate class), there are stored the types for the Document object, the MDI frame object, and the View object.

Given the information in the template, the MFC can create a new MDI child window. To do this, it needs to create a new document object of the specified type and then create a new view and frame object based on that document type. Most of this functionality is implemented in the OnFileNew method of the base CWinApp object. To get around this function, we need to do a little work of our own.

The first thing to do is to add a public constructor to the document object. This is necessary because the generated constructor for documents is protected and cannot be called from another class. We will need to construct a document on our own outside the framework, so it is necessary to have a constructor we can call. The constructor for this example simply accepts a character string, which is used as the title of the MDI window.

The next thing to do is to actually create a new document. This is done with the call to the new CCh91Doc method in OnNewMdiWindow. Following the construction, the method then calls the CreateNewFrame method of the document template. This method creates the new frame and view objects and initializes the window handles for each. Finally, we call the InitialUpdateFrame method of the template in order to put the MDI child window and its frame onto the MDI parent window. This method also takes care of initializing all of the internals of the document and view objects.

Once all of this is accomplished, the normal MFC processing takes place. The object is destroyed when a user closes it by double-clicking on the system menu or the close box. The object will respond normally to menu commands it knows about and accelerator keys built into the application. It will also be displayed on the Windows menu of the menu bar.

Comments

This method is a vast improvement over the OnFileNew/OnFileOpen method of creating new MDI child windows. It gives the programmer, not the MFC, the power of deciding what type of window to display, and it gives the program the flexibility to create multiple kinds of windows.

In order to extend this functionality, you should examine how the WM_MDICREATE message is processed. Look at the OnClientCreate method of the CMainFrame object for a start, and then examine the parameters passed through. You may find that you wish to override the creation process in different ways; for example, to maximize the child window every time it is created. This can be done in the OnClientCreate method.

COMPLEXITY
MODERATE

9.2 How do I...
Use a non-modal dialog box in an MDI window?

Problem

I would like the ability to display a form on the screen of my application. Although I could use a dialog box for this purpose, I would also like to have the ability to use the menus and accelerator keys in my form window.

I would prefer to have all of the windows on the MDI parent look the same, so I don't simply want to display a modeless dialog box. Is there a way in which I can embed a non-modal dialog in one of my Multiple Document Interface child windows?

Technique

There are several solutions to this problem. You could create a modeless dialog as a control window within your MDI window, but you will quickly find that this has problems. Modeless dialogs don't really have parent windows; they have owners. This causes the modeless dialog to be displayed incorrectly and to show up in the wrong place.

You could create a new MDI child window class based on the CDialog object. This method will certainly work but involves a substantial amount of work. Trapping for keystrokes, accelerator keys, and menu item commands are not jobs for the faint-hearted.

Fortunately, none of this is necessary. The MFC provides a class that encapsulates the functionality of the CDialog class within an MDI child window. This class is called the CFormView class and is supported directly (more or less) by the ClassWizard, AppStudio, and MFC elements.

We are not directly calling the API functions here, but it is interesting to note how the Windows API is involved in this procedure. A more complete discussion of the methodology employed by the MFC appears in the "How It Works" section of this How-To.

Steps

Open and run the Visual C++ application CH92.MAK from the CHAPT9\SAMPLES\CH92 directory on the CD that comes with this book. Select the main menu item Dialog and the menu item Display Form Window. You will see a new MDI child window displayed, as shown in Figure 9-2.

To reproduce this functionality in your own application, follow these steps:

1. Create a new project in Visual C++ using AppWizard. Give the application the name CH92.MAK. Enter AppStudio and create a new dialog. Add several static fields, edit boxes, and radio buttons to the dialog.

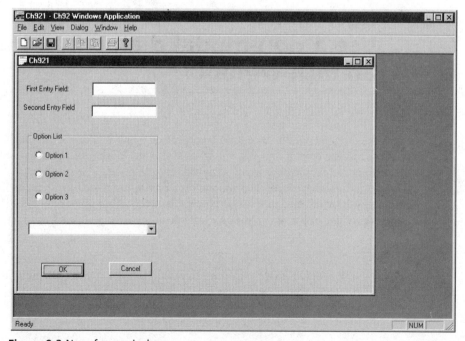

Figure 9-2 New form window

2. Double-click on the dialog box itself and select the Styles selection. Set the style combo box to be Child and the border combo box to be None. Make sure the Titlebar and Visible check boxes are not selected.

3. Select ClassWizard to create a new class for this dialog template. Name the class CDialogView and select the CFormView base class from the drop-down list. Accept the default names for the file names of the class and save the new class.

4. Select the CDialogView class source file (DIALOGVI.CPP) and add the following line marked in bold print to the message map of the file:

```
BEGIN_MESSAGE_MAP(CDialogView, CFormView)
  //{{AFX_MSG_MAP(CDialogView)
    ON_COMMAND(IDOK,OnOK)
  //}}AFX_MSG_MAP
END_MESSAGE_MAP()
```

5. Add the following class method to the CDialogView class:

```
void CDialogView::OnOK()
{
    GetParent()->PostMessage(WM_CLOSE);
}
```

6. Add the following declaration to the header file for the CDialogView class (DIALOGVI.H). Again, add only the line marked in bold print.

```
// Generated message map functions
  //{{AFX_MSG(CDialogView)
  virtual void OnOK();
  //}}AFX_MSG
  DECLARE_MESSAGE_MAP()
```

7. Select the CH92.CPP file from the project list. Add the following block of code to the InitInstance method of CCh92App:

```
pDocTemplate1 = new CMultiDocTemplate(
    IDR_CH92TYPE,
    RUNTIME_CLASS(CCh92Doc),
    RUNTIME_CLASS(CMDIChildWnd),        // standard MDI child frame
    RUNTIME_CLASS(CDialogView));
  AddDocTemplate(pDocTemplate1);
```

8. Next, reenter AppStudio. Select the main menu object from the menu list and add a menu with the caption Dialog. Add a new menu item to the Dialog menu. Give the new menu item the caption Display Form Window, and the identifier ID_DISPLAY_FORM_WINDOW. Save the menu and exit AppStudio.

9. Select the CCh92App object from the drop-down list in ClassWizard. Select the ID_DISPLAY_FORM_WINDOW object from the object list and the COMMAND message from the message list. Click on the Add Function button and accept the name OnDisplayFormWindow as the name of the new function. Add the following code to the OnDisplayFormWindow method of CCh92App:

```
void CCh92App::OnDisplayFormWindow()
{
    CCh92Doc *doc = new CCh92Doc("Form Window");
    CFrameWnd *wnd = pDocTemplate1->CreateNewFrame(doc, NULL);
    pDocTemplate1->InitialUpdateFrame(wnd, doc, TRUE);
}
```

10. Add the following include file line to the top of the CH92.CPP source file:

```
#include "dialogvi.h"
```

11. Enter the CCh92Doc object class definition in CH92DOC.H. Add the following declaration to the header file:

```
public:
    CCh92Doc(char *title);
```

12. Next, add the following code to the CH92DOC.CPP source file:

```
CCh92Doc::CCh92Doc(char *title)
{
    SetTitle(title);
}
```

13. Finally, select the CH92.H include file from the project list. Add the following declaration to the class definition for the CCh92App class:

```
CMultiDocTemplate* pDocTemplate1;
```

14. Compile and run the application.

How It Works

If you were to look at the source code for the Microsoft Foundation Classes, and specifically at the source code for the CFormView class, you would find that the Windows API figures prominently in the creation of the CFormView class. CFormView uses the CreateDialog Windows API function to create a new modeless dialog window. This window is then moved within the confines of the parent CView window to make it appear that the dialog is inside the view.

The modeless dialog is created by calling CreateDialog. This Windows API function has the following calling format:

```
HWND CreateDialog(hinst, lpszDlgTemp, hwndOwner, dlgprc)

HINSTANCE hinst;
LPCSTR lpszDlgTemp;
HWND hwndOwner;
DLGPROC dlgprc;
```

In the case of the CFormView, the hInst parameter is simply the instance of the application. The lpszDlgTemp is the name of the dialog template that is defined in the CFormView derived class CDialogView as IDD_DIALOG3. The hwndOwner parameter specifies the window that will "own" this modeless dialog and will be sent messages from the dialog. This is the form view window that is creating the dialog in the first place. Finally, the dlgprc parameter specifies the dialog procedure for this dialog. MFC passes

NULL for this parameter so that all dialog functions are simply routed to the standard dialog procedure.

Once we have the basics for creating the dialog within the window, the rest is easy. The dialog window is created invisibly and then moved into the client rectangle of the view that owns it. This is accomplished with the SetWindowPos API function. Finally, the accelerators and menu commands are processed the same way we did when we looked at using accelerators in a modeless dialog box back in Chapter 5.

Comments

It rarely makes sense to reinvent the wheel if someone has already done it for you. When you need to do something using the MFC that already exists, it makes a lot of sense to examine the underlying Windows API calls that accomplish the task and then look for MFC classes that support those Windows API calls. If you do this, your program will work more smoothly within the API and will be more portable between platforms.

COMPLEXITY
EASY

9.3   How do I...
Resize a list box or edit control with an MDI child window?

Problem

I would like the ability to have a list box or edit control in my MDI child window that will automatically resize itself when the size of the parent window changes. This is extremely useful for being able to do such things as create editing or listing windows that can be shown or hidden from the user at runtime without having a modal dialog box that the user must dismiss before continuing.

Technique

This is a quite common problem that occurs in many applications. You often wish to display a constant list box in one pane of a window or view and allow the user to make selections from that list at any point in the application. This means that you can't simply use a modal dialog box (since this would restrict the user to that dialog only), nor would you want to use a modeless dialog (since that would look out of place on the screen and would not appear in the window list). The solution then is to display the list box in a view window and have the normal Windows processing take care of updating and painting the region.

The idea here is that the list box should be "transparent" to the user. The user should not have to worry about the list box being too small or too big, which means that the list box should simply resize itself to the window in which it is embedded.

This How-To uses several Windows API functions, but the most notable one is the MoveWindow function. This function takes a window handle (the MFC version uses the window object) and a rectangle expressed in either the RECT structure or the coordinate values. The coordinates are used to map the window onto its parent window if one exists. Our technique, therefore, is to trap for window size messages (the WM_SIZE message) and to resize the list box to the size of the client window of the view. Along the way, you will learn how to create a control within the bounds of a view window as well.

Steps

Open and run the Visual C++ application CH93.MAK from the CHAPT9\SAM-PLES\CH93 directory on the CD that comes with this book. Select the main menu item Dialog and the drop-down menu item Resize List Window. You will see a new MDI child window displayed, as shown in Figure 9-3.

To reproduce this functionality in your own application, do the following:

1. Create a new project in Visual C++ using AppWizard. Enter ClassWizard and click on the Add Class button. Give the class the name CResizeView. Select CView as the base class for the new class. Save the class.

2. Still in ClassWizard, select the CResizeView class from the drop-down list. Select the CResizeView from the object list and the WM_CREATE message

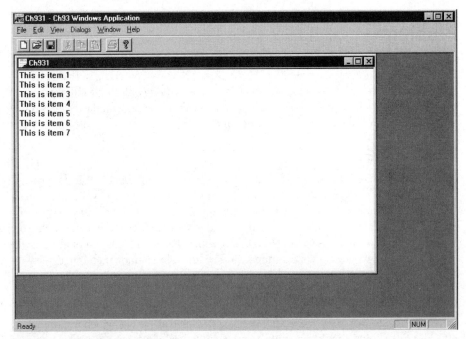

Figure 9-3 Resize list window

from the message list. Click on the Add Function button and add the following code to the OnCreate method of CResizeView:

```
int CResizeView::OnCreate(LPCREATESTRUCT lpCreateStruct)
{
  if (CView::OnCreate(lpCreateStruct) == -1)
    return -1;

  // Get the size of the client rectangle

  CRect r;
  GetClientRect(&r);

  // Create a list box object with this view

  list = new CListBox;
  list->Create(WS_CHILD | WS_VISIBLE | WS_VSCROLL, r, this, 1001 );

  // Add some items to the list

  list->AddString ( "This is item 1");
  list->AddString ( "This is item 2");
  list->AddString ( "This is item 3");
  list->AddString ( "This is item 4");
  list->AddString ( "This is item 5");
  list->AddString ( "This is item 6");
  list->AddString ( "This is item 7");

  return 0;
}
```

3. Next, again select the CResizeView object from the object list and the WM_SIZE message from the message list in ClassWizard. Click on the Add Function button. Enter the following code into the OnSize method of CResizeView:

```
void CResizeView::OnSize(UINT nType, int cx, int cy)
{
  CView::OnSize(nType, cx, cy);

  CRect r;
  GetClientRect(&r);
  list->MoveWindow(&r);

}
```

4. Finally, add this line to the destructor for the CResizeView, CResizeView::~CResizeView:

```
CResizeView::~CResizeView()
{
    delete list;
}
```

5. Add the following lines to the header file for CResizeView, RESIZEVI.H:

```
private:
  CListBox *list;
```

6. Next, add the following lines to the InitInstance method of CCh93App, the application object:

```
pResizeTemplate = new CMultiDocTemplate(
    IDR_CH93TYPE,
    RUNTIME_CLASS(CCh93Doc),
    RUNTIME_CLASS(CMDIChildWnd),        // standard MDI child frame
    RUNTIME_CLASS(CResizeView));
  AddDocTemplate(pResizeTemplate);
```

7. Go into AppStudio. Select the main menu object from the menu list. Add a new menu item with the caption Dialogs. To the Dialogs main menu entry, add a new drop-down menu item with the caption Resize List Window. Give the menu item the identifier ID_RESIZE_DLG.

8. Enter ClassWizard and select the CCh93App application object from the object list. Select the ID_RESIZE_DLG object from the object list and the COMMAND message from the message list. Click on the Add Function button and accept the name OnResizeDlg. Enter the following code into the OnResizeDlg method of CCh93App:

```
void CCh93App::OnResizeDlg()
{
    CCh93Doc *doc = new CCh93Doc("Resizable List Window");
    CFrameWnd *wnd = pResizeTemplate->CreateNewFrame(doc, NULL);
    pResizeTemplate->InitialUpdateFrame(wnd, doc, TRUE);
}
```

9. Add the following include file line to the top of the CH93.CPP source file:

```
#include "resizevi.h"
```

10. Now add these lines to the CH93.H header file:

```
private:
    CMultiDocTemplate* pResizeTemplate;
```

11. Enter the CCh93Doc object class definition in CH93DOC.H. Add the following declaration to the header file:

```
public:
    CCh93Doc(char *title);
```

12. Next, add the following code to the CH93DOC.CPP source file:

```
CCh93Doc::CCh93Doc(char *title)
{
    SetTitle(title);
}
```

13. Compile and run the application.

How It Works

When the view object is created, it creates a list box inside of its borders. This list box is created as a child of the view and is made visible within the view. Since the list box object is a child, the bounding rectangle for it is relative to the client area of the view window. Therefore, by simply getting the client rectangle in the OnCreate method of the view object, and moving the window to those coordinates, the list box appears to be in the full view window.

When the view is resized, the view object receives a WM_SIZE message. This message is caught by the OnSize method of the view object. In the OnSize method of the CResizeView object, the list is simply moved to the new client area of the view, therefore, making it the same size as the client window.

In the application object, we simply instantiate a new view class with the standard document class in a document template by using the CreateNewFrame method. Then we use that document template to instantiate a new copy of the view on the screen.

Comments

The same technique can be used for edit boxes in views. This is the method used by several framework vendors to create an edit view that is a full-screen editor. This method involves creating a multiline edit box within the view and then expanding or contracting the size of the edit box in response to size messages within the view.

You can use this technique with any control you might want to keep within the borders of a view. Property pages, for example, could be created within a view and resized based on users' preferences. This is preferable in the case of a property page that changes the text of its tabs and can grow too large to read comfortably at a given size.

An equivalent program could be written in Visual Basic as well. Here is an example of a Visual Basic form that allows you to automatically resize its controls:

1. First, create a new project or add a form to an existing project. Give the new project the name SIZE.MAK. Add a single list box to the form with the name List1.

2. Add the following code to the Form_Load method of the form:

```
Sub Form_Load ()
    List1.Top = 20
    List1.Height = Form1.Height
    List1.Left = 0
    List1.Width = Form1.Width

    For I = 1 To 20
        List1.AddItem "Item " + I
    Next I

End Sub
```

3. Add the following code to the Form_Resize method of the form:

```
Sub Form_Resize ()
    List1.Top = 0
    List1.Height = Form1.ScaleHeight
    List1.Left = 0
    List1.Width = Form1.ScaleWidth

End Sub
```

4. Save the project and run it.

COMPLEXITY
EASY

9.4   How do I...
Make a simple file viewer?

Problem

I need the capability to create a simple file viewer in a dialog in my application. The files displayed are not large (they consist of copyright information) and don't have any fancy formatting. I would really prefer not to have to write my own window object to do this, in which I would need to handle scrolling, painting, and so forth.

Is there any way I can use the Windows 95 API to create a very simple file viewer with a minimum of effort on my part?

Technique

Given the document/view architecture of the Microsoft Foundation Classes and the editor styling of Windows and Windows 95 in general, you would think that someone would have created a generalized file viewer by now. Unfortunately, if you look through the Windows API guide or the MFC guide, you will not find an example of a file viewer API call nor a file viewer class.

Fortunately, it turns out, the capability to display small (less than 32K of data) files exists in Windows 95 as well as in Windows 3.x. It is called the multiline edit box. The power of the edit box is vastly understated in most Windows applications and should be emphasized further. By using some of the capabilities of the common dialogs, and a single multiline edit field, we can build a fully functional file viewing dialog box in just minutes.

You don't believe the claim that a complex task such as this can be done in minutes? Read the following How-To.

Steps

Open and run the Visual C++ application CH94.MAK from the CHAPT9\SAM-PLES\CH94 directory on the CD that comes with this book. Select the main menu item Dialogs and the menu item File Viewer Dialog. You will see a dialog box displayed, as shown in Figure 9-4. Click on the Browse button and select a text file to view. Once you have selected a file, click on OK, and the file name will be displayed in the edit box at the top of the dialog. Click on the Load button, and the edit box will immediately begin to fill with text from the file.

You can mark and copy text in the edit box. If you try, you will find that you can also edit text in the edit box. Click on the Set Read Only check box and that capability will be removed. You will still be able to view, mark, and copy the text in the edit box, but will be unable to modify that text.

To reproduce this functionality in your own application, do the following:

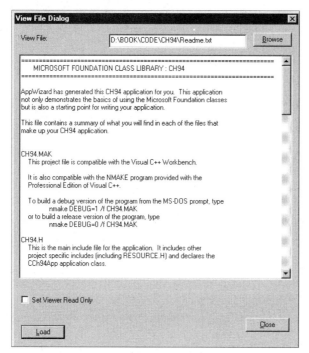

Figure 9-4 File viewer dialog

1. Create a new project inVisual C++ using AppWizard. Give the application the name CH94.MAK. Enter AppStudio and create a new dialog. At the top of the dialog add a static text field with the caption View File. Next to the static text field add a single-line edit box with the identifier IDC_EDIT2. Next, add a button aligned with the other two controls with the caption &Browse. Give this button the identifier IDC_BUTTON1.

2. Center an edit box in the dialog below the controls you just added. Delete the OK button from the dialog and give the Cancel button the new caption Close. Move the Close button to the bottom right corner of the dialog. Set the following styles for the multiline edit field. First, set the identifier to IDC_EDIT1. Next, set the style flags to "multiline" and "no hide sel" (click on these check boxes).

3. Enter ClassWizard and generate a new dialog class for this template. Give the new class the name CFileViewDlg. Accept all other defaults for the class and save it.

4. Exit AppStudio and save the resource file. Enter ClassWizard and select the CFileViewDlg from the drop-down list. Click on the IDC_BUTTON1 object in the object list and the BN_CLICKED message in the message list. Click on the

Add Function button and give the new function the name OnBrowse. Add the following code to the OnBrowse method of CFileViewDlg:

```
void CFileViewDlg::OnBrowse()
{
    CFileDialog dlg( TRUE, "txt", "*.txt");

    if ( dlg.DoModal() == IDOK ) {
        CEdit *edit = (CEdit *)GetDlgItem(IDC_EDIT2);
        edit->SetWindowText(dlg.GetPathName());
    }
}
```

5. Click on the IDC_BUTTON2 object in the object list and the BN_CLICKED message in the message list. Click on the Add Function button and give the new function the name OnLoad. Add the following code to the OnLoad method of CFileViewDlg:

```
const MAX_BUFFER_LEN = 256;

void CFileViewDlg::OnLoad()
{
    char fileName[_MAX_PATH];
    char buffer[MAX_BUFFER_LEN+1];
    CEdit *edit = (CEdit *)GetDlgItem(IDC_EDIT1);

    // Get the file to load

    GetDlgItem(IDC_EDIT2)->GetWindowText ( fileName, _MAX_PATH );

    // Load the file into the edit box

    FILE *fp = fopen ( fileName, "r" );
    if ( fp == (FILE *)NULL ) {
        MessageBox("Unable to open file", "Error", MB_OK );
        return;
    }

    // Clear out the edit box

    edit->SetWindowText ( "" );

    while ( !feof(fp) ) {

        // Get a line from the input file

        if ( fgets ( buffer, MAX_BUFFER_LEN, fp ) == NULL )
            break;

        // Clear off the carriage return at end of line

        if ( strlen(buffer) )
            buffer[strlen(buffer)-1] = 0;

        // Append CR/LF to make it appear nice
```

```
            strcat ( buffer, "\r\n" );

            edit->SetFocus ();

            // Set the caret to be at the end of the edit box

            int ndx = edit->GetWindowTextLength();
            edit->SendMessage(EM_SETSEL, ndx, ndx);

            // Append the text to the edit box

            edit->SendMessage(EM_REPLACESEL, 0, (LPARAM)(LPCSTR)buffer );

        }

        // Close the file

        fclose(fp);

    }
```

6. Click on the IDC_CHECK1 object in the object list and the COMMAND message in the message list. Click on the Add Function button and give the new function the name OnSetReadOnly. Add the following code to the OnSetReadOnly method of CFileViewDlg:

```
void CFileViewDlg::OnSetReadOnly()
{
    CButton *b = (CButton *)GetDlgItem(IDC_CHECK1);
    GetDlgItem(IDC_EDIT1)->SendMessage ( EM_SETREADONLY, b->GetCheck(), 0 );
}
```

7. Next, reenter AppStudio. Add a new menu item with the caption Dialogs. Add a new menu item to the Dialogs menu. Give the new menu item the caption File Viewer Dialog, and the identifier ID_FILE_VIEW_DLG. Save the menu and exit AppStudio.

8. Select the CCh94App object from the drop-down list in ClassWizard. Select the ID_FILE_VIEW_DLG object from the object list and the COMMAND message from the message list. Click on the Add Function button and accept the name OnFileViewDlg as the name of the new function. Add the following code to the OnFileViewDlg method of CCh94App:

```
void CCh94App::OnFileViewDlg()
{
    CFileViewDlg  dlg;
    dlg.DoModal();
}
```

9. Add the following include line to the top of the CH94.CPP source file:

```
#include "fileview.h"
```

10. Compile and run the application.

How It Works

When the dialog is initially displayed, there is nothing in either the edit box for the file name or the multiline edit box. When the user selects the Browse button, a dialog box (common file open dialog) is displayed The file name that is selected is copied into the edit box at the top of the dialog when the user selects the OK button in the common file open dialog.

When the user selects the Load button, the edit box with the file name is queried, and the file specified there is opened. This file is then read in, line by line, and the input buffer (line from the file) is then appended to the edit box. You do this by selecting the last character in the edit box by sending the edit box the command EM_SETSEL (to set the selection range) with the range set to -1, -1. This selects the end of the edit text. Then, send a EM_REPLACESEL command, which replaces the current selection. In this case, the text is simply appended to the end of the edit field.

The Set Read Only check box controls the read-only setting of the edit box. When it is selected, the checked flag for that field will be True, and therefore, the EM_SETREADONLY message in OnSetReadOnly will be passed the flag True. If it is not checked, the flag will be set to False, which turns off read-only mode.

COMPLEXITY
MODERATE

9.5 How do I...
Find and replace text?

Problem

I would like to give my users the ability to search for and replace text in an edit box in my application. Ideally, the procedure would require little work and even less coding on my part and use as many standard components of Windows as possible.

Does the Windows API provide the sort of functionality necessary for me to implement a search and replace feature in my application, or do I need to write one from scratch? It seems that with all of the search and replace functions in all of the programs available that someone must have solved this common problem by now.

Technique

As a matter of fact, this problem has been solved by hundreds of programmers over the years in hundreds of different ways. It is unlikely, though, that the problem was ever solved in as little code as we present in this How-To.

The edit box is a marvelous thing in the Windows 95 API. It combines flexibility and power with an amazing range of capabilities. In this How-To, we examine several of the messages available that you can send to an edit box to locate and replace a string in the edit text. In addition, we will show you how to create a standard Windows common find dialog box, which you can use to get user input to make the changes.

Steps

Open and run the Visual C++ application CH95.MAK from the CHAPT9\SAMPLES\CH95 directory on the CD that comes with this book. Select the main menu item Dialog and the menu item Find and Replace. You will see a dialog box displayed, as shown in Figure 9-5. Click on the Find and Replace button and enter terms to search for and replace in the common find dialog box. Once you have entered two terms, click on the Replace button, and the edit box will change to reflect the changes you have made if any were found.

To reproduce this functionality in your own application, do the following:

1. Create a new project in Visual C++ using AppWizard. Give the application the name CH95.MAK. Enter AppStudio and create a new dialog. Add a button to the new dialog with the caption Find and Replace. Accept the default identifier IDC_BUTTON1.

2. Add an edit box to the dialog with the style settings for multiline and No Hide Sel set to checked. Accept the default identifier IDC_EDIT1 for the name of the edit box.

3. Enter ClassWizard and create a new dialog class for the template you have just finished. Give the new dialog class the name CSearchAndReplaceDlg. Click on the CSearchAndReplaceDlg identifier in the object list and the WM_INITDIALOG

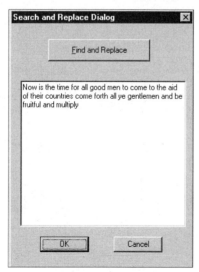

Figure 9-5 Find and replace
dialog box

message in the message list. Click on the Add Function button. Add the following code to the OnInitDialog method of CSearchAndReplaceDlg:

```
BOOL CSearchAndReplaceDlg::OnInitDialog()
{
  CDialog::OnInitDialog();

    // Add some text to the edit list

    CEdit *edit = (CEdit *)GetDlgItem(IDC_EDIT1);
    edit->SetWindowText("Now is the time for all good men to come to
                        the aid of their countries");
    CString s;
    edit->GetWindowText(s);
    int length = s.GetLength();
    edit->SetSel( length, length );
    edit->ReplaceSel( " come forth all ye gentlemen and be fruitful
                      and multiply");

  return TRUE;  // return TRUE  unless you set the focus to a control
}
```

4. Select the IDC_BUTTON1 identifier from the object list and the COMMAND message from the message list. Click on the Add Function button. Give the new function the name OnFindAndReplace. Add the following code to the OnFindAndReplace method of CSearchAndReplaceDlg:

```
void CSearchAndReplaceDlg::OnFindAndReplace()
{
    dlg = new CFindReplaceDialog;
    dlg->Create( FALSE, "", NULL, FR_DOWN, this );

}
```

5. Add the following line to the constructor for the dialog, CSearchAndReplaceDlg::CSearchAndReplaceDlg:

```
WM_FINDREPLACE = ::RegisterWindowMessage(FINDMSGSTRING);
```

Also, add this line to the top of the source file:

```
static UINT WM_FINDREPLACE;
```

6. Next, add the following line to the message map entries for the CSearchAndReplaceDlg class:

```
ON_REGISTERED_MESSAGE( WM_FINDREPLACE, OnFindReplace )
```

7. Add the following two functions to the source file for the CSearchAndReplaceDlg:

```
void CSearchAndReplaceDlg::ReplaceString ( const char *string, const
                                           char *replace )
{
    CString text;

    CEdit *edit = (CEdit *)GetDlgItem(IDC_EDIT1);
    edit->GetWindowText ( text );
```

```
    int idx = text.Find ( string );
    if ( idx == -1 ) { // Not found
        MessageBox("Not Found!", "Error", MB_OK | MB_ICONEXCLAMATION );
        return;
    }

    // Otherwise, set that selection point in the edit box

    edit->SetSel ( idx, idx + strlen(string) );

    // Now, replace that text with the replacement string

    edit->ReplaceSel ( replace );
}



LRESULT CSearchAndReplaceDlg::OnFindReplace(WPARAM wParam, LPARAM lParam)
{
    // If they don't want to terminate the dialog, check search parameters

    if ( !dlg->IsTerminating() ) {

        // See if they just want replace current item

        if ( dlg->ReplaceCurrent() ) {
            ReplaceString ( dlg->GetFindString(), dlg->GetReplaceString() );
        }


    }
    return 0L;
}
```

8. In the header file for the class, SEARCHAN.H, add the following lines to the
header file. Add only those lines marked in bold print.

```
class CSearchAndReplaceDlg : public CDialog
{
private:
    CFindReplaceDialog *dlg;

// Construction
public:
    CSearchAndReplaceDlg(CWnd* pParent = NULL); // standard constructor
    void ReplaceString ( const char *string, const char *replace );

// Dialog Data
    //{{AFX_DATA(CSearchAndReplaceDlg)
    enum { IDD = IDD_DIALOG1 };
        // NOTE: the ClassWizard will add data members here
    //}}AFX_DATA
```

continued on next page

continued from previous page

```
// Implementation
protected:
   virtual void DoDataExchange(CDataExchange* pDX);   // DDX/DDV support

   // Generated message map functions
   //{{AFX_MSG(CSearchAndReplaceDlg)
   virtual BOOL OnInitDialog();
   afx_msg void OnFindAndReplace();
   afx_msg LRESULT OnFindReplace(WPARAM wParam, LPARAM lParam);
   //}}AFX_MSG
   DECLARE_MESSAGE_MAP()
};
```

9. Next, reenter AppStudio. Select the main menu object from the menu list and add a menu with the caption Dialog. Add a new menu item to the Dialog menu. Give the new menu item the caption Find and Replace, and the identifier ID_FIND_REPLACE_DLG. Save the menu and exit AppStudio.

10. Select the CCh95App object from the drop-down list in ClassWizard. Select the ID_FIND_REPLACE_DLG object from the object list and the COMMAND message from the message list. Click on the Add Function button and accept the name OnFindReplaceDlg as the name of the new function. Add the following code to the OnFindReplaceDlg method of CCh95App:

```
void CCh95App::OnFindReplaceDlg()
{
    CSearchAndReplaceDlg dlg;
    dlg.DoModal();
}
```

11. Add the following include line to the top of the CH95.CPP source file:

```
#include "searchan.h"
```

12. Compile and run the application.

How It Works

You just implemented a complete search and replace system in under 30 lines of code. Not too bad, hmm? This example really shows the power that is built into the Windows API and exposed as functionality to the application programmer. Work that might take weeks for programmers to design, develop, and debug by themselves is encapsulated in things that are already available through the API functions and messaging system.

The example in this How-To uses the messaging system of the edit box control to do the majority of the work. When the user selects the Find and Replace button, a common dialog is displayed that prompts the user to enter the terms to search for and replace. This common dialog is built into Windows and will look the same in all applications. No work was necessary on your part to make this work.

Once the user selects the strings to find and to replace, the Windows API magic begins. The common dialog box posts messages to our application dialog box indicating that it would like us to change some text. How was this accomplished and how did we "know" to do the replacements? The answer lies in the RegisterWindowMessage call found in the constructor for the class. This API function takes a string and represents a unique number that will be returned by Windows when that message is posted by a window. The message is then "caught" by the ON_REGISTERED_MESSAGE macro in the message map. This macro will then call our own method, OnFindReplace.

In the OnFindReplace method, the various options of the common dialog control are checked. In this case, all we are looking for is the Replace button. We could also check whether the user selected case sensitivity and whether to match whole words only, but that was left out of this example to make it simpler. If the dialog is not telling us that it is going away (the IsTerminating function would indicate this), then we check if the user selected the Replace button. If so, the Find and Replace strings are sent to another function in our dialog, ReplaceString. Note that it is not necessary to check whether there is anything in the string to find since the common dialog will not permit you to select the Replace button until something is entered in this field.

In the ReplaceString method, we simply get the text from the multiline edit control into a CString variable. This class, CString, contains a method to search for text in the string. We find the position of the string in the text and hold onto it. This is then used to mark a selection area in the edit box control using the EM_SETSEL message (in the MFC, this is encapsulated in the SetSel function of CEdit). Next, the EM_REPLACESEL message, encapsulated in the ReplaceSel function, is called with the replacement string.

That's all there is to it!

Comments

This extremely useful technique is in no way limited to Visual C++ functionality. Here is an equivalent demonstration in Delphi:

1. Create a new project or add a new form to an existing project. To this form, add two static text fields aligned with two edit fields. Give the static text fields the captions Text To Find and Text To Replace.

2. Add an edit box to the middle of the form.

3. Add two buttons to the bottom of the form. Give the first button the caption Replace and the second button the caption Close.

4. Double-click on the form and add the following code to the FormCreate method:

```
procedure TForm1.FormCreate(Sender: TObject);
var
    i : Integer;
    Str : String;
begin
    for i := 1 to 100 do
        begin
            Str := 'This is line ' + IntToStr(i);
            Memo1.Lines.Add ( Str );
        end;
end;
```

5. Next, double-click on the button with the label Replace. Enter the following code for the Button1.Click method (if you called it other than Button1, change that reference in the code):

```
procedure TForm1.Button2Click(Sender: TObject);
var
    flag : Boolean;
    position : Integer;
begin
    { Assume best case }

    flag := True;

    { See if the find string is filled in }

    if ( Length(Edit1.Text) = 0 ) then
        begin
            MessageBox(0, 'Must enter a string to find!', 'Error', MB_OK );
            flag := False;
        end;

    if ( flag and (Length(Edit2.Text) = 0) ) then
        begin
            MessageBox(0, 'Must enter a string to replace!', 'Error',
                        MB_OK );
            flag := False;
        end;

    if ( flag ) then
        begin
            { Find the string in the memo field }

            position := Pos(Edit1.Text, Memo1.Text);

            { See if it was found }

            if ( position = 0 ) then
                begin
                    MessageBox (0, 'Not found', 'Error', MB_OK );
                    flag := False;
                end;
        end;

        { We now have the position in position }

        if ( flag = True ) then
            begin
                Memo1.SelStart := position - 1;
                Memo1.SelLength := Length(Edit1.Text);
                Memo1.SelText := Edit2.Text;
            end;
end;
```

6. Finally, add this code to the Button2.Click method by double-clicking on the Close button on the form:

```
procedure TForm1.Button1Click(Sender: TObject);
begin
   Close;
end;
```

COMPLEXITY
DIFFICULT

9.6   How do I...
Display files larger than 64K?

Problem

I have several very large files that I would like to be able to display for the user. The Windows edit control, however, only allows me to use about 32K of data before it runs out of space. I have learned of tricks that allow me to display up to about 64K of data in the edit control, but that is as big as it gets.

With the new 32-bit controls in Windows 95, isn't there some way for me to get around this limitation and display larger text files? If there is, how do I go about using it in one of my MDI applications?

Technique

There are several tricks that will allow you to display larger files in Windows edit controls, as you point out. None of them, however, will display very large files, nor will they allow you to format data in a "pretty" fashion.

With the advent of Windows 95, Microsoft has added several new controls to the arsenal of controls available in the API. One of these new controls is known as the Rich Text Edit control. This control allows you the capability to define formatting information for each of the characters or paragraphs in the edit control. You can control bold, italic, or underlined text (as well as strikethrough) and right-, left-, or center-justified paragraphs.

One of the other side effects of this control is that it behaves just like a normal edit control, with one important difference. Rich Text Edit controls can hold vastly more information than a standard edit control, and they allow you to display very large files with no problem.

In this How-To, we will create a new MFC view based on the new Rich Text Edit control and show you how to use that view to allow the user to change formatting information on-the-fly in the edit control by marking text and selecting menu items.

Steps

Open and run the Visual C++ application WORDRTF.MAK from the CHAPT9\SAM-PLES\CH96 directory on the CD that comes with this book. A new MDI window will be displayed on your application. Type some text into the new MDI window until you are comfortable that you have enough text for the test. Use the mouse to select a small section of the text and mark it. Next, select the Format menu item from the main menu and the Character drop-down item from the drop-down menu list. This menu cascades into another menu with several options on it. Select the Italic menu item from this list. You will see the text displayed in italic, as shown in Figure 9-6.

To reproduce this functionality in your own application, do the following:

1. Create a new project in Visual C++. Give the project the name WORDRTF.MAK and use the names CRTFView and CRTFDoc for the names of the documents and views. Save the project make file.

2. Create a new file in Visual C++ and add the following code to the file. Save this file as RTFVIEW.CPP. This will be the new base view class for the Rich Text Edit control view. You may reuse this file as often as necessary in other applications.

```
#include "stdafx.h"
#include "rtfview.h"
#include <ctype.h>

#ifdef AFX_CORE4_SEG
#pragma code_seg(AFX_CORE4_SEG)
#endif
```

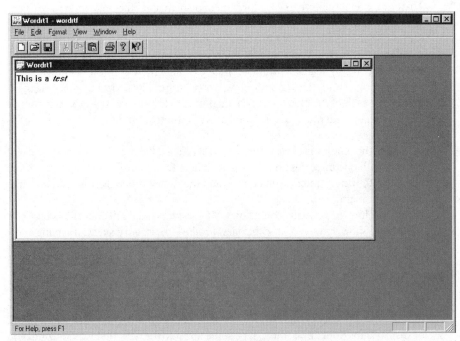

Figure 9-6 Italic text display in Rich Text Edit control window

```
#ifdef _DEBUG
#undef THIS_FILE
static char THIS_FILE[] = __FILE__;
#endif


////////////////////////////////////////////////////////////////////////
// CRTFEditView

#define new DEBUG_NEW

static const UINT nMsgFindReplace = ::RegisterWindowMessage(FINDMSGSTRING);

#ifdef _UNICODE
static HFONT hUnicodeFont;
struct _AFX_EDITVIEW_TERM
{
      ~_AFX_EDITVIEW_TERM()
   {
            AfxDeleteObject((HGDIOBJ*)&hUnicodeFont);
   }
};
static const _AFX_EDITVIEW_TERM editviewTerm;
#endif

BEGIN_MESSAGE_MAP(CRTFEditView, CView)
      //{{AFX_MSG_MAP(CRTFEditView)
      ON_WM_CREATE()
      ON_WM_PAINT()
      ON_EN_CHANGE(AFX_IDW_PANE_FIRST, OnEditChange)
      ON_UPDATE_COMMAND_UI(ID_EDIT_CUT, OnUpdateNeedSel)
      ON_UPDATE_COMMAND_UI(ID_EDIT_PASTE, OnUpdateNeedClip)
      ON_UPDATE_COMMAND_UI(ID_EDIT_SELECT_ALL, OnUpdateNeedText)
      ON_UPDATE_COMMAND_UI(ID_EDIT_UNDO, OnUpdateEditUndo)
      ON_COMMAND(ID_EDIT_CUT, OnEditCut)
      ON_COMMAND(ID_EDIT_COPY, OnEditCopy)
      ON_COMMAND(ID_EDIT_PASTE, OnEditPaste)
      ON_COMMAND(ID_EDIT_CLEAR, OnEditClear)
      ON_COMMAND(ID_EDIT_UNDO, OnEditUndo)
      ON_COMMAND(ID_EDIT_SELECT_ALL, OnEditSelectAll)
      ON_UPDATE_COMMAND_UI(ID_EDIT_FIND, OnUpdateNeedText)
      ON_UPDATE_COMMAND_UI(ID_EDIT_REPLACE, OnUpdateNeedText)
      ON_COMMAND(ID_EDIT_FIND, OnEditFind)
      ON_COMMAND(ID_EDIT_REPLACE, OnEditReplace)
      ON_UPDATE_COMMAND_UI(ID_EDIT_REPEAT, OnUpdateNeedFind)
      ON_COMMAND(ID_EDIT_REPEAT, OnEditRepeat)
      ON_UPDATE_COMMAND_UI(ID_EDIT_COPY, OnUpdateNeedSel)
      ON_UPDATE_COMMAND_UI(ID_EDIT_CLEAR, OnUpdateNeedSel)
      //}}AFX_MSG_MAP
      ON_REGISTERED_MESSAGE(nMsgFindReplace, OnFindReplaceCmd)

      // Standard Print commands (print only - not preview)
      ON_COMMAND(ID_FILE_PRINT, CView::OnFilePrint)
END_MESSAGE_MAP()
```

continued on next page

continued from previous page

```
const AFX_DATADEF DWORD CRTFEditView::dwStyleDefault =
    AFX_WS_DEFAULT_VIEW |
    WS_HSCROLL | WS_VSCROLL |
    ES_AUTOHSCROLL | ES_AUTOVSCROLL |
    ES_MULTILINE | ES_NOHIDESEL;

const AFX_DATADEF UINT CRTFEditView::nMaxSize = 1024U*1024U-1;

// class name for control creation
static const TCHAR szClassName[] = _T("RICHEDIT");

/////////////////////////////////////////////////////////////////////////////
// AFX_EDIT_STATE implementation

AFX_EDIT_STATE::AFX_EDIT_STATE()
{
    // Note: it is only necessary to initialize non-zero data.

    bNext = TRUE;
}

AFX_EDIT_STATE::~AFX_EDIT_STATE()
{
}

/////////////////////////////////////////////////////////////////////////////
// CRTFEditView construction/destruction

CRTFEditView::CRTFEditView()
{
    m_pShadowBuffer = NULL;
    m_nShadowSize = 0;
}

CRTFEditView::~CRTFEditView()
{
    ASSERT(m_hWnd == NULL);
    ASSERT(m_pShadowBuffer == NULL || afxData.bWin32s);
    delete m_pShadowBuffer;
}

BOOL CRTFEditView::PreCreateWindow(CREATESTRUCT& cs)
{
    ASSERT(cs.lpszClass == NULL);
    cs.lpszClass = szClassName;

    // map default CView style to default CRTFEditView style
    if (cs.style == AFX_WS_DEFAULT_VIEW)
        cs.style = dwStyleDefault;

    return CView::PreCreateWindow(cs);
}

int CRTFEditView::OnCreate(LPCREATESTRUCT lpcs)
{
```

```
        if (CView::OnCreate(lpcs) != 0)
            return -1;

        GetEditCtrl().LimitText(nMaxSize);
        return 0;
}


// EDIT controls always turn off WS_BORDER and draw it themselves
void CRTFEditView::CalcWindowRect(LPRECT lpClientRect, UINT nAdjustType)
{
    if (nAdjustType != 0)
    {
        // default behavior for in-place editing handles scrollbars
        DWORD dwStyle = GetStyle();
        if (dwStyle & WS_VSCROLL)
            lpClientRect->right += afxData.cxVScroll - CX_BORDER;
        if (dwStyle & WS_HSCROLL)
            lpClientRect->bottom += afxData.cyHScroll - CY_BORDER;
        return;
    }

    ::AdjustWindowRectEx(lpClientRect, GetStyle() | WS_BORDER, FALSE,
        GetExStyle() & ~(WS_EX_CLIENTEDGE));
}


/////////////////////////////////////////////////////////////////////////
// CRTFEditView document like functions

CRTFEdit& CRTFEditView::GetEditCtrl() const
{
        return *(CRTFEdit*)this;
}


void CRTFEditView::DeleteContents()
{
        ASSERT_VALID(this);
        ASSERT(m_hWnd != NULL);
        SetWindowText(NULL);
        ASSERT_VALID(this);
}


/////////////////////////////////////////////////////////////////////////
// CRTFEditView drawing

void CRTFEditView::OnPaint()
{
        // do not call CView::OnPaint since it will call OnDraw
        CWnd::OnPaint();
}


void CRTFEditView::OnDraw(CDC*)
{
        // do nothing here since CWnd::OnPaint() will repaint the EDIT
        // control
}
```

continued on next page

continued from previous page

```
///////////////////////////////////////////////////////////////////////
// CRTFEditView Printing support

///////////////////////////////////////////////////////////////////////
// CRTFEditView commands

void CRTFEditView::OnUpdateNeedSel(CCmdUI* pCmdUI)
{
        ASSERT_VALID(this);
        int nStartChar, nEndChar;
        GetEditCtrl().GetSel(nStartChar, nEndChar);
        pCmdUI->Enable(nStartChar != nEndChar);
        ASSERT_VALID(this);
}

void CRTFEditView::OnUpdateNeedClip(CCmdUI* pCmdUI)
{
        ASSERT_VALID(this);
        pCmdUI->Enable(::IsClipboardFormatAvailable(CF_TEXT));
        ASSERT_VALID(this);
}

void CRTFEditView::OnUpdateNeedText(CCmdUI* pCmdUI)
{
        ASSERT_VALID(this);
        pCmdUI->Enable(GetWindowTextLength() != 0);
        ASSERT_VALID(this);
}

void CRTFEditView::OnUpdateNeedFind(CCmdUI* pCmdUI)
{
        ASSERT_VALID(this);
        AFX_EDIT_STATE* pEditState = AfxGetEditState();
        pCmdUI->Enable(GetWindowTextLength() != 0 &&
                !pEditState->strFind.IsEmpty());
        ASSERT_VALID(this);
}

void CRTFEditView::OnUpdateEditUndo(CCmdUI* pCmdUI)
{
        ASSERT_VALID(this);
        pCmdUI->Enable(GetEditCtrl().CanUndo());
        ASSERT_VALID(this);
}

void CRTFEditView::OnEditChange()
{
        ASSERT_VALID(this);
        GetDocument()->SetModifiedFlag();
        ASSERT_VALID(this);
}

void CRTFEditView::OnEditCut()
{
```

```
        ASSERT_VALID(this);
        GetEditCtrl().Cut();
        ASSERT_VALID(this);
}

void CRTFEditView::OnEditCopy()
{
        ASSERT_VALID(this);
        GetEditCtrl().Copy();
        ASSERT_VALID(this);
}

void CRTFEditView::OnEditPaste()
{
        ASSERT_VALID(this);
        GetEditCtrl().Paste();
        ASSERT_VALID(this);
}

void CRTFEditView::OnEditClear()
{
        ASSERT_VALID(this);
        GetEditCtrl().Clear();
        ASSERT_VALID(this);
}

void CRTFEditView::OnEditUndo()
{
        ASSERT_VALID(this);
        GetEditCtrl().Undo();
        ASSERT_VALID(this);
}

void CRTFEditView::OnEditSelectAll()
{
        ASSERT_VALID(this);
        GetEditCtrl().SetSel(0, -1);
        ASSERT_VALID(this);
}

/////////////////////////////////////////////////////////////////////////////
// CRTFEditView attributes

LPCTSTR CRTFEditView::LockBuffer() const
{
        ASSERT_VALID(this);
        ASSERT(m_hWnd != NULL);
        if (afxData.bWin32s)
        {
                // under Win32s, it is necessary to maintain a shadow
                //   buffer. It is only updated when the control contents
                //   have been changed.
                if (m_pShadowBuffer == NULL || GetEditCtrl().GetModify())
                {
```

continued on next page

continued from previous page

```
                                        ASSERT(m_pShadowBuffer != NULL ||
                                          m_nShadowSize == 0);
                                        UINT nSize = GetWindowTextLength()+1;
                            if (nSize > m_nShadowSize)
                            {
                                    // need more room for shadow buffer
                                    CRTFEditView* pThis = (CRTFEditView*)this;
                                    delete m_pShadowBuffer;
                                    pThis->m_pShadowBuffer = NULL;
                                    pThis->m_pShadowBuffer = new TCHAR[nSize];
                                    pThis->m_nShadowSize = nSize;
                            }

                                    // update the shadow buffer with GetWindowText
                                    ASSERT(m_nShadowSize >= nSize);
                                    ASSERT(m_pShadowBuffer != NULL);
                                    GetWindowText(m_pShadowBuffer, nSize);

                                    // turn off edit control's modify bit
                                    GetEditCtrl().SetModify(FALSE);
                    }
                    return m_pShadowBuffer;
            }
            // else -- running under non-subset Win32 system
            HLOCAL hLocal = GetEditCtrl().GetHandle();
            ASSERT(hLocal != NULL);
            LPCTSTR lpszText = (LPCTSTR)LocalLock(hLocal);
            ASSERT(lpszText != NULL);
            ASSERT_VALID(this);
            return lpszText;
    }


void CRTFEditView::UnlockBuffer() const
{
            ASSERT_VALID(this);
            ASSERT(m_hWnd != NULL);
            if (afxData.bWin32s)
                return;
            HLOCAL hLocal = GetEditCtrl().GetHandle();
            ASSERT(hLocal != NULL);
            LocalUnlock(hLocal);
}


// this function returns the length in characters
UINT CRTFEditView::GetBufferLength() const
{
            ASSERT_VALID(this);
            ASSERT(m_hWnd != NULL);
            LPCTSTR lpszText = LockBuffer();
            UINT nLen = lstrlen(lpszText);
            UnlockBuffer();
            return nLen;
}


void CRTFEditView::GetSelectedText(CString& strResult) const
{
```

```
        ASSERT_VALID(this);
        LPSTR lpszText;
        GetEditCtrl().GetSelText(lpszText);
        strResult = lpszText;
        ASSERT_VALID(this);
}


//////////////////////////////////////////////////////////////////////////
// CRTFEditView Find & Replace

void CRTFEditView::OnEditFind()
{
        ASSERT_VALID(this);
        OnEditFindReplace(TRUE);
        ASSERT_VALID(this);
}


void CRTFEditView::OnEditReplace()
{
        ASSERT_VALID(this);
        OnEditFindReplace(FALSE);
        ASSERT_VALID(this);
}


void CRTFEditView::OnEditRepeat()
{
        ASSERT_VALID(this);
        AFX_EDIT_STATE* pEditState = AfxGetEditState();
        if (!FindText(pEditState->strFind,
            pEditState->bNext,
            pEditState->bCase))
        {
                OnTextNotFound(pEditState->strFind);
        }
        ASSERT_VALID(this);
}


void CRTFEditView::OnEditFindReplace(BOOL bFindOnly)
{
        ASSERT_VALID(this);
        AFX_EDIT_STATE* pEditState = AfxGetEditState();
        if (pEditState->pFindReplaceDlg != NULL)
        {
                if (pEditState->bFindOnly == bFindOnly)
                {
                        pEditState->pFindReplaceDlg->SetActiveWindow();
                        pEditState->pFindReplaceDlg->ShowWindow(SW_SHOW);
                        return;
                }
                else
                {
                        ASSERT(pEditState->bFindOnly != bFindOnly);
                        pEditState->pFindReplaceDlg->SendMessage(WM_CLOSE);
                        ASSERT(pEditState->pFindReplaceDlg == NULL);
                        ASSERT_VALID(this);
                }
```

continued on next page

489

continued from previous page

```
            }
            CString strFind;
            GetSelectedText(strFind);
            if (strFind.IsEmpty())
                    strFind = pEditState->strFind;
            CString strReplace = pEditState->strReplace;
            pEditState->pFindReplaceDlg = new CFindReplaceDialog;
            ASSERT(pEditState->pFindReplaceDlg != NULL);
            DWORD dwFlags = FR_HIDEWHOLEWORD;
            if (pEditState->bNext)
                    dwFlags |= FR_DOWN;
            if (pEditState->bCase)
                    dwFlags |= FR_MATCHCASE;
            if (!pEditState->pFindReplaceDlg->Create(bFindOnly, strFind,
                    strReplace, dwFlags, this))
            {
                    pEditState->pFindReplaceDlg = NULL;
                    ASSERT_VALID(this);
                    return;
            }
                ASSERT(pEditState->pFindReplaceDlg != NULL);
                pEditState->bFindOnly = bFindOnly;
                ASSERT_VALID(this);
    }


void CRTFEditView::OnFindNext(LPCTSTR lpszFind, BOOL bNext, BOOL bCase)
{
        ASSERT_VALID(this);
        AFX_EDIT_STATE* pEditState = AfxGetEditState();
        pEditState->strFind = lpszFind;
        pEditState->bCase = bCase;
        pEditState->bNext = bNext;

        if (!FindText(pEditState->strFind, bNext, bCase))
                OnTextNotFound(pEditState->strFind);
        ASSERT_VALID(this);
}


void CRTFEditView::OnReplaceSel(LPCTSTR lpszFind, BOOL bNext, BOOL bCase,
        LPCTSTR lpszReplace)
{
        ASSERT_VALID(this);
        AFX_EDIT_STATE* pEditState = AfxGetEditState();
        pEditState->strFind = lpszFind;
        pEditState->strReplace = lpszReplace;
        pEditState->bCase = bCase;
        pEditState->bNext = bNext;

        if (!InitializeReplace())
                return;

        GetEditCtrl().ReplaceSel(pEditState->strReplace);
        FindText(pEditState->strFind, bNext, bCase);
        ASSERT_VALID(this);
}
```

```
void CRTFEditView::OnReplaceAll(LPCTSTR lpszFind, LPCTSTR lpszReplace,
                                BOOL bCase)
{
        ASSERT_VALID(this);
        AFX_EDIT_STATE* pEditState = AfxGetEditState();
        pEditState->strFind = lpszFind;
        pEditState->strReplace = lpszReplace;
        pEditState->bCase = bCase;
        pEditState->bNext = TRUE;

        if (!InitializeReplace() &&
            !SameAsSelected(pEditState->strFind, pEditState->bCase))
        {
                // initial find was not successful
                return;
        }

        do
        {
                GetEditCtrl().ReplaceSel(pEditState->strReplace);
        } while (FindText(pEditState->strFind, 1, bCase));

        ASSERT_VALID(this);
}

BOOL CRTFEditView::InitializeReplace()
        // helper to do find first if no selection
{
        ASSERT_VALID(this);

        AFX_EDIT_STATE* pEditState = AfxGetEditState();

        // do find next if no selection
        int nStartChar, nEndChar;
        GetEditCtrl().GetSel(nStartChar, nEndChar);
        if (nStartChar == nEndChar)
        {
                if (!FindText(pEditState->strFind, pEditState->bNext,
                    pEditState->bCase))
                {
                   // text not found
                   OnTextNotFound(pEditState->strFind);
                }
                return FALSE;
        }

        if (!SameAsSelected(pEditState->strFind, pEditState->bCase))
        {
                if (!FindText(pEditState->strFind, pEditState->bNext,
                    pEditState->bCase))
                {
                   // text not found
                   OnTextNotFound(pEditState->strFind);
                }
                return FALSE;
```

continued on next page

continued from previous page

```
              }

              ASSERT_VALID(this);
              return TRUE;
      }

      LRESULT CRTFEditView::OnFindReplaceCmd(WPARAM, LPARAM lParam)
      {
              ASSERT_VALID(this);

              AFX_EDIT_STATE* pEditState = AfxGetEditState();
              CFindReplaceDialog* pDialog = CFindReplaceDialog::GetNotifier(lParam);
              ASSERT(pDialog != NULL);
              ASSERT(pDialog == pEditState->pFindReplaceDlg);
              if (pDialog->IsTerminating())
              {
                      pEditState->pFindReplaceDlg = NULL;
              }
              else if (pDialog->FindNext())
              {
                      OnFindNext(pDialog->GetFindString(),
                              pDialog->SearchDown(), pDialog->MatchCase());
              }
              else if (pDialog->ReplaceCurrent())
              {
                      ASSERT(!pEditState->bFindOnly);
                      OnReplaceSel(pDialog->GetFindString(),
                              pDialog->SearchDown(), pDialog->MatchCase(),
                              pDialog->GetReplaceString());
              }
              else if (pDialog->ReplaceAll())
              {
                      ASSERT(!pEditState->bFindOnly);
                      OnReplaceAll(pDialog->GetFindString(), pDialog-
                      >GetReplaceString(),
                              pDialog->MatchCase());
              }
              ASSERT_VALID(this);
              return 0;
      }

      typedef int (WINAPI* AFX_COMPARE_PROC)(LPCTSTR str1, LPCTSTR str2);

      BOOL CRTFEditView::SameAsSelected(LPCTSTR lpszCompare, BOOL bCase)
      {
              // check length first
              size_t nLen = lstrlen(lpszCompare);
              int nStartChar, nEndChar;
              GetEditCtrl().GetSel(nStartChar, nEndChar);
              if (nLen != (size_t)(nEndChar - nStartChar))
                      return FALSE;

              // length is the same, check contents
              CString strSelect;
              GetSelectedText(strSelect);
```

```
        return (bCase && lstrcmp(lpszCompare, strSelect) == 0) ||
                (!bCase && lstrcmpi(lpszCompare, strSelect) == 0);
}

BOOL CRTFEditView::FindText(LPCTSTR lpszFind, BOOL bNext, BOOL bCase)
{
        ASSERT_VALID(this);
        ASSERT(lpszFind != NULL);
        ASSERT(*lpszFind != '\0');

        UINT nLen = GetBufferLength();
        int nStartChar, nEndChar;
        GetEditCtrl().GetSel(nStartChar, nEndChar);
        UINT nStart = nStartChar;
        int iDir = bNext ? +1 : -1;

        // can't find a match before the first character
        if (nStart == 0 && iDir < 0)
                return FALSE;

        BeginWaitCursor();
        LPCTSTR lpszText = LockBuffer();

        if (iDir < 0)
        {
                // always go back one for search backwards
                nStart -= (lpszText+nStart) -
                        _tcsdec(lpszText, lpszText+nStart);
        }
        else if (nStartChar != nEndChar && SameAsSelected(lpszFind, bCase))
        {
                // easy to go backward/forward with SBCS
                if (_istlead(lpszText[nStart]))
                        nStart++;
                nStart += iDir;
        }

        // handle search with nStart past end of buffer
        size_t nLenFind = lstrlen(lpszFind);
        if (nStart+nLenFind-1 >= nLen)
        {
                if (iDir < 0 && nLen >= nLenFind)
                {
                        if (_afxDBCS)
                        {
                                // walk back to previous character n times
                                nStart = nLen;
                                int n = nLenFind;
                                while (n--)
                                {
                                        nStart -= (lpszText+nStart) -
                                                _tcsdec(lpszText, lpszText+nStart);
                                }
                        }
                        else
```

continued on next page

continued from previous page

```
                    {
                            // single-byte character set is easy and fast
                            nStart = nLen - nLenFind;
                    }
                    ASSERT(nStart+nLenFind-1 <= nLen);
            }
            else
            {
                    UnlockBuffer();
                    EndWaitCursor();
                    return FALSE;
            }
    }

    // start the search at nStart
    LPCTSTR lpsz = lpszText + nStart;
    AFX_COMPARE_PROC pfnCompare = bCase ? lstrcmp : lstrcmpi;

    if (_afxDBCS)
    {
            // double-byte string search
            LPCTSTR lpszStop;
            if (iDir > 0)
            {
                    // start at current and find _first_ occurrence
                    lpszStop = lpszText + nLen - nLenFind + 1;
            }
            else
            {
                    // start at top and find _last_ occurrence
                    lpszStop = lpsz;
                    lpsz = lpszText;
            }

            LPCTSTR lpszFound = NULL;
            while (lpsz <= lpszStop)
            {
                    if (*lpsz == *lpszFind &&
                            (!_istlead(*lpsz) || lpsz[1] == lpszFind[1]))
                    {
                            LPTSTR lpch = (LPTSTR)(lpsz + nLenFind);
                            TCHAR chSave = *lpch;
                            *lpch = '\0';
                            int nResult = (*pfnCompare)(lpsz, lpszFind);
                            *lpch = chSave;
                            if (nResult == 0)
                            {
                                    lpszFound = lpsz;
                                    if (iDir > 0)
                                            break;
                            }
                    }
                    lpsz = _tcsinc(lpsz);
            }
            UnlockBuffer();
```

```
            if (lpszFound != NULL)
            {
                    int n = (int)(lpszFound - lpszText);
                    GetEditCtrl().SetSel(n, n+nLenFind);
                    EndWaitCursor();
                    return TRUE;
            }
    }
    else
    {
        // single-byte string search
        UINT nCompare;
        if (iDir < 0)
                nCompare = (UINT)(lpsz - lpszText) + 1;
        else
                nCompare = nLen - (UINT)(lpsz - lpszText) - nLenFind + 1;

        while (nCompare > 0)
        {
                ASSERT(lpsz >= lpszText);
                ASSERT(lpsz+nLenFind-1 <= lpszText+nLen-1);

                LPSTR lpch = (LPSTR)(lpsz + nLenFind);
                char chSave = *lpch;
                *lpch = '\0';
                int nResult = (*pfnCompare)(lpsz, lpszFind);
                *lpch = chSave;
                if (nResult == 0)
                {
                    UnlockBuffer();
                    int n = (int)(lpsz - lpszText);
                    GetEditCtrl().SetSel(n, n+nLenFind);
                    ASSERT_VALID(this);
                    EndWaitCursor();
                    return TRUE;
                }

                // restore character at end of search
                *lpch = chSave;

                // move on to next substring
                nCompare--;
                lpsz += iDir;
        }
        UnlockBuffer();
    }

    ASSERT_VALID(this);
    EndWaitCursor();
    return FALSE;
}

void CRTFEditView::OnTextNotFound(LPCTSTR)
{
    ASSERT_VALID(this);
    MessageBeep(0);
```

continued on next page

continued from previous page

```
    }

        #undef new
        #ifdef AFX_INIT_SEG
        #pragma code_seg(AFX_INIT_SEG)
        #endif

        #ifndef _WINDLL
        AFX_DATADEF AFX_EDIT_STATE _afxEditState;
        #endif

        IMPLEMENT_DYNCREATE(CRTFEditView, CView)

//////////////////////////////////////////////////////////////////////////
```

3. Create a new file in Visual C++ and add the following code to the file. Save this file as RTFVIEW.H.

```
// rtfview.h  -  header file for CRTFEditView

#include "crtfedit.h"

#ifndef __RTFVIEW_H__
#define __RTFVIEW_H__


#undef AFX_DATA
#define AFX_DATA AFX_CORE_DATA

#define CX_BORDER    1
#define CY_BORDER    1
#define WS_EX_CLIENTEDGE         0x00000200L

// UNICODE/MBCS abstractions
#ifdef _MBCS
        extern const BOOL _afxDBCS;
#else
        #define _afxDBCS FALSE
#endif


//////////////////////////////////////////////////////////////////////////
// Auxiliary System/Screen metrics

struct AUX_DATA
{
        // system metrics
        int cxVScroll, cyHScroll;
        int cxIcon, cyIcon;

        int cxBorder2, cyBorder2;

        // device metrics for screen
        int cxPixelsPerInch, cyPixelsPerInch;
        int cySysFont;
```

```
        // solid brushes with convenient gray colors and system colors
        HBRUSH hbrLtGray, hbrDkGray;
        HBRUSH hbrBtnHilite, hbrBtnFace, hbrBtnShadow;
        HBRUSH hbrWindowFrame;
        HPEN hpenBtnHilite, hpenBtnShadow, hpenBtnText;

        // color values of system colors used for CToolBar
        COLORREF clrBtnFace, clrBtnShadow, clrBtnHilite;
        COLORREF clrBtnText, clrWindowFrame;

        // standard cursors
        HCURSOR hcurWait;
        HCURSOR hcurArrow;
        HCURSOR hcurHelp;              // cursor used in Shift+F1 help

        // special GDI objects allocated on demand
        HFONT   hStatusFont;
        HFONT   hToolTipsFont;
        HBITMAP hbmMenuDot;

        // other system information
        UINT    nWinVer;        // Major.Minor version numbers
        BOOL    bWin32s;        // TRUE if Win32s (or Windows 95)
        BOOL    bWin4;          // TRUE if Windows 4.0
        BOOL    bNotWin4;       // TRUE if not Windows 4.0
        BOOL    bSmCaption;     // TRUE if WS_EX_SMCAPTION is supported
        BOOL    bWin31;         // TRUE if actually Win32s on Windows 3.1
        BOOL    bMarked4;       // TRUE if marked as 4.0

        // special Windows API entry points
        int (WINAPI* pfnSetScrollInfo)(HWND, int, LPCSCROLLINFO, BOOL);
        BOOL (WINAPI* pfnGetScrollInfo)(HWND, int, LPSCROLLINFO);

// Implementation
        AUX_DATA();
        ~AUX_DATA();
        void UpdateSysColors();
        void UpdateSysMetrics();
};

extern AFX_DATA AUX_DATA afxData;


void AFXAPI AfxDeleteObject(HGDIOBJ* pObject);

/////////////////////////////////////////////////////////////////////////
// CRTFEditView - simple text editor view

class CRTFEditView : public CView
{
        DECLARE_DYNCREATE(CRTFEditView)

// Construction
public:
```

continued on next page

continued from previous page

```
        CRTFEditView();
        static AFX_DATA const DWORD dwStyleDefault;

// Attributes
public:
        // CRTFEdit control access
        CRTFEdit& GetEditCtrl() const;


        // other attributes
        void GetSelectedText(CString& strResult) const;

// Operations
public:
        BOOL FindText(LPCTSTR lpszFind, BOOL bNext = TRUE, BOOL bCase = TRUE);

// Overrideables
protected:
        virtual void OnFindNext(LPCTSTR lpszFind, BOOL bNext, BOOL bCase);
        virtual void OnReplaceSel(LPCTSTR lpszFind, BOOL bNext, BOOL bCase,
                                LPCTSTR lpszReplace);
        virtual void OnReplaceAll(LPCTSTR lpszFind, LPCTSTR lpszReplace,
                                BOOL bCase);
        virtual void OnTextNotFound(LPCTSTR lpszFind);

// Implementation
public:
        virtual ~CRTFEditView();
        virtual void OnDraw(CDC* pDC);
        virtual void DeleteContents();

        static AFX_DATA const UINT nMaxSize;
                // maximum number of characters supported

protected:
        LPTSTR m_pShadowBuffer;         // special shadow buffer only used
                                        // in Win32s
        UINT m_nShadowSize;

        CUIntArray m_aPageStart;        // array of starting pages

        // construction
        virtual BOOL PreCreateWindow(CREATESTRUCT& cs);

        // find & replace support
        void OnEditFindReplace(BOOL bFindOnly);
        BOOL InitializeReplace();
        BOOL SameAsSelected(LPCTSTR lpszCompare, BOOL bCase);

        // buffer access
        LPCTSTR LockBuffer() const;
        void UnlockBuffer() const;
        UINT GetBufferLength() const;
```

```
        // special overrides for implementation
        virtual void CalcWindowRect(LPRECT lpClientRect,
            UINT nAdjustType = adjustBorder);

        //{{AFX_MSG(CRTFEditView)
        afx_msg int OnCreate(LPCREATESTRUCT lpCreateStruct);
        afx_msg void OnPaint();
        afx_msg void OnUpdateNeedSel(CCmdUI* pCmdUI);
        afx_msg void OnUpdateNeedClip(CCmdUI* pCmdUI);
        afx_msg void OnUpdateNeedText(CCmdUI* pCmdUI);
        afx_msg void OnUpdateNeedFind(CCmdUI* pCmdUI);
        afx_msg void OnUpdateEditUndo(CCmdUI* pCmdUI);
        afx_msg void OnEditChange();
        afx_msg void OnEditCut();
        afx_msg void OnEditCopy();
        afx_msg void OnEditPaste();
        afx_msg void OnEditClear();
        afx_msg void OnEditUndo();
        afx_msg void OnEditSelectAll();
        afx_msg void OnEditFind();
        afx_msg void OnEditReplace();
        afx_msg void OnEditRepeat();
        afx_msg LRESULT OnFindReplaceCmd(WPARAM wParam, LPARAM lParam);
        //}}AFX_MSG
        DECLARE_MESSAGE_MAP()
};


#endif // __RTFEDIT_H_
```

4. Next, select the CRTFView source file, WORDRVW.CPP, and add the following code to the bottom of the file:

```
void CRTFView::OnInitialUpdate()
{
    CRTFEditView::OnInitialUpdate();

    // Force normal page size

    HDC hDC;
    CPrintDialog prtDlg(FALSE, PD_ALLPAGES | PD_USEDEVMODECOPIES |
                        PD_NOPAGENUMS | PD_HIDEPRINTTOFILE |
                        PD_NOSELECTION, NULL);
    prtDlg.GetDefaults();
    hDC = prtDlg.m_pd.hDC;
    if(!hDC)
    {
        // Printer DC Failed, Create one from the Display
        hDC = CreateCompatibleDC(NULL);
    }

    if(hDC)
    {
        if (!GetEditCtrl().SetTargetDevice(hDC, ((14400*85)/10)))
        {
            DeleteDC(hDC);
```

continued on next page

continued from previous page

```
        }
        else
        {
            m_hTargetDC = hDC;
        }
    }

    // Enable Notification Messages
    DWORD dwMask;
    dwMask = GetEditCtrl().GetEventMask();
    dwMask |= ENM_CHANGE | ENM_SELCHANGE;
    GetEditCtrl().SetEventMask(dwMask);
}
```

5. Enter the header file for the view class, WORDRVW.H, and add the following line to the file:

```
virtual void OnInitialUpdate();
```

6. Enter AppStudio and select the MDI menu from the menu list. Add a new main menu item to the menu with the caption Format. To this menu add two new menu items with the captions Character and Paragraph. Make the Character and Paragraph menus drop-down menus. To the Character menu, add four new drop-down menu items with the captions Bold, Italic, and Underline. Give these menu items the identifiers ID_FORMAT_BOLD, ID_FORMAT_ITALIC, and ID_FORMAT_UNDERLINE, respectively. To the Paragraph menu add three new menu items with the captions Right, Left, Center, and Bullet. Give these menu items the identifiers ID_FORMAT_RIGHT, ID_FORMAT_LEFT, ID_FORMAT_CENTER, and ID_FORMAT_BULLET, respectively. Save the menus and exit AppStudio.

7. Enter ClassWizard and select the CRTFView object from the drop-down list. Select the ID_FORMAT_BOLD object from the object list and the COMMAND message from the message list. Click on the Add Function button and accept the name OnFormatBold as the name of the new method. Add the following code to the OnFormatBold method of CRTFView:

```
void CRTFView::OnFormatBold()
{
    CHARFORMAT cf;
    cf.cbSize = sizeof(cf);

    GetEditCtrl().GetCharFormat(TRUE, &cf);

    if(cf.dwMask & CFM_BOLD)
        cf.dwEffects ^= CFE_BOLD;
    else
        cf.dwEffects |= CFE_BOLD;

    // Only look at BOLD bit

    cf.dwMask = CFM_BOLD;
```

```
        // Set the status for the selected text
        GetEditCtrl().SetCharFormat(SCF_SELECTION, &cf);
}
```

8. Enter ClassWizard and select the CRTFView object from the drop-down list. Select the ID_FORMAT_ITALIC object from the object list and the COMMAND message from the message list. Click on the Add Function button and accept the name OnFormatItalic as the name of the new method. Add the following code to the OnFormatItalic method of CRTFView:

```
void CRTFView::OnFormatItalic()
{
    CHARFORMAT cf;
    cf.cbSize = sizeof(cf);

    GetEditCtrl().GetCharFormat(TRUE, &cf);

    if(cf.dwMask & CFM_ITALIC)
        cf.dwEffects ^= CFE_ITALIC;
    else
        cf.dwEffects |= CFE_ITALIC;

    cf.dwMask = CFM_ITALIC;
    GetEditCtrl().SetCharFormat(SCF_SELECTION, &cf);

}
```

9. Enter ClassWizard and select the CRTFView object from the drop-down list. Select the ID_FORMAT_UNDERLINE object from the object list and the COMMAND message from the message list. Click on the Add Function button and accept the name OnFormatUnderline as the name of the new method. Add the following code to the OnFormatUnderline method of CRTFView:

```
void CRTFView::OnFormatUnderline()
{
    CHARFORMAT cf;
    cf.cbSize = sizeof(cf);

    GetEditCtrl().GetCharFormat(TRUE, &cf);

    if(cf.dwMask & CFM_UNDERLINE)
        cf.dwEffects ^= CFE_UNDERLINE;
    else
        cf.dwEffects |= CFE_UNDERLINE;

    cf.dwMask = CFM_UNDERLINE;
    GetEditCtrl().SetCharFormat(SCF_SELECTION, &cf);
}
```

10. Enter ClassWizard and select the CRTFView object from the drop-down list. Select the ID_FORMAT_RIGHT object from the object list and the COMMAND message from the message list. Click on the Add Function button and accept the name OnFormatRight as the name of the new method. Add the following code to the OnFormatRight method of CRTFView:

```
void CRTFView::OnFormatRight()
{
    PARAFORMAT pf;
    pf.cbSize = sizeof(pf);

    pf.dwMask = PFM_ALIGNMENT;
    pf.wAlignment = PFA_RIGHT;

    GetEditCtrl().SetParaFormat(&pf);
}
```

11. Enter ClassWizard and select the CRTFView object from the drop-down list. Select the ID_FORMAT_LEFT object from the object list and the COMMAND message from the message list. Click on the Add Function button and accept the name OnFormatLeft as the name of the new method. Add the following code to the OnFormatLeft method of CRTFView:

```
void CRTFView::OnFormatLeft()
{
    PARAFORMAT pf;
    pf.cbSize = sizeof(pf);

    pf.dwMask = PFM_ALIGNMENT;
    pf.wAlignment = PFA_LEFT;

    GetEditCtrl().SetParaFormat(&pf);
}
```

12. Enter ClassWizard and select the CRTFView object from the drop-down list. Select the ID_FORMAT_CENTER object from the object list and the COMMAND message from the message list. Click on the Add Function button and accept the name OnFormatCenter as the name of the new method. Add the following code to the OnFormatCenter method of CRTFView:

```
void CRTFView::OnFormatCenter()
{
    PARAFORMAT pf;
    pf.cbSize = sizeof(pf);

    pf.dwMask = PFM_ALIGNMENT;
    pf.wAlignment = PFA_CENTER;

    GetEditCtrl().SetParaFormat(&pf);
}
```

13. Enter ClassWizard and select the CRTFView object from the drop-down list. Select the ID_FORMAT_BULLET object from the object list and the COMMAND message from the message list. Click on the Add Function button and accept the name OnFormatBullet as the name of the new method. Add the following code to the OnFormatBullet method of CRTFView:

```
void CRTFView::OnFormatBullet()
{
    PARAFORMAT pf;
    pf.cbSize = sizeof(pf);
```

```
    GetEditCtrl().GetParaFormat(&pf);

    if(pf.dwMask & PFM_NUMBERING)
        pf.wNumbering ^= PFN_BULLET;
    else
        pf.wNumbering |= PFN_BULLET;

    // Only bulleted bit

    pf.dwMask = PFM_NUMBERING;

    GetEditCtrl().SetParaFormat(&pf);
}
```

14. Compile and run the application.

How It Works

It is truly beyond the scope of this book to explain how the CRTFEditView class works. This class is a clone of the CEditView class in the MFC and works in a completely similar manner to that class. It is, in fact, patterned after that class.

The CRTFView class simply encapsulates the functionality of the view of the Rich Text Edit class. As each character or paragraph formatting menu item is selected, the class method corresponding to that menu item is called.

Once a method for formatting is called, the procedure in each case is the same. First, the current character formatting information for the selected region is obtained. This is done by the GetCharFormat or GetParaFormat methods of the edit control class. This formatting information is then interrogated to see if the current formatting information includes the style bit (bold, italic, and so on) that was requested by the user.

If the style bit for the retrieved formatting information does not include the style, that style bit is then ORed into the style. If the style bit does include the style, it is XORed out of the style. The mask is then set to look only at that bit, and the SetCharFormat or SetParaFormat method of the edit control is called. This sends the Windows messages to the control, and they cause it to apply the new style to the marked text.

Comments

This How-To could be the basis for a complete text editor for the Windows 95 environment, or it could also be used to display anything from HTML documents to Word documents saved in Rich Text format.

One obvious use for this system would be in a tagged text file environment. You could simply write a preprocessor to load the text into the edit control by parsing the text tags and setting the appropriate style flags in the Rich Text Edit control. The reverse is true as well, writing out tags in place of style bits.

Finally, it should be noted that the Rich Text Edit control responds to all of the messages that a normal text control responds to. Thus, you can use all of the existing How-To's that we have discussed for edit controls with the Rich Text Edit control and expect them to work similarly. Although the normal messages, such as EM_SETSEL, only accept integer values for ranges, the Rich Text Edit control defines a set of messages of the form EM_SETSELEX, which can be used with long range values.

COMPLEXITY
EASY

9.7 How do I... Change the caret type in an edit control?

Problem

My users are often laptop users, who simply can't see the cursor in my edit fields on their tiny screens. How can I make the cursor larger for them to see more easily? Is there a general way to make the cursor a specific size, or maybe a more distinctive pattern, so that laptop users (and people with poor eyesight) can more easily figure out which edit control is the current one?

Technique

It is always nice when there is a simple solution to a complex problem. In this case the cursor (or *caret* as it is known in Windows programming parlance—the cursor is the mouse representation) can be quickly and easily changed to a bigger size or a more distinctive pattern through a simple Windows API call.

The CreateCaret and ShowCaret functions are the specific API functions we will be looking at in this How-To. While the Microsoft Foundation Classes provide an interface to some of the functionality of the Caret functions, this is a case where the API provides a richer and more easily understood method to do the job.

Steps

Open and run the Visual C++ application CH97.MAK from the CHAPT9\SAMPLES\CH97 directory on the CD that comes with this book. Select the main menu item Dialog and the menu item Change Caret Type. You will see a dialog like that displayed in Figure 9-7. Click on the Change Caret button and then click in the edit field. Notice that the caret is now a much thicker blinking line. Click on the Bitmap Caret button and then click in the edit field again. You will see a new kind of caret displayed that looks something like an I-beam.

To reproduce this functionality in your own application, follow these steps:

1. Create a new project in Visual C++. Give the application the name CH97.MAK. Enter AppStudio and create a new dialog. To this dialog add two buttons at the top of the window with the captions Change Caret and Bitmap Caret. Add an edit field in the middle of the dialog and move the OK and Cancel buttons to the bottom of the dialog.

Figure 9-7 Change caret dialog

2. Go into ClassWizard and create a new dialog class for the template you have just defined. Give this class the name CCaretDlg. In ClassWizard, select the CCaretDlg in the drop-down list. Select IDC_BUTTON1 from the object list and the BN_CLICKED message from the message list. Click on the Add Function button and give the new function the name OnChangeCaret. Enter the following code into the OnChangeCaret method of CCaretDlg:

```
void CCaretDlg::OnChangeCaret()
{
    caret_type = 1;
}
```

3. Again in ClassWizard, click on the IDC_BUTTON2 object in the object list and the BN_CLICKED message in the message list. Click on the Add Function button and give the new function the name OnBitmapCaret. Enter the following code into the OnBitmapCaret method of CCaretDlg:

```
void CCaretDlg::OnBitmapCaret()
{
    caret_type = 2;
}
```

4. Click on the IDC_EDIT1 object in the object list of ClassWizard and select the EN_SETFOCUS command. Click on the Add Function button and give the new function the name OnGetEditFocus. Enter the following code into the OnGetEditFocus method of CCaretDlg:

```
void CCaretDlg::OnGetEditFocus()
{
    switch ( caret_type ) {
        case 1:
            ::CreateCaret(GetDlgItem(IDC_EDIT1)->m_hWnd, NULL, 6, 4);
```

continued on next page

continued from previous page

```
                break;
            case 2:
                HBITMAP hBitmap = LoadBitmap(AfxGetInstanceHandle(),
                                        MAKEINTRESOURCE(IDB_BITMAP1));
                ::CreateCaret(GetDlgItem(IDC_EDIT1)->m_hWnd, hBitmap, 0, 0 );
                break;
        }

        if ( caret_type )
            ::ShowCaret(GetDlgItem(IDC_EDIT1)->m_hWnd);
    }
```

5. Click on the IDC_EDIT1 object in the object list of ClassWizard and the
EN_KILLFOCUS message in the message list. Click on the Add Function button and give the new function the name OnLoseEditFocus. Enter the
following code into the OnLoseEditFocus method of CCaretDlg:

```
void CCaretDlg::OnLoseEditFocus()
{
    if ( caret_type )
        DestroyCaret();
}
```

6. Finally, add this line to the constructor of the CCaretDlg:

```
caret_type = 0;
```

And while you are at it, add the following lines to the header file for CCaretDlg:

```
private:
    int caret_type;
```

7. Next, reenter AppStudio. Select the main menu object from the menu list and
add a menu with the caption Dialog. Add a new menu item to the Dialog
menu. Give the new menu item the caption Change Caret Type, and the identifier ID_CARET_DLG. Save the menu and exit AppStudio.

8. Select the CCh97App object from the drop-down list in ClassWizard. Select
the ID_CARET_DLG object from the object list and the COMMAND message
from the message list. Click on the Add Function button and accept the name
OnCaretDlg as the name of the new function. Then add the following code to
the OnCaretDlg method of CCh97App:

```
void CCh97App::OnCaretDlg()
{
    CCaretDlg dlg;
    dlg.DoModal();
}
```

9. Finally, add this line to the include list at the top of the CH9.CPP file:

```
#include "caretdlg.h"
```

10. Compile and run the application.

How It Works

When the user selects the Change Caret button or the Bitmap Caret button, all that happens is that a flag is set to a given value in the class. When the edit field is entered, the dialog class receives an EN_GETFOCUS message. This message is trapped in the OnGetEditFocus method, which uses the CreateCaret API function to create a new caret. The ShowCaret method is used to actually force the caret to display itself.

The Bitmap Caret button sets the caret type to be a bitmap. When you call CreateCaret, you can either pass the handle of a bitmap or a length and width. The bitmap handle is a reference to a bitmap that you have created in your application and loaded via the LoadBitmap function. This function is also part of the API.

In order to use the example in this How-To, create a bitmap using AppStudio and save it with the identifier IDB_BITMAP1. Bitmaps for carets can be any size, although an 8-by-8 grid works best for display purposes. If you are using larger fonts in your application, by all means use a wider and higher bitmap. One caveat to the process: the bitmap is inverted when it is displayed. Thus, only the white portions of your bitmap show up in the caret on the screen.

Comments

Custom carets are one of the least used parts of the Windows API system. Users would quite probably prefer to have carets displayed in special purposes, but applications rarely use this feature to accommodate them.

Laptop users and users with poor eyesight would certainly find a custom caret a welcome relief were it to show up in your application. Think about it carefully the next time you create a utility that might be used by one of these groups.

COMPLEXITY

EASY

9.8 How do I...
Change the speed at which the caret blinks?

Problem

For many of my users, the caret, or edit cursor, blinks either too fast or too slow for them to easily distinguish. I would really like to allow them to customize the speed at which the caret blinks so they might more easily read the text in edit boxes and find their positions.

How can I use the power of the Windows API to allow me to customize the blink speed of the caret? Is this even possible, or will I need to paint my own cursor and update it using some sort of timer?

Technique

In the ever customizable world of Windows 95, it would be truly tragic if there was something that users wanted to change but weren't permitted to by the operating system. Windows 95 was well enough thought out that this particular problem has been addressed through a simple, though poorly documented, API call known as SetCaretBlinkTime function.

The SetCaretBlinkTime function does exactly what the name implies. This function will change the rate at which the cursor in an edit field, known as the caret, blinks. A companion function, GetCaretBlinkTime, will tell you what the current setting is for the blink rate.

When you are working with system functions, such as SetCaretBlinkTime, it is usually "polite" for your application to restore the previous setting when you have finished working with a property. The caret blink rate is set for all applications in Windows, and you should respect this by resetting the previous, or default, setting when you lose the focus in your edit window.

In this How-To, we examine how you can slow down, or speed up, the caret blink rate in your application.

Steps

Open and run the Visual C++ application CH98.MAK from the CHAPT9\SAMPLES\CH98 directory on the CD that comes with this book. Select the main menu item Dialog and the drop-down menu item Change Caret Blink Speed. You will see a dialog like that displayed in Figure 9-8. Click on the Change Caret Blink button and then click in the

Figure 9-8 Change caret blink speed dialog

edit field. Notice that the caret is now blinking normally. Click on the Change Caret Blink several other times, clicking into the edit field after each change. Notice that the speed of the blink changes, and the text field next to the button indicates the speed.

To reproduce this functionality in your own application, follow these steps:

1. Create a new project in Visual C++ using AppWizard. Give the application the name CH98.MAK. Enter AppStudio and create a new dialog. In this new dialog add a button with the caption Change Caret Blink and a text field with the caption Speed: Normal. Add a single edit field to the dialog, moving the OK and Cancel buttons to the bottom of the dialog.

2. Go into ClassWizard and create a new dialog class for the template you have just defined. Give this class the name CBlinkDlg. In ClassWizard, select the CBlinkDlg in the drop-down list. Select the IDC_BUTTON1 from the object list and the BN_CLICKED message from the message list. Click on the Add Function button and give the new function the name OnChangeCursorSpeed. Enter the following code into the OnChangeCursorSpeed method of CBlinkDlg:

```
void CBlinkDlg::OnChangeCursorSpeed()
{
    // Three different options: Normal, Slow, Fast

    switch ( cur_setting ) {
        case 0: // Normal
            cur_setting = 1;
            SetCaretBlinkTime(old_time);
            GetDlgItem(IDC_TEXT1)->SetWindowText("Speed: Normal");
            break;
        case 1: // Slow
            cur_setting = 2;
            GetDlgItem(IDC_TEXT1)->SetWindowText("Speed: Slow");
            SetCaretBlinkTime(old_time*2);
            break;
        case 2: // Fast
            cur_setting = 0;
            GetDlgItem(IDC_TEXT1)->SetWindowText("Speed: Fast");
            SetCaretBlinkTime(old_time/2);
            break;

    }
}
```

3. Add the following lines to the constructor for the CBlinkDlg class:

```
old_time = GetCaretBlinkTime();
cur_setting = 0;
```

4. Now add these lines to the header file for the CBlinkDlg class, BLINKDLG.H:

```
private:
  UINT old_time;
  short cur_setting;
```

5. Next, reenter AppStudio. Select the main menu object from the menu list and add a new menu with the caption Dialog. Add a new menu item to the Dialog menu. Give the new menu item the caption Change Caret Blink Speed, and the identifier ID_CARET_SPEED. Save the menu and exit AppStudio.

6. Select the CCh98App object from the drop-down list in ClassWizard. Select the ID_CARET_SPEED object from the object list and the COMMAND message from the message list. Click on the Add Function button and accept the name OnCaretSpeed as the name of the new function. Now add the following code to the OnCaretSpeed method of CCh98App:

```
void CCh98App::OnCaretSpeed()
{
    CBlinkDlg  dlg;
    dlg.DoModal();
}
```

7. Finally, add this line to the include list at the top of the CH9.CPP file:

```
#include "blinkdlg.h"
```

8. Compile and run the application.

How It Works

When the user selects the dialog and clicks on the Change Caret Blink button, the dialog method OnChangeCursorSpeed is called. The current setting of the member variable cur_setting is checked, and that speed is set in the SetCaretBlinkTime method. In the constructor for the dialog, the original setting for the speed of the caret was obtained via the GetCaretBlinkTime function call. This speed is then either cut in half (to speed up the blink) or doubled (to slow down the blink). Note that the time to actually do a complete blink is twice as long as the setting, since the time is to turn off the cursor as well as to turn it on.

CHAPTER 10
PRINTING

10

PRINTING

How do I...

The printer is one of the most important peripherals available to the user. Unlike modems, scanners, or other hardware devices, most users are completely accustomed to dealing with printers. Mainframe users, typewriter users, and workstation users are all well aware of the printer and the value of printed output. It is somewhat ironic that in today's "paperless" office environment, we put a higher value on the quality and clarity of printed output than ever before in computer history.

Windows 95 is a full step above Windows 3.1 in the printing arena. Many printer drivers now support direct printing as well as better control over output and font selection through the operating system. Windows 95 is a quantum leap from the bad old days of MS-DOS when programs required hundreds of different pieces of code to deal with the multitude of printers available. Today, the Windows programmer need only concern himself or herself with the printer driver interface and the Windows API functions to deal with the printer. The hardware handshaking and printer control codes are all dealt with out of the sight of the programmer.

In this chapter, we will examine some of the API functions dealing with the printer and how you can use these API functions in your own applications. You will find out how to make your printouts look better, how to deal with cases where the user does not have a printer, and how to determine the capabilities of the printer being used in the system. Because Windows tries to present a single, consistent user interface for the end user, you will find out how to make your program use the same common dialog boxes as all of the professional programs.

10.1 Determine the Printer's Capabilities

It is a simple fact of life that different printers have different capabilities. For example, before you try to print graphics to a printer, it would be nice to know if the printer supports graphics. Printing outside the range of the currently installed printer is a certain way to annoy users. In this How-To, we show you how you can find out what the capabilities of the current printer are and what is and what is not supported by that printer.

10.2 Determine Page Size and Orientation of the Current Printer

When printing a document in Windows, it is quite nice to know how big the page is going to be on the printer. Also, a page that is printed in landscape mode will look quite different than a page printed in portrait mode. In this How-To, we will show you how you can find out what the current page size and orientation (landscape or portrait) is for the current printer.

10.3 Use the Common Printer Dialog Boxes

Users prefer to have the same interface presented to them for the same things. Windows 95 allows users to see certain dialogs in a certain consistent way. In this How-To, we examine the printer common dialog (which was present way back in Windows 3.x) and how you can use the common dialog to get printer information from the user.

10.4 Print to a File

It is not always guaranteed that users will have a printer handy when they want to capture their work. One of the realities of today's portable computing environment is that many laptop users would like to print a file, but do not have a printer handy. In this case, they will want to print to a file on their disk, allowing them to spool the file to the printer at a later time, perhaps when they are in the main office. In this How-To, we examine printing to a file and show you how you can modify your printout in some cases to take advantage of the fact that a print-to-file option was requested.

10.5 Determine Available Printer Fonts

When you are printing to a printer, some fonts simply look better than others. This occurs for a variety of reasons, but primarily because screen fonts simply don't look as good when they are "stretched" out to display on a printer. In this How-To, we will show you how to find out what fonts are supported and how to select them for a printer.

10.6 Determine the Print Queue Status

With Windows 95 and Windows NT came the ability to check printer queue statuses, a must in a networked environment. In this How-To, we will examine how to determine the status of a given printer queue.

Table 10-1 lists the Windows 95 API functions used in this chapter.

DeviceCapabilities	GetProfileString	GlobalAlloc
GlobalLock	GlobalUnlock	GlobalFree
GetPrinterDeviceDefaults	Escape	GetDeviceCaps
EnumFontFamilies	MakeProcInstance	FreeProcInstance
EnumPrinters	EnumJobs	OpenPrinter
LocalAlloc	LocalFree	

 Table 10-1 Windows 95 API functions used in Chapter 10

COMPLEXITY
MODERATE

10.1 How do I... Determine the printer's capabilities?

Problem

I need to know certain capabilities of the current printer in Windows. Actually, I would like to know all of the printers installed and the capabilities of whichever of the printers the user chooses. The information I need includes the page size (preferably in pixels) and the dimensions of the printer that the user selects.

How can I use the Windows API to find the printers installed, along with the page sizes and the dimensions of those printers?

Technique

To determine the printers installed under Windows, you need to be able to read the system information. This information is kept in the WIN.INI file in the Windows directory structure. Once you have this information, you can list the printers for the user. To determine the other information for a printer—the page size and dimensions—is more complex.

Each printer supported by Windows has a driver that implements the functionality required for that printer. This driver is actually a specialized form of a dynamic link library that Windows loads to access the printer-specific functions. This method of dynamic loading means that the programmer is freed from the responsibility of knowing how to communicate with each printer, and the operating system is freed from the need to hold all of the information for all of the supported printers in memory.

Communicating with the printer driver is a chore in and of itself. First, you must load the printer driver into memory. Next, to get the information out of the printer driver, a standard function, DeviceCapabilities, is located within the driver and queried for the information.

This How-To will take you through the steps necessary to find the list of installed printers, load the printer driver for the printer requested, and then get the information needed from the printer driver.

Steps

Open and run the Visual C++ application CH101.MAK from the CHAPT10\SAM-PLES\CH101 directory on the CD that comes with this book. Select the Dialog menu and the Printer Capabilities menu item from that menu. Select one of the printers (if there are more than one) listed in the list box on the left-hand side of the dialog. You will see a dialog similar to the one shown in Figure 10-1.

To duplicate the functionality of this example, follow this procedure:

1. Create a new project in Visual C++ using AppWizard. Give the new project the name CH101.MAK.

2. Enter AppStudio and create a new dialog template.

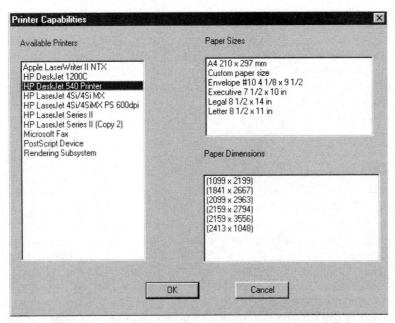

Figure 10-1 Dialog showing a selected printer and its capabilities

3. In the new dialog template, move the OK and Cancel buttons to the bottom of the dialog. Add a static text field with the caption Available Printers. Immediately below this static text field, add a list box.

4. Add a second static text field with the caption Paper Sizes and a list box below it. Add a third static text field with the caption Paper Dimensions and a third list box immediately below it.

5. Enter ClassWizard and generate a new dialog class for the dialog template you just created. Give the new class the name CPrinterCapDlg. Select the CPrinterCapDlg from the drop-down combo box in ClassWizard, and then select the CPrinterCapDlg object from the object list. Select the WM_INITDIALOG message and click on the Add Function button. Add the following code to the OnInitDialog method of CPrinterCapDlg:

```
BOOL CPrinterCapDlg::OnInitDialog()
{
        CDialog::OnInitDialog();

        char allDevices[4096];
        char *ptr;

    GetProfileString ("devices", NULL, "", allDevices, sizeof(allDevices) );

    // Add the names of the printer devices to the list box

    CListBox *list = (CListBox *)GetDlgItem(IDC_LIST1);

    // Get each name out of the device list

    ptr = allDevices;

    while (*ptr)
    {
        list->AddString ( ptr );
       ptr += strlen (ptr) + 1 ;
    }


        return TRUE;   // return TRUE unless you set the focus to a control
}
```

6. Select the CPrinterCapDlg from the drop-down combo box in ClassWizard. Select the IDC_LIST1 object from the object list and the LBN_SELCHANGE message from the message list. Click on the Add Function button and name the new function OnSelectPrinter. Add the following code to the OnSelectPrinter method of CPrinterCapDlg:

```
void CPrinterCapDlg::OnSelectPrinter()
{
    // Get the selected printer

    char printer[256];
    char driver[_MAX_PATH], driver_file[_MAX_PATH];
```

continued on next page

continued from previous page

```
char *ptr;
DWORD num_sizes, num_dimensions;
WORD FAR      *pawPaperList;
HANDLE        hPaperList, hPaperDims;
POINT FAR     *paptPaperList;

CListBox *list = (CListBox *)GetDlgItem(IDC_LIST1);
list->GetText ( list->GetCurSel(), printer );

GetProfileString("devices", printer, "", driver, sizeof(driver));

// Get the driver name out of the device string

ptr = strtok(driver, ",");
ptr = strtok(NULL, ",");

// Number of paper sizes
num_sizes = DeviceCapabilities (printer, "LPT1", (WORD)DC_PAPERS,
                                (LPSTR)NULL, (LPDEVMODE)NULL);

// Number of paper dimensions
num_dimensions = DeviceCapabilities (printer, "LPT1", (WORD)DC_PAPERSIZE,
                                (LPSTR)NULL, (LPDEVMODE)NULL);

// allocate space for paper sizes
hPaperList  = GlobalAlloc(GMEM_MOVEABLE, num_sizes*sizeof(WORD));
pawPaperList = (WORD FAR *) GlobalLock(hPaperList);

// allocate space for paper dimensions
hPaperDims   = GlobalAlloc(GMEM_MOVEABLE, num_dimensions*sizeof(POINT));
paptPaperList = (POINT FAR *) GlobalLock(hPaperDims);

// fill buffer with paper list
DeviceCapabilities (printer, "LPT1", (WORD)DC_PAPERS,
                (LPSTR)pawPaperList, (LPDEVMODE)NULL);

// fill buffer with paper dimensions
DeviceCapabilities (printer, "LPT1", (WORD)DC_PAPERSIZE,
                (LPSTR)paptPaperList, (LPDEVMODE)NULL);

// Load paper dimension list and paper size list

CListBox *list2 = (CListBox *)GetDlgItem(IDC_LIST2);
CListBox *list3 = (CListBox *)GetDlgItem(IDC_LIST3);

// Clear the lists first

list2->ResetContent();
list3->ResetContent();

char buffer[80];

for ( int i=0; i<(int)num_dimensions; ++i ) {

    // First the paper size
```

```
    if ((pawPaperList[i] < MAX_PAPERS) && (pawPaperList[i] > 0))
        list2->AddString ( szPaperList[pawPaperList[i]] );
    else
        list2->AddString ( szPaperList[0] );

    // Next the dimensions
    sprintf(buffer, "(%d x %d) ", paptPaperList[i].x, paptPaperList[i].y);
    list3->AddString ( buffer );
}

GlobalUnlock(hPaperList);
GlobalUnlock(hPaperDims);
GlobalFree(hPaperList);
GlobalFree(hPaperDims);


}
```

7. Add the following block of code to the top of the PRINTERC.CPP source file:

```
char   *szPaperList[] ={
                        "Custom paper size",
                        "Letter 8 1/2 x 11 in",
                        "Letter Small 8 1/2 x 11 in",
                        "Tabloid 11 x 17 in",
                        "Ledger 17 x 11 in",
                        "Legal 8 1/2 x 14 in",
                        "Statement 5 1/2 x 8 1/2 in",
                        "Executive 7 1/2 x 10 in",
                        "A3 297 x 420 mm",
                        "A4 210 x 297 mm",
                        "A4 Small 210 x 297 mm",
                        "A5 148 x 210 mm",
                        "B4 250 x 354",
                        "B5 182 x 257 mm",
                        "Folio 8 1/2 x 13 in",
                        "Quarto 215 x 275 mm",
                        "10x14 in",
                        "11x17 in",
                        "Note 8 1/2 x 11 in",
                        "Envelope #9 3 7/8 x 8 7/8",
                        "Envelope #10 4 1/8 x 9 1/2",
                        "Envelope #11 4 1/2 x 10 3/8",
                        "Envelope #12 4 3/4 x 11",
                        "Envelope #14 5 x 11 1/2",
                        "C size sheet",
                        "D size sheet",
                        "E size sheet"};
#define MAX_PAPERS   27
```

8. Enter AppStudio and select the menu resource list. Select the IDR_CH101TYPE
menu and add a new main menu entry with the caption Dialog. To the Dialog
menu add a new menu item with the caption Printer Capabilities and the identifier ID_PRINTER_CAP. Save the menu resource and the resource file.

9. Enter ClassWizard and select the CCh101App object from the drop-down combo box. Select the ID_PRINTER_CAP object from the object list and the COMMAND message from the message list. Click on the Add Function button and give the new function the name OnPrinterCap. Enter the following code into the OnPrinterCap method of CCh101App:

```
void CCh101App::OnPrinterCap()
{
    CPrinterCapDlg dlg;
    dlg.DoModal();
}
```

10. Add the following line to the top of the CH101.CPP source file:

```
#include "printerc.h"
```

11. Compile and run the application.

How It Works

When the user selects the Printer Capabilities menu item from the main menu, the dialog is created. This invokes the OnInitDialog method in response to the WM_INITDIALOG message from Windows. In this method the program retrieves the string from the WIN.INI file, which holds the names of the printers. This string is then parsed and the individual printer names are stored in the first list box.

When the list box selection changes by the user selecting a printer, the OnSelectPrinter method is called. This method then calls the DeviceCapabilities function for the requested printer. The number of paper sizes supported and the number of paper dimensions supported are then retrieved. Arrays of the proper sizes are allocated and then filled with additional calls to the DeviceCapabilities function.

Note that in Windows 3.x the DeviceCapabilities function was loaded from the printer driver. It is no longer necessary to load the printer driver function in Windows 95.

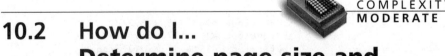

COMPLEXITY
MODERATE

10.2 How do I...
Determine page size and orientation of the current printer?

Problem

I would like to be able to know the page size (in inches) and the orientation (landscape or portrait) settings for the current printer. Is there any way I can directly find out this information through the Windows API functions?

Technique

It is quite possible to find the page size settings for the current printer as well as the currently set orientation. To do so, however, involves some manipulation of several printer settings and the need to actually create a device context (DC) for the printer in question.

In this How-To, we will show you how you can directly get a printer device context without the usual need to present the user with a common dialog box. Given that device context, we will then retrieve the information needed to calculate the page size in inches.

Steps

Open and run the Visual C++ application CH102.MAK from the CHAPT10\SAMPLES\CH102 directory on the CD that comes with this book. Select the Dialog menu and the Printer Statistics menu item from that menu. You will see a dialog similar to the one shown in Figure 10-2.

To duplicate the functionality of this example, follow this procedure:

1. Create a new project in Visual C++ using AppWizard. Give the new project the name CH102.MAK.

2. Enter AppStudio and create a new dialog template.

3. In the new dialog template, move the OK and Cancel buttons to the bottom of the dialog. Add a static text field with the caption Vertical Page Size (inches): to the dialog. Add a second text field with a blank caption aligned horizontally with the first field. Give this second text field the identifier ID_VERT_PAGE_SIZE.

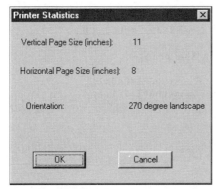

Figure 10-2 Dialog showing the page size and orientation for the currently selected printer

4. Add a static text field below, and aligned with the left side of, the Vertical Page Size (inches): static text field. Give this text field the caption Horizontal Page Size (inches):. Add a text field immediately to the right of this field with a blank caption and the identifier ID_HORZ_PAGE_SIZE.

5. Add a third vertical static text field on the left-hand side of the dialog, immediately below the Horizontal Page Size (inches): text field. Give this field the caption Orientation:. Add another static text field next to this Orientation: field and give it a blank caption. Assign the identifier ID_ORIENTATION to the new text field.

6. Enter ClassWizard and generate a new dialog class for the dialog template you have just created. Give the new dialog class the name CPrinterStatDlg. Select the CPrinterStatDlg object from the object list and the WM_INITDIALOG message from the message list. Enter the following code into the OnInitDialog method of CPrinterStatDlg:

```
BOOL CPrinterStatDlg::OnInitDialog()
{
    CDialog::OnInitDialog();

    // Get the device context for the printer

    CDC *printer_dc = new CDC;
    CPrintDialog dlg( FALSE );
    if (!AfxGetApp()->GetPrinterDeviceDefaults(&dlg.m_pd))
    {
        return(FALSE);
    }

    HDC hdcPrint = dlg.CreatePrinterDC();

    printer_dc->Attach ( hdcPrint );

    // Next, get the physical page size for the printer

    POINT p;
    Escape(printer_dc->m_hDC, GETPHYSPAGESIZE, NULL, NULL, &p);

    // Now get the physical size for the printer

    int log_x = printer_dc->GetDeviceCaps(LOGPIXELSX);
    int log_y = printer_dc->GetDeviceCaps(LOGPIXELSY);

    // Get the real size

    int x_size = p.x / log_x;
    int y_size = p.y / log_y;

    // Set those static text fields

    char buffer[80];
    sprintf(buffer, "%d", x_size);
    GetDlgItem(ID_HORZ_PAGE_SIZE)->SetWindowText(buffer);
```

```
    sprintf(buffer, "%d", y_size);
    GetDlgItem(ID_VERT_PAGE_SIZE)->SetWindowText(buffer);

    // Get the default printer from Win.INI

    char temp[256];
    GetProfileString("windows", "device", ",,,", temp, 256);

    char *printer_name, *driver_name, *port_name;

    printer_name = strtok(temp,(const char *) ",");
    driver_name = strtok ((char *) NULL, (const char *) ", ");
    port_name = strtok ((char *) NULL, (const char *) ", ");

    // Get the orientation

    int orientation = DeviceCapabilities( printer_name, port_name,
                                 DC_ORIENTATION, NULL, NULL );

    // Set the static text field based on the return from the function

    switch ( orientation ) {
      case 0:
        GetDlgItem(ID_ORIENTATION)->SetWindowText ( "Portrait" );
      break;
      case 90:
        GetDlgItem(ID_ORIENTATION)->SetWindowText ( "90 degree Landscape" );
      break;
      case 270:
        GetDlgItem(ID_ORIENTATION)->SetWindowText ( "270 degree landscape" );
      break;
        default:
        GetDlgItem(ID_ORIENTATION)->SetWindowText ( "Unknown" );
      break;
    }

    // Free up the memory

    delete printer_dc;

    return TRUE;  // return TRUE  unless you set the focus to a
                  // control
}
```

7. Enter AppStudio and add a new menu to the IDR_CH102TYPE menu. Give the new menu the caption Dialog. Add a new menu item to the Dialog menu with the caption Printer Statistics. Give the new menu item the identifier ID_PRINT_STATISTICS.

8. Enter ClassWizard and select the CCh102App object from the drop-down combo box. Select the ID_PRINTER_STATISTICS object from the object list and the COMMAND message from the message list. Click on the Add Function button and give the new function the name OnPrinterStatistics. Enter the following code into the OnPrinterStatistics method of CCh102App:

```
void CCh102App::OnPrintStatistics()
{
    CPrinterStatDlg dlg;
    dlg.DoModal();
}
```

9. Add the following line to the top of the CH102.CPP source file:

```
#include "printers.h"
```

10. Compile and run the application.

How It Works

The printer device context can return many interesting and informative pieces of data about the current printer settings. In this case, what we are interested in is the logical and physical mapping of the printer as well as the orientation setting. The first step in this process is to obtain a handle to a device context for the printer. This is done by using the common dialog box class, CPrintDialog, to create a new printer device context using the current settings for the printer.

Once a device context is created, the program then uses that DC to get the physical size of the printer page. This is done via the Escape function of the Windows API. The printer's horizontal and vertical resolutions are obtained by calling the GetDeviceCaps method of the printer DC. By dividing the physical page resolution by the logical page size for the printer, we obtain the size of the printed page in inches.

The orientation is obtained by calling the Escape Windows API function with the GETSETPRINTORIENT parameter. The returned value will normally be either 1 for portrait (normal print layout) or 2 for landscape (turned sideways print) mode.

Once all of the data is obtained, it is stored in the static text fields allocated for that purpose, using the SetWindowText API function.

COMPLEXITY
EASY

10.3 How do I... Use the common printer dialog boxes?

Problem

I would like to be able to use the common dialog boxes for printers in my application, but with some customization in order to be able to use them. The printer setup dialog is fine, but the print dialog itself has some options I do not support in my application. Also, in some cases, I would like to allow certain options, such as the Selection radio button for selecting a range of pages, but other times, I do not want such a selection (it doesn't make sense in all cases).

How can I use the Windows API to customize the common print dialog box? Is it necessary to implement all of this functionality myself to get pieces of it to work?

Technique

The common dialog boxes would hardly be useful if they required you to adhere to exactly the same standards for each and every program. Many programs, such as yours, either do not need the functionality of the entire dialog or require that certain functions be disabled for certain cases. The Windows 95 common dialog boxes fit all of these criteria. The common printer dialog box can be customized by simply passing a set of flags to the creation routine for the dialog.

In this How-To, we will examine the configurable portions of the common printer dialog and how you can set these options in your own application. We will show you a dialog that lists all of the configurable options and allows you to immediately view the results of various selections in that option set.

Steps

Open and run the Visual C++ application CH103.MAK from the CHAPT10\SAMPLES\CH103 directory on the CD that comes with this book. Select the Dialog menu and the Printer Dialog Options menu item from that menu. You will see a dialog similar to the one shown in Figure 10-3. Select (click on) the check boxes for Hide Print To File, Disable Page Numbers, and Disable Selection. Click on the Show Dialog button. You will see the dialog displayed in Figure 10-4.

To duplicate the functionality of this example, follow this procedure:

1. Create a new project in Visual C++ using AppWizard. Give the new project the name CH103.MAK.

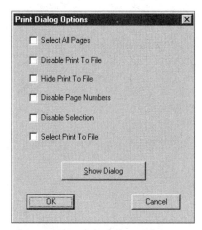

Figure 10-3 Dialog showing options to configure the common printer dialog box

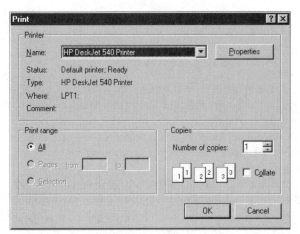

Figure 10-4 Common printer dialog reflecting the options selected in the Print Dialog Options dialog

2. Enter AppStudio and create a new dialog template. Add six check boxes to the dialog, aligned vertically in the center of the dialog. Give the check boxes the following captions: Select All Pages, Disable Print To File, Hide Print To File, Disable Page Numbers, Disable Selection, and Select Print To File, respectively.

3. Add a new command button to the dialog. Give the button the caption &Show Dialog.

4. Move the OK and Cancel buttons to the bottom of the dialog and give the dialog the caption Print Dialog Options.

5. Select ClassWizard and generate a new dialog class for the dialog template you have just finished creating. Give the new dialog class the name CPrintDlgOptions.

6. In ClassWizard, select the CPrintDlgOptions class from the drop-down combo box. Select the IDC_BUTTON1 object from the object list and the BN_CLICKED message from the message list. Click on the Add Function button and name the new function OnShowDialog. Enter the following code into the OnShowDialog method of CPrintDlgOptions:

```
void CPrintDlgOptions::OnShowDialog()
{
    // Get the options from the checkboxes.

    DWORD options = 0;

    // First, check the all pages

    CButton *check = (CButton *)GetDlgItem(IDC_CHECK1);
    if ( check->GetCheck() )
        options |= PD_ALLPAGES;
```

```
      // Check the print to file item

      check = (CButton *)GetDlgItem(IDC_CHECK3);
      if ( check->GetCheck() == 0 )
         options |= PD_DISABLEPRINTTOFILE;

      // The Hide Print To File Item

      check = (CButton *)GetDlgItem(IDC_CHECK4);
      if ( check->GetCheck() )
         options |= PD_HIDEPRINTTOFILE;

      // Disable Page Numbers

      check = (CButton *)GetDlgItem(IDC_CHECK5);
      if ( check->GetCheck() )
         options |= PD_NOPAGENUMS;

      // Disable selection

      check = (CButton *)GetDlgItem(IDC_CHECK6);
      if ( check->GetCheck() )
         options |= PD_NOSELECTION;

      // Select Print to File

      check = (CButton *)GetDlgItem(IDC_CHECK7);
      if ( check->GetCheck() )
         options |= PD_PRINTTOFILE;

      CPrintDialog dlg( FALSE, options, this );
      dlg.DoModal();
}
```

7. Enter AppStudio and select the menu resource list. Select the IDR_CH103TYPE
menu and add a new main menu entry with the caption Dialog. To the Dialog
menu add a new menu item with the caption Printer Dialog Options and the
identifier ID_PRINT_OPTIONS. Save the menu resource and the resource file.

8. Enter ClassWizard and select the CCh103App object from the drop-down
combo box. Select the ID_PRINT_OPTIONS object from the object list and
the COMMAND message from the message list. Click on the Add Function
button and give the new function the name OnPrinterOptions. Enter the following code into the OnPrinterOptions method of CCh103App:

```
void CCh103App::OnPrintOptions()
{
   CPrintDlgOptions dlg;
   dlg.DoModal();
}
```

9. Add the following line to the top of the CH103.CPP source file:

```
#include "printdlg.h"
```

10. Compile and run the application.

How It Works

The common printer dialog box accepts a flags parameter that contains a set of configurable options encoded as bits in the parameter to indicate which options the programmer would like to appear on the final output dialog.

By checking the check boxes in the dialog, the user indicates which of the common printer dialog options he or she would like to see appear in the final dialog. Note that some of the options are mutually exclusive. For example, it makes little sense to select the Select Print To File option as well as the Hide Print To File option. Although this is contradictory, the common printer dialog will accept it, selecting a hidden check box on the dialog.

Comments

Since this is a quite common dialog to need and even more common to customize, you can also create such a dialog in Delphi and Visual Basic. Here is how you go about it. First, the Delphi example:

1. Create a new project in Delphi and give it the name PRNTDLG.DPR. Add a new common dialog box for the printer to the form for the project. In addition to the common dialog, add four check boxes to the form.

2. Give the check boxes the following captions: Disable Print To File, Hide Print To File, Disable Page Numbers, Disable Selection.

3. Add two new buttons to the form, Show Dialog and Close. Double-click on the Show Dialog button and add the following code to the TForm1.Button1Click method of the form:

```
procedure TForm1.Button1Click(Sender: TObject);
begin

   if ( CheckBox2.Checked ) then
      begin
         PrintDialog1.Options := PrintDialog1.Options + [poPrintToFile];
         PrintDialog1.PrintToFile := True;
      end;
   if ( CheckBox3.Checked ) then
      PrintDialog1.Options := PrintDialog1.Options + [poDisablePrintToFile];
   if ( CheckBox4.Checked ) then
      PrintDialog1.Options := PrintDialog1.Options - [poPageNums];
   if ( CheckBox5.Checked ) then
      PrintDialog1.Options := PrintDialog1.Options - [poSelection];
PrintDialog1.Execute;
end;
```

4. Double-click on the Close button and add the following code to the TForm1.Button2Click method:

```
procedure TForm1.Button2Click(Sender: TObject);
begin
   Close;
end;
```

5. Compile and run the application.

Now, here is how you would do it in Visual Basic:

1. Create a new project in Visual Basic. Give the new project the name PRTCOM.MAK. Create a new form with the name PRTCOM.FRM.

2. Add new check boxes to the form with the captions Enable Print All Pages, Disable Print To File, Hide Print To File, Enable Page Numbers, Disable Selection, and Set Print To File.

3. Add a command button to the form with the caption Show Dialog. Double-click on the Show Dialog button and add the following code to the Command1_Click function:

```
Private Sub Command1_Click()
    If Check1.Value Then
        CMDialog1.Flags = CMDialog1.Flags Or PD_ALLPAGES
    Else
        CMDialog1.Flags = CMDialog1.Flags And Not PD_ALLPAGES
    End If
    If Check3.Value Then
        CMDialog1.Flags = CMDialog1.Flags Or PD_DISABLEPRINTTOFILE
    Else
        CMDialog1.Flags = CMDialog1.Flags And Not PD_DISABLEPRINTTOFILE
    End If
    If Check4.Value Then
        CMDialog1.Flags = CMDialog1.Flags Or PD_HIDEPRINTTOFILE
    Else
        CMDialog1.Flags = CMDialog1.Flags And Not PD_HIDEPRINTTOFILE
    End If
    If Check5.Value Then
        CMDialog1.Flags = CMDialog1.Flags Or PD_NOPAGENUMS
    Else
        CMDialog1.Flags = CMDialog1.Flags And Not PD_NOPAGENUMS
    End If
    If Check6.Value Then
        CMDialog1.Flags = CMDialog1.Flags Or PD_NOSELECTION
    Else
        CMDialog1.Flags = CMDialog1.Flags And Not PD_NOSELECTION
    End If
    CMDialog1.ShowPrinter
End Sub
```

4. Add the following to the General section of the form:

```
Attribute VB_Name = "Form1"
Attribute VB_Creatable = False
Attribute VB_Exposed = False
Const PD_ALLPAGES = &H0&
Const PD_SELECTION = &H1&
Const PD_PAGENUMS = &H2&
Const PD_NOSELECTION = &H4&
Const PD_NOPAGENUMS = &H8&
Const PD_COLLATE = &H10&
Const PD_PRINTTOFILE = &H20&
Const PD_PRINTSETUP = &H40&
Const PD_NOWARNING = &H80&
Const PD_RETURNDC = &H100&
```

continued on next page

continued from previous page

```
Const PD_RETURNIC = &H200&
Const PD_RETURNDEFAULT = &H400&
Const PD_SHOWHELP = &H800&
Const PD_USEDEVMODECOPIES = &H40000
Const PD_DISABLEPRINTTOFILE = &H80000
Const PD_HIDEPRINTTOFILE = &H100000
```

5. Compile and run the application.

COMPLEXITY
EASY

10.4 How do I...
Print to a file?

Problem

In my application, I am often printing reports from a database to an output device. Under normal circumstances, this output device is the printer. On occasion, however, the output device is for a user of a laptop, who would like a permanent record of his or her report but has no printer to output the data onto. If the user simply uses the Print To File option, my program doesn't recognize that the output goes elsewhere, and Windows displays a Printer Not Ready message (or other error).

How can I print to a file when the user requests it?

Technique

The process of printing to a file is rather subjective but is quite easy to implement. The basic strategy is that you create a common printer dialog box, allow the user to enter information into it, and check the return flags. If the print to file flag is set, ask the user for an output file name and then do whatever work is necessary to create a disk-based printout rather than a printer-based printout.

In this How-To, we will perform this process. The user will have a common print dialog box displayed and will be given the opportunity to check the Print To File check box in the dialog. If the check box is checked on output, the program will then display a common File Save As dialog box. Once the user has entered a file name to save the report to, the file will be opened and a set of records written to the file. The file will then be closed and the process will terminate.

The important features of this code include common dialog boxes for printing and saving files, checking the return flags from the printer common dialog, and using the result of the common File Save As dialog to create a new file.

Steps

Open and run the Visual C++ application CH104.MAK from the CHAPT10\SAM-PLES\CH104 directory on the CD that comes with this book. Select the File menu and

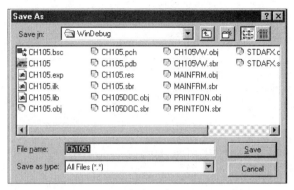

Figure 10-5 Common dialog for saving a file

the Print menu item from that menu. The printer common dialog box will be displayed. Click on the Print To File check box and then select the OK button. A Save As common dialog will be displayed, as shown in Figure 10-5. Enter a file name to save the report under and click OK. The report will then be written to the disk-based file you specified.

To duplicate the functionality of this example, follow this procedure:

1. Create a new project in Visual C++ using AppWizard. Give the new project the name CH104.MAK.

2. Enter ClassWizard and select the view object for this project, CCh104View, from the drop-down combo box. Click on the ID_FILE_PRINT object in the object list and the COMMAND message in the message list. Click on the Add Function button.

3. Accept the name OnFilePrint for the name of the new function and add the following code to the OnFilePrint method of CCh104View:

```
void CCh104View::OnFilePrint()
{
    // Put up a print dialog

    CPrintDialog dlg(FALSE, PD_ALLPAGES | PD_USEDEVMODECOPIES  );

    if ( dlg.DoModal() == IDOK ) {

        // See if they wanted to print to file or print to printer

        if ( dlg.m_pd.Flags & PD_PRINTTOFILE ) {

            // Get the output file here.

            CFileDialog fdlg(FALSE);

            if ( fdlg.DoModal() == FALSE )
                return;
```

continued on next page

continued from previous page

```
// Open the output file here

CString outFile = fdlg.GetPathName();

FILE *fp = fopen ( outFile, "w" );
if ( fp == (FILE *)NULL ) {
    MessageBox("Unable to create/open output file", "Error", MB_OK );
    return;
}

for ( int i=0; i<10; ++i ) {
    fprintf(fp, "Record %d Line 1\n", i);
    fprintf(fp, "Record %d Line 2\n", i);
    fprintf(fp, "Record %d Line 3\n\n", i);
}

fclose(fp);
    }
  }
}
```

4. Compile and run the application.

How It Works

When the printer common dialog box is created, the Flags field is checked to see if the Print To File option should be included in the dialog. In this case, we have told the common dialog to include the Print To File option by not specifying the PD_HIDEPRINTTOFILE flag in the option flags. See How-To 10.3 for more on setting up the common dialog.

Once the user has clicked on the OK button for the printer common dialog, the Flags field for the dialog is reset to the new settings that the user has requested. If the user selected the Print To File option, the PD_PRINTTOFILE flag will be set in the Flags field. At this point, the program knows that the user would like to print the output to a disk-based file, rather than the printer itself.

Once you determine that the Print To File check box was selected, it is necessary to get an output file name from the user in which to store your output. This is accomplished using the common file dialog. By specifying FALSE as the first argument to the common file dialog, this dialog becomes a Save As dialog. If we had specified TRUE for this argument, the common dialog would have looked like a File Open common dialog. This is similar to the print common dialog, which can appear as either a Print Dialog (argument is FALSE) or a Print Setup dialog (argument is TRUE).

Once the user enters a file name into the common file dialog and selects the OK button, the program retrieves the file name from the dialog with its complete path and attempts to create or open and truncate that file. If this is not possible, an error message is displayed. If it was possible, the program loops through the "records" and outputs the data to the file.

COMPLEXITY
MODERATE

10.5   How do I...
Determine available printer
fonts?

Problem

I would like to be able to find out which fonts are available for the printer before I send any output to the printer. This is necessary as I do not wish my output to look similar to what I intended, but rather exactly what I intended. Only by getting the output printer fonts can I exactly match the screen display to what it will look like on the printer.

How can I use the power of the Windows 95 API functions to obtain a list of the available printer fonts for the current default printer?

Technique

One of the nicest things you can do for a user today is to make sure that the fonts you are using in your program are available on his or her computer. This ensures that the printouts you create for the user are readable. There are few things quite as annoying as looking at a screen full of data that is perfectly readable and having that represented on the printer as a series of squiggly lines that are incomprehensible.

In this How-To, we examine the process necessary to find all of the available fonts for a given printer. To accomplish this, we make use of the Windows API function EnumFontFamilies, along with the MakeProcInstance, FreeProcInstance, and common printer dialog functions.

Steps

Open and run the Visual C++ application CH105.MAK from the CHAPT10\SAMPLES\CH105 directory on the CD that comes with this book. Select the Dialog menu and the List Printer Fonts menu item from that menu. You will see a dialog similar to the one shown in Figure 10-6, showing the available printer fonts for the current printer.

To duplicate the functionality of this example, follow this procedure:

1. Create a new project in Visual C++ using AppWizard. Give the new project the name CH105.MAK.

2. Enter AppStudio and create a new dialog template. Move the OK and Cancel buttons to the bottom of the dialog. Add a list box to the dialog and save the dialog template.

3. Select ClassWizard and generate a new dialog class for the dialog template you have just finished creating. Give the new dialog class the name CPrintFontDlg.

4. Select the CPrinterFontDlg from the drop-down combo box in ClassWizard, and then select the CPrinterFontDlg object from the object list. Select the

Figure 10-6 Dialog showing available printer fonts

WM_INITDIALOG message and click on the Add Function button. Add the following code to the OnInitDialog method of CPrinterFontDlg:

```
BOOL CPrintFontDlg::OnInitDialog()
{
    CDialog::OnInitDialog();

    // Get the device context for the printer

    CDC *printer_dc = new CDC;
    CPrintDialog dlg( FALSE );
    if (!AfxGetApp()->GetPrinterDeviceDefaults(&dlg.m_pd))
    {
        return(FALSE);
    }
    HDC hdcPrint = dlg.CreatePrinterDC();

    printer_dc->Attach ( hdcPrint );

    CListBox *list = (CListBox *)GetDlgItem(IDC_LIST1);


    FARPROC EnumFontProc = MakeProcInstance ( (FARPROC)EnumFontsFunc,
                                            AfxGetInstanceHandle() );

    ::EnumFontFamilies( printer_dc->m_hDC, NULL ,
                    (OLDFONTENUMPROC)EnumFontProc, (LPARAM)list);

    FreeProcInstance ( EnumFontProc );
```

```
    return TRUE;  // return TRUE  unless you set the focus to a control
}
```

5. Add the following code to the PRINTFON.CPP source file above the
OnInitDialog method:

```
int CALLBACK EnumFontsFunc(LOGFONT FAR *lplf, NEWTEXTMETRIC FAR *lpntm,
int FontType, LPARAM lpData)
{
    CListBox *list = (CListBox *)lpData;

    list->AddString ( lplf->lfFaceName );
    return 1;
}
```

6. Enter AppStudio and select the menu resource list. Select the IDR_CH105TYPE
menu and add a new main menu entry with the caption Dialog. To the Dialog
menu add a new menu item with the caption List Printer Fonts and the identifier ID_LIST_FONTS. Save the menu resource and the resource file.

7. Enter ClassWizard and select the CCh105App object from the drop-down
combo box. Select the ID_LIST_FONTS object from the object list and the
COMMAND message from the message list. Click on the Add Function button and give the new function the name OnListFonts. Enter the following
code into the OnListFonts method of CCh105App:

```
void CCh105App::OnListFonts()
{
    CPrintFontDlg dlg;
    dlg.DoModal();
}
```

8. Add the following line to the top of the CH105.CPP source file:

```
#include "printfon.h"
```

9. Compile and run the application.

How It Works

The EnumFontFamilies function of the Windows 95 API accepts a callback function,
which will be called once for each family of fonts supported by the output device context. In order to make sure that we are only getting fonts for the printer, we create a
device context for the printer specifically and pass that device context to the
EnumFontFamilies function. This will then call our callback function with each of the
font families, and the callback function will then store the names of these font families in the output list box.

In order to create a printer device context, we must first get the information about
the default printer. In the MFC, this is accomplished by calling the GetPrinterDeviceDefaults
method of the application object. You could also have obtained information on all of
the printer devices by getting the "devices" information out of the WIN.INI file. This
would allow you to check fonts for all installed printers.

Once the printer information is obtained, the device context is created and attached to the printer DC object. The callback function is created using the API function MakeProcInstance and cast to the appropriate type for the EnumFontFamilies function. The EnumFontFamilies function allows you to pass application-specific data to the callback function in the last parameter of the function. In our case, we pass a pointer to the list box in our dialog so that the callback function knows where to store the font names.

It is important to remember to return a non-zero value from your EnumFont callback function. Returning 0 from this function terminates the enumeration and will leave you with only a single font in the list box.

Comments

This is only the first step in the process of showing the user what will be represented on the output device. The next stage would be to make sure that only fonts that can be printed would be displayed on the screen as well.

COMPLEXITY
DIFFICULT

10.6   How do I...
Determine the print queue
status?

Problem

I would like to be able to display for users the status of print jobs in various printer queues around their system. I cannot seem to find a way to find out which printers are currently available and what jobs are running on those printers.

How can I use the Windows API functions to find out the printers and their jobs statuses?

Technique

With the release of Windows NT and then again with Windows 95, a whole new set of API functions was added specifically for dealing with printers and their status queues. In this How-To, we will examine the EnumPrinters and EnumJobs API functions, which will give you the information you need to determine the status of print jobs.

The EnumPrinters function, added with Windows 95, will list the available running printers with their names and identifiers. This function can be used to list the printers to which the user has access, whether they are running locally or on a network to which the user has access. In this example, we only consider the local printer case.

The EnumJobs function, also added with the new Windows 95 API set, will list the jobs running on a specified printer. In order to use the EnumJobs function, you must have a handle to a printer for which we use yet another API function, OpenPrinter.

Note that because this API functionality is only available under Windows 95 and Windows NT, you must use Visual C++ 2.1 (or greater) to compile this project.

Steps

Open and run the Visual C++ 2.1 application CH106.MAK from the CHAPT10\SAMPLES\CH106 directory on the CD that comes with this book. Select the Dialog menu and the Printer Jobs menu item. You will see a dialog showing the available printers. Select one of the printers in the first list box, and a list of jobs for that printer will be displayed in the second list box. Figure 10-7 shows an example printer selected with a single print job running.

To duplicate the functionality of this example, follow this procedure:

1. Create a new project in Visual C++ 2.x using AppWizard. Give the new project the name CH106.MAK.

2. Enter AppStudio and create a new dialog template. Move the OK and Cancel buttons to the bottom of the dialog. Add two list boxes to the dialog. Add two static text fields above the list boxes with the captions Available Printers and Jobs: and save the dialog template.

3. Select ClassWizard and generate a new dialog class for the dialog template you have just finished creating. Give the new dialog class the name CPrintQDlg.

4. Select the CPrintQDlg from the drop-down combo box in ClassWizard, and then select the CPrintQDlg object from the object list. Select the WM_INITDIALOG

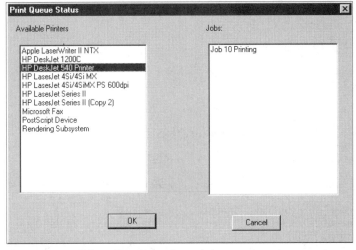

Figure 10-7 Dialog showing printer job queue and status

message and click on the Add Function button. Add the following code to the
OnInitDialog method of CPrintQDlg:

```
BOOL CPrintQDlg::OnInitDialog()
{
        CDialog::OnInitDialog();

        int size = 4096;
        unsigned long sizeNeeded = 0;
        unsigned long numPrinters;
        PPRINTER_INFO_1 pPrinters;

        pPrinters = (PPRINTER_INFO_1)LocalAlloc((LMEM_FIXED |
                    LMEM_ZEROINIT), size );

    int ret = EnumPrinters( PRINTER_ENUM_LOCAL, NULL, 1,
                            (LPBYTE)pPrinters, size, &sizeNeeded,
                            &numPrinters);

        CListBox *list = (CListBox *)GetDlgItem(IDC_LIST1);

        for ( int i=0; i<(int)numPrinters; ++i ) {
           list->AddString ( pPrinters[i].pName );
        }

        LocalFree ( pPrinters );

        return TRUE; // return TRUE unless you set the focus to a control
                     // EXCEPTION: OCX Property Pages should return FALSE
}
```

5. Select the CPrintQDlg from the drop-down combo box in ClassWizard. Select
the IDC_LIST1 object from the object list and the LBN_SELCHANGE message
from the message list. Click on the Add Function button and give the new
function the name OnSelectPrinter. Add the following code to the
OnSelectPrinter method of CPrintQDlg:

```
void CPrintQDlg::OnSelectPrinter()
{
    HANDLE handle;
    JOB_INFO_1 jobs[10];

    // Get the string from the list box

    CListBox *list = (CListBox *)GetDlgItem(IDC_LIST1);
    char buffer[256];
    list->GetText ( list->GetCurSel(), buffer );

    // First, open the printer to get a handle to it

    if ( !OpenPrinter(buffer, &handle, NULL ) ) {
        MessageBox ( "Could not open printer", "Error", MB_OK );
            return;
    }
```

```
// Enumerate the jobs

DWORD size = sizeof(jobs);
DWORD numBytes = 0;
DWORD numEntries = 0;

int ret = EnumJobs( handle, 0, 10, 1, (LPBYTE)jobs, size,
                    &numBytes, &numEntries );

// Add the results to the jobs list

CListBox *list2 = (CListBox *)GetDlgItem(IDC_LIST2);

for ( int i=0; i<(int)numEntries; ++i ) {
    char buffer[80];
        sprintf(buffer, "Job %ld", jobs[i].JobId );
        if ( jobs[i].pStatus != NULL )
            strcat ( buffer, jobs[i].pStatus );
    else {
        switch ( jobs[i].Status ) {
          case JOB_STATUS_PAUSED:
              strcat ( buffer, " Paused");
                break;
          case JOB_STATUS_PRINTED:
              strcat ( buffer, " Printed");
                break;
          case JOB_STATUS_PRINTING:
              strcat ( buffer, " Printing");
                break;
          case JOB_STATUS_SPOOLING:
              strcat ( buffer, " Spooling");
                break;
        }
    }
    list2->AddString ( buffer );
  }
}
```

6. Enter AppStudio and select the menu resource list. Select the IDR_CH106TYPE menu and add a new main menu entry with the caption Dialog. To the Dialog menu add a new menu item with the caption Printer Jobs and the identifier ID_PRINTER_JOBS. Save the menu resource and the resource file.

7. Enter ClassWizard and select the CCh106App object from the drop-down combo box. Select the ID_PRINTER_JOBS object from the object list and the COMMAND message from the message list. Click on the Add Function button and give the new function the name OnPrinterJobs. Enter the following code into the OnPrinterJobs method of CCh106App:

```
void CCh106App::OnPrinterJobs()
{
    CPrintQDlg dlg;
    dlg.DoModal();
}
```

8. Add the following line to the top of the CH106.CPP source file:

```
#include "printqdl.h"
```

9. Compile and run the application.

How It Works

The EnumPrinters function takes quite a few parameters. The important ones, however, are the first and fourth arguments to the function. The first argument specifies which printers you are interested in looking at. In this case, we only request local printers that are physically attached to this computer. An alternate parameter would specify network printers, which means all printers attached to any network that this machine knows about.

The fourth parameter to EnumPrinters is an allocated buffer of structures that will return information about the printers. If this buffer is not allocated with enough entries, the EnumPrinters function will fail and the API function GetLastError will return not enough room. In this case, the sizeNeeded parameter will hold the amount of space needed to return all of the information.

Once the printer list is set, the memory is cleared and the data is stored in the list box in the dialog. The user can then select a printer from the list, which will invoke the OnSelectPrinter method. This method uses the OpenPrinter API function to retrieve a handle to the selected printer. If your program does not have permission to access this printer, the function will fail. If it succeeds, the printer handle is passed to the EnumJobs API function, which returns a block of printer jobs up to the number specified in the size parameter. This function can return either of two types of structures. The simpler structure is the JOB_INFO_1 type, while a more detailed and complex structure is the JOB_INFO_2 type. The type of structure requested is passed into the function as the fourth parameter.

Once the EnumJobs function returns successfully, the printer job IDs are listed in the list box along with the status of those jobs. If no status is found, it is left blank. One note concerning the EnumJobs function: Some documentation lists the second parameter, the starting job number, as one based. This is untrue. The jobs are zero-based, and you will "lose" a job from the queue if you pass a value greater than 0 in this second parameter.

CHAPTER 11

COMMUNICATING WITH OTHER APPLICATIONS

COMMUNICATING
WITH OTHER
APPLICATIONS

How do I...

One of the most useful and overlooked aspects of the original Windows operating system was the ability not only to run multiple programs at the same time but to communicate between those programs. The Windows Clipboard was the original way for programs to communicate. Later, this was replaced by the ability to use dynamic data exchange (DDE) between programs. In Windows 3.1, the developers at Microsoft brought us yet a newer and better way to have multiple programs communicate—Object Linking and Embedding (OLE).

In this chapter, we examine the various methods you can use to get information from one program to another. We look at dragging and dropping from the File Manager to your program, as well as from your program to other programs. We will look at the early kind of data exchange, DDE, from both the client and server ends. Finally, we will examine the concept of object embedding, as used in OLE applications.

In today's world, few Windows programs truly "stand alone." They require interaction with other programs, devices, and capabilities. When you send a file to the print spooler, or use a device driver to access a scanner, or use OLE to embed a Microsoft Excel spreadsheet in your application, you are communicating. Communication between applications will become a required part of Windows applications. It behooves you then, as a developer of cutting-edge applications, to learn about this important facet of Windows 95.

11.1   Support Drag and Drop into My Application

In this How-To, you will learn how you can accept file names that are dragged and dropped from the File Manager into your application. You will find out how to accept these file names while your application is running, and how you can tap into this hidden resource to run your applications, given a file name from File Manager or Windows Explorer.

11.2   Support Drag and Drop from My Application

In this How-To, you will learn how you can drag and drop file names into other applications and run them, or drag an existing file into a running application in order to open it. You will learn how to find out if a program instance supports drag-and-drop and how to send drag-and-drop messages to other running applications.

11.3   Check the Contents of the Clipboard

When the user selects Paste from your Edit menu, what really happens in your application? Did you know that the clipboard supports multiple kinds of data to be stored on it? This How-To shows you how you can examine the contents of the clipboard and find out if there is any data of the type you would like to paste into your application.

11.4   Use Cut, Copy, and Paste to and from the Clipboard

Once the user has selected data in your application, he or she may want to cut, copy, or paste it. In this How-To, we examine how you can use the clipboard to support all of these operations in your own applications through simple use of the Windows 95 API.

11.5   Write a Dynamic Data Exchange Client

It is often nice to be able to use the functionality of other applications in your own. Microsoft Word, for example, has several abilities that are extremely nice to use but very difficult to implement. Why not leverage the Word functionality in your own application? In this How-To, we look at how you can implement DDE client services to ask other applications to perform tasks for you.

11.6   Write a Dynamic Data Exchange Server

Wouldn't it be nice if you could have a single engine running on the Windows desktop and "hang" multiple applications on that engine in order to perform related tasks? Database transactions, print services, data lookups, and hardware interfaces can all be implemented as a DDE server device that allows the programs running to take advantage of a single instance of an "engine" to perform tasks. In this How-To, we look at the requirements for a basic DDE server and how to put those requirements into your application.

11.7   Support the System Topic in Dynamic Data Exchange

The System topic in DDE is quite useful for client programs to inquire of a DDE server as to what capabilities are present in that server. You can find out what services a server implements as well as what other topics are available. In this How-To, we look at the requirements for the System topic in DDE and how you can implement one in your application.

11.8   Make Files Object Linking and Embedding (OLE) Compatible

If you want your files to be usable in an OLE environment, they need to conform to the OLE specifications for compound documents. In this How-To, we examine what is necessary to use compound documents and how you can use this functionality in your own application.

11.9   Create an OLE Server Object

In this How-To, we take on the difficult task of writing an OLE server object. This object can be embedded in other applications and yet perform the tasks for your own application. We will examine, step by step, how you create an OLE server and what is necessary to get it all to work together in Windows 95.

Table 11-1 lists the Windows 95 API functions used in this chapter.

DragAcceptFiles	DragQueryFile	SetCapture
GetAsyncKeyState	ReleaseCapture	MessageBox
SendMessage	ScreenToClient	GlobalFree

continued on next page

continued from previous page

PostMessage	GlobalAlloc	GlobalLock
GlobalUnlock	GlobalReAlloc	OpenClipboard
IsClipboardFormatAvailable	GetClipboardData	MakeProcInstance
DdeInitialize	DdeCreateStringHandle	DdeConnect
DdeGetLastError	DdeDisconnect	DdeFreeStringHandle
DdeUninitialize	DdeClientTransaction	DdeGetData
DdeCmpStringHandles	DdeCreateDataHandle	DdeNameService
DdePostAdvise	StgOpenStorage	StgCreateDocfile

Table 11-1 Windows 95 API functions used in Chapter 11

COMPLEXITY
MODERATE

11.1 How do I... Support drag-and-drop into my application?

Problem

I would like to be able to accept file names that have been dragged and dropped from other applications, such as Windows Explorer or File Manager (in Windows 3.x). What I would like to do is accept a list of file names and then process each one in turn. The MFC only seems to have a function for turning on accepting of files but no function to process them. How can I use the power of the Windows 95 API to get the file names that the user has "dropped" on my window?

Technique

The power of dragging and dropping files has proved to be quite successful in both Windows 3.x and Windows 95—so successful, in fact, that the whole basis for file manipulation in Windows 95 has turned toward drag-and-drop.

To put the file drag-and-drop into your application so that your windows can accept dropped files is quite easy once you understand how the process works. The MFC seems to have only one function for the DragAcceptFiles portion of the process, which simply notifies Windows that this window will accept files dropped onto it.

The second part of the process is to handle the resulting Windows message, WM_DROPFILES, which indicates that Windows is trying to drop a file onto your window. This How-To will show you how you can use this message in your own windows as well.

Steps

Open and run the Visual C++ application CH1101.MAK from the CHAPT11\SAM-PLES\CH1101 directory on the CD that comes with this book. Start the program and select the second document template displayed in the list box at startup. You will see a view with a blank list box embedded in it. Next, open Windows Explorer and select a file from the directory displayed. Drag the file into your window by selecting it and holding the left mouse button down. With the left mouse button down, move the mouse cursor so that it is somewhere within the bounds of the view window displayed. Release the left mouse button, and you will see the file name displayed in the list box in the view, as shown in Figure 11-1.

To reproduce this functionality in your own application, perform the following steps:

1. Create a new project in Visual C++ using AppWizard. Give this project the name CH1101.MAK. Go into the resource editor and create a new dialog. Set the following style bits for the new dialog: Not Visible, Child Window, No Border. Put a single list box in the dialog.

2. Select ClassWizard for the new dialog template. Generate a new dialog class for the dialog template and give it the name CDragView. Set the base class for the new class to be CFormView. Save the class and exit ClassWizard.

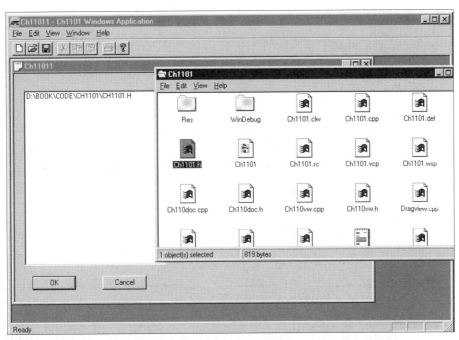

Figure 11-1 Drag-and-drop view with file dropped from Windows Explorer

3. Add a new function to the CDragView class called OnInitialUpdate. Enter the following code into the OnInitialUpdate method of CDragView:

```
void CDragView::OnInitialUpdate(void)
{
    CView::OnInitialUpdate();
    DragAcceptFiles();
}
```

4. Add a new entry in the message map for the CDragView class with the following syntax. Add only the line marked with bold print.

```
BEGIN_MESSAGE_MAP(CDragView, CFormView)
  //{{AFX_MSG_MAP(CDragView)
    ON_WM_DROPFILES()
    // NOTE - the ClassWizard will add and remove mapping macros here.
  //}}AFX_MSG_MAP
END_MESSAGE_MAP()
```

5. Next add the following method definition to the CDragView source file:

```
void CDragView::OnDropFiles(HDROP hDropInfo)
{
    char fileName[_MAX_PATH];

    // Assign the list box object

    CListBox *list = (CListBox *)GetDlgItem(IDC_LIST1);

    // First, determine how many files are dropped.

    UINT numFiles = DragQueryFile(hDropInfo, -1, NULL, 0);

    // Next, loop through and add the files to the listbox

    for ( UINT i=0; i<numFiles; ++i ) {

        // Get the file name

        DragQueryFile(hDropInfo, i, fileName, _MAX_PATH);

        // Store it in the list box

        list->AddString ( fileName );
    }

}
```

6. Add the following declarations to your header file for CDragView, DRAGVIEW.H. Again, add only the line marked with bold print.

```
protected:
  virtual void OnInitialUpdate(void);

  virtual ~CDragView();
  virtual void DoDataExchange(CDataExchange* pDX);  // DDX/DDV support
```

```
// Generated message map functions
//{{AFX_MSG(CDragView)
    afx_msg void OnDropFiles(HDROP hDropInfo);
```

7. Add the following lines to the application object, CCh1101App, InitInstance method. Add these lines immediately below the pDocTemplate creation in InitInstance:

```
pDocTemplate = new CMultiDocTemplate(
    IDR_CH1101TYPE,
    RUNTIME_CLASS(CCh1101Doc),
    RUNTIME_CLASS(CMDIChildWnd),        // standard MDI child frame
    RUNTIME_CLASS(CDragView));
  AddDocTemplate(pDocTemplate);
```

8. Finally, add the following line to the top of the CCh1101App source file, CH1101.CPP:

```
#include "dragview.h"
```

9. Compile and run the application.

How It Works

When you call the DragAcceptFiles method, Windows will mark your window with the WS_EX_ACCEPTFILES style bit. This bit indicates to Windows that when a file is dragged to your window and the mouse button released, a message should be sent to your window indicating this.

When the mouse button is released, the WM_DROPFILES message is sent to the window under which the mouse cursor is found. This message has a single parameter stored in the wParam element of the message structure. This parameter contains a handle to the drop information structure stored within Windows.

When you receive a WM_DROPFILES message with the drop structure, you can do several things. First, you can call the DragQueryFile function to find out how many files are stored in the structure. This is accomplished by passing a value of -1 for the index parameter in the function call.

Once you know how many files are stored in the structure, you can call the DragQueryFile function multiple times to extract each file name from the structure and deal with it as you choose. In this case, the file names are simply stored in the list box embedded in the view window.

That's really all there is to it!

Comments

This How-To could be the basis for a number of different applications, depending on how you choose to deal with the dropped file names. For example, an editor might use the dropped file names to load the files into the editor buffer and display it in an editor window. A filter might accept file names and use them to filter out certain user-defined words from the text.

This How-To is central to understanding all other drag-and-drop operations in Windows. It is critical that you understand the process involved before you can go further in working with drag-and-drop files in Windows 95.

COMPLEXITY

DIFFICULT

11.2   How do I...
Support drag-and-drop from my application?

Problem

I have read the previous How-To, explaining how I can drag and drop files from Windows Explorer into a window in my application. How can I drag things out of my application into other windows? I would like the ability to drag and drop not only into my windows, but between two windows in my application as well.

How does the Windows 95 API allow me to drag and drop files from a window?

Technique

How does Windows Explorer manage to drop the files into your application? The answer is that the Windows Explorer application sends a WM_DROPFILES message to your application when the user selects files and drags them over your application window.

This same technique can be used within your application to drag files from one window to another. Additionally, other programs that recognize the WM_DROPFILES message can be sent this same message to let the user drag files to those applications. This technique, which we will explore in more depth in this How-To, makes it possible to create "filters" of programs. Filters operate on a file and then allow the user to "chain" the results of that filter into other applications with a simple drag operation.

In this How-To, we examine the structure behind the WM_DROPFILES message and how you can create compatible instances of that structure.

Steps

Open and run the Visual C++ application CH1101.MAK from the CHAPT11\SAMPLES\CH1101 directory on the CD that comes with this book. Start the program and select the second document template displayed in the list box at startup. You will see a view with a blank list box embedded in it.

Next, open and run the Visual C++ application CH1102.MAK from the CHAPT11\SAMPLES\CH1102 directory on the CD that comes with this book. Select the File | New menu item or the New File icon in the toolbar. Select the second document template and click on the OK button. A view with a filled list box will be displayed.

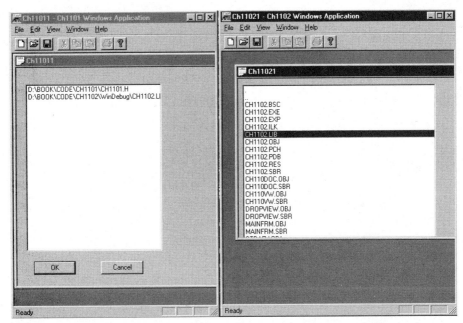

Figure 11-2 Drag-and-drop view with file dropped from a second view in the application

Select a file from the list box, and then move the mouse into the remainder of the view window (outside the list box). Press the left mouse button and move the mouse to the first (empty list) view. Release the left mouse button, and you will see the file name displayed in the list box in the view, as shown in Figure 11-2.

To reproduce this functionality in your own application, perform the following steps:

1. Create a new project in Visual C++ using AppWizard. Give this project the name CH1102.MAK. Go into the resource editor and create a new dialog. Set the following style bits for the new dialog: Not Visible, Child Window, No Border. Put a single list box in the dialog.

2. Select ClassWizard for the new dialog template. Generate a new dialog class for the dialog template and give it the name CDropView. Set the base class for the new class to be CFormView. Save the class and exit ClassWizard.

3. Add a new function to the CDropView class called OnInitialUpdate. Enter the following code into the OnInitialUpdate method of CDropView:

```
void CDropView::OnInitialUpdate(void)
{
    WIN32_FIND_DATA fileinfo;
    // Get the list box

    CListBox *list = (CListBox *)GetDlgItem(IDC_LIST1);
```

continued on next page

551

continued from previous page

```
        // Add the files in the current directory to it

        HANDLE hdl = FindFirstFile( "*.*", &fileinfo );
        int ret = TRUE;
        if( hdl == INVALID_HANDLE_VALUE )
           ret = FALSE;

        while ( ret ) {
           list->AddString ( fileinfo.cFileName );
           ret = FindNextFile( hdl, &fileinfo );
      }
    }
```

4. Next, enter ClassWizard and select the CDropView from the drop-down list. Select the CDropView object from the object list and the WM_LBUTTONDOWN message from the message list. Click on the Add Function button. Add the following code to the OnLButtonDown method of CDropView:

```
void CDropView::OnLButtonDown(UINT nFlags, CPoint point)
{
    char szDropPathName[200];
    BOOL fCallDefProc = FALSE, fInNonClientArea, fOkToDrop;
    HDROP hDrop, hDropT;
    LONG lResult = 0;
    POINT ptMousePos;
    HWND hWndSubject;

    // Capture mouse movements

    SetCapture();

    // Wait for mouse to be released

    do {
    } while (GetAsyncKeyState(VK_LBUTTON) & 0x8000);
    ReleaseCapture();

    // See if it is in a valid window

    ::GetCursorPos(&ptMousePos);
    hWndSubject = ::WindowFromPoint(ptMousePos);

    if (!IsWindow(hWndSubject))
{
        fOkToDrop = FALSE;
        }
    else
        {
        fOkToDrop = TRUE;
        }


    if (!fOkToDrop) {
        ::MessageBox(NULL, "Not a window", "Error", MB_OK );
        return;
    }
```

```
// Is the cursor in the window's non-client area?
fInNonClientArea = (HTCLIENT !=
        ::SendMessage(hWndSubject, WM_NCHITTEST, 0,
        (LONG) MAKELONG(ptMousePos.x, ptMousePos.y)));


// Create drop-file memory block and initialize it
::ScreenToClient(hWndSubject, &ptMousePos);
hDrop = DragCreateFiles(&ptMousePos, fInNonClientArea);
if (hDrop == NULL)
    {
    ::MessageBox(NULL,
                "Insufficient memory to drop file(s).",
                "Error", MB_OK);
    return;
    }


// Add the file by getting the text from the list box

CListBox *list = (CListBox *)GetDlgItem(IDC_LIST1);
int idx = list->GetCurSel();
list->GetText ( idx, szDropPathName );

// Get the current directory name

char buffer[_MAX_DIR];
char temp[_MAX_PATH];

_getcwd ( buffer, _MAX_DIR );

sprintf(temp, "%s\\%s", buffer, szDropPathName );

hDropT = DragAppendFile(hDrop, temp);

if (hDropT == NULL)  {
        ::MessageBox(NULL,
                    "Insufficient memory to drop file(s).",
                    "Error", MB_OK);
        GlobalFree(hDrop);
        hDrop = NULL;
        return;
 }
 else {
        hDrop = hDropT;
}

if (hDrop != NULL)
{
    // All pathnames appended successfully,
    // post the message
    // to the drop-file client window

    ::PostMessage(hWndSubject, WM_DROPFILES, (WPARAM)hDrop, 0L);
```

continued on next page

continued from previous page

```
            // Don't free the memory,
            // the Dropfile client will do it
        }


    CFormView::OnLButtonDown(nFlags, point);
}
```

5. Next, add the following block of code functions to the top of the
DROPVIEW.CPP file, just below the IMPLEMENT_DYNCREATE macro call:

```
typedef struct {
        WORD    wSize;                  // Size of data structure
        POINT   ptMousePos;            // Position of mouse cursor
        BOOL    fInNonClientArea;      // Was the mouse in the
                                       // window's non-client area
} DROPFILESTRUCT, FAR *LPDROPFILESTRUCT;


HDROP FAR DragCreateFiles (LPPOINT lpptMousePos,
                           BOOL fInNonClientArea)
{

    HGLOBAL hDrop;
    LPDROPFILESTRUCT lpDropFileStruct;

    // GMEM_SHARE must be specified because the block will
    // be passed to another application
    hDrop = GlobalAlloc(GMEM_SHARE | GMEM_MOVEABLE | GMEM_ZEROINIT,
                    sizeof(DROPFILESTRUCT) + 1);

    // If unsuccessful, return NULL
    if (hDrop == NULL) return((HDROP)hDrop);

    // Lock block and initialize the data members
    lpDropFileStruct = (LPDROPFILESTRUCT) GlobalLock(hDrop);
    lpDropFileStruct->wSize = sizeof(DROPFILESTRUCT);
    lpDropFileStruct->ptMousePos = *lpptMousePos;
    lpDropFileStruct->fInNonClientArea = fInNonClientArea;
    GlobalUnlock(hDrop);
    return((HDROP)hDrop);
}


HDROP FAR DragAppendFile (HGLOBAL hDrop, LPCSTR szPathname)
{
    LPDROPFILESTRUCT lpDropFileStruct;
    LPCSTR lpCrnt;
    WORD wSize;

    lpDropFileStruct = (LPDROPFILESTRUCT) GlobalLock(hDrop);

    // Point to first pathname in list
    lpCrnt = (LPSTR) lpDropFileStruct + lpDropFileStruct->wSize;
```

```
// Search for a pathname where first byte is a zero byte
while (*lpCrnt)          // While the 1st char of path is non-zero
    {
    while (*lpCrnt) lpCrnt++;    // Skip to zero byte
    lpCrnt++;
    }

// Calculate current size of block
wSize = (WORD) (lpCrnt - (LPSTR) lpDropFileStruct + 1);
GlobalUnlock(hDrop);

// Increase block size to accommodate new pathname being appended
hDrop = GlobalReAlloc(hDrop, wSize + lstrlen(szPathname) + 1,
                GMEM_MOVEABLE | GMEM_ZEROINIT | GMEM_SHARE);

// Return NULL if insufficient memory
if (hDrop == NULL) return((HDROP)hDrop);

lpDropFileStruct = (LPDROPFILESTRUCT) GlobalLock(hDrop);
// Append the pathname to the block
lstrcpy((LPSTR) lpDropFileStruct + wSize - 1, szPathname);
GlobalUnlock(hDrop);
return((HDROP)hDrop);   // Return the new handle to the block
}
```

6. Add the following declarations to your header file for CDropView, DROPVIEW.H.

```
protected:
  virtual void OnInitialUpdate(void);
```

7. Add the following lines to the application object, CCh1102App, InitInstance method. Add these lines immediately below the pDocTemplate creation in InitInstance:

```
pDocTemplate = new CMultiDocTemplate(

    IDR_CH1102TYPE,
    RUNTIME_CLASS(CCh1102Doc),
    RUNTIME_CLASS(CMDIChildWnd),      // standard MDI child frame
    RUNTIME_CLASS(CDropView));
  AddDocTemplate(pDocTemplate);
```

8. Finally, add the following line to the top of the CCh1102App source file, CH1102.CPP:

```
#include "dropview.h"
```

9. Compile and run the application.

How It Works

First, the user selects a file from the list box in the MFC window, or view. Then, the user presses the left mouse button somewhere in the client area of the view. This fires off the OnLButtonDown method of the view class.

The OnLButtonDown method simply waits until the user has released the left mouse button by setting the capture for the window (so that Windows will continue to send us mouse messages outside the range of the window borders) and waiting until the mouse button is no longer pressed (the GetAsyncKeyState function does this). Once the user releases the mouse button, the GetCursorPos function is called to retrieve the screen coordinates of the mouse cursor. Then the WindowFromPoint function is called to determine which window, if any, is under the mouse cursor at that point. If no window is found, the function simply returns.

Once a window is found, the DragCreateFiles function is called. This function sets up a global memory block with the GMEM_SHARED flag. This flag indicates that other applications can use this block of memory, as well as the operating system and the program that allocated it. The structure is then initialized with the window we found above and a flag indicating whether or not the mouse was in the non-client area of the window. This block of memory is then unlocked and the resultant handle returned to the calling function.

Next, the program finds the correct list entry and grabs the text for the list entry. This text is then passed to the DragAppendFile function, which does the work of adding this file to the list of files to be passed to the window on which we dropped the mouse cursor. Finally, the whole structure (via the handle) is sent to the window in the form of a PostMessage call. It is quite important to use PostMessage rather than SendMessage, as the latter will cause an infinite loop.

One final note: Do not free up the global memory once you have allocated it and sent it to the other application for dropping files. It is now the property of the other window and the operating system to deal with.

COMPLEXITY

EASY

11.3 How do I...
Check the contents of the clipboard?

Problem

I need to know if there is any text pasted to the clipboard in my application. I would like to enable and disable copy and paste functionality within a dialog based on whether there is any text to copy. For example, I would like the ability to enable a Copy button if there is text selected and disable it if there is no text selected.

Technique

The clipboard functions are an excellent inroad toward learning more about the way communication works in Windows. By using the clipboard functions, you can share information between two applications quite simply without the overhead of, say, DDE or OLE, or one of those other acronym things.

In this How-To, we explore how you can see what is available on the clipboard and how you can extract that information. Further, we will show you how you can directly paste the contents of the clipboard text to an edit control in one easy line of code!

Although none of the functionality of this How-To is difficult, putting it together and understanding the order of events occurring can be tedious. Pay careful attention to the way in which things are allocated and deallocated, and locked and unlocked, to ensure that you do not crash your system.

Steps

Open and run the Visual C++ application CH1103.MAK from the CHAPT11\SAMPLES\CH1103 directory on the CD that comes with this book. Select the Dialog main menu and the menu item Clipboard Dialog. You will see a new dialog window displayed, as shown in Figure 11-3. If there is something on the clipboard, you will see the Copy button enabled and the text of the clipboard displayed in the static text field at the top of the dialog. If there is nothing in text format on the clipboard, you will see nothing in the static text field, and the Copy button will be grayed.

To reproduce this functionality in your own application, follow these steps:

1. Create a new project in Visual C++ using AppWizard. Give the application the name CH1103.MAK. Enter the resource editor and select the main menu from the menu list. Add a new main-level menu with the caption Dialog. To the Dialog main menu add a new menu item with the caption Clipboard Dialog. Give this drop-down menu item the identifier ID_CLIP_DLG.

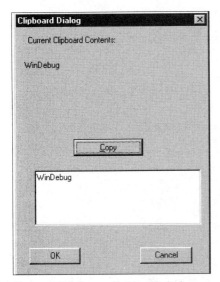

Figure 11-3 Copy clipboard dialog

2. Next, create a new dialog template by clicking on the Dialog resource in the resource list and then clicking on the New button. Move the OK and Cancel buttons to the bottom of the dialog. Add a static text field to the top of the dialog with the caption Current Clipboard Contents. Below this text field add a second static text field with no caption and an identifier of IDC_CLIP_CONTENTS.

3. Add a button below the blank static text field. Give the button the identifier IDC_BUTTON1 and the caption &Copy.

4. Add an edit field to the dialog immediately below the button. Remove any caption from the edit field.

5. Enter ClassWizard and generate a new dialog class for the template you have just created. Give the new class the name CClipDlg. Click on the CClipDlg identifier in the object list of ClassWizard and the message WM_INITDIALOG from the message list. Click on the Add Function button and add the following code to the OnInitDialog method of CClipDlg:

```
BOOL CClipDlg::OnInitDialog()
{
    CDialog::OnInitDialog();

    CenterWindow();

    // First, open the clipboard

    OpenClipboard();

    // See if the format is available

    if ( !IsClipboardFormatAvailable(CF_TEXT) ) {

        // NO data available. Disable copy button.

        GetDlgItem(IDC_BUTTON1)->EnableWindow(FALSE);
    }
    else {
        // Data available. Enable copy button
        GetDlgItem(IDC_BUTTON1)->EnableWindow(TRUE);

        // Get the data
        HANDLE hData = GetClipboardData(CF_TEXT);

        // Unlock the handle

        LPSTR lpData = (LPSTR)GlobalLock(hData);

        // Allocate a block of this size

        char *str = new char[GlobalSize(hData)];

        // Copy it into the string

        lstrcpy ( str, lpData );
```

```
    // Set the static text field to be this data

    GetDlgItem(IDC_CLIP_CONTENTS)->SetWindowText ( str );

    // Clean up after ourselves

    delete str;
    GlobalUnlock ( hData );

  }

  CloseClipboard();

  return TRUE;
}
```

6. Next, in ClassWizard, click on the IDC_BUTTON1 object in the object list and the BN_CLICKED message in the message list. Click on the Add Function button and give the new function the name OnCopyFromClipboard. Enter the following code into the OnCopyFromClipboard method of CClipDlg:

```
void CClipDlg::OnCopyFromClipboard()
{
    CEdit *edit = (CEdit *)GetDlgItem(IDC_EDIT1);

    edit->SendMessage(WM_PASTE);
}
```

7. Select the CCh1103App object from the drop-down list in ClassWizard. Select the ID_CLIP_DLG object from the object list and the COMMAND message from the message list. Click on the Add Function button and give the new function the name OnClipDlg. Enter the following code into the OnClipDlg method of CCh1103App:

```
void CCh1103App::OnClipDlg()
{
    CClipDlg dlg;
    dlg.DoModal();
}
```

8. Add the following line to the include list at the top of CH1103.CPP:

```
#include "clipdlg.h"
```

9. Compile and run the application.

How It Works

When the dialog is first displayed, the OnInitDialog method is called. This method first opens the clipboard for reading and writing by calling the OpenClipboard function. The next function to be called is the IsClipboardFormatAvailable. Since we are looking solely for text, we call this function with the CF_TEXT format as its parameter. This function will scan the clipboard to see if there are any entries with the format specified (text). If so, it returns a TRUE value; otherwise, it returns a FALSE value.

If there is no text on the clipboard, the OnInitDialog method simply disables the Copy button. If there is text on the clipboard, the method then gets a handle to that text using the GetClipboardData function. This function returns a handle to global memory. This memory can be accessed by "locking" the memory via the GlobalLock function. This function returns a temporary pointer to the data, which can be used to access the actual text in that handle. This pointer is used to copy the data into a local buffer, which is then passed to the static text control to display the text on the clipboard. Finally, we clean up after ourselves by relocking the handle and freeing the locally allocated data.

When the user presses the Copy button, the OnCopyFromClipboard function is called. This function simply sends a message to the edit control, telling it to copy the contents of the clipboard into its own buffer.

Note that once the data is copied, it is now separate from the clipboard data. Changes made to the edit field are not reflected in the clipboard and vice versa. To show this, modify the text in the edit field and then click on the Copy button again. More text will be shown in the edit field, overwriting your changes.

Comments

The clipboard is the simplest method to communicate between applications. This method is best for passing simple text or bitmaps between two applications by having the user do cuts and pastes in the two applications.

Although it is simple, the clipboard is an important part of the Windows API functionality. Users might respect (or fear) DDE and OLE communications between applications with visual editing and asynchronous communications, but they have come to understand and need the copy/cut/paste functions provided by the clipboard.

COMPLEXITY
EASY

11.4   How do I...
Use cut, copy, and paste to and from the clipboard?

Problem

I would like to be able to use the cut, copy, and paste commands in an edit control in one of my dialog boxes. Although I am aware that I can simply allow the user to use the CTRL-X, CTRL-C, and CTRL-Z keyboard commands to accomplish this, I would prefer not to make the user go through this exercise.

How can I create buttons in my dialog that I can use for these commands, instead of relying on the keyboard commands?

Technique

It is true that the keyboard shortcuts for the cut, copy, and paste commands are somewhat less than intuitive. These commands harken back to the days of Windows 2.x and were never really intended for today's users.

In many edit views, you can simply use a menu command that implements the shortcuts for the edit commands. In an earlier How-To, we discussed how you could use accelerator keys to work within modal dialogs.

As it turns out, however, using buttons within the dialog is the simplest way to implement the solution to the problem! In this How-To, we look at how you can use the dialogs to communicate with the edit boxes, which in turn talk to the Windows Clipboard. Although that sounds like a lot of work, you will find that it is implemented in only a few lines of code.

Steps

Open and run the Visual C++ application CH1104.MAK from the CHAPT11\SAMPLES\CH1104 directory on the CD that comes with this book. Select the Cut, Copy and Paste menu option from the Dialog menu. You will see a new dialog window displayed, as shown in Figure 11-4. Type a few lines into the edit box at the top of the dialog, and then select some of the text. Click at a new cursor position in the edit box. Click on the Copy button and then the Paste button. You should then see the text duplicated at the current cursor position. Play with the Cut, Copy, and Paste combinations to see what the various buttons do.

To reproduce this functionality in your own application, follow these steps:

1. Create a new project in Visual C++ using AppWizard. Give the application the name CH1104.MAK. Enter the resource editor and select the main menu from

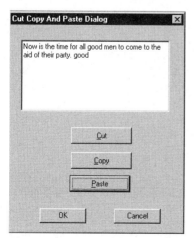

Figure 11-4 Cut, copy, and paste dialog

the menu list. Add a new main menu item with the caption Dialog. To the Dialog main menu add a new menu item with the caption Cut Copy Paste. Give this drop-down menu item the identifier ID_EDIT_FUNCS.

2. Next, create a new dialog template by clicking on the Dialog resource in the resource list and then clicking on the New button. Move the OK and Cancel buttons to the bottom of the dialog. Add an edit box to the top of the dialog and three buttons below the edit box.

3. Give the first button the caption &Cut. Give the second button the identifier &Copy, and give the third button the caption &Paste.

4. Enter ClassWizard and generate a new dialog class for the template you have just created. Give the new class the name CEditFuncDlg.

5. Click on the IDC_BUTTON1 identifier in the object list of ClassWizard and the BN_CLICKED message in the message list. Click on the Add Function button and give the function the name OnCut. Enter the following code into the OnCut method of the CEditFuncDlg class:

```
void CEditFuncDlg::OnCut()
{
    CEdit *edit = (CEdit *)GetDlgItem(IDC_EDIT1);
    edit->SendMessage(WM_CUT);
}
```

6. Click on the IDC_BUTTON2 identifier in the object list of ClassWizard and the BN_CLICKED message in the message list. Click on the Add Function button and give the function the name OnCopy. Enter the following code into the OnCopy method of the CEditFuncDlg class:

```
void CEditFuncDlg::OnCopy()
{
    CEdit *edit = (CEdit *)GetDlgItem(IDC_EDIT1);
    edit->SendMessage(WM_COPY);
}
```

7. Click on the IDC_BUTTON3 identifier in the object list of ClassWizard and the BN_CLICKED message in the message list. Click on the Add Function button and give the function the name OnPaste. Enter the following code into the OnPaste method of the CEditFuncDlg class:

```
void CEditFuncDlg::OnPaste()
{
    CEdit *edit = (CEdit *)GetDlgItem(IDC_EDIT1);
    edit->SendMessage(WM_PASTE);
}
```

8. Select the CCh1104App object from the drop-down list in ClassWizard. Select the ID_EDIT_FUNCS object from the object list and the COMMAND message from the message list. Click on the Add Function button and give the new function the name OnCutCopyPasteDlg. Enter the following code into the OnCutCopyPasteDlg method of CCh1104App:

```
void CCh1104App::OnCutCopyPasteDlg()
{
    CEditFuncDlg  dlg;
    dlg.DoModal();
}
```

9. Add the following line to the include list at the top of CH1104.CPP:

```
#include "editfunc.h"
```

10. Compile and run the application.

How It Works

This is, quite possibly, the simplest How-To in the entire book. All that occurs is that when the buttons are pressed, the class methods for those buttons are called. These buttons simply send the Windows API commands WM_CUT, WM_COPY, and WM_PASTE to the edit controls.

What happens "behind the scenes," however, is a whole different ball game. The edit controls receive the commands and communicate with the clipboard either to put data onto the clipboard (for the Copy and Cut commands) or to get information from the clipboard (in the case of the Paste command). Although, in this case, the data is being processed from a single application, there is nothing preventing you from copying or cutting to the clipboard in one application and pasting into another application. This is really a more complete example of potential interprocess communication than the previous How-To and better illustrates how much work the Windows API functions can do for you.

Comments

The same program can be written in Visual Basic as well. Here's how you go about it:

1. Create a new project or add a new form to an existing project. Add a multiline edit box at the top of the form with three buttons beneath the edit box.

2. Give the first button the caption Cut. Give the second button the caption Copy and the third button the caption Paste.

3. Add the following declarations to the "general" section of the form:

```
Private Declare Function SendMessage Lib "user32" Alias "SendMessageA"
(ByVal hwnd As Long, ByVal wMsg As Long, ByVal wParam As Long, lParam
As Long) As Long
Const WM_CUT = &H300
Const WM_COPY = &H301
Const WM_PASTE = &H302
```

4. Double-click on the Cut button and add the following code to the Command1_Click method of the form:

```
Private Sub Command1_Click()
    x = SendMessage(Text1.hwnd, WM_CUT, 0, 0)
End Sub
```

5. Double-click on the Copy button and add the following code to the Command2_Click method of the form:

```
Private Sub Command2_Click()
    x = SendMessage(Text1.hwnd, WM_COPY, 0, 0)

End Sub
```

6. Double-click on the Paste button and add the following code to the Command3_Click method of the form:

```
Private Sub Command3_Click()
    x = SendMessage(Text1.hwnd, WM_PASTE, 0, 0)


End Sub
```

7. Run the application. The results will be the same as the Visual C++ example in the How-To.

11.5 How do I...
Write a dynamic data exchange client?

Problem

I would like to be able to write a client for dynamic data exchange (DDE). Preferably, I would like the ability to exchange data with the Program Manager in Windows or other system servers for DDE.

How do I use the Windows API functions to create a DDE client?

Technique

DDE is an excellent way to communicate between applications without the overhead of OLE and at a more complex level than using the clipboard. In short, it is a good compromise between functionality and complexity in interapplication communication.

In this How-To, we examine how you can use the basics of the DDE library functions (actually, the DDEML library) to communicate with the Program Manager application. In this example, we will show you how to connect to the Program Manager as a server, how to list the groups that are shown in the programs section of your start menu, and how to disconnect from the server when you are done.

Steps

Open and run the Visual C++ application CH1105.MAK from the CHAPT11\SAMPLES\CH1105 directory on the CD that comes with this book. You will see a new dialog window displayed, as shown in Figure 11-5. Click on the Connect button, and the status indicator will change to indicate that you are now connected. Click on the Show Groups button, and a message box will be displayed showing you the groups currently installed in Program Manager (as shown in Figure 11-6). Finally, click on the Disconnect button, and the dialog will show the status indicator, indicating that you have disconnected from the server.

To reproduce this functionality in your own application, follow these steps:

1. Create a new project in Visual C++ using AppWizard. Give the application the name CH1105.MAK. Enter the resource editor and select the main menu from the menu list. Add a new main menu item with the caption Dialog. To the Dialog main menu add a new menu item with the caption Dde Dialog. Give this drop-down menu item the identifier ID_DDE_DLG.

2. Next, create a new dialog template by clicking on the Dialog resource in the resource list and then clicking on the New button. Move the OK and Cancel buttons to the bottom of the dialog. Add a static text box to the top of the dialog as well as a blank static text box next to it. Add three buttons below the text boxes.

3. Give the first static text box the caption Status: and the identifer IDC_STATIC. Give the second static text box a blank caption and the identifier IDC_STATUS.

4. Give the first button the caption Connect. Give the second button the caption Disconnect and the third button the caption Show Groups.

5. Enter ClassWizard and generate a new dialog class for the template you have just created. Give the new class the name CDDeDialog.

6. Click on the IDC_BUTTON1 identifier in the object list of ClassWizard and the BN_CLICKED message in the message list. Click on the Add Function

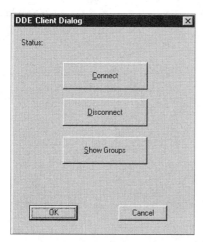

Figure11-5 DDE dialog box

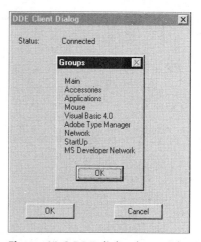

Figure 11-6 DDE dialog box with message box showing groups in program start menu

button and give the function the name OnConnect. Enter the following code
into the OnConnect method of the CDDeDialog class:

```
void CDDeDialog::OnConnect()
{
  FARPROC callBack = MakeProcInstance ( (FARPROC)DdeCallBack,
AfxGetInstanceHandle() );

  switch (DdeInitialize(&InstId, (PFNCALLBACK)callBack,
        APPCMD_CLIENTONLY, 0)) {
    case DMLERR_NO_ERROR :

         // Create string handles for topic and service

       Service = DdeCreateStringHandle(InstId, "PROGMAN", CP_WINANSI);
       Topic   = DdeCreateStringHandle(InstId, "PROGMAN", CP_WINANSI);

       if (Service && Topic) {
         HConv = ::DdeConnect(InstId, Service, Topic, 0);

         switch (DdeGetLastError(InstId)) {
           case DMLERR_NO_ERROR :
             GetDlgItem(IDC_STATUS)->SetWindowText("Connected");
             return;
           default :
             MessageBox ( "Unable to connect to ProgMan", "Error", MB_OK );
             return;
         }
       } else {
         MessageBox ( "Unable to create string handles!", "Error", MB_OK );
         return;
       }

    default :
      MessageBox ( "Error initializing DDE system!", "Error", MB_OK );
      return;
  }
}
```

7. Click on the IDC_BUTTON2 identifier in the object list of ClassWizard and
the BN_CLICKED message in the message list. Click on the Add Function
button and give the function the name OnDisconnect. Enter the following
code into the OnDisconnect method of the CDDeDialog class:

```
void CDDeDialog::OnDisconnect()
{
  if (HConv)
    DdeDisconnect(HConv);

  GetDlgItem(IDC_STATUS)->SetWindowText("Disconnected");

  if (InstId) {
    DdeFreeStringHandle(InstId, Service);
    DdeFreeStringHandle(InstId, Topic);
```

```
      DdeUninitialize(InstId);
   }
}
```

8. Click on the IDC_BUTTON3 identifier in the object list of ClassWizard and
the BN_CLICKED message in the message list. Click on the Add Function
button and give the function the name OnShowGroups. Enter the following
code into the OnShowGroups method of the CDDeDialog class:

```
void CDDeDialog::OnShowGroups()
{
  DWORD len;
  char   commands[1024];
  char   *TempText;

  sprintf(commands, "Groups");
  if (TempStringHandle)
    DdeFreeStringHandle(InstId, TempStringHandle);

  TempStringHandle = DdeCreateStringHandle(InstId, commands,
                              CP_WINANSI);
  hProgData = ::DdeClientTransaction(NULL, 0, HConv, TempStringHandle,
                              CF_TEXT, XTYP_REQUEST, 5000, NULL);
  len = ::DdeGetData(hProgData, NULL, 0,  0);
  TempText = new char[len];
  len = ::DdeGetData(hProgData, TempText, len,  0);
  MessageBox( TempText, "Groups", MB_OK );
}
```

9. Add the following code above the constructor for the CDDeDialog class:

```
static CDDeDialog *theDialog = NULL;

HDDEDATA FAR PASCAL _export DdeCallBack(WORD type, WORD, HCONV, HSZ,
                              HSZ, HDDEDATA, DWORD, DWORD)
{
  switch (type) {
    case XTYP_DISCONNECT:
        if ( theDialog )
          theDialog->GetDlgItem(IDC_STATUS)-
>SetWindowText("Disconnected");
      break;

    case XTYP_ERROR:
        MessageBox(NULL, "A critical DDE error has occurred.", "Error",
                MB_ICONINFORMATION);
  }

  return 0;
}
```

10. Add the following code to the constructor for the CDDeDialog class. Add all
lines marked in bold.

```
CDDeDialog::CDDeDialog(CWnd* pParent /*=NULL*/)
  : CDialog(CDDeDialog::IDD, pParent)
```

continued on next page

continued from previous page

```
{
    theDialog = this;
    InstId = 0;

    //{{AFX_DATA_INIT(CDDeDialog)
        // NOTE: the ClassWizard will add member initialization here
    //}}AFX_DATA_INIT
}
```

11. Add the following lines to the header file for the CDDeDialog class, DDEDIA-LO.H. In addition, include the standard include file DDEML.H.

```
private:
    DWORD       InstId;
    HCONV       HConv;
    HSZ         Service;
    HSZ         Topic;
    HSZ         TempStringHandle;
    HDDEDATA    hProgData;
```

12. Select the CCh1105App object from the drop-down list in ClassWizard. Select the ID_DDE_DLG object from the object list and the COMMAND message from the message list. Click on the Add Function button and give the new function the name OnDdeDialog. Enter the following code into the OnDdeDialog method of CCh1105App:

```
void CCh1105App::OnCDDeDialog()
{
    CDDeDialog  dlg;

    dlg.DoModal();
}
```

13. Add the following line to the include list at the top of CH1105.CPP:

```
#include "ddedialo.h"
```

14. Add the DDEML.LIB Windows library to your project. Compile and run the application.

How It Works

When the user selects the Dde Dialog from the menu, the CDDeDialog class is created. This invokes the constructor that initializes the instance handle for the DDE conversation to 0. This is very important to remember because the DDE system will crash if this value is non-zero when the DdeInitialize function is called.

When the user clicks on the Connect button, the following events occur. First, the dialog class creates a callback function handler by calling the MakeProcInstance function of the API. Next, the DdeInitialize API function is called to initialize the DDE system. If there was no error, two string handles are created. String handles are global memory blocks that are passed back and forth between applications. Since memory for a given application is local to that application, only global blocks can be used to share between applications.

Once all of this is completed successfully, the DDE system is now connected to the Program Manager server. When the user clicks on the Show Groups button, the system then uses the handle it obtained from the DdeInitialize call to send the command "Groups" to the server. This is accomplished by sending a XTYP_REQUEST command to the server, which indicates that the client would like some data back. This data is returned in the form of a global handle, which is then used to obtain the data. The DdeGetData function is called twice to obtain the data. First, the function is called with a NULL pointer for the returned data space. This indicates to the function that the caller wants only the size of the data. A block of that size is allocated, and the function is called again with that block as the pointer value. The DdeGetData function fills the data into the block and returns it to the application, where it is displayed.

Finally, the Disconnect button simply disconnects this dialog box from the Program Manager server and frees up the string handles that were allocated earlier.

Comments

Dynamic data exchange is an often overlooked method to communicate between programs. It is considerably easier to understand and debug than OLE and provides more power than the clipboard.

COMPLEXITY
DIFFICULT

11.6 How do I...
Write a dynamic data exchange server?

Problem

I would like to be able to create a DDE server that I can use in my application to service other applications' requests for data. How can I write one in a way in which I can use the code in different applications easily?

Technique

Writing a DDE server is a tricky and complex operation. Rather than simply writing a server, we will actually create a generic skeleton that you can use in your own application. We will then discuss a step-by-step procedure for implementing your own information in the server.

Steps

This How-To code can be found on the disk that accompanies this book in the directory CH11\SAMPLES\CH1106.

In order to create a server for DDE, first create a new file in your application. Give this file the name SERVER.CPP.

1. Enter the following code into the SERVER.CPP file:

```cpp
#include <stdafx.h>
#include "ddeml.h"

const TOPICS = 2;
const ITEMS  = 2;

class CDdeServer {
private:
    FARPROC   lpfnDdeCallBack;        // Callback function
    HSZ       ghszDDEMLDemo;          // Service name
    HSZ       ghszTopics[TOPICS];     // topics the server supports
    HSZ       ghszItems[ITEMS];       // items the server supports
    DWORD     idInst;                 // instance identifier
    BOOL      bAdviseLoopActive;      // Flag for advise loop


public:

    CDdeServer(void);
    BOOL Initialize(void);
    int  Uninitialize(void);
    void SetAdvise(BOOL flag) { bAdviseLoopActive = flag; };
    int  Advise(int whichTopic, int whichItem);
    DWORD GetDdeInstance(void) { return idInst; };
    HSZ   GetTopic(int i) { return ghszTopics[i]; };
    HSZ   GetItem(int i) { return ghszItems[i]; };
    HSZ   GetTopicHandle(void) { return ghszDDEMLDemo; };
};

static CDdeServer *theServer = NULL;

HDDEDATA EXPENTRY DdeCallBack(WORD      wType,
                             WORD      wFmt,
                             HCONV     hConv,
                             HSZ       hsz1,
                             HSZ       hsz2,
                             HDDEDATA  hDDEData,
                             DWORD     dwData1,
                             DWORD     dwData2)
{
   int     i, j;
   switch(wType)
   {
     case XTYP_ADVSTART:
           // Tell object to set advise flag to on

           theServer->SetAdvise(TRUE);
           return (HDDEDATA)TRUE;
```

```
case XTYP_ADVREQ:
    // Return a global handle to your information here
    return NULL;


case XTYP_ADVSTOP:
    theServer->SetAdvise(FALSE);
    return (HDDEDATA)NULL;


case XTYP_CONNECT:
    // The server gets an XTYP_CONNECT when the client requests a
    // conversation (via DdeConnect). The server should return TRUE
    // if it supports the topic, and FALSE otherwise.

    for (i = 0; i < TOPICS; i++)
    {
      if (!DdeCmpStringHandles(hsz1, theServer->GetTopic(i) ))
          return (HDDEDATA)TRUE;
    }
    return FALSE;   // None found to match


case XTYP_WILDCONNECT:

    // Return a pair of topic/items for each supported.

    HSZPAIR ahszp[(TOPICS + 1)];   // for the HSZPAIRS that we need
                                   // to return to the DDEML.

    if ((hsz2 != theServer->GetTopicHandle()) && (hsz2 != NULL))
    {
        // we only support the DDEMLDemo service
        return (HDDEDATA)NULL;
    }

    // scan the topic table and create hsz pairs

    j = 0;

    for (i = 0; i < TOPICS; i++)
    {
        if (!DdeCmpStringHandles(hsz1, theServer->GetTopic(i) ))
        {
            ahszp[j].hszSvc = theServer->GetTopicHandle();
            ahszp[j].hszTopic = theServer->GetTopic(i);
            j++;
        }
    }

    // The array of hszpairs should end with NULL string handles
    ahszp[j].hszSvc = ahszp[j].hszTopic = NULL;
    j++;
```

continued on next page

continued from previous page

```
            // send it back
            return(DdeCreateDataHandle(theServer->GetDdeInstance(),
                              (LPBYTE)&ahszp[0],
                              sizeof(HSZPAIR) * j,
                              0L,
                              0,
                              wFmt,
                              0));


    case XTYP_REQUEST:
        // The server gets an XTYP_REQUEST when the client requests
        // information via DdeClientTransaction(...XTYP_REQUEST).
        // This transaction must be handled differently for each
        // topic and format.


        // Is this a request on the System topic?
        if (!DdeCmpStringHandles(hsz1, theServer->GetTopic(0)))
        {
            return (HDDEDATA)NULL;   // no match
        }

        // Is this a CF_TEXT-format request on the item?
        if ((wFmt == CF_TEXT) && (!DdeCmpStringHandles(hsz2,
                              theServer->GetTopic(1))))
        {
            HDDEDATA hReturn;
            int       nValue = 256;    // Value to return

            // Create data handle for the number the user selected to
            // pass on to the client.
            hReturn = DdeCreateDataHandle(theServer->GetDdeInstance(),
                                  // instance identifier
                         (LPBYTE)&nValue,   // source buffer
                         sizeof(int),       // length of object
                         0,                 // offset into source buffer
                         theServer->GetItem(1),
                         wFmt,              // clipboard data format
                         0);                // creation flags
            if (!hReturn)
            {
                WORD wError;
                char szBuffer[128];

                wError = DdeGetLastError(theServer->GetDdeInstance());
                wsprintf(szBuffer, "DdeCreateDataHandle failed. Error
                        #%#0x", wError);
                MessageBox(NULL, szBuffer, "Error", MB_OK);
                return (HDDEDATA)NULL;
            }

            // send handle to the requested data back to client
            return hReturn;
        }
```

```
        // Is this a CF_BITMAP-format request on the GENERAL topic?
        if ( (wFmt == CF_BITMAP) && (!DdeCmpStringHandles(hsz2,
                                     theServer->GetItem(1))) )
        {
            return (HDDEDATA)NULL;
        }

        else
        {
            // Request on unsupported topic and/or format.
            return (HDDEDATA)NULL;
        }
        return (HDDEDATA)NULL;


    case XTYP_CONNECT_CONFIRM:
        return (HDDEDATA)NULL;

    case XTYP_POKE:
        return (HDDEDATA)DDE_FNOTPROCESSED;

    case XTYP_REGISTER:
        return (HDDEDATA)NULL;

    case XTYP_UNREGISTER:
        return (HDDEDATA)NULL;

    case XTYP_DISCONNECT:
        return (HDDEDATA)NULL;

    case XTYP_EXECUTE:
        return DDE_FNOTPROCESSED;

    default:
            return (HDDEDATA)NULL;

    }

}


CDdeServer::CDdeServer(void)
{
    idInst = 0;
    ghszDDEMLDemo = NULL;
    lpfnDdeCallBack = NULL;
    bAdviseLoopActive = FALSE;
    theServer = this;
}


BOOL CDdeServer::Initialize()
{
    lpfnDdeCallBack = MakeProcInstance((FARPROC)DdeCallBack,
                                     AfxGetInstanceHandle());

    // Initialize the system
```

continued on next page

continued from previous page

```
        if(DdeInitialize(&idInst, (PFNCALLBACK)lpfnDdeCallBack,
                        APPCLASS_STANDARD, 0L))
            return FALSE;

        // Create string handle for the Service name

        ghszDDEMLDemo = DdeCreateStringHandle(idInst, "Demo Service",
                                            CP_WINANSI);

        if (!ghszDDEMLDemo)
            return FALSE;

        // Create string handles to the Topic names
        ghszTopics[0] = DdeCreateStringHandle(idInst, "Sample", CP_WINANSI);
        ghszTopics[1] = DdeCreateStringHandle(idInst, SZDDESYS_TOPIC,
                                            CP_WINANSI);

        // Create string handles for the Item names
        ghszItems[0] = DdeCreateStringHandle(idInst, "Item1", CP_WINANSI);
        ghszItems[1] = DdeCreateStringHandle(idInst, "Item2", CP_WINANSI);

        // Register the service
        if (!DdeNameService(idInst, ghszDDEMLDemo, NULL, DNS_REGISTER))
            return FALSE;

        return TRUE;
    }

    int CDdeServer::Uninitialize()
    {
        // Unregister the service
        DdeNameService(idInst, ghszDDEMLDemo, NULL, DNS_UNREGISTER);

        // terminate all conversations
        DdeUninitialize(idInst);

        return 0;
    }

    int CDdeServer::Advise(int whichTopic, int whichItem)
    {
        if (bAdviseLoopActive) {

            // send XTYP_ADVREQ to own callback

            if (!DdePostAdvise(idInst, ghszTopics[whichTopic],
    ghszItems[whichItem]))
                return FALSE;

            return TRUE;
        }
        return FALSE;
    }
```

2. The first option to change is the number and name of the topics. In the Initialize function of the class, you can specify the topics using the ghszTopics array. This array holds the topic names for the server. The items are stored in the ghszItems array. By adding or modifying these arrays, you can change the server topics and items.

3. The name of the service as registerd with DDE is currently Demo Service. This name can be changed by simply modifying the call to DdeCreateStringHandle in the Initialize function. This is the very first call to the DdeCreateStringHandle function.

4. That's all the customization that is necessary in the Initialize and UnInitialize functions. In the callback function, you can modify the following behavior. The XTYP_ADVREQ case returns data to the calling function, assuming that the advise request setting is TRUE and that the data has changed. Use this case to return a global handle to the caller with the new information. The global handle is obtained using the following code:

```
hData = DdeCreateDataHandle(idInst,
        (LPBYTE)&data,          // The data to pass
        sizeof(data),           // The size of the data to pass
        0,                      // The offset from the beginning
                                //  of the data
        ghszItems[whichData],   // The item to use
        wFmt,                   // Format of the data on the
                                //  clipboard (CF_TEXT or CF_BITMAP).
        HDATA_APPOWNED);        // Indicates that the data is
                                //  owned bythe server
```

5. The XTYP_REQUEST case is shown with a simple example of how to pass back a number to the calling client program. You can use the XTYP_REQUEST case to expand on the data returned. Simply create an instance of the data you want to send and pass it as in the example.

How It Works

It is beyond the scope of this book to explain how DDE works. Instead, we will focus on the example and how each step works. First, the DDE system is initialized. This is a required step in any DDE system. Next, the server is registered with the DDE system. This is also required for any DDE server.

After the initialization and registration phases, the optional portions of the system begin. Normally, the system allocates string handles for all of the topics and items that are supported. A topic might be something akin to "Stock Prices" or "PLU values." An item might be a specific service, such as "price" or "name." If you were using DDE in a point-of-sale system, for example, the topic might be PLU values and the items could be "price," "quantity on hand," and "taxable flag." These could then be sent from the server to the client.

The server uses a callback function to accept all new DDE commands. The commands that you must process are XTYP_CONNECT, XTYP_WILDCONNECT, and XTYP_REQUEST. These indicate the basic functionality necessary to implement the server.

The advise statements (XTYP_ADVSTART, XTYP_ADVREQ, XTYP_ADVSTOP) are used to create a "warm" link between the client and the server. When a client posts an advise start message, the server will "advise" the client of any changes in that data.

For more information about the DDE commands, please consult your DDE reference manual.

Comments

Writing a DDE server is a difficult undertaking that should not be taken lightly. Many of the functions that you might want in a server already exist in the Windows API functions or in other server applications. Before you consider writing a full-blown server, you might seriously consider using OLE in your application and making the application an OLE server.

If you would really, really like to create a DDE server, we recommend you use the "ez-server" code that Microsoft provides for free and is included in the next How-To. This code implements a generic DDE server that can be embedded in your application and contains complete code to do System topics, callbacks, and all other features of DDE servers.

COMPLEXITY
DIFFICULT

11.7 How do I...
Support the System topic in dynamic data exchange?

Problem

I would like to be able to write a complete DDE server with support for the System topic, like the server found in Microsoft Word and Excel. The System topic seems to contain all of the information that I need as a developer to find out what services are supplied by the DDE server, and I would like to give that same functionality to users of my application.

How can I use the power of the DDE API functions to implement a server that contains a complete System topic handler?

Technique

This particular problem comes up again and again. It comes up so frequently, in fact, that Microsoft decided that they would personally help the developer to overcome the inherent problems in writing DDE servers.

Microsoft provides, free of charge or royalty, a simple generic DDE server file that contains support for all of the basic system functions in DDE. This file can be included in your applications and does all of the basic work of implementing a DDE server with System topic support.

In this How-To, we will take a look at this generic DDE server and examine how it uses the Windows API functions to implement a generic System topic support server. We will also explain how you can use this generic API in your own applications to add the functionality you need with little or no effort on your part.

When the name of the game is getting a working product on the market, there is no room for the "Not Invented Here" mentality. This code may not have been written by your company, but it does the job and works well. We strongly suggest that you take advantage of it in your applications.

Steps

Open and run the Visual C++ application CH1107.MAK from the CHAPT11\SAMPLES\CH1107 directory on the CD that comes with this book. Select the main menu item DDE Initialize. You will see a message box indicating that the DDE system has been set up with the System topic supported. This program is shown in Figure 11-7.

To reproduce a fully functional DDE server in your own application, follow this procedure:

1. Create a new application project make file in Visual C++ using AppWizard. Give this project the name CH1107.MAK.

2. Enter the resource editor and add a new main menu item to the project main menu. Give the menu the caption DDE. Add a new menu item to this menu with the identifier ID_DDE_INIT. Give the new drop-down menu the caption DDE Initialize.

3. Close the resource editor, saving the resource file. Enter ClassWizard and select the CCh1107App object from the drop-down list. Select the ID_DDE_INIT object from the object list and the COMMAND message from the message list. Click on the Add Function button and give the new function the name OnDdeInit. Enter the following code into the OnDdeInit method of CCh1107App:

```
void CCh1107App::OnDdeInit()
{
    if ( InitializeDDE(AfxGetInstanceHandle(),
```

continued on next page

Figure 11-7 DDE initialized
message box

continued from previous page

```
                              "DDE Demo Service",
                              NULL,
                              NULL,
                              APPCLASS_STANDARD) == TRUE ) {
        MessageBox ( NULL, "DDE Server Initialized for Server DDE Demo
                    Service", "Info", MB_OK );
    }
    else
        MessageBox ( NULL, "Unable to initialize server!", "Error",
                    MB_OK );
}
```

4. Next, reenter the resource editor and add a second menu item to the DDE main menu. Give this menu item the identifier ID_DDE_UNINT and the caption DDE Uninitialize.

5. Enter ClassWizard and select the CCh1107App object from the drop-down list. Select the ID_DDE_UNINIT object from the object list and the COMMAND message from the message list. Click on the Add Function button and accept the name OnDdeUninit as the name of the new function. Add the following code to the OnDdeUninit method of CCh1107App:

```
void CCh1107App::OnDdeUninit()
{
    UninitializeDDE();
}
```

6. Add the following lines to the top of the CH1107.CPP source file:

```
extern "C" {
#define _NODEFINEHSZ
#include "stddde.h"
};
```

7. Next, you will need to go to the CD-ROM enclosed with this book. Find the CH11\SAMPLES\CH1107 subdirectory in the code directory and copy the STDDDE.H and STDDDE.CPP files into your application's subdirectory for the CH1107.MAK application. These files are not reproduced here in the interests of space.

8. Add the STDDDE.CPP file to your project file.

9. You will need to modify one file that comes with your Visual C++ include set. The DDEML.H file is not set up properly to work with C++ files, although it works fine with C files. Locate the line that reads DECLARE_HANDLE32(HSZ) in the file and add the following line above it:

```
#ifndef _NODEFINEHSZ
```

Now add the following line below DECLARE_HANDLE32(HSZ):

```
#endif
```

10. Add the DDEML Windows library to your project link options. Your application should now compile and run properly.

How It Works

For more information about DDE's inner workings, look at How-To's 11.5 and 11.6. Here, we will talk a little about what it means to support the DDE System topic and how this code will aid you in that endeavor.

The DDE System topic is a standard method for DDE servers to indicate to their clients what sorts of things are supported in the server and what topics and items are available for the client to use.

The System topic supports the following items for a client to browse: Topics, SysItems, Formats, TopicItemList, Help, Status, and ReturnMessage. If a DDE server supports all of these items, it is considered in compliance with the System topic requirements.

The Topics item returns to the client a tab-delimited list of the topics supported by the DDE server. This list can change at any time, depending on the state of the server and the application.

SysItems returns a list of the System topic items that are supported from this list. A true server will support all of the listed topics, and the STDDDE.CPP code does exactly this.

Formats indicates to the calling client what clipboard formats are supported by this application. CF_TEXT is required and is the only one supported by this code.

TopicItemList returns a list of server-dependent topics for this server. In the case of our example program, there are no server-dependent topics. The STDDDE.CPP file contains a function AddDDEItem, which has the following syntax:

```
PDDEITEMINFO AddDDEItem(LPSTR lpszTopic,
                        LPSTR lpszItem,
                        LPWORD lpFormatList,
                        PDDEREQUESTFN lpReqFn,
                        PDDEPOKEFN lpPokeFn)
```

This function will add a new DDE topic and item to the server list and register a callback function for this item in case the client sends the topic and item request. The lpszTopic parameter specifies the name of the topic, and the lpszItem specifies the item within the topic. The lpFormatList parameter specifies the list of formats that this topic supports. The lpReqFn function handles request calls, while the lpPokeFn function handles DDE_POKE calls.

Help returns a help message for the indicated portion of the server.

Status returns the status of the last operation with the server over a given channel. This message is useful for DDE functions that only return a success or failure flag.

Finally, the ReturnMessage returns the status and message for the last DDE_ACK message, indicating whether or not the last message to the server was acknowledged properly.

Comments

Although this particular DDE server does nothing but support the System topic, it is an excellent starting point for a complete DDE server. All of the basic functionality is there to make a server that supports any number of topics and items and returns information to the caller in a server-dependent fashion.

You may include the STDDDE.CPP and STDDDE.H files in your application with no royalty or other charge.

11.8   How do I...
Make files Object Linking and Embedding (OLE) compatible?

Problem

I would like to get my application moving toward being OLE compatible but don't know where to start. I realize that the MFC contains many new classes for working with OLE, but I would prefer to dip my toes into the OLE waters cautiously.

Is there any way that I can simply make the storage files for my application compatible with OLE without dropping the rest of the system in as well? The OLE compound documents seem like an excellent way to work with structured files.

Technique

The *compound document* portion of OLE2 is a discrete element of the system and an excellent starting point for adding OLE support to your own applications. Compound documents are simply aggregates of data stored in a hierarchical format on disk. In essence, a compound document is a small file system. In this How-To, we examine how you create OLE compound documents and "streams" within those compound documents in order to save your data to disk and be able to recall it easily later.

The OLE compound document is almost a complete disk system of its own. It contains its own File Allocation Table (FAT) as well as directory entries and data. It will work concurrently with both the DOS-based FAT system or the new Windows 95/NT NTFS file system. For this reason, it makes perfect sense to get your feet wet with OLE using compound documents first.

Steps

Open and run the Visual C++ application CH1108.MAK from the CHAPT11\SAMPLES\CH1108 directory on the CD that comes with this book. Select the main menu Dialog and the menu item OLE File Dialog. You will see a new dialog window displayed, as shown in Figure 11-8. Type a string into the edit box and click on the Add button in the dialog. Repeat this process until you have several strings displayed in the list box. When you are satisfied with the list, click on the Save button in the dialog.

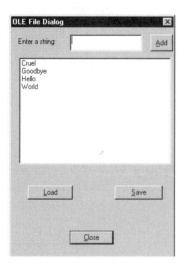

Figure 11-8 OLE file dialog box

Next, click on the Load button in the dialog, and the list will reappear in the list box. It is now stored on disk in a compound document and can be recalled into your application at any time.

To reproduce this functionality in your own application, follow these steps:

1. Create a new project in Visual C++. Give the application the name CH1108.MAK. In the options for the project, select OLE options and click on the Container radio button. This will create the base functionality to work with OLE containers. Enter the resource editor and select the main menu from the menu list. Add a new menu item with the caption Dialog. To the Dialog main menu add a new drop-down menu with the caption OLE File Dialog. Give this drop-down menu item the identifier ID_OLE_FILE_DLG.

2. Move the OK button to the bottom of the dialog and give it the caption Close. Delete the Cancel button from the dialog. Add a new static text field with the caption "Enter a string:". Immediately to the right of the text field add an edit box and immediately to the right of the edit box add a button. Give the button the caption &Add.

3. Add a list box to the dialog below the controls you have just entered.

4. Add two buttons below the list box with the captions Load and Save.

5. Enter ClassWizard and generate a new dialog class for the template you have just defined. Give the new class the name COleFileDlg. Save the new class definition.

6. Click on the IDC_BUTTON1 object in the object list of ClassWizard and the BN_CLICKED message in the message list. Click on the Add Function button and give the new function the name OnAdd. Enter the following code into the OnAdd method of COleFileDlg:

```
void COleFileDlg::OnAdd()
{
    // Get the edit text

    char s[80];
    CEdit *edit = (CEdit *)GetDlgItem(IDC_EDIT1);
    memset ( s, 0, 80 );
    edit->GetWindowText ( s, 80 );

    // If there was anything there, put it into the list box

    if ( strlen(s) ) {
        CListBox *list = (CListBox *)GetDlgItem(IDC_LIST1);
        list->AddString ( s );
    }

    // Clear the edit field text

    edit->SetWindowText ( "" );

    // Reset the focus to the edit field for more typing

    edit->SetFocus();
}
```

7. Click on the IDC_BUTTON2 object in the object list of ClassWizard and the
BN_CLICKED message in the message list. Click on the Add Function button
and give the new function the name OnLoad. Enter the following code into
the OnLoad method of COleFileDlg:

```
void COleFileDlg::OnLoad()
{
    LPSTORAGE pStorage;
    LPSTREAM  pStream;
    USHORT szwFile[512], szwInfo[512];

    // Try to open the storage device.

     // Make a Unicode copy of the filename.
     mbstowcs(szwFile, "test.doc", sizeof(szwFile));
     mbstowcs(szwInfo, "INFO", sizeof(szwFile));

    HRESULT hResult = StgOpenStorage(szwFile, NULL, STGM_READ |
                                STGM_SHARE_EXCLUSIVE |
                                STGM_DIRECT,NULL, NULL, &pStorage);

    if ( hResult != S_OK ) {

        // Couldn't open it.

        MessageBox ( "Couldn't open storage device!", "Error", MB_OK );
        return;
    }

    // Try to open the stream for input
```

```
        hResult = pStorage->OpenStream ( szwInfo, NULL, STGM_READ |
    STGM_SHARE_EXCLUSIVE | STGM_DIRECT, NULL, &pStream );

    if ( hResult != S_OK ) {

        // Couldn't open it, create it.

        hResult = pStorage->CreateStream ( szwInfo, STGM_READWRITE |
                STGM_SHARE_EXCLUSIVE | STGM_DIRECT | STGM_CREATE,
                NULL, NULL, &pStream );

        if ( hResult !=S_OK ) {

        MessageBox( "Couldn't create stream!", "Error", MB_OK );
        return;
    }

    // All went well. Read in elements and place in list box

    CListBox *list = (CListBox *)GetDlgItem(IDC_LIST1);
    list->ResetContent();
    int numElements = 0;
    char buffer[80];
    unsigned long  cb;

    pStream->Read ( &numElements, sizeof(numElements), &cb );

    for ( int i=0; i<numElements; ++i ) {
        memset ( buffer, 0, 80 );
        pStream->Read ( buffer, sizeof(buffer), &cb );
        list->AddString ( buffer );
    }

    // Close the stream

    pStream->Release();
    pStorage->Release ();
}
```

8. Click on the IDC_BUTTON3 object in the object list of ClassWizard and the BN_CLICKED message in the message list. Click on the Add Function button and give the new function the name OnSave. Enter the following code into the OnSave method of COleFileDlg:

```
void COleFileDlg::OnSave()
{
    LPSTORAGE pStorage;
    LPSTREAM  pStream;

    USHORT szwFile[512], szwInfo[512];

    // Try to open the storage device.

    // Make a Unicode copy of the filename.
     mbstowcs(szwFile, "test.doc", sizeof(szwFile));
     mbstowcs(szwInfo, "INFO", sizeof(szwFile));
```

continued on next page

continued from previous page

```
         // Try to open the storage device.

         if ( hResult != S_OK ) {

            // Couldn't open it. Create it.

            hResult = StgCreateDocfile( szwFile, STGM_READWRITE |
                     STGM_SHARE_EXCLUSIVE | STGM_DIRECT | STGM_CREATE,NULL,
                     &pStorage);

            if ( hResult != S_OK ) {
               MessageBox ( "Couldn't create storage device!", "Error", MB_OK );
               return;
            }
         }

         // Try to open the stream for output

         hResult = pStorage->OpenStream ( szwInfo, NULL, STGM_READ |
                  STGM_SHARE_EXCLUSIVE | STGM_DIRECT, NULL, &pStream );

         if ( hResult != S_OK ) {

            // Couldn't open it, create it.

            hResult = pStorage->CreateStream ( szwInfo, STGM_READWRITE |
                     STGM_SHARE_EXCLUSIVE | STGM_DIRECT | STGM_CREATE,
                     NULL, NULL, &pStream );

            if ( hResult != S_OK ) {
               MessageBox( "Couldn't create stream!", "Error", MB_OK );
               return;

            }

         }

         // All went well. Get elements from list box and write out

         CListBox *list = (CListBox *)GetDlgItem(IDC_LIST1);
         int numElements = list->GetCount();
         char buffer[80];
         unsigned long  cb;

         pStream->Write ( &numElements, sizeof(numElements), &cb );

         for ( int i=0; i<numElements; ++i ) {
            memset ( buffer, 0, 80 );
            list->GetText ( i, buffer );
            pStream->Write ( buffer, sizeof(buffer), &cb );
         }

         // Close the stream

         pStream->Release();
         pStorage->Release ();
      }
```

9. Add the following include file line to the top of the OLEFILED.CPP source file:

```
#include "ole2.h"
```

10 Select the CCh1108App object from the drop-down list in ClassWizard. Select the ID_OLE_FILE_DLG object from the object list and the COMMAND message from the message list. Click on the Add Function button and give the new function the name OnOleFileDlg. Enter the following code into the OnOleFileDlg method of CCh1108App:

```
void CCh11App::OnOleFileDlg()
{
    COLEFileDlg  dlg;
    dlg.DoModal();
}
```

11. Add the following line to the include list at the top of CH11.CPP:

```
#include "olefiled.h"
```

12. Compile and run the application.

How It Works

The OLE compound document routines are composed of two major class elements, the IStorage element and the IStream element. The IStorage element represents a "storage device" for OLE to store information into. This device can reside on disk or in memory and acts the same way in either case. Basically, the storage device is a file system that is imprinted on whatever the OLE system determines it should be stored in (memory or disk).

The IStream class represents a single "file" in the storage device. A stream is simply what it sounds like, a single "run" of bytes of data stored in a way that the program understands. While the IStorage class completely understands the representation of the file system on disk or in memory, the IStream class simply understands that there is a certain amount of raw data available in a given "file" in the storage device.

In order to work with storage devices, you must first either open or create one. This is accomplished by calling the StgOpenStorage function or creating (or truncating) a storage file by calling the StgCreateDocFile function. In either case, you pass the function the name of a storage device, which may be NULL. If the name is NULL, the OLE compound document functions will create a temporary storage device that will be deleted upon program exit or the storage device closing. The functions return a pointer to a IStorage class item, which is then used for all further reference to this storage device.

Once a storage device is open, you must open or create a stream within the storage device. This is the equivalent of a DOS open or create call for a file in a directory structure. The functions that accomplish this task are CreateStream and OpenStream. In either case, the stream is given a name that you can refer to later and a set of flags that determine access rights to the stream. The Open and Create functions return a pointer to an IStream class variable, which is then used for all subsequent access to the stream.

Once a stream is opened or created, it can be written to or read from exactly as a file is read or written. In this case, we store the number of elements in the list that we are writing to disk, followed by the elements themselves. When reading back the data, we simply open the stream and read in the number of elements, and then loop through those elements to read in each item. These items are then stored in the list box to complete the cycle.

Comments

The next How-To will explore the OLE2 functionality a bit more, but this How-To gets you started down the OLE road. With more and more applications becoming OLE compatible, it behooves you as a developer to create applications that can be used with OLE. Adding file compatibility is a good start.

One of the better advantages to using the OLE compound document file structure is that it is guaranteed to be compatible no matter what system it is run on. If you are concerned with direct disk access in NTFS systems, for example, you might seriously consider the use of compound documents to store your data. Not only will you gain the advantage of finding your data more quickly, but the file system underneath will not affect how your program runs.

COMPLEXITY
EASY

11.9 How do I...
Create an OLE server object?

Problem

I need to be able to write a complete OLE server for my application. This means that I must not only handle the case of my application running on its own, but also the case when an object from my application is embedded in another application's OLE container.

What is the easiest way to accomplish this with minimal duplication of code between the server and the application?

Technique

What if we told you that there was a way to have no duplication of code whatsoever between the application portion and the OLE server portion? You would probably jump for joy, wouldn't you?

Start jumping! The MFC provides a simple mechanism for implementing OLE servers that has almost no intrusiveness into your application design. In this How-To, we will create a simple OLE server that implements a simple editor that can be used either in a stand-alone mode or as an embedded OLE object with no code changes. Best of all, the whole thing only requires a few lines of code.

Steps

Open and run the Visual C++ application CH1109.MAK from the
CHAPT11\SAMPLES\CH1109 directory on the CD that comes with this book. Type
some characters into the editor window by clicking on the view and then typing.
Notice that the editor behaves like a normal editor in this application. Now, close
the application and start an OLE-compatible container application, such as Microsoft
Word for Windows. Select the Insert Object from the Edit menu of the application
and select the Ch11 Document from the list. Click on OK in the dialog, and the editor will be displayed in a small window running inside of Word. This can be seen
in Figure 11-9.

To reproduce this functionality in your own application, do the following:

1. Create a new application project make file in Visual C++ using AppWizard.
Give this project the name CH1109.MAK. In the options for the project, select
OLE options and click on the Full Server radio button. This will create the
base functionality to work with OLE servers.

2. Enter ClassWizard and select the CCh1109View from the drop-down list.
Select the CCh1109View object from the object list and the WM_CREATE
message from the message list. Click on the Add Function button. Enter the
following code into the OnCreate method of CCh1109View:

```
int CCh1109View::OnCreate(LPCREATESTRUCT lpCreateStruct)
{
  if (CView::OnCreate(lpCreateStruct) == -1)
```

continued on next page

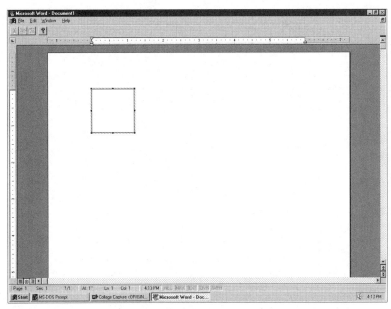

Figure 11-9 OLE server example using Microsoft Word for Windows

continued from previous page

```
            return -1;

   // Get the client rectangle for the entire view

   CRect r;
   GetClientRect(&r);

   // Create an edit control of that size

   if ( m_Edit.Create ( WS_CHILD | WS_VISIBLE | ES_MULTILINE |
       ES_UPPERCASE, r, this, 1001 ) == FALSE )
     MessageBox("Cannot create edit box!", "Error", MB_OK );
   return 0;
}
```

3. Next, in ClassWizard, select the CCh1109View object in the object list and the WM_SIZE message from the message list. Click on the Add Function button. Enter the following code into the OnSize method of CCh1109View:

```
void CCh1109View::OnSize(UINT nType, int cx, int cy)
{
   CView::OnSize(nType, cx, cy);

   // Get the client rectangle for the entire view

   CRect r;
   GetClientRect(&r);

   // Resize the edit control to that size

   m_Edit.MoveWindow(&r);
   m_Edit.SetFocus();

}
```

4. Add the following lines to the header file for the view object, CH11VW.H:

```
private:
   CEdit m_Edit;
```

5. Compile and run the application.

How It Works

As you will notice from the preceding code listings, there is no work whatsoever to do to create an application that functions as either an OLE server or a stand-alone application. The MFC classes for the views and documents automatically generate the required background code to make the application work in either setting.

In this application, we are creating a multiline edit box in the client area of the view window. Since this client area is not dependent on whether the program is running as a server or a stand-alone application, there is nothing to change in either case. The edit box simply collects data for the application.

CHAPTER 12
SOUND EFFECTS AND MUSIC

SOUND EFFECTS
AND MUSIC

How do I...

From a simple beep to request a new disk, to the sound effects in a computer game, sounds are a nonvisual cue that will make your Windows applications easier and more fun to use. In this chapter you will learn how to add the important sound and musical multimedia effects that will make your application a true Windows 95 application. The How-To's in this chapter will demonstrate simple methods of making sound effects and playing music from an audio CD. For those who want to develop the next great game, this chapter will also show you how to play MIDI files in the background.

12.1   Play Sound Effects

Every application, from a business application to a game, requires a simple method of playing a sound effect. This How-To will demonstrate how you can add sound effects to your applications with the minimum coding effort. It also discusses some ideas for distributing sound effects with or inside your application.

12.2   Read Track Information from a Compact Disc

Write your own database for tracking your CD collection! Or, replace the Windows CD player. This How-To provides the foundation for writing applications to manage audio CDs. It shows you how to get track information from the CD and provides some innovative ideas for using that information.

12.3   Play Music from a Compact Disc

This How-To will teach you to play tracks from an audio CD, so that your applications can become truly multimedia aware.

12.4   Play MIDI Music

For those who prefer some background music for their application, who are writing the next hot computer game, or who intend to write their own MIDI sequencer, this How-To will get you up and running. You will learn how to produce music from your application with minimal processor overhead, and you will write a small application that plays a MIDI file in the background.

Table 12-1 lists the Windows APIs covered in this chapter.

PlaySound	mciSendString
mciSendCommand	mciGetErrorString
MM_MCINOTIFY	GetOpenFileName

 Table 12-1 Windows APIs covered in Chapter 12

COMPLEXITY
EASY

12.1   How do I...
Play sound effects?

Problem

I want to add some simple sound effects to my application, but I don't want to have to write a complete music system. Is there a way I can add sound effects with a small amount of code?

Technique

Sound effects for Windows applications are typically stored as sampled sound wave data in a .WAV wave file. You can easily add sound effects to your application by using the PlaySound API function to play back these wave files. The PlaySound function is a high-level audio function, meaning that it enables you to use the PC speaker or a sound card in a highly device-independent manner, and with little code. The corollary to this is that you have little direct control over the way a sound is played. The PlaySound routine plays the sound effect in the best way, given the rate at which the sound was sampled and the rate at which the sound card can play it back. You cannot change this using the API (although the user can control some of these settings using the Control Panel). Similarly, you cannot mix or pause sounds played with the PlaySound API.

Despite these limitations, the PlaySound function provides enough flexibility for it to be useful in all but the most demanding applications. In the following steps you will learn how you can incorporate sounds into your application using this API function.

The PlaySound function takes three arguments. The syntax of the routine is

```
BOOL PlaySound(LPCTSTR lpszName,    // sound string
               HANDLE hModule,      // sound resource
               DWORD fdwSound);     // sound type
```

The first argument is a pointer supplied by the application. Usually this argument points to the name of a wave file to be played. You can also use this argument to pass the name of a resource or an alias, such as the system exclamation sound. The second argument is a HINSTANCE handle to an instance of an executable file. You only need to use this argument if you are using the SND_RESOURCE flag to request that a sound is loaded from a resource.

The third argument is a flag word. You can use this flag word to tell the PlaySound function where to play the sound from and how you want it played. Table 12-2 lists the options for these flags.

VALUE	MEANING
SND_ALIAS	The lpszName parameter specifies an entry in the [sounds] section of the registry. Do not use with SND_FILENAME or SND_RESOURCE.
SND_ASYNC	PlaySound returns as soon as the sound starts playing. Do not use with SND_SYNC.
SND_FILENAME	The name parameter specifies the name of a wave file. Do not use with SND_ALIAS or SND_RESOURCE.
SND_NODEFAULT	Do not play the system default sound if the requested sound cannot be found.
SND_NOWAIT	Do not wait for an available wave device. Fail the call if the wave device is busy or unavailable.
SND_RESOURCE	The name parameter specifies the name of a resource. Do not use with SND_ALIAS or SND_FILENAME.
SND_SYNC	The PlaySound function will not return until the sound has finished playing. Do not use with SND_ASYNC.

Table 12-2 Flags for the PlaySound function

Steps

Open and run the SOUNDFX application, which you will find in the CHAPTER12\SOUNDFX directory on the accompanying disc. When you run the application, you will see a small dialog like that shown in Figure 12-1. The dialog has two buttons, a Close button that closes the application and a Play Sound button. If you click the Play Sound button, the application will play a sound effect.

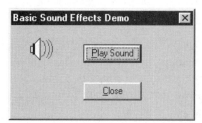

Figure 12-1 SOUNDFX application

Note: You will need to have a sound card, or similar hardware, and the necessary drivers installed. If in doubt, consult your Windows manuals for instructions about how to set up your sound card drivers.

The following steps will guide you through producing this simple application.

1. Start by creating a directory and naming it SOUNDFX. Use this directory as your working directory for the project, and place all the source files in this directory.

2. Create a text file, and save it as SOUNDFX.RC. Add the following lines to this file. This is the resource script that defines the dialog.

```
/* ---------------------------------------------------------------- */
/*                                                                  */
/* MODULE: SOUNDFX.RC                                               */
/* PURPOSE: This is the resource script which defines the dialog    */
/*          and icon for the application.                           */
/*                                                                  */
/* ---------------------------------------------------------------- */

#include <windows.h>
#include "soundfx.rh"

IDD_PLAYSOUND DIALOG 78, 62, 157, 71
STYLE DS_MODALFRAME | WS_POPUP | WS_VISIBLE | WS_CAPTION |
      WS_SYSMENU | DS_3DLOOK
CAPTION "Basic Sound Effects Demo"
FONT 8, "MS Sans Serif"
{
    DEFPUSHBUTTON "&Play Sound", ID_PLAYSOUND, 63, 14, 50, 14,
                BS_DEFPUSHBUTTON | WS_TABSTOP
    PUSHBUTTON "&Close", IDCANCEL, 63, 43, 50, 14, WS_TABSTOP
    ICON IDI_SOUNDS, IDI_SOUNDS, 15, 8, 18, 20
}

IDI_SOUNDS ICON "sounds.ico"
```

3. Create another file, and name it SOUNDFX.RH. This file will be included by both the resource script that you have just created and the main program source. The identifiers in this file are used to refer to the resources in the dialog. Add the following code to this file.

```
#ifndef __SOUNDFX_RH
/* -------------------------------------------------------------- */
/*                                                                */
/* MODULE: SOUNDFX.RH                                             */
/* PURPOSE: This include file defines the resource IDs used in the */
/*          application.                                          */
/*                                                                */
/* -------------------------------------------------------------- */
#define __SOUNDFX_RH

#define IDI_SOUNDS      1001
#define IDD_PLAYSOUND   200
#define ID_PLAYSOUND    101

#endif /* not __SOUNDFX_RH */
```

4. You will also need an icon for this application, as an icon is displayed in the dialog. Copy the file SOUNDS.ICO from the CHAPTER12\SOUNDFX directory on the CD. Alternatively, you can use a resource editor to create a simple icon file for the application. If you do this, create a 32-by-32-pixel icon, and save the file as SOUNDS.ICO.

5. Now it is time to create the main source file for the application. Create a new file, and save it as SOUNDFX.C. Add the following comments and declarations at the top of the file. Note particularly that this program includes the file MMSYSTEM.H along with the other Windows header files. MMSYSTEM.H is the main include file for the Windows multimedia extensions. This file declares the prototype for the PlaySound function and also defines the constants that you will use when you call this function.

```
/* -------------------------------------------------------------- */
/*                                                                */
/* MODULE: SOUNDFX.C                                              */
/* PURPOSE: This module demonstrates how you can use the PlaySound */
/*          API function to play sound effects from a file or     */
/*          from your application's resources.                    */
/*                                                                */
/* -------------------------------------------------------------- */

#define STRICT

#include <windows.h>
#include <winnt.h>
#include <mmsystem.h>
#include "soundfx.rh"
```

6. Now add the following code to the code you have already entered. The PlaySoundEffect function calls PlaySound to play the sound. The example application uses the SND_ASYNC flag to tell the function to return as soon as it has started playing the sound effect. If you want the application to pause

until the sound is completed, use the SND_SYNC flag instead. The
SND_SYNC flag tells PlaySound not to return control to the application until
it has finished playing the sound.

The application tests the return code from the PlaySound function. If a FALSE
result is returned, the application displays a dialog indicating that there was an
error playing the sound.

```
/* ------------------------------------------------------------------ */
/* This function plays a sound file using the PlaySound function.    */
/* This API function also allows waves to be played from a resource, */
/* or directly from a buffer in memory.                              */
/* ------------------------------------------------------------------ */
void PlaySoundEffect(HWND hWnd)
{
    BOOL ok;

    ok = PlaySound("DEMO.WAV",NULL,SND_ASYNC | SND_FILENAME |
                SND_NODEFAULT);
    if (!ok)
        MessageBox(hWnd,"Unable to play DEMO.WAV","PlaySound",
                MB_ICONEXCLAMATION | MB_OK);
}
```

7. Add the HandleDialog function, shown next, to the source file. This function
handles Windows messages sent to the dialog while it is active. The function
responds to WM_COMMAND messages to process the button clicks, calling
PlaySoundEffect when the Play button is clicked, and closing the dialog when
the Close button is clicked.

```
/* ------------------------------------------------------------------ */
/* This function handles the messages sent to the dialog. When the   */
/* dialog receives the IDCANCEL command, the dialog is closed. When  */
/* the function receives the ID_PLAYSOUND command, the              */
/* PlaySoundEffect function is called.                               */
/* ------------------------------------------------------------------ */
BOOL CALLBACK HandleDialog(HWND hWnd, UINT message,
                        WPARAM wParam, LPARAM lParam)
{
    switch (message)
    {
        case WM_INITDIALOG:
            return TRUE;
        case WM_COMMAND:
            if (wParam == IDCANCEL)
            {
                DestroyWindow(hWnd);
                return TRUE;
            }
            else
                if (wParam == ID_PLAYSOUND)
                {
                    PlaySoundEffect(hWnd);
```

```
                    return TRUE;
                }
            break;
        case WM_DESTROY:
            PostQuitMessage(0);
            return TRUE;
    }
    return FALSE;
}
```

8. Add the following code to the source file. The WinMain function is the entry point or starting point for C Windows applications. The code creates the dialog and then uses GetMessage, IsDialogMessage, TranslateMessage, and DispatchMessage in a loop to receive the messages from Windows and send them to the handler for the dialog.

```
/* ------------------------------------------------------------------ */
/* Our main function - set up and run the application.               */
/* ------------------------------------------------------------------ */
int PASCAL WinMain(HINSTANCE hInstance, HINSTANCE hPrevInstance,
                   LPSTR lpCmdLine, int nCmdShow)
{
    MSG   msg;
    HWND  hWnd;

    if ((hWnd = CreateDialog(hInstance,MAKEINTRESOURCE(IDD_PLAYSOUND),
                             NULL,HandleDialog)) == NULL)
        return FALSE;

    while (GetMessage(&msg,NULL,NULL,NULL))
        if (!IsDialogMessage(hWnd, &msg))
        {
            TranslateMessage(&msg);
            DispatchMessage(&msg);
        }

    return msg.wParam;
}
```

9. One more file is needed before you can successfully run the application. The application expects a file called DEMO.WAV to be in the current directory when it goes to play the sound effect. Copy the file DEMO.WAV from the CHAPTER12\SOUNDFX directory on the CD into your working directory. If you prefer, you can copy a .WAV file from another application instead, or perhaps a standard Windows sound from the WINDOWS\MEDIA directory on your system.

Comments

The PlaySound function provides a good level of functionality with minimal programming effort. Another consideration when writing an application that uses sounds is how the wave files will be distributed. The example application that you developed in this

How-To looked in the current directory to find the sound effect to play. In commercial applications, you might look in the directory where the application resides to find the file. Both of these methods require the wave file to be present or distributed with the application. A better method might be to encapsulate the waveform within the executable file as a resource. You can then call PlaySound with the SND_RESOURCE flag set, and specify the name of the resource in the name argument.

COMPLEXITY

MODERATE

12.2 How do I...
Read track information from a compact disc?

Problem

I would like to write a database to keep track of my CDs. Is there any method for reading at least some of the information from the CDs themselves?

Technique

While audio CDs do not store all the details about the tracks on the CD in a way that a Windows application can easily retrieve them, you can at least identify the number of tracks on a disc and the length of each track in minutes and seconds.

Such information is available through the Media Control Interface (MCI), an application programming interface to the multimedia features of Windows 95. The MCI provides high-level access to the features of compact discs, video discs, MIDI, animation, and wave devices. There are two ways to access MCI functions. You can use mciSendString to send string messages such as "play cdaudio from track 5." This is useful for high-level languages that are string oriented, such as Visual Basic. The other method uses the mciSendCommand function, which uses C-style structures and constants. The examples that you will encounter in this chapter use mciSendString, as this makes the code easier to read, and it is portable to most programming languages.

You can query a CD by opening the CD audio device, asking it for the number of tracks on the CD, and then asking for the length of each track. The MCI functions also allow you to specify what format position and length the information should be interpreted with. Probably the most useful format will be TMSF, which returns the information in tracks, minutes, seconds, and frames. For sound technology such as a CD track, the term "frames" does not seem to make sense—it is something that you might expect to find in the video world. For the purpose of this exercise with CD tracks, consider a frame to be one 75th of a second.

Using the mciSendCommand Function

The example applications throughout this chapter use the mciSendString command to interact with the Media Control Interface. This API allows you to use strings of English-like commands to communicate with the system. While this aids in producing clear code, some C programmers may feel that the production and translation of these strings uses too much overhead. As an alternative, you could use the mciSendCommand function in your applications. This command takes integer commands and flags, and pointers to structures when required. The syntax of the command is as follows:

```
MCIERROR mciSendCommand(
        MCIDEVICEID IDDevice,    // device ID
        UINT  uMsg,              // command to send
        DWORD fdwCommand,        // specific flags
        DWORD dwParam);          // structure pointer
```

The IDDevice parameter is used to pass a handle to the multimedia device. This handle is returned in a MCI_OPEN_PARAMS structure when the device is opened. The uMsg parameter contains the command to be executed. The MCI_OPEN command is used to open a device, MCI_CLOSE is used to close a device, MCI_PLAY plays a track or sequence, and MCI_STATUS retrieves track and status information. The third argument is used to pass extra flags for the operation. Using MCI_NOTIFY in this argument causes the command to operate asynchronously, with the MCI sending a notification to your application when it is complete.

The final argument, dwParam, may be used to pass the address of a structure. Certain MCI commands require a structure that defines any additional parameters—track number or device aliases are examples. For more information about using the mciSendCommand function, see your API reference guide.

Steps

Open and run the TRACKINF application, which you will find in the CHAPTER12\TRACKINF directory on the disc that accompanies this book. This application displays a small dialog such as that shown in Figure 12-2. The list of tracks and lengths will only be displayed if you have a CD player installed and an audio CD in the drive. If this is not the case, the application will display an error message when you execute it, and the list box will remain empty. You can change the track information listed by inserting another CD and clicking the Refresh button. This causes the application to read the data from the current compact disc. Clicking the Close button closes the application.

The following steps will lead you through the construction of this application.

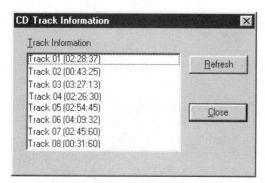

Figure 12-2 TRACKINF application

Note: You will need to have a CD player and the necessary drivers installed. If in doubt, consult your Windows manuals for instructions about how to set up your sound card and/or CD player drivers.

1. First, create a directory and call it TRACKINF. Use this directory as your working directory while you build this application, and place the source files into it.

2. A good next step is the creation of a resource script that defines the dialog. Although this could be easily accomplished through a resource editor, it is more useful in this case to enter it as a text file. Create a file called TRACKINF.RC, and enter the following lines in the file. This script includes the TRACKINF.RH file, then defines the dialog to be displayed.

```
/* -------------------------------------------------------------------- */
/*                                                                      */
/* MODULE: TRACKINF.RC                                                  */
/* PURPOSE: This is the resource script which defines the dialog        */
/*          and icon for the application.                               */
/*                                                                      */
/* -------------------------------------------------------------------- */

#include <windows.h>
#include "trackinf.rh"

IDD_TRACKINFO DIALOG 78, 62, 207, 112
STYLE DS_MODALFRAME | DS_3DLOOK | WS_POPUP | WS_VISIBLE |
      WS_CAPTION | WS_SYSMENU
CAPTION "CD Track Information"
FONT 8, "MS Sans Serif"
{
    LTEXT "&Track Information", -1, 11, 7, 59, 8
    LISTBOX IDL_TRACKLIST, 11, 19, 133, 81, LBS_NOTIFY | WS_BORDER |
        WS_BORDER | WS_VSCROLL
    PUSHBUTTON "&Refresh", ID_REFRESH, 152, 20, 50, 14, WS_TABSTOP
    DEFPUSHBUTTON "&Close", IDCANCEL, 152, 57, 50, 14,
                BS_DEFPUSHBUTTON | WS_TABSTOP
}
```

3. Next you should define the resource identifiers used by the resource script. Create a text file and name it TRACKINF.RH. Add the following definitions to the file:

```
#ifndef __TRACKINF_RH
/* ------------------------------------------------------------------ */
/*                                                                    */
/* MODULE: TRACKINF.RH                                                */
/* PURPOSE: This include file defines the resource IDs used in the    */
/*          application.                                              */
/*                                                                    */
/* ------------------------------------------------------------------ */
#define __TRACKINF_RH

#define IDD_TRACKINFO    200
#define IDL_TRACKLIST    102
#define ID_REFRESH       103

#endif /* not __TRACKINF_RH */
```

4. Now it is time to create the C program that drives the application. Create a new file and call it TRACKINF.C. Add the following comments and the #include statements. Notice that this application includes MMSYSTEM.H as well as the other Windows include files. This file defines the function prototypes and constants for the multimedia and MCI application programming interface.

```
/* ------------------------------------------------------------------ */
/*                                                                    */
/* MODULE: TRACKINF.C                                                 */
/* PURPOSE: This application demonstrates the use of the              */
/*          mciSendCommand API function to retrieve information       */
/*          about the tracks on a CD.                                 */
/*                                                                    */
/* ------------------------------------------------------------------ */

#define STRICT

#include <windows.h>
#include <winnt.h>
#include <mmsystem.h>
#include <stdlib.h>
#include "trackinf.rh"
```

5. Add the following function to this same source file. Function GetTrackInfo opens the CD audio device. If successful, it uses the "status cdaudio number of tracks" command to ask for the number of tracks on the CD, then loops for that number of tracks. For each track, it uses the "status cdaudio length track" command, specifying the track to query. It uses the returned string together with the track number to make a line of text, which is then inserted into the list box. Notice the call to mciSendString with the "set cdaudio time format TMSF" command. This command ensures that the return value from the length query will be in the expected format.

```
/* ------------------------------------------------------------------ */
/* This function attempts to read the track information for the CD    */
/* Audio device, and inserts the information as strings into a list   */
/* box. The function returns TRUE if successful, or FALSE if there    */
/* is no CD in the drive.                                             */
/* ------------------------------------------------------------------ */
BOOL GetTrackInfo(HWND hWnd)
{
    HWND                hWndList;
    char                retBuf[60], trackDesc[60];
    char                buf[256];
    DWORD               numTracks, track;
    MCIERROR            mciError;

    /* Get the handle of the listbox to add the items to. */
    hWndList = GetDlgItem(hWnd,IDL_TRACKLIST);

    mciError = mciSendString("open cdaudio",retBuf,
                        sizeof(retBuf),NULL);
    if (mciError == 0)
    {
        mciError = mciSendString("status cdaudio number of tracks",
                        retBuf,sizeof(retBuf),NULL);
        if (mciError == 0)
        {
            /* Set the type of time information to be returned. */
            mciError = mciSendString("set cdaudio time format TMSF",
                        NULL,0,NULL);
            /* Loop through and retrieve info for each track. */
            numTracks = atoi(retBuf);
            for (track = 1; ((mciError == 0) &&
                        (track <= numTracks)); track++)
            {
                // Get the length of each track, and add the info
                // to the listbox.
                wsprintf(trackDesc,"status cdaudio length track %d",
                        track);
                mciError = mciSendString(trackDesc,retBuf,
                                    sizeof(retBuf),NULL);
                if (mciError == 0)
                {
                    wsprintf(buf,"Track %02ld (%s)",track,retBuf);
                    SendMessage(hWndList,LB_ADDSTRING,0,(LPARAM)buf);
                }
            }
        }
        // Close the device for the moment.
        mciSendString("close cdaudio",NULL,0,NULL);
    }

    // Return TRUE if successful, otherwise display the error
    // and return FALSE.
    if (mciError == 0)
        return TRUE;
    else
    {
```

```
            mciGetErrorString(mciError,buf,sizeof(buf));
            MessageBox(hWnd,buf,"Track Info",MB_ICONSTOP | MB_OK);
            return FALSE;
        }
}
```

6. Add the HandleDialog function shown next. This function responds to the Windows messages that are sent to the dialog window. In particular, it responds to the WM_INITDIALOG message by filling in the list box, and also performs this in response to the ID_REFRESH command message. In the latter case, it has to clear the list box contents before adding new track information. The function also responds to the IDCANCEL message by closing the dialog, and to the WM_DESTROY message by shutting down the application.

```
/* ------------------------------------------------------------ */
/* This function handles the messages sent to the dialog.       */
/* ------------------------------------------------------------ */
BOOL CALLBACK HandleDialog(HWND hWnd, UINT message,
                           WPARAM wParam, LPARAM lParam)
{
    switch (message)
    {
        case WM_INITDIALOG:
            GetTrackInfo(hWnd);
            return TRUE;
        case WM_COMMAND:
            if (wParam == IDCANCEL)
            {
                DestroyWindow(hWnd);
                return TRUE;
            }
            else
                if (wParam == ID_REFRESH)
                {
                    // The user clicked the Refresh button. Clear
                    // the contents of the list box and refresh
                    // the list.
                    SendDlgItemMessage(hWnd,IDL_TRACKLIST,
                                       LB_RESETCONTENT,0,0);
                    GetTrackInfo(hWnd);
                }
            break;
        case WM_DESTROY:
            PostQuitMessage(0);
            return TRUE;
    }
    return FALSE;
}
```

7. Finally, add the following code to the source file. This is the WinMain function, which is called by Windows when the application commences. The function sets up the dialog, then pumps messages in a loop until the application completes.

```
/* ---------------------------------------------------------------- */
/* Our main function - set up and run the application.              */
/* ---------------------------------------------------------------- */
int PASCAL WinMain(HINSTANCE hInstance, HINSTANCE hPrevInstance,
                   LPSTR lpCmdLine, int nCmdShow)
{
    MSG  msg;
    HWND hWnd;

    if ((hWnd = CreateDialog(hInstance,MAKEINTRESOURCE(IDD_TRACKINFO),
                             NULL,HandleDialog)) == NULL)
        return FALSE;

    while (GetMessage(&msg,NULL,NULL,NULL))
        if (!IsDialogMessage(hWnd, &msg))
        {
            TranslateMessage(&msg);
            DispatchMessage(&msg);
        }

    return msg.wParam;
}
```

Comments

The track information status commands provided in the MCI library are probably of little use by themselves. Possible useful applications include providing a moving gauge when playing a track from a CD, and the construction of a database of information about the user's compact disc library. The user would insert the disc and simply fill in the artist and title information beside the track information obtained directly from the disc.

COMPLEXITY
MODERATE

12.3 How do I...
Play music from a compact disc?

Problem

How can I play music from an audio CD? Can this be done in the background while I am working?

Technique

You can use the Media Control Interface (MCI) functions to play an entire CD, or selected tracks from a CD, using very simple, high-level code. The MCI is a set of APIs that allow you to write high-level, device-independent code. Commands from your code are interpreted by the MCI and passed on to the device drivers that interface with the hardware itself. There are two ways to use the MCI. The mciSendCommand function is used to send commands to the system and receive the results. Communication is via a series of C-type structures and constants. A simpler method of implementing the functionality of the API is through the mciSendString interface. This function expects a string containing a pseudo-English command, and it returns its results in a string. This approach is more readable and also easily portable across programming languages and environments.

There are three simple steps involved in playing an audio CD:

1. Open the device.

2. Play the CD.

3. Close the CD.

You could implement a simple program that used the mciSendString function and commands that looked very similar to those just listed, and you would have a simple CD player. To be useful, however, your CD player needs to allow you to select the tracks and play the music in the background, so you can work while you listen. Thus, a useful application would need two additional steps; so the list might look like this:

1. Open the device.

2. Retrieve track information for the user to select.

3. Play the CD or specific tracks.

4. Wait for the CD to finish playing.

5. Close the CD.

How-To 12.2 shows in detail how you can retrieve the track information from an audio CD and display it for the user. Opening, playing, and closing the CD are simple commands, so the remaining problem is how to wait for the CD to finish playing without locking up the computer. In Windows 95, we could just use a separate thread and have our main application start this thread to play the CD. However, there is an even simpler method than this. By adding the keyword "notify" to the end of a command sent with mciSendString, the command becomes asynchronous, returning control to the application once the process has started. The application receives a message, MM_MCINOTIFY, when the process has completed, or been aborted.

In the following steps you will learn how you can implement each of these components to make a simple CD player.

Steps

Open and run the PLAYCD application. You will find this application in the CHAPTER12\PLAYCD subdirectory on the CD-ROM that accompanies this book. The application initially displays the dialog shown in Figure 12-3. To the left is a list of the tracks on the currently inserted CD, and below it are Play and Stop buttons. Initially, the Play button is enabled, and the Stop button is disabled. When you click on a track and click the Play button, the application plays the selected track on the CD. While the CD is playing, the Play button is grayed, but you can click the Stop button to halt

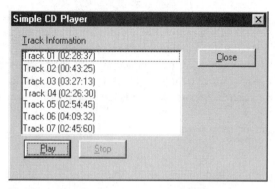

Figure 12-3 PLAYCD example application

the music. Once the music stops, the Play button is enabled again, and the Stop button is disabled.

The following steps will lead you through the production of this example application.

> Note: You will need to have a CD player and the necessary drivers installed. If in doubt, consult your Windows manuals for instructions about how to set up your sound card and/or CD player drivers.

1. Create a new directory and call it PLAYCD. You will use this as your working directory for this application. Place all the source files for the application in this directory.

2. Create a resource script that defines the dialog for the application. To do this, create a new file with a text editor, and save it as PLAYCD.RC. Type the following resource compiler commands into the file. These commands define the dialog box used to play the CD. It contains a list box for track selection, Play and Stop buttons, and a Close button to shut down the application. The Play and Stop buttons are initially disabled.

```
/* ----------------------------------------------------------------- */
/*                                                                   */
/* MODULE: PLAYCD.RC                                                 */
/* PURPOSE: This is the resource script which defines the dialog     */
/*          and icon for the application.                            */
/*                                                                   */
/* ----------------------------------------------------------------- */

#include <windows.h>
#include "playcd.rh"

IDD_PLAYCD DIALOG 34, 35, 220, 116
```

```
STYLE DS_MODALFRAME | DS_3DLOOK | WS_POPUP | WS_VISIBLE |
    WS_CAPTION | WS_SYSMENU
CAPTION "Simple CD Player"
FONT 8, "MS Sans Serif"
{
    LTEXT "&Track Information", -1, 9, 6, 58, 8
    LISTBOX IDL_TRACKLIST, 9, 18, 139, 68, LBS_STANDARD
    DEFPUSHBUTTON "&Play", ID_PLAYTRACK, 11, 87, 41, 14,
                  BS_DEFPUSHBUTTON | WS_TABSTOP
    PUSHBUTTON "&Close", IDCANCEL, 161, 16, 50, 14, WS_TABSTOP
    PUSHBUTTON "&Stop", ID_STOP, 59, 87, 41, 14, WS_DISABLED | WS_TABSTOP
}
```

3. Now create an include file, and place in it the resource identifiers used by the resource compiler script. These identifiers will also be referenced by the application when it changes the state of the buttons and fills in and queries the list box. Create a new file, and call it PLAYCD.RH. Add the following definitions:

```
#ifndef __PLAYCD_RH
/* ------------------------------------------------------------ */
/*                                                              */
/*                                                              */
/* MODULE: PLAYCD.RH                                            */
/* PURPOSE: This include file defines the resource IDs used in the */
/*          application.                                        */
/*                                                              */
/* ------------------------------------------------------------ */
#define __PLAYCD_RH

#define IDD_PLAYCD       200
#define IDL_TRACKLIST    101
#define ID_PLAYTRACK     102
#define ID_STOP          103

#endif /* not __PLAYCD_RH */
```

4. Having created the include file, you can now write the source code for the application. Create another new file, and save it as PLAYCD.C. Type the following comments and statements into the top of the file. Notice particularly the #include statements. As well as the conventional Windows include files, this application includes MMSYSTEM.H. This file is required for all multimedia applications, defining constants and prototyping functions that compose the interface to MCI and other multimedia systems.

```
/* ------------------------------------------------------------ */
/*                                                              */
/* MODULE: PLAYCD.C                                             */
/* PURPOSE: This application demonstrates the use of the        */
/*          mciSendCommand API function to retrieve information  */
/*          about the tracks on a CD.                           */
/*                                                              */
/* ------------------------------------------------------------ */

#define STRICT

#include <windows.h>
```

continued on next page

continued from previous page

```
#include <winnt.h>
#include <mmsystem.h>
#include <stdlib.h>
#include "playcd.rh"
```

5. Now add the following function to the same source file. The GetTrackInfo
function attempts to open the "cdaudio" device. If opening the device is successful, it asks the device how many tracks are on the currently inserted CD.
The code iterates through the tracks, asking for the length in TMSF format
(tracks, minutes, seconds, and frames) for each track. The result of each query
is placed into the list box as a string.

```
/* ---------------------------------------------------------------- */
/* This function attempts to read the track information for the CD  */
/* Audio device, and inserts the information as strings into a list */
/* box. The function returns TRUE if successful, or FALSE if there  */
/* is no CD in the drive.                                           */
/* ---------------------------------------------------------------- */
void GetTrackInfo(HWND hWnd)
{
    HWND            hWndList;
    char            retBuf[60], trackDesc[60];
    char            buf[256];
    DWORD           numTracks, track;
    MCIERROR        mciError;

    // Get the handle of the listbox to add the items to.
    hWndList = GetDlgItem(hWnd,IDL_TRACKLIST);

    mciError = mciSendString("open cdaudio",retBuf,
                        sizeof(retBuf),NULL);
    if (mciError == 0)
    {
        mciError = mciSendString("status cdaudio number of tracks",
                            retBuf,sizeof(retBuf),NULL);
        if (mciError == 0)
        {
            // Set the type of time information to be returned.
            mciError = mciSendString("set cdaudio time format TMSF",
                            NULL,0,NULL);
            // Loop through and retrieve info for each track.
            numTracks = atoi(retBuf);
            for (track = 1; ((mciError == 0) &&
                            (track <= numTracks)); track++)
            {
                // Get the length of each track, and add the info to
                // the listbox.
                wsprintf(trackDesc,"status cdaudio length track %d",
                        track);
                mciError = mciSendString(trackDesc,retBuf,
                                    sizeof(retBuf),NULL);
                if (mciError == 0)
                {
                    wsprintf(buf,"Track %02ld (%s)",track,retBuf);
                    SendMessage(hWndList,LB_ADDSTRING,0,(LPARAM)buf);
```

```
                    }
                }
            }
            // Close the device for the moment.
            mciSendString("close cdaudio",NULL,0,NULL);
    }

    // Display the error if one occurred.
    if (mciError != 0)
    {
        mciGetErrorString(mciError,buf,sizeof(buf));
        MessageBox(hWnd,buf,"Play CD",MB_ICONSTOP | MB_OK);
    }
}
```

6. The next function starts the CD playing. It retrieves the number of the selected item in the list of tracks, and also the total number of tracks listed in the list box. There are three possible combinations with the MCI "play" command. The "play cdaudio" command starts playing at the current position on the CD, and plays until the end of the disc. Adding a track to play from, such as "play cdaudio from 3," plays from that track until the end of the disc. Finally, you can add the track to play to; for instance, "play cdaudio from 3 to 4" plays from the start of track three to the start of track four. If track four does not exist, MCI returns an error.

The following code plays from the requested track to the start of the next track, unless the requested track is the last track on the disc. In this case, the code plays to the end of the disc. In any case, only a single track is played.

```
/* ---------------------------------------------------------------- */
/* This function opens the CD Audio device and plays the selected   */
/* track. The function specifies the NOTIFY option, so a message    */
/* will be sent when the track is completed.                        */
/* ---------------------------------------------------------------- */
void PlayTrack(HWND hWnd)
{
    char        buf[60];
    MCIERROR    mciError;
    LRESULT     trackID;
    HWND        hWndList;
    DWORD       numTracks;

    // See if there is a track selected in the list box. If there
    // is, play that track, otherwise display an error and exit.
    hWndList = GetDlgItem(hWnd,IDL_TRACKLIST);
    if (hWndList)
        trackID = SendMessage(hWndList,LB_GETCURSEL,0,0);
    else
        trackID = LB_ERR;

    if (trackID == LB_ERR)
    {
        MessageBox(hWnd,"Please select a track to play","Play CD",
                MB_ICONEXCLAMATION | MB_OK);
```

continued on next page

continued from previous page

```
            return;
        }

    // Open the device.
    mciError = mciSendString("open cdaudio",buf,sizeof(buf),NULL);
    if (mciError == 0)
    {
        // Set the type of time information used.
        mciSendString("set cdaudio time format TMSF",
                    NULL,0,NULL);

        mciSendString("status cdaudio number of tracks",
                    buf,sizeof(buf),NULL);
        numTracks = atoi(buf);

        // Play the specified track. Using the word notify
        // tells the MCI interface to send a notification message
        // to the specified window when done.
        trackID++;
        if (trackID < numTracks)
          wsprintf(buf,"play cdaudio from %ld to %ld notify",
                    trackID,trackID + 1);
        else
          wsprintf(buf,"play cdaudio from %ld notify",trackID);
        mciError = mciSendString(buf,NULL,0,hWnd);
        if (mciError == 0)
        {
          // Enable the Stop button and gray the Play button.
          EnableWindow(GetDlgItem(hWnd,ID_PLAYTRACK),FALSE);
          EnableWindow(GetDlgItem(hWnd,ID_STOP),TRUE);
        }
        else // Close the device if playing failed.
            mciSendString("close cdaudio",NULL,0,NULL);
    }

    // Display the error if one occurred.
    if (mciError != 0)
    {
        mciGetErrorString(mciError,buf,sizeof(buf));
        MessageBox(hWnd,buf,"Play CD",MB_ICONSTOP | MB_OK);
    }
}
```

> Note that the code above does not close the CD audio device if the call is successful. A successful call starts the CD playing, and the application will be sent a message once the track completes.

7. Function TrackDone is called in response to a MM_MCINOTIFY message. This message is sent when an asynchronous MCI command completes, either successfully, or aborted by an error or another command. Add this function to the same source file.

```
/* ---------------------------------------------------------------- */
/* This function handles the message sent to the dialog when the    */
/* cd is finished playing.                                          */
/* ---------------------------------------------------------------- */
void TrackDone(HWND hWnd)
{
    // Enable the Play button and gray the Stop button.
    EnableWindow(GetDlgItem(hWnd,ID_PLAYTRACK),TRUE);
    EnableWindow(GetDlgItem(hWnd,ID_STOP),FALSE);

    // Close the CD device.
    mciSendString("close cdaudio",NULL,0,NULL);
}
```

8. Add the following code to the PLAYCD.C source file also. This function is
called when the user clicks the Stop button. The code will be executed if the
user clicks the button when the CD is playing, and it will also be called when
the application closes. For this reason, the code ensures that the Stop button
genuinely is enabled before using the mciSendString function to send a "stop
cdaudio" message to the CD player.

```
/* ---------------------------------------------------------------- */
/* This function responds when the user clicks the stop button. It  */
/* checks to ensure that the stop button is enabled (which tells us */
/* that the CD is playing), and stops the CD device.                */
/* ---------------------------------------------------------------- */
void StopButtonClicked(HWND hWnd)
{
    HWND     hWndStop;
    MCIERROR mciError;
    char     buf[100];

    hWndStop = GetDlgItem(hWnd,ID_STOP);
    if ((hWndStop) && (IsWindowEnabled(hWndStop)))
    {
        // Tell the CD to stop playing.
        mciError = mciSendString("stop cdaudio",NULL,0,NULL);

        // Display the error if one occurred.
        if (mciError != 0)
        {
            mciGetErrorString(mciError,buf,sizeof(buf));
            MessageBox(hWnd,buf,"Play CD",MB_ICONSTOP | MB_OK);
        }
    }
}
```

9. Now add the HandleDialog function, shown next, to the source file. This
function is a callback function, which will be called by Windows whenever
there is a message to be processed for the dialog box. The function responds to
a number of Windows messages. The first message it processes is the
WM_INITDIALOG message. In response to this message, the code loads the
track information from the CD into the list box for display. When the function
receives the ID_PLAYTRACK command message, it calls the PlayTrack

function that you wrote earlier, which starts the selected track playing. It responds to the ID_STOP command by calling StopButtonClicked to interrupt the music, and it also calls StopButtonClicked when the dialog is closed.

The most interesting message to be processed is the MM_MCINOTIFY message. This message is sent because you specified "notify" with the mciSendString function call in the PlayTrack function. The MM_MCINOTIFY message informs you that the command (in this case playing a track) has completed, aborted, or been interrupted. The LPARAM argument will contain the device ID that sent the message, and the WPARAM argument will contain a code explaining the reason for the message. In this example, there is only one device sending the message, and the reason code is ignored. Instead, the application calls the TrackDone function to change which buttons are enabled and disabled.

```
/* ---------------------------------------------------------------- */
/* This function handles the messages sent to the dialog. When the  */
/* dialog receives the IDCANCEL command, the dialog is closed.      */
/* ---------------------------------------------------------------- */
BOOL CALLBACK HandleDialog(HWND hWnd, UINT message,
                            WPARAM wParam, LPARAM lParam)
{
    switch (message)
    {
        case WM_INITDIALOG:
            GetTrackInfo(hWnd);
            return TRUE;
        case WM_COMMAND:
            switch (wParam)
            {
                case IDCANCEL:
                    DestroyWindow(hWnd);
                    return TRUE;
                case ID_PLAYTRACK:
                    PlayTrack(hWnd);
                    return TRUE;
                case ID_STOP:
                    StopButtonClicked(hWnd);
                    return TRUE;
                default:
                    break;
            }
            break;
        case MM_MCINOTIFY:
            TrackDone(hWnd);
        break;
        case WM_DESTROY:
            StopButtonClicked(hWnd);
            PostQuitMessage(0);
            return TRUE;
    }
    return FALSE;
}
```

10. Finally, you need to add a WinMain function. This function, called when the application is first loaded, is responsible for initializing the dialog and pumping messages so that the application can run. Add the following code to the bottom of the source file, PLAYCD.C.

```
/* ------------------------------------------------------------- */
/* Our main function - set up and run the application.           */
/* ------------------------------------------------------------- */
int PASCAL WinMain(HINSTANCE hInstance, HINSTANCE hPrevInstance,
                   LPSTR lpCmdLine, int nCmdShow)
{
    MSG  msg;
    HWND hWnd;

    if ((hWnd = CreateDialog(hInstance,MAKEINTRESOURCE(IDD_PLAYCD),
                             NULL,HandleDialog)) == NULL)
        return FALSE;

    while (GetMessage(&msg,NULL,NULL,NULL))
        if (!IsDialogMessage(hWnd, &msg))
        {
            TranslateMessage(&msg);
            DispatchMessage(&msg);
        }

    return msg.wParam;
}
```

Comments

The PLAYCD sample application demonstrates how you can use the Windows Media Control Interface to play specific tracks on a CD. You can expand on the functionality offered here to play entire CDs. You could even combine this application with the track information application discussed in How-To 12.2, to provide a CD player with a database. The user could select which tracks he or she liked and disliked, and your CD player could play only the preferred music. Alternatively, you could write a minimal application that simply played random tracks in the background while the user worked on another task.

COMPLEXITY
MODERATE

12.4 How do I... Play MIDI music?

Problem

I want to play music in the background while my application is running, but the wave data necessary to do this would make my application huge. Is there any way I can use the MIDI support in most sound cards to play background music with a much smaller disk and memory footprint?

Technique

Conventional Windows sound effects produce reasonable quality output on most sound cards and certainly allow you to produce exciting and useful sounds. Arguably, this same technique could be used to play background music for a game or other multimedia application. However, the amount of wave data required for even a few seconds of sampled music is huge. In addition to the obvious problem of finding disk storage space for such a large quantity of data, there is the requirement of processor time to load and prepare such data for the sound card.

The solution to these problems is to use synthesized music rather than sampled sound. Synthesized music is stored and played using the Musical Instrument Digital Interface, or MIDI for short. Most sound cards support a prebuilt range of standard synthesized instrument sounds, which means that the cards themselves store the entire waveform necessary to generate the sound, or at least an algorithm that approximates the waveform. All that is required for your application is a .MID file, which stores the pitch, duration, and instrument to be used to play each note. This data is much smaller and requires less processor time to manipulate.

So how do you use the MIDI capabilities of a sound card? Traditionally, the answer to this question has varied from manufacturer to manufacturer, and even at times from one sound card to another. With Microsoft Windows 3.1, Microsoft added the Multimedia System API, providing a generic way to get at the MIDI capabilities without having to know about the exact interface to the sound card. The example that you will see in this How-To uses the Windows Multimedia API to play a MIDI file in the background.

Playing a MIDI file is similar to playing any other multimedia device—it requires opening the appropriate device and sending a play command with the necessary information to play the file. There are two API functions that allow you to send commands to multimedia devices. The function traditionally used by C programmers is the mciSendCommand function, which uses C structures and constants to do its work. The other function is mciSendString. This command uses a string syntax that is more easily accessible to people programming with other languages. It also aids readability, so this How-To will use this API function to communicate with the MIDI device.

The second technique to grasp is how to leave the MIDI device playing in the background while your application performs some other, more useful function. The key to this is the use of the "notify" keyword. Adding this keyword to a multimedia system function causes Windows to return control to your application as soon as the music has started playing, service the MIDI device in the background, and inform your application when the music has finished. In the following steps you will see how to use this method to play a MIDI file.

Figure 12-4 PLAYMIDI sample application

Steps

Compile and run the PLAYMIDI application from the CHAPTER12\PLAYMIDI directory on the compact disc accompanying this book. Click the Browse button and look for a MIDI file to play. You will find a file called 95DEMO.MID (the .MID extension may be hidden by Windows) in the CHAPTER12\PLAYMIDI directory on the CD. Open this file by double-clicking it, or by clicking the Open button in the standard File Open dialog.

Once you have selected a MIDI file, the file name will be displayed in the dialog, and the Play button will be enabled. Figure 12-4 shows how you can expect the application to look at this stage. You can play the selected file by clicking the Play button. While the file is playing, the Play button will be grayed, and the Stop button will be enabled. You can wait until the music finishes, or click the Stop button to stop the music early. In either case, the Play button will be enabled again, and the Stop button will be grayed. Click the Close button when you are ready to close the example application.

The following steps will guide you through the construction of this sample application. Along the way, you will learn how to use the Multimedia System API to play MIDI files and how to play music in the background.

> Note: You will need to have a sound card that supports MIDI playback and the necessary drivers installed. If in doubt, consult your Windows manuals for instructions about how to set up your sound card drivers and the MIDI mapper.

1. Start by creating a directory where you will place the files for this application. Call the directory PLAYMIDI.

2. Next create a text file to hold the resource script for the application. Call this file PLAYMIDI.RC. Add the following lines to the file. These lines define the dialog that you see on screen when the application runs.

```
/* ------------------------------------------------------------ */
/*                                                              */
/* MODULE: PLAYMIDI.RC                                          */
/* PURPOSE: This is the resource script which defines the dialog */
/*          and icon for the application.                       */
/*                                                              */
/* ------------------------------------------------------------ */
```

continued on next page

continued from previous page

```
#include <windows.h>
#include "playmidi.rh"

IDD_PLAYMIDI DIALOG 30, 62, 233, 70
STYLE DS_MODALFRAME | DS_3DLOOK | WS_POPUP | WS_VISIBLE |
    WS_CAPTION | WS_SYSMENU
CAPTION "MIDI Player Demo"
FONT 8, "MS Sans Serif"
{
    GROUPBOX "MIDI File", ID_GROUPBOX1, 9, 3, 219, 33, BS_GROUPBOX
    LTEXT "", ID_FILENAME, 16, 18, 152, 8
    DEFPUSHBUTTON "&Browse", ID_BROWSE, 174, 15, 50, 14,
                    BS_DEFPUSHBUTTON  | WS_TABSTOP
    PUSHBUTTON "&Play", ID_PLAY, 33, 43, 31, 14, WS_DISABLED | WS_TABSTOP
    PUSHBUTTON "&Stop", ID_STOP, 67, 43, 31, 14, WS_DISABLED | WS_TABSTOP
    PUSHBUTTON "&Close", IDCANCEL, 150, 43, 50, 14, WS_TABSTOP
}
```

3. The resource script that you defined uses some identifiers to represent the internal numbers of controls. Create an include file to define these identifiers, so that the controls can be accessed by the C source code of the application as well. To do this, create a new text file called PLAYMIDI.RH, then add the following definitions to this file.

```
#ifndef __PLAYMIDI_RH
/* ------------------------------------------------------------ */
/*                                                              */
/* MODULE: PLAYMIDI.RH                                          */
/* PURPOSE: This include file defines the resource IDs used in the */
/*          application.                                        */
/*                                                              */
/* ------------------------------------------------------------ */
#define __PLAYMIDI_RH

#define IDD_PLAYMIDI     200
#define ID_GROUPBOX1     101
#define ID_FILENAME      102
#define ID_BROWSE        103
#define ID_PLAY          104
#define ID_STOP          105

#endif /* not __PLAYMIDI_RH */
```

4. Having finished the prerequisites, you are ready to start on the main task—writing the C source code for the application. Create a file called PLAYMIDI.C, and add the following lines. These lines include the header files needed by the application. Note especially the inclusion of MMSYSTEM.H. This file provides the constants, structures, and function prototypes necessary to use the Windows multimedia functions.

```
/* ------------------------------------------------------------------ */
/*                                                                     */
/*                                                                     */
/* MODULE: PLAYMIDI.C                                                  */
/* PURPOSE: This application demonstrates how you can use the          */
/*          multimedia system API to play MIDI files using the MIDI    */
/*          mapper.                                                    */
/*                                                                     */
/* ------------------------------------------------------------------ */

#define STRICT

#include <windows.h>
#include <winnt.h>
#include <commdlg.h>
#include <mmsystem.h>
#include "playmidi.rh"
```

5. Now add the following code to the same source file. Function BrowseClicked
   displays a standard File Open dialog to retrieve the name of the MIDI file from
   the user. It does this by initializing an OPENFILENAME structure, then calling
   the GetOpenFileName Windows API function. If you usually program using
   an application framework, or a language such as Delphi or Visual Basic, you
   would instead use the capabilities of your environment to display this dialog
   and retrieve a file name.

```
static char *FileNameFilter = "Midi Sequences (*.mid)\0*.MID\0All Files
                              (*.*)\0*.*\0";

/* ------------------------------------------------------------------ */
/* This function is called when the Browse button is clicked. It       */
/* uses a file open common dialog box to get the name of a MIDI        */
/* sequence file. If a valid file name is returned, the function       */
/* sets the ID_FILENAME static text to the name of the file. If the    */
/* user chooses Cancel, the previous string is retained (which may     */
/* be an emtpy string).                                                */
/* ------------------------------------------------------------------ */
void BrowseClicked(HWND hWnd)
{
    char                    fileName[255];
    OPENFILENAME            ofStruct;

    // Get the previous file name, if any.
    fileName[0] = 0;
    GetDlgItemText(hWnd,ID_FILENAME,fileName,sizeof(fileName));

    // Initialize the open file structure.
    ofStruct.lStructSize = sizeof(OPENFILENAME);
    ofStruct.hwndOwner = hWnd;
    ofStruct.hInstance = 0;
    ofStruct.lpstrFilter = (LPSTR)FileNameFilter;
    ofStruct.lpstrCustomFilter = NULL;
    ofStruct.nMaxCustFilter = 0;
    ofStruct.nFilterIndex = 1;
    // Stores the result in this variable.
    ofStruct.lpstrFile = fileName;
```

continued on next page

continued from previous page

```
        ofStruct.nMaxFile = sizeof(fileName);
        ofStruct.lpstrFileTitle = NULL;
        ofStruct.nMaxFileTitle = 0;
        ofStruct.lpstrInitialDir = NULL;
        ofStruct.lpstrTitle = "Choose a MIDI sequence file";
        ofStruct.Flags = OFN_FILEMUSTEXIST | OFN_HIDEREADONLY |
                         OFN_PATHMUSTEXIST;
        ofStruct.nFileOffset = 0;
        ofStruct.nFileExtension = 0;
        ofStruct.lpstrDefExt = "*";
        ofStruct.lCustData = NULL;
        ofStruct.lpfnHook = NULL;
        ofStruct.lpTemplateName = NULL;

        /* Call the common dialog routine, then store the new
           file name if the user clicks OK, and enable or disable
           the Play button depending upon whether there is a file
           currently specified. */
        if (GetOpenFileName(&ofStruct))
        {
            SetDlgItemText(hWnd,ID_FILENAME,fileName);
            EnableWindow(GetDlgItem(hWnd,ID_PLAY),TRUE);
        }
        else
            if (fileName[0] == 0)
                EnableWindow(GetDlgItem(hWnd,ID_PLAY),FALSE);
}
```

6. Add function PlayClicked, listed next, to the source file. This function is the heart of the code to play the MIDI file. It uses mciSendString to open the specified file. The "type sequencer" option tells MCI that the file supplied is a MIDI file and should be played with the sequencer. This is necessary in case the file does not have a .MID extension. When the device is open, the code uses the mciSendString function again, this time with the command "play myseq notify." This starts the music playing and returns immediately to the application. The multimedia system will send a MM_MCINOTIFY message to the application window when the music completes.

```
/* ------------------------------------------------------------ */
/* This function uses the MIDI sequencer device to open the     */
/* specified file and play it. By specifying the notify keyword, */
/* control is returned to the application as soon as the sequence */
/* begins playing, and the application will be notified when it is */
/* complete.                                                    */
/* ------------------------------------------------------------ */
void PlayClicked(HWND hWnd)
{
    char        inBuf[300], outBuf[60], fileName[255];
    MCIERROR    mciError;

    /* Retrieve the file name from the static text control.
       The fileName must be valid; otherwise the Play button
       would not be enabled. */
    GetDlgItemText(hWnd,ID_FILENAME,fileName,sizeof(fileName));
```

```
// Open the device.
wsprintf(inBuf,"open %s type sequencer alias myseq",fileName);
mciError = mciSendString(inBuf,outBuf,sizeof(outBuf),NULL);
if (mciError == 0)
{
    /* Play the MIDI file. Using the word notify
        tells the MCI interface to send a notification
        message to the specified window when done. */
    mciError = mciSendString("play myseq notify",NULL,0,hWnd);
    if (mciError == 0)
    {
        // Enable the Stop button and gray the Play button.
        EnableWindow(GetDlgItem(hWnd,ID_PLAY),FALSE);
        EnableWindow(GetDlgItem(hWnd,ID_STOP),TRUE);
    }
    else // Close the device if playing failed.
        mciSendString("close myseq",NULL,0,NULL);
}

// Display any error messages.
if (mciError != 0)
{
    mciGetErrorString(mciError,inBuf,sizeof(inBuf));
    MessageBox(hWnd,inBuf,"Play MIDI",MB_ICONSTOP | MB_OK);
}
}
```

7. Add the MIDINotify function shown next. This function will be called from the message-handling function for the dialog when the dialog receives a MM_MCINOTIFY message from Windows. The code enables the Play button, grays the Stop button, and closes the MIDI device.

```
/* ---------------------------------------------------------------- */
/* This function handles the message sent to the dialog when the    */
/* sequence is finished playing.                                    */
/* ---------------------------------------------------------------- */
void MIDINotify(HWND hWnd)
{
    // Enable the Play button and gray the Stop button.
    EnableWindow(GetDlgItem(hWnd,ID_PLAY),TRUE);
    EnableWindow(GetDlgItem(hWnd,ID_STOP),FALSE);

    // Close the device.
    mciSendString("close myseq",NULL,0,NULL);
}
```

8. Add function StopClicked to the source file. The following code will be called when the user clicks the Stop button. The application will usually only receive this message while a MIDI file is playing, as it is only during this time that the Stop button is enabled. This function is also called when the user clicks the Close button to close the application. In this way, you can ensure that the MIDI device is freed when the application finishes. In response to this message, the code sends a "stop" message to the sequencer, using the mciSendString API function. In response to this message, the multimedia system will stop playing the MIDI music file and will send a notification message to the dialog window.

```
/* ------------------------------------------------------------ */
/* This function is called when the user clicks the Stop button, */
/* and also when the application is about to shut down. It checks */
/* to see if the MIDI device is still playing, and if so, stops it */
/* ------------------------------------------------------------ */
void StopClicked(HWND hWnd)
{
    HWND       hWndStop;
    MCIERROR   mciError;
    char       buf[100];

    hWndStop = GetDlgItem(hWnd,ID_STOP);
    if ((hWndStop) && (IsWindowEnabled(hWndStop)))
    {
        // Tell MCI to stop playing the sequence.
        mciError = mciSendString("stop myseq",NULL,0,NULL);

        // Display any error message if it failed.
        if (mciError != 0)
        {
            mciGetErrorString(mciError,buf,sizeof(buf));
            MessageBox(hWnd,buf,"Play MIDI",MB_ICONSTOP | MB_OK);
        }
    }
}
```

9. Now you can add the main message handler for the dialog, and thus, the application. Add the following code to the end of the PLAYMIDI.C source file. HandleDialog processes the WM_INITDIALOG message to initialize the dialog, setting the file name to blank and disabling the Play and Stop buttons. In response to the ID_BROWSE command message, this code calls the BrowseClicked function that you added before, letting the user select a file to be played and enabling the Play button. In response to the ID_PLAY command message, the code calls PlayClicked to start the selected MIDI file playing and enable the Stop button. In response to ID_STOP, the function calls StopClicked to stop the MIDI device playing. These are all WM_COMMAND command messages, and nothing out of the ordinary.

The interesting message handled in this function is the MM_MCINOTIFY message. This message will be sent to the dialog window when the MIDI device finishes playing the music, because the code in the PlayClicked function used the keyword "notify" when starting playing. The WPARAM argument of this message specifies the reason for the message (the reason why playing has ceased), and the LPARAM argument supplies a device ID of the device sending the message. While the device ID is not used in this application, it might be useful for an application that supported a number of simultaneous multimedia devices (for instance, using .WAV sound effects and MIDI at the same time). Table 12-3 lists the possible reasons returned in the WPARAM argument.

FLAG	MEANING
MCI_NOTIFY_ABORTED	The device received a command that prevented the current callback conditions from being met. This might occur if a new command interrupts the current command and it also requests notification.
MCI_NOTIFY_SUCCESSFUL	Playback completed successfully.
MCI_NOTIFY_SUPERSEDED	The device received another command with the "notify" flag set.
MCI_NOTIFY_FAILURE	A device error occurred while the device was executing the command.

Table 12-3 Reasons for MM_MCINOTIFY messages

```
/* ------------------------------------------------------------------ */
/* This function handles the messages sent to the dialog. When the    */
/* dialog receives the IDCANCEL command, the dialog is closed.        */
/* ------------------------------------------------------------------ */
BOOL CALLBACK HandleDialog(HWND hWnd, UINT message, WPARAM wParam, LPARAM lParam)
{
    switch (message)
    {
        case WM_INITDIALOG:
            // Set the initial state of the controls.
            SetDlgItemText(hWnd,ID_FILENAME,"");
            EnableWindow(GetDlgItem(hWnd,ID_PLAY),FALSE);
            EnableWindow(GetDlgItem(hWnd,ID_STOP),FALSE);
            return TRUE;
        case WM_COMMAND:
            switch (wParam)
            {
                case IDCANCEL:
                    DestroyWindow(hWnd);
                    return TRUE;
                case ID_BROWSE:
                    BrowseClicked(hWnd);
                    return TRUE;
                case ID_PLAY:
                    PlayClicked(hWnd);
                    return TRUE;
                case ID_STOP:
                    StopClicked(hWnd);
                    return TRUE;
                default:
                    break;
            }
            break;
        case MM_MCINOTIFY:
            MIDINotify(hWnd);
            break;
        case WM_DESTROY:
            StopClicked(hWnd);
            PostQuitMessage(0);
            return TRUE;
    }
    return FALSE;
}
```

10. Finally, add the WinMain function, listed next, to the source file. This function
is called when Windows runs the application. It sets up the dialog and pumps
messages for the life of the application.

```
/* -------------------------------------------------------------------- */
/* Our main function - set up and run the application.                  */
/* -------------------------------------------------------------------- */
int PASCAL WinMain(HINSTANCE hInstance, HINSTANCE hPrevInstance,
                   LPSTR lpCmdLine, int nCmdShow)
{
    MSG   msg;
    HWND  hWnd;

    if ((hWnd = CreateDialog(hInstance,MAKEINTRESOURCE(IDD_PLAYMIDI),
                             NULL,HandleDialog)) == NULL)
        return FALSE;

    while (GetMessage(&msg,NULL,NULL,NULL))
        if (!IsDialogMessage(hWnd, &msg))
        {
            TranslateMessage(&msg);
            DispatchMessage(&msg);
        }

    return msg.wParam;
}
```

Comments

As you can see, playing a MIDI file can be accomplished by executing the appropriate commands with the mciSendCommand API function. Using the MM_MCINOTIFY
message and the "notify" flag allows the playing to be carried out in the background,
separate from your application. You can no doubt imagine some useful applications
for this technique. A good example would be the creation of a game with background
music. You could initialize the MIDI device when the user started playing, send the
"play" command to start the music, and then send the "stop" and "close" commands
when the user exits the game or ends the level. By responding to the MM_MCINOTIFY
command, you can start the MIDI music playing again each time that it finishes.

CHAPTER 13
WORKING WITH WINDOWS

WORKING WITH WINDOWS

How do I...

Of all the components in the Windows 95 API, none is as important as the window. Windows are the basic building blocks for all controls, graphics, and user interaction. In Windows 95, windows can be used for application views, dialogs, message boxes, and controls.

In this chapter, we examine some of the more interesting uses for windows and windowing systems in Windows 95. Using the functions listed in Table 13-1, we will look at how to create screen savers, how to create windows without titles, and how to change the way windows look, whether they are visible or minimized on the screen.

13.1   Write a Screen Saver

In this How-To, we will examine what is necessary to write a screen saver using Visual C++, and how the Windows API works with screen savers. We will also look at text positioning as a means of using the screen saver to occupy the screen.

13.2   Create a Window with No Title Bar

Windows with plain borders are useful for a number of things. In this How-To, we examine how you can use a window with a simple border and no title bar to display text in the center of a dialog box. The window will act as a child of the dialog box and will work as a "super" static text field, with multiple lines, fonts, and colors.

13.3   Keep a Window on Top of All Other Windows

For many utility programs, the ability to have a window "float" above all other windows on the desktop is paramount to providing a constant information source for the user. In this How-To, we look at how you can force a window to always remain on top, even if the user selects another window to be "above" it.

13.4   Move a Window to the Bottom of All Other Windows

Similar to the previous How-To, it is quite often a useful feature to have a window that is "below" other windows. Panels in dialogs have this functionality. Other reasons might include having a "provider" application running, which should never be seen by the user. Putting this window at the bottom of the display order can accomplish this.

13.5   Change the Shape of the Mouse Cursor

When working in Windows, it is often necessary to indicate to the user the state of the application. The well-known hourglass mouse cursor from Windows 3.x is an example of the type of functionality that users have come to expect in applications. Alternatively, you might want the cursor to display as a circle with a line through it to indicate that a given operation is not allowed at some point. In this How-To, we look at the predefined mouse cursor shapes and how you can create your own cursor shape.

13.6   Change My Application's Icon When Minimized

In Windows 3.x when an application's main window is minimized, the icon displayed tells the user what kind of application it is and what state it might be in. In Windows 95, the application's title indicates this on the task bar. We will look at how you can modify the icon that is displayed when the window is minimized, which also works in Windows 95 as the icon that is displayed in the Explorer window for the application.

13.7   Load Icons from Another Application

When you are working with icons in your application, it is often nice to be able to "steal" icons from other applications in order to use them in your own. This saves you the effort of actually reproducing them in a paint or other program and also provides a consistent interface for the user. In this How-To, we examine how you can extract icons from other applications on the system for use in your own program.

13.8 Move and Size Windows Within My Application

When you are working with resizable forms or dialogs in your application, it is often necessary to resize and move controls in order to make the window appear the same regardless of the size it is expanded to by the user. In this How-To, we use the power of the Windows API to make controls respond to their parent windows in order to be moved to new positions and sizes.

Table 13-1 lists the Windows 95 API functions used in this chapter.

GetClientRect	SelectObject	PatBlt
GetSystemMetrics	GetDC	SetTextColor
SetBkColor	TextOut	ReleaseDC
InvalidateRect	CreateEx	SetCursor
SetTimer	GetCursorPos	PostMessage
SetCursorPos	KillTimer	GetWindowRect
Create	CreateWindowEx	CreateFont
SetWindowPos	ShowWindow	DestroyCursor
SetClassWord	LoadCursor	LoadIcon
DestroyIcon	SetClassLong	SetWindowText
SendDlgItemMessage	MoveWindow	

 Table 13-1 Windows 95 API functions used in Chapter 13

COMPLEXITY
MODERATE

13.1 How do I... Write a screen saver?

Problem

I would like to be able to write a screen saver. Although I understand the basics of the process involved (blank the screen, do something until the user presses a key), I do not understand the specifics of how I create a screen saver and how it is called by Windows. How do I use the API and the MFC to create a screen saver?

Technique

There are only a few special things to know in order to write a screen saver using the MFC. First, you need to be able to create a main window that occupies the entire screen and does not contain a border or a caption. This is accomplished through the CreateWindow API function (indirectly in the case of the MFC). Next, you need to know how to blank the screen to a specific color. We accomplish this by handling the WM_ERASEBKGND windows API message and "painting" the screen to black. Finally, you need to be able to do something to catch the user's attention until he or she presses a key or moves the mouse.

In our example screen saver, which is admittedly quite crude, we draw a text string at random locations on the screen until the mouse is moved or a key is pressed. Every 100 text draws results in the screen being cleared, to avoid ugly screens.

Steps

Open and run the Visual C++ application CH131.MAK from the CHAPT13\SAM-PLES\CH131 directory on the CD that comes with this book. Use the Debug | Options screen to set the command line arguments for the application to "-s". This indicates to the program that it is running as a screen saver. Run the application and watch the text draw at random locations on the screen. You should see a screen much like that displayed in Figure 13-1. When you are satisfied with the display, press a key or move the mouse around to end it.

To write your own screen saver application based on this example, follow this procedure:

1. Create a new application make file in Visual C++ using AppWizard. Call the application CH131.MAK. Select the Options button in AppWizard and turn off Multiple Document Interface, Initial Toolbar, Print Preview, Custom VBX controls, and Context Sensitive Help.

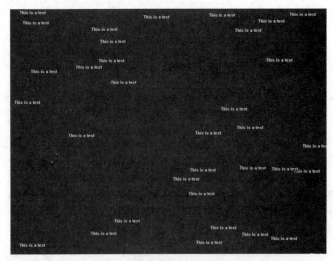

Figure 13-1 Screen Saver application in action

2. Enter ClassWizard and select the Add Class button. Give the class the name CScreenSaverWnd and select generic CWnd as the base class for the new class.

3. Select the CScreenSaverWnd object from the object list in ClassWizard and the WM_ERASEBKGND message from the message list. Click on the Add Function button and add the following code to the OnEraseBkgnd function of CScreenSaverWnd:

```
BOOL CScreenSaverWnd::OnEraseBkgnd(CDC* pDC)
{
    COLORREF rgbBkColor = RGB(0,0,0);
    //
    // Erase only the area needed
    //
    CRect rect;
    GetClientRect(&rect) ;

    //
    // Make a brush to erase the background.
    //
    CBrush NewBrush(rgbBkColor) ;

    pDC->SetBrushOrg(0,0) ;

    CBrush* pOldBrush = (CBrush*)pDC->SelectObject(&NewBrush);

    //
    // Paint the Background....
    //
    pDC->PatBlt(rect.left, rect.top, rect.Width(),
                rect.Height(),PATCOPY);

    pDC->SelectObject(pOldBrush);

    return TRUE;
}
```

4. Select the CScreenSaverWnd from the object list and the WM_TIMER message from the message list in ClassWizard. Click on the Add Function button and add the following code to the OnTimer method of CScreenSaverWnd:

```
void CScreenSaverWnd::OnTimer(UINT nIDEvent)
{
    static int counter = 0;

    int x = rand() % ::GetSystemMetrics ( SM_CXSCREEN );
    int y = rand() % ::GetSystemMetrics ( SM_CYSCREEN );

    // Draw a new text string at the random coordinates.

    CDC *dc = GetDC();
    dc->SetTextColor ( RGB(255,255,255) );
    dc->SetBkColor ( RGB(0,0,0) );
    dc->TextOut ( x, y, "This is a test", strlen("This is a test"));
```

continued on next page

629

continued from previous page

```
        ReleaseDC(dc);

        // Allow 100 text messages to be displayed. After that clear the screen

        counter ++;
        if ( counter == 100 ) {
            counter = 0;
            InvalidateRect(NULL);
        }

        CWnd::OnTimer(nIDEvent);
    }
```

5. Add the following methods to the CScreenSaver class at the bottom of the source file:

```
BOOL CScreenSaverWnd::Create()
{
    const char* pszClassName
        = AfxRegisterWndClass(CS_HREDRAW|CS_VREDRAW|
                              CS_SAVEBITS|CS_DBLCLKS);;

    return CWnd::CreateEx(WS_EX_TOPMOST,
                          pszClassName,
                          "",
                          WS_POPUP | WS_VISIBLE,
                          0, 0,
                          ::GetSystemMetrics(SM_CXSCREEN),
                          ::GetSystemMetrics(SM_CYSCREEN),
                          NULL,
                          NULL);
}

void CScreenSaverWnd::PostNcDestroy()
{
    delete this;
}

LRESULT CScreenSaverWnd::WindowProc(UINT nMsg, WPARAM wParam, LPARAM lParam)
{
    static BOOL      fHere = FALSE;
    static POINT     ptLast;
    POINT            ptCursor, ptCheck;

    switch (nMsg){
    case WM_SYSCOMMAND:
        if ((wParam == SC_SCREENSAVE) || (wParam == SC_CLOSE)) {
            return FALSE;
        }
        break;

    case WM_DESTROY:
        PostQuitMessage(0);
        break;
```

```
case WM_SETCURSOR:
    SetCursor(NULL);
    break;

case WM_NCACTIVATE:
    idTimer = SetTimer(1, 100, NULL);
    if (wParam == FALSE) {
        return FALSE;
    }
    break;

case WM_ACTIVATE:
case WM_ACTIVATEAPP:
    if(wParam != FALSE) break;
    // Only fall through if we are losing the focus...

case WM_MOUSEMOVE:
    if(!fHere) {
        GetCursorPos(&ptLast);
        fHere = TRUE;
    } else {
        GetCursorPos(&ptCheck);
        if(ptCursor.x = ptCheck.x - ptLast.x) {
            if(ptCursor.x < 0) ptCursor.x *= -1;
        }
        if(ptCursor.y = ptCheck.y - ptLast.y) {
            if(ptCursor.y < 0) ptCursor.y *= -1;
        }
        if((ptCursor.x + ptCursor.y) > MAXMOVE) {
            PostMessage(WM_CLOSE, 0, 0l);
        }
    }
    break;

case WM_LBUTTONDOWN:
case WM_MBUTTONDOWN:
case WM_RBUTTONDOWN:
    GetCursorPos(&ptCursor);
    ptCursor.x ++;
    ptCursor.y ++;
    SetCursorPos(ptCursor.x, ptCursor.y);
    GetCursorPos(&ptCheck);
    if(ptCheck.x != ptCursor.x && ptCheck.y != ptCursor.y)
    ptCursor.x -= 2;
    ptCursor.y -= 2;
    SetCursorPos(ptCursor.x,ptCursor.y);

case WM_KEYDOWN:
case WM_SYSKEYDOWN:
    PostMessage(WM_CLOSE, 0, 0l);
    break;
}
return CWnd::WindowProc(nMsg, wParam, lParam);
}
```

6. Next, add the following lines to the header file for the CScreenSaverWnd
class, SCREENSA.H:

```
const MAXMOVE = 100;
private:
  UINT idTimer;
public:
BOOL Create();

protected:
  virtual LRESULT WindowProc(UINT nMsg, WPARAM wParam, LPARAM lParam);
  virtual void PostNcDestroy();
```

7. Next, modify the InitInstance method of the application object, CCh131App,
to read as follows:

```
BOOL CCh131App::InitInstance()
{
    if ((((!lstrcmpi(m_lpCmdLine,"/s") || !lstrcmpi(m_lpCmdLine,"-s")) ||
!lstrcmpi(m_lpCmdLine,"s"))) {
        // Run as screen saver.
        CScreenSaverWnd* pWnd = new CScreenSaverWnd;
        pWnd->Create();
        m_pMainWnd = pWnd;
        return TRUE;
    } else {
        // Configuration option.

        return FALSE;
    }
}
```

8. Add the following line to the top of the CH131.CPP application object source
file:

```
#include "screensa.h"
```

9. If you wish, you may now remove from the project the MAINFRM.CPP,
MAINFRM.H, and document/view files, since they are no longer used.

10. Modify the definition file, CH131.DEF, for the application with the following
line:

```
DESCRIPTION   'SCRNSAVE : My Screen Saver'
```

11. Build the executable. In order to run the executable and allow it to be found as
a screen saver, you must rename it to a .SCR file (CH131.SCR) and move it
into the Windows directory on your system. Control Panel will then find it (by
the name listed in the DESCRIPTION line of the definition file) and will allow
you to select it as the current screen saver.

How It Works

A Windows screen saver is simply an executable file that has been renamed to a .SCR extension file. It accepts two kinds of command line arguments—a run command (-s) and a configure command (-c). Our screen saver ignores the configure command, but you could easily add a dialog to configure the settings such as the text string to display and the number of items to display before blanking the screen.

When Windows starts a screen saver, it sends it the command line argument to start, -s, and then simply follows standard window rules. The InitInstance method of the application creates a new instance of the CScreenSaverWnd class and then sets the main window variable to point at that class. The entire logic portion of this application resides solely in the CScreenSaverWnd class.

When the CScreenSaverWnd class is created, the Create method is invoked. This method creates a new window using the Windows API function CreateEx. This function will allow you to create main-level windows in the desktop without a parent to hold them. The Window is created with no border or caption, and the size is specified to be the entire screen using the GetSystemMetrics API function.

The new window uses a window procedure, WindowProc, to manage all messages sent to the window. It handles only a few of the messages, most notably the mouse move and button down messages and the keyboard notification messages. Moving the mouse more than a tiny bit will close the window, as will pressing any key.

The OnEraseBkgnd method of the class is called in response to the Windows message WM_ERASEBKGND. This message indicates to the window that it should clear its own background. In this case, we simply use the GDI functions SelectObject (to obtain and set a new colored brush) and the PatBlt function to clear the background to black.

The OnTimer function is called in response to creating a timer in the NcActivate case of the WindowProc. This function is called each 50 milliseconds and will simply find a new point on the screen, using the random number generator, and then output a string. The string is put on the screen using the TextOut function. Note that the background and foreground colors have been set previously using the GDI functions SetTextColor and SetBkColor.

Finally, the timer method checks to see if 100 strings have been output. If so, it forces the window to repaint itself by calling the InvalidateRect API function.

Comments

This How-To is a very simple, but quite complete, example of how you can create screen savers. It doesn't do anything fancy, such as paint fractals or other objects, but in all other respects it is a complete screen saver.

To flesh out the screen saver, you might want to add the ability to handle multiple fonts or text rotations and to vary the string selected. You would also want to add the ability to configure the screen saver in response to the configure command (-c) from Windows.

COMPLEXITY
MODERATE

13.2 How do I... Create a window with no title bar?

Problem

I would like to be able to create a window with no title bar or caption for use in one of my dialog boxes. Basically, what I would like is a static text window that is capable of displaying multiple lines of text along with different fonts for those lines of text.

How do I create such a window and how do I position it in my dialog where I would like it at design time?

Technique

In this How-To, we examine how you can vary the parameters to the Windows API function CreateWindowEx in order to create child windows that contain no caption or title bar. We will use the dialog class to hold the child window, and then we'll use the child window to display text in different fonts.

In order to use a child window in a dialog at design time, you need to leave space for it when you are designing the dialog template in the resource editor (or whatever dialog editor you choose). In this example, we create a static text field "placeholder" that will position our new window when it is created.

Steps

Open and run the Visual C++ application CH132.MAK from the CHAPT13\SAMPLES\CH132 directory on the CD that comes with this book. Select the Dialogs main menu and the "Dialog with captionless window" menu item. You will see a dialog like the one displayed in Figure 13-2. Notice that the three lines of the dialog's static text field in the center of the dialog are displayed in different type fonts and sizes.

To reproduce this functionality in your own application, do the following:

1. Create a new application in Visual C++ using AppWizard. Give the new project the name CH132.MAK. Using the resource editor, create a new dialog box for the application. Give the new dialog the caption Test Captionless Window Dialog.

2. Add a static text field at the top of the dialog with the caption Multi-Line Multi-Font Text Box. Immediately below that static text field, add a second text field much larger in both horizontal and vertical scale. Give this second text field the identifier ID_PLACEHOLDER and no caption.

3. Enter ClassWizard and generate a new dialog class for the dialog template you
have just created. Give the new dialog class the name CNoCaptionDlg. Select
the CNoCaptionDlg object from the object list in ClassWizard and the message WM_INITDIALOG. Click on the Add Class button and add the following
code to the OnInitDialog method of CNoCaptionDlg:

```
BOOL CNoCaptionDlg::OnInitDialog()
{
  CDialog::OnInitDialog();

  // Create a new window for this dialog in place of the "placeholder"
  // static text field

  CWnd *w = GetDlgItem(IDC_PLACEHOLDER);
  CRect r, dr;
  w->GetWindowRect ( &r );
  GetWindowRect ( &dr );

  r.top -=  dr.top;
  r.left -= dr.left;
  r.bottom -= dr.top;
  r.right -= dr.left;

  wnd = new CFancyTextWnd;
  wnd->Create( NULL, "", WS_VISIBLE | WS_BORDER | WS_CHILD, r, this, 1010, NULL );
  wnd->ShowWindow(SW_SHOW);
```

Figure 13-2 Dialog box with
captionless window embedded in it

```
    return TRUE;   // return TRUE  unless you set the focus to a control
}
```

4. Add the following to the destructor for the CNoCaptionDlg class:

```
CNoCaptionDlg::~CNoCaptionDlg(void)
{
    delete wnd;
}
```

5. Finally, add the following lines to the header file for the CNoCaptionDlg,
NOCAPTIO.H. Add only the lines marked in bold print.

```
#include "fancytex.h"

class CNoCaptionDlg : public CDialog
{
// Construction
public:
    CNoCaptionDlg(CWnd* pParent = NULL); // standard constructor
private:
    CFancyTextWnd *wnd;
public:
~CNoCaptionDlg();
```

6. Enter ClassWizard again and select the Add Class button. Give the new class
the name CFancyTextWnd and the base class of generic CWnd. Select the
CFancyTextWnd class from the ClassWizard object list and the WM_PAINT
message from the message list. Add the following code to the OnPaint method
of CFancyTextWnd:

```
void CFancyTextWnd::OnPaint()
{
    CPaintDC dc(this); // device context for painting

    dc.SetTextColor ( RGB(255,255,255) );
    dc.SetBkColor ( GetSysColor(COLOR_BTNFACE) );

    dc.SelectObject ( &f1 );
    dc.TextOut ( 0,0, "This is a test", strlen("This is a test"));
    dc.SelectObject ( &f2 );
    dc.TextOut ( 0,24, "This is a test", strlen("This is a test"));
    dc.SelectObject ( &f3 );
    dc.TextOut ( 0,40, "This is a test", strlen("This is a test"));
}
```

7. Next, add the following code to the constructor for the class,
CFancyTextWnd::CFancyTextWnd:

```
CFancyTextWnd::CFancyTextWnd()
{
    f1.CreateFont ( -14, 0, 0, 0, FW_NORMAL, 0, 0, 0, 0, 0, 0, 0, 0, NULL );
    f2.CreateFont ( -16, 0, 0, 0, FW_NORMAL, TRUE, 0, 0, 0, 0, 0, 0, 0, NULL );
    f3.CreateFont ( -18, 0, 0, 0, FW_BOLD, 0, 0, 0, 0, 0, 0, 0, 0, NULL );
}
```

8. Add the following declarations to the header file for the class, FANCYTEX.H:

```
private:
    CFont f1;
    CFont f2;
    CFont f3;
```

9. Now, reenter the resource editor and add a new main-level menu with the caption Dialogs. To the Dialogs main menu, add the menu item "Dialog with captionless window." Give this new menu item the identifier ID_NO_CAPTION. Save the menu and exit the resource editor.

10. Select ClassWizard and the CCh132App object from the drop-down list. Select the ID_NO_CAPTION object from the object list and the COMMAND message from the message list. Click on the Add Function button and give the new function the name OnNoCaption. Enter the following code into the OnNoCaption method of CCh132App:

```
void CCh132App::OnNoCaption()
{
    CNoCaptionDlg  dlg;
    dlg.DoModal();

}
```

11. Add the following include file line to the top of the CH132.CPP source file:

```
#include "nocaptio.h"
```

12. Compile and run the application.

How It Works

When the dialog class is instantiated by the user selecting the "Dialog with captionless window" menu item from the menu, the dialog object is created, which calls the OnInitDialog method of the CNoCaptionDlg class.

This method creates a new window by calling the Create method of CWnd, which is a direct call to the Windows API function CreateWindowEx. This function creates a new window handle and places the new window on the screen. This method informs the Windows system of the styles that it would like assigned to the window. Normally, the styles for a window include WS_CAPTION, WS_CHILD, WS_VISIBLE, and WS_BORDER. In this case, however, by omitting the WS_CAPTION style bit, we produce a window with no caption or title bar.

COMPLEXITY
EASY

13.3 How do I...
Keep a window on top of all other windows?

Problem

I need the ability to force my application's main window to remain on top of all other windows on the desktop. My application is a simple utility that displays information for the user, and it is not of much use if the user cannot see the information at all times.

How can I force my main window to remain on top of the stack of windows displayed?

Technique

Windows 95, as well as all other versions of Windows, have the concept of a Z order, which indicates the order in which windows are displayed on the screen. The lowest window in the Z order is displayed at the bottom, while the highest window in the Z order is displayed at the top of the stack.

The SetWindowPos API function can be used to affect the Z order of any window that is currently displayed on the desktop. In this How-To, we look at a simple method to use the SetWindowPos API function to force a window to remain on top of other windows at all times.

Steps

Open and run the Visual C++ application CH133.MAK from the CHAPT13\SAMPLES\CH133 directory on the CD that comes with this book. Select the main menu Dialog and the menu item "Always on top window." Move other windows on the desktop over the window, and you will find that they always move behind the window so that your application is always displayed. This application is shown in Figure 13-3.

To reproduce this functionality in your own application, do the following:

1. Create a new project in Visual C++ using AppWizard. Give this project the name CH133.MAK. Enter the resource editor.

2. Add a new main menu with the caption Dialog. To the Dialog main menu item, add a new menu item with the caption "Always on top window." Give this new drop-down menu the identifier ID_TOP_WINDOW.

3. Enter ClassWizard and select the application object for this application, CCh133App. Click on the ID_TOP_WINDOW object in the object list and the COMMAND message from the message list. Click on the Add Function button in ClassWizard.

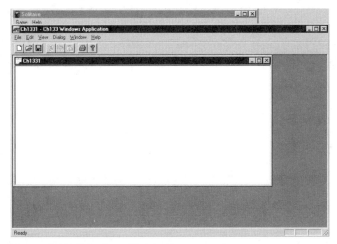

Figure 13-3 Window that is always on top

4. Give the new function the name OnTopWindow and add the following code to the OnTopWindow function of CCh133App:

```
void CCh133App::OnTopWindow()
{
    ::SetWindowPos(AfxGetMainWnd()->m_hWnd, HWND_TOPMOST, -1, -1, -1, -1,
            SWP_NOMOVE | SWP_NOSIZE );
}
```

5. Compile and run the application.

How It Works

The SetWindowPos function takes seven arguments, but we are only using three in this example. First, the initial parameter specifies the window handle of the window whose position you would like to change. In this case, we use the built-in MFC function to obtain a pointer to the main window and then get the public member variable that holds the handle for that window. Next, the window position variable is set to HWND_TOPMOST. This parameter specifies the window handle after which this window should be displayed. The special value HWND_TOPMOST indicates to the Windows 95 operating system that this window should always be displayed as the topmost window.

The next four arguments specify a new position for the window. Since we are only affecting the Z order position of the window, we do not need these arguments. The final argument is a set of flags that indicate which parameters to use and which to ignore. In this case, we set the SWP_NOMOVE flag, indicating that the first two position arguments are not to be used. We also set the SWP_NOSIZE flag, indicating that the last two position arguments are not to be used either.

Comments

Here is how you would accomplish the same thing in Visual Basic:

1. Create a new project or add a new form to an existing project. Add a single button to the form as well as any other controls you wish (we added a radio button).

2. Set the caption on the button to Close and add the following code to the Command1_Click function by double-clicking on the button:

```
Private Sub Command1_Click()
    End
End Sub
```

3. Add the following code to the Form_Load function by double-clicking on the form itself:

```
Private Sub Form_Load()
    Dim Flags As Integer

    Flags = &H1
    Flags = Flags Or &H2
    Call SetWindowPos(hWnd, -1, 0, 0, 0, 0, Flags)

End Sub
```

4. Finally, add the following line to the general section of the form:

```
Private Declare Sub SetWindowPos Lib "User32" (ByVal hWnd As Integer,
ByVal hWndInsertAfter As Integer, ByVal X As Integer, ByVal Y As Integer,
ByVal cx As Integer, ByVal cy As Integer, ByVal wFlags As Integer)
```

5. Run the application. Note how the form always remains on top regardless of what you might call up.

COMPLEXITY

EASY

13.4 How do I...
Move a window to the bottom of all other windows?

Problem

I would like to be able to move my main window to the bottom of the window stack and thus have it temporarily disappear from the screen while another application is running. My application spawns another task, and I would like the ability to make that other task run in front of my window so that the user only sees the other application.

How do I move my window to the back of all other windows?

Technique

Similar to the previous How-To, we can use the SetWindowPos API function to move a window to the back of the window Z order. In the previous How-To, we used the special setting of HWND_TOPMOST to make sure that a window was always on top of all other windows.

There is no true corresponding setting that forces a window to stay on the bottom. The setting HWND_BOTTOM will force a window initially to the bottom, but the window can then be moved back to the top of the Z order by clicking on it with the mouse. At no time, however, will a window without the HWND_TOPMOST setting ever move on top of a window that does have the HWND_TOPMOST setting.

In this How-To, we examine another facet of the SetWindowPos function and show you how to move a window to the bottom of the Z order stack temporarily.

Steps

Open and run the Visual C++ application CH134.MAK from the CHAPT13\SAMPLES\CH134 directory on the CD that comes with this book. Select the main menu Dialog and the menu item Move Window To Bottom. You will notice that the window will immediately drop behind all other windows that occupy any portion of the space this window occupies. This application is displayed in Figure 13-4.

To reproduce this functionality in your own application, do the following:

1. Create a new project in Visual C++ using AppWizard. Give the project the name CH134.MAK. Enter the resource editor.

2. Add a new main menu with the caption Dialog. To the Dialog main menu, add a new menu item with the caption Move Window To Bottom. Give this new drop-down menu the identifier ID_BOTTOM_WINDOW.

Figure 13-4 Window moved to the back

3. Enter ClassWizard and select the application object for this application, CCh134App. Click on the ID_BOTTOM_WINDOW object in the object list and the COMMAND message from the message list. Click on the Add Function button in ClassWizard.

4. Give the new function the name OnBottomWindow and add the following code to the OnBottomWindow function of CCh134App:

```
void CCh134App::OnBottomWindow()
{
    ::SetWindowPos(AfxGetMainWnd()->m_hWnd, HWND_BOTTOM, -1, -1, -1, -1,
SWP_NOMOVE | SWP_NOSIZE );
}
```

5. Compile and run the application.

How It Works

When the user selects the Move Window To Bottom menu command, the application calls the SetWindowPos API function for that window handle, giving it the HWND_BOTTOM flag. This indicates that the window is to be moved to the bottom of the current window stack. While the window will not always be at the bottom of the stack, it is reasonable to assume that, until other windows are created or this window is brought to the top of the stack, it will remain at the bottom of the desktop.

COMPLEXITY
EASY

13.5   How do I...
Change the shape of the
mouse cursor?

Problem

I would like to be able to change the shape of the mouse cursor depending on the state of my application. For example, if I am doing heavy background printing, I might want to display an hourglass cursor. If I am working in editing mode, I would like the I-beam cursor. Also, I would like the ability to define my own shapes and display them at certain times.

How do I use the power of the Windows 95 API to make the cursor shape change while still using the environment I am accustomed to?

Technique

This problem is slightly more complicated than it sounds, for all the wrong reasons. Although it is a trivial task to load and show cursors of various types, including user-defined cursors, it is not quite as easy to integrate those changes into the environment in which you are working.

When using Visual C++, for example, changing the cursor appears to be a one-line procedure. Unfortunately, the built-in functionality of the Visual C++ system wants to change the cursor back to its default shape as soon as you move the mouse. This makes it difficult to keep the cursor in the shape you originally intended it to be.

The designers of Windows, however, thought the problem out quite well, as you will see in this example. Not only did they give you the functionality you need to modify the shape of the mouse cursor on the screen, but they also gave you a Windows message that allows you to reset the cursor whenever the mouse moves.

In this How-To, we examine the LoadCursor and SetCursor API functions as well as the Windows message WM_SETCURSOR.

Steps

Open and run the Visual C++ application CH135.MAK from the CHAPT13\SAMPLES\CH135 directory on the CD that comes with this book. You will see a normal Multiple Document Interface window (or View in MFC parlance). Select the Cursor main menu item and one of the drop-down items under the Cursor menu. Your options are Hourglass, I-Beam, Cross, or User Defined. After selecting one of these options, move the mouse back into the MDI window. You will notice that the mouse cursor changes to the shape you selected from the menu. The MDI window and the menu for cursor selection is shown in Figure 13-5.

To reproduce this functionality in your own application, do the following:

1. Create a new project in Visual C++ using AppWizard. Give the project the name CH135.MAK. Enter the resource editor.

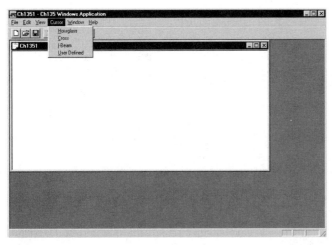

Figure 13-5 MDI window showing mouse cursor options menu

2. Add a new main menu with the caption Cursor. To the Cursor main menu item, add new menu items with the captions Hourglass, I-Beam, Cross, and User Defined.

3. Give the Hourglass menu item the identifier ID_HOURGLASS. Give the I-Beam menu item the identifier ID_IBEAM. Give the Cross menu item the identifier ID_CROSS. Finally, give the User Defined menu item the identifier ID_USER_CURSOR.

4. In the resource editor, create a new menu item. Select Cursor from the dialog box that requests the type of resource to create. When the cursor box is displayed, draw a cursor of your own liking. Give the cursor the identifier IDC_MOUSE_CURSOR in the Properties screen.

5. Exit the resource editor and save the new resources. Select ClassWizard and click on the CCh135View from the drop-down list.

6. Click on the ID_HOURGLASS object identifier and the COMMAND message. Click on the Add Function button and give the new function the name OnHourglass. Enter the following code into the OnHourglass function of CCh135View:

```
void CCh135View::OnHourglass()
{
    curCursor = ::LoadCursor(NULL, IDC_WAIT);
}
```

7. Click on the ID_CROSS object identifier and the COMMAND message. Click on the Add Function button and give the new function the name OnCross. Enter the following code into the OnCross function of CCh135View:

```
void CCh135View::OnCross()
{
    curCursor = ::LoadCursor(NULL, IDC_CROSS);
}
```

8. Click on the ID_IBEAM object identifier and the COMMAND message. Click on the Add Function button and give the new function the name OnIbeam. Enter the following code into the OnIbeam function of CCh135View:

```
void CCh135View::OnIbeam()
{
    curCursor = ::LoadCursor(NULL, IDC_IBEAM);
}
```

9. Click on the ID_USER_CURSOR object identifier and the COMMAND message. Click on the Add Function button and give the new function the name OnUserCursor. Enter the following code into the OnUserCursor function of CCh135View:

```
void CCh135View::OnUserCursor()
{
    curCursor = hMouseCursor;
}
```

10. Next, click on the CCh135View object in the object list and the WM_SETCURSOR message in the message list. Click on the Add Function button and enter the following code into the OnSetCursor method of CCh135View:

```
BOOL CCh135View::OnSetCursor(CWnd* pWnd, UINT nHitTest, UINT message)
{
    ::SetCursor(curCursor);
    return TRUE;
}
```

11. Add the following code to the constructor for the CCh135View class:

```
CCh135View::CCh135View()
{
  // Load the special cursor for our application

  hMouseCursor = ::LoadCursor(AfxGetInstanceHandle(),
MAKEINTRESOURCE(IDC_MOUSE_CURSOR));
  curCursor = ::LoadCursor ( NULL, IDC_IBEAM );
}
```

12. Finally, add a destructor for the class and add the following code to the destructor:

```
CCh135View::~CCh135View()
{
    ::DestroyCursor ( hMouseCursor );

}
```

13. Add the following lines to the header file for the CCh135View class, CH135VIEW.H:

```
private:
  HCURSOR hMouseCursor;
  HCURSOR curCursor;
```

14. Compile and run the application.

How It Works

The LoadCursor function of the Windows 95 API loads a cursor resource from a given instance handle. If the instance handle passed to the function is NULL or 0, the LoadCursor function will look for a standard windows cursor, such as hourglass, cross, or I-beam. Once the cursor resource is found, a handle to the cursor is retrieved for the application to use.

The SetCursor function of the API uses the cursor handle returned by the LoadCursor function in order to actually display the cursor in the window for which it is called. It sets the cursor for any window that does not specifically set the cursor itself (which means that the desktop is affected). Once the handle to the cursor is retrieved from the LoadCursor function, the SetCursor function will display that cursor.

Finally, the DestroyCursor function is needed for any cursors that are loaded from the actual instance handle of the application. When we created a new cursor resource in the resource editor and loaded it with the LoadCursor function call, it became necessary to destroy the cursor resource and free the memory when the window was closed.

When Windows 95 wants to set the current cursor value, it sends a WM_SETCURSOR message to the window. This includes changing the cursor or moving the mouse. The window receives this message and is expected to reset the cursor shape to whatever it would like to display. In our case, the individual menu items simply set a member variable of the view class to be the cursor we want to display. Then in the OnSetCursor method (which is the response method for the WM_SETCURSOR message), the cursor is shown to the user.

If you do not override the WM_SETCURSOR handling in your window, the operating system will change the cursor as soon as the user moves the mouse, which will cause the cursor to look as though it never changed.

COMPLEXITY
MODERATE

13.6   How do I...
Change my application's icon when minimized?

Problem

In the good old days of the Windows 3.x SDK and C programming, I could change the icon that was displayed when my application was minimized. All I needed to do was to specify the icon that appeared in the Windows registration call RegisterWindowClass. If I wanted to create a window and change the icon whenever the window was minimized, I could specify a NULL icon in the registration process and then paint the icon myself in the handler for the WM_PAINT.

With the advent of the Microsoft Foundation Classes, Delphi, and Visual Basic, however, some of this functionality seems to have gotten away from the application programmer. I can find no way, using the MFC, to accomplish what used to be a handful of lines of code. Is this a sad reflection on frameworks, or can I still change the application icon via the API functions?

Technique

Before you get too melancholy over the missing functionality of the new toolkits, try to remember that it also used to take 100 lines of code to create a window and put it on the screen.

In spite of this, it is still quite possible to use the Windows API to accomplish what you want to do. The process of registering a window does, in fact, specify the icon that will be displayed when the window is minimized. It is also possible, however, to modify that icon at runtime after the window class is registered. This is the entire purpose, in fact, behind the SetClassLong function of the Windows 95 API library.

Using the SetClassLong function, we will change the icon for the class to be the icon you wish displayed when minimized (as well as in the corner of a Windows 95 window).

Still nostalgic for the "good old days"?

Steps

Open and run the Visual C++ application CH136.MAK from the CHAPT13\SAM-PLES\CH136 directory on the CD that comes with this book. You will see a normal Multiple Document Interface window (or View in MFC parlance). Click on the minimize button of the MDI window to reduce it to an iconic form. You will see the customized icon appear, as shown in Figure 13-6.

To reproduce this functionality in your own application, do the following:

Figure 13-6 Minimized MDI window showing customized icon

1. Create a new project in Visual C++ using AppWizard. Give the new project the name CH136.MAK. Enter ClassWizard.

2. Click on the Add Class button. Name the new class CMyFrame and select CMDIChildWnd for the base class of the new class. Accept the other defaults and generate the new class definition.

3. Select the CMyFrame class from the drop-down list in ClassWizard. Select the class name CMyFrame from the object list and the WM_CREATE message from the message list. Click on the Add Function button. Enter the following code into the OnCreate method of CMyFrame:

```
int CMyFrame::OnCreate(LPCREATESTRUCT lpCreateStruct)
{
  SetClassLong( m_hWnd, GCL_HICONSM, (LONG)theIcon );
  if (CMDIChildWnd::OnCreate(lpCreateStruct) == -1)
    return -1;

  // TODO: Add your specialized creation code here

  return 0;
}
```

4. Add the following code to the constructor for the class, CMyFrame::CMyFrame:

```
CMyFrame::CMyFrame()
{

    theIcon = ::LoadIcon ( AfxGetInstanceHandle(), MAKEINTRESOURCE(IDI_ICON1) );
}
```

5. Add the following code to the destructor for the class, CMyFrame::~CMyFrame:

```
CMyFrame::~CMyFrame()
{
    DestroyIcon(theIcon);
}
```

6. Add the following lines to the header file for the CMyFrame class, MYFRAME.H:

```
private:
  HICON    theIcon;
```

7. Select the CH136.CPP file from the project list. Modify the document template line for the CCh136View template instantiation to read as follows:

```
CMultiDocTemplate* pDocTemplate;
  pDocTemplate = new CMultiDocTemplate(
    IDR_CH136TYPE,
    RUNTIME_CLASS(CCh136Doc),
    RUNTIME_CLASS(CMyFrame),           // standard MDI child frame
    RUNTIME_CLASS(CCh136View));
  AddDocTemplate(pDocTemplate);
```

8. Add the following line to the top of the CCh136App source file, CH136.CPP:

```
#include "myframe.h"
```

9. In the resource editor, create a new icon resource. Draw whatever shape you would like to see appear in the minimized icon and save it with the identifier IDI_ICON1.

10. Compile and run the application.

How It Works

Windows automatically deals with showing the iconized version of a window when it is minimized. It does this by inspecting the class word for the window and extracting the icon from that position in the extra bytes of the window structure. All we are doing in this example is setting the class word to be our own icon so it is the picture that is displayed when minimized.

Note that it is necessary to create our own frame window to make all of this happen. The frame window is created in ClassWizard and connected to the document/view architecture through the document template.

Comments

It should be noted that the Win32 API also allows you to use the WM_SETICON message to accomplish the same task.

COMPLEXITY
MODERATE

13.7 How do I...
Load icons from another application?

Problem

I would like to be able to allow the user to browse through other application's icons in order to select an icon to display in my own application. I know that this is possible, because File Manager in Windows 3.x could do it and so can Windows Explorer in Windows 95.

I could not find a way to do it using the Microsoft Foundation Classes. Is there a way I can use the power of the Windows 95 API to accomplish this task? If so, how is it done?

Technique

The Microsoft Foundation Classes encompass a large portion of the Windows API and provides considerable functionality for those functions. Unfortunately, it was simply impossible for all API functions to fit neatly into classes, and therefore, several of the API functions were simply ignored. Others were deemed inappropriate for use in a class library and were also ignored. The function we need to use here is in the latter class. The ExtractIcon function provides exactly the functionality you are looking for in your application.

To use the ExtractIcon function, you need only have the name of an executable, dynamic link library, or library file that resides somewhere on an accessible disk. Many such programs, libraries, and DLLs exist, which contain a multitude of resources such as icons that you can use in your own application.

In this How-To, we explore the furthest reaches of the Windows API as we discover not only how to find out what icons exist in an executable or dynamic link library but also how to load them into your own application and display them in a dialog.

Steps

Open and run the Visual C++ application CH137.MAK from the CHAPT13\SAMPLES\CH137 directory on the CD that comes with this book. Select the main menu Dialogs and the menu item Browse Icons. A dialog will be displayed like the one in Figure 13-7. Click on the Select File button and a standard Windows File Open dialog will be displayed. Navigate to the WINDOWS subdirectory and select a DLL to examine. A good choice is the MORICONS.DLL file. When you select the file in the File Open dialog, the name will be placed in a text field at the top of the file. The number of icons will be displayed in another text field below the Select File button.

Enter a number between 1 and the number of icons shown in the text field in the edit field next to the prompt View Icon Number:. Click on the View button, and the icon will be displayed below the edit field. An example of a viewed icon from the MORICONS.DLL file is shown in Figure 13-8.

To reproduce this functionality in your own application, do the following:

1. Create a new project in Visual C++ using AppWizard. Give the new project the name CH137.MAK. Enter the resource editor.

2. Create a new dialog class. Add a static text field at the top of the dialog with the caption Browsing File:. Next to this static text field, add a second text field with no caption and the identifier ID_FILE_NAME.

3. Add a command button to the dialog below the two text fields you have added. Give the button the caption Select File. Below the command button add a static

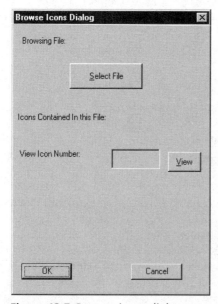

Figure 13-7 Browse icons dialog

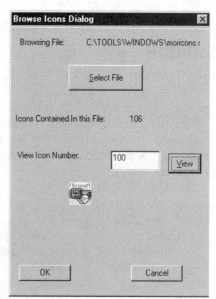

Figure 13-8 Browse icons dialog showing icon from MORICONS.DLL

text field with Icons contained in this file: as the caption. Next to the static text field add a second text field with the identifier ID_NUM_ICONS and no caption.

4. Below the two static text fields for the number of icons, add another text field with the caption View Icon Number: and an edit field next to it. Beside the edit field, add a button with the caption View.

5. Finally, add an icon to the dialog below the edit field by adding a picture field at this position and setting its type to ICON.

6. Select ClassWizard and generate a new dialog class for the template you have just created. Give the new class the name CBrowseIconsDlg.

7. Select the IDC_BUTTON1 object from the object list and the BN_CLICKED message from the message list. Click on the Add Function button and give the new function the name OnSelectFile. Add the following code to the OnSelectFile method of CBrowseIconsDlg:

```
void CBrowseIconsDlg::OnSelectFile()
{
    // Get the file name from the user

    CFileDialog fd(TRUE);

    if ( fd.DoModal() == IDOK ) {
        CString theFile = fd.GetPathName();
        UpdateIcons(theFile);
        GetDlgItem(IDC_EDIT1)->EnableWindow(TRUE);
        GetDlgItem(ID_FILE_NAME)->SetWindowText ( theFile );
        fileName = theFile;
    }

}
```

8. Select the IDC_BUTTON2 object from the object list and the BN_CLICKED message from the message list. Click on the Add Function button and give the new function the name OnViewIcon. Add the following code to the OnViewIcon method of CBrowseIconsDlg:

```
void CBrowseIconsDlg::OnViewIcon()
{
    // Get the string from the edit box

    char buffer[80];
    GetDlgItem(IDC_EDIT1)->GetWindowText ( buffer, 80);

    // Change to a number

    int idx = atoi(buffer);

    // See how many are in the file

    GetDlgItem(ID_NUM_ICONS)->GetWindowText ( buffer, 80 );
    int numIcons = atoi(buffer);
```

continued on next page

continued from previous page

```
        if ( numIcons < idx ) {
            MessageBox("Not that many icons in file", "Error", MB_OK );
            return;
        }

        // Extract that icon from the file

        HICON hIcon = ExtractIcon( AfxGetInstanceHandle(), fileName, idx );

        // Update the text box with this icon

        HICON hOldIcon = (HICON)::SendDlgItemMessage( m_hWnd,
                            IDC_ICON_PLACEHOLDER, STM_SETICON, (WPARAM)hIcon, 0 );
}
```

9. Select the CBrowseIconsDlg object from the object list and the WM_INITDIA-LOG message from the message list. Click on the Add Function button and add the following code to the OnInitDialog method of CBrowseIconsDlg:

```
BOOL CBrowseIconsDlg::OnInitDialog()
{
    CDialog::OnInitDialog();

    // Set window to be disabled.

    GetDlgItem(IDC_EDIT1)->EnableWindow(FALSE);

    return TRUE;  // return TRUE  unless you set the focus to a control
}
```

10. Add the following method definition to the class:

```
void CBrowseIconsDlg::UpdateIcons(CString& s)
{
    // Step 1: Try to get number of icons

    int numIcons = (int)ExtractIcon( AfxGetInstanceHandle(), s, -1 );

    char buffer[80];
    sprintf(buffer, "%d", numIcons);
    GetDlgItem(ID_NUM_ICONS)->SetWindowText(buffer);

}
```

11. Add the following declarations to the header file for CBrowseIconsDlg, BROWSEIC.H:

```
private:
CString fileName;

// Construction
public:
void UpdateIcons(CString& s);
```

12. Now, reenter the resource editor and add a new main-level menu with the caption Dialogs. To the Dialogs menu, add the menu item with the caption Browse Icons. Give this new menu item the identifier ID_BROWSE_ICONS. Save the menu and exit the resource editor.

13. Select ClassWizard and the CCh137App object from the drop-down list. Select the ID_BROWSE_ICONS object from the object list and the COMMAND message from the message list. Click on the Add Function button and give the new function the name OnBrowseIcons. Enter the following code into the OnBrowseIcons method of CCh137App:

```
void CCh137App::OnBrowseIcons()
{
    CBrowseIconsDlg dlg;

    dlg.DoModal();
}
```

14. Add the following line to the top of the CCh137App source file, CH137.CPP:

```
#include "browseic.h"
```

15. Compile and run the application.

How It Works

When the dialog is initially displayed, there is no data to load, so the dialog is blank. Once the user selects the Select File button, a common File Open dialog box is displayed. When the user selects a file, the ExtractIcon function is called for that file with the current instance handle and a parameter of -1 for the index of the icon to select. This -1 parameter indicates to the function that it should return the number of icon resources found in the file. When this is done, that number is displayed in the static text field using the SetWindowText API function.

When the user enters a value in the edit box and selects the View button, the program checks the current value of the number of icons available in the file and determines whether the index given by the user is valid. If the index is invalid, the program displays an error message and continues. If the index is valid, the ExtractIcon function is called again with the index of the icon requested, the current instance handle, and the name of the file to extract from. If successful, this function will return a handle to the icon.

When the icon handle is returned to the dialog box, the SendDlgItemMessage function is called with the STM_SETICON windows message. This message indicates to a static text field that it should display the icon passed in the wparam field of the message. Once this is done, the icon should be visible to the user.

COMPLEXITY

MODERATE

13.8   How do I...
Move and size windows within my application?

Problem

I have a dialog box that I would like to be able to let the user resize and view. Unfortunately, the dialog box contains controls that would then need to be moved around and possibly resized to make them fit into the new size arrangements of the dialog.

How do I move and resize windows within my dialog, and generally within my application, to put them where I want them?

Technique

In this How-To, we will use several different Windows API functions to accomplish our goal. First, we will look at the GetWindowRect function, which is used to return a bounding rectangle in screen coordinates for a window. Next, we will consider the GetSystemMetrics function to obtain certain data about dialog boxes. Finally, we will use the MoveWindow API function to actually resize and move the controls in the dialog box.

This technique can be used in a similar method for windows on the screen, such as views, pop-ups, and so forth. The actual parameters may vary, as controls are child windows relative to their parent dialog box and require some special processing to get them into the correct position.

Steps

Open and run the Visual C++ application CH138.MAK from the CHAPT13\SAMPLES\CH138 directory on the CD that comes with this book. Select the main menu Dialogs and the menu item Move and Resize Dialog. A dialog will be displayed like the one in Figure 13-9. You will notice that the window border is of a resizable type, allowing you to drag it into new sizes. Move the border around until you are satisfied with the position and size of the dialog. Release the mouse, and the controls will resize and move themselves into relative positions in the dialog.

To reproduce this functionality in your own application, do the following:

1. Create a new project in Visual C++ using AppWizard. Give the new project the name CH138.MAK. Enter the resource editor.

2. Create a new dialog class. Add a static text field at the top of the dialog with the caption "Enter List Choice:". Create an edit field next to the static text field.

3. Add a list box immediately below the static text field and the edit field.

Figure 13-9 Move and resize dialog

4. Move the OK and Cancel buttons to the bottom of the dialog.

5. Select ClassWizard and generate a new dialog class for the template you have just created. Give the new class the name CMoveResizeDlg. Select the CMoveResizeDlg object from the object list in ClassWizard and the WM_SIZE message from the message list. Click on the Add Function button and add the following code to the OnSize method of CMoveResizeDlg:

```
void CMoveResizeDlg::OnSize(UINT nType, int cx, int cy)
{
  CDialog::OnSize(nType, cx, cy);

  CRect er, r, rt;

  // First, get the current size of the dialog box

  GetWindowRect( &r );

  CWnd *edit1 = GetDlgItem(IDC_EDIT1);
  if ( edit1 == NULL )
     return;
  CWnd *btn1 = GetDlgItem(IDOK);
  if ( btn1 == NULL )
     return;
  CWnd *btn2 = GetDlgItem(IDCANCEL);
  CWnd *list1 = GetDlgItem(IDC_LIST1);

  // The "pivot" point is the first edit field. This determines the high point
  // of the dialog. Use it to resize and move all other fields

  edit1->GetWindowRect( &er );

  // Move the OK button to be just above the bottom of the dialog box

  btn1->GetWindowRect( &rt );

  int height = rt.bottom - rt.top;
```

continued on next page

continued from previous page

```
            int width  = rt.right - rt.left;

            // Reset rectangle

            rt.bottom = r.bottom - height - 10 - r.top;
            rt.top    = rt.bottom - height;
            rt.left   = GetSystemMetrics(SM_CXFRAME) + 10;
            rt.right  = rt.left + width;

            btn1->MoveWindow( &rt );

            // Do the same for the CANCEL button

            btn2->GetWindowRect ( &rt );

            height = rt.bottom - rt.top;
            width  = rt.right - rt.left;

            // Reset rectangle

            rt.bottom = r.bottom - height - 10 - r.top;
            rt.top    = rt.bottom - height;
            rt.right  = r.right - r.left - 10;
            rt.left   = rt.right - width;

            int bottom_of_list = rt.top - 10;

            btn2->MoveWindow( &rt );

            // Hold onto the top and bottom parts

            rt.top = er.bottom - r.top + 10;
            rt.bottom = bottom_of_list;
            rt.left = 10;
            rt.right = r.right - r.left - 10;

            list1->MoveWindow( &rt );

        }
```

6. Now, reenter the resource editor and add a new main-level menu with the caption &Dialogs. To the Dialogs main menu, add a menu item with the caption Move and Resize Dialog. Give this new menu item the identifier ID_MOVE_DLG. Save the menu and exit the resource editor.

7. Select ClassWizard and the CCh13App object from the drop-down list. Select the ID_MOVE_DLG object from the object list and the COMMAND message from the message list. Click on the Add Function button and give the new function the name OnMoveDlg. Enter the following code into the OnMoveDlg method of CCh13App:

```
void CCh13App::OnMoveDlg()
{
    CMoveResizeDlg dlg;
```

```
    dlg.DoModal();
}
```

8. Add the following line to the top of the CCh138App source file, CH138.CPP:

```
#include "moveresi.h"
```

9. Compile and run the application.

How It Works

When the dialog is resized, a WM_SIZE message is sent to the dialog class. This is caught by the OnSize method. The OnSize method then gets the window rectangle for the dialog box itself by calling the GetWindowRect API function. This rectangle is then used to reposition the other controls in the dialog.

When repositioning controls in a dialog, you use the MoveWindow function. Unfortunately, for child controls, MoveWindow uses the relative window position within the parent frame (in this case the dialog). Therefore, to convert from the window coordinates to the client coordinates for a window, we subtract the top and left of the dialog frame position from all other coordinates. In addition, we need to modify the x coordinate by the dialog frame width (the resizable border). Once all of this is accomplished, the MoveWindow function is called to reposition and/or resize the control.

In this example, the OK and Cancel buttons always retain their original size and are simply moved about in the dialog. The list box in the center of the dialog is not only moved but resized so that it falls between the OK button and the top edit box.

Comments

The same technique can be used in Delphi. Here is an example of such a form:

1. Create a new project in Delphi or add a new form to an existing project. To this form add a static text field with the caption Enter Selection. Add an edit field immediately to the right of this static text field.

2. Add a list box and two command buttons to the form below the static text field and edit box.

3. Click on the OnResize event in the Events page of the Property Inspector and enter the name FormResize for the new event handler. Enter the following code into the FormResize method of the form:

```
procedure TForm1.FormResize(Sender: TObject);
var
    fr,r,r1 : TRect;
    height, width : Integer;
begin
    { Get the position of the edit box }
    GetWindowRect ( Edit1.handle, r );
```

continued on next page

continued from previous page

```
{ Get current position of OK box }
GetWindowRect ( Button1.handle, r1 );

{ Get size of form }
GetWindowRect( Form1.Handle, fr );

{ Move OK button }
height := r1.bottom - r1.top;
width  := r1.right - r1.left;

Button1.Top := fr.bottom - 10 - height - fr.top -
               GetSystemMetrics(SM_CYCAPTION);
Button1.Left := 10;

{ Move Cancel button }
GetWindowRect ( Button2.handle, r1 );
height := r1.bottom - r1.top;
width  := r1.right - r1.left;

Button2.Top := fr.bottom - 10 - height - fr.top -
               GetSystemMetrics(SM_CYCAPTION);
Button2.Left := fr.right - width - 20 - fr.left;

{ Now, move the list box }

ListBox1.Top := Edit1.Top + Edit1.Height + 10;
ListBox1.Height := Button1.Top - 10 - ListBox1.Top;
ListBox1.Width := Button2.Left + Button2.Width - ListBox1.Left;

end;
```

CHAPTER 14

PROGRAMMING TIPS
AND TRICKS

PROGRAMMING TIPS AND TRICKS

How do I...

In any programming environment, there are the little things that make the difference between experienced programmers and programmers that just get along. In the Windows world, there are hundreds of these "little things" that make up the Windows API function library. Many of these functions are rarely used because they are simply too specialized for the majority of Windows applications. Other functions are rarely used because they are simply not well understood by programmers.

In this chapter, we examine some of the more esoteric elements of Windows API programming. These little tips and tricks will make you a better Windows programmer, but more importantly, they will give you a better understanding of the Windows programming environment.

In the How-To sections of this chapter, you will learn about defensive programming, extensible programming, and user-friendly programming, using the functions listed in Table 14-1. All of these features are of paramount importance to the user and thus to your continued success in the programming profession.

14.1   Determine Whether a Pointer Is Valid

The vast majority of Windows users' complaints stem from general protection faults (GPFs) while applications are running. Of these GPFs, the majority could have been avoided if some care had gone into the design and implementation of the underlying functionality of the application. For programmers, most GPFs are caused by pointers that are pointing at invalid areas of memory. Using these pointers to access or write to the memory pointed at will cause Windows to GPF or hang, upsetting the user. In this How-To, we look at a built-in pointer checking routine in Windows. The method is the same one used to generate the GPF message and can be used by your program to validate pointers before they cause any grief.

14.2   Determine Whether a String Is Valid

The second leading cause of program crashes is the use of invalid string pointers. Pointers in your application that are used to display, format, or print strings can be checked for validity before a usage that would cause a program crash. In this How-To, we will look at the Windows API function responsible for this check and how you can use it in your own applications to prevent crashes.

14.3   Place Version Information in My Application

There is little more annoying in the Windows world than using a resource that is out of date. Program crashes, unreproducible results, and strange behavior are often caused by the fact that VBXs, dynamic link libraries, and other executables do not match the version you are expecting in your own application. Earlier in the book, we examined how you could check the version information in other people's DLLs and executables. In this How-To, we will show you how you can place that version information for other people to use in your own applications and DLLs.

14.4   Write a Dynamic Link Library

A dynamic link library is a reusable component of Windows that can be loaded independent of executables and need not be bound in a compile and link time. DLLs, as they are called, are extremely simple ways to contain updatable components without requiring the shipment of entirely new versions of executables. In addition, DLLs can be a valuable way to encapsulate differences in functionality between different types of code. For example, you might have ten different kinds of data that can be read by your application. The method for reading differs for each, as does the interpretation of the data, but the majority of the code is the same for all ten types. In this case, you might place the different code types in DLLs and only load the particular version of the read and interpret DLL that you need. This saves memory by requiring only one version of the code at a time, instead of ten different versions all bound into the executable.

14.5   Use a Dynamic Link Library

In this How-To, we will examine how you use the string dynamic link library from the previous How-To to provide the ability to subclass a running program and trap its window messages in a log file.

14.6 Create Applications That Can Display in All Resolutions

Windows is a supposedly device-independent graphical user interface. Unfortunately, many Windows applications make assumptions about the resolution of the graphic display. In this How-To, we use the Windows API functions to determine the size of the screen and display our windows in the proper places based on the size of the actual display monitor (in pixels, of course).

Table 14-1 lists the Windows 95 API functions used in this chapter.

IsBadWritePtr	IsBadStringPtr	LocalAlloc
LocalLock	LocalUnlock	LocalFree
GetFileVersionInfoSize	GetFileVersionInfo	VerQueryValue
MoveWindow	LoadLibrary	GetProcAddress
FreeLibrary	EnumWindows	GetSystemMetrics

 Table 14-1 Windows 95 API functions used in Chapter 14

COMPLEXITY
EASY

14.1 How do I... Determine whether a pointer is valid?

Problem

I would like to be able to determine at runtime whether a pointer in my application is valid. Is there any way to find out if the pointer is really pointing at something in my application, without accessing it and getting a general protection fault?

Technique

After giving this a moment of thought, it should occur to you that since Windows is able to determine that a pointer is invalid (which is why it displayed the general protection fault message in the first place) it should be possible for your application to determine this as well.

Fortunately, the wonderful people who wrote Windows included in the API a set of functions to determine whether pointers legitimately point at something in memory. There is actually a complete set of these functions for checking pointers to readable memory and writable memory as well as memory that holds executable code. For the purpose of this How-To, though, we will concentrate on the most important aspect—the writable pointer to data.

In the majority of your C and C++ code, you check for the validity of pointers by comparing them to NULL. In Delphi, you compare pointers to Nil. Visual Basic, of course, doesn't have pointers. The problem lies in the fact that most C and C++ compilers do not initialize pointers to the NULL value. Forgetting to initialize a pointer is the basic problem behind many pointer-related GPFs. In this How-To, we use the IsBadWritePtr API function to determine whether a pointer is valid.

Steps

Open and run the Visual C++ application CH141.MAK from the CHAPTER14\SAMPLES\CH141 directory on the CD that comes with this book. Select the menu Validate and the menu item Valid Pointer. A message box should appear with the string "Pointer is Good" in the message portion. Next, select the menu item Invalid Pointer from the Validate menu. You will see the message box displayed in Figure 14-1 indicating that this is, in fact, an invalid pointer reference. Notice that the program did not crash on selecting the invalid pointer.

To duplicate the functionality of this example, follow this procedure:

1. Create a new project in Visual C++ using AppWizard. Give the new project the name CH141.MAK. Select the options for the project in AppWizard and turn off the Multiple Document Interface, Toolbar, and Print and Print Preview check boxes.

2. Enter the resource editor and select the menu resource from the resource list. Select the IDR_MAINFRAME menu (which should be the only menu present) and add a new main-level menu entry with the caption Validate.

3. Add a menu item to the Validate menu with the caption Valid Pointer and the identifier ID_VALID_PTR.

4. Add another menu item to the Validate menu with the caption Invalid Pointer and the identifier ID_INVALID_PTR. Exit the resource editor, saving the resource file when prompted.

5. Enter ClassWizard and select the application object, CCh141App from the drop-down combo box. Select the ID_VALID_PTR object from the object list and the COMMAND message from the message list. Click on the Add Function button and accept the name OnValidPtr for the name of the new function. Add the following code to the OnValidPtr method of the CCh141App class:

Figure 14-1 Message box indicating an invalid pointer reference

```
void CCh141App::OnValidPtr()
{
    int *p = new int[20];

    if ( IsBadWritePtr(p, 20*sizeof(int) ) )
        MessageBox(NULL, "Pointer is Bad!", "Error", MB_OK );
    else
        MessageBox(NULL, "Pointer is Good!", "Info", MB_OK );

    delete [] p;

}
```

6. Enter ClassWizard again and select the application object CCh141App from the drop-down combo box. Select the ID_INVALID_PTR object from the object list and the COMMAND message from the message list. Click on the Add Function button and accept the name OnInvalidPtr for the name of the new function. Add the following code to the OnInvalidPtr method of the CCh141App class:

```
void CCh141App::OnInvalidPtr()
{
    int far *p;    // This pointer doesn't point at anything!

    if ( IsBadWritePtr(p, 20*sizeof(int)) )
        MessageBox(NULL, "Pointer is Bad!", "Error", MB_OK );
    else
        MessageBox(NULL, "Pointer is Good!", "Info", MB_OK );

}
```

7. Compile and run the application.

How It Works

The IsBadWritePtr validates two things for a pointer. First, it makes sure that the pointer actually points to something in the valid data space for the application. Since most stray pointers are not pointing at a valid segment of memory, the IsBadWritePtr function will catch most uninitialized pointers.

The second thing that the IsBadWritePtr function validates is that the memory contained by the pointer points to an object block of at least the size specified in the function call to IsBadWritePtr and that the memory is writable. Memory overwrites can also be caught this way by checking to see that the allocated pointer points to something big enough to hold the memory you want to store in that block of memory.

When the IsBadWritePtr function is called in the first example (OnValidPtr), the pointer is a perfectly legitimate block of memory that is contained in a writable area of memory. Thus the function fails, indicating that the block is a good pointer.

When the IsBadWritePtr function is called in the second example (OnInvalidPtr), the pointer is not pointing at anything. Thus the function succeeds, indicating that the pointer is bad and should not be used.

Comments

This procedure will only catch uninitialized or invalid pointers that point outside of your data space. It will not catch pointers that are pointing at a deleted object or pointers that are pointing at the NULL memory address. Be sure to check for NULL before using any pointer in your application.

COMPLEXITY
EASY

14.2   How do I...
Determine whether a string is valid?

Problem

I would like to be able to determine at runtime whether a string I have allocated in my application is valid. Is there any way to find out if the string has been allocated and if it is pointing at a valid string in memory?

Technique

It is quite possible to determine whether a string pointer (LPSTR in Windows lingo) has been allocated by your program and whether the string it is pointing to is still valid. Combined with a check for a NULL pointer, this How-To will make your applications bulletproof with respect to bad string pointers.

In this How-To, we use the IsBadStringPtr API function to determine whether a string is pointing at anything in your application data space and whether the thing it is pointing at is a valid string.

Steps

Open and run the Visual C++ application CH142.MAK from the CHAPTER14\SAMPLES\CH142 directory on the CD that comes with this book. Select the menu Validate and the menu item Valid String. A message box should appear with the string "String is Good!" in the message portion. Next, select the menu item Invalid String from the Validate menu. You will see the message box displayed in Figure 14-2

Figure 14-2 Message box indicating an invalid string (LPSTR) reference

indicating that this is, in fact, an invalid string reference. Notice that the program did not crash on selecting the invalid string pointer.

To duplicate the functionality of this example, follow this procedure:

1. Create a new project in Visual C++ and name it CH142.MAK. Select the options for the project in AppWizard and turn off the Multiple Document Interface, Toolbar, and Print and Print Preview check boxes.

2. Enter the resource editor and select the menu resource from the resource list. Select the IDR_MAINFRAME menu (which should be the only menu present) and add a new main-level menu entry with the caption Validate.

3. Add a menu item to the Validate menu with the caption Valid String and the identifier ID_VALID_STRING.

4. Add another menu item to the Validate menu with the caption Invalid String and the identifier ID_INVALID_STRING. Exit the resource editor, saving the resource file when prompted.

5. Enter ClassWizard and select the application object, CCh142App from the drop-down combo box. Select the ID_VALID_STRING object from the object list and the COMMAND message from the message list. Click on the Add Function button and accept the name OnValidString for the name of the new function. Add the following code to the OnValidString method of the CCh142App class:

```
void CCh142App::OnValidString()
{
    HANDLE hStr = LocalAlloc(LPTR, 256);
    LPSTR string = (LPSTR)LocalLock(hStr);

    if ( IsBadStringPtr(string, 256)  )
        MessageBox(NULL, "String is Bad!", "Error", MB_OK );
    else
        MessageBox(NULL, "String is Good!", "Info", MB_OK );

    LocalUnlock ( hStr );
    LocalFree ( hStr );
}
```

6. Enter ClassWizard again and select the application object CCh142App from the drop-down combo box. Select the ID_INVALID_STRING object from the object list and the COMMAND message from the message list. Click on the Add Function button and accept the name OnInvalidString for the name of the new function. Add the following code to the OnInvalidString method of the CCh142App class:

```
void CCh142App::OnInvalidString()
{
    LPSTR string;

    if ( IsBadStringPtr(string, 256)  )
```

continued on next page

continued from previous page

```
        MessageBox(NULL, "String is Bad!", "Error", MB_OK );
    else
        MessageBox(NULL, "String is Good!", "Info", MB_OK );
}
```

7. Compile and run the application.

How It Works

When Windows creates a string variable using the LocalAlloc function, a portion of memory is set aside at the start of the memory block indicating the status and size of the memory block. A handle is then created that references this block in memory. Windows uses these handles to manipulate memory in your program indirectly so that the actual memory blocks can be moved around to create new space.

The IsBadStringPtr function simply checks to see if the string is still valid and if it points to something that could legitimately be considered a string. In this case, the valid string menu item handle allocates a string of 256 bytes and then validates it through the function. Unless the alloc fails, the returned pointer will be valid and the IsBadStringPtr function will fail.

In the case of the invalid string pointer, the new string pointer is never allocated, which causes the memory it points at to be garbage. Windows checks this in the IsBadStringPtr function and indicates to the calling program that the string pointer is invalid.

Comments

This procedure will only catch uninitialized strings or those that do not point at valid strings. It will not catch pointers that are pointing at a deleted object or pointers that are pointing at the NULL memory address. Be sure to check for NULL before using any pointer in your application.

COMPLEXITY
EASY

14.3   How do I...
Place version information in
my application?

Problem

My company is having severe problems with versions of the application changing. Users are calling with technical support questions and do not know which version they are running. This leads to headaches, as problems that exist in one version do not exist in others. The technical support people are screaming for a solution.

Is there an easy way for me to quickly add version information that programmers can use in the application to determine which version of the executable is running?

Technique

The problem of versions in computer software has been a chronic pain in the neck for many years. As mentioned, problems that exist in one version of an application can "go away" (hopefully by being fixed) in other versions. For technical support people, this means the difference between simply saying, "We will ship you an updated version" and saying, "We have no idea why that doesn't work for you; it works fine here." As you can imagine, users prefer the first approach over the second.

In this How-To, we examine the version resource that Windows allows you to embed in your application. This resource allows you to put the executable name, the version number, and other descriptive information into the executable itself. We will also look at how you can display that information for the user in an About box that tells users exactly which version of the software they are running.

Steps

Open and run the Visual C++ application CH143.MAK from the CHAPTER14\SAMPLES\CH143 directory on the CD that comes with this book. Select the menu Help and the menu item About. You will see the About box shown in Figure 14-3 displaying the current version number for the executable.

Figure 14-3 About box for Ch143 example showing current version number of executable

To duplicate the functionality of this example, follow this procedure:

1. Create a new project in Visual C++ using AppWizard. Give the new project the name CH143.MAK. Select the options for the project in AppWizard and turn off the Multiple Document Interface, Toolbar, and Print and Print Preview check boxes.

2. Select the CH143.RC2 file from the project list and edit it. Enter the following block of text into the file:

```
/////////////////////////////////////////////////////////////////////
// Version stamp for this .EXE

#include "winver.h"

VS_VERSION_INFO     VERSIONINFO
FILEVERSION         1, 0
PRODUCTVERSION      1, 0
```

continued on next page

continued from previous page

```
FILEFLAGSMASK           VS_FFI_FILEFLAGSMASK
FILEFLAGS               (VS_FF_PRERELEASE | VS_FF_DEBUG)
FILEOS                  VOS_DOS_WINDOWS16
FILETYPE                VFT_APP
FILESUBTYPE             VFT2_UNKNOWN
BEGIN
 BLOCK "VarFileInfo"
 BEGIN
    VALUE "Translation", 0x0409, 1252
 END
 BLOCK "StringFileInfo"
 BEGIN
    BLOCK "040904E4"
    BEGIN
        VALUE "CompanyName",      "The Waite Group\0"
        VALUE "FileDescription", "Chapter 14 How To Number 3.\0"
        VALUE "FileVersion",      "1.92\0"
        VALUE "InternalName",     "Version Resource Example\0"
        VALUE "LegalCopyright",   "Copyright (c) 1995 The Waite Group.
                                   All rights reserved.\0"
        VALUE "LegalTrademarks", "None.\0"
        VALUE "OriginalFilename", "ch143.exe\0"
        VALUE "ProductName",      "Version Resource Example Ch143.exe\0"
        VALUE "ProductVersion",   "1.00\0"
    END
 END
END
```

3. Enter the resource editor and select the Dialog resource list. Click on the ID_ABOUTBOX entry. In the displayed dialog box template, edit the displayed string to remove the 1.0 following the Version string. In place of the 1.0, add a new static text field. Give this text field the identifier ID_FILE_VERSION and blank the caption. Exit the resource editor, saving the resource file.

4. Enter ClassWizard and select the CAboutDlg class from the drop-down list. Click on the CAboutDlg class in the object list and the WM_INITDIALOG message in the message list. Click on the Add Function button. Enter the following code into the OnInitDialog method of CAboutDlg:

```
BOOL CAboutDlg::OnInitDialog()
{
  CDialog::OnInitDialog();

  UpdateVersionInformation();

  return TRUE;  // return TRUE  unless you set the focus to a control
}
```

5. Add the following code to the bottom of the CH143.CPP file:

```
void CAboutDlg::UpdateVersionInformation()
{
    BYTE       block[1024];
    DWORD FAR  *translation;
```

```
DWORD FAR    *buffer;
DWORD        handle;
UINT         bytes;
static char *fileName = "ch143.exe";

char         name[512];        // StringFileInfo data block.
char         data[256];

// Get the actual size of the information block.

bytes = (UINT)GetFileVersionInfoSize(fileName, &handle);

if (bytes)
{
    // Get the actual block for the version information

    if (GetFileVersionInfo(fileName, handle, bytes, block))
    {
        if (VerQueryValue(block, "\\VarFileInfo\\Translation", (VOID FAR *
            FAR *)&translation, (UINT FAR *)&bytes)) {

            // The File Version for this file

            wsprintf(name, "\\StringFileInfo\\%04x%04x\\FileVersion",
                    LOWORD(*translation), HIWORD(*translation));

            if (VerQueryValue(block, name, (VOID FAR * FAR *)&buffer, (UINT
                FAR *)&bytes)) {
                lstrcpy(data, (char far *)buffer);
                GetDlgItem(ID_FILE_VERSION)->SetWindowText(data);
            }
        }
        else {
          MessageBox ( "Unable to get translation type", "Error", MB_OK );
        }
    }
}
```

6. Add the following declaration to the CAboutDlg class, found in CH143.CPP:

```
protected:
  void UpdateVersionInformation();
```

7. Add the following line to the top of the CH143.CPP file in the include file list:

```
#include "winver.h"
```

8. In Visual C++, edit the project libraries to include the Windows library VERSION.LIB. Edit the Project | Files to include the directory from the LIB directory of your Visual C++ installation (if you selected MSVC20, for example, this would be \MSVC20\LIB\VERSION.LIB) .

9. Compile and run the application.

How It Works

When Windows executables are created, the resource file specified for the executable is bound into the actual executable file. This resource data is then available to the rest of the Windows system using the FindResource and LoadResource API functions. In addition, version information can be retrieved using the GetFileVersionInfoSize and GetFileVersionInfo API functions.

In this example, we first embed the data into the resource file using the VERSIONINFO resource statement. The available data for the VERSIONINFO statement includes lines containing the text "FileVersion", "ProductName", and so forth. The strings that follow these statements are the data that can be retrieved from the executable. Using Windows Explorer, you can view this information from the desktop.

When the About menu item is selected from the Help menu, the dialog is created. This, in turn, calls the OnInitDialog method of the dialog class. This method loads the data from the resource data stored in the file and puts it into the text field we added to the dialog. From this point on, any change made to the resource statement in the resource file will automatically be reflected in the dialog. This allows programmers to update the version information or other strings without requiring the rest of the system to be aware of what the current version number is currently set to.

COMPLEXITY
MODERATE

14.4   How do I...
Write a dynamic link library?

Problem

I need to be able to write a dynamic link library for use with my application. I understand how to write all of the underlying Windows calls to get the thing to work, but I don't understand how to write a DLL.

What are the components I need to get started and which are required? How do I use an integrated environment tool to work with a DLL?

Technique

Writing a dynamic link library was once a horrible chore. There were all sorts of entries to remember, definition files to update, memory requirements to worry about, and other nightmares for the programmer. Newer environments, such as Visual C++ and Delphi, allow you to create dynamic link libraries (DLLs) easily without worrying about many of the problems that plagued programmers in the past.

In this How-To, we will create a simple DLL that allows you to save and restore the position of a window of a running application. Because this is a task that could be shared among many different applications (to save the desktop appearance, for example), this is a job that is well suited for a DLL.

Figure 14-4 Dialog to save and restore the position of a window

Steps

Open and run the Visual C++ application CH144.MAK from the CHAPTER14\SAMPLES\CH144 directory on the CD that comes with this book. Select the menu DLL Test and the menu item Save Window Position. You will see the dialog box shown in Figure 14-4, listing the available windows to save. Select one and click on OK. Move to that application and move the window to a new location on the desktop. When you are finished, reselect the CH144 application and select the menu item Restore Window Position from the DLL Test menu.

Note that the example here is the underlying functionality contained within the DLL. If you would like to re-create the application that is running the DLL shown here, look at How-To 14.5.

To duplicate the functionality of this example, follow this procedure:

1. Create a new project in Visual C++ using the Project | New command. Name the new application's make file INTFCE.MAK. Select Windows Dynamic Link Library (DLL) from the type list and click on the OK button. In the next dialog (select files) simply click on OK.

2. Create a new file in Visual C++ and add the following code to the file. Save this file as LIBMAIN.CPP.

```
#define  STRICT
#include <windows.h>

// Turn off warning: Parameter '' is never used
#ifdef _BORLANDC_
#pragma argsused
#endif
```

continued on next page

continued from previous page

```
BOOL DllEntryPoint (
    HANDLE      hDLL,
    DWORD       dwReason,
    LPVOID      lpReserved)
{

    switch (dwReason)
        {
        case DLL_PROCESS_ATTACH:
            break;
        case DLL_PROCESS_DETACH:
            break;
        case DLL_THREAD_ATTACH:
        case DLL_THREAD_DETACH:
        default:
            break;
        }
    return TRUE;
}
```

3. Create a new file in Visual C++ and add the following code to the file. Save this file as SAVEPOS.CPP.

```
#define  STRICT
#include <windows.h>
#include <stdio.h>
#include <stdlib.h>
#include <string.h>

extern "C" {
void SaveWindow(HWND hWnd)
{
    RECT rect;

    // Get the current window rectangle

    ::GetWindowRect ( hWnd, &rect );

    // Write it to a file

    FILE *fp = fopen ( "win.pos", "w" );
    fprintf(fp, "%d, %d, %d, %d\n", rect.left, rect.top, rect.right,
            rect.bottom );
}

void RestoreWindow(HWND hWnd)
{
    RECT rect;

    // Try to open the file

    FILE *fp = fopen ( "win.pos", "r" );

    // If successful, read position

    if ( fp != (FILE *)NULL ) {
```

```
fscanf(fp, "%d, %d, %d, %d", &rect.left, &rect.top, &rect.right,
        &rect.bottom );

// And move the window there

MoveWindow ( hWnd, rect.left, rect.top, (rect.right-rect.left),
        (rect.bottom-rect.top), TRUE);
}

fclose(fp);

}
}
```

4. Create a new file in Visual C++ and enter the following lines into it. Save this file as CH144.DEF.

```
LIBRARY    CH144
EXETYPE    WINDOWS
CODE       PRELOAD MOVEABLE DISCARDABLE
DATA       PRELOAD MOVEABLE SINGLE
HEAPSIZE   8192
EXPORTS
        SaveWindow
        RestoreWindow
```

5. Select the menu item Edit from the Project menu. Add the LIBMAIN.CPP and SAVEPOS.CPP files to the application. In addition, add the CH144.DEF module definition file to the project. Save the application.

6. Compile the application. It will create a new dynamic link library along with the import library needed to use the DLL in other applications. This DLL can then be called from other applications by including the function prototypes for SaveWindow and RestoreWindow in a header file and loading the functions from the CH144.DLL link library.

How It Works

Dynamic link libraries consist of three discrete sections. First, the link library is initialized. This occurs in the LIBMAIN.CPP file's DllEntryPoint function. This is the standard entry and exit point for all dynamic link libraries. This is a simple skeleton DLL and requires no initialization for the work done.

After the initialization, the next part of the DLL to understand is the end of the line, when the DLL is unloaded from memory. In Windows 3.x, this occurred in the WEP (or Windows Exit Procedure), and in Windows 95 this also occurs in the DllEntryPoint function. Here, all cleanup and deallocation work is done for the DLL. In our case, there is nothing to clean up or deallocate, so the function does nothing.

Finally, there is the meat of the DLL—the actual functionality contained in the library. In this section, we have the SAVEPOS.CPP file. This file contains two exportable functions, SaveWindow and RestoreWindow. In our module definition file, CH144.DEF, we define these functions as exported. This indicates to Windows 95 that these functions may be loaded from external programs.

When Windows loads a dynamic link library, the table of functions that is exported can be loaded by an application. This table is then consulted by name for the actual entry points of the function. When the application wants to load a function, it simply links in an import library for the DLL and uses a prototype for that function to call it from the DLL.

In our case, the DLL simply takes a window handle and saves the position of that window to a file. This occurs in the SaveWindow function. When the RestoreWindow function is called, the file is reopened and the old position read in. The window is then moved back to the old position.

Comments

The application's dynamic link library as presented does not do much. It is possible, however, using the power of the Windows API, to do much more with other applications. The important point of this example is the skeleton necessary to implement a DLL, and the lack of special-purpose code within the DLL.

COMPLEXITY
MODERATE

14.5 How do I...
Use a dynamic link library?

Problem

I need to be able to load functions from a dynamic link library (DLL) without having an import library to use to do this. I don't understand how I can get back a pointer to the functions stored in the library without knowing where in memory the code resides.

How do I use the Windows API functions to get this information and load functions dynamically from a DLL?

Technique

The idea of loading a function from an external library without "knowing" what the function is at compile time is a rather intriguing one. You always need to know, of course, the calling convention for the function—that is something that is required. It is possible, however, to load a function from a dynamic link library knowing nothing more than the parameters to pass and the name of the function.

The Windows API provides several functions for dealing with dynamic link libraries and the functions within them. In this How-To, we will look at two specific functions of the API: LoadLibrary and GetProcAddress. A companion function to LoadLibrary, FreeLibrary, will also be considered and used.

The technique we will employ in this How-To may seem confusing, but it follows a logical series of steps. First, a library will be loaded from the disk into memory via the LoadLibrary call. Next, we will "load" a function from the library using the GetProcAddress function. Finally, we will call the function through a pointer using the specified arguments.

Steps

Before running this example, copy the CH144.DLL file from the CHAPTER14\SAMPLES\CH144 directory on the CD that comes with this book into your WINDOWS\SYSTEM directory. Open and run the Visual C++ application CH145.MAK from the CHAPTER14\SAMPLES\CH145 directory on the CD that comes with this book. Select the menu DLL Test and the menu item Save Window Position. A dialog will be displayed with available application windows to select. Select one and click on OK. Move to that application and move the window to a new location on the desktop. When you are finished, reselect the CH145 application and select the menu item Restore Window Position from the DLL Test menu.

Although this program was discussed in How-To 14.4, in this case, we are considering the program calling the DLL, rather than the DLL itself.

To duplicate the functionality of this example, follow this procedure:

1. Create a new project in Visual C++ and name it CH145.MAK. Select the options for the project in AppWizard and turn off the Multiple Document Interface, Toolbar, and Print and Print Preview check boxes.

2. Enter the resource editor and select the menu resource from the resource list. Select the IDR_MAINFRAME menu (which should be the only menu present) and add a new main-level menu entry with the caption DLL Test.

3. Add a menu item to the DLL Test menu with the caption Save Window Position and the identifier ID_SAVE_WINDOW_POS.

4. Add a menu item to the DLL Test menu with the caption Restore Window Position and the identifier ID_RESTORE_WINDOW_POS.

5. Exit the resource editor, saving the resource file in the process.

6. Enter ClassWizard and select the application object, CCh145App from the drop-down combo box. Select the ID_SAVE_WINDOW_POS object from the object list and the COMMAND message from the message list. Click on the Add Function button and accept the name OnSaveWindowPos for the name of the new method. Add the following code to the OnSaveWindowPos method of CCh145App:

```
void CCh145App::OnSaveWindowPos()
{
    CSelectWindow dlg;

    if ( dlg.DoModal() == IDOK ) {
        SaveWindowCallback ptr;
        FARPROC f;
```

continued on next page

```
    hLib = LoadLibrary ( "ch144.dll" );

    f = GetProcAddress( hLib, "SaveWindow");
    ptr = (SaveWindowCallback)f;
    theHandle = dlg.WindowHandle();

    (*ptr)(theHandle);

  FreeLibrary ( hLib );

  }
}
```

7. Enter ClassWizard and select the application object, CCh145App from the
drop-down combo box. Select the ID_RESTORE_WINDOW_POS object
from the object list and the COMMAND message from the message list. Click
on the Add Function button and accept the name OnRestoreWindowPos for
the name of the new method. Add the following code to the
OnRestoreWindowPos method of CCh145App:

```
void CCh145App::OnRestoreWindowPos()
{
    if ( hLib ) {
        RestoreWindowCallback ptr;
        FARPROC f;

        hLib = LoadLibrary ( "ch144.dll" );

        f = GetProcAddress( hLib, "RestoreWindow");
        ptr = (RestoreWindowCallback)f;

        (*ptr)(theHandle);

    }
}
```

8. Enter the resource editor and create a new dialog template. Add a single list
box to the template and move the OK and Cancel buttons to the bottom of the
template. Give the new dialog the identifier IDD_DIALOG2.

9. Select ClassWizard and generate a new dialog class for the dialog template you
have just created. Give the new class the name CSelectWindow. Select the
CSelectWindow object from the drop-down combo box in ClassWizard. Select
the CSelectWindow object from the object list and the WM_INITDIALOG
message from the message list. Click on the Add Function button and add the
following code to the OnInitDialog method of CSelectWindow:

```
BOOL CSelectWindow::OnInitDialog()
{
    CDialog::OnInitDialog();

    CListBox *list = (CListBox *)GetDlgItem(IDC_LIST1);

    EnumWindows ( EnumWindowsProc, (LPARAM)list );
```

```
    UpdateData();

    return TRUE;  // return TRUE  unless you set the focus to a control
}
```

10. Select the CSelectWindow object from the drop-down combo box in
ClassWizard. Select the IDOK object from the object list and the
BN_CLICKED message from the message list. Click on the Add Function button and accept the OnOK name for the new method. Add the following code
to the OnOK method of CSelectWindow:

```
void CSelectWindow::OnOK()
{
    // Get the text and window selected

    CListBox *list = (CListBox *)GetDlgItem(IDC_LIST1);
    int idx = list->GetCurSel();

    if ( idx != LB_ERR ) {
        list->GetText(idx, window_text );
        window_handle = (HWND)list->GetItemData ( idx );
        CDialog::OnOK();
    }
    else
        MessageBox("You must make a selection to continue", "Error", MB_OK );
}
```

11. Add the following lines to the header file for the CSelectWindow class,
SELECTWI.H:

```
private:
    CString window_text;
    HWND      window_handle;
public:
     CString& WindowText() { return window_text; };
     HWND      WindowHandle() { return window_handle; };
```

12. Add the following lines to the header file for the application object
CCh145App, Ch145.H:

```
class CCh145App : public CWinApp
{
private:
  HINSTANCE hLib;
  HWND        theHandle;
public:
    virtual int  ExitInstance();
```

13. Next, add the following method definition to the source file for the application
object, CH145.CPP:

```
int CCh145App::ExitInstance()
{
```

continued on next page

continued from previous page

```
    if ( hLib )
        FreeLibrary(hLib);
    return 0;
}
```

14. Modify the CH145.CPP to add the following lines. Lines to be added are marked in bold print.

```
typedef void (*SaveWindowCallback)(HWND hWnd);
typedef void (*RestoreWindowCallback)(HWND hWnd);

CCh145App::CCh145App()
{
   hLib = NULL;
}

/////////////////////////////////////////////////////////////////////
// The one and only CCh145App object

CCh145App NEAR theApp;

/////////////////////////////////////////////////////////////////////
// CCh145App initialization

BOOL CCh145App::InitInstance()
{
   hLib = NULL;
```

15. Compile and run the application.

How It Works

When the DLL Test menu item is selected, the program attempts to load the DLL containing the functions for window positioning. If the DLL is not present or cannot be loaded, the return from LoadLibrary will be NULL. In this case, we do nothing. If the library was successfully loaded, the function then "extracts" a function pointer from the library by calling the GetProcAddress. Notice that since we compiled the DLL functions as extern "C", it is not necessary to worry about the C++ name mangling for these functions.

Once the function is "loaded" from the library, it is then called indirectly via the pointer we just received. In this case, we know that the function takes only one parameter, a window handle. This parameter is passed to the DLL, which does all of the work of getting the application window position and saving it to a file.

In the RestoreWindow case, we again load a function from the DLL, again with only a single parameter. The function is again called indirectly through the pointer, and the window position is restored.

Comments

Calling functions from a DLL is a powerful programming technique in Windows 95. This technique allows you to modify the functionality of your own application without having the necessary code residing in your own executable.

Some uses for DLLs in real-world applications could include specialized drivers for hardware, internationalization support (using resource-only DLLs), and any other occasion in which code may vary for different reasons.

COMPLEXITY
EASY

14.6 How do I... Create applications that can display in all resolutions?

Problem

I would like my application always to be displayed in the same percentage of the screen, centered within the borders. Unfortunately, with the differences in screen resolutions among various monitors and video cards, the program appears in different places on different systems.

How can I generalize my program so that it appears in the same approximate location on each and every system?

Technique

The idea of a device-independent graphical user interface seems ideal. Windows tries to provide graphics without the pain of knowing where the screen memory was located and what sort of video drivers were installed. This was the plan, anyway.

Unfortunately, many video drivers take advantage of specialized processing in the video cards to do effects. Others allow the user to specify screen resolutions that are well beyond the "normal" capabilities of Windows (for example 1024-by-768 resolution for many SVGA boards).

To make your program truly device independent, you must first understand the API functions that allow you the luxury of not worrying about how big the monitor is. In this How-To, we examine the GetSystemMetrics and MoveWindow functions, which when combined, allow us to specify exactly where an application window will appear and how much screen space it will take up on any monitor.

The most surprising thing about this How-To is that with all that it is doing, it requires only three lines of code!

Steps

Open and run the Visual C++ application CH146.MAK from the CHAPTER14\SAMPLES\CH146 directory on the CD that comes with this book. You will see the window displayed in Figure 14-5. No matter what monitor or video card this program is run on, it will look the same to the user!

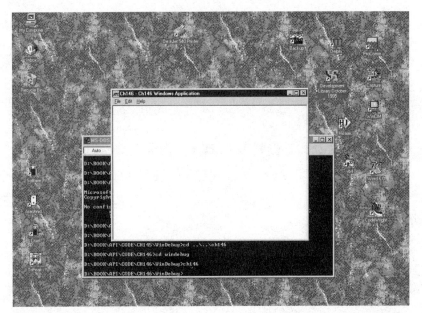

Figure 14-5 A device-independent application window at a specified position

To duplicate the functionality of this example, follow this procedure:

1. Create a new project in Visual C++ using AppWizard. Give the new project the name CH146.MAK. Select the options for the project in AppWizard and turn off the Multiple Document Interface, Toolbar, and Print and Print Preview check boxes.

2. Add the following lines to the CCh146App object source file in the InitInstance function. The new lines to add are marked in bold print.

```
// create a new (empty) document
  OnFileNew();

  if (m_lpCmdLine[0] != '\0')
  {
    // TODO: add command line processing here
  }

  // Set the window size to be half the size of the screen.

  int width = GetSystemMetrics(SM_CXSCREEN);
  int height = GetSystemMetrics(SM_CYSCREEN);

  m_pMainWnd->MoveWindow(width/4, height/4, width/2, height/2 );

  return TRUE;
}
```

3. Compile and run the application. That's all there is to it!

How It Works

When the application starts, the InitInstance method of the application object is called. The first calls to the GetSystemMetrics retrieve the screen width and height in pixels. These two values are then used to calculate how big a window should be to take up exactly half of the screen and be centered in the middle of the desktop window.

When writing applications for Microsoft Windows 95, it is quite important that you consider the user's screen resolution before you start moving windows and dialogs around on the screen. Use the GetSystemMetrics function to determine the screen resolution of the current screen settings.

Comments

Although simple, this How-To provides a very important basis for your Windows 95 applications. Users are quite accustomed to windows that are the correct size for their desktop without the strange look and feel of applications written for specific screen resolutions. Carefully consider the different resolutions available when writing applications, designing dialogs, and displaying information on the screen.

CHAPTER 15

THE POLISHED APPLICATION

15

THE POLISHED APPLICATION

How do I...

Writing Windows applications is a difficult process. It involves understanding a good deal about the internals of Windows as well as the application-specific tasks you want the program to accomplish. Once the program is "finished," however, the real work begins. In too many cases, programs are released before they are completely polished, without all of the bells and whistles that make the program attractive to users.

In this chapter we consider the job of polishing an application. Polishing is adding the pieces of the application that users have become accustomed to and that make the program richer and easier to use. Toolbars are a standard part of the Windows program pieces that users have grown accustomed to. Other components that "must" be in the application include status bars, splash screens, and background bitmaps. In this chapter we show you the secrets behind all of these tasks.

15.1   Implement Context-Sensitive Help

If you had to pick one feature in the Windows system to add to your application, it should certainly be context-sensitive help. Users love the ability to click on a Help button or press F1 and receive a screen filled with helpful information about the task they are currently working on. In this How-To, we show you how to use the power of the Windows API to launch Windows Help and allow the user to immediately view just the right help topic for the information they are working on at that moment.

15.2   Create a Status Bar

Status bars are another important bit of Windows functionality that programs should not be without. The MFC automatically adds status bars to your main window, but did you know that you can add them to any window?

15.3   Make a Toolbar

Similar to the status bar, the toolbar is important to the user. Instead of navigating your way through a complex morass of menus and submenus, you can let the user simply click on a button to perform a task by implementing a toolbar in your application. Again, we will show you how you can add a toolbar to any window, not just the main window. Also, we will look at floating toolbars or *toolboxes*.

15.4   Allow the User to Modify the Toolbar On-the-Fly

Having a toolbar for an application is a necessity, but having a toolbar that the user can customize is something that most programmers simply dream about. In this How-To, we examine how you can implement customizable toolbars that users can modify while your program is still running!

15.5   Display Demonstrations Within Online Help

Windows Help allows you to do many things, including the ability to call external functions from the Help system. In this How-To, we will show you how you can use external functions to create outside demonstrations of functionality.

15.6   Display an About Box When My Application Starts

Many applications display an About box when they start. Visual C++ does, as does Microsoft Word, Borland's Delphi, and others. This About box usually contains information about the application, which is displayed until the user dispatches it. In this How-To, we will show you how you can display an About box that remains on the screen until the user sends it away. This dialog will be displayed before your program starts, giving the user something to look at while the remainder of the program loads.

15.7   Display a Splash Screen

Splash screens are a specialized type of window that remains until either a certain period of time has gone by or the user presses a mouse button or keyboard key. In this How-To, we will take you through the steps necessary to create a splash screen and make it disappear when you are done with it.

15.8   Find Out About My Program's Icons

It is useful to find out which icons are displayed when your program (or another program) is minimized. Windows 95 has different icons which are displayed when the program is shown on the screen and when it is minimized to the task bar. This How-To will show you how to use Windows 95 API functions to find out what icons will be displayed under different circumstances of a program.

15.9   Display a Bitmap as a Window or Dialog Background

Wouldn't it be nice to be able to use the background of a window or dialog to display something other than the boring gray colors that Windows uses? It would be especially interesting to be able to display a bitmap on the background to really liven up your application. This How-To shows you the steps and API functions you need to get the job done.

Table 15-1 lists the Windows 95 API functions used in this chapter.

GetFocus	GetDlgCtrlID	MessageBox
GetClientRect	MoveWindow	ShowWindow
LoadBitmap	SetButtons	FindWindow
PostMessage	UpdateWindow	GetCurrentTime
BringWindowToTop	DestroyWindow	CreateCompatibleDC
SelectObject	StretchBlt	GetObject
GetSystemMetrics	SHGetFileInfo	ImageList_GetIcon
SendDlgItemMessage	SetBkMode	DeleteObject

 *Table 15-1* Windows 95 functions used in Chapter 15

COMPLEXITY

MODERATE

15.1 How do I...
Implement context-sensitive help?

Problem

I need to be able to implement context-sensitive help in my form-based application for Windows. Specifically, I would like to be able to determine exactly which field in a form the user is presently editing and to trap for the F1 key when it is pressed.

The program should then display a help message or help file entry based on which field the user is working with. How do I use the Windows API functions to help me out of this jam?

Technique

This is a very nice feature to offer users. When users are working in a form (or CFormView in MFC parlance), the last thing they want to do is page through a Help file looking for the entry that corresponds to the specific field they are working on.

In this How-To, we will examine using the GetFocus and GetDlgCtrlID functions of the Windows API to determine exactly which field the user is working on. At that point, the field is determined and the specific help message you wish to display can be loaded and shown to the user. For this example, we will simply display a message box containing the field-specific help.

Steps

Open and run the Visual C++ application CH151.MAK from the CHAPT15\SAMPLES\CH151 directory on the CD that comes with this book. You will see a form displayed on the screen with a number of fields to enter. Click the mouse in the Name edit field and press F1. You will see the form with the message box displayed in Figure 15-1.

To duplicate the functionality of this example, follow this procedure:

1. Create a new project in Visual C++ using AppWizard. Give the new project the name CH151.MAK.

2. Enter the resource editor and create a new dialog template.

3. To the dialog box add a group field and within the group field add three radio buttons. Give the radio buttons the captions Active Customer, InActive Customer, and Prospect, respectively.

4. To the dialog add six sets of prompts for static text fields and edit fields. Give the static text fields the following captions: Name, Address, City, State,

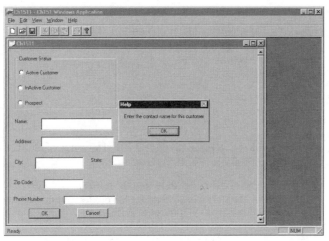

Figure 15-1 Context-sensitive help for the Name edit field of the form

Zip Code, and Phone Number. Give the edit fields blank captions with the identifiers IDC_EDIT1, IDC_EDIT2, IDC_EDIT3, IDC_EDIT4, IDC_EDIT5, and IDC_EDIT6, respectively.

5. Enter ClassWizard and create a new class for this dialog template. Give the new class the name CContactView and the base class type CFormView. Select the IDD_DIALOG1 dialog template identifier as the dialog on which to base this class.

6. Reenter the resource editor and select the Accelerator resource entry. Add a new accelerator for the F1 key by entering F1 into the Key edit field and ID_HELP into the ID edit field. Save the accelerator table and exit the resource editor.

7. Select the CONTACTV.CPP source file for the CContactView class and add the line marked in bold to the message map for the class:

```
BEGIN_MESSAGE_MAP(CContactView, CFormView)
 //{{AFX_MSG_MAP(CContactView)
    // NOTE - the ClassWizard will add and remove mapping macros here.
  ON_COMMAND(ID_HELP, OnHelp)
 //}}AFX_MSG_MAP
END_MESSAGE_MAP()
```

8. Add the following code to the CONTACTV.CPP source file:

```
void CContactView::OnHelp()
{
    // Get active control

    CWnd *wnd = GetFocus();
```

continued on next page

continued from previous page

```
// Get id of control

int id = wnd->GetDlgCtrlID();

// Determine what to do based on Id

switch ( id ) {
    case IDOK: // Ok Button
        MessageBox("The Ok button will close the form", "Help", MB_OK );
        break;
    case IDCANCEL: // Cancel Button
        MessageBox("The Cancel Button will cancel the edit and close the
                   form", "Help", MB_OK );
        break;
    case IDC_RADIO1: // Active Customer Radio Button
        MessageBox("Select this option for active customers\nthat have
                   ordered recently", "Help", MB_OK );
        break;
    case IDC_RADIO2: // Inactive Customer Radio Button
        MessageBox("Select this option for inactive customers\nthat have NOT
                   ordered recently", "Help", MB_OK );
        break;
    case IDC_RADIO3: // Prospect Radio Button
        MessageBox("Select this option for prospects\nthat have never
                   ordered", "Help", MB_OK );
        break;
    case IDC_EDIT1: // Name
        MessageBox("Enter the contact name for this customer", "Help",
                   MB_OK );
        break;
    case IDC_EDIT2: // Address
        MessageBox("Enter the contact address for this customer", "Help",
                   MB_OK );
        break;
    case IDC_EDIT3: // City
        MessageBox("Enter the city for this customer", "Help", MB_OK );
        break;
    case IDC_EDIT4: // State
        MessageBox("Enter the state for this customer", "Help", MB_OK );
        break;
    case IDC_EDIT5: // Zip Code
        MessageBox("Enter the 9 digit zip code for this customer",
                   "Help", MB_OK );
        break;
    case IDC_EDIT6: // Phone
        MessageBox("Enter the phone number (with area code)\n for this
                   customer", "Help", MB_OK );
        break;
    }
}
```

9. Add the following line to the header file for the CContactView class,
CONTACTV.H. Add only the line marked in bold.

```
// Generated message map functions
  //{{AFX_MSG(CContactView)
    // NOTE - the ClassWizard will add and remove member functions here.
  afx_msg void OnHelp(void);
  //}}AFX_MSG
  DECLARE_MESSAGE_MAP()
```

10. Finally, make modifications to the CH151.CPP source file for the application. First, add the header file for the new view to the include file list, as follows:

```
#include "contactv.h"
```

11. Next, modify the document template definition for the application by changing the following lines. Changes are marked in bold.

```
// Register the application's document templates.  Document templates
  //  serve as the connection between documents, frame windows and views.

  CMultiDocTemplate* pDocTemplate;
  pDocTemplate = new CMultiDocTemplate(
    IDR_CH151TYPE,
    RUNTIME_CLASS(CCh151Doc),
    RUNTIME_CLASS(CMDIChildWnd),              // standard MDI child frame
    RUNTIME_CLASS(CContactView));
  AddDocTemplate(pDocTemplate);
```

12. Compile and run the application.

How It Works

When you add a new entry to the accelerator table for an application, it automatically makes that keystroke into a command for your application, exactly as if you had added a menu entry with that identifier and selected the menu. In this case, we are adding a new command to our application that maps the F1 key to the command ID_HELP.

In our view class, we trap for the ID_HELP command by adding a message map entry for that command. This is done via the MFC message mapping system but could just as easily be done using the message tracking system defined in WINDOWSX.H. Once the F1 key is pressed, the OnHelp function will be called.

In the OnHelp function the real meat of the procedure takes place. First, the current control is identified by using the GetFocus function. GetFocus returns the window that currently has the input focus. Since a key was pressed, the current input focus also identifies the control that the user was in when the F1 key was pressed.

After determining which control has the input focus, it is necessary to get the identifier for the control so that the application has something it can compare known identifiers with. This is accomplished via the GetDlgCtrlID function of the API. This function returns the defined control identifier for a window.

Once the identifier is known for the current control, it is a simple matter to display a message box showing the user the context-sensitive help for that control, as defined by the application.

Comments

Although this particular example simply displays a message box to indicate the help message for the control, it would be quite easy to display a help page for each control. This book would be quite cluttered if we had to add the complete text for the help file for the entries, but actually implementing such a system is easy.

To implement context-sensitive help topics in a help file, do the following. First, create a new help file with a help topic for each entry in the dialog. Note the help topic identifiers for each page and create a header file with these constants. Next, modify the switch statement in the OnHelp function of the CContactView class to replace each MessageBox with an entry of the form,

```
::WinHelp(m_hWnd, "helpfile.hlp", HELP_CONTEXT, identifier);
```

where the "helpfile.hlp" parameter should be replaced by the actual name of the help file you created, and the identifier parameters should be replaced by the identifier for the specific control you are interested in.

COMPLEXITY
MODERATE

15.2   How do I...
Create a status bar?

Problem

I need to be able to add a status bar to my normal views as well as to the main window of my application. It seems quite easy to add a status bar to the bottom of my main window (the MFC does it for me), but how can I add status bars to the other windows in my application?

Technique

The status bar window was added as a standard control in Windows 95, but status bars have been around since Windows 3.1. The Microsoft Foundation Classes contain a "wrapper" class that encapsulates the functionality of the status bar in either 16-bit Windows 3.1 or 32-bit Windows 95, so we will use that class in our example. If you are interested in how to create status bars using direct API calls, simply create a window with the class name of "status" in your application.

To create a status bar in your view windows, you simply instantiate an object of the type CStatusBar and manipulate it so that it is displayed at the top of your window. How do you manipulate the status bar? Ah, well, that's the rub, isn't it? In this How-To, we show you the steps you need to take to get a status bar to be created and shown in any window (although we chose view windows for our example).

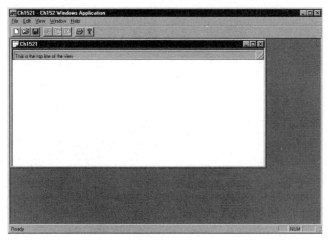

Figure 15-2 MFC view showing a top status bar with
sample text

Steps

Open and run the Visual C++ application CH152.MAK from the
CHAPT15\SAMPLES\CH152 directory on the CD that comes with this book. You will
see a view displayed with a status bar shown at the top, as in Figure 15-2.

To duplicate the functionality of this example, follow this procedure:

1. Create a new project in Visual C++ using AppWizard. Give the new project the
name CH152.MAK.

2. Enter ClassWizard and select the CCh152View class from the drop-down list.
Select the CCh152View object from the object list and the WM_CREATE
message from the message list. Click on the Add Function button. Add the
following code to the OnCreate method of CCh152View:

```
int CCh152View::OnCreate(LPCREATESTRUCT lpCreateStruct)
{
  if (CView::OnCreate(lpCreateStruct) == -1)
    return -1;

    if ( !topStatusBar.Create( this, WS_CHILD | WS_VISIBLE | CBRS_TOP |
WS_BORDER )  )
    {
        MessageBox("Unable to create status bar!", "Error", MB_OK );
        return -1;      // fail to create
    }

    if ( !topStatusBar.SetIndicators(indicators,1) )
    {
```

continued on next page

continued from previous page

```
            MessageBox("Unable to set status bar indicators!", "Error", MB_OK );
              return -1;
          }

          topStatusBar.SetPaneText(0,"This is the top line of the view",TRUE);
       return 0;
    }
```

3. Next, enter ClassWizard and again select the CCh152View class from the drop-down combo box. Select the CCh152View object from the object list and the WM_SIZE message from the message list. Click on the Add Function button and add the following code to the OnSize method of CCh152View:

```
void CCh152View::OnSize(UINT nType, int cx, int cy)
{
    CView::OnSize(nType, cx, cy);

    CRect r;
    GetClientRect(&r);
    r.bottom = 25;

    topStatusBar.MoveWindow(&r);
    UINT nID;
    UINT nStyle;
    int  cxWidth;
    topStatusBar.GetPaneInfo( 0, nID, nStyle, cxWidth );
    topStatusBar.SetPaneInfo( 0, nID, SBPS_STRETCH, cxWidth);

}
```

4. Select the CH152VW.H file from the project list and add the following declaration to the class definition for CCh152View:

```
private:
    CStatusBar topStatusBar;                  // Top line status bar
```

5. Select the CH152VW.CPP file from the project list and add the following lines to the top of the file:

```
static UINT BASED_CODE indicators[] =
{
    ID_SEPARATOR,            // status bar indicator
    ID_INDICATOR_CAPS,
    ID_INDICATOR_NUM,
    ID_INDICATOR_SCRL,
};
```

6. Compile and run the application.

How It Works

The status bar class in the MFC, CStatusBar, simply encapsulates the status bar control type in Windows 95. In this example, we are simply creating a new status bar as a child of another window (a view window in this example, but it could be any kind of window). If you have tried this on your own, you will find that the status bar seems to be created normally but never displays itself on the child window.

The trick to creating a window on the child lies in the OnSize method of the window. Here we reposition the status bar window so that it falls at a specific place in the view window. This is necessary because the status bar window is normally automatically repositioned by the parent window in the application. In this case, however, it is not possible for the status bar window to be repositioned automatically, so we need to do the work for the window.

There are a few things to notice about this particular example. Here we are using a status window with none of the usual "panes" that users are accustomed to seeing. Normally, the status bar is displayed at the bottom of the window with panes for the Control, Caps Lock, Num Lock, and other keys. In addition, you might see the line and column values representing the position of the cursor in the window. In this example we are simply using a status bar as a display for static text—probably the title of some document or other information.

In addition to the lack of secondary panes, this status bar also has another peculiarity. The only pane stretches across the entire width of the status bar. Status bars work with "panes" of text that normally occupy a fixed amount of the bar across the width of the window. It is possible, however, to use the SBPS_STRETCH setting for a given pane in the status bar to make that pane stretch the remaining distance of the status bar. This is done in the OnSize method of the view.

Comments

You can also create status bars in Delphi. To do so, follow this procedure:

1. Create a new project in Delphi or add a new form to an existing application.

2. Add a panel component to the top of the form. Set the align property to alTop and the alignment property to taLeftJustify.

3. Set the caption of the panel component to whatever you would like it to be. To set the component caption at runtime, use the following code in the TForm1.FormCreate method of the form:

```
Panel1.Caption := 'This is a top view status bar';
```

4. Compile and run the application.

COMPLEXITY
MODERATE

15.3   How do I...
Make a toolbar?

Problem

I would like to be able to create a toolbar control in a window other than the main window. Although it is quite easy, using the MFC, to create a toolbar for the main window, I can find no way to create one in a child window.

Is there some way to automatically create a toolbar in a child window in my application?

Technique

There is no direct way to automatically create a toolbar control in a window other than the main window for an MFC view. This is a limitation of the tools, however, not a limitation of the Foundation Class library. It is quite possible for an MFC view window to have a toolbar, but not quite as straightforward as you might like.

To add a toolbar to an MFC view window, you must first override the frame window for the view and add the toolbar creation and initialization there. This is necessary because the MDI window that Windows actually deals with is the frame window (a CMDIChildWindow) rather than the actual view window (CView).

In this How-To, we will show you how you can add a toolbar to an existing view without any changes to the view class itself. First, we will create a new frame window for the view to reside in, and then we will show you how to define a toolbar for that frame window so that it appears when the view is created.

Steps

Open and run the Visual C++ application CH153.MAK from the CHAPT15\SAMPLES\CH153 directory on the CD that comes with this book. You will see a view displayed with a toolbar shown at the top, as shown in Figure 15-3.

To duplicate the functionality of this example, follow this procedure:

1. Create a new project in Visual C++ using AppWizard. Give the new project the name CH153.MAK.

2. Enter ClassWizard and select the Add Class button. Give the new class the name CTBFrame. Give the class a base class of CMDIChildWindow. Generate the new class definition.

3. In ClassWizard, select the CTBFrame object from the object list and the WM_CREATE message from the message list. Add the following code to the OnCreate method of CTBFrame:

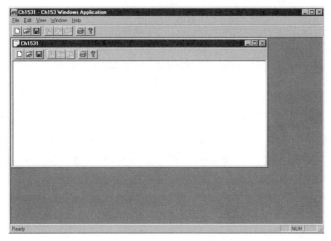

Figure 15-3 MFC view showing a toolbar

```
int CTBFrame::OnCreate(LPCREATESTRUCT lpCreateStruct)
{
   if (CMDIChildWnd::OnCreate(lpCreateStruct) == -1)
      return -1;

   if (!m_wndToolBar.Create(this) ||
       !m_wndToolBar.LoadBitmap(IDR_MAINFRAME) ||
       !m_wndToolBar.SetButtons(buttons, (sizeof(buttons) /
sizeof(buttons[0]))) )
   {
      TRACE("Failed to create toolbar\n");
      return -1;       // fail to create
   }


   m_wndToolBar.ShowWindow(SW_SHOW);

   return 0;
}
```

4. Add the following lines to the top of the TBFRAME.CPP source file:

```
static UINT BASED_CODE buttons[] =
{
   // same order as in the bitmap 'toolbar.bmp'
   ID_FILE_NEW,
   ID_FILE_OPEN,
   ID_FILE_SAVE,
      ID_SEPARATOR,
   ID_EDIT_CUT,
   ID_EDIT_COPY,
   ID_EDIT_PASTE,
      ID_SEPARATOR,
```

continued on next page

continued from previous page

```
        ID_FILE_PRINT,
        ID_APP_ABOUT,
};
```

5. Next, add the following declaration to the header file for the CTBFrame class, TBFRAME.H:

```
private:
    CToolBar      m_wndToolBar;
```

6. Select the CH153.CPP source file for the application object. Modify the document template definition by changing the following block of code. Note that the line to change is marked in bold.

```
CMultiDocTemplate* pDocTemplate;
  pDocTemplate = new CMultiDocTemplate(
    IDR_CH153TYPE,
    RUNTIME_CLASS(CCh153Doc),
    RUNTIME_CLASS(CTBFrame),
    RUNTIME_CLASS(CCh153View));
  AddDocTemplate(pDocTemplate);
```

7. Now add the following include line to the include list at the top of the CH153.CPP source file:

```
#include "tbframe.h"
```

8. Compile and run the application.

How It Works

When the MFC creates a new MDI child window, it first creates an MDI frame window. This MDI frame window will be the "container" object for the document and view objects in your application. The MDI frame window contains the view window as well as the border and any nonclient area for the view. It is within this nonclient area that the toolbar window is created. The toolbar in this example simply uses the same bitmaps (and commands) as the main frame window for the application.

In the MFC, the toolbar window is dependent on the version of Windows being run. The toolbar class is a wrapper for a toolbar control built into the operating system.

In our frame window we create the toolbar window when the frame window itself is done creating. This allows the toolbar to be positioned at the correct location at the top of the frame window. An interesting note is that the toolbar will move automatically with the parent window when the parent window is moved or resized. The MFC Tech Notes tell you that this is accomplished via private messages within the MFC.

Comments

This example shows you how you can add a toolbar to a view window in your application. Unfortunately, this example simply uses the same toolbar bitmaps that the main application uses. It is more likely that the user would want specialized toolbar buttons for a view in your application. You would be better off creating a new toolbar bitmap in the resource editor and using this new bitmap with new commands for your view toolbars.

You can also create and modify toolbars in Visual Basic. Here is an example of how to do it:

1. Create a new project in Visual Basic. Give the new project the name toolbar. Add a toolbar control to the form for the project. In addition, add an image list control to the form.

2. Double-click on the form and add the following code to the Form_Load method of the form:

```
Private Sub Form_Load()
' Create object variable for the ImageList.
    Dim imgX As ListImage

' Load pictures into the ImageList control.
    Set imgX = ImageList1.ListImages. _
    Add(, "open", LoadPicture("bitmaps\tlbr_w95\open.bmp"))    ' 1
    Set imgX = ImageList1.ListImages. _
    Add(, "save", LoadPicture("bitmaps\tlbr_w95\save.bmp"))    ' 2
    Toolbar1.ImageList = ImageList1


' Create object variable for the Toolbar.
    Dim btnX As Button
    ' Add button objects to Buttons collection using the
    ' Add method. After creating each button, set both
    ' Description and ToolTipText properties.
    Set btnX = Toolbar1.Buttons.Add(, , , tbrSeparator)
    Set btnX = Toolbar1.Buttons.Add(, "open", , tbrDefault, "open")
    btnX.ToolTipText = "Open File"
    btnX.Description = btnX.ToolTipText
    Set btnX = Toolbar1.Buttons.Add(, "save", , tbrDefault, "save")
    btnX.ToolTipText = "Save File"
    btnX.Description = btnX.ToolTipText

End Sub
```

3. Double-click on the toolbar control. Add the following code to the Toolbar1_ButtonClick method of the form:

```
Private Sub Toolbar1_ButtonClick(ByVal Button As Button)
    If Button.Key = "open" Then
        MsgBox "Open Button Selected"
    Else
        If Button.Key = "save" Then
            MsgBox "Save Button Selected"
        End If
    End If
End Sub
```

4. Compile and run the application. The toolbar will appear with two buttons showing. Tool-tips will also be displayed for the toolbar buttons. Clicking on either button will display a message box indicating which button was clicked.

COMPLEXITY
MODERATE

15.4 How do I...
Allow the user to modify the toolbar on-the-fly?

Problem

I would like to allow the user to configure the toolbar as he or she would like it to appear on the screen. Unfortunately, I can't figure out how to dynamically move toolbar buttons into and out of the toolbar to allow the user to configure them.

How can I make a toolbar appear on-the-fly as the user requests?

Technique

Toolbars are an important part of a Windows 95 application. Without them, users must navigate their way through an increasingly large number of menus and submenus to find the commands they are looking for.

The ability to customize toolbars, however, sets apart the really professional Windows 95 application from the mass of clutterware that occupies the store shelves. In this How-To, we look at the functionality of the Windows 95 toolbar and how you can use the power of the MFC combined with the control to accomplish the task of a dynamic toolbar that reflects user preferences.

Steps

Open and run the Visual C++ application CH154.MAK from the CHAPT15\SAMPLES\CH154 directory on the CD that comes with this book. You will see a view displayed with a toolbar shown at the top, as in Figure 15-4. Select the Configure menu and the Toolbar menu item from the menu. You will then see the dialog for customizing the toolbar displayed in Figure 15-5. Select the first item in the left-hand list box (File New) and click on the right-pointing arrow (->). The item will move over into the right-hand list box. Repeat this procedure for the first three items in the left-hand list box. Click on OK. The toolbar will change to the view shown in Figure 15-6, reflecting the new preferences.

To duplicate the functionality of this example, follow this procedure:

1. Create a new project in Visual C++ using AppWizard. Give the new project the name CH154.MAK.

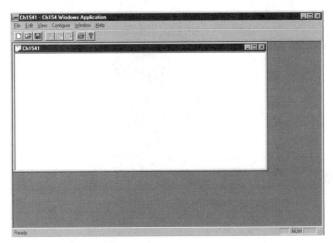

Figure 15-4 MFC view showing a standard toolbar

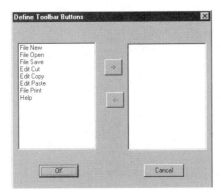

Figure 15-5 The toolbar
customization dialog

2. Enter the resource editor and create a new dialog template. Move the OK and Cancel buttons to the bottom of the dialog. Add two new list boxes at the left and right-hand sides of the top of the dialog.

3. Add two buttons to the dialog between the two list boxes. Give the first button the caption -> and the second button the caption <-. Save the dialog template.

4. Enter ClassWizard and generate a new dialog class for the dialog template you have just created. Give the new dialog class the name CToolbarDlg. Select the CToolbarDlg class from the drop-down combo box in ClassWizard and in the object list. Select the WM_INITDIALOG message from the message list and click on the Add Function button. Enter the following code into the OnInitDialog method of CToolbarDlg:

Figure 15-6 MFC view showing the new customized
toolbar reflecting user preferences

```
BOOL CToolbarDlg::OnInitDialog()
{
   CDialog::OnInitDialog();
   CListBox *list = (CListBox *)GetDlgItem(IDC_LIST1);

   for ( int i=0; buttons[i].string[0]; ++i ) {
      list->AddString ( buttons[i].string );
   }

   CenterWindow();

   return TRUE;   // return TRUE  unless you set the focus to a control
}
```

5. Select the IDC_BUTTON1 object from the object list in ClassWizard and the
    BN_CLICKED message from the message list. Click on the Add Function but-
    ton and give the new function the name OnMoveToList. Enter the following
    code into the new OnMoveToList method of CToolbarDlg:

```
void CToolbarDlg::OnMoveToList()
{
   CListBox *list1 = (CListBox *)GetDlgItem(IDC_LIST1);
   CListBox *list2 = (CListBox *)GetDlgItem(IDC_LIST2);

   // See if there is anything selected

   if ( list1->GetCurSel() == LB_ERR ) {
      MessageBeep(0);
      return;
   }

   // Yes. Get the selection string
```

```
        CString sel_string;

        list1->GetText ( list1->GetCurSel(), sel_string );

        // Append it to the second list box

        list2->AddString ( sel_string );

        // Remove it from the first list box

        list1->DeleteString ( list1->GetCurSel() );
}
```

6. Select the IDC_BUTTON2 object from the object list in ClassWizard and the BN_CLICKED message from the message list. Click on the Add Function button and give the new function the name OnMoveFromList. Enter the following code into the new OnMoveFromList method of CToolbarDlg:

```
void CToolbarDlg::OnMoveFromList()
{
    CListBox *list1 = (CListBox *)GetDlgItem(IDC_LIST1);
    CListBox *list2 = (CListBox *)GetDlgItem(IDC_LIST2);

    // See if there is anything selected

    if ( list2->GetCurSel() == LB_ERR ) {
        MessageBeep(0);
        return;
    }

    // Yes. Get the selection string

    CString sel_string;

    list2->GetText ( list2->GetCurSel(), sel_string );

    // Append it to the second list box

    list1->AddString ( sel_string );

    // Remove it from the first list box

    list2->DeleteString ( list2->GetCurSel() );

}
```

7. Select the IDOK object from the object list in ClassWizard and the BN_CLICKED message from the message list. Click on the Add Function button and accept the name OnOK. Enter the following code into the new OnOK method of CToolbarDlg:

```
void CToolbarDlg::OnOK()
{
    // Initialize flags array
```

continued on next page

continued from previous page

```
for ( int k=0; k<MAX_TOOLBAR_ENTRIES; ++k )
    flags[k] = FALSE;

// Get all of the selected items and check them in our list

CListBox *list2 = (CListBox *)GetDlgItem(IDC_LIST2);
CString  string;

for ( int i=0; i<list2->GetCount(); ++i ) {

    // Get the string

    list2->GetText ( i, string );

    // See which it is in our list

    int idx = -1;

    for ( int j=0; buttons[j].string[0]; ++j )
       if ( !strcmp(string, buttons[j].string) )
           idx = j;

    // Set that flag to TRUE

    flags[idx] = TRUE;
}

CDialog::OnOK();
}
```

8. Add the following new method to the CToolbarDlg source file, TOOLBARD.CPP:

```
BOOL CToolbarDlg::GetToolFlag(int cmd)
{
    for ( int i=0; buttons[i].string[0]; ++i )
       if ( buttons[i].id == cmd )
           return flags[i];
    return FALSE;
}
```

9. Add the following lines to the header file for the CToolbarDlg class, TOOLBARD.H. The lines to add are marked in bold.

```
const MAX_TOOLBAR_ENTRIES = 9;

class CToolbarDlg : public CDialog
{
private:
  BOOL flags[MAX_TOOLBAR_ENTRIES];
public:
  BOOL GetToolFlag(int cmd);
```

10. Enter the resource editor and select the menu for the MDI child windows, IDR_CH154TYPE. Add a new menu with the caption Configure and a new menu item to the Configure menu with the caption Toolbar. Save the resource file and exit the resource editor.

11. In ClassWizard, select the CMainFrame class. Click on the ID_CONFIGURE_TOOLBAR object in the object list and the COMMAND message in the message list. Click on the Add Function button and give the new function the name OnConfigureToolbar. Enter the following code into the new OnConfigureToolbar method of CMainFrame:

```
void CMainFrame::OnConfigureToolbar()
{
    CToolbarDlg  dlg;
    int          id = 0;

    if ( dlg.DoModal() == IDOK ) {

        int which = 0;

        for ( int i=0; i<(sizeof(buttons)/sizeof(buttons[0])); ++i ) {
            if ( dlg.GetToolFlag(buttons[i]) == TRUE )
                m_wndToolBar.SetButtonInfo( id++, buttons[i], TBBS_BUTTON, which );
            if ( buttons[i] != ID_SEPARATOR )
                which ++;
        }
        for ( i=id; i<(sizeof(buttons)/sizeof(buttons[0])); ++i )
            m_wndToolBar.SetButtonInfo( i, 0, TBBS_SEPARATOR, 12 );

        m_wndToolBar.InvalidateRect(NULL);
    }

}
```

12. Compile and run the application.

How It Works

The MFC toolbar control is a simple Windows 95 control that responds to certain commands. One of the commands it understands is the ability to set and reset the buttons that are displayed. There are two basic kinds of buttons on a toolbar. Command buttons contain an image and a command ID. When the user clicks on a command button, the current window is sent the command ID via a WM_COMMAND message. The other kind of toolbar button is a separator. Separators are simply there to take up space and do not respond to users' button clicks.

In this example we configure the toolbar by selecting the toolbar buttons that the user wishes to see on the toolbar display. When the user clicks on the OK button in the configure dialog, a flag array is set up with a TRUE flag for each item the user wants in the toolbar. For each item not wanted, FALSE is stored in the flag. The main window then queries the flag array from the dialog and sets each of the toolbar buttons to be either the toolbar button desired or a separator indicating that no button was desired for that command.

Comments

The program in this How-To provides a simple technique for customizing toolbars, but it is by no means complete. Initially, the toolbar buttons remain in the same order in which they were originally designed. A beginning customization would allow the user to select not only the items they want to display but the order in which they would like them to appear.

Another possible customization for this is to implement an owner-drawn list box for the toolbar selection dialog that contains not only the command name but the actual image used for the toolbar button.

Finally, a drag-and-drop interface between the two list boxes in the customization dialog would be a nice touch. Don't forget that a snappy user interface that is customizable is the hallmark of a good Windows 95 application.

COMPLEXITY
MODERATE

15.5 How do I...
Display demonstrations within online help?

Problem

I would like the ability to interact with my program while the user is in a help file for my application. What I am looking for here is a way to create a Wizardlike application with the help file driving my application.

Is there any way to use the Windows API functions to communicate between my help file and my application?

Technique

The Windows Help system is a marvelous invention. It provides a standard interface between users and help information and allows application developers to worry about the content of their help information rather than the presentation of it. There are times, however, when you need capabilities beyond those provided in standard help commands. This is one of those times.

In this case we are trying to call external programs from within Windows Help. This is possible by defining an external function in a DLL to do whatever it is you wish to do. We will show you a step-by-step process to accomplish this in this How-To.

Steps

Open and run the Visual C++ application CH155.MAK from the CHAPT15\SAMPLES\CH155 directory on the CD that comes with this book. Select the Help menu and the Index menu item. You will see the help screen shown in Figure 15-7. Click on the highlighted text, Click Here To Run Dialog. You will need to copy the MYHELP.DLL file from the CD to your WINDOWS\SYSTEM directory. A dialog box will be displayed in the application running beside the help file, as shown in Figure 15-8. You can also view the dialog by selecting Dialog | Show Dialog from the menu in the CH155 application.

To duplicate the functionality of this example, follow this procedure:

1. Create a new project in Visual C++ using AppWizard. Give the new project the name CH155.MAK.

2. Enter the resource editor and create a new dialog. Add several fields to the dialog including a static text field, an edit field, and three radio buttons. Give the static text field the caption Input String #1. Give the radio buttons the captions Customer Type 1, Customer Type 2, and Customer Type 3.

3. Select ClassWizard and generate a new dialog class for the dialog template you have just created. Give the new dialog class the name CMyDialog.

4. In the resource editor, select the menu resource IDR_MAINFRAME. Add a new main menu item with the caption Dialog and a menu item with the caption Show Dialog. Give the Show Dialog menu item the identifier ID_SHOW_DIALOG.

Figure 15-7 Help screen for the CH155 application

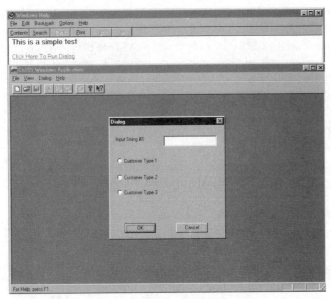

Figure 15-8 Dialog displayed via the help screen in CH155
application

5. In ClassWizard, select the application object for the project, CCh155App.
Select the ID_SHOW_DIALOG object from the object list and the COMMAND
message from the message list. Click on the Add Function button and accept
the name OnShowDialog for the new function. Enter the following code into
the OnShowDialog method of CCh155App:

```
void CCh155App::OnShowDialog()
{
    CMyDialog dlg;

    dlg.DoModal();
}
```

6. Add the following line to the include file list at the top of CH155.CPP:

```
#include "mydialog.h"
```

7. Remove the OnFileNew call in the InitInstance method of CCh155App. This
will prevent the application from opening a new view.

8. Save and compile the CH155.MAK application.

9. Next, create a new project with the name MYHELP.MAK. Use the Project |
New command to create the project and make it a Windows dynamic link
library.

10. Add a new file in Visual C++ and enter the following code into it. Save this file
as LIBMAIN.CPP:

```
#define  STRICT
#include <windows.h>

// Turn off warning: Parameter '' is never used
#ifdef _BORLANDC_
#pragma argsused
#endif

BOOL DllEntryPoint (
     HANDLE      hDLL,
     DWORD       dwReason,
     LPVOID      lpReserved)
{

     switch (dwReason)
        {
        case DLL_PROCESS_ATTACH:
             break;
        case DLL_PROCESS_DETACH:
             break;
        case DLL_THREAD_ATTACH:
        case DLL_THREAD_DETACH:
        default:
             break;
        }
     return TRUE;
}
```

11. Finally, add a third new file to the project and enter the following code into it. Save this file as SHOWDIAL.CPP.

```
#define STRICT
#include "windows.h"

extern "C" {

BOOL ShowDialog(char FAR *str)
{
    HWND hWnd = FindWindow(NULL, "Ch155 Windows Application");
    if ( hWnd )
       ::PostMessage(hWnd, WM_COMMAND, 32771, OL );
    return TRUE;
}

}
```

12. Add LIBMAIN.CPP and SHOWDIALOG.CPP to the project. Compile the new DLL.

13. Create a new file with the name CH155.RTF and enter the following text into the file:

```
{\rtf1\ansi \deff0
{\fonttbl{\f0\froman Tms Rmn;}{\f1\fdecor Symbol;}{\f2\fswiss Helv;}
{\f3\fmodern Courier;\f4\fswiss MS Sans Serif;\f5\fswiss Helvitica;}
```

continued on next page

continued from previous page

```
{\f6\fswiss Arial;\f7\fswiss Arial Super;\f8\fswiss MS Serif;}
{\f9\froman Times;\f10\froman Times New Roman;}
}
{\colortbl;

\red0\green0\blue127;
\red0\green127\blue0;
\red0\green127\blue127;
\red127\green0\blue0;
\red127\green0\blue127;
\red127\green127\blue0;
\red127\green127\blue127;

\red192\green192\blue192;
\red0\green0\blue255;
\red0\green255\blue0;
\red0\green255\blue255;
\red255\green0\blue0;
\red255\green0\blue255;
\red255\green255\blue0;
\red255\green255\blue255;}
\f2\fs20
{#{\footnote # Test}
K{\footnote K test;contents}
${\footnote $ Test}
+{\footnote + General}
{\b \fs24 This is a simple test}\par\pard
\par{{\uldb Click Here To Run Dialog}{\v !ShowDialog("MyDialog")}
}\par\pard
}\page
}
```

14. Next, create a new file with the name CH155.HPJ (a Windows Help project file). Add the following text into this file:

```
[OPTIONS]
  ERRORLOG = error.log
  COMPRESS = No
[BUILDTAGS]

[FILES]
  CH155.RTF

[BITMAPS]

[ALIAS]
[CONFIG]
  BrowseButtons()
  RegisterRoutine("myhelp.dll", "ShowDialog", "S" )
[WINDOWS]
[BAGGAGE]
```

15. Build a new Windows Help file using the CH155.RTF and CH155.HPJ files.

16. Run the application.

How It Works

When the application launches a help file, WinHelp (the Windows Help system) looks at the registered functions found in the CONFIG section of the help project file (.HPJ). All functions in this section are listed with the DLL they are found in as well as the calling parameters they will accept.

In the help file, the function is called by invoking it as a macro for WinHelp. The Windows Help system then looks through the list of defined functions for one that matches this one and attempts to load the function from the DLL. Once this is accomplished successfully, the function is called.

In our DLL, the function ShowDialog looks for the window of our application. It knows that the application has a window title of the form CH155 Windows Application. Once the window is found, it is as simple as posting (not sending) a message to that window indicating that a command has been invoked. This brings up the dialog and displays it for the user.

Comments

This is obviously a simple example of calling application functionality through a Windows Help file, but it is also a quite powerful technique. Using this method, you can do any exposed functionality in your application through outside help files. You could run sample dialogs, bring up displays, display graphics, or any other function that is possible to reach through a COMMAND message.

In addition to calling outside programs, you can do considerable work in a DLL-based function for WinHelp. Internal parameters allow you to specify the window handle of the help screen, which allows you to display animations, change the background, or any other task you deem necessary for your help system.

COMPLEXITY
MODERATE

15.6   How do I...
Display an About box when my application starts?

Problem

I need to be able to display an About box before my application loads and for a few seconds after the main window is shown. Examples of this can be seen in many professional Windows applications, and my application needs it as well. I would also like the About box to go away after a fixed period of time or when the user clicks in the main window of my application.

How can I create an About box that does all of this using the Windows API?

Technique

The idea of an About box that displays for a few seconds before the program begins is not a new idea. This is the basis for a splash screen, which displays a colorful picture for the user to view while the program is loading. In this case, however, we are interested only in displaying textual information such as copyright or ownership data.

To create an About box that goes away on its own requires that you create the dialog modelessly. A modeless dialog is one that has no owner and is not "modal," which means that other applications can run at the same time the dialog is displayed.

Steps

Open and run the Visual C++ application CH156.MAK from the CHAPT15\SAMPLES\CH156 directory on the CD that comes with this book. You will see the About box dialog displayed, as shown in Figure 15-9. Click anywhere in the client area of the main window when it appears, and the dialog will disappear. If you wait five seconds, the dialog will also disappear.

To duplicate the functionality of this example, follow this procedure:

1. Create a new project in Visual C++ using AppWizard. Give the new project the name CH156.MAK.

2. Enter ClassWizard and select the Add Class button. Name the new class CSplash and select CDialog as the base class for the class. Ignore the warning about not defining a dialog template identifier for the class. Generate the new class.

3. Select the CSplash class from the drop-down combo box in ClassWizard. Select the object CSplash in the object list and the WM_INITDIALOG message in the message list. Click on the Add Function method. Add the following code to the OnInitDialog method of CSplash:

```
BOOL CSplash::OnInitDialog()
{
   CDialog::OnInitDialog();

   CenterWindow();
   return TRUE;  // return TRUE  unless you set the focus to a control
}
```

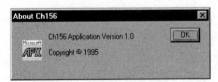

Figure 15-9 About box dialog
displayed at startup

4. Add the following code to the SPLASH.CPP file:

```
BOOL CSplash::Create(CWnd* pParent)
{
  //{{AFX_DATA_INIT(CSplashWnd)
    // NOTE: the ClassWizard will add member initialization here
  //}}AFX_DATA_INIT

  if (!CDialog::Create(CSplash::IDD, pParent))
  {
    TRACE0("Warning: creation of CSplashWnd dialog failed\n");
    return FALSE;
  }

  return TRUE;
}
```

5. Add or modify the following lines marked in bold in the SPLASH.H header file:

```
class CSplash : public CDialog
{
// Construction
public:
  CSplash(CWnd* pParent = NULL);   // standard constructor
  ~CSplash();                       // standard destructor
  BOOL Create(CWnd* pParent);

// Dialog Data
  //{{AFX_DATA(CSplash)
  enum { IDD = IDD_ABOUTBOX };
    // NOTE: the ClassWizard will add data members here
  //}}AFX_DATA

// Implementation
protected:
  virtual void DoDataExchange(CDataExchange* pDX);   // DDX/DDV support

  // Generated message map functions
  //{{AFX_MSG(CSplash)
  virtual BOOL OnInitDialog();
    // NOTE: the ClassWizard will add member functions here
  //}}AFX_MSG
  DECLARE_MESSAGE_MAP()
};
```

6. Select the CH156.H file from the project list. Add the following lines to the class definition for CCh156App. Once again, the lines to add are marked in bold.

```
#include "splash.h"

class CCh156App : public CWinApp
{
```

continued on next page

continued from previous page

```
private:
   CSplash m_splash;
   DWORD m_dwSplashTime;
public:
   CCh156App();

// Overrides
   virtual BOOL InitInstance();
   virtual BOOL OnIdle(LONG lCount);
   virtual BOOL PreTranslateMessage(MSG* pMsg);
```

7. Select the CH156.CPP source file from the project list. Make the following modifications (marked in bold) to the InitInstance method of the CCh156App class:

```
BOOL CCh156App::InitInstance()
{
    if (m_splash.Create(m_pMainWnd)) {
        m_splash.ShowWindow(SW_SHOW);
        m_splash.UpdateWindow();
    }
    m_dwSplashTime = ::GetCurrentTime();

    // Standard initialization
    // If you are not using these features and wish to reduce the size
    // of your final executable, you should remove from the following
    // the specific initialization routines you do not need.

    SetDialogBkColor();          // Set dialog background color to gray
    LoadStdProfileSettings();    // Load standard INI file options
                                 // (including MRU)

    // Register the application's document templates.  Document templates
    // serve as the connection between documents, frame windows and views.

    CMultiDocTemplate* pDocTemplate;
    pDocTemplate = new CMultiDocTemplate(
       IDR_CH156TYPE,
       RUNTIME_CLASS(CCh156Doc),
       RUNTIME_CLASS(CMDIChildWnd),          // standard MDI child frame
       RUNTIME_CLASS(CCh156View));
    AddDocTemplate(pDocTemplate);

    // create main MDI Frame window
    CMainFrame* pMainFrame = new CMainFrame;
    if (!pMainFrame->LoadFrame(IDR_MAINFRAME))
       return FALSE;
    m_pMainWnd = pMainFrame;

    // create a new (empty) document
    OnFileNew();

    if (m_lpCmdLine[0] != '\0')
    {
       // TODO: add command line processing here
    }
```

```
    // The main window has been initialized, so show and update it.
    pMainFrame->ShowWindow(m_nCmdShow);
    pMainFrame->UpdateWindow();
    m_splash.BringWindowToTop();

    return TRUE;
}
```

8. Add the following function to the CH156.CPP source file:

```
BOOL CCh156App::OnIdle(LONG lCount)
{
    // call base class idle first
    BOOL bResult = CWinApp::OnIdle(lCount);

    // then do our work
    if (m_splash.m_hWnd != NULL) {
        if (::GetCurrentTime() - m_dwSplashTime > 5000) {
            // timeout expired, destroy the splash window
            m_splash.DestroyWindow();
            m_pMainWnd->UpdateWindow();

            // NOTE: don't set bResult to FALSE,
            //   CWinApp::OnIdle may have returned TRUE
        }
        else {
            // check again later...
            bResult = TRUE;
        }
    }
    return bResult;
}
```

9. Add the following function to the source file CH156.CPP:

```
BOOL CCh156App::PreTranslateMessage(MSG* pMsg)
{
    BOOL bResult = CWinApp::PreTranslateMessage(pMsg);

    if (m_splash.m_hWnd != NULL &&
        (pMsg->message == WM_KEYDOWN ||
         pMsg->message == WM_SYSKEYDOWN ||
         pMsg->message == WM_LBUTTONDOWN ||
         pMsg->message == WM_RBUTTONDOWN ||
         pMsg->message == WM_MBUTTONDOWN ||
         pMsg->message == WM_NCLBUTTONDOWN ||
         pMsg->message == WM_NCRBUTTONDOWN ||
         pMsg->message == WM_NCMBUTTONDOWN)) {
        m_splash.DestroyWindow();
        m_pMainWnd->UpdateWindow();
    }

    return bResult;
}
```

10. Compile and run the application.

How It Works

The dialog box for the About box is created modelessly when the application begins in the InitInstance method of the application object class. Once it is created, it is automatically brought to the front of the window when the main window is created. The dialog then simply stays there until the user either waits five seconds (5 * 1000 milliseconds), clicks the mouse, or presses a key.

If the user clicks the mouse or presses a key, the PreTranslateMessage method of the application object is called. This method checks to see if the window is present for the About box and, if so, destroys it. The main window is updated and the program continues.

If the user waits five seconds, the OnIdle method will be called for the application object. This method will be called whenever there is time to do idle processing for the application. In this case, the OnIdle method checks to see if enough time has elapsed to destroy the window. If so, it destroys the About box window, and program execution continues.

Comments

You can accomplish the same task using Delphi. Here is how you go about it:

1. Create a new project in Delphi. Select the New Form button from the toolbar. From the gallery of forms, select the About Box form.

2. Double-click on the first form in your project (form1) and add the following code to the Form1.FormCreate method:

```
procedure TForm1.FormCreate(Sender: TObject);
begin
    SetWindowPos ( AboutBox.handle, HWND_TOPMOST, 0, 0, 0, 0, SWP_NOSIZE Or
SWP_NOMOVE );
end;
```

3. Using the Object Inspector, add a method for the OnClick method for Form1. Give the new method the name DoClick. Add the following code to the DoClick method of Tform1:

```
procedure TForm1.DoClick(Sender: TObject);
begin
    if AboutBox <> Nil then
        begin
            AboutBox.Hide;
            AboutBox.Free;
            AboutBox := Nil;
        end;

end;
```

4. Using the Object Inspector, add a new method for the OnKeyDown message. Give the new method the name DoKeyDown. Add the following code to the DoKeyDown method of TForm1:

```
procedure TForm1.DoKeyDown(Sender: TObject; var Key: Word;
   Shift: TShiftState);
begin
    if AboutBox <> Nil then
       begin
          AboutBox.Hide;
          AboutBox.Free;
          AboutBox := Nil;
       end;

end;
```

5. Add a timer object to the TForm1 form. Select the OnTimer method in Object Inspector for Form1, and create a new method called DoTimer to handle this message. Add the following code to the DoTimer method of TForm1:

```
procedure TForm1.DoTimer(Sender: TObject);
begin
    if AboutBox <> Nil then
       begin
          AboutBox.Hide;
          AboutBox.Free;
          AboutBox := Nil;
          Timer1.Enabled := False;
       end;

end;
```

6. Edit the project source file by selecting the View | Project Source menu item from the main menu. Modify the project source as follows. The modified or added lines are marked in bold print.

```
program Splash;

uses
   Forms,
   Splsh in 'SPLSH.PAS' {Form1},
   Splsh2 in 'SPLSH2.PAS' {AboutBox},
   Winprocs;

{$R *.RES}

begin
   AboutBox := TAboutBox.Create(Application);
   AboutBox.Show;
   AboutBox.Update;
   Application.CreateForm(TForm1, Form1);
   Application.Run;
end.
```

7. Compile and run the application.

15.7 How do I...
Display a splash screen?

Problem

I need to be able to display a splash screen when my application begins. Basically, what users want is a pretty bitmap that displays itself for a few seconds and then goes away when the program is ready to start. I would prefer to be able to let the user cancel the screen with a mouse click or keystroke.

Technique

Splash screens have become an integral part of the user interface of professional applications. Users have become accustomed to seeing the screens display and in some cases even look forward to a pretty graphic or bitmap.

In this How-To we will examine the graphic bitmap functions, window creation functions, and several miscellaneous functions of the Windows 95 API. This How-To presents a generic splash window class for Visual C++ that can display any bitmap stored in a .BMP file on disk. In addition, we will show you how to find the size of the bitmap and to stretch the bitmap, if necessary, to a larger or smaller size than originally defined.

Steps

Open and run the Visual C++ application CH157.MAK from the CHAPT15\SAMPLES\CH157 directory on the CD that comes with this book. You will see the splash screen showing the Windows logo, as shown in Figure 15-10. Click anywhere in the splash window when it appears or in the client area of the main window and the splash window will disappear. Also, if you wait five seconds, the splash window will disappear on its own.

> Note: If you are using Visual C++ 4.0, the Component Gallery contains a working Splash Screen component that can simply be dropped into your application. It is recommended that you use that component in Visual C++ 4.0.

To duplicate the functionality of this example, follow this procedure:

1. Create a new project in Visual C++ using AppWizard. Give the new project the name CH157.MAK.

2. Enter ClassWizard and select the Add Class button. Name the new class CSplashWnd and select CWnd as the base class for the class. Generate the new class.

Figure 15-10 Splash screen displayed at startup showing the Windows logo bitmap

3. Select the CSplashWnd class from the drop-down combo box in ClassWizard, and then select it again in the objects list. Select WM_PAINT from the message list. Click on the Add Function button and add the following code to the OnPaint method of CSplashWnd:

```
void CSplashWnd::OnPaint()
{
    CPaintDC dc(this); // device context for painting

    CDC memDC;
    memDC.CreateCompatibleDC(&dc);

    CBitmap* pOld = memDC.SelectObject(bitmap);

    if (pOld == NULL)
        return;      // destructors will clean up

    dc.StretchBlt(0, 0, m_winWidth, m_winHeight, &memDC, 0, 0, m_wndWidth,
                m_wndHeight, SRCCOPY);
    memDC.SelectObject(pOld);

    // Do not call CWnd::OnPaint() for painting messages
}
```

4. Next, add a new method to the CSplashWnd class for the creation of the window. Add the following code to the CSplashWnd class in SPLSHWND.CPP:

```
BOOL CSplashWnd::Create()
{
    BITMAP bm;
    bitmap->GetObject(sizeof(BITMAP), &bm);

    // Get the size of the splash window
    m_wndWidth = bm.bmWidth;
    m_wndHeight = bm.bmHeight;
```

continued on next page

continued from previous page

```
        // Get the size of the screen
        int screenWidth = GetSystemMetrics(SM_CXSCREEN);
        int screenHeight = GetSystemMetrics(SM_CYSCREEN);

        // If they didn't give us a size, use the bitmap size.

        if ( m_winHeight == 0.0 )
            m_winHeight = m_wndHeight;
        if ( m_winWidth == 0.0 )
            m_winWidth = m_wndWidth;

        // get top/left coord to center the splash window
        int top = (screenHeight - m_winHeight)/2;
        int left = (screenWidth - m_winWidth)/2;

        return CWnd::CreateEx(WS_EX_TOPMOST, "AfxWnd", "", WS_POPUP | WS_VISIBLE,
            left, top, m_winWidth, m_winHeight, NULL, NULL);
}
```

5. Add the following code to the constructor (CSplashWnd::CSplashWnd) for the class:

```
CSplashWnd::CSplashWnd(int resId, double width_ratio, double
height_ratio)
{
    bitmap = new CBitmap;
    bitmap->LoadBitmap ( resId );

    // Get the size of the screen
    int screenWidth = GetSystemMetrics(SM_CXSCREEN);
    int screenHeight = GetSystemMetrics(SM_CYSCREEN);


    m_winWidth  = (int)((double)screenWidth * width_ratio);
    m_winHeight = (int)((double)screenHeight * height_ratio);
}
```

6. Next, add a destructor (CSplashWnd::~CSplashWnd) to the class and add the following code to it:

```
CSplashWnd::~CSplashWnd()
{
    delete bitmap;
}
```

7. Select the SPLSHWND.H file and modify it as follows. Lines to modify are marked in bold.

```
#ifndef _SPLSHWND_H_
#define _SPLSHWND_H_

/////////////////////////////////////////////////////////////////////
// CSplashWnd window

class CSplashWnd : public CWnd
{
```

```
private:
    CBitmap *bitmap;

// Construction
public:
    CSplashWnd(int resId, double width_ratio, double height_ratio);

// Attributes
public:
  virtual BOOL Create();

// Operations
public:

// Implementation
public:
  virtual ~CSplashWnd();

protected:
  int m_wndWidth;
  int m_wndHeight;
  int m_winWidth;
  int m_winHeight;

  // Generated message map functions
  //{{AFX_MSG(CSplashWnd)
  afx_msg void OnPaint();
  //}}AFX_MSG
  DECLARE_MESSAGE_MAP()
};

#endif
```

8. Select the CH157.CPP file and the CCh157App class from the project list. Modify the constructor for the class (CCh157App::CCh157App) to read as follows. Modified lines are marked in bold.

```
CCh157App::CCh157App()
{
    m_pwndSplash = NULL;
}
```

9. Next, modify the InitInstance method of CCh157App as follows. Add all lines marked in bold.

```
BOOL CCh157App::InitInstance()
{
    m_dwSplashTime = ::GetCurrentTime();
    m_pwndSplash = new CSplashWnd("c:\\windows\\winlogo.bmp",
0.8,0.8);
    if ( m_pwndSplash->Create() == FALSE ) {
       delete m_pwndSplash;
       m_pwndSplash = NULL;
    }
    else {
```

continued on next page

continued from previous page

```
        m_pwndSplash->ShowWindow(SW_SHOW);
        m_pwndSplash->UpdateWindow();
        ASSERT(m_pwndSplash != NULL);
    }

    // Standard initialization
    // If you are not using these features and wish to reduce the size
    //  of your final executable, you should remove from the following
    //  the specific initialization routines you do not need.

    SetDialogBkColor();          // Set dialog background color to gray
    LoadStdProfileSettings();    // Load standard INI file options
                                 // (including MRU)
```

10. Add a new entry to the class for the OnIdle method. Enter the following code into the OnIdle method of CCh157App:

```
BOOL CCh157App::OnIdle(LONG lCount)
{
    // call base class idle first
    BOOL bResult = CWinApp::OnIdle(lCount);

    // then do our work
    if (m_pwndSplash != NULL)
    {
        if (m_pwndSplash->m_hWnd != NULL)
        {
            if (::GetCurrentTime() - m_dwSplashTime >= 5000)
            {
                // timeout expired, destroy the splash window
                m_pwndSplash->DestroyWindow();
                delete m_pwndSplash;
                m_pwndSplash = NULL;
                m_pMainWnd->UpdateWindow();
                // NOTE: don't set bResult to FALSE,
                //   CWinApp::OnIdle may have returned TRUE
            }
            else
            {
                // check again later...
                bResult = TRUE;
            }
        }
    }

    return bResult;
}
```

11. Add a new entry to the class for the PreTranslateMessage method. Add the following code to the PreTranslateMethod of CCh157App:

```
BOOL CCh157App::PreTranslateMessage(MSG* pMsg)
{
    BOOL bResult = CWinApp::PreTranslateMessage(pMsg);
```

```
    if (m_pwndSplash != NULL)
    {
        if (pMsg->message == WM_KEYDOWN ||
            pMsg->message == WM_SYSKEYDOWN ||
            pMsg->message == WM_LBUTTONDOWN ||
            pMsg->message == WM_RBUTTONDOWN ||
            pMsg->message == WM_MBUTTONDOWN ||
            pMsg->message == WM_NCLBUTTONDOWN ||
            pMsg->message == WM_NCRBUTTONDOWN ||
            pMsg->message == WM_NCMBUTTONDOWN)
        {
            if (pMsg->hwnd == m_pwndSplash->m_hWnd) m_dwSplashTime -= 5000;
            else
            {
                m_pwndSplash->DestroyWindow();
                delete m_pwndSplash;
                m_pwndSplash = NULL;
                m_pMainWnd->UpdateWindow();
            }
        }
    }

    return bResult;
}
```

12. Add the following include file line to the top of the CH157.CPP source file:

```
#include "splshwnd.h"
```

13. Modify the header file for the CCh157App class, CH157.H, as follows.
Modified or added lines are marked in bold.

```
// ch157.h : main header file for the CH157 application
//

#ifndef __AFXWIN_H__
    #error include 'stdafx.h' before including this file for PCH
#endif

#include "resource.h"        // main symbols

/////////////////////////////////////////////////////////////////////
// CCh157App:
// See ch157.cpp for the implementation of this class
//

class CSplashWnd;

class CCh157App : public CWinApp
{
private:
    CSplashWnd *m_pwndSplash;
    DWORD m_dwSplashTime;
```

continued on next page

continued from previous page

```
public:
    CCh157App();

// Overrides
    virtual BOOL InitInstance();
        virtual BOOL OnIdle(LONG lCount);
        virtual BOOL PreTranslateMessage(MSG* pMsg);

// Implementation

    //{{AFX_MSG(CCh157App)
    afx_msg void OnAppAbout();
        // NOTE - the ClassWizard will add and remove member functions here.
        //      DO NOT EDIT what you see in these blocks of generated code !
    //}}AFX_MSG
    DECLARE_MESSAGE_MAP()
};
```

///

14. Compile and run the application.

How It Works

When the application starts, it will create an instance of the CSplashWnd class. The PreTranslateMessage and OnIdle functions will work to check whether the user presses a key, clicks the mouse, or enough time has expired (currently five seconds) to destroy the window.

The window is actually created in the CSplashWnd class. The height ratio and width ratio parameters to the constructor determine what portion of the screen the bitmap will take up. If these parameters are set to 0.0, the bitmap will be displayed at the size at which it was created. The Create method first loads the bitmap from the executable resources.

Once the bitmap is loaded, the window is set up for the correct size, based on either the size of the bitmap or the ratio of the screen size specified by the user. The bitmap window is centered, and the actual Windows 95 window is created using the CreateEx API function.

When the window receives a Paint message, the bitmap is selected into the device context for the window, and the device context is then rendered to the screen. The bitmap is stretched or shrunk to the proper ratio for display in the window.

When all of this is completed, the window is displayed on the screen. It will remain there until five seconds have passed or the user clicks the mouse or presses a key.

15.8 How do I...
Find out about my program's icons?

Problem

I would like to be able to find out which icons are displayed when my program (or another program) is minimized. Windows 95 seems to display different icons when the program is shown on the screen and when it is minimized to the task bar.

How can I use the Windows 95 API functions to find out what icon will be displayed under different circumstances for a program?

Technique

Windows 95 introduces the new idea of "big icons" and "small icons." Big icons are displayed in the upper-left corner of the window when the program is running. This is the icon that holds the system menu for the window. Windows 95 actually supports a third, larger icon (48 by 48) for use on high-resolution monitors. In this case, the "big" icons become "medium" icons.

When the program is minimized, however, a different icon appears next to the name of the application on the task bar. Although these icons are usually the same (or similar) in appearance, they need not be.

The new Windows 95-only API function SHGetFileInfo can retrieve information about the icons that are displayed for a given program or dynamic link library. In this How-To, we examine how you can use the SHGetFileInfo to retrieve and display icon information for any executable file.

Steps

Open and run the Visual C++ application CH158.MAK from the CHAPT15\SAMPLES\CH158 directory on the CD that comes with this book. Select the Dialogs menu and the View Program Icons menu item. In the resulting dialog, select the Select File button and select an executable file from the File Open dialog. The dialog will then display the large and small icons for that executable file, as shown in Figure 15-11.

To duplicate the functionality of this example, follow this procedure:

1. Create a new project in Visual C++ using AppWizard. Give the new project the name CH158.MAK.

2. Create a new dialog in the resource editor. Add a static text field with the caption Enter File Name:. Add an edit field next to the static text field. Add a button to the right of the edit field with the caption &View.

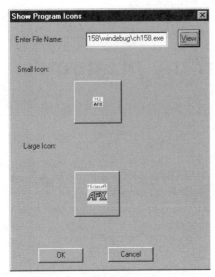

Figure 15-11 Dialog showing small and large icons for a specified application

3. Add two buttons to the dialog. Accept the identifiers IDC_BUTTON2 and IDC_BUTTON3. Enter ClassWizard and generate a new class definition for the dialog. Give the new class the name CPgmIconDlg.

4. Enter ClassWizard and select the CPgmIconDlg from the drop-down list. Select the IDC_BUTTON1 object from the object list and the BN_CLICKED message from the message list. Click on the Add Function button. Give the new function the name OnViewIcons. Add the following code to the OnViewIcons method of CPgmIconDlg:

```
void CPgmIconDlg::OnViewIcons()
{
    HICON    hIconSmall, hIconLarge;
    HIMAGELIST hSysImageList;
    SHFILEINFO  shfi;
    char buffer[_MAX_PATH];

    // Get the file name from the edit box

    GetDlgItem(IDC_EDIT1)->GetWindowText ( buffer, _MAX_PATH );
    if ( !strlen(buffer) ) {
        MessageBox("You must enter a file name!", "Error", MB_OK );
        return;
    }
```

```
hSysImageList = (HIMAGELIST)SHGetFileInfo(buffer,
                                0,
                                &shfi,
                                sizeof (SHFILEINFO),
                                SHGFI_SYSICONINDEX | SHGFI_SMALLICON);
if (hSysImageList)
{
hIconSmall = ImageList_GetIcon (hSysImageList,
                                shfi.iIcon,
                                ILD_NORMAL);
 // Set the icon in the dialog

::SendDlgItemMessage(m_hWnd, IDC_BUTTON2, BM_SETIMAGE,
                (WPARAM)IMAGE_ICON,(LPARAM)hIconSmall);

}
else
{
// SHGetFileInfo failed...
}

hSysImageList = (HIMAGELIST)SHGetFileInfo(buffer,
                                0,
                                &shfi,
                                sizeof (SHFILEINFO),
                                SHGFI_SYSICONINDEX | SHGFI_LARGEICON);
if (hSysImageList)
{
hIconLarge = ImageList_GetIcon (hSysImageList,
                                shfi.iIcon,
                                ILD_NORMAL);
 // Set the icon in the dialog

::SendDlgItemMessage(m_hWnd, IDC_BUTTON3, BM_SETIMAGE,
                (WPARAM)IMAGE_ICON, (LPARAM)hIconLarge);

}
else
{
// SHGetFileInfo failed...
}

}
```

5. Add a new main menu item in the resource editor. Give the new menu the caption Dialogs. Add a new menu item to the Dialogs menu. Give the new menu item the caption View Program Icons and the identifier ID_VIEW_PGM_ICONS.

6. Enter ClassWizard and select the CCh158App object from the drop-down list. Select the ID_VIEW_PGM_ICONS object from the object list and the COMMAND message from the message list. Click on the Add Function button and give the new function the name OnViewPgmIcons. Add the following code to the OnViewPgmIcons method of CCh158App:

```
void CCh158App::OnViewPgmIcons()
{
    CPgmIconDlg dlg;
    dlg.DoModal();
}
```

7. Add the following include file line to the top of the CH158.CPP source file:

```
#include "pgmicond.h"
```

8. Compile and run the application.

How It Works

The user selects a program into the edit box by typing in the name of the executable file and clicking on the View button of the dialog. The SHGetFileInfo function is then called for the executable file name. This new Windows 95-only API function returns a wealth of information about the executable file. One of the things it returns is the image list used to display the large and small icons for the application. The large icon is the one used in the top left corner of the main window. The small icon is the icon that appears next to the program name when the application is minimized to the toolbar.

The SHGetFileInfo function returns differing information based on the value of the last parameter passed to it. In this case, we are asking for the image list from the file. Within the image list is stored the actual displayable icon that is retrieved using the ImageList_GetIcon function of the API. This process is then repeated for the large icon, and the two are displayed in the dialog box.

It is worth noting that the icons are displayed using the new Windows 95 message BM_SETIMAGE to the button. This message makes it simpler to display either icons or bitmap images on buttons in Windows 95. In previous versions of Windows (and in the current version of Windows NT), it was necessary to set the BS_ICON style bit when creating the button to accomplish this task.

COMPLEXITY
MODERATE

15.9 How do I...
Display a bitmap as a window
or dialog background?

Problem

I would like to replace the boring gray background in my dialogs with a more interesting bitmap in my application. I would prefer to have the bitmap look like wallpaper on the dialog without interfering with the dialog controls or static text.

I cannot seem to find a simple way to change the background of the window. Is there a method using the Windows API that will allow me to change the background of a dialog to a specified bitmap?

Technique

It is not all that difficult to change the background of the dialog to a specified bitmap. What is required is an understanding of how dialogs and windows set their background colors and how you can modify that behavior to change what it is that is displayed.

When Windows wants to color the background of a dialog, two messages are normally sent to the dialog. The first message is a WM_ERASEBKGND. This message indicates to the dialog that it should paint the background color for the dialog in order to "erase" anything that was on the screen where the dialog is to appear.

The next message that you need to know about is the WM_CTLCOLOR message. This message is sent to a dialog or window to indicate that Windows needs to know what color to make the controls on the dialog.

In this How-To, we override the processing for the WM_ERASEBKGND message in order to draw a bitmap into the background of a window. Further, we override the WM_CTLCOLOR message so that dialog controls do not "bleed" onto our bitmap. The final result is a background for a dialog that appears to be painted in the background with the controls "above" the background bitmap.

Steps

Open and run the Visual C++ application CH159.MAK from the CHAPT15\SAMPLES\CH159 directory on the CD that comes with this book. Select the Dialog menu and the Bitmap Background menu item from the menu. You will see a dialog displayed (shown in Figure 15-12) that has a background bitmap and a number of controls showing.

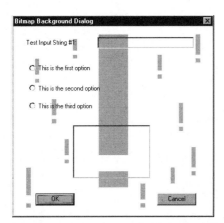

Figure 15-12 Dialog with background bitmap displayed

To duplicate the functionality of this example, follow this procedure:

1. Create a new project in Visual C++ using AppWizard. Give the new project the name CH159.MAK.

2. Enter the resource editor and create a new dialog template. Add a few static text fields and edit fields to the dialog as well as radio buttons and a list box. The actual composition of the dialog does not matter so long as you are satisfied that the layout will cover a portion of the bitmap.

3. Select ClassWizard and generate a new dialog class for the dialog template you have just created. Give the new class the name CBitmapBkgdDlg.

4. Still in the resource editor, create a new bitmap. In our example, the bitmap is simply a large exclamation point surrounded by smaller exclamation points. You can use your artistic talents to create whatever bitmap you desire. When you have finished your masterpiece, give it the identifier IDB_BITMAP1 and save the resource file. Exit the resource editor.

5. Enter ClassWizard and select the CBitmapBkgdDlg from the drop-down combo box. Select the CBitmapBkgdDlg from the object list and the WM_INITDIALOG message from the message list. Click on the Add Function button and add the following code to the OnInitDialog method of CBitmapBkgdDlg:

```
BOOL CBitmapBkgdDlg::OnInitDialog()
{
   CDialog::OnInitDialog();

   CBitmap * pBmpOld;
   RECT rectClient;

   VERIFY( m_brush = (HBRUSH)GetStockObject( HOLLOW_BRUSH ) );
   VERIFY( m_Bitmap.LoadBitmap( IDB_BITMAP1 ) );

   m_Bitmap.GetObject( sizeof(BITMAP), &m_bmInfo );
   GetClientRect( &rectClient );
   m_size.cx = rectClient.right;
   m_size.cy = rectClient.bottom;
   m_pt.x = rectClient.left;
   m_pt.y = rectClient.top;
   CClientDC dc(this);
   VERIFY( m_dcMem.CreateCompatibleDC( &dc ) );
   VERIFY( pBmpOld = m_dcMem.SelectObject( &m_Bitmap ) );
   VERIFY( m_hBmpOld = (HBITMAP) pBmpOld->GetSafeHandle() );
   return TRUE;  // return TRUE  unless you set the focus to a control
}
```

6. Next, select CBitmapBkgdDlg from the object list in ClassWizard and the WM_CTLCOLOR message from the message list. Click on the Add Function button and add the following code into the OnCtlColor method of CBitmapBkgdDlg:

```
HBRUSH CBitmapBkgdDlg::OnCtlColor(CDC* pDC, CWnd* pWnd, UINT nCtlColor)
{
```

```
    // Have text and controls be painted smoothly over bitmap
    // without using default background color
    pDC->SetBkMode( TRANSPARENT );
    return m_brush;
}
```

7. Next, select CBitmapBkgdDlg from the object list in ClassWizard and the WM_DESTROY message from the message list. Click on the Add Function button and add the following code into the OnDestroy method of CBitmapBkgdDlg:

```
void CBitmapBkgdDlg::OnDestroy()
{
    CDialog::OnDestroy();

    // Select old bitmap into memory dc (selecting out circle bitmap)
    // Need to create a temporary pointer to pass to do this
    ASSERT( m_hBmpOld );
    VERIFY( m_dcMem.SelectObject( CBitmap::FromHandle(m_hBmpOld) ) );

    // Need to DeleteObject() bitmap which was loaded
    m_Bitmap.DeleteObject();
}
```

8. Edit the message map for the CBitmapBkgdDlg to look like the following. The new line to add is marked in bold print.

```
BEGIN_MESSAGE_MAP(CBitmapBkgdDlg, CDialog)
  //{{AFX_MSG_MAP(CBitmapBkgdDlg)
    ON_WM_ERASEBKGND()
  ON_WM_CTLCOLOR()
  ON_WM_DESTROY()
  //}}AFX_MSG_MAP
END_MESSAGE_MAP()
```

9. Add a new method for the CBitmapBlgdDlg source file, BITMAPBK.CPP, as follows:

```
BOOL CBitmapBkgdDlg::OnEraseBkgnd(CDC* pDC)
{
  pDC->StretchBlt( m_pt.x, m_pt.y, m_size.cx, m_size.cy,
            &m_dcMem, 0, 0, m_bmInfo.bmWidth-1, m_bmInfo.bmHeight-1,
            SRCCOPY );

  return TRUE;     // No more background painting needed
}
```

10. Select the BITMAPBK.H header file from the project list. Make the following modifications to the file, marked in bold print:

```
// bitmapbk.h : header file
//
```

continued on next page

continued from previous page

```
////////////////////////////////////////////////////////////////////
// CBitmapBkgdDlg dialog

class CBitmapBkgdDlg : public CDialog
{
protected:
    CDC m_dcMem;               // Compatible Memory DC for dialog
    CBitmap m_Bitmap;          // Bitmap to display
    HBITMAP m_hBmpOld;         // Handle of old bitmap to save

    HBRUSH m_brush;            // Handle of background brush

    BITMAP m_bmInfo;           // Bitmap Information structure
    CPoint m_pt;               // Position for upper left corner of bitmap
    CSize m_size;              // Size (width and height) of bitmap

// Construction
public:
    CBitmapBkgdDlg(CWnd* pParent = NULL); // standard constructor

// Dialog Data
    //{{AFX_DATA(CBitmapBkgdDlg)
    enum { IDD = IDD_DIALOG1 };
        // NOTE: the ClassWizard will add data members here
    //}}AFX_DATA

// Implementation
protected:
    virtual void DoDataExchange(CDataExchange* pDX);   // DDX/DDV support

    // Generated message map functions
    //{{AFX_MSG(CBitmapBkgdDlg)
    afx_msg HBRUSH OnCtlColor(CDC* pDC, CWnd* pWnd, UINT nCtlColor);
    afx_msg void OnDestroy();
    virtual BOOL OnInitDialog();
    virtual BOOL OnEraseBkgnd(CDC* pDC);
    //}}AFX_MSG
    DECLARE_MESSAGE_MAP()
};
```

11. Enter the resource editor and add a new menu item to the IDR_CH159TYPE
menu. Give the new menu the caption Dialog. Add a new menu item to the
Dialog menu with the caption Bitmap Background and the identifier
ID_BITMAP_BKGD. Exit the resource editor, saving the resource file.

12. Enter ClassWizard and select the CCh159App object from the drop-down
combo box. Select the ID_BITMAP_BKGD object from the object list and the
COMMAND message from the message list. Click on the Add Function button and accept the name OnBitmapBkgd for the name of the new function.
Enter the following code into the OnBitmapBkgd method of CCh159App:

```
void CCh159App::OnBitmapBkgd()
{
    CBitmapBkgdDlg  dlg;
```

```
    dlg.DoModal();
}
```

13. Add the following line to the top of the CH159.CPP source file:

```
#include "bitmapbk.h"
```

14. Compile and run the application.

How It Works

When Windows initializes a dialog box, it sends a WM_ERASEBKGND message to the window handle for the dialog. You can trap this message in order to erase the background yourself. In this How-To, we trap the erase message and then use the API function StretchBlt to copy the bitmap we loaded from the resource file onto the background of the dialog box.

The OnCtlColor method of the dialog makes sure that the controls do not "bleed" onto the bitmap by setting the background brush to be hollow. This allows the bitmap to look as though it was painted onto the dialog without the annoying white space caused by the background of the static controls.

INDEX

Books have a substantial influence on the destruction of the forests of the Earth. For example, it takes 17 trees to produce one ton of paper. A first printing of 30,000 copies of a typical 480 page book consumes 108,000 pounds of paper which will require 918 trees!

Waite Group Press™ is against the clear-cutting of forests and supports reforestation of the Pacific Northwest of the United States and Canada, where most of this paper comes from. As a publisher with several hundred thousand books sold each year, we feel an obligation to give back to the planet. We will therefore support organizations which seek to preserve the forests of planet Earth.

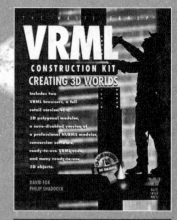

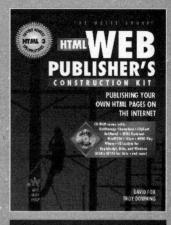

LIMITED WARRANTY

The following warranties shall be effective for 90 days from the date of purchase: (i) The Waite Group, Inc. warrants the enclosed disk to be free of defects in materials and workmanship under normal use; and (ii) The Waite Group, Inc. warrants that the programs, unless modified by the purchaser, will substantially perform the functions described in the documentation provided by The Waite Group, Inc. when operated on the designated hardware and operating system. The Waite Group, Inc. does not warrant that the programs will meet purchaser's requirements or that operation of a program will be uninterrupted or error-free. The program warranty does not cover any program that has been altered or changed in any way by anyone other than The Waite Group, Inc. The Waite Group, Inc. is not responsible for problems caused by changes in the operating characteristics of computer hardware or computer operating systems that are made after the release of the programs, nor for problems in the interaction of the programs with each other or other software.

THESE WARRANTIES ARE EXCLUSIVE AND IN LIEU OF ALL OTHER WARRANTIES OF MERCHANTABILITY OR FITNESS FOR A PARTICULAR PURPOSE OR OF ANY OTHER WARRANTY, WHETHER EXPRESS OR IMPLIED.

EXCLUSIVE REMEDY

The Waite Group, Inc. will replace any defective disk without charge if the defective disk is returned to The Waite Group, Inc. within 90 days from date of purchase.

This is Purchaser's sole and exclusive remedy for any breach of warranty or claim for contract, tort, or damages.

LIMITATION OF LIABILITY

THE WAITE GROUP, INC. AND THE AUTHORS OF THE PROGRAMS SHALL NOT IN ANY CASE BE LIABLE FOR SPECIAL, INCIDENTAL, CONSEQUENTIAL, INDIRECT, OR OTHER SIMILAR DAMAGES ARISING FROM ANY BREACH OF THESE WARRANTIES EVEN IF THE WAITE GROUP, INC. OR ITS AGENT HAS BEEN ADVISED OF THE POSSIBILITY OF SUCH DAMAGES.

THE LIABILITY FOR DAMAGES OF THE WAITE GROUP, INC. AND THE AUTHORS OF THE PROGRAMS UNDER THIS AGREEMENT SHALL IN NO EVENT EXCEED THE PURCHASE PRICE PAID.

COMPLETE AGREEMENT

This Agreement constitutes the complete agreement between The Waite Group, Inc. and the authors of the programs, and you, the purchaser.

Some states do not allow the exclusion or limitation of implied warranties or liability for incidental or consequential damages, so the above exclusions or limitations may not apply to you. This limited warranty gives you specific legal rights; you may have others, which vary from state to state.

SATISFACTION REPORT CARD

Please fill out this card if you wish to know of future updates to *Windows 95 API How-To,* or to receive our catalog.

First Name: _____   **Last Name:** _____

Street Address: _____

City: _____   **State:** _____   **Zip:** _____

E-mail Address _____

Daytime Telephone: (_____) _____

Date product was acquired: Month _____ **Day** _____ **Year** _____   **Your Occupation:** _____

Overall, how would you rate *Windows 95 API How-To?*

☐ Excellent   ☐ Very Good   ☐ Good
☐ Fair   ☐ Below Average ☐ Poor

What did you like MOST about this book? _____
_____
_____

What did you like LEAST about this book? _____
_____
_____

Please describe any problems you may have encountered with installing or using the disk: _____
_____

How did you use this book (problem-solver, tutorial, reference...)?
_____

What is your level of computer expertise?

☐ New   ☐ Dabbler   ☐ Hacker
☐ Power User   ☐ Programmer   ☐ Experienced Professional

What computer languages are you familiar with? _____
_____

Please describe your computer hardware:

Computer _____ Hard disk _____
5.25" disk drives _____ 3.5" disk drives _____
Video card _____ Monitor _____
Printer _____ Peripherals _____
Sound Board _____ CD ROM _____

Where did you buy this book?

☐ Bookstore (name): _____
☐ Discount store (name): _____
☐ Computer store (name): _____
☐ Catalog (name): _____
☐ Direct from WGP   ☐ Other _____

What price did you pay for this book? _____

What influenced your purchase of this book?

☐ Recommendation   ☐ Advertisement
☐ Magazine review   ☐ Store display
☐ Mailing   ☐ Book's format
☐ Reputation of Waite Group Press ☐ Other

How many computer books do you buy each year? _____

How many other Waite Group books do you own? _____

What is your favorite Waite Group book? _____
_____

Is there any program or subject you would like to see Waite Group Press cover in a similar approach? _____
_____

Additional comments? _____
_____
_____

Please send to: **Waite Group Press**
                       200 Tamal Plaza
                       Corte Madera, CA 94925

☐ **Check here for a free Waite Group catalog**

STOP!

BEFORE YOU OPEN THE DISK OR CD-ROM PACKAGE ON THE FACING PAGE, CAREFULLY READ THE LICENSE AGREEMENT.

Opening this package indicates that you agree to abide by the license agreement found in the back of this book. If you do not agree with it, promptly return the unopened disk package (including the related book) to the place you obtained them for a refund.